UNIX® System V Network Programming

Addison-Wesley Professional Computing Series

Brian W. Kernighan, Consulting Editor

Ken Arnold/John Peyton, *A C User's Guide to ANSI C*

Tom Cargill, *C++ Programming Style*

David Curry, *UNIX System Security: A Guide for Users and System Administrators*

Robert B. Murray, *C++ Strategies and Tactics*

Scott Meyers, *Effective C++: 50 Specific Ways to Improve Your Programs and Designs*

Radia Perlman, *Interconnections: Bridges and Routers*

David Piscitello/A. Lyman Chapin, *Open Systems Networking*

Stephen A. Rago, *UNIX System V Network Programming*

W. Richard Stevens, *Advanced Programming in the UNIX Environment*

UNIX® System V Network Programming

Stephen A. Rago

◆
▼▼

ADDISON-WESLEY PUBLISHING COMPANY

Reading, Massachusetts   Menlo Park, California   New York   Don Mills, Ontario
Wokingham, England   Amsterdam   Bonn   Paris   Milan   Madrid   Sydney   Singapore   Tokyo
Seoul   Taipei   Mexico City   San Juan

The programs and applications presented in this book have been included for their instructional value. They have been tested with care, but are not guaranteed for any particular purpose. The publisher does not offer any warranties or representations, nor does it accept any liabilities with respect to the programs or applications.

The publisher offers discounts on this book when ordered in quantity for special sales. For more information please contact:

Corporate & Professional Publishing Group
Addison-Wesley Publishing Company
One Jacob Way
Reading, Massachusetts 01867

Library of Congress Cataloging-in-Publication Data

Rago, Stephen A.
    UNIX System V network programming/Stephen A. Rago.
        p. cm. (Addison-Wesley professional computing series)
    Includes index.
    ISBN 0-201-56318-5 (hard)
    1. Operating systems (Computers). 2. Unix System V (Computer
file). 3. Computer networks. I. Title. II. Series.
QA76.76.063R34   1993
005.7' 11—dc20   92-45276
                                                        CIP

ISBN 0-201-56318-5
Text printed on recycled and acid-free paper.
1 2 3 4 5 6 7 8 9 10 MU 96959493
First Printing, June 1993

To Patricia

Contents

Preface   xi

PART 1: Background Material   1

1. Introduction to Networks   3
   1.1. Background   3
   1.2. Network Characteristics   4
   1.3. Networking Models   10
   Summary   18
   Bibliographic Notes   18

2. UNIX Programming   19
   2.1. Overview   19
   2.2. Concepts   20
   2.3. Conventions   25
   2.4. Writing Programs   26
   Summary   89
   Exercises   90
   Bibliographic Notes   90

PART 2: User-level Network Programming   93

3. STREAMS   95
   3.1. STREAMS Background   95
   3.2. STREAMS Architecture   96
   3.3. System Calls   101
   3.4. Nonblocking I/O and Polling   113
   3.5. Service Interfaces   128

3.6. IPC with STREAMS Pipes   131
3.7. Advanced Topics   143
Summary   147
Exercises   147
Bibliographic Notes   148

4. The Transport Layer Interface   149
4.1. Introduction   149
4.2. Transport Endpoint Management   151
4.3. Connectionless Service   165
4.4. Connection-oriented Service   174
4.5. TLI and Read/Write   207
Summary   214
Exercises   214
Bibliographic Notes   215

5. Selecting Networks and Addresses   217
5.1. Introduction   217
5.2. Network Selection   218
5.3. Name-to-Address Translation   229
5.4. Name-to-Address Library Design   243
Summary   259
Exercises   259
Bibliographic Notes   259

6. The Network Listener Facility   261
6.1. The Service Access Facility   261
6.2. Port Monitors   265
6.3. The Listener Process   267
6.4. One-shot Servers   267
6.5. Standing Servers   274
6.6. The NLPS Server   285
Summary   288
Exercises   288
Bibliographic Notes   289

7. Sockets   291
7.1. Introduction   291
7.2. Socket Management   294
7.3. Connection Establishment   301
7.4. Data Transfer   306
7.5. UNIX Domain Sockets   313
7.6. Advanced Topics   323
7.7. Comparison with the TLI   330
7.8. Name-to-Address Translation   334

Summary   352
Exercises   352
Bibliographic Notes   353

8. Remote Procedure Calls   355
   8.1. Introduction   355
   8.2. XDR   359
   8.3. High-level RPC Programming   373
   8.4. Low-level RPC Programming   382
   8.5. rpcgen   403
   8.6. Advanced RPC Features   412
   Summary   421
   Exercises   422
   Bibliographic Notes   422

PART 3: Kernel-level Network Programming   423

9. The STREAMS Subsystem   425
   9.1. The Kernel Environment   425
   9.2. The STREAMS Environment   439
   9.3. STREAMS Messages   446
   9.4. STREAMS Queues   455
   9.5. Communicating with Messages   462
   9.6. Message Types   464
   Summary   477
   Exercises   477
   Bibliographic Notes   477

10. STREAMS Drivers   479
   10.1. Introduction   479
   10.2. Driver Entry Points   481
   10.3. The Data Link Provider Interface   489
   10.4. Ethernet Driver Example   495
   Summary   537
   Exercises   537
   Bibliographic Notes   537

11. STREAMS Modules   539
   11.1. Introduction   539
   11.2. Module Entry Points   542
   11.3. The Terminal Interface   546
   11.4. Network TTY Emulator Example   550
   Summary   575
   Exercises   575

Bibliographic Notes   575

12. STREAMS Multiplexors   577
   12.1. Introduction   577
   12.2. How Multiplexors Work   579
   12.3. The Transport Provider Interface   585
   12.4. Transport Provider Example   596
   Summary   673
   Exercises   673
   Bibliographic Notes   674

PART 4: Design Project   675

13. Design Project: Implementing SLIP   677
   13.1. Introduction to SLIP   677
   13.2. Software Architecture   678
   13.3. User-level Components   683
   13.4. Kernel-level Components   720
   Summary   750
   Exercises   750
   Bibliographic Notes   750

Bibliography   753

Index   761

Preface

This book is for programmers who are interested in learning how to use the networking interfaces in UNIX System V Release 4 (SVR4). We use real-life examples to demonstrate how interfaces are used and techniques are applied. All too often in the workplace we find ourselves faced with new assignments for which we have little background. In these situations, we must educate ourselves as quickly as possible so that we can competently undertake the task at hand. Although technical manuals usually provide the information necessary to complete a task, they often lack the background, motivation, and explanation that help us to understand more clearly what we're doing and why we're doing it.

Intended as a practical reference, this book contains very little coverage of theory, and details better dealt with through manual pages are omitted, although references are used liberally. It could, however, be used to complement a graduate or advanced undergraduate course in networking.

As a prerequisite to reading this book, you should be familiar with the UNIX environment and the C programming language so that the examples can be understood. Some background in data structures and algorithms would be helpful, but is not required.

References to SVR4 manual pages are in the running text, appearing as the command name or function name, followed by the section of the manual in which the page is found, as in open(2). Here, we are referring to the open manual page in Section 2 of the system manuals.

Originally, there was only one manual for the system. With the introduction of each new release of the system, the manual grew in size until it had to be split up into separate manuals. In UNIX System V Release 3, there was one manual for users, one manual for programmers, and one manual for system administrators.

In SVR4, however, the manual pages were redistributed by functional area. The user commands are no longer in a single manual, nor can you find all the programming interfaces in one place. This new organization has proven difficult to navigate by novices and experts alike. The following summary should aid in the process of locating the desired manual pages.

Programmer's Reference Manual
> (1)   Commands relating to source code management, compilation, and loading
> (2)   System calls
> (3, 3C, 3S, 3E, 3G, 3M, 3X)   Most library routines
> (4)   File formats
> (5)   Miscellany (commonly used constants, data structures, and macros)

Programmer's Guide: Networking Interfaces
> (1, 1M)   Networking commands
> (3, 3C, 3N)   Network-related library routines
> (4)   Network-related file formats
> (5)   Miscellany, including network-related environment variables
> (7)   Networking drivers and modules

Programmer's Guide: STREAMS
> (1, 1M)   STREAMS-related commands
> (2)   STREAMS-specific system calls
> (3C)   STREAMS-specific library routines
> (7)   STREAMS modules and drivers

User's Reference Manual
> (1)   Commands any user might want to run

System Administrator's Reference Manual
> (1M)   Administrative commands
> (4)   Administrative file formats
> (5)   Miscellaneous facilities
> (7)   Special files (devices)
> (8)   Administrative procedures

You might find it helpful if these manuals are close by when you read this book.

Background

The first standard network interface incorporated in the UNIX system was the socket mechanism. This mechanism was provided in the 4.2 release of the Berkeley Software Distribution (BSD) version of the UNIX operating system from the University of California at Berkeley. With it was an implementation of the Internet protocol suite (TCP, UDP, IP, et al.). These became available in 1983.

AT&T did not address standard networking interfaces in System V until 1985, when it ported Dennis Ritchie's Streams mechanism from the Version 8 Research UNIX System to UNIX System V Release 2.0p, the unreleased predecessor to System V Release 3.0 (SVR3). With the release of SVR3 in 1986, STREAMS, the framework for networking in System V, became generally available, along with the Transport Layer Interface (TLI) library. Ironically, SVR3 was released without including any networking protocols.

In 1988, X/OPEN, a consortium dedicated to enhancing application portability through standards endorsements, specified its own transport layer interface library, based on AT&T's TLI library. The X/OPEN specification, called the X/OPEN Transport Interface (XTI), is effectively a superset of TLI. In 1990 the Portable

Operating System Interface (POSIX) committee of the Institute of Electrical and
Electronics Engineers (IEEE) created the 1003.12 working group to standardize portable networking interfaces for application programs. As of this writing, the 1003.12
working group's efforts are still underway, but it looks as though both sockets and
XTI will be included in the standard.

SVR4 is unique in that it includes support for many standards in one operating
system. Unlike other versions of UNIX that support dual-universe environments,
SVR4 provides applications with one environment consisting of features from previous versions of the System V, SunOS, BSD, Xenix, SCO, and Research UNIX systems, as well as some new features of its own. Support for POSIX 1003.1 (the system application programming interface) is also provided. The major networking
interfaces provided include STREAMS, TLI, sockets, and remote procedure calls.

Organization

The material covered in this book pertains mainly to SVR4, although some features
were present in earlier releases of UNIX System V. This book is divided into four
sections: background material, user-level network programming, kernel-level network programming, and a design example.

Both user-level and kernel-level networking components are described to
present a complete picture of network programming in UNIX System V. Although
not everyone will be interested in both environments, knowledge of one environment
makes programming in the other easier. Instead of just blindly following the instructions in the manuals, it enables the programmer to understand the effects of his or her
actions and make better design decisions.

The first two chapters provide some background that will make the rest of the
book more useful to readers with less experience. More experienced readers can skip
these introductory chapters without much loss of context. Chapter 1 provides a brief
introduction to networking concepts, and Chapter 2 provides an overview of application programming in the UNIX System V environment. In particular, Chapter 2 contains example functions that are used throughout the rest of this text. If you skip
Chapter 2, you might want to refer back to individual examples as you come across
these functions in later chapters.

Chapter 3 is the first chapter concerned with network programming per se. It
covers the STREAMS programming environment. Since the STREAMS mechanism
is the basis for most of the communication facilities in System V, understanding its
services and system call interface is a prerequisite to discussing any System V networking facility.

Chapter 4 covers the Transport Layer Interface library. This is the interface
applications use to access the services provided by the transport layer of a computer
network. Emphasis is placed on application design to support network independence.

Chapter 5 describes the network selection and name-to-address translation facilities, which further extend the ability of a programmer to design network-
independent applications. Chapter 6 covers the network listener process. Using the

listener simplifies the design of server processes. The Service Access Facility (SAF), the administrative framework in which the listener operates, is also discussed.

Chapter 7 gives a brief description of the BSD socket interface and its corresponding implementation in SVR4. The socket and TLI mechanisms are contrasted and compared. Chapter 8 discusses remote procedure calls and the external data representation used to develop distributed applications. This ends the user-level section of the text.

The next four chapters are dedicated to kernel-level network programming. Chapter 9 describes the kernel environment, its utility routines, and the interfaces to the STREAMS environment. Chapter 10 describes how to write STREAMS drivers, centering around the design of a simple Ethernet driver. Chapter 11 describes how to write STREAMS modules, centering around the design of a module that can be used to emulate a terminal over a network connection. Chapter 12 describes how to write STREAMS multiplexing drivers. It uses a simple connection-oriented transport provider as a detailed example.

Finally, the last section of the book, Chapter 13, covers the design of a SLIP package for SVR4, including both the user-level and kernel-level components. It illustrates the application of much from the preceding 12 chapters and, in essence, ties the book together.

Much of the interesting material lies in the examples. You are encouraged to work through each until it is understood.

Acknowledgements

This book was produced on an Intel i386-based system running UNIX System V Release 4.0, Version 3. The text editor `sam` was used to create and update the text. The pictures were created with `xcip`, a newer version of `cip`, on an AT&T 630MTG terminal. The output for the book was produced with `eqn`, `tbl`, `pic`, `troff`, and `dpost` from the Documenter's WorkBench, Version 3.2.

I would like to thank the following reviewers for their invaluable input: Steve Albert (Unix System Laboratories), Maury Bach (IBM Scientific and Technical Center), George Bittner (Programmed Logic Corporation), Steve Buroff (AT&T Bell Labs), Jeff Gitlin (AT&T), Ron Gomes (Morgan Stanley & Company), Peter Honeyman (University of Michigan), Brian Kernighan (AT&T Bell Labs), Dave Olander (Unix System Laboratories), Dennis Ritchie (AT&T Bell Labs), Michael Scheer (Plexus Systems), Rich Stevens (independent consultant), and Graham Wheeler (Aztec Information Management). In particular, both Brian Kernighan and Rich Stevens read every chapter and freely shared their knowledge, experience, and formatting macros and shell scripts. They have greatly increased the quality of the book.

Many people helped by answering questions where written history was vague or incomplete. In addition to the reviewers, this group includes Guy Harris (Auspex Systems), Bob Israel (Epoch Systems), Hari Pulijal (Unix System Laboratories), Usha Pulijal (Unix System Laboratories), Glenn Skinner (SunSoft), Ken Thompson (AT&T Bell Labs), and Larry Wehr (AT&T Bell Labs).

Rich Drechsler (AT&T Bell Labs) provided the PostScript program that increased the width of the constant-width font used throughout this book. Both he and Len Rago (AT&T Bell Labs) helped in debugging problems with the laser printer used during the typesetting of this book. Thanks to them both. Thanks to Dick Hamilton (Unix System Laboratories) for making an early copy of SVR4.2 documentation available. Also, thanks to Gus Amegadzie (Programmed Logic Corporation), who helped test the SLIP software presented in Chapter 13. Special thanks to John Wait (Addison-Wesley) for his advice and encouragement during the last two years.

Finally, I want to thank my family, without whom this book wouldn't have been possible. They have supported me and helped to pull up the slack created by the amount of time I devoted to writing this book. My parents instilled in me the work ethic necessary to get it done (as well as provided their baby-sitting services), and my wife worked harder to give me the time to write it.

Part 1
Background Material

1
Introduction
to Networks

This chapter discusses the motivation behind networking and some of the characteristics of various networks that we will encounter throughout the rest of this book.

1.1 BACKGROUND

A network can be loosely defined as *the hardware and software that enable two entities to communicate*. Humans can communicate over a telephone network. Central processing units in a multiprocessor can communicate over internal system buses. While these systems can be considered networks, this text is concerned only with communicating entities that are independent computer systems (often called *hosts*).

Computer networks are popular for many reasons. They provide a cost-effective alternative to large computing facilities. Rather than place all users and their files on a large mainframe, the users can be distributed among smaller, less expensive computers. By connecting these smaller machines with a network, the same level of sharing can be attained as if everyone were on one big machine.

Networks allow the separate computers to share files, devices such as printers and plotters, and other computing facilities, such as processing ability. Users can exchange electronic mail over a network. Computer systems can be administered remotely, over a network.

Because of networks, computers can be placed in the locations that best fit the organizations that use them, instead of the other way around. Geographical freedom allows organizations to structure themselves in ways that allow them to accomplish their goals more effectively.

Reliability is another benefit of using computer networks. While one computer is unavailable for processing, because it is either overloaded or out of service, processing can be redirected to another computer on the network. Services previously provided by a single computer can be distributed over several.

1.2 NETWORK CHARACTERISTICS

Networks are classified by their different characteristics. This section gives a short overview of some of these characteristics.

Transmission Medium

There are many diverse media used to transmit data in a computer network. They vary in cost, transmission speed, bandwidth, and applicable transmission techniques and distances. The medium forms the communication path, often called a *channel*, between nodes in a network. A *node* can be a host computer or an intermediate communications processor, such as a circuit switch, bridge, or router.

The most common transmission medium is copper wire. Twisted pair wire is the least expensive alternative, but its transmission speeds are limited because the wire is subject to electrical interference. Shielded twisted pair wire provides better isolation from electrical interference, supporting higher data rates. Coaxial cabling provides better isolation from electrical interference than twisted pair, resulting in even higher transmission speeds, but coaxial cabling costs more.

Fiber optic cabling is becoming one of the more promising alternatives to copper wire for network media. Although it is expensive now, as technological advances are made, the price will decrease. The main advantages of fiber optic cabling are its higher transmission speed and its immunity to electrical interference.

Transmission media need not be tangible to be useful in a computer network. Wireless media include radio waves, microwaves, and infrared waves. Cable-style media are called *bounded* media, while wireless media are referred to as *unbounded* media.

Network Topology

The physical structure of a network is called its *topology*. Topology is important because it affects how messages are transferred within the network. Each node in a network is connected to the others (either physically with cabling, or logically via airwaves) in one of two ways.

A point-to-point connection is an individual communication channel between two nodes. It is usually impractical for all nodes in a network to have point-to-point connections to all the other nodes. When no direct connection exists between two nodes, intermediate nodes assist in the communication by passing messages along in the network. Each time a message travels from one node to another, the message is said to have taken a ''hop.''

A multipoint connection involves multiple nodes connected to the same communication channel. In a multipoint connection, message transfer occurs via *broadcasts*, where all nodes can receive the same message. Addressing information in the message indicates the intended destination nodes.

A bus topology is shown in Figure 1.1. Each node, represented by a small circle, is attached to the same physical communication medium. The ends of the medium are terminated to prevent the signal from being reflected.

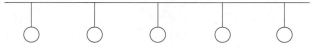

Fig. 1.1. Bus Topology

In a ring topology (see Figure 1.2) each node is connected to the next, with the entire network forming a closed circle. Within this point-to-point network, the connections between pairs of nodes are electronically isolated from other nodes on the network. Each station acts as a repeater of the signal, regenerating it as it is received. The network-interface hardware contains a switch that can be thrown in the event of node failure, thus allowing the signal to pass through.

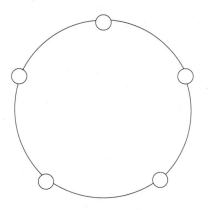

Fig. 1.2. Ring Topology

In a star topology (see Figure 1.3) each node is connected to a special node at the center, called the *hub*. The hub can be either passive, providing only a path for the messages to traverse, or active, regenerating the electrical signals it receives. Hubs can also be intelligent, participating in the selection of the paths that the messages will take.

Many other topologies can be found, from trees (see Figure 1.4), to fully connected graphs (called meshes), to hybrids consisting of multiple interconnected structures. Regular structures are easier to model mathematically than hybrid ones. For example, in a point-to-point network with a tree topology, we know that the maximum number of hops a message might take is bounded by $2h$, where h is the height of the tree.

It is important to distinguish the physical layout of a network from the way signals are transmitted on it. For example, even though a network might be a bus in the electrical sense, if all nodes are connected to a single hub in the center (as in Figure 1.3), then the topology is said to be a star.

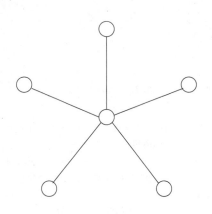

Fig. 1.3. Star Topology

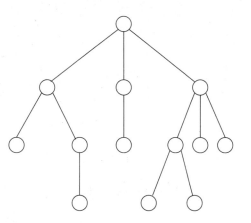

Fig. 1.4. Tree Topology

Another potential point of confusion is the access method (discussed shortly). One can find examples in the literature where a token-passing bus network is described as a physical bus and as a logical ring. Just because the access method used is similar to that of a ring network, a logical structure is imposed on the network, clouding the meaning of topology. Topology is not the same as access method, although the two can be related.

Transmission Method

Signals can be sent over the transmission medium in many ways. Between two stations transmission can be unidirectional (*simplex*), bidirectional with one station transmitting at a time (*half-duplex*), or bidirectional with two stations transmitting at the same time (*full-duplex*). For example, Ethernet uses half-duplex communication techniques since any station can transmit a message, but only one station can transmit at a time.

Another aspect of the transmission method is whether the sender and receiver are synchronized with each other. With synchronous communication, the sending and receiving clocks are synchronized. Data are transmitted at fixed intervals. With asynchronous communication, the sending and receiving clocks are unrelated and data are transmitted at arbitrary intervals. To compensate for this, extra information (called *framing* information) is added to each message to allow the receiver to identify the message boundaries. The framing information also allows the receiver to synchronize its clock with the message so the contents can be retrieved. Since it identifies the message boundaries, the framing information is placed both before and after the message. For example, RS-232 serial communication uses one *start bit* and one or two *stop bits* to frame each byte transmitted.

Signals can be transmitted over physical cables using either digital or analog techniques. Digital, or *baseband*, transmission involves sending pulses on the cable. Although any station can transmit the signal, only one station can transmit at a time. Multiple stations share the medium by using time-division multiplexing: signals from multiple stations are interleaved over time.

Analog techniques, called *broadband* transmission, use multiple frequencies to transmit and receive signals. The communication medium is shared among multiple stations by using frequency-division multiplexing, time-division multiplexing, or both. For example, a coaxial cable might be divided into several frequency ranges, with separate conversations occurring in each range. Each frequency range, in turn, might be shared among several conversations through the use of time-division multiplexing.

Transmission Speed

When network speeds are compared, the words *speed* and *bandwidth* are often used interchangeably. Bandwidth is *not* the same as transmission speed, although the two are related. The bandwidth of any medium is a measure of that medium's capacity to carry analog signals. In other words, bandwidth is a measure of the range of frequencies that can be transmitted. Bandwidth is measured in units of *hertz* (Hz).

In contrast, the transmission speed is measured in terms of the number of bits per second (bps) that can be transmitted. Bandwidth is a measure of analog quantities, whereas speed is a measure of digital quantities. As such, baseband networks are rated in bits per second, and broadband networks are measured in hertz.

For example, baseband coax supports transmission speeds between 10 to 15 megabits per second (Mbps). Broadband coax has a usable bandwidth between 300 and 400 megahertz (MHz). Fiber optic cable can transmit data at several gigabits per second (Gbps). The theoretical limit of transmission speed can be calculated from the bandwidth using Shannon's theorem for noisy channels:

$$\text{max speed in bps} = B \, \log_2(1 + S/N)$$

where B is the bandwidth in Hz, S is the signal power, and N is the noise power. S/N is known as the *signal-to-noise ratio*. The signal-to-noise ratio is usually expressed in decibels (dBs) as $10 \log_{10}(S/N)$. For a fixed signal-to-noise ratio, it is easy to see that as bandwidth increases, so does transmission speed.

Access Method

When communication channels are shared, rules must be followed to determine who may transmit on the channel. Even so, it is still possible for simultaneous transmission attempts by more than one node to result in *collisions*. When a collision occurs, the data in the messages are no longer usable, and bandwidth is wasted.

Three common classifications of channel access methods are *centralized polling*, *decentralized polling*, and *contention*. Each approaches the problem of time-division multiplexing in a different way.

Centralized polling involves one node on the network acting as the master. Its job is to determine the node that can transmit next. The master can use a simple round-robin policy, or a more complicated method. For example, the master could use a table with priorities for each node so that some nodes are favored over others.

Decentralized polling removes the need for a master node. One example of decentralized polling is *token passing*. A small message, called a *token*, is passed around the network. As each node receives the token, the node can tell if it has permission to transmit, depending on whether the token is marked free or busy. If it is free, the node can mark it busy, append its data, and transmit the message. Otherwise, the token is just passed along. When a transmitting node receives the message it has just sent, it regenerates the free token, allowing the next node to transmit.

Contention-based access methods can only be used with broadcast networks. The basic principle behind this class of access methods is that nodes transmit when they want, and collisions occur when more than one node transmits at the same time. As one might expect, many variations exist to try to minimize the number of collisions.

One such variation is nonpersistent Carrier Sense Multiple Access (CSMA). In this method, each node senses the channel before transmitting. If the channel is free, a node will immediately try to transmit. If the channel is busy, or if a collision occurs, sensing stops and the node waits for a random amount of time before sensing again.

Another variation is to have the node continue to monitor the channel after transmission begins. If a collision is detected, the transmission can be aborted so time is not wasted. This method is known as Carrier Sense Multiple Access with Collision Detection (CSMA/CD).

Operating Distance

Networks are commonly labeled according to the distance they cover. Distance is important because it places limitations on the kinds of hardware and software used. Signals can be transmitted only so far before they attenuate or disperse. As the distance between nodes increases, so does the delay between the time a message is transmitted and the time it arrives. This limits the algorithms that can be used to control communications.

For example, in a broadcast network where transmission delays are small, medium access control policies can employ carrier sense techniques. On the other hand, if the transmission delay is large, as in satellite-based communications, sensing the state of the channel is impractical because the information is stale by the time it is used. Other access control techniques must be applied.

Excluding the networks used to connect processing elements in multiprocessors and multicomputers, computer networks are split into three broad categories based on the distance they cover. A local area network (LAN) provides communication for nodes within a room, a building, or a collection of closely located buildings, such as a campus. A metropolitan area network (MAN) provides communication for nodes within a larger radius, such as within a city. A wide area network (WAN), also called a *long-haul* network, provides communication for nodes within a larger radius still, such as across countries or continents.

Switching Style

A network's switching style determines how data paths are created between the transmitting node and the receiving node.

A circuit-switched network creates a dedicated path between the sending and receiving nodes. The path, or circuit, exists for the duration of the transmission, providing a constant delay and the sequential delivery of data. Call setup times are usually long, and bandwidth is wasted between intervals of transmission.

A message-switched network does not necessarily have a direct physical path between the sender and the receiver. The message contains addressing information used to help nodes route the message to its destination. Delays can vary, and nodes need to have enough memory to store entire messages until they can be forwarded on to the next node. This technique is also called *store-and-forward*. Bandwidth is not wasted, since messages from different pairs of communicating nodes are interleaved over the same circuits.

A packet-switched network is like a message-switched one, but the message is segmented into smaller units called *packets*. The goal of packet-switching is to try to obtain the benefits of both circuit-switched and message-switched networks. The smaller units of data transfer allow for fairer sharing of the channel, so delays do not vary as much as with message-switching. Although less memory is needed to store packets at each node, more work is needed to reassemble packets into messages at the receiving node, especially if the packets arrive in a different order from which they were sent.

Networks with point-to-point connections can use any switching technique. Networks with multipoint connections use packet-switching because it is fairest. As with all network characteristics, hybrid switching methods can be found.

Modes of Service

Networks can provide several different modes of service. The modes are classified as either *connection-oriented* service or *connectionless* service.

With connection-oriented service, the network provides users with a way to transmit messages over connections to other nodes. The connections can be physical, as in circuit-switching, but most often a *virtual circuit* is provided. Virtual circuits provide services similar to physical circuits, except that there is no underlying dedicated path for the connection. The illusion of the circuit is provided through software.

The connection-oriented service mode provides reliable, sequenced delivery of data between nodes. Before applications try to use a virtual circuit, the connection must be established. After this point, applications do not need to specify addressing information when transmitting data, because the address of the destination is implicitly identified by the circuit.

With connectionless service, the network provides a simple data-transfer facility. Each data-transfer request requires the user to specify the destination address and is treated independently from other transfer requests. There is no guarantee that multiple data units will arrive in the order in which they were sent. In fact, there is no guarantee they will arrive at all. This type of service is called *datagram* service.

A modification of the datagram service that tries to improve these conditions is *reliable datagram* service. Reliable datagrams are just like normal datagrams, except that packet delivery is guaranteed to be reliable and in sequence. Applications still must specify the addressing information with each transfer request, however.

Connection-oriented service is usually better for long-lived transactions, and connectionless service is usually better for short transactions. One determining factor is the amount of time required to establish a connection compared to the amount of time required to complete the transaction. The longer a transaction takes, the less important the time to create the connection becomes. Of course, applications using unreliable datagrams must be able to withstand data loss and delivery out of sequence.

Another factor to consider when choosing between the two modes of service is the throughput required by the application. Connection-oriented service affords protocols the opportunity to allocate resources for the connection, potentially improving throughput. Virtual-circuit protocols, however, are usually more complex than connectionless ones, resulting in lower throughput.

1.3 NETWORKING MODELS

Programs written to use the facilities provided by networks usually follow and support several networking models. We cover the more popular ones here.

The Transparency Model

The main goal of applications that follow the transparency model is to hide the presence of the network. The programs want to provide transparent access to the resources on the network. One example of an application that fits this model is a remote file system, such as AT&T's RFS or Sun's NFS. Remote file systems make files on remote machines appear as if the files were stored on the local machine.

Applications that hide the network are often called *distributed applications* or *distributed systems*. In contrast, a *networked application* is one that uses the services of a network, but may or may not hide its presence. (A distributed application is a special case of a networked application.) With a distributed file system, one can use standard commands, such as cp(1), to transfer files between machines. rcp(1), on the other hand, is not considered to be a distributed application because the presence of separate machines connected via a network is not hidden from the users.

The Client–Server Model

By far, the most popular model for networking software is the client–server model. This model involves processes (servers) on selected machines providing services to processes (consumers, or clients) on other machines. A client process will contact a server process and request a particular service. Then the server will perform the service on behalf of the client. For example, an application that copies files between machines on a network is divided into two parts. The client-side part is invoked by the user on the local machine to initiate the transfer. The server-side part resides on the remote machine that assists in the transmission of the file.

Even applications that do not appear to be oriented toward a client–server architecture often use the client–server model. Depending on which part of the application is initiating the request for service, individual steps in a transaction can exhibit client–server relationships. Consider a distributed database system where, ordinarily, all processes work in unison, performing similar roles. A single transaction, such as an update request, can be broken down into several steps. The node that receives the initial request from the user acts as a server with respect to the user's program. Once the request is verified, the node might farm it out to additional nodes on the network where the request will be executed. During this step, however, the original node takes on the role of a client, since it is now the one requesting a service.

The OSI Reference Model

The Open Systems Interconnection (OSI) reference model, developed by the International Organization for Standardization (ISO), provides one useful way to view networks by dividing them up into separate layers based on functionality. Some doubt the commercial success of OSI-based networks, mainly because many existing networks do not map well to the model, and partitioning networks into so many levels is thought to be inefficient. Nevertheless, the OSI reference model is still of value because it gives us a foundation from which we can discuss the functions performed in networks.

The OSI reference model divides a network into seven logical layers (see Figure 1.5). Each layer performs functions associated with specific tasks and provides these functions as a service to the layer above it. The goal behind the functional break-down is to enhance interoperability among products from different vendors. As long as the interface between layers remains fixed, the actual implementation of the layers can change without affecting other parts of the network.

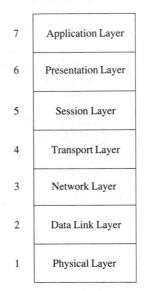

Fig. 1.5. OSI Reference Model

At the interface between layers in the model, a provider–consumer relationship exists (see Figure 1.6). The lower layer provides a set of services to the upper layer. With two communicating applications, the upper layer of one application communicates with its peer by using the services of the lower layer (see Figure 1.7). The only physical communication that occurs is at the lowest layer. Between the other layers, communication is virtual (hence the dotted lines).

Each horizontal line corresponds to a different *protocol*, a set of rules to be followed to enable communication. The ISO specifies two kinds of standards: one for the interfaces and another for the protocols. The reference model itself is only concerned with the interface standards. ISO 7498 describes the OSI reference model.

Data are transferred from layer to layer, until the bottom of the stack is reached, at which point the data are transmitted across the communication medium and received on the destination end of the channel. Here, the data travel up the protocol stack until they arrive at the sender's peer layer.

As a message travels down the stack, each layer adds its own information to the message. The information can be placed in a header before the rest of the message, or it can be placed in a trailer at the end of the message. As the message travels up

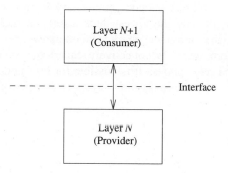

Fig. 1.6. Layered Provider–Consumer Relationship

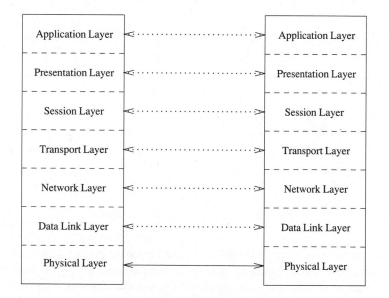

Fig. 1.7. Peer-to-Peer Communication

the stack on the receiving end, each layer removes its information from the message before passing it to the layer above.

In OSI terminology, each layer deals with two kinds of messages. A *service data unit* is the amount of information whose identity is preserved from a transmitting layer to its receiving peer layer. A *protocol data unit* is the amount of information actually transmitted in one message to the peer. One service data unit can be transmitted in one or more protocol data units.

The lower four layers are concerned with the network, and the upper three layers are concerned with the applications using the network. Intermediate switching nodes, whose responsibilities include routing and storing messages sent between hosts, are composed of only the lowest three layers, as shown in Figure 1.8. The intermediate nodes that provide communication between hosts (along with their interconnections) form what is collectively called the *subnet*. The intermediate nodes are also called *relay nodes*. It is possible for host nodes to act as relay nodes too, but in this case, only the lower three layers of the network are involved in communication.

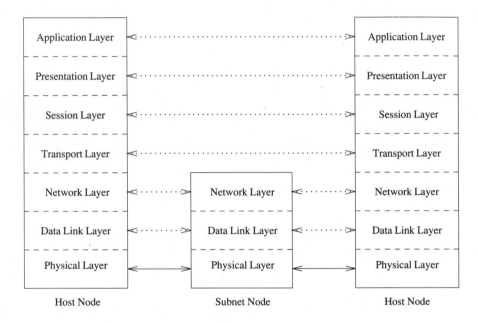

Fig. 1.8. Subnet Nodes in the OSI Model

The lowest layer in the OSI reference model is called the *physical layer*. Its job is to control the transmission of data in a format suitable for the transmission medium, such as electrical signals or pulses. The specifications for the physical layer include the mechanical and electrical characteristics.

The physical layer provides the data link layer with services primarily concerned with the transmission of physical service data units, usually some number of bits. The physical layer also provides the service of bit sequencing, ensuring that bits are delivered in the same order in which they were transmitted. If an error occurs, the physical layer detects the error and notifies the data link layer.

Some examples of physical layer standards are the International Telegraph & Telephone Consultative Committee's (CCITT) V-series interfaces (like V.22 bis and V.32), the Electronic Industry Association's (EIA) RS-232-C interface, and CCITT's X.21 interface. The IEEE standards for local area networks (802.3 for CSMA/CD networks, 802.4 for token bus networks, and 802.5 for token ring networks) include the specification of the physical layer for their respective media. They have been adopted by ISO as international standards.

The *data link layer* sits just above the physical layer. It is in charge of transmitting messages over the physical connection, detecting errors, and possibly trying to correct some types of errors. The IEEE has divided the data link layer into two sublayers: the Logical Link Control (LLC) and the Medium Access Control (MAC), as depicted in Figure 1.9.

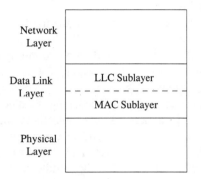

Fig. 1.9. LLC and MAC Sublayers

The MAC sublayer mediates access to the medium, encapsulating all knowledge of the medium, so that the LLC sublayer can ignore the issues of medium control. The LLC sublayer provides connectionless and connection-oriented interfaces for the network layer, independent of the type of medium. The connectionless service provides for communication over *logical data links*. The connection-oriented service provides for communication over *data link connections*. In both cases the link is the communication path between nodes; the nodes are not necessarily the original source or final destination.

The data link layer provides services such as delimiting the flow of bits from the physical layer (a process called *framing*), error notification, message sequencing, and flow control. Flow control allows the network layer to regulate the rate at which data link service data units (DLSDUs) are received. Flow control and message sequencing are only available with connection-oriented service.

ISO 8802-2 (adopted from IEEE's 802.2 standard) defines the LLC sublayer interface and services. ISO 8802-3 (IEEE 802.3), 8802-4 (IEEE 802.4), and 8802-5 (IEEE 802.5) include the MAC sublayer specifications for their respective transmission media.

The *network layer* is the topmost layer concerned with the subnet. Its job is to relay and route messages between nodes, in ways that are transparent to the upper layers. The network layer also handles addressing of nodes in the network and congestion control. Like the data link layer, the network layer supports both connectionless and connection-oriented modes of service.

Other services that the network layer can optionally provide with connection-oriented service are flow control, expedited data, resets, and receipt confirmation. Flow control allows the transport layer to stop transfer of data from the network layer. The flow control may or may not be propagated to the other end of the network connection. Expedited data service gives the transport layer a way to send important data out-of-band, at a higher priority than normal data transmission. Resets allow the transport layer to discard data queued by the network layer. Receipt-confirmation service allows the transport layer to verify that messages have been received successfully.

Messages sent to the network layer from the transport layer might undergo *segmenting* or *blocking* by the network layer. Segmenting is the process of splitting a message (network service data unit, NSDU) up into multiple segments (network protocol data units, NPDUs) prior to transmission. The inverse function of segmenting is called *reassembling*. Blocking is the process of packing multiple messages into a single segment. The inverse operation of blocking is called *unblocking*.

The ISO has divided the network layer into three sublayers (see Figure 1.10). The topmost sublayer, the subnet independent convergence protocol (SNICP), provides the mechanisms for routing packets and isolates the transport layer from the details of each underlying subnetwork. The middle sublayer, the subnet dependent convergence protocol (SNDCP), can be used to provide services missing in some subnetworks, so that the same services can be found on all subnetworks. The bottommost sublayer, the subnet access sublayer (SNAcP), contains the subnet-dependent services for data transfer and connection management.

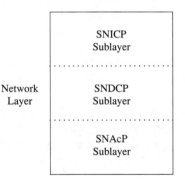

Fig. 1.10. Sublayers of the Network Layer

ISO 8348 defines the services of the network layer. ISO 8473 defines a connectionless network layer protocol (SNICP sublayer). CCITT's X.25 standard includes the specification of a network protocol (SNAcP sublayer) to be used to access public data networks. ISO 8878 defines the SNDCP sublayer functions needed to provide the services of an X.25 subnetwork over older X.25 subnetworks, which support fewer features. IP, the internetworking protocol used with TCP and UDP, is another example of a network layer protocol (SNICP sublayer).

The *transport layer* provides a network-independent message transfer facility. The transport layer is important because it is the lowest layer that provides an interface that is independent of the subnet. Both connectionless and connection-oriented service modes are available.

For connection-oriented service, flow control is provided from host to host. Reliable message delivery and end-to-end error detection and recovery are also provided. Besides the normal data-transfer service, the transport layer optionally supports an expedited data-transfer service.

The transport layer might use message segmenting and blocking. It might also use *concatenation*, which is similar to blocking, except that multiple transport protocol data units (TPDUs) are packed into a single NSDU. The opposite of concatenation is called *separation*. Transport connections can be *multiplexed* over a single network connection, mapped one-to-one with network connections, or a single transport connection can be *split* over multiple network connections, whichever is appropriate.

The transport layer service definition is given in ISO 8072. The transport protocol specifications can be found in ISO 8073. Five connection-oriented protocol classes are defined (TP0 through TP4), each providing more features than the last. Another example of a connection-oriented transport protocol is the Transmission Control Protocol (TCP), used in many UNIX systems. Examples of connectionless transport protocols include ISO 8602 and the Internet's User Datagram Protocol (UDP).

The *session layer* provides services to organize, synchronize, and regulate the exchange of data. These services include session connection establishment and release (both orderly and abortive), normal and expedited data transfer, exception reporting, interaction management, synchronization, and quarantine. The interaction management service allows presentation users to control whose turn it is to communicate. The interaction might be simplex, half-duplex, or full-duplex. The synchronization service allows the presentation layer to define and identify synchronization points during the session and reset the session connection to a state defined by a synchronization point. The quarantine service allows the sending presentation user to control when (and if) the data are available to its peer.

The session layer handles flow control between it and the transport layer. If a transport connection fails, the session layer can reestablish the transport connection so that the session connection can persist.

ISO 8326 provides the service definition for the session layer. ISO 8327 is the session layer protocol specification.

The *presentation layer* handles data syntax conversions. The local data representation, called the *abstract syntax*, may not match that used by the peer. Therefore, an agreed-upon *transfer syntax* (also called *concrete syntax*) is used during transmission. The sending presentation layer converts the application's data from the local syntax to the transfer syntax before sending it to the session layer. The receiving presentation layer converts the data from the transfer syntax to the local syntax before delivering it to the application layer.

The presentation layer provides the same services as the session layer, in addition to the negotiation and transformation of syntax. Transformation examples include data compression, encryption, and conversion between different data formats (from ASCII to EBCDIC, for example).

ISO 8822 defines the services provided by the presentation layer. ISO 8824 specifies a language for describing abstract syntaxes, commonly known as Abstract Syntax Notation One (ASN.1). ISO 8825 specifies how to describe data unambiguously; it is commonly known as the Basic Encoding Rules (BERs).

The *application layer* provides applications with access to the OSI environment. Services are partitioned into groups called *application service elements* (ASEs), each with its own set of standards. For example, the Association Control Service Element (ACSE) supports the establishment, maintenance, and termination of associations between applications. ISO 8649 provides the service definition, and ISO 8650 provides the protocol specification.

Another ASE is the Reliable Transfer Service Element (RTSE), which provides reliable data transfer between applications. ISO 9066-1 provides its service definition, and ISO 9066-2 provides its protocol specification. Other ASEs include message handling, virtual terminal service, file transfer, concurrency and recovery control, electronic mail service, directory service, and network management service.

Summary

We have presented a brief introduction to network characteristics and terminology. The OSI reference model has been discussed, and several network standards that embody the reference model have been mentioned. Throughout the rest of this book, we will refer back to various layers in the OSI reference model, since many of the networking interfaces in SVR4 were designed with the reference model in mind.

Bibliographic Notes

Tanenbaum [1989] provides a broad overview of networking, along with the discussion of protocols and, in some cases, theoretical analyses. Lathi [1983] discusses basic communication theory.

Comer [1991] describes the Internet protocols and architecture. Martin [1989] provides an overview of networking products and protocols.

For those readers who find poring through the OSI standards a daunting task, Black [1991] summarizes things nicely. Otherwise, OSI standards are available from the American National Standards Institute (ANSI).

2

UNIX Programming

This chapter will give a brief overview of the UNIX programming environment. Although examples from this chapter are used throughout the rest of the book, readers familiar with this topic can skip to the next chapter without loss of continuity. The material in this chapter is intended to make the examples in the remainder of the book easier to understand. A more thorough treatment of the subject can be found in many of the the books listed at the end of the chapter.

2.1 OVERVIEW

Figure 2.1 shows the architecture of the UNIX system. At the center is the *kernel*, the operating system core. It controls the computer's resources. *Drivers* are the parts of the operating system that control peripheral devices, such as terminals, printers, and disk drives. Although, strictly speaking, drivers are not part of the kernel proper, they are closely linked to the kernel and are considered part of the operating system. Drivers use the facilities provided by the kernel. In turn, the kernel relies on some drivers to provide vital services, such as access to devices used during system start-up. The terms "kernel" and "operating system" are often used interchangeably in the literature.

The operating system provides services to user applications through the *system call* interface. Each system call implements a basic service, for example input or output. Descriptions of each system call can be found in Section 2 of the *Programmer's Reference Manual*.

More elaborate functions are available in *library routines*, found in Section 3. These provide either enhanced versions of system calls, or facilities not found in system calls. An example of the former is the standard input/output (I/O) routines, which provide, among other things, buffering of data during input and output. An example of the latter is mathematical functions like `sqrt(3M)` and `sin(3M)`.

There are over 120 system calls in System V Release 4 (SVR4). There are even more library routines. We will not cover all the interfaces here. Instead, we shall

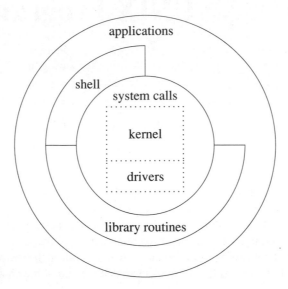

Fig. 2.1. UNIX System Architecture

give a brief overview of some of the more common ones, so that the rest of the examples in this book are more understandable. Some examples in later chapters will use functions introduced in this chapter.

The *shell* is a program that acts as the command interpreter for users. It provides a way for users to run programs and to interact more easily with the rest of the system. The shell sets up the environment in which users' programs are run. Three common shells are available: the System V shell (sh, a derivative of the Bourne shell), the C shell (csh), and the Korn shell (ksh, also a derivative of the Bourne shell).

To program effectively in the UNIX environment, it is necessary to understand a few basic concepts and the conventions that programs follow to interact in the environment.

2.2 CONCEPTS

The UNIX system is built around two fundamental concepts: *files* and *processes*. Most system calls and library routines deal with one or the other. Files provide storage for data and access to devices and special services. Processes provide the framework in which programs execute.

Processes

When a program runs in the UNIX system, it executes in the context of a *process*. A process consists of some state information, a scheduling handle, a stack, and the text (instructions) and data (initialized and uninitialized) of a program.

A process can create a copy of itself by *forking*. It can then overlay its executable image with that of another program by using the `exec` system call. The process that calls `fork(2)` is called the *parent*. The new process is called the *child*. Processes are uniquely identified in the system by their *process IDs*.

Each process has an identity associated with a user in the system. This is represented by a *user ID*. Furthermore, users can be grouped into different classes for the purposes of sharing files, so each process also has a *group ID*. Although a process only has one group ID in effect at any given time, it can optionally have other group IDs representing other groups to which it can belong. These are called its *supplementary* group IDs.

Besides the supplementary group IDs, each process has three other kinds of user and group IDs: real, effective, and saved-set. The *real* user and group IDs identify the owner of the process. Since processes are the means by which programs are executed, the real IDs identify the person who is running the program.

From time to time processes may need to acquire special privileges (to access files they do not own, for example). Processes do this through system calls that change the IDs [see `setuid(2)` and `setgid(2)`], or by executing programs with the *set-user-ID* or *set-group-ID* attribute enabled. In the latter case, the process will have its *effective* user or group ID changed to the corresponding ID that is associated with the owner of the file. The effective user and group IDs are used for permission checks in the operating system. They are initially equal to the real IDs when a user login session starts.

So that a set-ID program can change effective IDs back and forth between the real ID and the ID associated with the program file's owner, processes also have a *saved-set-user ID* and a *saved-set-group ID*. When executing a set-ID program, the saved-set ID of the process is set to the corresponding ID of the file's owner, so it contains the same value as the corresponding effective ID. Using `setuid`, a process can change its effective user ID to either its real user ID or its saved-set-user ID. Similarly, a process can change its effective group ID to either its real group ID or its saved-set-group ID using `setgid`.

If a program does not have a set-ID attribute enabled, the saved-set-ID of the process does not change. When the super-user executes `setuid` or `setgid`, all three IDs are changed.

When a process begins execution, it is placed in a *session* so it can be associated with other programs run from the same terminal. Processes are further grouped into *process groups* within a session for the purposes of signal delivery. The *foreground* process group is the set of processes that can read from and write to the user's terminal at will. These processes are sent signals from the terminal driver when the user types the interrupt or quit key.

Processes in background process groups have limited access to the terminal until they are brought into the foreground by the shell's *job control* commands. Job control is a feature that allows users to suspend and restart groups of commands at will. With a job control shell, processes running in the background cannot read from the terminal, but optionally can write to it. If a shell does not support job control, all processes in the session are in the same process group, and background processes can write to the terminal, but cannot read from it.

One process is designated as the *session leader*. It has the power to allocate a *controlling terminal* device from which signals will be sent. The controlling terminal is shared by all processes in the session and is usually the same device on which the user has logged in. The controlling terminal for a session is different from other terminal devices in that it has the ability to send signals to the foreground process group associated with it. Processes can access their controlling terminal by opening the special file /dev/tty.

Each process in the system keeps track of where it is in the file system. This location is known as the *current working directory*. It is used to resolve relative pathnames (described shortly). Each process also has a *root directory* that specifies the location from which absolute pathnames (also described shortly) are evaluated. Processes can change their locations in the file system through the use of the chdir system call. They can change their root directories with the chroot system call.

Files

Almost every object in the UNIX system can be accessed as a file. Each file has a type that defines what service it provides and how it can be used. Data and programs are stored in regular files. The lists of files in directories are stored in directory files. Interprocess communication facilities are available through *pipe special* files. Devices can be accessed via *character special* files and *block special* files. Even processes can be accessed through files.

Files are stored in *file systems*. Each file system has a type that determines the services provided. For example, S5 is a file system type that provides access to files stored in the traditional System V format. Multiple file systems are combined to form a tree structure in the UNIX system. The entire tree is often referred to as the "file system," with ambiguity removed by the surrounding context.

The semantics of each file are determined by the file's type and the underlying file system type that contains it. Usually the system does not place structure on the content of most regular files. They are treated as sequences of bytes. Programs using the files usually place the structure, if any, on the data. One notable exception to this is executable files, whose format must be understood by the operating system to enable the address space of a process to be overlaid by the contents of the executable file.

Directories are special files that contain information about other files. Directory files have a format defined by the file system. The format includes the file's name and a number that uniquely identifies the file in the file system containing it. Historically, this number has been called the *inode number*. It maps to an *inode* containing file attributes, such as file size, modification time, and the location of the file data.

Files have permissions that determine who may read, write, or execute them. For directory files, the execute permissions are used to determine who can search the directory, since directory files cannot be executed. Files also have ownership that qualifies these permissions. Each file is associated with a user ID and a group ID in the system. These specify the individual owner and the group owner of the file, resulting in three ownership categories: user, group, and everyone else in the world.

Access to a file is obtained by opening it. Data can then be read or written. Access to a file is relinquished by closing it. When a program ends, any files it had open are automatically closed by the system.

Ordinarily, nothing stops two or more processes from accessing the same file at the same time, potentially overwriting each other's data. System V supports file and record locking to ensure the consistency of files that are manipulated by multiple processes simultaneously. Two forms are available: advisory and mandatory. With advisory file and record locking, processes cooperate to serialize access to sections of a file. Arbitrary segments of a file can be locked, or the entire file can be locked.

The locks are reader–writer locks: only one writer is allowed access to a segment at one time, but multiple readers can access the same segment at the same time. Readers block out writers, and writers block out readers and other writers.

Advisory locking relies on processes to follow the rules, locking before reading or writing the file. If a process does not follow the advisory record-locking rules, nothing prevents it from accessing parts of a file that are locked by others. This is why the method is called ''advisory.''

Mandatory file and record locking, on the other hand, relies on enforcement from the operating system. A mode bit associated with a file can be set to enable mandatory locking. When enabled, selected system calls can fail or block when they try to access locked segments of the file.

Filenames and Namespaces

Each file has a filename. It is the handle by which programs gain access to the file. The file system namespace is hierarchical: it forms a tree starting at the *root* directory, named / (forward slash). The forward slash is also used to separate filenames in a *pathname*.

A pathname is the concatenation of filenames that represent a given file. All but the last filename must represent a directory. The pathname can be either absolute, starting from the root, or relative, starting from the current directory. Figure 2.2 shows an example of part of the file system tree. The pathname /usr/include/stdio.h is an example of an absolute pathname. If our current working directory was /usr, we could also access the same file via the relative pathname include/stdio.h.

Besides /, there are two other reserved filenames. The name . (dot) represents the current directory. The name .. (dot-dot) represents the parent directory in the hierarchy. The pathname include/stdio.h is equivalent to the pathname ./include/stdio.h since all relative pathnames are interpreted starting at the current directory. If our current directory were instead /usr/include/sys, we

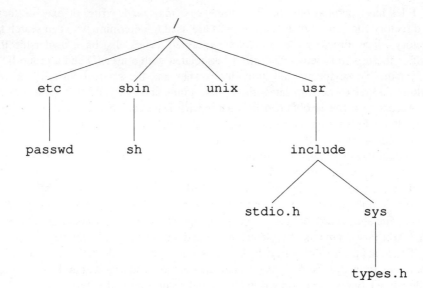

Fig. 2.2. File System Hierarchy

could use the relative pathname `../stdio.h` to refer to the same file. At the root, dot and dot-dot refer to the same file — the root. In other words, the root's parent is the root itself.

Multiple names in the file system can refer to the same file. Each name accounts for an additional reference to the file's *link count*. These aliases are called "hard" links, to distinguish them from symbolic links.

Symbolic links provide another way to create aliases for files. They are a special file type that results in a pathname substitution occurring when they are evaluated. In contrast, pathname evaluation of hard links occurs when they are made. Hard links cannot span multiple file systems, but symbolic links can.

There are several advantages to using the file system namespace to access objects and services. We can often use existing tools to manipulate the objects and services since they appear as files. Also, the need for special-purpose system calls is removed: operations on the objects and services are implemented as file system operations. For example, the `/proc` file system provides access to active process images through the file system interface. It has made `ptrace(2)` obsolete and has removed the need for `ps(1)` to read the kernel's memory image to search for process information.

2.3 CONVENTIONS

As with any system, programs must follow several conventions to interact with the UNIX environment.

Program Interface

Most UNIX programs are written in a dialect of the C programming language, such as K&R C or ANSI C, although this is by no means the only programming language available. When C programs are run, transfer of control passes to the function named `main`. This function has two optional arguments:

```
main(int argc, char *argv[])
{
}
```

The first argument, `argc`, is the number of arguments to the program, including the name of the program itself. `argv` is an array of pointers to character strings composing the program's name and command-line arguments. By convention, `argv[0]` contains a pointer to the program name.

Most UNIX systems also provide a third argument to `main` that describes the shell environment at the time the program is run. This third argument, however, is not defined by the ANSI C standard, and POSIX specifies that the environment be accessible through the global symbol `environ`, instead. `environ` is the beginning of an array of pointers to character strings describing the shell environment. The strings are in the format of "parameter=value."

File Descriptors

Files are accessed using small, nonnegative integers, numbered starting at 0, called *file descriptors*. Initially there are three valid file descriptors when a program starts. File descriptor 0 is open to the *standard input*, file descriptor 1 is open to the *standard output*, and file descriptor 2 is open to the *standard error*. These are the default places to and from which a program can perform I/O. Data can be read from the standard input, and written to the standard output. Error messages can be directed to the standard error. All three are usually associated with the user's terminal unless redirected from the shell.

Each process is limited in the number of file descriptors it can use at one time. The limit can be obtained using the `getrlimit` system call and changed (up to a maximum limit) with the `setrlimit` system call. The default values for the limits are configurable on a per-system basis.

Exit Values

When a program exits, the process executing it is destroyed. Notification of the process's death is sent to the parent process that created it. The exit status, passed to `exit(2)`, indicates the disposition of the process. By convention, zero means that the program succeeded, and a nonzero value indicates that the program ran into an error and might not have been able to accomplish its task.

Header Files

Header files contain common function declarations, macro definitions, and structure templates needed when using system calls and libraries. The default location where they can be found is /usr/include. Alternate header file directories can be specified with the −I option to the C compiler.

Table 2.1 summarizes the purpose of some commonly used header files.

Table 2.1. Common Header Files

Header File	Description
<ctype.h>	Character-processing macros.
<errno.h>	Error numbers and variables.
<fcntl.h>	open flags and fcntl definitions.
<limits.h>	System limits.
<math.h>	Mathematical function declarations.
<memory.h>	Byte-processing function declarations.
<signal.h>	Signal numbers and function declarations.
<stdio.h>	Standard I/O library declarations.
<stdlib.h>	General utility declarations and macros.
<string.h>	Character-string management function declarations.
<time.h>	Time-handling declarations.
<unistd.h>	POSIX declarations and macros.
<sys/stat.h>	File attribute declarations and macros.
<sys/types.h>	System typedefs.

2.4 WRITING PROGRAMS

UNIX programs can be partitioned into two broad categories: *user commands* and *daemons*. User commands are the programs that users run from their shells. Some user commands just perform a single task and then exit, while others are interactive in nature, requiring further input from the user. cc(1), ls(1), and vi(1) are examples of user commands.

Users have the choice of running commands in the *foreground* or *background*. The shell will wait for commands that are run in the foreground to complete. However, commands that are run in the background will execute asynchronously to the user's shell (i.e., the shell will not wait for them to complete).

Daemons are actually a special type of command not associated with a particular user's login session. Thus, daemons cannot be interactive. They run in the background, invoked either as a side effect of a user command, or by a system process, so that their execution is usually invisible to the user.

For example, the cron(1M) daemon provides a batch scheduling facility by allowing users to register commands to be run at specified times. listen(1M) is a general-purpose network daemon capable of relieving server applications from the details of transport-level connection establishment.

Compiling Programs

To create an executable image, a program's C source file has to be compiled. The simplest form

```
cc prog.c
```

will create a file called a.out in the current directory. The compiler will create an object file from the source file, and then invoke the link editor [ld(1)] to link the object file with the necessary startup glue to create an executable image. We can change the name of the executable image using mv(1), or we can just use the −o option to tell the compiler to tell the link editor the desired name, as in

```
cc -o prog prog.c
```

The compiler is smart enough to tell the link editor to link the executable with the C library, if needed. Any other libraries must be specified with the −l flag. For example, to include the math library, we would use

```
cc -o prog prog.c -lm
```

Like the −o option, the −l flag is passed on to the link editor. Note that any libraries to be linked with the program must appear after the source files. The order in which files are link-edited is the order in which they appear on the command line. The link editor knows to include a particular library routine by noticing its use in the object files that it has previously processed. If the libraries were specified before the source or object files, the link editor would not have had a chance to identify any library routines to include when processing the libraries.

Argument Processing

The first program we will look at will illustrate some of the program conventions discussed earlier.

Example 2.4.1. The following simple program prints the arguments passed to it from the command line. The arguments are printed on the standard output, usually attached to the user's terminal.

```c
/*
 * printargs.c, version 1.
 */
#include <stdlib.h>
#include <stdio.h>

void
main(int argc, char *argv[])
{
    int i;

    /*
     * Print the number of arguments followed by each
```

```
         * argument on a separate line.
         */
        printf("argc = %d\n", argc);
        for (i = 0; i < argc; i++)
            printf("argv[%d] = %s\n", i, argv[i]);
        exit(0);
}
```

There are several things we can learn by running the program. (Whenever interactive sessions are displayed throughout the book, we use a boldface constant-width font for user input to distinguish it from text printed by the computer.)

```
$ ./printargs
argc = 1
argv[0] = ./printargs
$ pwd
/tmp
$ /tmp/printargs
argc = 1
argv[0] = /tmp/printargs
$ /tmp/printargs abc
argc = 2
argv[0] = /tmp/printargs
argv[1] = abc
$ printargs abc def
argc = 3
argv[0] = printargs
argv[1] = abc
argv[2] = def
$ printargs "abc def"
argc = 2
argv[0] = printargs
argv[1] = abc def
$
```

Note that the first argument includes the entire pathname of the command, in the same format as it was invoked. If we use a relative pathname, the command's pathname is passed to the program as a relative pathname. If we use an absolute pathname, the command's pathname is passed to the program as an absolute pathname.

The next thing to note is that the arguments typed are interpreted according to the shell's conventions for argument handling and quoting. Command arguments are separated by white space, except strings included in quotes are treated as one argument.

The program prints the number of arguments, followed by the arguments themselves, on the standard output using printf(3S). printf is a function in the standard I/O library that takes a format string and optional arguments, processes the arguments according to the format, and writes the result to the file descriptor associated with the standard output. All programs that use the standard I/O library should include <stdio.h>. The function prototype for printf is

```
#include <stdio.h>

int printf(const char *format, .../* args */);
```

The format string contains characters to be copied to the standard output, special escape sequences that represent cursor controls, such as \b for backspace and \n for newline, and conversion specifications that determine how the optional arguments will be printed. Conversion specifications begin with the percent sign (%). Commonly used conversion specifications are ''d'' for decimal integers, ''o'' for octal integers, ''x'' for hexadecimal integers, ''f'' for floating-point numbers, ''c'' for single characters, and ''s'' for character strings.

printf returns the number of characters printed, or −1 on error. Most callers ignore the return value.

We use exit(2) to terminate the program.

```
#include <stdlib.h>

void exit(int status);
```

The argument status is used to indicate the result of the program's execution: success or failure. On a successful exit, we return 0 to the shell as the exit value. On error, we return a nonzero value (1). In the next example, we will see how users can check the exit status of the commands they run.

Before terminating the program, exit will attempt to print any data buffered for writing by prior calls to standard I/O functions.   □

In the previous example, we could have changed main to return an integer and replaced the call to exit with a return statement. Returning from the main procedure of a program will cause the program to exit, using the return value as the exit status. If no return value is specified, the exit status is indeterminate.

The ability to register functions to be called before exiting is provided through atexit(3C). Calling _exit instead of exit will bypass their execution. Because of this, and because signals can terminate a program, functions registered with atexit cannot be depended upon to execute before program termination.

By using _exit, we also bypass the writing out of any buffered data previously written using the standard I/O library. The function prototype for _exit is similar to the one for exit:

```
#include <unistd.h>

void _exit(int status);
```

In the real world, most programs need to include some sort of error checking. Error messages are printed on the standard error instead of the standard output, allowing error messages to be separated from a program's normal output. This is most useful when the standard output of a program is piped to another command because, unless redirected, error messages will still appear on the user's screen. In the next example, we will add some simple error handling to our program.

Example 2.4.2. To illustrate simple error handling, we will change Example 2.4.1, making it an error case if the command is invoked without any arguments.

```c
/*
 * printargs.c, version 2.
 */
#include <stdlib.h>
#include <stdio.h>
#include <string.h>

void
main(int argc, char *argv[])
{
    int i;
    char *cmd;

    /*
     * Find the last occurrence of "/" in the command
     * name. If "/" does not appear in the name, just
     * set cmd to the beginning of the name.  Otherwise,
     * set cmd to point one character past the "/".
     */
    if ((cmd = strrchr(argv[0], '/')) == NULL)
        cmd = argv[0];
    else
        cmd++;

    /*
     * Validate the number of command-line arguments.
     */
    if (argc == 1) {
        fprintf(stderr, "usage: %s args...\n", cmd);
        exit(1);
    }

    /*
     * Print the number of arguments followed by each
     * argument on a separate line.
     */
    printf("argc = %d\n", argc);
    for (i = 0; i < argc; i++)
        printf("argv[%d] = %s\n", i, argv[i]);
    exit(0);
}
```

Sample output obtained by running the program is shown below.

```
$ ./printargs
usage: printargs args...
$ pwd
/tmp
$ /tmp/printargs
usage: printargs args...
$ /tmp/printargs abc def
argc = 3
```

```
argv[0] = /tmp/printargs
argv[1] = abc
argv[2] = def
$ printargs abc def
argc = 3
argv[0] = printargs
argv[1] = abc
argv[2] = def
$
```

Since commands can be grouped in shell scripts or pipelines, it is often convenient to include the command name in the error message. When a command is invoked with the wrong arguments, a helpful error message will include a terse summary of the proper usage. We could hard-code the name of the command in the error messages, but a more flexible option is to use the command name found in argv[0]. Then, if someone creates a hard link to the program, the error message will contain the name of the command as it was invoked, not some fixed, seemingly unrelated name.

Because the first argument contains the entire pathname of the command, we need to strip everything but the last component of the pathname (also called the *basename*). This can be done by using strrchr(3C).

```
#include <string.h>

char *strrchr(const char *s, int c);
```

Given a character and a pointer to a string, strrchr will return a pointer to the last occurrence of the character in the string, or NULL if the character is not contained in the string. In the example, we set cmd to point to the last forward slash in the command name. If there is no such character, then the caller is in the same directory as the command, has "." in the search path, and invoked the command using only the command name. In this case we set cmd to point to the first argument, argv[0]. Otherwise, we set cmd to point to the character after the last slash that appears in argv[0].

If this version of the command is invoked without arguments, we write a message to the standard error using fprintf(3S).

```
#include <stdio.h>

int fprintf(FILE *fp, const char *format, .../* args */);
```

fprintf is similar to printf, but the caller must specify the file stream identifier associated with the location (file descriptor) to which the output is to be written. printf(...) is equivalent to fprintf(stdout, ...).

After we verify that there are indeed arguments to be printed, we print the number of arguments, followed by the arguments themselves, on the standard output, just as in the original version of the command.

On success, we return 0 to the shell for the exit value. On error, we return a nonzero value (1). Users can check the results of their program execution through shell parameters as follows:

```
$ printargs
usage: printargs args...
$ echo $?
1
$ printargs abc
argc = 2
argv[0] = printargs
argv[1] = abc
$ echo $?
0
$
```

The return values can be used to chain commands together, conditionally executing successive commands on success or failure, as in

```
$ printargs && echo command succeeded
usage: printargs args...
$ printargs || echo command failed
usage: printargs args...
command failed
$ printargs abc && echo command succeeded
argc = 2
argv[0] = printargs
argv[1] = abc
command succeeded
$ printargs abc || echo command failed
argc = 2
argv[0] = printargs
argv[1] = abc
$
```

□

The shell environment variables are available as a means of conveying per-user configuration information to programs. They are a side-door communications path between users and programs. The next example illustrates the format of environment variables and how programs can access them.

Example 2.4.3.

```
/*
 * printenv.c
 */
#include <stdlib.h>
#include <stdio.h>

extern char **environ;

void
main()
{
    int i;

    /*
     * Print the number of arguments followed by each
```

```
    * environment variable on a separate line.
    */
   for (i = 0; environ[i]; i++)
       printf("%s\n", environ[i]);
   exit(0);
}
```

Nothing new is presented in this example. We just print all the environment variable strings. The list is terminated by a NULL pointer. When run, the program produces output similar to

```
$ ./printenv
EDITOR=vi
HOME=/home/sar
HZ=100
LOGNAME=sar
MAIL=/usr/mail/sar
PAGER=pg
PATH=/home/sar/bin:/usr/bin:/usr/ucb
PS1=$
PS2=>
SHELL=/sbin/sh
TERM=630
TZ=EST5EDT
$                                                                       □
```

As an alternative to environ, C programs can use getenv(3C) to access shell environment variables. Given the name of an environment variable, getenv will return a pointer to the value of the variable, if it exists. This interface is often more convenient than explicitly searching the environment array.

Common environment variables that applications can expect to find are listed in environ(5). Others are listed on the manual page to which they pertain. For example, the environment variables used by the shell are listed in sh(1).

Conventions used for command argument formats are specified in intro(1). They should be followed so that users can be presented with a consistent interface to all commands. This allows users to expect certain behavior from commands when presented with the same input. The getopt(3C) routine extends these conventions further. For example, one convention is to use the option -? to force a command to print its usage statement.

One other useful convention supported by getopt is the use of "--" to indicate the end of the options. See what happens when we create a file whose name begins with a dash.

```
$ cd /var/tmp
$ ls -l
total 0
$ >-g      # create a file named "-g"
$ ls -l
total 0
-rw-r-----   1 sar        unixdev       0 Nov 30 21:26 -g
$ rm -g
```

```
rm: illegal option -- g
usage: rm [-fir] file ...
$ rm *
rm: illegal option -- g
usage: rm [-fir] file ...
$ rm -- -g
$ ls -l
total 0
$
```

We cannot easily remove the file. There are other ways of removing it, but the simplest is to use −− to separate the command options from the filenames.

Besides providing a greater degree of consistency, the getopt function simplifies the task of processing command arguments.

```
#include <stdlib.h>
#include <stdio.h>

int getopt(int argc, char *const *argv, const char *opts);

extern char *optarg;
extern int optind, opterr, optopt;
```

The parameters argc and argv are the same ones passed to main. The idiom char *const * means that argv is a pointer to an array of constant character strings, not that argv is itself constant. The opts parameter points to a character string containing all the option letters the command supports. Each option that has a corresponding argument is followed by a colon (:) in the string.

getopt will return a character corresponding to one of the characters in opts, or EOF when all the options have been processed. When an option letter is returned that has a corresponding argument, optarg will point to that argument. getopt sets optind to the index of the next argument in argv to be processed. The opterr flag controls whether getopt prints an error message when either an invalid option letter is specified or an argument is missing. Applications that want to suppress the error message can set opterr to zero. On error, optopt will contain the character of the option that caused the error.

Example 2.4.4. The following program strips nonprintable characters from text files. It can be used to remove control characters from files. It exhibits use of getopt to handle options in a standard way.

The program accepts input from its standard input or from multiple files specified on the command line. It supports the convention of using ''−'' as an alias for the standard input [see intro(1)]. Output is directed to the standard output.

Two options are available: −x <char> will exclude the specified character from being stripped. The character should be specified as a decimal integer corresponding to the ASCII value for the character. The second option, −v, places the command in verbose mode, causing a message to be printed to the standard error summarizing the number of characters cleaned. (This prevents the summary from being mixed up with the normal output.)

```
/*
 * clean.c
 */
#include <stdio.h>
#include <ctype.h>
#include <string.h>
#include <errno.h>
#include <stdlib.h>

int clean(FILE *, int);

void
main(int argc, char *argv[])
{
    int c, i, err, verbose, xchar;
    FILE *fp;
    char *fname;

    opterr = err = verbose = 0;
    xchar = EOF;

    /*
     * Process command-line options.
     */
    while ((c = getopt(argc, argv, "vx:")) != EOF) {
        switch(c) {
        case 'v':
            /*
             * Use verbose mode.
             */
            verbose++;
            break;

        case 'x':
            /*
             * Don't strip the specified character.
             * Only one exception is allowed.
             */
            if (xchar != EOF) {
                err++;
                break;
            }
            xchar = atoi(optarg);
            if ((xchar > 255) || (xchar < 0)) {
                fprintf(stderr, "-x value out of range\n");
                exit(1);
            }
            break;

        default:
            /*
             * All other options constitute an error.
             */
            err++;
```

```
        }
    }
    if (err) {
        fprintf(stderr,
            "usage: clean [-v] [-x char] [files]\n");
        exit(1);
    }

    /*
     * If no files were specified on the command line,
     * use stdin.
     */
    if (optind == argc) {
        c = clean(stdin, xchar);
        if (verbose)
            fprintf(stderr, "stdin: %d chars cleaned\n", c);
        exit(0);
    }

    /*
     * Strip each file given on the command line.
     */
    for (i = optind; i < argc; i++) {
        /*
         * "-" is a special alias for stdin.
         */
        if ((argv[i][0] == '-') && (argv[i][1] == '\0')) {
            fp = stdin;
            fname = "stdin";
        } else {
            fname = argv[i];
            fp = fopen(fname, "r");
            if (fp == NULL) {
                fprintf(stderr, "Cannot open %s: %s\n",
                    fname, strerror(errno));
                err++;
                continue;
            }
        }
        c = clean(fp, xchar);
        if (verbose)
            fprintf(stderr, "%s: %d chars cleaned\n",
                fname, c);

        /*
         * Don't close stdin -- we might need it again.
         */
        if (fp != stdin)
            fclose(fp);
    }
    exit(err);
}
```

We start out by disabling error messages from getopt by setting opterr to zero. After initializing the error and verbose state variables to zero, we set the extra character variable (xchar) to EOF, an invalid value for a character. Then we call getopt until all options are processed. Since the −v option does not require an argument, there is no colon following it in the options string.

If the user specifies the −v flag, getopt will return v, and we increment the verbose flag. If the user specifies the −x flag, we make sure that the user has not already used the flag on the command line, since we only support prevention of one extra character from being stripped. Then we call atoi (3C) [see strtol (3C)] to convert the argument from a string to an integer.

```
#include <stdlib.h>

int atoi(const char *s);
```

The return value is the decimal equivalent of the number represented by the string s. Conversion stops at the point where the first nondecimal character is found. This does not provide the error checking on the argument that one may need, but in this example we do not care. If we invoked the command with the arguments −x 2a, then we would pass the string 2a to atoi, which would return the value 2. After calling atoi, we make sure the character value is within bounds. If it is not, we print an error message on the standard error and exit.

Any other return value from getopt is treated as an error, so we increment the error flag. When we are done processing the options, if the error flag is nonzero, we print a usage message on the standard error and exit. Otherwise, if no filename arguments are specified on the command line, optind will be equal to argc, and we process the standard input. If verbose mode is enabled, we print the number of characters cleaned, returned to us from the function clean (described shortly). Then we exit with a successful exit status.

If optind is not equal to argc, the user has specified filenames on the command line. We process each one in order. We first check the filename to see if it matches the alias "−", representing the standard input. If so, we set fp to stdin, the file pointer for the standard input. All file stream identifiers, here called file pointers to distinguish them from file descriptors, are of type FILE * (defined in <stdio.h>).

If a filename is used, we call fopen (3S) to get a file pointer for it.

```
#include <stdio.h>

FILE *fopen(const char *fname, const char *type);
```

fname is the name of the file to be opened, and type is a string indicating how the file pointer will be used. Table 2.2 summarizes the possible values for type. The "b" in the string enables the caller to differentiate between text and binary files, but in UNIX there is no difference as far as the operating system is concerned. This capability is provided for portability with non-UNIX systems that support the standard I/O library.

On success, fopen returns a file pointer. On failure, it returns NULL. If we cannot open the specified file, we print an error message on the standard error and

Table 2.2. Possible Values for `type` String

String	Description
r or rb	Open for reading.
w or wb	Open for writing. If file exists, truncate to zero length, else create it.
a or ab	Open for append (write at EOF). If file does not exist, create it.
r+, rb+, or r+b	Open for update (reading and writing).
w+, wb+, or w+b	Open for update. If file exists, truncate to zero length, else create it.
a+, ab+, or a+b	Open for update at EOF. If file does not exist, create it.

continue processing other files. The function `strerror(3C)` will return a string that describes an error number passed to it.

```
#include <string.h>

char *strerror(int errnum);
```

The error number we pass to it is contained in `errno`, defined in `<errno.h>`. The convention is for any system call or library routine to set `errno` to the number of an error describing the reason for failure before returning a failure indication. `errno` is not reset to zero in system calls or library routines, so applications should be careful to clear it if needed. Otherwise it might contain a value from a previously ignored failure.

After opening the file, we process it and, if the file pointer is not `stdin`, we close it before continuing on to the next file. The synopsis for `fclose(3S)` is

```
#include <stdio.h>

int fclose(FILE *fp);
```

`fp` is the file pointer to be closed. Before closing, `fclose` will force any written data that have been buffered by the standard I/O library to be written out to the underlying file. On success, `fclose` returns 0; on error, it returns EOF. Because `fclose` actually may write data, applications using the standard I/O library to write files should use `ferror(3S)` to check if the write was successful if `fclose` returns EOF.

When all the files have been processed, we exit with a status value set to `err`, which will be zero if no errors were encountered, or otherwise the number of files we could not open. The function used to strip the unprintable characters follows:

```
int
clean(FILE *fp, int xchar)
{
    int c, np;
```

```
            np = 0;
            while ((c = getc(fp)) != EOF)
                if (isprint(c) || (c == '\n') || (c == '\t')
                  || (c == xchar))
                    putchar(c);
                else
                    np++;
            return(np);
}
```

We use np to count the number of characters not printed. The function getc(3S) returns one character from the file.

```
            #include <stdio.h>

            int getc(FILE *fp);
```

getc will return EOF when no more characters are available from the file. Because the standard I/O library does buffering, calls to read or write one character are more efficient than if the system calls had been used. The library tries to read and write in larger units.

We use isprint(3C) to determine if the character is printable [see ctype(3C)].

```
            #include <ctype.h>

            int isprint(int c);
```

If the character passed in c is printable, a nonzero value is returned. Zero is returned if the character is not printable.

We also treat newline (\n) and tab (\t) as printable. If the character returned from getc matches the character specified with the −x option, then we treat it as printable, as well. Recall that we initialized xchar to EOF, so if the −x option was not used, the value of xchar will still be EOF. Since we never execute the if statement when getc returns EOF, the test (c == xchar) is safe; it will never be true if xchar equals EOF.

Any printable character is printed on the standard output using putchar(3S) [see putc(3S)].

```
            #include <stdio.h>

            int putchar(int c);
```

c contains the character to be written. On success, putchar returns the character written; on failure, EOF is returned. putchar(c) is a macro for putc(c, stdout). Similarly, getchar() is a macro for getc(stdout).

After processing all the characters in the file, clean returns the number of characters not printed.   □

Error Handling

Most robust programs contain a considerable amount of error checking and reporting. To decrease the amount of editing and simplify the programming process, programmers often use their own error-reporting functions. Here we provide two that will be used in the examples throughout the rest of this book.

The C library provides one function, `perror(3C)`, that prints a user-supplied string on the standard error stream, followed by a description of the error based on the value of `errno`. `perror` is useful, but it is limited because it only takes one argument. If the string is made up of several components, the caller is forced to build the string before calling `perror`, as in

```
char errbuf[256];

sprintf(errbuf, "%s: cannot open %s", argv[0], filename);
perror(errbuf);
```

`sprintf` is like `fprintf`, but instead of the string being copied to a file stream, the string is copied to a memory location (`errbuf` in the example above). One other annoying thing about `perror` is if it is called when `errno` is zero, the string `: Error 0` is printed after the caller's message.

Example 2.4.5. This example illustrates a simple error-handling facility. Two public routines are provided: one for nonfatal error reporting and one for fatal error reporting.

The functions provide for a variable number of arguments that can be of different types [see `stdarg(5)`]. The definitions supporting this facility can be found in `<stdarg.h>`. The type `va_list` is used to represent the list of arguments. An argument of this type is initialized with the `va_start` macro. Individual arguments are accessed using the `va_arg` macro. Before returning from a function that uses variable arguments, `va_end` should be called to clean up anything that `va_start` might have left behind.

```
#include <stdio.h>
#include <string.h>
#include <stdarg.h>
#include <stdlib.h>
#include <errno.h>

static void _cmnerr(const char *, va_list);

void
error(const char *fmt, ...)
{
       va_list ap;

       va_start(ap, fmt);
       _cmnerr(fmt, ap);
       va_end(ap);
}
```

```
static void
_cmnerr(const char *fmt, va_list ap)
{
    int err;

    /*
     * Save the value of errno just in case one of the
     * functions we call changes it.
     */
    err = errno;

    /*
     * Print the caller's message, the system error
     * message if an error has occurred, and a newline.
     */
    vfprintf(stderr, fmt, ap);
    if (err != 0)
        fprintf(stderr, ": %s", strerror(err));
    putc('\n', stderr);
}
```

The `error` function is just a wrapper that calls `_cmnerr` to do the real work. The arguments to `error` are a format string similar to that supported by `printf(3S)` and any arguments to be printed according to the format.

In `_cmnerr`, we save the value of `errno`, in case any function we use changes `errno` before we call `strerror`. We use `vfprintf(3S)` [see `vprintf(3S)`] to print the error message on the standard error.

```
#include <stdio.h>
#include <stdarg.h>

int vfprintf(FILE *fp, const char *format, va_list ap);
```

`vfprintf` is like `fprintf`, except that `vfprintf` takes a `va_list` argument describing the variable number of arguments instead of the arguments themselves.

After the caller's message is printed, if our routine was entered with `errno` set, we print a colon and a space, followed by the error message corresponding to the error number, on the standard error. In either case, we print a newline at the end of the message using `putc`.

The next function is used for fatal errors. It is an exact copy of `error`, with the addition of a call to `exit` at the end.

```
void
fatal(const char *fmt, ...)
{
    va_list ap;

    va_start(ap, fmt);
    _cmnerr(fmt, ap);
    va_end(ap);
    exit(1);
}
```

□

Low-Level I/O

So far, all of the I/O we have seen has been through library routines. But applications can use the lower-level system calls instead, if the added functionality and portability of the library routines are not needed.

To gain access to a file, we use open(2).

```
#include <sys/types.h>
#include <sys/stat.h>
#include <fcntl.h>

int open(const char *path, int oflag, .../* mode_t mode */);
```

path points to the pathname of the file to be opened; oflag specifies how we want to access the file; and mode, used only during file creation, contains the file permissions to be given to the new file. The open flags must contain one of the following flags:

O_RDONLY	Open file for reading only
O_WRONLY	Open file for writing only
O_RDWR	Open file for both reading and writing

In addition, the open flags can contain any of the following flags, logically ORed with the previous ones:

O_APPEND	All writes occur at end of file
O_NDELAY	Old-style ''nodelay'' mode (System V)
O_NONBLOCK	New-style ''nonblocking'' mode (POSIX)
O_SYNC	Make all writes synchronous
O_CREAT	If the file does not exist, create it
O_EXCL	With O_CREAT, fail if the file exists
O_TRUNC	Truncate the file to zero length
O_NOCTTY	Do not allocate a controlling terminal

For each open file, the system maintains the location at which the next I/O operation will occur. The O_APPEND flag guarantees that all writes to the file will occur at the end of the file. This is used to prevent data loss when multiple processes are writing to the same file at the same time.

The O_NDELAY and O_NONBLOCK flags change the behavior of I/O-related system calls by causing them to return instead of blocking. In some cases the O_NDELAY semantics are ambiguous; applications should use O_NONBLOCK for clarity and portability. For devices, open can block, at the discretion of the driver, until the device is ready (for terminal drivers this usually means when carrier is present). If either O_NDELAY or O_NONBLOCK is used, then open will return without waiting for the device to become ready (again, at the discretion of the driver).

The O_SYNC flag, when used with a regular file, will cause all writes to wait for the data to be written to disk before returning. This can be used by applications that need to guarantee the integrity of their file contents and can withstand the performance degradation inherent in synchronous I/O.

Normally open is used to gain access to an existing file, but applications can also use it to create a file if it does not already exist. The O_CREAT flag is used for this purpose. The optional third parameter (mode) should be set to the bitmask of flags that represent the desired file permissions as follows:

S_IRUSR	Individual owner read permission
O_IWUSR	Individual owner write permission
S_IXUSR	Individual owner execute permission
S_IRGRP	Group owner read permission
S_IWGRP	Group owner write permission
S_IXGRP	Group owner execute permission
S_IROTH	Others read permission
S_IWOTH	Others write permission
S_IXOTH	Others execute permission
S_ISUID	Set user ID on execution
S_ISGID	Set group ID on execution
S_ISVTX	Save text image after execution
S_ENFMT	Enable mandatory file and record locking

Note that the permissions of the newly created file may not match those as specified by the caller because the file creation mask of the process might restrict the permissions further. (The file creation mask is discussed at the end of the chapter.)

When a file is created, the individual owner of the file is set to the effective user ID of the process. Similarly, the group owner is set to the process's effective group ID. If, however, the set-group-ID bit is on for the directory containing the file, the group owner of the file is inherited from the group owner of the directory.

The O_CREAT flag can be combined with the O_EXCL flag to prevent the open from succeeding if the file already exists. This is useful when files are used as synchronization mechanisms between multiple processes. open with O_EXCL | O_CREAT provides a kind of atomic test-and-set: if the file already exists, open fails; otherwise, the file is created, analogous to acquiring a lock. For devices, O_EXCL might be interpreted by the driver in an implementation-dependent manner. This usually translates to the driver failing the open if the device is already in use, if the driver supports such a facility.

The O_NOCTTY flag can be used to prevent controlling terminal allocation when opening a terminal device. In System V, whenever a session leader without a controlling terminal opens a terminal device that is not already allocated as a controlling terminal to another session, that terminal is allocated as the controlling terminal for the process's session.

The O_TRUNC flag can be used to truncate regular files to zero bytes when they are opened. On success, open returns a file descriptor for the file. On failure, −1 is returned.

Once a file is opened for reading, we can use read(2) to retrieve data from the file.

```
#include <sys/types.h>
#include <unistd.h>

ssize_t read(int fd, void *buf, size_t nbyte);
```

The file descriptor, `fd`, is used as a handle to identify the file. The data are copied to contiguous memory locations starting at the address specified by `buf`. The number of bytes to copy is given by `nbyte`. On success, `read` will return the number of bytes read, or −1 on error. It is possible for `read` to return fewer bytes than requested. This can happen, for instance, if the caller asks for more bytes than are currently available in the file.

By convention, if `read` returns zero, then the end of the file has been reached. There is no special character to mark the end of a file.

Once a file is open for writing, we can use `write(2)` to transfer data to the file. If we are at the end of the file when we write to it, the file will grow by the number of bytes written. Otherwise, we will overwrite the contents of the file at the location specified by the current file offset.

```
#include <sys/types.h>
#include <unistd.h>

ssize_t write(int fd, const void *buf, size_t nbyte);
```

`fd` is the file descriptor for the file, `buf` is the starting address of the contiguous memory locations from which the data will be copied, and `nbyte` is the number of bytes to write. On success, `write` will return the number of bytes written, or −1 on error. It is possible for `write` to return fewer bytes than requested. For example, if there is not enough space left on the underlying device, only a partial `write` would be possible.

As we read and write a file, the file offset is incremented by the amount of data transferred. We can manipulate the file offset ourselves with `lseek(2)`. This is often done to ''rewind'' a file, setting the file offset to 0 so that we can begin reading from the start of the file.

```
#include <sys/types.h>
#include <unistd.h>

off_t lseek(int fd, off_t offset, int whence);
```

`fd` is the file descriptor for the file, `offset` is either an absolute or relative offset, and `whence` determines how `offset` is used.

If `whence` is set to `SEEK_SET`, then the file offset is set to the value of `offset`. If `whence` is set to `SEEK_CUR`, then the file offset is incremented by `offset`. If `whence` is set to `SEEK_END`, then the file offset is set to the end of the file plus `offset`.

On success, `lseek` returns the new file offset, measured in bytes from the beginning of the file. On failure, `lseek` returns −1 and sets `errno` to indicate the reason for failure. Some devices are incapable of seeking, and when `lseek` is applied to them, it succeeds, but the file offset is actually ignored by the driver. To seek to the beginning of a file, one can use

```
lseek(fd, 0L, SEEK_SET);
```

When a program is done using a file, it should use close (2) to relinquish access to the file, thereby freeing up the file's resources.

```
#include <unistd.h>

int close(int fd);
```

When a program exits, all files it had open are automatically closed for it by the operating system. close returns 0 on success and −1 on failure. Most programs ignore the return value from close because even if it fails, the file is still closed. There is little recovery possible other than notifying the user.

Example 2.4.6. The following program presents a simple implementation of the cat (1) command. It does not support any options. Nor does it read from the standard input if filenames are absent from the command line. Nevertheless, it does catenate the contents of the files specified on the command line.

```
#include <sys/types.h>
#include <stdlib.h>
#include <stdio.h>
#include <fcntl.h>
#include <unistd.h>
#include <errno.h>

#define BUFSIZE   (8*1024)
static char buf[BUFSIZE];

extern void error(const char *fmt, ...);
void catreg(int);

void
main(int argc, char *argv[])
{
     int i, fd;

     /*
      * Process each file named on the command line.
      */
     for (i = 1; i < argc; i++) {
         if ((fd = open(argv[i], O_RDONLY)) < 0) {
             error("cat: cannot open %s", argv[i]);
             continue;
         }
         catreg(fd);
         close(fd);
     }
     exit(0);
}

void
```

```
catreg(int fd)
{
    int nr, nw;

    for (;;) {
        /*
         * Read a chunk of the file.
         */
        nr = read(fd, buf, BUFSIZE);
        if (nr > 0) {
            /*
             * Write the chunk just read.  Clear errno
             * to silence error() on short writes.
             */
            errno = 0;
            nw = write(1, buf, nr);
            if (nw != nr) {
                if (nw < 0)
                    error("cat: write failed");
                else
                    error("cat: short write");
                break;
            }
        } else {
            if (nr != 0)
                error("cat: read failed");
            break;
        }
    }
}
```

For each file named on the command line, we print its contents on the standard output (file descriptor 1). We use open to gain access to the file in read-only mode. Then we iterate, reading at most BUFSIZE bytes at a time and writing them on the standard output, until there are no bytes left in the file, at which point read will return 0. If we encounter an error at any point, we print an error message using the function described in Example 2.4.5, close the file, and continue on with the next one.

Note that before calling write, we set errno to 0. This is because an open might have failed for a previous file and if we encounter a short write, the error message will be misleading, corresponding to the error from open.   □

The previous example illustrated the use of the basic I/O system calls, but SVR4 also provides more advanced means of I/O. Most disk-based file systems support the ability to map portions of a file into a process's address space. This feature is optional, however.

When a file is mapped into the address space of a process, I/O occurs implicitly through data references, instead of explicitly through system calls. A memory load is analogous to a call to read, and a memory store is analogous to a call to write. Unlike read and write, however, the I/O occurs in quantities equal to the system's page size.

The advantage to using mmap instead of read and write is that it can often be more efficient. It avoids extra system calls necessary when reading and writing files in units smaller than the file size. It also avoids the copy operation needed by read and write to transfer the data between the user's buffer and a kernel buffer.

To map a file into our address space, we use mmap(2):

```
#include <sys/types.h>
#include <sys/mman.h>

caddr_t mmap(caddr_t addr, size_t len, int prot, int flags,
        int fd, off_t off);
```

addr is a hint from the process of where in the address space the file should be mapped. If successful, the system call will map len bytes of the file, starting from the offset specified by off. The return value is the address at which the mapping has been made, or −1 on error.

fd is the file descriptor of the file to be mapped. prot specifies the access permissions for the pages being mapped. It is comprised of the bitwise-OR of PROT_READ for read permission, PROT_WRITE for write permission, and PROT_EXEC for execute permission, or it can be set to PROT_NONE for no permission.

The flags parameter controls how the mapping is made. If it is set to MAP_SHARED, then changes to the mapping are shared among all the processes mapping the file, and any changes to the data will be written to the underlying file. If flags is set to MAP_PRIVATE, then the process still shares the mapping, but if it tries to change the data, a private copy is made for the process and the mapping is changed to refer to the private copy. In this case, the underlying file remains unchanged.

The MAP_PRIVATE and MAP_SHARED flags are mutually exclusive; one of the two must be specified when using mmap. MAP_FIXED, on the other hand, is an optional flag that may be used with either of the others. If MAP_FIXED is set, then addr is taken to be the fixed address at which the mapping should be made. If the mapping cannot be made at addr, then mmap fails. If MAP_FIXED is not set, then addr is merely a hint. A value of 0 for addr indicates the caller does not care where the mapping is made, leaving the decision up to the system. This is the most common use because it improves portability by leaving system-specific knowledge of the address-space layout out of the application.

A mapping can be released with munmap(2):

```
#include <sys/types.h>

int munmap(caddr_t addr, size_t len);
```

addr is the start of the mapping, and len is its length in bytes. munmap returns 0 on success and −1 on failure.

Example 2.4.7. The following program is a modification of the one from Example 2.4.6. The main routine is the same, except that we first try to access the file by mapping it. If the file system does not support mapped files, then we revert to using the read system call, as in Example 2.4.6.

```c
#include <sys/types.h>
#include <sys/mman.h>
#include <sys/stat.h>
#include <stdlib.h>
#include <stdio.h>
#include <fcntl.h>
#include <unistd.h>
#include <errno.h>

extern void error(const char *fmt, ...);
int catmap(int);
void catreg(int);

void
main(int argc, char *argv[])
{
    int i, fd;

    /*
     * Process each file named on the command line.
     */
    for (i = 1; i < argc; i++) {
        if ((fd = open(argv[i], O_RDONLY)) < 0) {
            error("cat: cannot open %s", argv[i]);
            continue;
        }

        /*
         * Try mapping the file first.  If that fails,
         * fall back to using read(2).
         */
        if (catmap(fd) < 0)
            catreg(fd);
        close(fd);
    }
    exit(0);
}

int
catmap(int fd)
{
    int nw;
    caddr_t addr;
    struct stat sbuf;

    /*
     * Get the file size and try to map the whole file.
     */
    if (fstat(fd, &sbuf) < 0)
        return(-1);
    addr = mmap(0, sbuf.st_size, PROT_READ, MAP_PRIVATE,
      fd, 0);
```

```
        if (addr == (caddr_t)-1) /* mmap failed */
            return(-1);

        /*
         * Write the file just mapped.  Clear errno
         * to silence error() on short writes.
         */
        errno = 0;
        nw = write(1, addr, sbuf.st_size);
        if (nw != sbuf.st_size) {
            if (nw < 0)
                error("cat: write failed");
            else
                error("cat: short write");
        }

        /*
         * Undo the mapping.
         */
        munmap(addr, sbuf.st_size);
        return(0);
    }
```

Since we must tell mmap the amount of data to map into our address space, we first use fstat(2) [see stat(2)] to gather statistics about the file to be printed. fstat is one of a set of functions that return file statistics. The others are stat, which takes a pathname instead of a file descriptor, and lstat, which is similar to stat, except that if the pathname refers to a symbolic link, lstat will return information about the link itself, instead of the file to which it refers. (stat "follows" the link, whereas lstat does not.)

```
    #include <sys/types.h>
    #include <sys/stat.h>

    int stat(const char *path, struct stat *sbuf);
    int lstat(const char *path, struct stat *sbuf);
    int fstat(int fd, struct stat *sbuf);
```

If successful, these functions return 0 and fill the memory referenced by sbuf with a stat structure containing at least the following fields:

st_mode	is a bitmask containing the file type and access permissions. These are described in stat(5).
st_ino	is a number that uniquely identifies the file in the file system.
st_dev	is a number that uniquely identifies the mounted file system; it is not necessarily the device number of the device containing the file system.
st_rdev	is the device number for character special and block special files.
st_nlink	is the number of hard links to the file.
st_uid	is the user ID of the file's owner.
st_gid	is the group ID of the file's owner.
st_size	is the size of the file in bytes.

`st_atime`   is the time the file was last accessed.
`st_mtime`   is the time the file was last modified.
`st_ctime`   is the time the file's inode was last changed.
`st_blksize` is the file's recommended block size for performing I/O.
`st_blocks`   is the number of disk blocks in sectors (a sector is 512 bytes in
                     UNIX; see `NBPSCTR` in `<sys/param.h>`).

On error, the functions return −1 and set `errno` to indicate the reason for failure.

We use the `st_size` member of the `stat` structure as the amount of data to
map, thus creating a mapping for the entire file. Since we only want to read the file,
we use `PROT_READ` for the access permissions on the pages. We create a private
mapping because it is equivalent to a shared mapping if we do not change the data.

If `mmap` succeeds, we write the data from the location in our address space to
the standard output. As each new page is referenced, a page fault occurs, and the
system fills the page with the contents of the file corresponding to that page's offset.
Then we can continue writing the data to the standard output. When finished printing the file, we unmap it using `munmap`.

We can map the entire file without worrying too much about its size because the
maximum mappable amount is large, although configurable, and we only access the
file one page at a time. Because SVR4 is a paging-based virtual memory system, it
can steal and reuse pages as needed, so once we have written a page, it can be reused,
if necessary, for the next page.   □

Logging

Generating error messages is a necessary task for most programs, but daemons cannot usually write an error message on the standard error since they are not associated
with a terminal or login session. It makes more sense for daemons to log the errors
to a file for later inspection by an administrator.

Example 2.4.8. The following function shows how a daemon can create a log file
for recording information about its operation, such as errors it encounters. It returns
0 on success and −1 on failure.

```
#include <sys/types.h>
#include <sys/stat.h>
#include <unistd.h>
#include <fcntl.h>
#include <errno.h>
#include <grp.h>

#define LOGPERM   (S_IRUSR|S_IWUSR|S_IRGRP|S_IWGRP)

int logfd = -1;

int
initlog(const char *logfile)
{
```

```
struct stat sbuf;
struct group *gp;
int fl;

/*
 * Open the log file, creating it if it isn't
 * present.
 */
logfd = open(logfile, O_WRONLY|O_APPEND|O_CREAT,
  LOGPERM);
if (logfd < 0)
    return(-1);

/*
 * Set the close-on-exec flag.
 */
fl = fcntl(logfd, F_GETFD, 0);
if ((fl < 0) ||
  (fcntl(logfd, F_SETFD, fl|FD_CLOEXEC) < 0)) {
    close(logfd);
    logfd = -1;
    return(-1);
}

/*
 * Get the group ID for group "daemon."
 */
gp = getgrnam("daemon");
if (gp == NULL) {
    close(logfd);
    logfd = -1;
    errno = EINVAL;
    return(-1);
}

/*
 * If the file isn't owned by the super-user or group
 * daemon, change the file's user and group IDs.
 */
if (fstat(logfd, &sbuf) < 0) {
    close(logfd);
    logfd = -1;
    return(-1);
}
if ((sbuf.st_uid != 0) || (sbuf.st_gid != gp->gr_gid))
    fchown(logfd, 0, gp->gr_gid);
return(0);
}
```

We have seen the use of open before, but here we use it to create the log file if that file does not exist. If we do create the file, the permissions used are specified by LOGPERM, which we have set to allow read and write access by the individual and group owners.

We open the log file in append mode so that multiple daemons writing to the log file at the same time will not have their messages garbled by intermixing the characters from both messages. If the `open` succeeds, we set the close-on-exec flag for the file descriptor. This ensures that the file descriptor will be closed if the daemon must `fork` and `exec` any other programs. We use `fcntl(2)` to set the flag:

```
#include <sys/types.h>
#include <unistd.h>
#include <fcntl.h>

int fcntl(int fd, int cmd, ... /* void *arg */);
```

`fd` is the file descriptor to which the control operation applies, `cmd` determines the operation, and `arg` is an optional third argument whose type depends on the command. `fcntl` can be used for a variety of file-based operations, as summarized in Table 2.3.

Table 2.3. `fcntl` Operations

Command	Description
F_DUPFD	Duplicate `fd` using a file descriptor greater than or equal to the integer specified by `arg`.
F_GETFD	Get the file descriptor flags. The only one defined is `FD_CLOEXEC`.
F_SETFD	Set the file descriptor flags to the integer specified by `arg`.
F_GETFL	Get the file flags (`O_RDWR`, for example).
F_SETFL	Set the file flags to the integer specified by `arg`.
F_FREESP	Free space in a file represented by the `flock` structure pointed to by `arg`.
F_SETLK	Set or clear a record lock described by the `flock` structure pointed to by `arg`.
F_SETLKW	Same as `F_SETLK`, but block until the lock can be set.
F_GETLK	Get information on possible locks set on a file.
F_RSETLK	Special-purpose version of `F_SETLK` to communicate with the NFS lock daemon.
F_RSETLKW	Special-purpose version of `F_SETLKW` to communicate with the NFS lock daemon.
F_RGETLK	Special-purpose version of `F_GETLK` to communicate with the NFS lock daemon.

Note the distinction between the file descriptor flags and the file flags. Each file descriptor has its own flag word, currently containing the close-on-exec flag. Each file also has a set of flags corresponding to the access mode (like read-only) and other special properties (like append mode and nonblocking mode). Duplicated file descriptors have different file descriptor flags, but they share the same file flags. For more detailed information on the other commands provided by `fcntl`, see `fcntl(2)` and `fcntl(5)`.

Next we use `fstat` to read the file statistics and check the user and group IDs of the log file to make sure that they are correct for our application. Most applications should not hard-code the IDs, but the super-user's ID is always 0, so this is an acceptable exception.

We want the group ID of the log file to be set such that other applications in the group `daemon` can write to the log file. We cannot be guaranteed that the group ID of the process starting the daemon will be what we want, and if we create the log file, it will inherit the effective group ID of the process. We use `getgrnam(3C)` [see `getgrent(3C)`] to find the group ID associated with group `daemon`:

```
#include <grp.h>

struct group *getgrnam(const char *name);
```

On success, `getgrnam` returns a pointer to the `group` structure corresponding to the group named `name`. On failure, `getgrnam` returns `NULL`. The `group` structure describes the format of entries in `/etc/group`, and contains the following fields:

```
char    *gr_name;    /* group name */
char    *gr_passwd;  /* encrypted group password */
gid_t   gr_gid;      /* numerical group ID */
char    **gr_mem;    /* list of group members */
```

If the IDs do not match, we use `fchown(2)` to change them back to their proper values. `fchown` is similar to `chown(2)`, but uses a file descriptor to identify the file instead of a pathname.

```
#include <unistd.h>
#include <sys/stat.h>

int chown(const char *path, uid_t owner, gid_t group);
int lchown(const char *path, uid_t owner, gid_t group);
int fchown(int fd, uid_t owner, gid_t group);
```

`owner` is the user ID and `group` is the group ID. By default, `chown` follows a symbolic link; `lchown` can be used to change the ownership of the link itself. On success, the functions return 0, and on failure, they set `errno` and return −1.

If either `owner` or `group` is set to −1, then the corresponding ID is not changed. To change a file's ownership, the effective user ID of the process must match that of either the file or the super-user. In other words, if you are not the super-user, you can give away only files that you own.

SVR4 allows an administrator to restrict this behavior so that only the super-user can change the file's user ID, and file owners can only change the group IDs of their files to their effective group IDs or IDs of groups that appear in their supplementary group lists. Even though the file system has final say over whether this restriction is in effect or not, most file systems just call a common function that uses a tunable parameter to determine if the `chown` functions are restricted.   □

With compile-time options and limits, applications can conditionally compile code based on values specified in system header files. But how can applications function reliably in an environment where limits and capabilities can change based on configurable parameters? The answer is the system provides three functions that return information about tunable system parameters. Thus, applications can check if operations are supported before attempting them. Two functions deal with file-based options [see `fpathconf(2)`], and one deals with system-wide options [see `sysconf(3C)`].

The file-based functions need either a file descriptor or a pathname. If the file is a directory, the parameter usually applies to any file created in that directory.

```
#include <unistd.h>

long fpathconf(int fd, int name);
long pathconf(const char *path, int name);
```

`name` represents an option or limit listed in Table 2.4.

Table 2.4. `pathconf` and `fpathconf` Option and Limit Names

Name	Description
_PC_LINK_MAX	Maximum value of a file's link count.
_PC_NAME_MAX	Maximum number of bytes in a filename, excluding terminating NULL.
_PC_PATH_MAX	Maximum number of bytes in a pathname, excluding terminating NULL.
_PC_NO_TRUNC	If supported, pathnames greater than NAME_MAX generate an error instead of being silently truncated.
_PC_CHOWN_RESTRICTED	If supported, the chown functions are restricted as described in Example 2.4.8.
_PC_PIPE_BUF	Maximum number of bytes that can be written to a pipe without fragmenting the data with that of other writers.
_PC_MAX_CANON	Maximum number of bytes in a terminal's canonical input queue.
_PC_MAX_INPUT	Maximum number of bytes in a terminal's (raw) input queue.
_PC_VDISABLE	If supported, the value of a character that can be used to disable terminal special characters.

Both functions return the value associated with the option, or −1 if the option is not supported or an invalid value for `name` is given. If the option is not supported, `errno` will not be changed. If `name` is invalid, `errno` will be set to `EINVAL`.

The function that returns information about system-wide options and limits is `sysconf`:

```
#include <unistd.h>

long sysconf(int name);
```

Like the other functions, `name` represents the option or limit being queried. An invalid value for `name` will cause the function to return −1 with `errno` set to `EINVAL`. If the option is not supported, −1 is returned without changing the value of `errno`. Otherwise, the value associated with the option is returned. `name` can take on the values listed in Table 2.5.

Table 2.5. `sysconf` Option and Limit Names

Name	Description
_SC_ARG_MAX	Maximum length in bytes for `exec` arguments and environment variables.
_SC_CHILD_MAX	Maximum number of simultaneous processes per real user ID.
_SC_NGROUPS_MAX	Maximum number of simultaneous supplementary group IDs per process.
_SC_OPEN_MAX	Maximum number of files a process can have open at one time.
_SC_PASS_MAX	Maximum number of characters in a password.
_SC_LOGNAME_MAX	Maximum number of characters in a login name.
_SC_JOB_CONTROL	If defined, system supports job control.
_SC_SAVED_IDS	If defined, each process has a saved-set-user ID and saved-set-group ID.
_SC_CLK_TCK	Number of clock ticks per second.
_SC_PAGESIZE	The size of a page of memory in bytes.
_SC_VERSION	An integer defining the version of ISO/IEC 9945-1 (also known as POSIX 1003.1) to which the system conforms.
_SC_XOPEN_VERSION	The version of the X/OPEN Portability Guide to which the system conforms.

In Example 2.4.8, it does not matter if `fchown` is restricted. Even if the daemon ran with an unprivileged user ID and tried to change the ownership of the log file, the daemon will ignore the return value from `fchown` without any problems because the ownership of the file does not affect the correctness of the daemon as long as the daemon can open the file for writing.

Example 2.4.9. Continuing with the logging example (Example 2.4.8), the following function provides a way for daemons to write messages to a log file.

```
#include <sys/types.h>
#include <sys/stat.h>
#include <unistd.h>
```

```
#include <time.h>
#include <stdarg.h>
#include <string.h>

#define BUFSZ 1024
#define MAXLOGSZ 100000

static char buf[BUFSZ];
extern int logfd;

void
log(const char *fmt, ...)
{
    time_t t;
    char *tm;
    struct stat sbuf;
    va_list ap;

    /*
     * Get the current time and convert it to a
     * human-readable string.
     */
    time(&t);
    tm = ctime(&t);

    /*
     * Change newline to tab.  24 is location
     * of newline.  25 is end of string.  Then
     * copy the string to the buffer.
     */
    tm[24] = '\t';
    strncpy(buf, tm, 25);

    /*
     * Append the caller's string to the buffer.
     */
    va_start(ap, fmt);
    vsprintf(buf+25, fmt, ap);
    va_end(ap);

    /*
     * Add a newline.
     */
    strcat(buf, "\n");

    /*
     * If the log file is too large, truncate it to 0.
     */
    if (fstat(logfd, &sbuf) == 0) {
        if (sbuf.st_size > MAXLOGSZ)
            ftruncate(logfd, 0);
    }

    /*
```

```
      * Write the log message.
      */
     write(logfd, buf, strlen(buf));
  }
```

We start out by getting the current system time so we can add a timestamp to the message we are about to write to the log file. We use `time(2)` to get the system time.

```
  #include <sys/types.h>
  #include <time.h>

  time_t time(time_t *tloc);
```

If `tloc` is nonzero, it points to the location to store the time. The time is also returned by the system call on success. On failure, −1 is returned, and `errno` is set to indicate the reason for failure. The time value returned is in seconds since 00:00:00 UTC (Coordinated Universal Time), 1 January 1970.

Once we have the time, we need to convert it into a format that is easier for people to read. For this, we use the `ctime(3C)` function:

```
  #include <time.h>

  char *ctime(const time_t *tloc);
```

`tloc` is a pointer to a time value in seconds since 00:00:00 UTC, 1 January 1970. The return value is a pointer to a 26-character string of the format

```
  DDD MMM dd hh:mm:ss yyyy\n\0
```

where `DDD` is a three-letter abbreviation for the day of the week, `MMM` is a three-letter abbreviation for the month, `dd` is the day of the month expressed as a two-digit number, `hh` is the hour of the day expressed as a two-digit number, `mm` is the number of minutes past the hour expressed in two digits, `ss` is the number of seconds expressed in two digits, and `yyyy` is the year expressed as a four-digit number. The string is ended by a newline followed by a `NULL`.

The character string represents the time after correcting for the proper time zone and daylight savings time. The string is stored in a fixed location whose contents are overwritten by each call to `ctime`.

After we convert the time to a printable string, we change the newline to a tab and copy the string to our private buffer using `strncpy(3C)` [see `string(3C)`]. We copy everything but the `NULL` byte.

```
  #include <string.h>

  char *strncpy(char *s1, const char *s2, size_t n);
```

This function copies the null-terminated string pointed to by s2 to the memory location pointed to by s1. At most, n characters are copied. If string s2 is longer than n characters, then string s1 will not be null-terminated. If string s2 is shorter than n characters, then string s1 will be padded with `NULL` characters until n characters have been copied.

We could have used `strcpy` instead, but we would have overwritten the null character in the next step. In it, we copy the caller's format string and arguments to the location in the buffer immediately after the tab using `vsprintf` [see `vprintf(3S)`], the variable argument version of `sprintf`. We end our processing of the string by adding a newline to the end using `strcat(3C)` [see `string(3C)`].

```
#include <string.h>

char *strcat(char *s1, const char *s2);
```

`strcat` copies string `s2` to the end of `s1`, overwriting the null byte at the end of `s1`. The null byte at the end of `s2` is the last character to be copied. A pointer to the result (`s1`) is returned.

Before we write the message to the log file, we check if the file has grown too large (greater than `MAXLOGSZ` bytes in this example). If so, we truncate the file to zero bytes using `ftruncate(3C)`:

```
#include <unistd.h>

int truncate(const char *path, off_t length);
int ftruncate(int fd, off_t length);
```

The file represented by the file descriptor (or the pathname) is changed so that its new size is `length` bytes. If the original size was greater than `length`, the bytes after `length` are made inaccessible. If the original size was less than `length`, the space between the previous end of file and `length` will read back as zeros.

By truncating the file periodically, we remove the need for it to be monitored by the system administrator. We also remove the possibility of it growing so large that we either reach our file size limit or use up all the space in the file system.

When writing the message to the log file, we use `strlen` to calculate the number of bytes in the message:

```
#include <string.h>

size_t strlen(const char *s);
```

`strlen` returns the number of characters in the string pointed to by `s`, not including the terminating null character.   □

Signals

Signals are the software equivalent of hardware interrupts. Signals can be sent to processes from other processes or from the kernel. The purpose of signals is to notify processes of events of interest, optionally causing the processes to exit. When sent between processes, signals become a crude form of interprocess communication containing one bit of information (that the signal occurred).

When a signal is sent to a process, the signal is said to have been *posted* to (or *generated* for) the process. When the process finally receives notification that the signal occurred, the signal is said to have been *delivered* to the process. During the time between the posting of a signal and its delivery, the signal is said to be *pending*.

A process has the ability to control how signals will affect it. This is called the *signal disposition*. Signals can be ignored, so the process never receives notification of the signal delivery. Signals can be defaulted, causing the process to act according to the default action for the specific signal (the action is usually either ignore or terminate). Or the process can catch the signal, resulting in the execution of a program-specified function when the signal is delivered. There can be a different function with each signal, or one function can handle multiple signals.

Some signals create a *core file* when they terminate a process. The core file is a copy of a process's memory image and can be used to debug the program to identify the reason for termination. The core file is created in the process's current working directory, if permissions allow. See `core(4)` for more details.

Processes also have the ability to *hold* signals. This is not really a disposition, since it is a status that can be set independently from the disposition. Holding a signal results in the signal remaining in the pending state, if it is posted to the process, until it is *released*. While a signal is held, it is also said to be *blocked*. Similarly, if a signal is released, it is said to be *unblocked*.

If the same signal is posted to a process multiple times before the signal is delivered, the process will only see one occurrence of the delivery. The kernel only keeps track of whether or not the signal is pending; no count is associated with the signal. Therefore, signals are inadequate for counting discrete events.

SVR4 defines 31 distinct signals. A complete list can be found in `signal(5)`. Table 2.6 summarizes the signals most frequently used by applications.

Table 2.6. Commonly Used Signals

Signal	Description
SIGHUP	Controlling terminal hangup.
SIGINT	Interrupt the process.
SIGQUIT	Quit execution.
SIGKILL	Kill the process (cannot be caught or ignored).
SIGPIPE	Write on a pipe with no reader.
SIGALRM	Alarm clock has gone off.
SIGTERM	Software termination signal.
SIGUSR1	Application-defined signal.
SIGUSR2	Application-defined signal.
SIGCHLD	Child status change.
SIGPOLL	Pollable event occurred.

Four distinct interfaces are provided in SVR4 for dealing with signals. The original mechanism dates back to the fourth edition of the research version of UNIX. The second mechanism was added in System V Release 3 to solve problems associated with the use of the original one. POSIX developed yet another interface, which was added in SVR4. The fourth is the BSD interface, available in the BSD compatibility library in SVR4. We will only cover the first three.

The original signal interface offers a simple way to set the disposition of a signal:

```
#include <signal.h>

void (*signal(int sig, void (*disp)(int)))(int);
```

signal is a system call that returns the address of a function that takes an integer argument and has no return value. sig is the signal number (SIGINT, for example). disp is either the address of a signal-handling function to be called when the signal is delivered (this is called *catching* the signal), or a constant specifying that the signal should be ignored (SIG_IGN) or defaulted (SIG_DFL).

On success, signal returns the previous disposition; on error, it returns SIG_ERR. The signal system call is maintained for compatibility with older applications that use it. It has been made obsolete by newer interfaces because of the unreliable semantics it provides. The following example illustrates one of the problems.

Example 2.4.10. When signal is used to install a signal handler, the disposition of the signal is reset to SIG_DFL before entering the signal handler. Thus, if the signal handler needs to catch multiple occurrences of a signal, it must reinstall itself immediately. Even so, there is a window between the time that the handler disposition is set to default and the time that the handler runs and changes the disposition to catch the signal when another occurrence of the signal will take the default behavior. Most signals have a default behavior to terminate the process.

To illustrate this window, the following program will reinstall the signal handling function in the handler itself, but only after sleeping for one second. We purposely increase the timing window so we can see the effect of delivering the signal at the wrong time.

```
#include <unistd.h>
#include <signal.h>
#include <stdio.h>

void
main()
{
    int i;
    void handler(int);

    /*
     * Install the signal handler.
     */
    signal(SIGINT, handler);

    /*
     * Pause 10 times.  Only interrupted by signals.
     */
    for (i = 0; i < 10; i++)
        pause();
}
```

```
void
handler(int sig)
{
    printf("got SIGINT\n");

    /*
     * Open up a timing window.
     */
    sleep(1);

    /*
     * Reinstall the signal handler.
     */
    signal(SIGINT, handler);
}
```

We start out by installing a signal handler for SIGINT. Then we iterate, calling pause(2) 10 times. The pause system call will suspend the execution of the calling process until a signal is received. A signal must not be ignored if we intend it to cause pause to return.

```
#include <unistd.h>

int pause(void);
```

The return value for pause is always −1, with errno set to EINTR. Of course, if the action of the signal is to cause the process to terminate, pause does not return.

The signal handler prints a message to indicate that the signal has been caught, sleeps for one second, and then reinstalls itself as the signal handler for SIGINT. The sleep function puts the process to sleep for at least the specified number of seconds [see sleep(3C)].

```
#include <sys/types.h>
#include <unistd.h>

uint_t sleep(uint_t nsec);
```

nsec is the number of seconds to sleep. The return value is the number of seconds that were not slept because the function was interrupted by the delivery of a signal.

If we run the program, every time we hit the interrupt key on our terminal, the message got SIGINT is printed on the screen. If the time between successive keystrokes is less than one second, however, the execution of the program is interrupted and the process exits. (The default action for SIGINT is to terminate the process.)   □

Another problem with the signal interface is that it only provides one way to make a process immune to signals. Processes must ignore signals that they do not want to affect their execution. This has the effect, however, of causing the process to miss the signal entirely. There are times when it is desirable to defer the delivery of the signal until a process is ready to deal with it.

The sigset system call was added in System V Release 3 to fix the drawbacks associated with the signal system call.

```
#include <signal.h>

void (*sigset(int sig, void (*disp)(int)))(int);
```

The arguments are the same as for `signal`; however, `disp` may take on an additional value.

If `disp` is set to `SIG_HOLD`, the signal disposition is unchanged and the signal specified by `sig` is added to the process's *signal mask*. The signal mask is the set of signals that are currently held for the process. While held, if a signal is posted to the process, the signal is not delivered, but remains pending until the signal is removed from the signal mask. Once removed, if the signal is pending, it is delivered to the process.

On success, if the signal was previously held, `sigset` returns `SIG_HOLD`. Otherwise, the previous disposition of the signal is returned. On error, `SIG_ERR` is returned, and `errno` is set to indicate the reason for failure.

When the signal handler is called, the disposition of the signal remains unaltered. In addition, before the signal handler is called, the signal being delivered is automatically added to the process's signal mask. When the signal handler returns, the signal mask is set to its previous state. This removes the need for the process to reinstall the handler from within the handler, thus closing the timing window.

Example 2.4.11. This example is similar to the previous one, except that we are using `sigset` instead of `signal`.

```
#include <unistd.h>
#include <signal.h>
#include <stdio.h>

void
main()
{
        int i;
        void handler(int);

        /*
         * Install the signal handler.
         */
        sigset(SIGINT, handler);

        /*
         * Pause 10 times.  Only interrupted by signals.
         */
        for (i = 0; i < 10; i++)
            pause();
}

void
handler(int sig)
{
        printf("got SIGINT\n");
```

```
    /*
     * Open up a timing window.   No need to reinstall
     * the signal handler.
     */
    sleep(1);
}
```

When we run this program and continually hit the interrupt key, we get exactly 10 got SIGINT messages. No matter how rapidly in succession we press the interrupt key, we cannot cause the program to terminate early.

Notice that if we hit the interrupt key twice within a second, we will get one message followed by a second message about one second later. This is a result of the second interrupt being held while we sleep inside the signal handler. When we return from the signal handler, the system removes SIGINT from our signal mask, notices that SIGINT is pending, adds SIGINT to the signal mask, and calls our handler again.

If we manage to hit the interrupt key three times in one second, we see the same behavior. This confirms our understanding that multiple occurrences of the same signal are only seen once by the process before the signal is delivered.   □

In addition to sigset, several other interfaces were added in SVR3 to simplify the management of signals.

```
#include <signal.h>

int sighold(int sig);
int sigrelse(int sig);
int sigignore(int sig);
int sigpause(int sig);
```

sighold adds the specified signal to the process's signal mask. sigrelse removes the specified signal from the signal mask. sigignore sets the disposition of the specified signal to SIG_IGN. sigpause removes the specified signal from the process's signal mask and causes the process execution to suspend until any signal is received. All four functions return 0 on success and −1 on failure.

Signal handlers are often used to manipulate global data structures that are also manipulated by the main paths of the program. This can cause problems with the consistency of the data structures since the main paths in the program are interrupted asynchronously by the delivery of signals. The areas of code that manipulate these shared data structures are called *critical regions*. These are code paths that must execute without being interrupted by the signal handler lest the data structures become corrupted. sigset and its related set of signal-management functions can be used to protect critical regions, as illustrated in the following example.

Example 2.4.12. The following program, described in two sections, prints a linked list of integers. During the printing stage, we force a signal handler to interrupt the main execution path and remove an element from the list. We will see what happens when we run the program after we describe it.

```
#include <sys/types.h>
#include <stdlib.h>
#include <unistd.h>
#include <stdio.h>
#include <signal.h>

#define LISTSZ    20

struct list {
    struct list *next;
    int         val;
} list[LISTSZ];
struct list *head;

void handler(int);
void printlist(int);

void
main(int argc, char *argv[])
{
    int i, n;

    if (argc == 2)
        n = atoi(argv[1]);
    else
        n = 0;

    /*
     * Install a signal handler for SIGINT.
     */
    sigset(SIGINT, handler);

    /*
     * Build a linked list.
     */
    for (i = LISTSZ-1; i >= 0; i--) {
        list[i].val = i+1;
        list[i].next = head;
        head = &list[i];
    }

    /*
     * Print the list, generating SIGINT when we
     * reach element "n".
     */
    printlist(n);

    /*
     * Print the list without generating signals.
     */
    printlist(0);
    exit(0);
}
```

The list data structure contains a link pointer for the next element in the list and an integer to store the value of the element. There are 20 elements in the list, numbered from 1 to 20. The `head` variable is used as the beginning of the list. The two auxiliary functions declared are shown following this description.

The program expects to be called with a single command-line argument corresponding to an element in the list. When searching the list, we will send a signal to ourselves when we reach the specified element. If no arguments are given, an invalid list element (0) is used, preventing the signal generation

We use `sigset` to install a signal handler for `SIGINT`. Then we build the list from element 20 to element 1 (the index, `i`, goes from 19 to 0 since arrays in C start at index 0). Once the list is built, we print it, passing the printing function the element number to be used as the flag indicating when the signal should be sent. We then print the list again without generating a signal, so that we can see the effect of the signal handler.

```
void
printlist(int n)
{
      struct list *p;

      /*
       * Print the value of each element in the list.
       */
      for (p = head; p != NULL; p = p->next) {
          printf("%d ", p->val);

          /*
           * If we've reached the specified element,
           * send ourselves SIGINT.
           */
          if (p->val == n)
              kill(getpid(), SIGINT);
      }
      printf("\n");
}

void
handler(int sig)
{
      struct list *p, *op;

      /*
       * Search the list and remove element 12.
       */
      op = NULL;
      for (p = head; p != NULL; p = p->next) {
          if (p->val == 12) {
              if (op != NULL)
                  op->next = p->next;
              else
                  head = p->next;
              p->next = NULL;
```

```
            break;
        }
        op = p;
    }
}
```

The `printlist` function traverses the linked list, printing each element as it is found. When we reach an element whose value equals the argument to the function, we send ourselves `SIGINT`. Then we continue printing the list and end it with a newline. We use `getpid(2)` to identify our process ID:

```
#include <sys/types.h>
#include <unistd.h>

pid_t getpid(void);
```

The return value is our process ID. We use this to identify the process to receive the signal. We use `kill(2)` to send the signal:

```
#include <sys/types.h>
#include <signal.h>

int kill(pid_t pid, int sig);
```

`pid` is the process ID of the process to receive the signal, and `sig` is the signal number, or 0. If `sig` is 0, no signal is generated, and `kill` returns with an indication of whether the process specified by `pid` exists (0 if the process exists, −1 with `errno` set to `ESRCH` if it does not).

The caller must have the proper permissions to send a signal to another process. Since we are sending the signal to ourselves in this example, we pass the permissions check. If `pid` is negative, the signal is sent to the process group whose ID matches the absolute value of `pid`. If `pid` is −1, the signal is sent to all processes whose real user ID equals the effective user ID of the caller. If `pid` is −1 and the caller is the super-user, then the signal is sent to all processes [except processes 0 and 1 because they are special system processes; see `init(1M)`]. On success, `kill` returns 0; on failure, it returns −1.

The signal handler walks the linked list and removes element 12. The execution of this program (called `cr1`) follows:

```
$ ./cr1
1 2 3 4 5 6 7 8 9 10 11 12 13 14 15 16 17 18 19 20
1 2 3 4 5 6 7 8 9 10 11 12 13 14 15 16 17 18 19 20
$ ./cr1 11
1 2 3 4 5 6 7 8 9 10 11 13 14 15 16 17 18 19 20
1 2 3 4 5 6 7 8 9 10 11 13 14 15 16 17 18 19 20
$ ./cr1 12
1 2 3 4 5 6 7 8 9 10 11 12
1 2 3 4 5 6 7 8 9 10 11 13 14 15 16 17 18 19 20
$ ./cr1 13
1 2 3 4 5 6 7 8 9 10 11 12 13 14 15 16 17 18 19 20
1 2 3 4 5 6 7 8 9 10 11 13 14 15 16 17 18 19 20
$
```

If we run the command without any arguments, the list is printed twice. No signal is generated, so element 12 remains in the list. If we generate the signal when we reach element 11, then we are able to traverse the list successfully both times. When we generate the signal at element 12, however, the signal handler runs and sets the twelfth element's next pointer to NULL when the element is removed from the list. Unfortunately, the main code path in printlist is about to use the next pointer to continue on in the list and mistakenly assumes the end of the list has been reached. We see that the list is actually intact, with element 12 removed, when we print it the second time.

Finally, if we generate the signal when we reach element 13, we see the list as whole the first time and as missing element 12 the second time. This is as it should be, since we were past the element to be removed when the signal was generated.

We could attempt to solve the problem of finding the incorrect end of the list by ignoring SIGINT while we search the list. We call this version of the program cr2. The only function to change is printlist:

```
void
printlist(int n)
{
        struct list *p;
        void (*fn)(int);

        /*
         * Ignore SIGINT.
         */
        fn = sigset(SIGINT, SIG_IGN);

        /*
         * Print the value of each element in the list.
         */
        for (p = head; p != NULL; p = p->next) {
            printf("%d ", p->val);

            /*
             * If we've reached the specified element,
             * send ourselves SIGINT.
             */
            if (p->val == n)
                kill(getpid(), SIGINT);
        }

        /*
         * Restore the original disposition of SIGINT.
         */
        sigset(SIGINT, fn);
        printf("\n");
}
```

The results of running cr2 should not be surprising. Since we ignored SIGINT, the handler never receives delivery of the signal:

```
$ ./cr2 11
```

```
1 2 3 4 5 6 7 8 9 10 11 12 13 14 15 16 17 18 19 20
1 2 3 4 5 6 7 8 9 10 11 12 13 14 15 16 17 18 19 20
$ ./cr2 12
1 2 3 4 5 6 7 8 9 10 11 12 13 14 15 16 17 18 19 20
1 2 3 4 5 6 7 8 9 10 11 12 13 14 15 16 17 18 19 20
$ ./cr2 13
1 2 3 4 5 6 7 8 9 10 11 12 13 14 15 16 17 18 19 20
1 2 3 4 5 6 7 8 9 10 11 12 13 14 15 16 17 18 19 20
$
```

Finally, if we were to hold the signal during the printing of the list, the signal handler would get a chance to run when we were through. Again, only the `printlist` function changes:

```c
void
printlist(int n)
{
    struct list *p;

    /*
     * Block SIGINT.
     */
    sighold(SIGINT);

    /*
     * Print the value of each element in the list.
     */
    for (p = head; p != NULL; p = p->next) {
        printf("%d ", p->val);

        /*
         * If we've reached the specified element,
         * send ourselves SIGINT.
         */
        if (p->val == n)
            kill(getpid(), SIGINT);
    }

    /*
     * Unblock SIGINT.
     */
    sigrelse(SIGINT);
    printf("\n");
}
```

The output from running the third version of this program is consistent. Regardless of when the signal is generated, the first pass through the list sees the list in its entirety, and the second pass sees it minus element 12:

```
$ ./cr3 11
1 2 3 4 5 6 7 8 9 10 11 12 13 14 15 16 17 18 19 20
1 2 3 4 5 6 7 8 9 10 11 13 14 15 16 17 18 19 20
$ ./cr3 12
1 2 3 4 5 6 7 8 9 10 11 12 13 14 15 16 17 18 19 20
1 2 3 4 5 6 7 8 9 10 11 13 14 15 16 17 18 19 20
```

```
$ ./cr3 13
1 2 3 4 5 6 7 8 9 10 11 12 13 14 15 16 17 18 19 20
1 2 3 4 5 6 7 8 9 10 11 13 14 15 16 17 18 19 20
$
```

We have seen that the critical region in this example program is the time during which we are traversing the list inside the `printlist` function. Note that the `printf` of the newline is not inside the critical region since it is independent of the structure of the list.   ⊓

The third signal interface is the one specified in the POSIX P1003.1 standard. It was designed because existing ones had the potential for races when blocking multiple signals, and because the limit to the number of signals that could be defined had almost been reached. The 4.2BSD signal interface addressed the former problem, but not the latter one. The System V `signal` and `sigset` interfaces addressed neither. The POSIX signal interface, based on the 4.2BSD signal interface, provides a superset of the functionality available with the other interfaces, attempting to address deficiencies where possible.

The POSIX signal interface deals with signals in sets. A set of signals is represented by the data structure type `sigset_t`. The following functions are defined to initialize and manipulate signal sets [see `sigsetopts(3C)`]:

```
#include <signal.h>

int sigemptyset(sigset_t *set);
int sigfillset(sigset_t *set);
int sigaddset(sigset_t *set, int sig);
int sigdelset(sigset_t *set, int sig);
int sigismember(sigset_t *set, int sig);
```

`sigemptyset` clears the set such that no signals are contained in it. `sigfillset` initializes the set to contain all the signals defined in the system. `sigaddset` adds the signal specified by `sig` to the set specified by `set`. Similarly, `sigdelset` removes the specified signal from the set. These functions return 0 on success and −1 on error.

The `sigismember` function tests if the specified signal is in the given set. If so, 1 is returned. Otherwise, 0 is returned. On error, −1 is returned.

The `sigaction` system call is used to change the disposition of a signal, obtain the current disposition of a signal, or both.

```
#include <signal.h>

int sigaction(int sig, const struct sigaction *act,
    struct sigaction *oact);
```

`sig` is the signal whose disposition is being fetched, changed, or both. `act` is the address of a structure describing the new disposition, or NULL if the current disposition is only being retrieved. `oact` is the address of a structure where the previous disposition is to be placed, or NULL if the caller is not interested in the previous disposition. `sigaction` returns 0 on success and −1 on failure.

The `sigaction` structure minimally defines the following members:

```
void      (*sa_handler)();
sigset_t  sa_mask;
int       sa_flags;
```

The signal disposition is specified by `sa_handler`. It can be `SIG_IGN`, `SIG_DFL`, or the address of a signal-handling function. If a handler is specified, then `sa_mask` defined the set of signals to be blocked (added to the process's signal mask) during the execution of the handler. The signal being delivered is automatically added to the signal mask by the operating system, so it does not need to be specified in `sa_mask`. The `sa_flags` field controls the behavior of the signal handler. It is a bitmask composed of the flags listed in Table 2.7. The only flag defined by POSIX is `SA_NOCLDSTOP`; the others are System V extensions.

Table 2.7. `sigaction` Flags

Flag	Description
SA_ONSTACK	If an alternate signal stack has been declared with `sigaltstack(2)`, run the signal handler using that stack. Otherwise use the same stack as the main program.
SA_RESETHAND	Reset the signal disposition to `SIG_DFL` and do not add the signal to the signal mask before calling the handler.
SA_NODEFER	Do not add the signal to the signal mask before calling the handler.
SA_RESTART	Transparently restart any system call interrupted by the delivery of this signal, instead of the system call returning −1 with `errno` set to `EINTR`.
SA_SIGINFO	Instead of only passing the signal number to the handler, pass additional information to the handler [see `siginfo(5)` and `ucontext(5)`].
SA_NOCLDWAIT	If `sig` is `SIGCHLD`, do not create zombie processes when children of the calling process exit.
SA_NOCLDSTOP	If `sig` is `SIGCHLD`, do not generate the signal when children stop or continue.

The `sigprocmask` system call can be used to retrieve the current signal mask, change the signal mask, or both.

```
#include <signal.h>

int sigprocmask(int how, const sigset_t *set,
    sigset_t *oset);
```

how can be set to one of three values. If it is set to `SIG_BLOCK`, then `set` is added to the signal mask. If `how` is set to `SIG_UNBLOCK`, then `set` is removed from the signal mask. If `how` is set to `SIG_SETMASK`, `set` replaces the signal mask. If `set` is NULL, then `how` is ignored. If `oset` is non-NULL, then the previous signal mask is stored in the signal set to which it points. If set is NULL, then oset can be used to obtain the current signal mask.

The sigpending system call can be used to return the set of signals that are currently blocked, but pending.

```
#include <signal.h>

int sigpending(sigset_t *set);
```

set specifies the location to store the set of pending signals. Both sigprocmask and sigpending return 0 on success and −1 on failure.

The sigsuspend system call atomically replaces the signal mask and suspends the process until a signal is delivered.

```
#include <signal.h>

int sigsuspend(const sigset_t *set);
```

set specifies the new signal mask to install before suspending the process. sigsuspend always returns −1, since it will either fail or be interrupted by a signal. On return, the signal mask of the process is restored to the state it was in before calling sigsuspend.

Example 2.4.13. The relevant portions of the program from Example 2.4.12 are shown in this example, but the signal interface has been changed to use the POSIX functions.

```
void
main(int argc, char *argv[])
{
    int i, n;
    struct sigaction sa;

    if (argc == 2)
        n = atoi(argv[1]);
    else
        n = 0;

    /*
     * Install a signal handler for SIGINT.
     */
    sa.sa_handler = handler;
    sigemptyset(&sa.sa_mask);
    sa.sa_flags = 0;
    sigaction(SIGINT, &sa, NULL);

    /*
     * Build a linked list.
     */
    for (i = LISTSZ-1; i >= 0; i--) {
        list[i].val = i+1;
        list[i].next = head;
        head = &list[i];
```

```
        }

        /*
         * Print the list, generating SIGINT when we
         * reach element "n".
         */
        printlist(n);

        /*
         * Print the list without generating signals.
         */
        printlist(0);
        exit(0);
}

void
printlist(int n)
{
        struct list *p;
        sigset_t s, os;

        /*
         * Clear the signal set, add SIGINT to it,
         * and block SIGINT.
         */
        sigemptyset(&s);
        sigaddset(&s, SIGINT);
        sigprocmask(SIG_BLOCK, &s, &os);

        /*
         * Print the value of each element in the list.
         */
        for (p = head; p != NULL; p = p->next) {
            printf("%d ", p->val);

            /*
             * If we've reached the specified element,
             * send ourselves SIGINT.
             */
            if (p->val == n)
                kill(getpid(), SIGINT);
        }

        /*
         * Restore the original signal mask, unblocking
         * SIGINT.
         */
        sigprocmask(SIG_SETMASK, &os, NULL);
        printf("\n");
}
```

In this version (called cr4), we see that the output is correct, matching that of the
final version in Example 2.4.12.

```
$ ./cr4 11
1 2 3 4 5 6 7 8 9 10 11 12 13 14 15 16 17 18 19 20
1 2 3 4 5 6 7 8 9 10 11 13 14 15 16 17 18 19 20
$ ./cr4 12
1 2 3 4 5 6 7 8 9 10 11 12 13 14 15 16 17 18 19 20
1 2 3 4 5 6 7 8 9 10 11 13 14 15 16 17 18 19 20
$ ./cr4 13
1 2 3 4 5 6 7 8 9 10 11 12 13 14 15 16 17 18 19 20
1 2 3 4 5 6 7 8 9 10 11 13 14 15 16 17 18 19 20
$
```
□

Using Multiple Processes

As we have mentioned before, one process can create another process by forking.
The original process is called the parent, and the new process is called the child. Initially the child is an exact copy of the parent, sharing the same text and data. Most
process characteristics are inherited, including the real and effective user and group
IDs, the supplementary group IDs, the environment variables, the open files and their
flags, the signal dispositions and signal mask, the process group and session IDs, the
controlling terminal, the current and root directories, the file mode creation mask,
and the resource limits.

There are, however, some characteristics that differ between parent and child.
The child process gets a different process ID and has a different parent process ID.
The child gets its own copy of the file descriptors, so files can be closed in either the
parent or the child without affecting each other's open files. In addition, the child
process times are set to zero, since it has just begin to run. The alarm time is set to
zero, and any pending signals are cleared. The child does not inherit record locks.

The `fork` system call is used to create another process.

```
#include <sys/types.h>
#include <unistd.h>

pid_t fork(void);
```

`fork` is the only system call that returns twice — once in the child and once in the
parent. The parent's return value is the process ID of the child, and the child's return
value is 0 (an impossible process ID for a child process since process 0 is a system
process). This way, programs can optionally provide separate execution paths for
each process. If `fork` fails, it only returns once (to the parent). In this case the
return value is −1, with `errno` set to indicate the reason for failure.

Historically, `EAGAIN` has been used as the error code that indicates a failure
because the system is temporarily out of process slots. This can be used as an indication to try again later, so if you want your program to be robust, you might delay for
a random amount of time and try to fork again (the shell does this). Most other
errors from system calls are more decisive, with no hope of succeeding if tried later.

Over the years, `EAGAIN` has been borrowed for other temporary failure cases in
several system calls. For example, if a device is in *nonblocking* mode (described in
Section 3.4), a read when no data are immediately available will return −1 with

errno set to EAGAIN, instead of blocking until data are available. The error message printed by strerror(3C) and perror(3C) has never been updated to reflect this usage, however. The message is still No more processes.

Why would one want to create another process? There are two reasons. First, it is often convenient to structure a job so that multiple threads of control can work together to accomplish the task. For example, when we compile a program, the cc command forks and execs each stage in the compilation process: compiling, optimizing, assembling, and link editing. Based on command-line arguments, different stages are optionally performed. The stages are separate programs that can be updated and replaced independently.

Second, we need a way to execute another program without destroying our process context. Since exec(2) overlays our program with a new one, we need to create a second process through which the new program can execute, leaving our original process intact.

As implied by the names, there is a special relationship between a parent process and its children. When a child terminates, the operating system creates a record containing information about the reason the child terminated, and then notifies the parent of the child's death. The parent can optionally retrieve the status information. This allows the parent to take different actions depending on whether or not the child succeeded in its task.

When a child stops or continues because of job control, and when a child terminates, the operating system sends the SIGCHLD signal to the parent process. The default disposition for SIGCHLD is to ignore the signal, but a process can catch the signal and obtain the status of its children. The status can be obtained through wait(2) or waitpid(2). (A third interface, waitid(2), can also be used. It provides extended information about the reason for the status change. See waitid(2) and siginfo(5) for more information.)

The synopses for wait and waitpid are

```
#include <sys/types.h>
#include <wait.h>

pid_t wait(int *status);
pid_t waitpid(pid_t pid, int *status, int options);
```

wait suspends the calling process until one of its children either terminates or stops. If all children are stopped or terminated, wait immediately returns −1 with errno set to ECHILD. If the status of a child is available, wait returns the process ID of the child, and the integer pointed to by status is set to the child's termination status. If the parent process is uninterested in the termination status, status can be set to NULL.

The termination status can be evaluated using the macros described in wstat(5). The macros are listed in Table 2.8. Note that stat is the integer status, not the address of the integer as in the system calls.

waitpid is similar to wait, but it provides greater flexibility to the caller. If pid is −1, the status requested will be from any of the caller's children. If pid is greater than 0, the status requested will be from the child whose process ID matches

Table 2.8. Macros Used to Evaluate the Exit Status of a Process

Macro	Description
WIFEXITED(stat)	Evaluates to nonzero if the child terminated normally.
WEXITSTATUS(stat)	If WIFEXITED is nonzero, this evaluates to the child's exit code.
WIFSIGNALED(stat)	Evaluates to nonzero if the child terminated because of a signal.
WTERMSIG(stat)	If WIFSIGNALED is nonzero, this evaluates to the signal number that caused the child to terminate.
WCOREDUMP(stat)	If WIFSIGNALED is nonzero, this evaluates to nonzero if a core image of the child was created.
WIFSTOPPED(stat)	Evaluates to nonzero if the child is stopped.
WSTOPSIG(stat)	If WIFSTOPPED is nonzero, this evaluates to the signal number that caused the child to stop.
WIFCONTINUED(stat)	Evaluates to nonzero if the child has continued.

pid. If pid is 0, the status requested will be from any child in the same process group as the caller. Finally, if pid is less than −1, the status requested will be from any child whose process group ID matches the absolute value of pid.

Further flexibility is available through the options argument. It is a bitmask of flags that affect the operation of waitpid, as described in Table 2.9. Both wait and waitpid return −1 on error.

Table 2.9. waitpid Flags

Flag	Description
WCONTINUED	Report the status of children that have not had their status reported since being continued.
WNOHANG	Do not suspend the caller if a child's status is not immediately available. This can cause waitpid to return 0 if none of the children's statuses is available.
WNOWAIT	Peek at the status, but do not obtain it, so that we may wait for it again.
WUNTRACED	Report the status of children that have not had their status reported since being stopped.

The call

```
pid = wait(&status);
```

is equivalent to

```
pid = waitpid(-1, &status, WUNTRACED);
```

If a process does not wait for its children, the children become *zombies* when they terminate. A zombie is a defunct process whose process slot cannot be reclaimed until its parent either retrieves its status, or exits. The creation of zombies can be avoided by explicitly setting the disposition of SIGCHLD to SIG_IGN in the parent process. Although the default is ignore already, this action serves as an indication to the system that the process does not intend to obtain the termination status of its children.

The ability of a parent process to prevent the creation of zombies by explicitly ignoring SIGCHLD is only provided as a compatibility mechanism for older System V applications that use this feature. For portability, long-lived processes that create children should use one of the wait functions to obtain the exit statuses of their terminated children.

We have mentioned the exec system call several times, but there is no system call named exec. When we speak of the exec system call, we are referring to a system call family. There are actually six separate variations making up the exec family:

```
#include <unistd.h>

int execl(const char *path, const char *arg, ...);
int execle(const char *path, const char *arg, ...,
    char *const envp[]);
int execlp(const char *file, const char *arg, ...);
int execv(const char *path, char *const argv[]);
int execve(const char *path, char *const argv[],
    char *const envp[]);
int execvp(const char *file, char *const argv[]);
```

All functions replace the text and data of the current process with that of the program specified by path or file. None has a successful return because on success, the new program begins execution, having replaced the program that called exec. The file specified by path or file must be either an executable object file or an interpreter data file. In the latter case, the file should begin with the sequence

```
#! pathname [arg]
```

where pathname is the pathname of the interpreter, and arg is a single, optional argument. The pathname is passed as the first argument to the interpreter, followed by arg if it is present, then followed by any remaining arguments specified in the call to exec. The #! line is limited in length to at most 256 characters.

execl, execle, and execlp can be used when the number of arguments is known in advance. The arguments are passed to the main function of the executable file. The argument strings should be null-terminated, with the first one containing the basename of the command to be executed, and the last one set to NULL.

If the number of arguments is not known in advance, execv, execve, and execvp are more convenient because argv can be assembled on the fly. They take an array of argument strings, the first of which should be set to the basename of the command to execute, and the last of which should be set to NULL.

execle and execve allow the caller explicit control over the environment of the executable. The `envp` array contains the new environment, with each null-terminated string specifying a separate environment variable in the form "parameter=value." With the other four variants, the executable inherits the environment specified by the caller's `environ` pointer.

`execlp` and `execvp` differ in two ways from `execl` and `execv`. First, the `file` parameter is not necessarily a pathname. If it contains slashes, it is interpreted as a pathname. Otherwise, it is interpreted as a file that exists in a directory specified by the caller's `PATH` environment variable. Second, if the file is not an executable object file, it is passed as input to the shell.

Before passing control to the new program, `exec` restores any signals being caught to a default disposition. Other signal dispositions remain in effect when the new program begins execution.

If the set-user-ID attribute is enabled for the executable file, the effective user ID of the process is changed to the owner of the file. Similarly, if the set-group-ID attribute is enabled, the effective group ID of the process is changed to the file's group ID.

If any file descriptors have their close-on-exec flag set, they are closed before control is passed to the new program. Otherwise, the file descriptors remain open. All other process attributes are retained, including the process mask, the pending signals, and the pending alarm clock (if it exists).

The next two examples will demonstrate the usage of `fork`, `exec`, and `waitpid`.

Example 2.4.14. This example illustrates how a process can create a child for the purposes of executing a command. It accepts commands typed on a terminal and executes them inside a shell. Details about how to handle interactive programs are discussed following the example.

```
#include <sys/types.h>
#include <stdio.h>
#include <stdlib.h>
#include <unistd.h>
#include <errno.h>
#include <wait.h>

#define INPUTSIZ 256

void doshell(char *);
extern void error(const char *fmt, ...);
extern void fatal(const char *fmt, ...);

void
main()
{
        char buf[INPUTSIZ];

        /*
         * Print the initial prompt.
         */
```

```
        printf("> ");

        /*
         * While the user is providing input, read a command,
         * execute it in a subshell, and print the next prompt.
         */
        while (fgets(buf, INPUTSIZ, stdin) != NULL) {
            doshell(buf);
            printf("> ");
        }
        exit(0);
}

void
doshell(char *cmd)
{
        pid_t pid;

        /*
         * Create a child process to execute the command.
         */
        if ((pid = fork()) < 0) {
            error("fork failed");
            return;
        }
        if (pid == 0) {
            /*
             * The child executes the command in a
             * subshell.  This implies the command
             * can be a shell script.
             */
            execl("/sbin/sh", "sh", "-c", cmd, NULL);
            fatal("exec failed");
        }

        /*
         * The parent waits for the child to exit
         * before returning.
         */
        if (waitpid(pid, NULL, 0) < 0)
            fatal("waitpid failed");
}
```

We start by printing a prompt on the user's terminal using the standard output stream. Then we read one line of input from the standard input stream and pass the string to doshell to execute the string as a shell command. We use fgets(3S) [see gets(3S)] to read from the terminal.

```
#include <stdio.h>

char *fgets(char *buf, int n, FILE *fp);
```

fgets(3S) will read at most n characters from the stream specified by fp until either a newline is read or the end-of-file is reached. The bytes read are copied to the memory location referenced by `buf`. On error or EOF, NULL is returned. On success, `buf` is returned.

Continuing with the example, in `doshell` we create a child process using `fork(2)`. The child executes `/sbin/sh`, passing `cmd` to the shell as the command to be executed. Meanwhile, the parent waits for the child using `waitpid(2)`. The parent does not need the termination status of the child, so we pass NULL for the status pointer.   □

There are several problems when interactive programs use `fork`, `exec`, and `wait`. All the problems are caused by interactions with signals. The user has the ability to terminate the program using the interrupt or quit key. If the user hits either, a signal is sent to the foreground process group that has the terminal as its controlling terminal. In Example 2.4.14 the signal will terminate both the parent and the child (assuming the program is not running in the background).

This problem can be solved by having the parent ignore SIGINT and SIGQUIT, while the child lets the signals take their default actions. This arrangement, however, is awkward because pressing the interrupt or quit key will usually cause data we have typed to be discarded if we have not typed the newline yet. If this happens, it would be more user-friendly to have the parent print the prompt again, so we will need to catch SIGINT and SIGQUIT. This happens to be convenient because signals that are caught have their disposition reset to default during an `exec` — we do not need to do anything special in the child.

Merely catching the signals is not enough to function properly, however. When `fgets` is interrupted by a signal, it returns without having read any data, and the parent will exit. This can be solved with a nonlocal jump from the signal handler to just before the `while` loop in `main`. `sigsetjmp` and `siglongjmp` [see `sigsetjmp(3C)`] provide a nonlocal `goto` capability.

```
#include <setjmp.h>

int sigsetjmp(sigjmp_buf env, int savemask);
void siglongjmp(sigjmp_buf env, int val);
```

`env` is a structure used to save and restore state information about the execution environment of the program. `savemask` can be used to control whether the process's signal mask and scheduling state [see `priocntl(2)`] are also saved; a nonzero value causes them to be saved, and a value of 0 does not.

`sigsetjmp` is used to save the state, and `siglongjmp` is used to jump to the location following the `sigsetjmp` corresponding to `env`, but the action will appear as if `sigsetjmp` had returned the value specified by `val`. If `sigsetjmp` returns 0, a normal return is considered to have occurred. Otherwise, a nonzero return from `sigsetjmp` is only possible from a call to `siglongjmp`. If `val` is 0, `sigsetjmp` will return 1.

`sigsetjmp` and `siglongjmp` are similar to `setjmp` and `longjmp` [see `setjmp(3C)`], except that `setjmp` and `longjmp` do not allow you to control signal masks. You can obtain `setjmp` and `longjmp` behavior with `sigsetjmp` and `siglongjmp`, so it is better to use `sigsetjmp` and `siglongjmp` instead.

These functions are complex to use properly. After a nonzero return from
sigsetjmp, all global and static variables have values as of the time
siglongjmp was called. Also, the values of register and automatic variables are
undefined, unless declared as volatile. Therefore, these functions should be used
sparingly. Structured programming advocates deplore the use of goto statements
because goto statements can potentially decrease the understandability and correctness of computer programs. Imagine how they feel about nonlocal goto statements.

Example 2.4.15. This example is a revision of the previous one, but it includes the
logic necessary when performing interactive I/O. Many programs, such as vi (1),
allow users to "escape" from the current program to execute another command. The
following program illustrates how this can be done.

```c
#include <sys/types.h>
#include <signal.h>
#include <setjmp.h>
#include <stdio.h>
#include <stdlib.h>
#include <unistd.h>
#include <errno.h>
#include <wait.h>

#define INPUTSIZ 256

static sigjmp_buf env;

static void catcher(int);
static void nop(int);
void doshell(char *);
extern void error(const char *fmt, ...);
extern void fatal(const char *fmt, ...);

void
main()
{
    struct sigaction sa;
    char buf[INPUTSIZ];

    /*
     * Protect against a siglongjmp before the real
     * sigsetjmp is done.
     */
    if (sigsetjmp(env, 0)) {
        fprintf(stderr, "Interrupted\n");
        exit(1);
    }

    /*
     * Print the initial prompt.
     */
    printf("> ");
```

```
        /*
         * Set up a signal handler for SIGINT and SIGQUIT.
         */
        sa.sa_handler = catcher;
        sigemptyset(&sa.sa_mask);
        sigaddset(&sa.sa_mask, SIGINT);
        sigaddset(&sa.sa_mask, SIGQUIT);
        sa.sa_flags = 0;
        if (sigaction(SIGINT, &sa, NULL) < 0)
            fatal("sigaction failed"),
        if (sigaction(SIGQUIT, &sa, NULL) < 0)
            fatal("sigaction failed");

        /*
         * This is the real sigsetjmp.  If it returns a
         * nonzero value, then the signal handler called
         * siglongjmp.  Redisplay the prompt in this case.
         */
        if (sigsetjmp(env, 1))
            printf("\n> ");

        /*
         * While the user is providing input, read a command,
         * execute it in a subshell, and print the next prompt.
         */
        while (fgets(buf, INPUTSIZ, stdin) != NULL) {
            doshell(buf);
            printf("> ");
        }
        exit(0);
}

/*
 * Signal handler for SIGINT and SIGQUIT.
 */
static void
catcher(int sig)
{
        /*
         * Flush the input and output, and jump back to
         * print the prompt again.
         */
        fflush(stdout);
        fflush(stdin);
        siglongjmp(env, 1);
}
```

The main function is similar to that in Example 2.4.14, except here we have
added the code to install a signal handler for SIGINT and SIGQUIT, and we have
added two calls to sigsetjmp. In the first call, we close the timing window that
could cause a longjump using an uninitialized jump buffer. This window would
otherwise be open between the time we call sigaction to install the signal handler
and the time we call sigsetjmp with savemask set to 1. The error is triggered

by the signal arriving during the window, causing the signal handler to call
siglongjmp before the jump buffer was initialized. Instead, if a signal comes in
during this window, we print an error message and exit cleanly.

The second call to sigsetjmp is the real one intended to enable us to
redisplay the prompt properly after the user interrupts the execution of the program.
When called the initial time, sigsetjmp returns 0 and we fall into the while
loop. If we receive SIGINT or SIGQUIT, we execute the signal handler called
catcher.

In catcher, we use fflush(3S) [see fclose(3S)] to flush the standard
input and output streams to make sure they are in a sane state.

```
#include <stdio.h>

int fflush(FILE *fp);
```

fp is the standard I/O stream to flush. By flush, we mean that any buffered data not
yet written will be forced out to the device, and any data not yet read will be discarded. fflush returns 0 on success and EOF on failure.

After flushing the standard input and output, we use siglongjmp to jump
back into main. It will appear as if sigsetjmp returned 1, and we will print a
new prompt (preceded by a newline just in case we interrupted an incomplete line).
Then we will begin reading terminal input again.

While in the handler for one signal, we block the other. This further ensures the
sanity of the standard I/O data structures, since they are globally accessible.

```
void
doshell(char *cmd)
{
    pid_t pid, wpid;
    struct sigaction sigi, osigi;
    struct sigaction sigq, osigq;

    /*
     * Install a dummy signal handler so we don't jump
     * back to print the prompt until we are done.
     */
    sigemptyset(&sigi.sa_mask);
    sigi.sa_handler = nop;
    sigi.sa_flags = 0;
    if (sigaction(SIGINT, &sigi, &osigi) < 0)
        fatal("sigaction failed");
    sigemptyset(&sigq.sa_mask);
    sigq.sa_handler = nop;
    sigq.sa_flags = 0;
    if (sigaction(SIGQUIT, &sigq, &osigq) < 0)
        fatal("sigaction failed");

    /*
     * Create a child process to execute the command.
     */
    if ((pid = fork()) < 0) {
        error("fork failed");
```

```
                /*
                 * Restore the prior signal dispositions.
                 */
                if (sigaction(SIGINT, &osigi, NULL) < 0)
                    fatal("sigaction failed");
                if (sigaction(SIGQUIT, &osigq, NULL) < 0)
                    fatal("sigaction failed");
                return;
            }
        if (pid == 0) { /* child */
            /*
             * The child executes the command in a
             * subshell.  This implies the command
             * can be a shell script.
             */
            execl("/sbin/sh", "sh", "-c", cmd, NULL);
            fatal("exec failed");
        }

        /*
         * The parent waits for the child to exit before
         * restoring the prior signal dispositions and
         * returning.
         */
        while ((wpid = waitpid(pid, NULL, 0)) != pid)
            if ((wpid == -1) && (errno != EINTR))
                fatal("waitpid failed");
        if (sigaction(SIGINT, &osigi, NULL) < 0)
            fatal("sigaction failed");
        if (sigaction(SIGQUIT, &osigq, NULL) < 0)
            fatal("sigaction failed");
    }

    /*
     * This is a dummy signal handler.
     */
    static void
    nop(int sig)
    {
    }
```

This version of doshell is more complicated because of the subtle interaction with signals that leads us to swap the catcher signal handler for the stub nop. When we are waiting for the child to complete, we do not want to longjump back to main without retrieving the termination status of the child if it is interrupted by the user. If we were to do this by leaving catcher installed, we would end up creating a zombie process for each interrupted child. The zombies would waste system resources until the parent exited.

The parent must wait for the child process in a loop in case waitpid is interrupted by a signal. If waitpid returns −1 with errno set to any value other than EINTR, then a real error occurred, so we call fatal to print a message and exit.

Before the parent returns from `doshell`, it restores the previous dispositions for `SIGINT` and `SIGQUIT`.   □

Creating Daemons

As we have explained before, daemons are noninteractive commands that run in the background performing services for users, but usually go unnoticed by users. Because daemons run in the background, they cannot maintain an association with a terminal where a user can notice error messages, so daemons usually log errors to files for later inspection by system administrators.

If a daemon can be invoked as a member of a session with a controlling terminal (from a user's terminal, for instance), then the daemon needs to disassociate itself from the controlling terminal. This prevents signals from the terminal from affecting the daemon and allows the terminal to be reallocated as the controlling terminal for later sessions.

Disassociation can be performed by creating a new session for which the daemon will be the session leader. By leaving the old session, the daemon process forces the disassociation between itself and the old session's controlling terminal. The one drawback with this course of action is the next terminal device that the daemon opens will be allocated as the daemon's controlling terminal, as long as the device is not already some other session's controlling terminal. This can be avoided by specifying the O_NOCTTY flag to `open`.

The function used to create a new session is `setsid(2)`:

```
#include <sys/types.h>
#include <unistd.h>

pid_t setsid(void);
```

`setsid` will create a new session and process group for the calling process and set the process group ID and session ID to the caller's process ID. In addition, the caller's controlling terminal is released. This is not to say the caller loses access to file descriptors open to the terminal, merely that the terminal no longer bears the special relationship of a controlling terminal.

If the calling process is already a process group leader, then `setsid` fails. On success, `setsid` returns the calling process's new session ID; on failure −1 is returned, with `errno` set to indicate the reason for failure.

Because daemons run in the background in their own session and process group, they can linger around after the user that started them has logged off. When a process starts, it inherits the current working directory of its parent, so if a daemon is started from a user's shell, the daemon's current working directory will be whatever directory the user was in when the command that started the daemon was executed. This can cause unexpected results like being unable to unmount the file system because the daemon process still retains a reference to the directory where it was started. Also, if the daemon encounters an error and creates a core file, it will be created in the current directory, thus littering random directories.

The solution is for the daemon to change the current directory to either a well-known directory associated with its use, such as /var/spool/uucp for the uucp daemons, or to the root, so that it does not interfere with unmounting file systems. The chdir system call can be used to change the current working directory of a process.

```
#include <unistd.h>

int chdir(const char *path);
```

path represents the pathname of the new current working directory. A process must have search permissions on the directory to use it for the current working directory. On success, 0 is returned. On failure, the current working directory is unchanged and −1 is returned, with errno set to indicate the reason for failure.

Example 2.4.16. This example shows a general-purpose initialization routine that will transform a process into a daemon.

```
#include <sys/types.h>
#include <sys/resource.h>
#include <sys/stat.h>
#include <stdlib.h>
#include <stdio.h>
#include <fcntl.h>
#include <unistd.h>
#include <errno.h>
#include <string.h>
#include <signal.h>

extern int logfd;
extern void log(const char *fmt, ...);
extern void fatal(const char *fmt, ...);

void
daemonize(const char *cmd)
{
    int i;
    pid_t pid;
    struct rlimit rl;
    char filename[256];

    /*
     * Clear file creation mask.
     */
    umask(0);

    /*
     * Create the log file.
     */
    sprintf(filename, "/tmp/%s.log", cmd);
    if (initlog(filename) < 0)
        fatal("%s: cannot create log file", cmd);
```

```c
    /*
     * Get the maximum number of files we can open.
     */
    if (getrlimit(RLIMIT_NOFILE, &rl) < 0)
        fatal("%s: cannot get file limit", cmd);

    /*
     * Become a session leader to lose our
     * controlling terminal.
     */
    if ((pid = fork()) < 0)
        fatal("%s: cannot fork", cmd);
    else if (pid != 0)  /* parent */
        exit(0);
    setsid();

    /*
     * Ensure that future opens won't allocate
     * controlling terminals.
     */
    sigset(SIGHUP, SIG_IGN);
    if ((pid = fork()) < 0)
        fatal("%s: cannot fork", cmd);
    else if (pid != 0)  /* parent */
        exit(0);

    /*
     * Close all open file descriptors, except for
     * the log file.  Choose a reasonable limit if
     * the limit is currently infinite.
     */
    if (rl.rlim_max == RLIM_INFINITY)
        rl.rlim_max = 1024;
    for (i = 0; i < rl.rlim_max; i++)
        if (i != logfd)
            close(i);
    errno = 0;  /* set from close of invalid fd */

    /*
     * Change the current directory to the root of
     * the file system tree so other file systems can
     * be unmounted while we're running.
     */
    if (chdir("/") < 0) {
        log("cannot chdir to /: %s", strerror(errno));
        exit(1);
    }

    /*
     * Attach file descriptors 0, 1, and 2 to /dev/null.
     * Applications expect them to be at least open.
     */
    if ((i = open("/dev/null", O_RDWR)) != 0) {
        if (i < 0)
```

```
                    log("error opening /dev/null: %s",
                        strerror(errno));
                else
                    log("open /dev/null: expected fd 0, got %d",
                        i);
                exit(1);
        }
        if ((i = dup(0)) != 1) {
            if (i < 0)
                log("dup failed: %s", strerror(errno));
            else
                log("dup(0) expected fd 1, got %d", i);
            exit(1);
        }
        if ((i = dup(0)) != 2) {
            if (i < 0)
                log("dup failed: %s", strerror(errno));
            else
                log("dup(0) expected fd 2, got %d", i);
            exit(1);
        }
}
```

The first step in becoming a daemon is to change the process's file creation mask so any files created will contain the permissions specified during the creation, instead of qualifying the permissions based on the inherited file creation mask. This is done by setting the mask to 0 with the umask system call.

```
#include <sys/types.h>
#include <sys/stat.h>

mode_t umask(mode_t mask);
```

mask is the new file mode creation mask. The previous value of the process's file mode creation mask is returned.

After setting the file mode creation mask, we create a log file for the daemon to record error messages or significant events. If this fails, we print an error message and exit. We try to organize things so that operations that may fail during initialization occur before we fork. This allows us to report the error to the user. If something fails after forking, we have to report the error to the log file.

The next step is to obtain the maximum number of open files we can have at one time, in preparation for closing them. There is no way in System V to obtain the highest-numbered file descriptor in use for a process, so the best we can do is obtain the maximum for the process. This is flawed because it is possible to lower the limits, leaving file descriptors in use that have greater values than the maximum. getrlimit(2) gives us the process's limits:

```
#include <sys/time.h>
#include <sys/resource.h>

int getrlimit(int resource, struct rlimit *rlp);
```

where `resource` identifies one of the process's resources, and `rlp` points to an `rlimit` structure containing the following fields:

```
rlim_t rlim_cur;
rlim_t rlim_max;
```

The current limit, also called the "soft" limit, is stored in `rlim_cur`. The hard limit, `rlim_max`, is the upper bound on the current limit. The current limit can be modified up to the hard limit using `setrlimit(2)`. Unprivileged processes can raise or lower their soft limits and irreversibly lower their hard limits. Only privileged processes (those with an effective user ID of the super-user) can raise their hard limits. The special value `RLIM_INFINITY` is used to represent an infinite limit. The limits are summarized in Table 2.10.

Table 2.10. Per-Process Resource Limits

Limit	Description
RLIMIT_CORE	Maximum size in bytes of a core file the process can create.
RLIMIT_CPU	Maximum time in CPU seconds the process can use.
RLIMIT_DATA	Maximum size in bytes of the process's heap.
RLIMIT_FSIZE	Maximum size in bytes of a file the process can create.
RLIMIT_NOFILE	Maximum number of simultaneous open file descriptors a process can have.
RLIMIT_STACK	Maximum size in bytes of the process's stack.
RLIMIT_VMEM	Maximum size in bytes of the process's mapped address space.

Continuing with the example, if we are unable to obtain the limits for the number of open files, we print an error message and exit. Otherwise, we fork, and the parent immediately exits. The function continues in the child.

The first thing we do in the child process is to use `setsid` to create a new session and process group. Because we forked and the parent exited, we are guaranteed that the child is not a process group leader, so we know `setsid` will have the proper effect. At this point, we no longer have a controlling terminal. The next terminal we open, however, will be allocated as our new controlling terminal (as long as it is not already allocated as a controlling terminal for another session) because we are a session leader. To prevent this, we ignore `SIGHUP` and fork again. Then the session leader exits. This leaves us with the (second) child process in a session that has no leader. Since the child is not the leader, it can open terminal devices without having to worry about unintentionally allocating a controlling terminal. Ignoring `SIGHUP` is necessary because when the session leader exits, all processes in the foreground process group are sent `SIGHUP`.

Next we proceed to close all open file descriptors, except the one open to the log file. If the hard limit for the process was infinite, we assume a limit of 1024 to prevent the `for` loop from taking too long. This is a weak heuristic, but about the best we can do until a system call is added to return the value of the highest-numbered file descriptor in use.

Since we probably had fewer than the maximum number of open files, `errno` is probably set to `EBADF` after the `for` loop. We reset it back to 0 to prevent misleading log messages. Then we change directory to the root of the file system. If this fails, we log a message and exit.

When we closed all the file descriptors, that included the ones used for the standard input, output, and error. When we open a file, the kernel selects the lowest-numbered free file descriptor for use. If the daemon opens any files and calls a library routine that tries to perform I/O on `stdin`, `stdout`, or `stderr`, then the library routine will be using the wrong file. To prevent this, we reserve file descriptors 0, 1, and 2 by opening `/dev/null` and duplicating the file descriptor returned. `/dev/null` is a pseudo-driver that forces `read` to return 0 and `write` to return as if the entire amount requested had been written. This makes library routines that use file descriptors 0, 1, and 2 harmless.

When we open `/dev/null`, we expect a successful return to be 0, since we know file descriptor 0 is closed. If any other positive value is returned, it is a logic error in our function, so we log a message and exit. If a negative value is returned, we encountered an error opening the file and so log an error message.

We use `dup(2)` to make a copy of file descriptor 0.

```
#include <unistd.h>

int dup(int fd);
```

`fd` is the file descriptor to be duplicated. On success, a nonnegative file descriptor is returned. On failure, −1 is returned and `errno` is set to indicate the reason for failure.

The returned file descriptor refers to the same file as `fd` and shares the same file entry in the kernel. This means the file flags and offset are shared as well. The file descriptor flags, on the other hand, are not shared. The returned file descriptor will always have its close-on-exec flag turned off.

Like `open`, `dup` returns the lowest-numbered available file descriptor. The call

```
fd2 = dup(fd1);
```

is equivalent to the call

```
fd2 = fcntl(fd1, F_DUPFD, 0);
```
                                                                              □

Summary

This chapter has been a crash course in UNIX programming. We only touched on topics that you will come across throughout the rest of the book. Several of the example functions are used in examples in other chapters.

Exercises

2.1 Modify the program in Example 2.4.4 to print an error message and fail if the argument to the −x option contains any illegal characters.

2.2 Modify the program in Example 2.4.6 to read from the standard input if no arguments are specified. Then modify it to include the argument ''−'' as an alias for the standard input.

2.3 Rewrite `initlog` from Example 2.4.8 taking into account that `fchown` might be restricted on the system. How can you ensure that the log file will be created with the correct user and group IDs?

2.4 Assume multiple copies of the same daemon can be running at any given time. Modify Example 2.4.9 to include the process ID of the daemon creating the log message.

2.5 If we were to replace the `printlist` function from Example 2.4.12 with the following version, would it work properly? Explain why.

```
void
printlist(int n)
{
        struct list *p;

        sighold(SIGINT);
        p = head;
        while (p != NULL) {
            sighold(SIGINT);
            printf("%d ", p->val);
            if (p->val == n)
                kill(getpid(), SIGINT);
            p = p->next;
            sigrelse(SIGINT);
        }
        printf("\n");
}
```

2.6 In Example 2.4.15, hard-coding the size of `buf` to 256 is not portable. Improve the program so the size of `buf` is set at run-time based on the maximum number of characters it is possible to read from a terminal. [Hint: see `malloc(3C)`.]

Bibliographic Notes

Ritchie and Thompson [1974] introduce the UNIX system in the classic ACM article. Thompson [1978] describes the implementation of the UNIX system. These articles are valuable because they show us the original UNIX system through the eyes of its originators.

The C programming language (''classic C,'' also known as ''K&R C'') is described by Kernighan and Ritchie [1978]. In the second edition, Kernighan and Ritchie [1988] describe the ANSI version of the C programming language.

Kernighan and Pike [1984] provide a comprehensive introduction to the UNIX programming environment. Rochkind [1985] presents a more advanced treatment of the same subject. Although somewhat dated, both of these texts are still useful thanks to the compatibility maintained by System V

Pike and Kernighan [1984] discuss the philosophical issues related to UNIX program design. These issues are no less relevant today.

Stevens [1992] provides an excellent introduction to programming in a standards-based UNIX environment. His text contains many examples and notes the differences between the SVR4 and 4.4BSD implementations of the UNIX system.

Williams [1989] describes the implementation of job control, session management, and process groups in SVR4. Lennert [1987] discusses the ins and outs of writing daemons in both the System V and BSD environments.

Part 2
User-level Network Programming

3
STREAMS

The STREAMS mechanism in UNIX System V Release 4 provides the framework on which communication services can be built. These services include communication between terminals and a host computer, between processes on the same computer, and between processes on different computers. This chapter will describe what makes up the STREAMS mechanism and how applications can use it to build communication services.

3.1 STREAMS BACKGROUND

The STREAMS subsystem [not to be confused with the streams returned by `fopen(3C)`] was designed to unify disparate and often ad hoc mechanisms that previously existed in the UNIX operating system to support different kinds of character-based I/O. In particular, it was intended to replace the `clist` mechanism that provided support for terminal I/O in previous releases.

In the `clist`-based terminal subsystem, each terminal line could have one processing element, called a *line discipline*, associated with it. The line discipline handled all special character processing. If a user needed some nonstandard processing of the terminal data stream, he or she could change the line discipline, but only one line discipline could be associated with a terminal at a time.

STREAMS provides a variation on this theme: users can add (''push'') and remove (''pop'') intermediate processing elements, called *modules*, to and from the data stream at will. The modules can be stacked so that more than one can be used in the data stream at a time. This fundamental change allows independent modules that perform simple tasks to be combined in interesting ways to perform more complex tasks, in much the same way as UNIX commands are connected via shell pipelines.

Data transfer in a stream occurs by passing messages between adjacent processing elements. Only pointers to the messages are passed, avoiding the costly overhead of data copying. Messages are typed and have an associated priority, both indicating how they should be processed. Using message-passing to perform I/O creates another fundamental difference between STREAMS and previous character-based subsystems: data transfer in a stream is data-driven rather than demand-driven.

In previous I/O subsystems, when a user wanted to read data from a device, the driver's `read` routine was invoked. Similarly, when a user wanted to write data, the driver's `write` routine was invoked. In STREAMS, drivers usually do not know when users are reading from or writing to the stream. A read will block until data are available, and a write will result in messages being sent to the driver.

The original Streams [*sic*] mechanism was invented by Dennis Ritchie at AT&T Bell Laboratories around 1982 to unify and improve the character I/O subsystem, improve performance, and decrease system size. It was included in Version 8 of the Research UNIX System. Between 1984 and 1985, AT&T's development organization "productized" Streams, adding a new message structure and support for multiplexing, and capitalizing the name. STREAMS was first generally available in UNIX System V Release 3.0 in 1986. Ironically, full terminal support did not appear until System V Release 4.0, four years later.

3.2 STREAMS ARCHITECTURE

A simple *stream* provides a bidirectional data path between a process at user level and a device driver in the kernel (see Figure 3.1). Data written by the user process travel *downstream* toward the driver, and data received by the driver from the hardware travel *upstream* to be retrieved by the user. Even though data travel up and down the stream in messages, drivers and modules can treat the data flow as a byte stream.

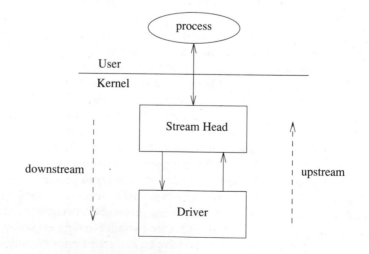

Fig. 3.1. A Simple Stream

A simple stream consists of two processing elements: the *stream head* and a driver. The stream head consists of a set of routines that provide the interface between applications in user space and the rest of the stream in kernel space. When an application makes a system call with a STREAMS file descriptor, the stream head routines are invoked, resulting in data copying, message generation, or control operations being performed. The stream head is the only component in the stream that can copy data between user space and kernel space. All other components effect data transfer solely by passing messages and thus are isolated from direct interaction with users of the stream.

The second processing element is the driver, found at the end, or tail, of the stream. Its job is to control a peripheral device and transfer data between the kernel and the device. Since it interacts with hardware, this kind of driver is called a *hardware driver*. Another kind of driver, called a *software driver*, or *pseudo-driver*, is not associated with any hardware. Instead, it provides a service to applications, such as emulating a terminal-like interface between communicating processes.

The stream head cannot be replaced in the same way that a driver can. Drivers can be added to the kernel simply by linking their object files with the kernel object files. The stream head, on the other hand, is provided with the kernel proper and is fixed. The same stream head processing routines are used with every stream in the system. Each stream head, however, is customizable to a small extent by changing the processing options it supports.

The fundamental building block in a stream is the *queue* (see Figure 3.2). It links one component to the next, thereby forming the stream. Each component in the stream contains at least one pair of queues: one queue for the read side (upstream) and one for the write side (downstream). The queue serves as a location to store messages as they flow up and down the stream, contains status information, and acts as a registry for the routines that will be used to process messages.

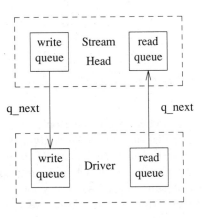

Fig. 3.2. STREAMS Queues

When one component wants to pass a message along in the stream, the queue is used to identify the next component. Then, the next component's queue is used to identify the function to call to pass the message to that component. In this manner, each component's queue provides an interface between the component and the rest of the stream.

A module on a stream is shown in Figure 3.3. A module is an intermediate processing element that can be dynamically added to, or removed from, the stream. Modules are structurally similar to drivers, but usually perform some kind of filter processing on the messages passing between the stream head and the driver. For example, a module might perform data encryption or translation between one interface and another.

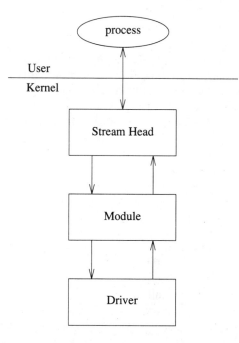

Fig. 3.3. A Module on a Stream

Adding and removing modules are not the only ways a user can customize a stream. A user can also establish and dismantle multiplexing configurations. Multiple streams can be *linked underneath* a special kind of software driver called a *multiplexing driver*, or *multiplexor* (see Figure 3.4). The multiplexing driver will route messages between upper streams opened to access the driver, and lower streams linked underneath the driver. Multiplexing drivers are well suited to implementing windowing systems and networking protocols. Windowing systems multiplex data between multiple windows and the physical terminal. Networking protocols multiplex messages between multiple users and possibly multiple transmission media.

As we have seen, streams can be used to connect processes with devices, but this is not their only use. Streams are also used to connect processes with other

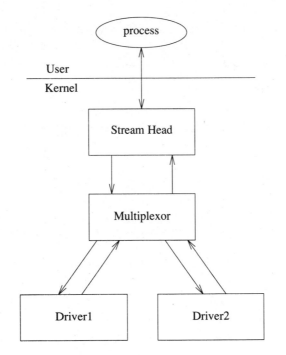

Fig. 3.4. A Multiplexing Driver

processes. Pipes are implemented as streams in UNIX System V Release 4. There are two kinds of pipes: unnamed pipes and named pipes. An unnamed pipe (also called an "anonymous pipe") is so called because it has no entry in the file system namespace. The `pipe` system call creates an unnamed pipe by allocating two stream heads and pointing the write queue of each at the read queue of the other (see Figure 3.5).

Before pipes were implemented using streams, they could only be used for uni-directional data transfer. On successful return, `pipe` would present the user with a file descriptor for one end of the pipe open for reading and a file descriptor for the other end open for writing. In contrast, pipes in SVR4 are full-duplex connections; both pipe ends are open for reading and writing.

A named pipe (also called a "FIFO" because data are retrieved in a first-in–first-out manner) is created via the `mknod` system call. It has a name in the file system and can be accessed with the `open` system call. A named pipe is actually one stream head with its write queue pointing at its read queue (see Figure 3.6). Data written to a named pipe are available for reading from the same "end" of the pipe.

Two processes can use named pipes as rendezvous points, but since communication is unidirectional, their usefulness is limited. They are retained primarily to support applications that still use them. The *mounted streams* facility found in SVR4 makes named pipes obsolete by giving users a way to associate a name with an

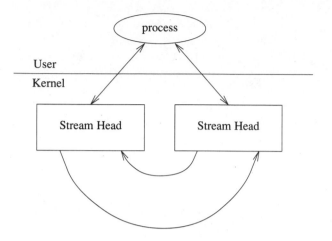

Fig. 3.5. An Anonymous Pipe

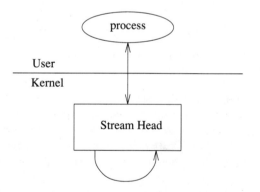

Fig. 3.6. A FIFO

anonymous pipe. Mounted streams are discussed in Section 3.6. Although strictly speaking, an anonymous pipe is also a FIFO, we will follow current conventions and use the term "FIFO" to refer to a named pipe and the term "pipe" to refer to an anonymous pipe.

There are several advantages to STREAMS-based pipes. First, local inter-process communication (IPC) now uses the same mechanisms as remote, or networked, IPC. This allows applications to treat local IPC connections the same as remote connections. Most operations that can be applied to a stream can now be applied to a pipe. For example, modules can be pushed onto pipes to obtain more functionality. Second, STREAMS-based pipes are full-duplex, allowing bidirectional communication between two processes with one pipe instead of two.

Now that we have seen the major components that make up a stream, we will briefly look at some of the characteristics of STREAMS messages that are of interest to user-level applications. All communication within a stream occurs by passing pointers to STREAMS messages. The messages are typed, and the type indicates both the purpose of the message and its priority. Based on the type, a message can be either high-priority or normal-priority. The normal-priority messages are further subdivided into *priority bands* for the purposes of flow control and message queueing.

Any data the user wants to transmit to the other end of the stream are packaged in M_DATA messages by the stream head. This is the most common message type. If the user needs to send or receive control information, then an M_PROTO message is used. Control information is intended for a module or driver in the stream, is interpreted by that component, and is usually not transmitted past the component. A special message type, M_PCPROTO, is reserved for high-priority control information, such as interface acknowledgements.

Simple messages are composed of one *message block*. More complex messages can be created by linking multiple message blocks together. These are then treated logically as larger messages. The data in one message block are viewed as being contiguous with the data in the next message block. The message structure is usually transparent to user-level applications. One exception to this is when dealing with a complex message including both control information and user data. In the next section, we shall see how messages like these can be generated and received.

Chapter 9 discusses the STREAMS kernel architecture, including message structure and types, in detail.

3.3 SYSTEM CALLS

Access to a stream is provided via the open and pipe system calls. In the former case, if a device is not already open, the open system call will build the stream. This involves allocating a stream head and allocating two pairs of queues, one pair for the stream head and one pair for the driver. The queues are linked together as shown in Figure 3.2, and the driver's open routine is called. If the driver open succeeds, a file descriptor referring to the stream is returned to the user. If the driver open fails, the structures are freed and the system call fails, returning −1 to the user.

Once the stream is constructed and the first open has completed successfully, another open of the same device will create a new file descriptor referring to the same stream. The driver open routine is called again, but there is no need to allocate the data structures since they are already set up. Pipes, when created, have their streams ''opened'' internally by the operating system. There is no driver to open.

Multiple processes using the same device also use the same stream. A device is uniquely identified by its *device number*. The device number is split into a *major number* and a *minor number*. The major number identifies the actual device and its associated driver. The minor number identifies a subdevice. For example, a serial ports board would be identified by its major device number, but an individual line on the board is identified by its minor device number.

For a network, minor devices are usually virtual entities since they are multi-plexed over one communication line. Instead of being limited by the number of lines, the minor devices are usually limited by tunable configuration parameters that correspond to the maximum number of simultaneous conversations.

Often, applications do not care what particular minor device they use. They just want one that is not already in use. To relieve the applications of the burden of searching for unused minor devices, drivers can be written to support special minors called *clones*. When an application opens the clone minor device of a particular driver, the driver selects a different, unused minor device to be used by the applica-tion. Clones are particularly well suited for network drivers and pseudo-drivers.

After a stream is opened, the user may apply to it almost any system call that takes a valid file descriptor. In addition, four system calls work only on file descrip-tors that refer to streams. These are `getmsg(2)`, `getpmsg(2)`, `putmsg(2)`, and `putpmsg(2)`. They deal with information that is separated into two classes: user data and control information.

The few system calls that will not work with streams are those that make restric-tions on the file type, such as `getdents(2)`, which only works with directories, or those that support a conflicting paradigm, like `mmap(2)`. `mmap` and streams do not work together, because mapping a STREAMS driver into the address space of a pro-cess would enable direct I/O to the device through loads from and stores into the mapped address range, and the entire stream would be bypassed. No messages would be created, and modules would not get a chance to process the data.

Data can be written to the stream using either `write` or `putmsg`. With `write`, the stream head will copy the user's data into (possibly multiple) STREAMS messages of type `M_DATA` and send them downstream. Data are frag-mented according to the *maximum packet size* of the topmost module or driver in the stream. The maximum packet size is a parameter specified by each module and driver that determines the size of the largest STREAMS data message that the com-ponent can accept.

If there are too many bytes of data in the messages on the write queues down-stream, a stream is said to be *flow-controlled* on the write side. When this condition occurs, `write`s to the stream will block until flow-control restrictions are lifted. If, however, the file descriptor is in nonblocking mode, `write` will return −1 with `errno` set to `EAGAIN` instead of blocking. Flow control protects the system from any one stream using too much memory for messages.

Example 3.3.1. Assume the module on the top of the stream has a maximum packet size of 4096 bytes. Then the line

```
write(fd, buf, 4097);
```

will send two STREAMS messages downstream. The first message will have 4096 bytes of data in it, and the second message will contain the last byte of data. If, on the other hand, the maximum packet size is larger than 4097 bytes, the `write` will generate only one message.

Actually, a global tunable parameter, STRMSGSZ, can be set by a system administrator to limit the largest STREAMS message created. By default, STRMSGSZ is set to 0 to indicate that the limit is infinite. In this case, write behaves as described. If STRMSGSZ is set to a nonzero value, however, the size of messages created by write is limited by the smaller of the maximum packet size of the module on top of the stream and the value of STRMSGSZ.   □

With putmsg, the stream head will try to create exactly one message from the user's buffers. This system call can be used to send control information, data, or both. An M_DATA, M_PROTO, or M_PCPROTO message can be generated, depending on whether the user supplies a control buffer and what flags the user specifies, as summarized in Table 3.1.

Table 3.1. putmsg Argument Combinations

Control Buffer	Data Buffer	Flag	Message Type
No	Yes	0	M_DATA
Yes	Don't care	0	M_PROTO
Yes	Don't care	RS_HIPRI	M_PCPROTO

The synopsis for putmsg is

```
#include <stropts.h>

int putmsg(int fd, const struct strbuf *ctlp,
      const struct strbuf *datp, int flag);
```

fd is a file descriptor referring to a stream, ctlp is a pointer to a structure describing an optional control buffer to be transmitted, and datp is a pointer to an optional data buffer to be transmitted. If a control buffer is provided, flag will determine whether the resulting message is a normal protocol message (M_PROTO) or a high-priority protocol message (M_PCPROTO; "PC" stands for Priority Control). The only valid values for flag are 0 for a normal protocol message and RS_HIPRI for a high-priority protocol message. If no control buffer is provided, then flag must be set to 0, or an error will result.

If a data buffer is provided, then there will be one or more M_DATA blocks linked to the protocol message block. If a data buffer is provided, but no control buffer is provided, then a single M_DATA message block is generated.

To describe the control and data portions of the generated message, the strbuf structure is used, defined in <sys/stropts.h> as:

```
struct strbuf {
      int      maxlen;
      int      len;
      char     *buf;
};
```

maxlen is ignored by putmsg. It is used to specify the size of the user's buffer in calls to getmsg. len indicates the amount of control information or data to be transmitted. `buf` contains the address of the buffer containing the control information or data.

On success, `putmsg` returns 0; on error, it returns −1. If the size of the data is either greater than the maximum packet size or less than the minimum packet size of the topmost module or driver in the stream, then the system call will fail with `errno` set to `ERANGE`.

Example 3.3.2. Assume you have to communicate with a network driver that expects user data to be presented to it with control information describing the identity of the recipient of the data. The recipient is known by its network address. The control information is stored in an `M_PROTO` message block, and the user data is stored in `M_DATA` blocks linked to the `M_PROTO` block. The driver expects the `M_PROTO` message to contain the following structure:

```
struct data_req {
      long        primitive;     /* identifies message */
      ushort_t    addr_len;      /* destination address */
      ushort_t    addr_offset;   /* location in message */
};

#define DATA_REQUEST 1       /* data request primitive */
```

The `data_req` structure and the recipient's address are both stored as control information. The address location in the buffer is given by `addr_offset`. To use the least amount of space, we will choose the address to follow immediately after the `data_req` structure.

We can use the following function to request that the driver transmit a message:

```
#include <sys/types.h>
#include <stropts.h>
#include <stdlib.h>
#include <memory.h>

int
senddata(int fd, char *buf, uint_t blen, char *addr,
     ushort_t alen)
{
      struct data_req *reqp;
      struct strbuf ctl, dat;
      char *bp;
      int size, ret;

      /*
       * Allocate a memory buffer large enough to hold
       * the control information.
       */
      size = sizeof(struct data_req) + alen;
      if ((bp = malloc(size)) == NULL)
          return(-1);

      /*
       * Initialize the data_req structure.
```

```
     */
    reqp = (struct data_req *)bp;
    reqp->primitive = DATA_REQUEST;
    reqp->addr_len = alen;
    reqp->addr_offset = sizeof(struct data_req);

    /*
     * Copy the address to the buffer.
     */
    memcpy(bp + reqp->addr_offset, addr, alen);
    ctl.buf = bp;
    ctl.len = size;
    dat.buf = buf;
    dat.len = blen;

    /*
     * Send the message downstream, free the memory
     * allocated for the control buffer, and return.
     */
    ret = putmsg(fd, &ctl, &dat, 0);
    free(bp);
    return(ret);
}
```

The arguments to `senddata` are a file descriptor referring to the stream, the address of a data buffer, the amount of data in the buffer, the destination address, and the address length. We allocate enough memory for the control buffer to hold the `data_req` structure plus the destination address. We then populate the `data_req` structure with the necessary information and initialize the `strbuf` structures describing the control and data information. After we call `putmsg` to create the message and send it downstream, we free the memory we allocated and return the value returned by `putmsg`.   □

Early in the implementation of System V STREAMS, `putmsg` was actually called `send`. Similarly, `getmsg` was called `recv`. Before released, the names were changed to their present ones to avoid conflicting with the 4BSD system calls used for data transfer over sockets. Somehow, the definition of the flag for `getmsg` and `putmsg` was never changed, hence it retains its original name, `RS_HIPRI`. The "R" stands for "receive," and the "S" stands for "send."

Data can be obtained from the stream using either the `read` or `getmsg` system call. `read` treats the data flow as a byte stream and, by default, only operates on M_DATA messages. This means the data returned by `read` may span message boundaries. If a `read` is attempted from a stream with an M_PROTO or M_PCPROTO message at the head of its read queue, the `read` will fail with `errno` set to EBADMSG. There are options to change the default behavior of `read`. They will be discussed later in this chapter.

Since `read` is byte-stream-oriented, applications have to do something extra to determine when all the data have been received. Three common methods are

1. Use fixed-size messages. Both the writer and the reader agree in advance on the size of each message passed.
2. Always start each message with a field describing the size of the message.
3. Always end each message with a special character or sequence of characters.

The application determines which method is appropriate.

Example 3.3.3. This example illustrates a function that reads exactly the amount asked. It can be used to implement method (1) discussed previously.

```c
#include <unistd.h>
#include <errno.h>

int
mread(int fd, char *buf, int len)
{
    int n;

    while (len > 0) {
        n = read(fd, buf, len);
        if (n <= 0) {
            if (n == 0) /* unexpected EOF */
                errno = EPROTO;
            return(-1);
        }
        len -= n;
        buf += n;
    }
    return(0);
}
```

Since we have to read exactly `len` bytes, if we receive less than that, we treat it as an error. If `read` returns 0, we treat it as an end-of-file condition and return an error. On success, we return 0 instead of the number of bytes read since the caller knows we have read as much as we were asked.   □

`getmsg`, like `putmsg`, deals with only one message at a time. It can process both user data and control information, retrieving an M_DATA, M_PROTO, or M_PCPROTO message from the front of the stream head read queue.

```c
#include <stropts.h>

int getmsg(int fd, struct strbuf *ctlp,
    struct strbuf *datp, int *flagp);
```

`fd` is a file descriptor referring to a stream, `ctlp` is a pointer to a structure describing an optional control buffer to be received, and `datp` is a pointer to an optional data buffer to be received. Information in the M_PROTO or M_PCPROTO portion of the message is stored in the control buffer described by an `strbuf` structure, shown earlier. The `maxlen` field indicates the size of the buffer. On return, the `len` field indicates the amount of information received and placed in the buffer. Information in the M_DATA portion of the message is processed in a similar manner.

The `flagp` field is a *pointer* to an integer, unlike the `flag` field in `putmsg`. A common mistake is to pass a flag in this field, resulting in `getmsg` failing with `errno` set to `EFAULT` (although the stronger type-checking done by ANSI C compilers has reduced the likelihood of this error).

If the flag pointed to by `flagp` is set to 0, the first message on the stream head read queue will be retrieved. If the flag is set to `RS_HIPRI`, then `getmsg` will wait until an `M_PCPROTO` message arrives at the stream head and will retrieve it instead. On return, the flag will be set to `RS_HIPRI` if an `M_PCPROTO` message has been received, and 0 otherwise.

On success, if an entire message is retrieved, `getmsg` returns 0. If only part of the message is retrieved (because the caller's buffer was too small), then `getmsg` will return nonnegative values. If there is more control information, `MORECTL` is returned. If there are more data, `MOREDATA` is returned. If both remain, then (`MORECTL | MOREDATA`) is returned. On error, −1 is returned.

Example 3.3.4. Assume the same driver used in Example 3.3.2 responds with an acknowledgement every time it receives a request to transmit a message. The acknowledgement does not contain user data, but it does contain control information. It can be implemented as an `M_PCPROTO` message containing the following structure in its data buffer:

```
struct data_ack {
      long    primitive;   /* identifies message */
      long    status;      /* success or failure */
};
#define DATA_ACK 2         /* data request acknowledgement */
```

The `primitive` field identifies the message as a `DATA_ACK`. The `status` field contains an error number if the data request failed, or 0 if it succeeded.

The following routine retrieves the `M_PCPROTO` message from the front of the stream head read queue. It returns 0 if an acknowledgement was received and indicates success. If either the acknowledgement cannot be received or the acknowledgement indicates the request failed, it returns −1.

```
#include <sys/types.h>
#include <stropts.h>
#include <unistd.h>
#include <errno.h>

int
getack(int fd)
{
      struct data_ack ack;
      struct strbuf ctl;
      int fl = RS_HIPRI;
      int ret;

      /*
       * Initialize the control buffer and retrieve the
       * acknowledgement message.
```

```
        */
        ctl.buf = (caddr_t)&ack;
        ctl.maxlen = sizeof(struct data_ack);
        ret = getmsg(fd, &ctl, NULL, &fl);
        if (ret != 0) {
            /*
             * ret shouldn't be greater than 0, but if it
             * is, then the message was improperly formed.
             */
            if (ret > 0)
                errno = EPROTO;
            return(-1);
        }
        if (ack.primitive != DATA_ACK) {
            /*
             * The message we just obtained was not the
             * acknowledgement we expected.
             */
            errno = EPROTO;
            return(-1);
        }

        /*
         * The status field of the message contains an error
         * number if the request failed, or 0 otherwise.
         */
        errno = ack.status;
        return(errno ? -1 : 0);
}
```

We start out by setting up the control buffer. Using `getmsg` with the RS_HIPRI flag, we block until an M_PCPROTO message is received. If we get a message with more control information than we asked for, MORECTL will be returned. If the message had data in it (i.e., was linked to an M_DATA message), MOREDATA will be returned since we do not specify a buffer to be used for data. Either of these cases is an error in this example, so we set `errno` to EPROTO and return failure notification.

If the primitive is not a data acknowledgement, then there has been a protocol error, so we again set `errno` to EPROTO and return −1. If the message is a DATA_ACK, we set `errno` to indicate the status of the previous data request and return 0 on success or −1 on failure.   □

Why use `getmsg` and `putmsg` when `read` and `write` will do? The fact is most people probably will not have to use `getmsg` or `putmsg`, at least not directly. `getmsg` and `putmsg` were implemented to enable user-level applications to communicate with networking drivers and modules that export message-based interfaces. These interfaces (called *service interfaces*) use M_PROTO and M_PCPROTO messages to implement their service primitives and events.

With the `read` and `write` system calls, applications would have to work harder to distinguish between service parameters and user data because `read` and write provide a byte-stream interface and only one buffer is involved. This means applications might have to make multiple system calls to send or receive a single message. In addition, read and write provide only one band of data flow, so high-priority primitives, such as interface acknowledgements and out-of-band data, which ideally would take precedence over other primitives, will be queued behind existing data.

The getmsg and putmsg system calls solve these problems. They provide a message-oriented interface with separate buffers for control information and user data. For more information on service interfaces, see Section 3.5.

The ioctl system call is used to perform I/O control operations on the stream.

```
int ioctl(int fd, int command, ... /* arg */);
```

The particular control operation is identified by command. An optional third argument whose type and semantics vary based on the command is usually included. Almost any file-based operation can be implemented as an ioctl command. For this reason, ioctl has often been described as the "garbage can" system call.

There are two classes of commands that can be used. One class is a command directed at a module or driver in the stream. The other class is directed at the stream head. This latter class is the set of "generic" stream head ioctl commands described in streamio(7).

Example 3.3.5. A module can be "pushed" onto the stream with the I_PUSH ioctl command. Even though it appears to the user as if the module is on the top of the stream, the module is actually inserted between the stream head and the top-most module or driver in the stream. Even so, the conventions are to say, "the module has been pushed on the stream," and "the module is on top of the stream."

```
ioctl(fd, I_PUSH, "module_a");
ioctl(fd, I_PUSH, "module_b");
```

After this sequence of calls, the module named module_b is on the top of the stream. After each module is pushed onto the stream, its open routine is called so that it can allocate any necessary data structures. Each push of a module on a stream invokes a different instance of the module, analogous to the way each minor device provides access to a different instance of a driver.

The topmost module on the stream can be popped off with the I_POP ioctl command:

```
ioctl(fd, I_POP, 0);
```

If this follows the previous two calls, then the module named module_a will be left on the top of the stream. When a module is popped off the stream, its close routine is called so that it may deallocate any data structures associated with that instance of the module.   □

The stream head ioctl commands are summarized in Table 3.2. The class of module and driver ioctl commands is further subdivided into two categories: I_STR and *transparent*. The I_STR type derives its name from the

Table 3.2. Stream Head `ioctl` Commands

Command	Description
I_NREAD	Get the number of messages and the size of the first message on the stream head read queue.
I_PUSH	Push a module on a stream.
I_POP	Remove the top module from a stream.
I_LOOK	Get the name of the top module on a stream.
I_FLUSH	Flush (discard) data on queues.
I_SRDOPT	Set read options.
I_GRDOPT	Get read options.
I_STR	Driver/module `ioctl` commands.
I_SETSIG	Enable SIGPOLL generation.
I_GETSIG	Get events that generate SIGPOLL.
I_FIND	Verify if a module is in a stream.
I_LINK	Create a multiplexor link.
I_UNLINK	Remove a multiplexor link.
I_PEEK	Peek at data in the first message on the stream head read queue.
I_FDINSERT	Send information about another stream.
I_SENDFD	Pass a file descriptor.
I_RECVFD	Receive a file descriptor.
I_SWROPT	Set write options.
I_GWROPT	Get write options.
I_LIST	List the modules and driver in a stream.
I_PLINK	Create a persistent multiplexor link.
I_PUNLINK	Remove a persistent multiplexor link.
I_FLUSHBAND	Flush banded data on queues.
I_CKBAND	Check if a message with the given band is on the stream head read queue.
I_GETBAND	Get the band of the first message on the stream head read queue.
I_ATMARK	Check if the first message on the stream head read queue is "marked."
I_SETCLTIME	Set the close delay time.
I_GETCLTIME	Get the close delay time.
I_CANPUT	Check if the given band is writable.

command used to implement it. The caller packages the real `ioctl` command and argument in an `strioctl` structure and passes the address of the structure as the third argument to `ioctl`, as in:

```
struct strioctl {           /* defined in <sys/stropts.h> */
      int     ic_cmd;       /* command */
      int     ic_timout;    /* timeout value */
      int     ic_len;       /* length of data */
      char    *ic_dp;       /* pointer to data */
};
struct strioctl str;
      :
      :
ioctl(fd, I_STR, &str);
```

The `strioctl` structure allows the user to specify one optional buffer to contain data to be sent along with the command. On success, data may be returned to the buffer.

The stream head translates the `strioctl` structure into a message sent downstream. If the command is recognized by a module or driver, the request is performed and an acknowledgement message is sent upstream to complete the system call. If the command is unrecognized by all processing elements in the stream, the driver responds by sending a negative acknowledgement message upstream, which causes the system call to fail.

This mechanism did not allow existing binary applications to use `ioctl` with STREAMS-based drivers or modules since the command and data had to be massaged into the `strioctl` structure. Nor did it support the use of more than one data buffer during `ioctl` processing. To solve these problems, transparent `ioctl`s were added to SVR3.2.

With transparent `ioctl`s, the stream head does not expect an `I_STR` command, nor does it know anything about the format of the data referenced by the third argument to `ioctl`. All unrecognized commands are treated as transparent by sending a specially tagged `ioctl` message downstream. If a module or driver recognizes the command, it will respond with the proper messages to complete the request. Otherwise, the driver will generate a negative acknowledgement, as with the `I_STR` type.

Note that users can specify a timeout with an `I_STR` `ioctl`. The `ic_timout` field contains the number of seconds to wait for the `ioctl` to complete before giving up. The special symbol `INFTIM` is used to wait indefinitely. Transparent `ioctl`s have no way to control the timeout. They will wait indefinitely.

Because modules and drivers stack in a stream, the first component to recognize an `ioctl` command will act on it. Modules pass along `ioctl` messages containing unrecognized commands. Drivers have the responsibility of failing unrecognized `ioctl` commands. More information on the details of `ioctl` processing can be found in Chapters 9 through 12.

Access to a stream is relinquished by calling the `close` system call with the file descriptor referring to the stream. The driver's close routine is only called on the last close of the stream. So if more than one process has opened the same stream, or if a STREAMS file descriptor has been duplicated [see dup(2)], the driver will not be notified that a close is occurring until the last file descriptor referring to the stream has been closed.

On last close, a stream is dismantled. Starting at the top of the stream, the system calls the close routine of each module before removing the module from the stream. When no modules are left, the system will call the driver's close routine and deallocate the data structures representing the stream.

Flushing Data

Since messages can be queued within a stream, applications have the ability to flush the data in it with the I_FLUSH ioctl command. By flush, we do not mean the ability to force that data to the tail of the stream. In this context, "flush" means to discard the data by freeing the messages.

The third parameter to the system call is a flag indicating which side of the stream to flush: FLUSHR for the read side, FLUSHW for the write side, and FLUSHRW for both sides. [FLUSHRW is equivalent to (FLUSHR|FLUSHW).]

When the I_FLUSH ioctl is used, the stream head sends a special message (of type M_FLUSH) containing the flags downstream that informs the modules and driver to flush their queues. As each module receives the message, it flushes its queues and passes the message on to the next component. When the driver receives the message and flushes its queues, if FLUSHR is set, the driver shuts off FLUSHW and sends the message back upstream. When it reaches the head of the stream, the stream head flushes its read queue and frees the message. If FLUSHR is not set, the driver frees the message instead.

Flushing can also occur from within a stream. As the result of an external event, a module or driver can generate an M_FLUSH message to flush the stream. In this case, the user is unaware that the flushing has occurred. The stream head takes care of the M_FLUSH message much in the same way the driver did, but the sense of the flags is reversed. If FLUSHW is set, the stream head shuts off FLUSHR and sends the message downstream. Otherwise, it frees the message. The shutting off of the FLUSHR flag by the stream head and the FLUSHW flag by the driver prevents the message from circulating in the stream indefinitely.

Error Handling

The separation of module and driver processing from the user's I/O requests presents problems for error reporting. This is partially because of the decoupling effect of message-based interfaces, and partially because of the ability of modules and drivers to defer processing messages by queueing them. By the time the module or driver detects an error, the application may no longer be performing the system call that caused the error. Errors can also result from the tail of a stream, unrelated to any specific action by the user.

This has led to the use of error semantics that, in most cases, make a stream unusable when an error occurs. Usually when a module or driver detects an unrecoverable error, the action taken is to inform the stream head of the error by sending a message upstream, placing the stream in *error mode*. Then, from that point on, all system calls except close and poll will fail with the error code specified in the message. The only way for a user to clear the error is to close the stream and reopen the device.

One exception to this type of error handling is `ioctl` failures. The processing of an `ioctl` in a stream is synchronous; the user waits until a message arrives acknowledging the completion of the `ioctl` command. Drivers and modules indicate success or failure in the completion message. There is no need to place the stream in error mode, although this can be done in extreme cases. Drivers and modules usually try to avoid placing a stream in error mode unless absolutely necessary, because of the severe consequences.

Drivers and modules have the option of placing just one side of a stream in error mode. If only the read side is in error mode, then only read-like system calls will fail. If only the write side is in error mode, then only write-like system calls will fail. If a system call is neither read-like nor write-like, then it will fail if either side is in error mode.

Drivers and modules can also put the stream in *hangup mode*. This might occur when the driver detects a problem with the communication line, for example. In hangup mode, `reads` will succeed, retrieving any data on the stream head read queue, until no more data are left. Then `read` will return 0. However, `write` will fail in hangup mode, setting `errno` to `EIO`.

3.4 NONBLOCKING I/O AND POLLING

Normally, a read from a stream will block until data are available. A write will block if the stream is flow-controlled. An alternative to this form of I/O is called *nonblocking I/O*. If a stream is opened with the `O_NDELAY` flag or the `O_NONBLOCK` flag, then `read` and `getmsg` will fail with `errno` set to `EAGAIN` if there are no data immediately available, and `write` and `putmsg` will fail with `errno` set to `EAGAIN` if the stream is flow-controlled. For `write`, if part of the data has been written before the stream is flow-controlled, then `write` will return the number of bytes written.

These semantics are useful to applications that do not want to wait for data to either arrive or drain. This might be the case if the application has a lower-priority task it can perform until I/O can be continued. In some cases, an application might be able to use nonblocking I/O to improve its response time.

Nonblocking I/O alone would be tedious to use: an application would have to check the file descriptors periodically to see if the state had changed. With the use of the `I_SETSIG` `ioctl` command, this is not necessary. `I_SETSIG` provides a way for the application to be signaled when data arrive or flow-control restrictions are removed. The application specifies a bitmask of events it is interested in, and the stream head sends the `SIGPOLL` signal to the process when any of the events occurs. Then the application can either handle the event right away, or note that it occurred and handle it at its convenience.

Table 3.3 summarizes the events of interest that can be registered with the stream head. (Out-of-band data are discussed in Section 3.7.)

Table 3.3. Stream Head `SIGPOLL` Events

Event	Description
S_INPUT	Data (other than high-priority) can be read.
S_HIPRI	High-priority data can be read.
S_OUTPUT	Write side is no longer flow-controlled for normal data.
S_MSG	Signal message is at head of stream head read queue.
S_ERROR	Stream is in error (M_ERROR message received).
S_HANGUP	Device has hung up stream.
S_RDNORM	Normal data (band 0) can be read.
S_WRNORM	Same as S_OUTPUT.
S_RDBAND	Out-of-band data can be read.
S_WRBAND	Write side is no longer flow-controlled for out-of-band data.
S_BANDURG	Modifier to S_RDBAND to generate SIGURG instead of SIGPOLL.

Normal data are packaged in M_DATA messages and have a priority band of zero. S_INPUT is equivalent to (S_RDNORM|S_RDBAND) because read and getmsg remove the first message from the stream head read queue, regardless of the message's band. S_WRNORM is the same as S_OUTPUT because write and putmsg (without the RS_HIPRI flag) generate messages in band zero. S_WRNORM was added only to maintain a consistent naming scheme. S_BANDURG is used by the socket library described in Chapter 7.

The default action for the SIGPOLL signal is to kill the process. This may seem severe, but the stream head will never generate SIGPOLL unless the process explicitly requests it by invoking the I_SETSIG ioctl command. Therefore, applications must be careful to install the signal handler for SIGPOLL before using the I_SETSIG ioctl.

In a way, the default disposition of SIGPOLL encourages proper use of I_SETSIG. If you ask for signals to be generated without being prepared to handle them, then you pay the price. There is one unfortunate side effect, however. If a program has arranged for SIGPOLL generation and then execs, the signal dispositions for signals with handlers are restored to their default values. If the process that calls exec is a descendant of the process that called I_SETSIG, then everything is fine because SIGPOLL is only sent to the process that requested it. On the other hand, if the process calling exec is the same one that requested SIGPOLL be generated, then the new program will be killed if it receives SIGPOLL. Thus, before execing, processes using SIGPOLL should either disable its generation, ignore the signal, or set the close-on-exec flag for the file descriptors associated with the streams that might generate the signal.

Example 3.4.1. Data transfer to a stream can be illustrated with the cat(1) command. Since terminals are streams, we can use the standard output as the example of a STREAMS file descriptor to which data will be written.

Consider the simplified implementation of cat from Example 2.4.6. It is fairly straightforward, reading from the file and writing to the standard output until either there is an error, or the end of the file has been reached.

But what would happen if the standard output flow-controlled? The application would block in the write until the flow control subsided and the rest of the data could be written. We could make better use of this time if we were able to read more of the file until the standard output could accept more data. This version of the program employs nonblocking I/O to do just that:

```c
#include <sys/types.h>
#include <stdlib.h>
#include <stdio.h>
#include <fcntl.h>
#include <unistd.h>
#include <errno.h>
#include <stropts.h>
#include <signal.h>

#define  BUFSIZE  (64*1024)
#define  RDSIZE   (BUFSIZE/8)

char buf[BUFSIZE];
int widx, ridx;        /* write and read indices */
int totwr, totrd;      /* total amounts read and written */
int flowctl;           /* 1 if flow-controlled, 0 if not */
int nfc;               /* number of times flow-controlled */

void catreg(int), cattostream(int);
int doread(int);
void dowrite(int), finwrite(void);
void setblock(int), setnonblock(int);

#ifdef FCBUG
void nop(int);
#endif

extern void error(const char *fmt, ...);
extern void fatal(const char *fmt, ...);

void
main(int argc, char *argv[])
{
      int i, fd, isoutstr;
#ifdef FCBUG
      struct sigaction sa;

      /*
       * If system contains flow-control bug,
       * install a signal handler for SIGALRM.
       */
      sa.sa_handler = nop;
      sigemptyset(&sa.sa_mask);
      sa.sa_flags = 0;
```

```
        if (sigaction(SIGALRM, &sa, NULL) < 0)
            fatal("cat: sigaction failed");
#endif

        /*
         * See if the standard output is a stream.  If
         * isastream fails, assume stdout is not a stream.
         */
        isoutstr = isastream(1);
        if (isoutstr == -1)
            isoutstr = 0;

        /*
         * Process each file named on the command line.
         */
        for (i = 1; i < argc; i++) {
            if ((fd = open(argv[i], O_RDONLY)) < 0) {
                error("cat: cannot open %s", argv[i]);
                continue;
            }

            /*
             * If the standard output is a stream, call
             * cattostream to print the file.  Otherwise
             * call catreg (see Example 2.4.6) to do it.
             */
            if (isoutstr)
                cattostream(fd);
            else
                catreg(fd);
            close(fd);
        }
#ifdef DEBUG
        printf("cat: number of flow controls = %d\n", nfc);
#endif
        exit(0);
}

#ifdef FCBUG
void
nop(int sig)
{
}
#endif
```

There are several differences between this version of cat and the one presented in Example 2.4.6. First, we have added a dummy signal handler, nop, for SIGALRM. It is only used if the symbol FCBUG is defined. nop is part of a work-around for a bug in STREAMS flow control found in versions of SVR4. (The bug has been fixed in SVR4.1 and SVR4.2.) The bug creates a window where the event that triggers the generation of SIGPOLL can be lost. The same bug can result in missing the event when using poll, too.

The second difference is the call to isastream(3C) to determine if the standard output is a stream. The synopsis for `isastream` is

```
int isastream(int fd);
```

`isastream` returns 1 if `fd` is a file descriptor associated with a stream, 0 if not, and −1 on error. If an error occurs, we assume the standard output is not a stream. We use `catreg`, from Example 2.4.6, if file descriptor 1 is not a stream. Otherwise, we call `cattostream` to copy the contents of the file to the standard output.

Notice that the buffer is larger, but the read size (RDSIZE) will still be the same as the previous version. This is because we will use the buffer in a circular fashion: as we are copying data from one part of it, we will copy data into another part, until we reach the end of the buffer, where we will jump back to the beginning of the buffer again, until no more data are left (see Figure 3.7).

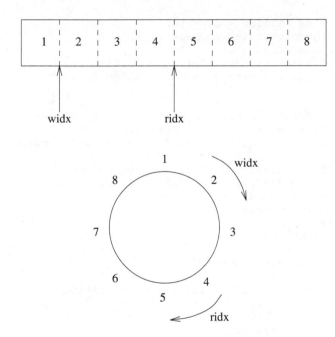

Fig. 3.7. Circular Buffer

Before writing to the stream, `cattostream` installs a signal handler for `SIGPOLL` and registers with the stream to be sent `SIGPOLL` whenever flow-control restrictions are removed. Then it places the stream in nonblocking mode by calling `setnonblock` (described shortly).

The basic flow is to read some data from the file, write the data to the terminal, and if flow control is asserted, continue reading from the file into the circular buffer until either there is no room left in the buffer or the `read` is interrupted by the delivery of `SIGPOLL`. We use `sigprocmask` to manage the critical sections of code where an error might occur if the execution is interrupted by the delivery of

SIGPOLL. If there is no room left in the buffer, we have nothing to do but wait for flow-control restrictions to be lifted, so we use sigsuspend.

```
void
cattostream(int fd)
{
    int n;
    struct sigaction sa;
    sigset_t s, os;

    sigemptyset(&s);
    sigaddset(&s, SIGPOLL);

    /*
     * Install a signal handler for SIGPOLL.
     */
    sa.sa_handler = dowrite;
    sigemptyset(&sa.sa_mask);
    sa.sa_flags = 0;
    if (sigaction(SIGPOLL, &sa, NULL) < 0)
        fatal("cat: sigaction failed");

    /*
     * Arrange to be notified when the standard output
     * is no longer flow-controlled.  Then place the file
     * descriptor for stdout in nonblocking mode.
     */
    if (ioctl(1, I_SETSIG, S_OUTPUT) < 0)
        fatal("cat: I_SETSIG ioctl failed");
    setnonblock(1);
    totrd = totwr = 0;
    ridx = widx = 0;
    flowctl = 0;
    for (;;) {
        if ((n = doread(fd)) == 0) {
            /*
             * End of file; finish writing.
             */
            finwrite();
            break;
        } else if (n < 0) {
            /*
             * Read was interrupted by SIGPOLL.
             */
            continue;
        } else {
            /*
             * Successfully read something.
             */
            totrd += n;
        }

        /*
         * Start critical section.  Block SIGPOLL.
```

```
                    * Then try to write what we've just read.
                    */
                   sigprocmask(SIG_BLOCK, &s, &os);
                   dowrite(0);
                   while (flowctl) {
                       if (ridx != widx) {
                           /*
                            * Allow read to be interrupted.
                            */
                           sigprocmask(SIG_UNBLOCK, &s, NULL);
                           if ((n = doread(fd)) == 0) { /* EOF */
                               finwrite();
                               return;
                           } else if (n > 0) { /* read data */
                               totrd += n;
                           }
                           sigprocmask(SIG_BLOCK, &s, NULL);
                       } else {
#ifdef FCBUG
                           /*
                            * Flow control bug -- might miss event.
                            */
                           alarm(1);
#endif
                           /*
                            * Atomically unblock SIGPOLL and
                            * wait to be interrupted.  On return,
                            * SIGPOLL is still blocked.
                            */
                           sigsuspend(&os);
#ifdef FCBUG
                           alarm(0);
                           if (ioctl(1, I_CANPUT, 0) != 0) {
                               /*
                                * Flow control lifted;
                                * continue writing.
                                */
                               flowctl = 0;
                               dowrite(0);
                               break;
                           }
#endif
                       }
                   }

                   /*
                    * End critical section.  Unblock SIGPOLL.
                    */
                   sigprocmask(SIG_UNBLOCK, &s, NULL);
               }
       }
```

We use `alarm` so that we do not block indefinitely if FCBUG is defined. To work around the flow-control bug, we use the `I_CANPUT` `ioctl` to check if we can write to the stream. If not, we just continue in the loop. If so, we clear the flowctl flag and call dowrite to continue writing to the stream. On systems that have fixed the flow-control bug, dowrite is called as the signal handler for SIGPOLL.

We use setnonblock to place a stream in nonblocking mode and setblock to restore it back to the default blocking behavior. Both functions get the current copy of the file flags for the stream and then turn the O_NONBLOCK flag either off or on. Modifying a copy of the current flags ensures that we do not change any of the flags already set; we just want to change the status of the O_NONBLOCK flag.

```
void
setnonblock(int fd)
{
    int fl;

    /*
     * Get the current file flags and turn on
     * nonblocking mode.
     */
    if ((fl = fcntl(fd, F_GETFL, 0)) < 0)
        fatal("cat: fcntl F_GETFL failed");
    if (fcntl(fd, F_SETFL, fl|O_NONBLOCK) < 0)
        fatal("cat: fcntl F_SETFL failed");
}

void
setblock(int fd)
{
    int fl;

    /*
     * Get the current file flags and turn off
     * nonblocking mode.
     */
    if ((fl = fcntl(fd, F_GETFL, 0)) < 0)
        fatal("cat: fcntl F_GETFL failed");
    if (fcntl(fd, F_SETFL, (fl&~O_NONBLOCK)) < 0)
        fatal("cat: fcntl F_SETFL failed");
}
```

When we have reached the end of the input file, read will return 0 and we call finwrite to finish writing the data to the standard output. In it, we attempt to cancel the SIGPOLL generation. If that fails, we just ignore SIGPOLL. The I_SETSIG should not fail, but we program defensively where we can. Then we disable nonblocking mode for the standard output and finish writing the data to the terminal.

```
void
finwrite(void)
{
```

```
        /*
         * Cancel SIGPOLL generation for stdout.
         */
        if (ioctl(1, I_SETSIG, 0) < 0) {
            struct sigaction sa;

            /*
             * I_SETSIG shouldn't have failed, but
             * it did, so the next best thing is to
             * ignore SIGPOLL.
             */
            sa.sa_handler = SIG_IGN;
            sigemptyset(&sa.sa_mask);
            sa.sa_flags = 0;
            if (sigaction(SIGPOLL, &sa, NULL) < 0)
                fatal("sigaction failed");
        }

        /*
         * Disable nonblocking mode and write last
         * portion to the standard output.
         */
        setblock(1);
        dowrite(0);
    }
```

In the circular buffer, `ridx` is the index of the next location into which we read data, and `widx` is the index of the next location from which we write data. The maximum data read at once is given by RDSIZE. If we are less than `ridx` bytes from the end of the buffer, then we read only as many bytes as can fit in the buffer.

After reading, we increment `ridx` by the number of bytes read and if it reaches the end of the buffer, we reset it to 0. If SIGPOLL comes in during the middle of the read, then we can get one of two results: either we transferred some data to the buffer and `read` will return the number of bytes transferred, or we did not transfer anything and `read` fails with `errno` set to EINTR. Any other failure is a real error.

```
int
doread(int fd)
{
    int n, rcnt;

    /*
     * Calculate the space left to read.
     * Read at most RDSIZE bytes.
     */
    rcnt = widx - ridx;
    if (rcnt <= 0) {
        /*
         * The writer is behind the reader
         * in the buffer.
         */
        rcnt = BUFSIZE - ridx;
        if (rcnt > RDSIZE)
```

```
            rcnt = RDSIZE;
    }

    /*
     * Read as much as we can.
     */
    n = read(fd, &buf[ridx], rcnt);
    if (n >= 0) {
        ridx += n;

        /*
         * If we've reached the end of the buffer,
         * reset the read index to the beginning.
         */
        if (ridx == BUFSIZE)
            ridx = 0;
    } else if (errno != EINTR) {
        fatal("cat: read failed");
    }
    return(n);
}
```

The routine that does the writing to the terminal, dowrite, is always called with SIGPOLL blocked. This is because the write might cause the stream to become flow-controlled, and we do not want the signal to be generated while we are still in dowrite or we could lose track of whether or not the stream is flow-controlled.

Consider what would happen if we did not block SIGPOLL and it came in after write failed because of flow control, but before flowctl was set to 1. dowrite would again be called, but this time as the handler for SIGPOLL. If it is able to write to the stream, it will set flowctl to 0. Then, when it returns to the original instance of dowrite, we continue by setting flowctl to 1, which is incorrect. If cattostream is able to read the remaining part of the file, then the error will be of no consequence, because cattostream will just call finwrite to write the contents of the buffer to the stream. If, however, the buffer fills without having read the entire file, then cattostream will call sigsuspend and never return because the stream is not really flow-controlled.

```
void
dowrite(int sig)
{
    int n, wcnt;

    while (widx >= ridx) {

        /*
         * Stop when the writer has caught up with
         * the reader.
         */
        if ((widx == ridx) && (totrd == totwr))
            break;
```

```
        /*
         * The writer is ahead of the reader in the
         * buffer.  Calculate the amount left to write,
         * and write it.
         */
        wcnt = BUFSIZE - widx;
        n = write(1, &buf[widx], wcnt);
        if (n < 0) {
            if (errno == EAGAIN) {
                /*
                 * The stream is flow-controlled.
                 */
                nfc++;
                flowctl = 1;
                return;
            } else {
                fatal("cat: write failed");
            }
        } else {
            totwr += n;
        }
        widx += n;

        /*
         * If the write index has reached the end
         * of the buffer, reset it to 0.
         */
        if (widx == BUFSIZE)
            widx = 0;
    }
    while (widx < ridx) {
        /*
         * The writer is behind the reader in the buffer.
         */
        wcnt = ridx - widx;
        n = write(1, &buf[widx], wcnt);
        if (n < 0) {
            if (errno == EAGAIN) {
                /*
                 * The stream is flow-controlled.
                 */
                nfc++;
                flowctl = 1;
                return;
            } else {
                fatal("cat: write failed");
            }
        } else {
            totwr += n;
        }
        widx += n;

        /*
         * If the write index has reached the end
```

```
    * of the buffer, reset it to 0.
    */
   if (widx == BUFSIZE)
        widx = 0;
}

/*
 * If we reach this point, write was able to
 * transmit everything, so we probably aren't
 * flow-controlled.
 */
flowctl = 0;
}
```

If `widx` is greater than `ridx`, then the most we can write is from `widx` to the end of the buffer. Otherwise, the most we can write is from `widx` to the next place to read, `ridx`. If `write` fails with `errno` set to `EAGAIN`, we set the `flowctl` flag to indicate flow control has been asserted. If it fails for any other reason, it is a real error, and we exit. If `write` succeeds, we increment `widx` by the number of bytes written. If `widx` goes past the end of the buffer, we set it back to 0. Note that if `widx` equals `ridx`, nothing is written (i.e., the ''writer'' has caught up with the ''reader'').

Although more complex, this version of the program can execute several times faster than the first. This is because the program does other useful work while the output is flow-controlled. However, if the output device is fast enough such that it never flow-controls, there will be no increase in speed.

On a 33 MHz i386, I timed different versions of `cat` over three terminal devices: the console (whose screen contents are essentially mapped into the kernel address space), the asynchronous serial line connected to an ASCII terminal running at 19,200 bps (using the ASY driver), and the same serial line with an AT&T 630MTG windowing terminal running `layers` (using the XT driver, with ASY linked underneath it). The results from printing a 100,000-byte file are summarized in Table 3.4. All times are in seconds.

Table 3.4. Timing Results Writing to Different Devices

Device	cat from /usr/bin	cat from Example 2.4.6	cat from This Example
Console	36	36	36
ASY	285	273	122
XT	381	369	247

During the tests, the console stream never flow-controlled, the ASY stream flow-controlled twice, and the XT stream flow-controlled three times. Note that no increase of speed is seen with the console. That is because the console driver merely has to copy the message contents to the memory location representing the console screen to display text. This is a good example of the output device being fast enough to prevent the stream from flow-controlling.

Although this example completed faster than the other versions when the serial driver was used, the amount of time actually needed to display the text on the screen was almost equivalent. This is because this version of cat simply wrote its data and exited. It did not make the display rate any higher. The stream buffered as much data as the drivers and modules would allow. The drivers and modules continued to process data even though the command had exited because the shell still held the stream open.   □

Polling

Applications that need to handle multiple file descriptors can use the poll system call to check pending conditions on multiple file descriptors at once. Rather than blocking in a system call on one of the file descriptors while events are occurring on others, applications can block waiting for events on any of a number of file descriptors. The synopsis for poll is

```
#include <sys/types.h>
#include <poll.h>
#include <stropts.h>

int poll(struct pollfd *parray, ulong_t nfds, int timeout);
```

An application supplies an array of pollfd structures, the number of entries in the array, and a timeout value. If nothing happens within the number of milliseconds specified by the timeout, the system call returns 0. The special timeout value of INFTIM (−1) causes the system call to block indefinitely until an event occurs on one of the file descriptors. The special timeout value of 0 prevents the poll from waiting (i.e., it peeks at the state of things and returns). The pollfd structure is defined as:

```
struct pollfd {
      int      fd;        /* file descriptor */
      short    events;    /* requested events */
      short    revents;   /* returned events */
};
```

An application sets the fd field to the file descriptor to be polled and the events field to the bitmask of events to be checked. On return, the revents field contains the subset of events that occurred, plus some that the system can set. The events about which the caller can request notification are listed in Table 3.5.

In addition to those events that the caller can request, three other events can be reported (see Table 3.6). The POLLERR, POLLHUP, and POLLNVAL events only apply to the revents field. An application cannot explicitly poll for these events by setting them in the events field.

Example 3.4.2. Most commands like cu(1) and rlogin(1) are implemented by forking, using one process to read from the terminal and write to the network, and the other process to read from the network and write to the terminal. This architecture

Table 3.5. Requestable `poll` Events

Event	Description
POLLIN	Data (other than high-priority) can be read.
POLLPRI	High-priority data can be read.
POLLOUT	Write side is no longer flow-controlled for normal data.
POLLRDNORM	Normal data (band 0) can be read.
POLLWRNORM	Same as POLLOUT.
POLLRDBAND	Out-of-band data can be read.
POLLWRBAND	Write side is no longer flow-controlled for out-of-band data.

Table 3.6. Nonrequestable `poll` Events

Event	Description
POLLERR	Stream is in error (M_ERROR message received).
POLLHUP	Device has hung up stream.
POLLNVAL	The file descriptor is invalid.

can be reimplemented using only one process and using `poll` to avoid blocking on either file descriptor. The following function illustrates how this might be done.

```
#include <poll.h>
#include <unistd.h>

extern void error(const char *fmt, ...);

void
comm(int tfd, int nfd)
{
    int n, i;
    struct pollfd pfd[2];
    char buf[256];

    pfd[0].fd = tfd;     /* terminal */
    pfd[0].events = POLLIN;
    pfd[1].fd = nfd;     /* network */
    pfd[1].events = POLLIN;
    for (;;) {

        /*
         * Wait for events to occur.
         */
        if (poll(pfd, 2, -1) < 0) {
            error("poll failed");
            break;
        }
```

```
        /*
         * Check each file descriptor.
         */
        for (i = 0; i < 2; i++) {
            /*
             * If an error occurred, just return.
             */
            if (pfd[i].revents&(POLLERR|POLLHUP|POLLNVAL))
                return;

            /*
             * If there are data present, read them from
             * one file descriptor and write them to the
             * other one.
             */
            if (pfd[i].revents&POLLIN) {
                n = read(pfd[i].fd, buf, sizeof(buf));
                if (n > 0) {
                    write(pfd[1-i].fd, buf, n);
                } else {
                    if (n < 0)
                        error("read failed");
                    return;
                }
            }
        }
    }
}
```

The comm function sets up the pollfd array and performs a poll that will block until data arrive on either file descriptor. The variable i indicates the file descriptor to check. If there was an error or hangup on the stream, we return. If there are data to be read, the POLLIN flag will be set and we read the data from the stream and write them to the other stream. Since we only have two indices, 0 and 1, the idiom 1-i gives us the other index. Then we perform the same task with the other stream. We continue this until there is an error.

Do not be misled by the example. Both cu and rlogin are a lot more complex than this example might imply. They are both complicated by signal handling and local command (''escapes'') processing. rlogin uses out-of-band data to implement end-to-end flow control and to propagate interrupts across the network. cu, on the other hand, transmits all characters in a single band, sometimes resulting in awkward delays between the time that special characters (such as interrupt and stop) are typed and the time that the remote computer reacts to them. This is mainly because other characters that were transmitted before the special ones might still be buffered, delaying the remote machine from interpreting the special ones. This behavior is because cu was not designed from the start to work over networks. It was designed to work primarily with asynchronous serial communication devices and was not converted to use the transport-level network interface until SVR3. Even now, it does not attempt to use out-of-band transmission services if the underlying communication facility supports them.   □

3.5 SERVICE INTERFACES

A *service interface* is the boundary between a user (called the "consumer") and the provider of a service. A service interface consists of the primitives that can be passed across the interface and the rules specifying the state transitions that occur when the primitives are generated and received. The state transitions imply an ordering of primitives; for example, an acknowledgement being sent in response to a request. The consumer can generate request primitives to obtain service from the provider. The provider, in turn, may answer a request with a response primitive. External events might cause the provider to notify the consumer with an event primitive (see Figure 3.8).

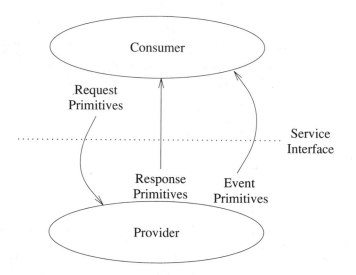

Fig. 3.8. Service Interface

Service interfaces are closely related to the OSI reference model discussed in Chapter 1. At each layer in the model, an interface exists between the upper and lower layers. Service interfaces are modeled after these interfaces. The layer beneath the interface provides a service to the layer above the interface.

The purpose of specifying a service interface is to allow consumers of services to be written independent of the providers of the service. This enhances the possibility for different consumers to be matched up with different providers, as long as they share a common service interface. The Transport Provider Interface (TPI) is one example of a service interface. It is discussed in detail in Chapter 12.

Consider an application (the consumer) that lets users remotely log in to different computers connected to a network. If the application conforms to a published service interface, then it is possible to have a variety of network protocols (the providers) that support remote login just by conforming to the same interface. Figure 3.9 illustrates this point. In it, TIMOD is a module that helps the transport interface library routines conform to the proper service interface, the TPI. Two transport providers are shown, each implementing a different protocol. TCP is the Internet's Transmission Control Protocol, and TP4 is ISO's class 4 transport protocol.

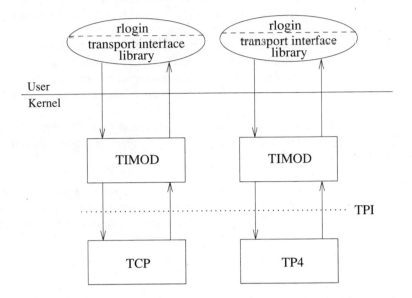

Fig. 3.9. Service Interfaces Promoting Software Reuse

Service interfaces can exist at the boundary between any two processing elements in a stream. The service interfaces provide the separation and isolation needed to implement layered protocols.

In System V, service interface primitives are implemented as STREAMS messages. Usually, primitives are constructed by creating M_PROTO message blocks containing control information, such as the primitive type and addressing information, and linking these to M_DATA message blocks containing the associated user data. By separating user data from control parameters, protocol-independent filtering modules can be used in the stream (they process only the M_DATA portions of messages). For example, you could write a module that encrypts data in M_DATA messages and push it on a network connection's stream. Both sides of the connection would have to push the same module and then inform the module of the correct key to use to encrypt and decrypt the data. The module could then operate by processing all M_DATA messages it receives, including the ones linked to M_PROTO and M_PCPROTO messages. The module would not have to know anything about the protocol used, because the module operates on user data only. Thus, the module could be used with different protocols.

The reason that the `getmsg` and `putmsg` system calls exist is to provide a means for user-level applications to communicate across service interfaces. The message-based service interface used in the kernel between processing elements in a stream is extended to applications running at user level by the ability of `getmsg` and `putmsg` to process both control information and user data.

A less obvious benefit of service interfaces is the ability to migrate protocols from the kernel to intelligent peripheral devices. Since applications deal with a fixed service interface, all that need be done is to provide a driver that presents the same service interface to users while communicating the primitives to the peripheral device where the real work is done. The system calls are unaffected by changes like this because they know nothing about the communication involved; they merely act as a message-transfer mechanism. Protocol processing can even migrate between user level and kernel level as long as the same service interfaces are provided for existing applications.

An example of a service primitive is a request to send data. The primitive type and addressing information would be contained in the control buffer, and the user data would be contained in the data buffer.

Example 3.5.1. A hypothetical (and inefficient) protocol might require that a positive or negative acknowledgement be sent to the consumer for every data request generated. Combining the routines from two previous examples (3.3.2 and 3.3.4), we can write a routine that implements this service interface.

```
#include <sys/types.h>
#include <unistd.h>
#include <signal.h>
#include <stropts.h>

int
send(int fd, char *buf, uint_t blen, char *addr,
    uint_t alen)
{
    sigset_t set, oset;

    /*
     * Block SIGPOLL.
     */
    sigemptyset(&set);
    sigaddset(&set, SIGPOLL);
    sigprocmask(SIG_BLOCK, &set, &oset);

    /*
     * Send the message.
     */
    if (senddata(fd, buf, blen, addr, alen) < 0) {
        sigprocmask(SIG_SETMASK, &oset, NULL);
        return(-1);
    }

    /*
     * Receive the acknowledgement.
     */
```

```
        if (getack(fd) < 0) {
            sigprocmask(SIG_SETMASK, &oset, NULL);
            return(-1);
        }

        /*
         * Restore the original signal mask.
         */
        sigprocmask(SIG_SETMASK, &oset, NULL);
        return(0);
    }
```

This is a simple example, but it illustrates a problem with library routines used to implement service interface primitives that require a response. The response message might generate SIGPOLL if the caller had previously called I_SETSIG and the message type of the response corresponds to an input event in which the caller was interested. If we ignore SIGPOLL in the library routine, the caller might miss the arrival of data. If we block (hold) SIGPOLL, then we might generate an event because of the arrival of the response message when there is really nothing for the caller to read.

Luckily, response primitives are usually M_PCPROTO messages, and applications are usually only interested in the arrival of normal and out-of-band data. This is because only one high-priority message is enqueued at one time on a stream head's read queue, so it is unlikely that M_PCPROTO messages are used for anything other than interface acknowledgements. (Otherwise, primitives would be lost when additional M_PCPROTO messages arrived.) In the event that the caller wants to be signaled when high-priority messages arrive, it is probably better that we generate a false event than to remain silent, so we choose to hold SIGPOLL instead of ignoring it.   □

Examples of more realistic service interfaces are discussed in later chapters.

3.6 IPC WITH STREAMS PIPES

We briefly introduced STREAMS-based pipes in Section 3.2. In this section we will explore the architecture of pipes, along with some of the side effects of this architecture. Then we will see how STREAMS pipes are used for interprocess communication.

A pipe is created with the pipe system call:

```
#include <unistd.h>

int pfd[2];

if (pipe(pfd) < 0) {
    perror("pipe failed");
    exit(1);
}
```

Figure 3.10 shows the structure of a pipe. Each file descriptor has its own stream head, with the write queue pointing at the other's read queue. Data written using one file descriptor will be packaged into messages by the stream head and placed on the read queue of the stream head at the other end of the pipe. These data are then available to be read using the other file descriptor.

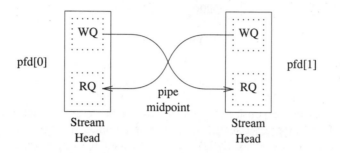

Fig. 3.10. Queue Linkage in a Pipe

If a module is pushed on one end of the pipe, it cannot be popped from the other end (see Figure 3.11). To be removed, it must be popped from the same end on which it was pushed. This is because the pipe is really two separate streams linked together. The point where the streams "twist" (where the write queues point to the read queues) is the midpoint of the pipe. Operations that are local to a stream will end here, such as searching for modules to pop, or listing the modules in the stream.

Recall that multiple processes that open the same device share the same stream. This is also true for pipes. Since a pipe is a stream, when more than one process is writing to the same end of a pipe at the same time, the data from one process will be interleaved with the data from the other processes.

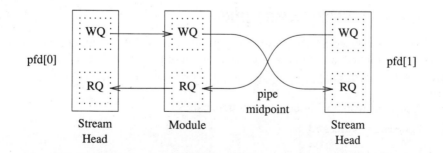

Fig. 3.11. A Module Pushed on a Pipe

Historically, pipe semantics have guaranteed that if a process writes no more than PIPE_BUF bytes, the data will not be fragmented and interleaved with data from other processes. In other words, if a process writes at most PIPE_BUF bytes in one system call, the process reading from the other end of the pipe (assuming it reads the same amount) will receive all the data written by the writer, without the data being intermixed with data from other writers. If, however, the writer sends the data with more than one write system call, data from other writers might be interleaved with the data from the separate system calls.

Different UNIX systems support different values for PIPE_BUF. Two common values are 4096 and 5120 bytes. POSIX_PIPE_BUF defines the minimum value that any POSIX-conforming system must support. Both constants are defined in <limits.h>. Portable applications should not assume that the value for PIPE_BUF is greater than POSIX_PIPE_BUF. A portable way does exist, however, to find the value of PIPE_BUF for a given system: use pathconf(2) or fpathconf(2).

For example, assume two processes, A and B, are writing to the same end of a pipe, and that $100 < $ PIPE_BUF $ < 10,000$. If process A writes 100 bytes and process B writes 100 bytes, then the reader will receive 100 bytes from one process, followed by 100 bytes from the other process, depending on who wrote first. Now, if process A decides to write 10,000 bytes, but process B only writes 100 bytes, the reader could receive the first PIPE_BUF from process A, then the 100 bytes from process B, followed by the remaining data $(10,000 - $ PIPE_BUF $)$ from process A. The order depends on a number of factors, such as process scheduling priority and availability of buffers for STREAMS messages.

If a module is pushed on one end of the pipe, these semantics are maintained as long as the module's maximum packet size is at least PIPE_BUF bytes. The maximum packet size determines how the data are fragmented when written. Of course, with modules on the pipe, the order of arrival might change depending on how the modules process the data.

Even though pipes are streams, they exhibit slightly different behavior during nonblocking I/O, because of older pipe semantics. For compatibility, if a pipe's stream is placed in nonblocking mode with the O_NDELAY flag, read will return 0 when no data are available, and write will block when the stream is flow-controlled. If the stream is placed in nonblocking mode with the O_NONBLOCK flag, read will return −1 with errno set to EAGAIN when no data are available, and write will return −1 with errno set to EAGAIN when the stream is flow-controlled.

If one end of a pipe is closed, then the other end is placed in hangup mode. Thus, processes cannot write to the open end, but they can still read from it. Processes will be sent SIGPIPE when they try to write to a pipe when the other end is not in use. The default action for SIGPIPE is to kill the process, so processes that do not want to be killed in this manner when using pipes should either catch or ignore SIGPIPE if there is a chance that one end will go away abruptly.

Flushing Data in a Pipe

An interesting problem occurs with flushing data in a pipe. Recall that flushing occurs by passing an M_FLUSH message through the stream. The message contains flags that specify the queues to flush (read-side, write-side, or both). At the point where the two streams forming the pipe meet, the read side of one stream becomes the write side of the other, and vice versa. So if only one side of the stream is flushed, the flag will refer to the opposite side after passing the midpoint of the pipe.

Referring back to Figure 3.10, let's look at what happens when we try to flush the stream using

```
ioctl(pfd[0], I_FLUSH, flag);
```

If flag is FLUSHR, then the stream head read queue referred to by pfd[0] will be flushed. If flag is FLUSHW, then the stream head read queue referred to by pfd[1] will be flushed, since data written to pfd[0] are placed on the read queue of pfd[1]. If flag is FLUSHRW, then both read queues are flushed. The stream head never enqueues messages on its write queue, so there is no need to flush it. Note that no message is generated to flush the pipe when no modules are present.

If there are modules on the stream pipe (see Figure 3.11), however, a message is used instead, in the same way as if there were a driver at the end of the stream. Now let's see what happens in this case. If only FLUSHR is set in the M_FLUSH message, the module would flush its read queue and pass the message to the stream head of pfd[1]. Then that stream head would flush its read queue, which is not what we intended. Since the read queue of pfd[1] holds messages we write to pfd[0], flushing the read queue of pfd[1] would only make sense if we had specified FLUSHW.

If only FLUSHW is set, the module would flush its write queue and pass the message to the stream head of pfd[1]. The stream head would then route the message down its write side, passing the message back to the module. The module would again flush its write queue and pass the message back to where it originated, the stream head of pfd[0]. This time, however, the stream head will not route the message back down the write side of the stream. It is smart enough to prevent the flush message from circulating more than once in the pipe.

The problem of flushing the wrong queues in a pipe exists because, at the midpoint, the side of the stream where processing is taking place changes, but the sense of the flags in the M_FLUSH message does not. To flush one side of a pipe correctly, we need to flip the sense of the flags. For example, to flush the write side, we should flush all the write queues from the stream head down to the midpoint, then switch and flush all the read queues on the other side from the midpoint up to the other stream head.

To solve this problem, a module (called PIPEMOD) is available to switch the sense of the flush flags. PIPEMOD performs no other function. If an application requires modules on the pipe and the ability to flush data, then PIPEMOD should be the first module pushed on the stream, closest to the midpoint. (It only needs to be on one side of the pipe.) Otherwise, it can be left off the stream. In addition to

PIPEMOD, other modules intended for use in pipes may incorporate the necessary logic to switch the sense of the flush flags.

Mounted Streams

When a process needs to communicate with one of its children, it usually does so through a pipe. The parent enables communication by creating a pipe before forking off the child. After the child is created, the parent will write to and read from one of the two file descriptors returned from the `pipe` system call. The child will use the other end of the pipe.

More interesting, however, is the use of pipes for communication between unrelated processes. By giving one end of a pipe a name in the file system, a process offers a way for other processes to communicate with it. FIFOs provide this capability, but communication is unidirectional. Mounted streams overcome this problem. Here's how: a process creates a pipe and mounts one end of it over an existing file using `fattach(3)`. Then, when other processes open the file, they gain access to the mounted end of the pipe instead of the preexisting file. Communication can occur as in the parent/child case, with the original process reading from and writing to the unmounted end of the pipe, and the other processes reading from and writing to the mounted end of the pipe.

The `fattach` library routine uses the `mount` system call and a special file system called NAMEFS to support mounted streams (also called ''named streams''). The synopsis for `fattach` is

```
int fattach(int fd, const char *path);
```

The process must own and have write permission on the file represented by `path`, or have super-user privileges. After the stream is attached, processes opening the file will gain access to the pipe. Any processes that have the file open before the call to `fattach` will still access the original file after the attach is made, but if they open the file again, they will access the pipe instead.

Example 3.6.1. One problem that arises with window systems is that they may render your login terminal device useless. Others cannot write to your terminal unless the windowing software has replaced the login terminal's entry in `/var/adm/utmp` with the name of the new device to which messages can be sent. Even though library routines exist to make this change easier [see `getut(3C)`], they can cause problems because they do not serialize access to the data files being changed.

Instead of changing the `utmp` entry, a windowing system can elect to display messages written to your terminal in the current window or in a reserved window by monitoring the end of the pipe returned by this function:

```
#include <sys/types.h>
#include <sys/stat.h>
#include <unistd.h>

#define TTYMODE   (S_IRUSR|S_IWUSR|S_IWGRP)
```

```
int
chgterm()
{
    int pfd[2];
    char *tty;

    /*
     * Get the name of the controlling terminal.
     */
    if ((tty = ttyname(0)) == NULL)
        return(-1);

    /*
     * Create a pipe and mount one end on top of
     * the terminal's device node.  Then change
     * the mode of the pipe to give it the same
     * permissions as terminals.
     */
    if (pipe(pfd) < 0)
        return(-1);
    if ((fattach(pfd[1], tty) < 0) ||
       (chmod(tty, TTYMODE) < 0)) {
        close(pfd[0]);
        close(pfd[1]);
        return(-1);
    }

    /*
     * Close the end of the pipe just mounted and
     * return the other end to the caller.
     */
    close(pfd[1]);
    return(pfd[0]);
}
```

On success, the function returns a file descriptor to be monitored, or −1 if it fails. It obtains the name of the terminal that was used to log in, creates a pipe, and mounts one end of the pipe over the name. Then it makes the name publicly writable. This does not change the mode of the on-disk file representing the terminal name, as you might expect. Instead, it changes the mode of the pipe while it is attached to the name, leaving the mode of the on-disk file unaltered. From the output of ls −l /dev/ttyXX, it will appear as if the terminal name is a pipe with permission 0620, but as soon as the pipe is unmounted, things will revert to the actual device mode and permissions.

One catch with using this method is that the terminal device will not act as a terminal when opened by other processes. Since many programs behave differently when they are writing to a terminal, it might be prudent for the windowing system to push a special module on the pipe to make the pipe appear as a terminal. Such a module is easy to write, as we shall see in Chapter 11.   □

A process can unmount a stream that has been attached to the file system namespace with `fdetach(3)`:

```
int fdetach(const char *path);
```

Unless both ends of a pipe are mounted, if one end of a pipe is closed while the other end is mounted, then the mounted end is automatically unmounted. This is why we do not have to call `fdetach` if `chmod` fails in the previous example.

Sharing and Passing File Descriptors

When two processes want to share file descriptors, they usually have to be related in some way. When a process forks, the child process has access to all file descriptors in use by the parent before the fork. Any files opened after the fork are private to the process that opened them. This is useful when the parent needs to fork off a child to perform some task.

Passing file descriptors between unrelated processes can be accomplished in this manner by having the child `exec` the program that is to receive the file descriptors. This approach is inconvenient because it restricts the types of programs that can make use of it. For example, processes already running would not be able to receive file descriptors since the passing can only be done at the creation of the process. Additionally, the file descriptors to be shared are limited to only those file descriptors in use before the `fork`.

The `I_SENDFD` and `I_RECVFD` `ioctl` commands improve this situation by allowing unrelated processes to pass file descriptors to each other. When a process wants to send a file descriptor to another process, it can use the `I_SENDFD` `ioctl` command in conjunction with a mounted pipe:

```
#include <stropts.h>

if (ioctl(pipefd, I_SENDFD, otherfd) < 0)
    perror("Cannot send file descriptor");
```

The first parameter, `pipefd`, must be a file descriptor of a stream pipe or a loop-back driver. The third parameter, `otherfd`, is the file descriptor to be sent. The only requirement is that it be a valid open file descriptor.

After sending `otherfd`, the process can close it if the file descriptor is not needed. The system will keep it open until the receiving process closes it. To pass a file descriptor, the stream head creates an `M_PASSFP` message, obtains a reference to the file pointer, places the file pointer and identification of the sender in the message, and enqueues the message on the stream head read queue at the other end of the pipe.

A process can then receive the file descriptor with the `I_RECVFD` `ioctl` command:

```
#include <stropts.h>

struct strrecvfd recv;

if (ioctl(pipefd, I_RECVFD, &recv) < 0)
    perror("Cannot receive file descriptor");
```

The third argument is a pointer to a `strrecvfd` structure that describes the new file descriptor:

```
struct strrecvfd {
      int      fd;
      uid_t    uid;
      gid_t    gid;
};
```

The `fd` field contains the new file descriptor. The `uid` field contains the effective user ID of the sending process. Similarly, the `gid` field contains the effective group ID of the sending process.

If an `M_PASSFP` message is at the front of the stream head read queue, any attempts to use `read` or `getmsg` on that stream will fail with `errno` set to `EBADMSG`.

Example 3.6.2. Suppose client applications must authenticate their network connections so they can obtain service. Instead of having every client application call a function to do the authentication, we can delegate a separate process on each machine to handle the authentication. Separating the authentication from the clients has the advantage that we can change the authentication scheme at any time without having to change all of the applications; we just replace the authenticator process instead. (A similar technique can be applied to server processes as well.)

One way to implement the interface to the authenticator process is to pass the network connection to the process, let it do the work, and then have it pass the file descriptor back to the client. For example, the authenticator might use the user ID found in the `strrecvfd` structure as an index into a database containing public and private keys (passwords) to be used in authentication. A function similar to the following can be used to exchange file descriptors with the authenticator:

```
#include <fcntl.h>
#include <unistd.h>
#include <stropts.h>
#include <errno.h>

int
auth(int netfd)
{
      int afd;
      struct strrecvfd recv;

      /*
       * Open a mounted stream pipe to the authenticator.
       */
      if ((afd = open("/var/.authpipe", O_RDWR)) < 0) {
          close(netfd);
          return(-1);
      }

      /*
       * Send the network connection to be authenticated.
```

```
        */
        if (ioctl(afd, I_SENDFD, netfd) < 0) {
            close(afd);
            close(netfd);
            return(-1);
        }

        /*
         * We don't need the network file descriptor.
         * The authenticator will pass us back the
         * file descriptor to use.
         */
        close(netfd);
        if (ioctl(afd, I_RECVFD, &recv) < 0) {
            recv.fd = -1;
        } else if (recv.uid != 0) { /* impostor */
            close(recv.fd);
            errno = EACCES;
            recv.fd = -1;
        }
        close(afd);
        return(recv.fd);
    }
```

The first step is to open the mounted pipe (`/var/.authpipe`) that the authentication server is using. It is usually a good idea to start pipe names with a period so people grepping around will not indefinitely block reading from the pipe. If the open fails, we close the network file descriptor since we cannot authenticate the connection, and we return failure.

If we can open the named pipe, we send the file descriptor to the authentication process. Then we close the network file descriptor since we do not need it anymore and receive the authenticated file descriptor from the authentication process. If the authenticator is not running with super-user privileges, we discard the file descriptor and set `errno` to EACCES to indicate a permissions problem. This limits the ability of someone being able to spoof the authentication facility.

If everything checks out, we close the pipe's file descriptor and return the file descriptor associated with the authenticated network connection.   □

Unique Connections

There is a bug in the previous example. If more than one process is trying to authenticate a connection at the same time, then we might end up with the authenticated file descriptors going to the wrong processes. With more than one process trying to receive a file descriptor from the same end of a pipe, the first process to run will get the file descriptor. This is the same problem that exists with both FIFOs and mounted streams: the reader cannot distinguish data from multiple writers, and multiple readers cannot contend for data from the same end of a pipe without some sort of synchronization.

This problem can be solved by using a special module called CONNLD. The server process can push CONNLD on the mounted end of the pipe. Then, whenever a process opens the pipe, it will get a unique connection to the server. The way this works is that CONNLD creates a second pipe and sends one end to the server process. Then it arranges to have the other end returned to the client process as the returned file descriptor from `open`. The client process will block until the server receives the file descriptor with the `I_RECVFD` ioctl command. Then both processes can communicate over the unique connection without interference from other processes.

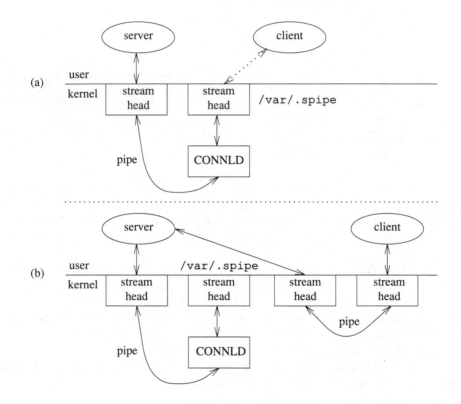

Fig. 3.12. Unique Connections with CONNLD

Figure 3.12 shows a process opening a pipe (with CONNLD on it) mounted on the file named `/var/.spipe`. In part (a), the client process attempts to open the pipe and goes to sleep. After CONNLD creates a new pipe and sends one end to the server process, the server receives it, waking up the client. Part (b) of the figure shows the end result. The server process has a new file descriptor that refers to one end of a pipe that goes directly to the client process. The client process does *not* gain access to the mounted pipe. Instead, the mounted pipe is replaced by the newly created pipe before `open` returns.

Example 3.6.3. The following two routines can be used by a server process to provide unique connections on a mounted pipe. The first routine creates the pipe, pushes CONNLD on one end, and then mounts that end in the file system. This is all the initialization needed to enable unique connections. The second routine is a stub for the authentication process discussed in the previous example.

```c
#include <sys/stat.h>
#include <unistd.h>
#include <fcntl.h>
#include <stropts.h>

#define PIPEPATH "/var/.authpipe"
#define ALLRD     (S_IRUSR|S_IRGRP|S_IROTH)
#define ALLWR     (S_IWUSR|S_IWGRP|S_IWOTH)
#define PIPEMODE  (ALLRD|ALLWR)

int pfd[2];

extern void fatal(const char *fmt, ...);

void
initialize()
{
    /*
     * Create a pipe.
     */
    if (pipe(pfd) < 0)
        fatal("cannot create pipe");

    /*
     * Push CONNLD on one end to enable unique
     * connections.
     */
    if (ioctl(pfd[1], I_PUSH, "connld") < 0)
        fatal("cannot push CONNLD");

    /*
     * Create a place to mount the pipe.
     */
    close(creat(PIPEPATH, PIPEMODE));

    /*
     * Mount the end of the pipe containing
     * CONNLD on PIPEPATH.
     */
    if (fattach(pfd[1], PIPEPATH) < 0)
        fatal("cannot attach pipe to file system");
}

void
serve()
{
    struct strrecvfd recv;
```

```
        struct strrecvfd conn;
        int okay;

        for (;;) {
            /*
             * Get the file descriptor of the pipe
             * connected to the local client process.
             */
            if (ioctl(pfd[0], I_RECVFD, &conn) < 0)
                continue;

            /*
             * Get the file descriptor to be authenticated.
             */
            if (ioctl(conn.fd, I_RECVFD, &recv) < 0) {
                close(conn.fd);
                continue;
            }

            /*
             * Authenticate the connection.
             */
            okay = doauth(recv.fd);

            /*
             * Send authenticated file descriptor back to
             * the client process.
             */
            if (okay)
                ioctl(conn.fd, I_SENDFD, recv.fd);

            /*
             * Close the file descriptors we no longer need.
             */
            close(conn.fd);
            close(recv.fd);
        }
    }
```

The second routine implements a sample service loop. The first I_RECVFD obtains the file descriptor for one end of the unique pipe connection to the client. The second I_RECVFD obtains the file descriptor of the network connection that is to be authenticated. If authentication succeeds, the authenticated file descriptor is passed back to the client. If authentication fails, the pipe is closed, resulting in the client's I_RECVFD ioctl request failing.   □

Another interesting problem occurs with using pipes for communication between unrelated processes. By placing a pipe in the file system namespace, applications can expose themselves to unwanted communication, through either error or mischief. If the access permissions of a mounted pipe are unrestrictive, as they often must be, processes other than those intended can attempt communication. Since they might not follow the proper protocol, server applications have to be less trusting.

For example, suppose an application were written to expect a message following a fixed format, and a client only wrote half of the message. Then the next process to write to the pipe would have the first part of its message interpreted as the second half of the previous (incomplete) message.

Applications can be made less susceptible to these types of errors by following a few simple rules:

1. If you read less than you expect to, discard the data.
2. Validate the data received, if possible.
3. If you are using `read` and get EBADMSG, there might be a protocol message or file-descriptor message on the stream head read queue. If it is a protocol message, retrieve it using `getmsg` and discard the information. If it is a file-descriptor message, use I_RECVFD to get the file descriptor and then close it right away. If you are using `getmsg` and get EBADMSG, then there is a file-descriptor message on the stream head read queue. As in the read case, receive it and close it.
4. Put the stream in *message discard* mode so any data remaining in the message after you have read what you needed are discarded (see the next section for more details).

3.7 ADVANCED TOPICS

This section will cover some less commonly used aspects of STREAMS, including read modes, write modes, and priority bands.

Read Modes

By default, `read(2)` treats data on the stream head read queue as a byte stream. This means it ignores message boundaries. If the user issues a `read` large enough, data will be retrieved from multiple messages on the queue until either the queue is empty or the `read` request size is satisfied. As discussed earlier, `read` only works if the message on the front of the stream head read queue is of type M_DATA.

These characteristics can be changed with the I_SRDOPT `ioctl` command. Of the six modes, three control how `read` processes data in messages on the queue and three control how `read` treats nondata messages. The current read modes in effect for a stream can be obtained with the I_GRDOPT `ioctl` command.

Usually, *byte stream mode* (RNORM, the default) will suffice for most applications, but there are two other mutually exclusive modes that applications can use. The first, *message discard mode* (RMSGD), will prevent `read` from returning data in more than one message if the amount requested is greater than the amount of data in the first message on the stream head read queue. If the application requests less, then the remainder of the message is discarded. This is useful when an application employs a protocol that uses fixed-size messages. If a process sends more data than required, the excess will be discarded when read by the application. If a process writes less than required, the read will not consume successive messages to satisfy the amount of data missing from the first message.

The second mode is *message nondiscard mode* (RMSGN). Like RMSGD mode, this mode will prevent read from returning data in more than one message if the amount requested is greater than the amount of data in the first message on the stream head read queue. Unlike RMSGD mode, however, if the application reads less than the amount of data in the first message, the remainder of the message is placed back on the front of the stream head read queue, to be obtained by the next read. This mode is useful when an application does not know how much data to expect, wants to do large reads for performance, and expects data to be written in one message. It is equivalent to getmsg without control information.

Three mutually exclusive modes control the treatment of protocol messages (M_PROTO and M_PCPROTO) by the read system call. The default mode, RPROTNORM, causes read to fail with errno set to EBADMSG when a protocol message is at the front of the stream head read queue. Applications can use this mode to recognize when protocol messages arrive.

The second mode is RPROTDIS, *protocol discard mode*. If an M_PROTO or M_PCPROTO message is at the front of the stream head read queue and a process tries to read it in this mode, the control portion is discarded and any data that were contained in M_DATA blocks linked to the protocol message are delivered to the process as the data that are read. This mode might be set by an application preparing a stream for reading by another application that has no knowledge of the service interface being used, as long as only data-transfer primitives are used.

The third mode is *protocol data mode*, RPROTDAT. In it, the protocol messages are converted to data messages and their contents are returned to the user as data when read is used. It has no immediate use, but was added to the system because it was a logical extension of the other modes, easily fell out of the design of read modes, and might prove useful in the future in implementing some applications found in other UNIX variants.

Write Modes

The two write(2) modes can be set with the I_SWROPT ioctl command and obtained with the I_GWROPT ioctl command.

The first mode only applies to pipes. For compatibility, a write of zero bytes to a pipe will have no effect. The SNDZERO option enables zero-length message generation. Applications usually use zero-length data messages to represent end-of-file, but some existing programs write zero bytes to their standard output. When used in a pipeline, these applications might not work as expected. So if an application wants to generate zero-length data messages on a pipe, it needs to enable the SNDZERO option explicitly.

The second write mode applies to both write and putmsg on any stream. If a stream is in either error mode or hangup mode, the SNDPIPE option will cause SIGPIPE to be sent to processes that try to use write or putmsg on the stream. This is used to support 4BSD socket semantics over STREAMS.

Priority Bands

Each STREAMS message belongs to a particular priority band for the purposes of flow control and message queueing. The priority band of a message determines where it is placed on a queue with respect to other messages. In addition, each priority band has a separate set of flow-control parameters. Users usually do not have to concern themselves with priority bands unless the service interface they are using requires it.

Priority bands are used for features like expedited data (out-of-band data), where one class of data message has a higher priority than another. The OSI definition of expedited data specifies that they are unaffected by the flow-control constraints of normal data. This was the primary motivation for the addition of priority bands. Rather than add a facility to support only expedited data (one out-of-band data path), a more general facility was implemented, supporting up to 256 bands of data flow. Normal data belong in band 0. Expedited data are implemented in band 1. It is not expected that many more bands than this will be used, but if the need ever arises, the operating system will not have to be changed again.

High-priority messages are always first in a queue. These are followed, in order of decreasing band number, by the other message types. Normal-priority (band 0) messages are found at the end of the queue.

Two system calls were added to deal with priority bands at the service interface between the user and the kernel. An application can use `putpmsg(2)` to generate a message in a particular priority band:

```
#include <stropts.h>

int putpmsg(int fd, const struct strbuf *ctlp,
        const struct strbuf *datp, int band, int flags);
```

The first three arguments are the same as in `putmsg`. The `band` argument specifies the priority band between 0 and 255, inclusive. If `flags` is set to `MSG_BAND`, then a message is generated in the priority band specified by `band`. Otherwise, if `flags` is set to `MSG_HIPRI`, `band` must be set to 0 and an `M_PCPROTO` message is generated. The call

```
putmsg(fd, ctlp, datp, 0);
```

is equivalent to the call

```
putpmsg(fd, ctlp, datp, 0, MSG_BAND);
```

An application can use `getpmsg(2)` to retrieve a message from a particular priority band:

```
#include <stropts.h>

int getpmsg(int fd, struct strbuf *ctlp,
        struct strbuf *datp, int *bandp, int *flagsp);
```

The integer referenced by `flagsp` can be one of `MSG_HIPRI`, `MSG_BAND`, or `MSG_ANY`, to retrieve a high-priority message, a message from *at least* the band specified by the integer referenced by `bandp`, or any message, respectively. If

MSG_BAND is set, it is possible to obtain a message from a band greater than requested, and it is possible to obtain a high-priority message. (This behavior is analogous to the way getmsg works if the RS_HIPRI flag is not used. Note that the flags are different between the original system calls and their priority band versions.) On return, bandp points to an integer containing the priority band of the message, and flagsp points to an integer indicating the message received was high-priority (MSG_HIPRI) or not (MSG_BAND). The call

```
int flags = 0;

getmsg(fd, ctlp, datp, &flags);
```

is equivalent to the call

```
int flags = MSG_ANY;
int band = 0;

getpmsg(fd, ctlp, datp, &band, &flags);
```

In addition to getpmsg and putpmsg, four ioctl commands were added to support priority band processing [see streamio(7) for more details]. Priority bands also became visible in the STREAMS event mechanisms, namely poll and signal generation.

Autopush

Usually when a stream is opened and the device is not already open, no modules are present in the stream. Applications have to push the modules they want explicitly. When the terminal subsystem was ported to STREAMS, this became a problem. In the clist-based implementation, when a terminal device was opened, a line discipline was already associated with the terminal line. Originally, this was not true with STREAMS-based TTY drivers. To avoid having to modify all applications that opened terminal devices, the *autopush* feature was developed.

The autopush feature allows administrators to specify a list of modules to be automatically pushed whenever a device is opened. The autopush(1M) command provides the administrative interface to configure devices for autopush. For a particular device, administrators have the choice of configuring all the minors, a range of minors, or individual minors.

If a device is configured for autopush, when it is opened the stream head will take care of pushing the modules on the stream before returning from the open system call. This way, applications can open terminal devices and automatically have a line discipline associated with the terminal line, maintaining compatibility.

However, there is a drawback to the autopush mechanism. After opening a driver, applications have no way of knowing *a priori* whether or not there are modules on the stream. If it matters to the applications, they must check explicitly for the presence of modules.

Example 3.7.1. This example illustrates how applications can check for the presence of modules on a stream. The function returns the number of modules on the stream on success, or a negative number on failure.

```
#include <sys/types.h>
#include <unistd.h>
#include <stropts.h>

int
nmod(int fd)
{
        int n;

        n = ioctl(fd, I_LIST, NULL);
        return(n - 1);
}
```

The I_LIST ioctl command is used to return a list of names of all the modules and the driver in the stream. With a NULL argument, however, it returns the number of names so that the caller can allocate the necessary space for the list. We use this to see if any modules are pushed on the stream. Since the driver is included in the list, we return one less than the number returned by I_LIST. If the ioctl fails, then we just return a negative number. The I_LIST ioctl should never return 0, so that case is treated as an error as well.   □

Summary

We have briefly covered the user-level interface to the STREAMS subsystem in System V. Those interested in more details of how the STREAMS mechanism works can refer to Chapter 9. Each of the next five chapters covers networking-related facilities that are built on top of the STREAMS subsystem.

Exercises

3.1 Write a routine that reads a message that always starts with an indication of the message's size.

3.2 Modify Example 3.4.2 to use nonblocking I/O in conjunction with polling.

3.3 Describe how to determine whether the message at the front of the stream head read queue is a protocol message or a file-descriptor message [hint: see streamio(7)].

3.4 Assume processes send you the following message over a pipe:

```
struct msg {
    uid_t   uid;
    pid_t   pid;
    char    text[256];
};
```

Write a routine that reads messages with this format, taking into account the four rules from Section 3.6 for guarding against corrupt and illegitimate data.

Bibliographic Notes

The Streams mechanism, invented by Dennis Ritchie, was introduced in the Eighth Edition Research UNIX System [Ritchie 1984]. STREAMS was first commercially available in UNIX System V Release 3.0 [AT&T 1986]. Presotto and Ritchie [1985, 1990] present Stream pipes, mounted streams, and CONNLD as they appeared in the Ninth Edition Research UNIX System.

Olander, McGrath, and Israel [1986] discuss the work done to provide support for service interfaces in System V STREAMS. Rago [1989] describes changes made to the STREAMS subsystem to provide support for multiple bands of data flow.

To contrast the `clist` mechanism with the STREAMS mechanism that replaced it, refer to Bach [1986].

4

The Transport
Layer Interface

The Transport Layer Interface (TLI) is the primary networking interface used in UNIX System V. It is accessed at user level through a library and at kernel level through a STREAMS message-based service interface. This chapter will present the transport interface as user-level applications view it.

4.1 INTRODUCTION

The Transport Layer Interface presents a generic view of a network, corresponding to the transport level in the OSI seven-layer model of a network (see Figure 4.1).

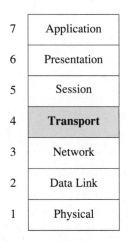

7	Application
6	Presentation
5	Session
4	**Transport**
3	Network
2	Data Link
1	Physical

Fig. 4.1. The OSI Model

The TLI was first provided in UNIX System V Release 3.0. A transport-level interface was chosen for two reasons. First, the transport layer is the lowest level

that operates end-to-end. This means that it is the first building block that applications can use to communicate over a network while remaining ignorant of the network topology. Second, the services provided by the transport layer correspond to
services provided by many common network protocols suites, such as TCP, XNS,
SNA, and ISO.

The TLI is composed of three parts (see Figure 4.2). The first component is a
user-level library containing the application-visible interface to the transport layer.
The library provides applications with functions that perform connection establishment, data transfer, and local management.

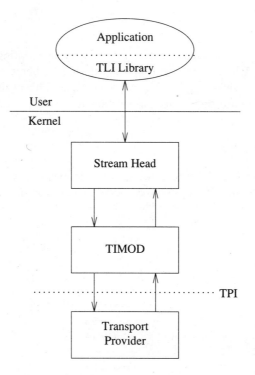

Fig. 4.2. The Composition of the TLI

The second component is the *transport provider*, so named because it provides
the transport service. The transport provider is usually implemented as a STREAMS
multiplexing driver (see Section 3.2). It implements the transport-level protocol used
for communication.

The third component is a STREAMS module, TIMOD, that sits between the
transport library and the transport provider. TIMOD helps map TLI primitives to
TPI primitives. The TPI (Transport Provider Interface) is a message-based service
interface that specifies the types and allowable sequences of messages passed
between the transport consumer (the application) and the transport provider. TIMOD

passes most messages along unchanged. Several primitives, however, are implemented as `ioctl` commands to take advantage of the way `ioctl` operations are
serialized in a stream. With these operations, TIMOD converts the `ioctl` message
into the corresponding TPI primitive before forwarding it to the transport provider.
When the acknowledgement is received from the transport provider, TIMOD converts it into the appropriate `ioctl` response message and forwards it upstream so
the system call can complete.

The major benefit of a clearly defined interface such as the TLI is that it lets
programmers develop applications that are independent of the underlying network.
That is not to say that any application using the TLI library will work with every network. Each network has its own set of specific options. If one is careful not to use
any network-specific features, however, then a network-independent application can
be developed. This style of program design alleviates the need for a separate version
of every application to be provided with each different network.

The TLI library can be included in a program by linking with the `-lnsl`
option. The TLI library is one part of a larger network services library (hence, it is
found in `libnsl`).

There are two basic modes of transport service: connection-oriented and connectionless. (Recall the discussion of datagrams and virtual circuits in Chapter 1.)
We will look at connectionless service before connection-oriented service since connectionless service is the simpler of the two. Before discussing modes of service,
however, we need to cover the steps necessary to access the services.

4.2 TRANSPORT ENDPOINT MANAGEMENT

An application accesses a transport provider through a *transport endpoint*. This is an
abstraction implemented as a file descriptor and some state information. For a transport endpoint to be usable, it must be initialized properly. This is usually a two-step
process:

1.   Open the transport provider to obtain an endpoint.
2.   Bind an address to the endpoint.

An address identifies a given transport endpoint in the network namespace.
Address formats are protocol- and implementation-dependent. The TLI library
places no constraints on the format of an address, nor does it attempt to interpret the
contents of any address field. The TLI library treats addresses as opaque sequences
of bytes to remain flexible. Throughout this chapter, we will avoid specifying explicit networks and addresses in the examples. Ways of handling network selection and
addressing are discussed in Chapter 5.

The `t_open(3N)` routine is used to create a transport endpoint:

```
#include <tiuser.h>
#include <fcntl.h>

int t_open(char *path, int oflag, struct t_info *infop);
```

path is the pathname of the device node corresponding to the transport provider to be opened, oflag is the set of open flags [see open(2) for the list] and must include at least O_RDWR, and infop points to a structure that, on return, will contain information that describes the transport provider's characteristics. The infop parameter can be NULL if the application is not interested in the information. The characteristics include the maximum size of the transport address and the service type, among other things. They are described in detail later.

On success, a nonnegative integer (a file descriptor) is returned that can be used with other TLI routines. On error, t_open returns −1 and sets t_errno to a TLI error number. If t_errno is set to TSYSERR, then errno will contain an error number that further describes why t_open failed.

To simplify error reporting, the TLI library provides a routine to print an error message based on the value of t_errno. This routine, called t_error(3N), is similar to perror(3C):

```
#include <tiuser.h>

extern int t_errno;
extern char *t_errlist[];
extern int t_nerr;

void t_error(char *errmsg);
```

Like perror, t_error will print the string errmsg on the standard error output, followed by a short description of the error. If t_errno has a value of TSYSERR, t_error will print the string System error: followed by a space and the same message that perror would have printed.

t_errlist is an array of error messages indexed by t_errno. t_nerr is the number of elements in the array.

The second step in initializing the transport endpoint involves using t_bind(3N) to associate an address with the endpoint.

```
#include <tiuser.h>

int t_bind(int fd, struct t_bind *reqp,
    struct t_bind *retp);
```

fd is a file descriptor obtained from t_open, reqp describes the requested address, and retp describes the address actually bound. In some cases, the address ultimately bound may be different than the one requested.

The transport provider has control over whether an alternate address is bound instead. Some transport providers will select an alternate address if the one requested is already bound to another transport endpoint. Other transport providers will allow duplicate addresses to be bound, as long as at most one of them is bound with a nonzero connect queue length (discussed below). This is possible when the transport provider uses some other mechanism, such as connection IDs, to identify connections.

The t_bind structure is used to describe the addresses:

```
struct t_bind {
     struct netbuf    addr;
     uint_t           qlen;
};

struct netbuf {
     uint_t   maxlen;
     uint_t   len;
     char     *buf;
};
```

The qlen field indicates the number of outstanding connect indications an application is willing to handle at one time. It is only used for connection-oriented endpoints on which connections will be accepted. Its use will be discussed in detail in Section 4.4. The addr field describes the buffer used to hold the address. The netbuf structure is used by many TLI routines to describe memory extents. It is similar to the strbuf structure described in the previous chapter.

In the netbuf structure, the maxlen field contains the length of the memory extent, the len field contains the length of the data in the buffer, and the buf field contains the address of the memory extent. Usually in netbuf structures containing information specified by the caller, only the buf and len fields need be initialized. In netbuf structures that are filled in on return from TLI functions, only buf and maxlen need be set by the caller. The len field will be set on return by the TLI functions.

If an application does not care what address is used, then reqp can be NULL, and the transport provider will select an address for the application. This is often the case with client processes that are concerned with the address of the server but that usually have no requirement on their own address. If an application needs to record its address for some reason, then retp should point to a t_bind structure so the bound address can be saved. Otherwise, it too can be NULL.

If an application knows the address that it wants bound, then the address should be specified with reqp. An application can verify that the address requested is actually the address bound by comparing the address requested with the address returned in retp. On success, t_bind returns 0; on error, it returns −1.

The TLI library provides a simple way to allocate data structures containing fields that refer to memory extents with sizes that vary based on the characteristics of the transport provider. t_alloc(3N) provides this service.

```
#include <tiuser.h>

char *t_alloc(int fd, int struct_type, int fields);
```

The fd parameter specifies the transport provider so that t_alloc can figure out the sizes of the buffers to allocate. The struct_type field specifies which TLI data structure is to be allocated. The possible values it can take on are listed in Table 4.1.

Table 4.1. Structure Types Allocated Via t_alloc

struct_type Value	Structure Allocated
T_BIND	t_bind
T_CALL	t_call
T_OPTMGMT	t_optmgmt
T_DIS	t_discon
T_UNITDATA	t_unitdata
T_UDERROR	t_uderr
T_INFO	t_info

The fields parameter is a bitmask indicating the netbuf structures that are to have buffers allocated. The values are derived from the union of types of netbuf structures that are used by TLI data structures. Flags exist for address, options, and user data, although not all TLI data structures use these types of fields. The flags are summarized in Table 4.2.

Table 4.2. Flags for fields Argument to t_alloc

fields Flag	netbuf Field Allocated
T_ADDR	addr, used for addresses.
T_OPT	opt, used for user options.
T_UDATA	udata, used for user data.
T_ALL	All fields of the given structure.

A pointer to the memory to be used for the requested data structure is returned on success. The memory will be cleared (set to zeros) on return. For each netbuf structure allocated, the buf field will point to the memory extent for that buffer and the maxlen field will be set to the length of the buffer. If memory cannot be allocated, t_alloc returns NULL.

Example 4.2.1. The following routine might be used by a client application to initialize a transport endpoint before communicating with a server application.

```
#include <tiuser.h>
#include <fcntl.h>

int
initclient(char *transport)
{
    int fd;

    /*
     * Open the transport provider.
     */
    if ((fd = t_open(transport, O_RDWR, NULL)) < 0) {
        t_error("Cannot open network");
```

```
            return (-1);
        }

        /*
         * Bind an arbitrary address to the transport
         * endpoint.
         */
        if (t_bind(fd, NULL, NULL) < 0) {
            t_error("Cannot bind address");
            t_close(fd);
            return (-1);
        }
        return (fd);
    }
```

The requested network is opened, ignoring the informational parameters available. Then an arbitrary address is bound and the network file descriptor is returned. If the t_bind fails, then t_close (3N) (described following this example) is used to free the state information and close the file descriptor allocated by t_open. After any failure, t_error is used to print an error message describing the reason for the failure.

A server process might use the following routine to initialize its transport endpoint:

```
#include <sys/types.h>
#include <tiuser.h>
#include <fcntl.h>
#include <stdio.h>
#include <memory.h>
#include <stdlib.h>

extern int t_errno;
extern char *t_errlist[];

extern void log(const char *, ...);

#define tlog(STR) log("%s: %s", (STR), t_errlist[t_errno])

int
initserver(char *transport, char *addr, uint_t alen,
    uint_t qlen)
{
    int fd;
    struct t_bind *reqp, *retp;

    /*
     * Open the transport provider.
     */
    if ((fd = t_open(transport, O_RDWR, NULL)) < 0) {
        tlog("Cannot open network");
        exit(1);
    }
```

```
    /*
     * Allocate t_bind structures for the requested and
     * returned addresses.
     */
    reqp = (struct t_bind *)t_alloc(fd, T_BIND, T_ADDR);
    retp = (struct t_bind *)t_alloc(fd, T_BIND, T_ADDR);
    if ((reqp == NULL) || (retp == NULL)) {
        tlog("Cannot allocate bind structures");
        exit(1);
    }

    /*
     * Copy the requested address to the t_bind structure
     * and bind the address to the transport endpoint.
     */
    memcpy(reqp->addr.buf, addr, alen);
    reqp->addr.len = alen;
    reqp->qlen = qlen;
    if (t_bind(fd, reqp, retp) < 0) {
        tlog("Cannot bind address");
        exit(1);
    }

    /*
     * Check that the transport provider bound the
     * address that we requested.
     */
    if ((retp->addr.len != alen) ||
      (memcmp(addr, retp->addr.buf, alen) != 0)) {
        log("Bound different address than requested\n");
        exit(1);
    }
    return(fd);
}
```

After opening the transport provider, two t_bind structures are allocated, one for the requested address and one for the returned address. The T_ADDR parameter to t_alloc tells the function to allocate only a netbuf buffer for the addr element of the t_bind structure. Since this is the only netbuf structure appearing in the t_bind structure, we could have also used T_ALL.

Note that, on error, no cleanup is performed before exiting. This is because the system will take care of freeing any allocated memory and closing any open files when the process exits.

Since servers usually are not associated with a terminal, t_error cannot be used directly. Instead, the server logs a message using the global array of TLI error messages and the global TLI error variable, t_errno.   □

As we have seen in the previous example, a process can close a transport endpoint with t_close(3N):

```
#include <tiuser.h>

int t_close(int fd);
```

`t_close` will free any state information associated with the transport enpoint and close the file descriptor to the transport provider. `t_close` returns 0 on success and −1 on error, although there is not much recovery possible if it fails. Most applications just ignore its return value. Programmers should avoid using `close(2)` with a transport endpoint because `close` does not clean up the library's state information.

If an address was bound to the transport endpoint when it was closed, the transport provider will disassociate the address from the endpoint. With the connection-oriented mode of service, closing a transport endpoint will result in the connection being released. Depending on the implementation, a transport provider may or may not guarantee delivery of data not yet received by the other transport endpoint. If a transport provider discards all data awaiting reception by a transport endpoint when the other end of the connection is closed, then the transport provider is said to have generated an *abortive release* when the close occurred. If, on the other hand, the transport provider reliably delivers all data to the transport endpoint still open, then the transport provider generated an *orderly release* when the other end was closed.

If an application just wants to break the association of an address with a transport endpoint, it can use `t_unbind(3N)`:

```
#include <tiuser.h>

int t_unbind(int fd);
```

This is useful when an application wants to bind a different address to an endpoint. `t_unbind` returns 0 on success and −1 on failure. Since the transport provider automatically unbinds an address from a transport endpoint when the endpoint is closed, it is unnecessary to call `t_unbind` if an application is about to close the transport endpoint or exit.

Another routine useful during cleanup processing is `t_free(3N)`. If data structures have been allocated via `t_alloc` and they will not be used anymore, but the process is not going to exit, then `t_free` can be used to free the data structures:

```
#include <tiuser.h>

int t_free(char *ptr, int struct_type);
```

Here, `ptr` is a pointer to the data structure, and `struct_type` identifies the type of data structure, just as it did in the call to `t_alloc`.

Example 4.2.2. The `initserver` routine from example 4.2.1 has a bug: it neglects to free the `t_bind` structures on successful return. Here is a more robust version:

```
#include <sys/types.h>
#include <tiuser.h>
#include <fcntl.h>
```

```c
#include <stdio.h>
#include <memory.h>
#include <stdlib.h>

extern int t_errno;
extern char *t_errlist[];

extern void log(const char *, ...);

#define tlog(STR) log("%s: %s", (STR), t_errlist[t_errno])

int
initserver(char *transport, char *addr, uint_t alen,
    uint_t qlen)
{
    int fd;
    struct t_bind *reqp, *retp;

    /*
     * Open the transport provider.
     */
    if ((fd = t_open(transport, O_RDWR, NULL)) < 0) {
        tlog("Cannot open network");
        exit(1);
    }

    /*
     * Allocate t_bind structures for the requested and
     * returned addresses.
     */
    reqp = (struct t_bind *)t_alloc(fd, T_BIND, T_ADDR);
    retp = (struct t_bind *)t_alloc(fd, T_BIND, T_ADDR);
    if ((reqp == NULL) || (retp == NULL)) {
        tlog("Cannot allocate bind structures");
        exit(1);
    }

    /*
     * Copy the requested address to the t_bind structure
     * and bind the address to the transport endpoint.
     */
    memcpy(reqp->addr.buf, addr, alen);
    reqp->addr.len = alen;
    reqp->qlen = qlen;
    if (t_bind(fd, reqp, retp) < 0) {
        tlog("Cannot bind address");
        exit(1);
    }

    /*
     * Check that the transport provider bound the
     * address that we requested.
     */
    if ((retp->addr.len != alen) ||
```

```
            (memcmp(addr, retp->addr.buf, alen) != 0)) {
                log("Bound different address than requested\n");
                exit(1);
        }

        /*
         * Free the memory for the t_bind structures we no
         * longer need.
         */
        t_free((char *)reqp, T_BIND);
        t_free((char *)retp, T_BIND);
        return(fd);
}
```

The only difference in this version is the addition of the t_free statements before the successful return.

We can write a different version of initserver that avoids duplicating the request address because the caller supplies it. We have to remember, however, to set the netbuf buffer address to NULL before calling t_free to prevent t_free from trying to free memory it did not allocate.

```
int
initserver(char *transport, char *addr, uint_t alen,
      uint_t qlen)
{
        int fd;
        struct t_bind *reqp, *retp;

        /*
         * Open the transport provider.
         */
        if ((fd = t_open(transport, O_RDWR, NULL)) < 0) {
                tlog("Cannot open network");
                exit(1);
        }

        /*
         * Allocate t_bind structures for the requested and
         * returned addresses.
         */
        reqp = (struct t_bind *)t_alloc(fd, T_BIND, 0);
        retp = (struct t_bind *)t_alloc(fd, T_BIND, T_ADDR);
        if ((reqp == NULL) || (retp == NULL)) {
                tlog("Cannot allocate bind structures");
                exit(1);
        }

        /*
         * Point the t_bind structure for the requested
         * address at the address passed to us and bind
         * the address to the transport endpoint.
         */
        reqp->addr.buf = addr;
        reqp->addr.len = alen;
```

```
        reqp->qlen = qlen;
        if (t_bind(fd, reqp, retp) < 0) {
            tlog("Cannot bind address");
            exit(1);
        }

        /*
         * Check that the transport provider bound the
         * address that we requested.
         */
        if ((retp->addr.len != alen) ||
           (memcmp(addr, retp->addr.buf, alen) != 0)) {
            log("Bound different address than requested\n");
            exit(1);
        }

        /*
         * Free the memory for the t_bind structures we no
         * longer need.  Don't let t_free free the address
         * buffer -- the caller might not be through with
         * it yet.
         */
        reqp->addr.buf = NULL;
        t_free((char *)reqp, T_BIND);
        t_free((char *)retp, T_BIND);
        return(fd);
    }
```

                                                                          □

The t_getinfo(3N) routine can be used to obtain the characteristics of the transport endpoint at any time during the endpoint's existence. t_getinfo returns the same information as the infop parameter to t_open.

```
#include <tiuser.h>

int t_getinfo(int fd, struct t_info *info);
```

The characteristics described by the t_info structure include the following:

addr   Maximum address size in bytes; −1 for no limit; −2 for no user access to addresses.

options   Maximum options size in bytes; −1 for no limit; −2 for no user-settable options.

tsdu   Maximum transport service data unit size in bytes; −1 for no limit; −2 for no support of normal data transfer.

etsdu   Maximum expedited transport service data unit size in bytes; −1 for no limit; −2 for no support of expedited data transfer.

connect   Maximum amount of user data that can be sent with a connect request; −1 for no limit; −2 for no support for user data on connect.

discon   Maximum amount of user data that can be sent with a disconnect request; −1 for no limit; −2 for no support for user data on disconnect.

servtype   The type of service provided by the endpoint (T_CLTS, T_COTS, or T_COTS_ORD).

Most of the characteristics are self-explanatory. A few, such as the service type, deserve further discussion.

A transport endpoint can provide only one service type. The service types currently defined are connectionless (T_CLTS), connection-oriented (T_COTS), and connection-oriented with orderly release (T_COTS_ORD). Other than the support of an orderly release facility, T_COTS service is identical to T_COTS_ORD service. Applications that want to verify the service type of the transport provider can check the infop->servtype field after opening the transport provider.

Instead of adding an additional mode of service, support of orderly release would have been better implemented as a separate capability specified in the t_info structure, for several reasons. First, there are really two pieces of information an application needs to know: whether the transport provider supports orderly release and, if so, what is the default action if the endpoint is closed without explicitly releasing the connection. Even though a transport provider supplies the ability to use orderly release, it also has to support an abortive release (also called a *disconnect*). The transport provider may default to either an orderly or abortive release.

Second, an application using an abortive release will still operate properly over a transport provider supporting orderly release. On the other hand, an application using orderly release will not work if the transport provider does not supply that capability. In contrast, applications written for connectionless service will not work with a connection-oriented transport provider, and vice versa. The service type is more clearly distinguished by mutually exclusive characteristics. The addition of different service types based on minor differences in service makes use of the service type more complex. Imagine if there were a separate type for every optional characteristic in the interface (for example, data sent with a connect, data sent with a disconnect, etc.).

The transport service data unit (TSDU) size is an interesting parameter. The TSDU size is properly defined as the maximum amount of data whose message boundaries are preserved from one transport endpoint to another. It is *not* the maximum amount of data that can be sent on a transport endpoint. The maximum amount of data that can be sent is the transport interface data unit (TIDU) size. It is defined as the maximum amount of data that can be passed between the transport user and the transport provider.

The two parameters are the source of much confusion for users of the transport interface. For example, in the version of TCP that is supplied with SVR4, the TSDU size is 0. This does not imply that data cannot be transmitted over TCP, but rather it reflects the byte-stream nature of the TCP protocol. TCP is not message-oriented and does not maintain the concept of message boundaries. The TIDU size for TCP is 16 KBytes. This is the maximum amount of data that can be sent from the transport user to the transport provider in one message.

Example 4.2.3. The following program can be used to display the TSDU size and TIDU size of a given transport provider.

```c
#include <sys/types.h>
#include <sys/stream.h>
#include <sys/tihdr.h>
#include <stropts.h>
#include <stdio.h>
#include <unistd.h>
#include <fcntl.h>
#include <stdlib.h>

/*
 * The T_info_ack structure defined prior to SVR4 contained
 * one long integer less than the current structure.
 */
#define OLDSIZE   (sizeof(struct T_info_ack)-sizeof(long))

char *errmsg =
  "tisz: Incorrect response from transport provider";

extern void fatal(const char *, ...);

void
main(int argc, char *argv[])
{
    int fd, ret;
    struct strbuf ctl;
    struct T_info_ack ack;
    struct T_info_req req;
    int flag = RS_HIPRI;

    if (argc != 2)
        fatal("usage: tisz device");
    if ((fd = open(argv[1], O_RDWR)) < 0)
        fatal("tisz: Cannot open transport provider");

    /*
     * Create an information request transport primitive
     * and send it to the transport provider.  The format
     * is one M_PCPROTO message block with no data blocks.
     */
    ctl.buf = (char *)&req;
    ctl.len = sizeof(struct T_info_req);
    req.PRIM_type = T_INFO_REQ;
    if (putmsg(fd, &ctl, NULL, RS_HIPRI) < 0)
        fatal("tisz: Cannot send request");

    /*
     * Receive the information acknowledgement from
     * the transport provider.  The format is one
     * M_PCPROTO message block with no data blocks.
```

```
        */
        ctl.buf = (char *)&ack;
        ctl.maxlen = sizeof(struct T_info_ack);
        if ((ret = getmsg(fd, &ctl, NULL, &flag)) != 0) {
            if (ret < 0)
                fatal("tisz: Cannot receive response");
            else
                fatal(errmsg);
        }

        /*
         * Validate the message and print the sizes.
         */
        if (((ctl.len != sizeof(struct T_info_ack)) &&
            (ctl.len != OLDSIZE)) ||
            (ack.PRIM_type != T_INFO_ACK))
                fatal(errmsg);
        printf("TIDU size = %d bytes\n", ack.TIDU_size);
        printf("TSDU size = %d bytes\n", ack.TSDU_size);
        exit(0);
    }
```

The program uses `putmsg` and `getmsg` to get the characteristics of the transport provider, as specified by the TPI. After opening the transport provider, we send a request for the provider characteristics. Then we receive the response, validate it, and print the values. Between SVR3.2 and SVR4.0 the size of the `T_info_ack` structure grew by the size of a `long`, so we need to check the amount of control information in the response against both the old and the new sizes.   □

Because the provider characteristics are returned from `t_open`, one might think that `t_getinfo` is not very useful. This is far from true. Some characteristics might change as a result of protocol-dependent negotiation between the transport user and the transport provider. In addition, with the ability to pass file descriptors between processes, one needs a way to be able to query the provider for the characteristics.

The function used to negotiate options with the transport provider is `t_optmgmt(3N)`:

```
#include <tiuser.h>

int t_optmgmt(int fd, struct t_optmgmt *reqp,
        struct t_optmgmt *retp);
```

`fd` is the file descriptor for the transport endpoint, and `reqp` and `retp` point to `t_optmgmt` structures:

```
struct t_optmgmt {
        struct netbuf    opt;
        long             flags;
};
```

The `reqp` argument is used to request the transport provider to take a specific action. The `retp` argument is used to return options from the transport provider to the user. In the request structure, `opt.buf` points to the options buffer, `opt.len` is the length of the options in the buffer, and `opt.maxlen` is unused. In the returned structure, `opt.buf` points to the options buffer, and `opt.maxlen` is the size of the buffer. The `opt.len` field is set on return to the size of the options returned in the buffer. The format of the options is implementation-dependent.

The `flags` field in the request structure specifies the action to be taken. It can be one of the following:

`T_NEGOTIATE`	Negotiate values specified by `reqp` with the transport provider. Accepted values will be returned through `retp`.
`T_CHECK`	Verify if options are supported by transport provider. On return, `retp->flags` will be set to `T_SUCCESS` if the options are supported, or `T_FAILURE` if not.
`T_DEFAULT`	Return the default options supported by the transport provider.

Currently, an address must be bound to the transport endpoint to be able to use `t_optmgmt`. This restriction is being considered for removal, though.

On success, `t_optmgmt` returns 0; on failure it returns −1. Since the options and their format are implementation-dependent, applications should generally not use this function if they want to remain portable. Of course, one could use this function and still remain network-independent by storing the options in a database file and designing the application to read the options and negotiate them without interpreting them. The drawback to this design is the addition of another file to be administered.

One undocumented function was added to the TLI library in SVR4. (The lack of documentation was unintentional.) The function, `t_getname(3N)`, can be used to get the local or remote address for a transport endpoint.

```
#include <tiuser.h>

int t_getname(int fd, struct netbuf *namep, int type);
```

`fd` is the file descriptor for the transport endpoint, `namep` is a pointer to a `netbuf` structure used to obtain the address, and `type` determines which address should be returned. If `type` is set to `LOCALNAME`, then the address bound to the transport endpoint is returned. If `type` is set to `REMOTENAME`, then the address of the transport endpoint at the other end of the connection is returned.

The `namep->buf` field should be initialized to a memory buffer used to store the address. The `namep->maxlen` field should be set to the length of the buffer in bytes. On return, `namep->len` will be set to the length of the address (also in bytes). `t_getname` returns 0 on success and −1 on failure.

The `t_getname` function was implemented as an `ioctl` call so as not to impact the TPI. Transport providers do not have to support the `ioctl` commands for the function to work, however. TIMOD will keep track of both the address bound to the endpoint and the address to which the endpoint is connected. The drawback is that `t_getname` will not work if TIMOD is popped off the stream and the transport provider does not support the `ioctl` commands.

With the ability to pass file descriptors between processes, `t_getname` is the only way a process can identify for itself the addresses associated with a given transport endpoint. With the LOCALNAME type, t_getname is equivalent to the getsockname(3N) routine. Similarly, with the REMOTENAME type, t_getname is equivalent to the getpeername(3N) socket routine. Sockets are discussed in Chapter 7.

Several other transport endpoint management routines exists. These will be covered during the discussion of connectionless and connection-oriented service modes.

4.3 CONNECTIONLESS SERVICE

The connectionless service has only three primitives: send a message, receive a message, and receive error notification. This is in contrast to the connection-oriented mode's 10 primitives. The relative spareness of the connectionless interface is a direct result of the absence of connection establishment and release. The state machine for connectionless mode, shown in Figure 4.3, is trivial.

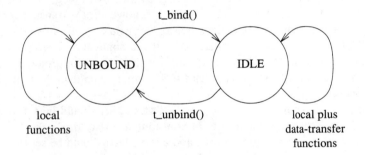

Fig. 4.3. Connectionless Mode State Diagram

While the transport endpoint is in the unbound state, only local management operations may be performed on it. However, once an address is bound to the endpoint, data transfer is possible. Messages sent and received are described by the t_unitdata structure:

```
struct t_unitdata {
        struct netbuf    addr;
        struct netbuf    opt;
        struct netbuf    udata;
};
```

The addr field describes the destination or source of the message, depending on which TLI routine is used. The udata field describes the data sent or received. The opt field is for implementation-specific options that an application might want to be associated with the message delivery. For example, if an application is about to send large amounts of data, it might want to specify an option to increase the high and low water marks. Applications intended to be network-independent should not use the opt field.

The t_sndudata(3N) function is used to send a message over a connection-less transport provider:

```
#include <tiuser.h>

int t_sndudata(int fd, struct t_unitdata *udp);
```

fd is the file descriptor for the transport endpoint, and udp points to the t_unitdata structure that describes the data to be sent. If an application uses t_alloc to allocate the t_unitdata structure's user data buffer, then the application might have a few surprises in store for it.

If the transport provider has a TSDU size of −1 (i.e., no limit to the number of bytes that can be sent), then t_alloc will allocate a buffer big enough to hold only 1024 bytes. If an application needs to send more data than this in one message, it would be best for the application to use its own buffer for the user data.

t_alloc uses the TSDU size to select the size of the buffer to allocate. It is reasonable for an application to assume that if t_alloc returned a t_unitdata structure containing a user data buffer udata.maxlen bytes long, then the application can send at most udata.maxlen bytes. If, however, the transport provider's TSDU size is larger than its TIDU size, then t_sndudata will fail with t_errno set to TSYSERR and errno set to EPROTO if the application attempts to send a message larger than the TIDU size. This error is usually used for protocol errors, but t_sndudata uses it when the caller tries to send more data than the transport provider can accept.

To send a datagram, udata.buf and udata.len should be set to the start and length, respectively, of the data to be transmitted. Also, addr.buf should be set to the start of the destination address, and addr.len should be set to its length. If no options are being used, then opt.len should be set to zero.

On success, t_sndudata returns 0, and on error it returns −1. If t_sndudata returns 0, an application should not assume that the message arrived at the peer, nor should it even assume that the transport provider processed the message successfully. An application should assume only that the message was delivered successfully to the transport provider.

t_sndudata uses putmsg(2) to deliver the message to the transport provider, according to the rules of the transport provider interface. If the stream is flow-controlled and in nonblocking mode, t_sndudata will fail, setting t_errno to TFLOW. Applications can use the same mechanisms presented in Chapter 3 to determine when it is possible to continue sending data.

The t_rcvudata(3N) function is used to receive a message from a connectionless transport provider:

```
#include <tiuser.h>

int t_rcvudata(int fd, struct t_unitdata *udp, int *flagp);
```

fd is the file descriptor for the transport endpoint, and udp points to the `t_unitdata` structure that describes the data received. `udp->addr.buf` contains the address of the transport endpoint that sent the data. The `flagp` parameter is a pointer to an integer that is set to 0 if all the data fit into the buffers on return, or `T_MORE` if only part of the message was retrieved.

Before using this function, the caller must make sure that the `buf` and `maxlen` fields in the `netbuf` structures are initialized properly. Even if the caller is not expecting options, a buffer for them should be allocated to handle them if present. This can be done easily by using `t_alloc` with the `T_ALL` flag to allocate the `t_unitdata` structure and its buffers.

On success, `t_rcvudata` returns 0, and on error, it returns −1. By default, `t_rcvudata` blocks until data are available. If the stream is in nonblocking mode and no data are available, then `t_rcvudata` will fail with `t_errno` set to `TNODATA`.

If there are option data present in the message and the caller does not provide a buffer for the options, or if the buffer is too small, `t_rcvudata` will fail with `t_errno` set to `TBUFOVFLW`. The same goes for the address buffer. Unfortunately, the message is lost in this case.

One other interesting error return is when `t_errno` is set to `TLOOK`. This indicates that an outstanding event is present that needs to be processed before the caller can receive any data. For connectionless service, the only outstanding event possible is an indication from the transport provider that an error occurred attempting to send a message generated by a previous call to `t_sndudata`. The caller can clear the event by using `t_rcvuderr(3N)`.

Before looking at `t_rcvuderr`, we should consider the implications of the `TLOOK` behavior. Why should a previous message transmission interfere with the receipt of other messages? The answer lies in the fact that a STREAMS queue is a FIFO (more or less). If a message representing an error is at the front of the stream head read queue, then an application cannot retrieve other messages until the error message is retrieved. This is the reason for the `TLOOK` pseudo-error. Note that if `t_error` is used when `t_errno` is set to `TLOOK`, the message is `An event requires attention`, not exactly the clearest of error messages.

Applications can use `t_rcvuderr(3N)` to clear the error condition when `t_rcvudata` fails with `t_errno` set to `TLOOK`:

```
#include <tiuser.h>

int t_rcvuderr(int fd, struct t_uderr *errp);
```

`fd` is the file descriptor for the transport endpoint, and `errp` points to the `t_uderr` structure that describes the error. The structure is defined as:

```
struct t_uderr {
    struct netbuf    addr;
    struct netbuf    opt;
    long             error;
};
```

where `addr` specifies the destination address of the message that could not be sent, `opt` specifies any protocol options associated with the transmission, and `error` specifies an implementation-dependent error code. If the user does not wish to get this information, `errp` can be NULL, in which case the only action taken will be to clear the error condition.

One must question the usefulness of such a primitive for a service that is inherently unreliable. Of what use is an error indication for a transmission that occurred in the past, when the data associated with the transmission cannot be identified (unless the user has only sent one message)? Given that delivery of the message is not guaranteed, why bother reporting some of the errors? Even curiouser is the fact that the transport provider is under no requirement to generate reliable error indications for messages that cannot be sent in connectionless mode. And the fact that the error code is implementation-dependent implies that applications wishing to remain independent of the protocol and its implementation can only record the error for later inspection. The existence of `t_rcvuderr` needlessly complicates the processing of data in connectionless mode.

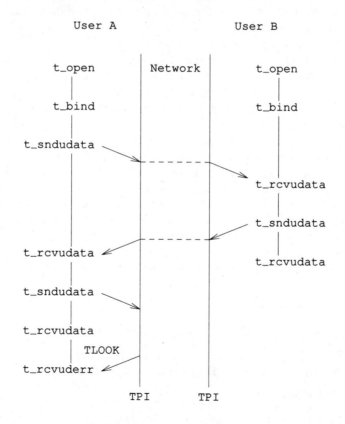

Fig. 4.4. Connectionless Primitives

Now that all the connectionless primitives have been described, we should look at how they relate to one another. Figure 4.4 shows a timeline of two transport users communicating over a connectionless transport provider. They both gain access to the transport provider and bind addresses to their transport endpoints. User A sends a message to User B. Then User B sends a response back to User A. Expecting a second message, User B blocks in t_rcvudata. When User A sends the second message, however, the transport provider encounters an error while processing the message and sends an error indication to the transport user. When User A tries to receive another message from User B, the error indication is recognized because t_rcvudata fails with t_errno set to TLOOK. Then User A clears the error condition by calling t_rcvuderr. Let's see how this sequence of events might be handled in a real application.

Example 4.3.1. One service that probably can withstand unreliable data delivery is something like a remote who(1) facility. Users can always repeat the command if they suspect errors. The following client routines can be used over connectionless transport providers as the basis for a simple version of rwho(1).

The client sends a datagram to a server on the specified machine. The server responds with several datagrams containing a list of the users currently logged in on the server. The client then prints the list on the standard output.

```c
#include <sys/types.h>
#include <stdio.h>
#include <stdlib.h>
#include <tiuser.h>
#include <string.h>
#include <signal.h>
#include <memory.h>
#include <unistd.h>

void timeout(int);
extern int t_errno;
extern int initclient(char *);

void
rwho(int argc, char *argv[], char *transport, char *addr,
     uint_t alen)
{
    int fd, i, flags;
    struct t_unitdata *udp;
    struct sigaction sa;

    if (argc < 2) {
        fprintf(stderr, "usage: rwho host [options]\n");
        exit(1);
    }

    /*
     * Create a client-style transport endpoint.
     */
    if ((fd = initclient(transport)) < 0)
        exit(1);
```

```
/*
 * Allocate the t_unitdata structure to be used to
 * send and receive data.
 */
udp = (struct t_unitdata *)t_alloc(fd, T_UNITDATA,
  T_ALL);
if (udp == NULL) {
    t_error("Cannot allocate unitdata");
    exit(1);
}

/*
 * Copy the destination address to the unitdata
 * request.
 */
memcpy(udp->addr.buf, addr, alen);
udp->addr.len = alen;

/*
 * Build the command string to send to the server.
 */
strcpy(udp->udata.buf, "who");
for (i = 2; i < argc; i++) {
    strcat(udp->udata.buf, " ");
    strcat(udp->udata:buf, argv[i]);
}
udp->udata.buf[strlen(udp->udata.buf)] = '\0';
udp->udata.len = strlen(udp->udata.buf)+1;

/*
 * Set an alarm so we don't block forever.
 */
sa.sa_handler = timeout;
sa.sa_flags = 0;
sigemptyset(&sa.sa_mask);
sigaction(SIGALRM, &sa, NULL);
alarm(20);

/*
 * Send the request.
 */
if (t_sndudata(fd, udp) < 0) {
    t_error("Cannot send request");
    exit(1);
}

/*
 * Receive response messages until we encounter an
 * error or receive the last message (a single byte
 * containing 0).
 */
for ( ; ; ) {
    if (t_rcvudata(fd, udp, &flags) < 0) {
        if (t_errno == TLOOK) {
```

```
                    /*
                     * Try to retrieve the error
                     * indication.
                     */
                    if (t_rcvuderr(fd, NULL) < 0) {
                        t_error("Cannot clear TLOOK");
                        exit(1);
                    }
                } else {
                    t_error("Cannot receive data");
                    exit(1);
                }
            } else {
                /*
                 * If this is the last message, exit.
                 */
                if ((udp->udata.len == 1) &&
                  (*udp->udata.buf == '\0'))
                    exit(0);

                /*
                 * Write the response on the standard output.
                 */
                write(1, udp->udata.buf, udp->udata.len);
            }
        }
    }

void
timeout(int sig)
{
    fprintf(stderr, "Command timed out\n");
    exit(1);
}
```

The command syntax specifies the first parameter to be the name of the remote host whose current user lognames should be printed. Then standard options to who(1) follow. The initclient routine was given in Example 4.2.1.

After a transport endpoint has been initialized, we allocate a t_unitdata structure to be used for communication. Since we will use the same structure for both sending and receiving, we allocate all valid fields. If we were to allocate only a buffer for user data, then the possibility exists for t_rcvudata to fail if the server sends protocol options, or if its address is longer than the client's address.

After copying the address to the addr field, we copy the command to be executed (who) to the udata buffer. For every optional parameter specified, we tack a space followed by the parameter onto the end of the command string we are building in the data buffer. Then we install a signal handler for SIGALRM and set an alarm for 20 seconds. If the command does not finish executing in 20 seconds, the alarm will go off and the timeout routine will print an error message and exit.

The command line is sent to the server using t_sndudata. Then we repeatedly call t_rcvudata to retrieve any messages. If we get the error TLOOK, we call t_rcvuderr to clear the error condition, but we ignore the error information. If we successfully retrieve a message, we print it on the standard output (file descriptor 1). The last message transmitted will consist of a single NULL byte. When we receive it, we exit successfully.   □

There is not much difference between a client application and a server application in terms of the transport primitives when a connectionless mode transport provider is used. The roles played by the applications determine whether each is a client or a server.

Example 4.3.2. The server side of the remote who command presented in Example 4.3.1 follows:

```
#include <sys/types.h>
#include <stdio.h>
#include <fcntl.h>
#include <tiuser.h>
#include <string.h>
#include <unistd.h>

extern int t_errno;
extern char *t_errlist[];

extern void log(const char *, ...);
extern int initserver(char *, char *, uint_t, uint_t);

#define tlog(STR) log("%s: %s", (STR), t_errlist[t_errno])

void
rwhod(char *transport, char *addr, uint_t alen)
{
    int fd;
    struct t_unitdata *udp;
    FILE *fp;
    int flags;

    /*
     * Create a server-style transport endpoint.
     */
    fd = initserver(transport, addr, alen, 0);

    /*
     * Allocate the t_unitdata structure to be used to
     * send and receive data.
     */
    udp = (struct t_unitdata *)t_alloc(fd, T_UNITDATA,
      T_ALL);
    if (udp == NULL) {
        tlog("Cannot allocate unitdata");
        return;
    }
```

```
    /*
     * Receive request messages, execute the command, and
     * send the output back to the client.
     */
    for ( ; ; ) {
        if (t_rcvudata(fd, udp, &flags) < 0) {
            if (t_errno == TLOOK) {
                /*
                 * Try to retrieve the error
                 * indication.
                 */
                if (t_rcvuderr(fd, NULL) < 0) {
                    tlog("Cannot clear TLOOK");
                    break;
                }
            } else {
                tlog("Cannot receive data");
            }
            break;
        } else {
            /*
             * Execute the command.  fp is open to the
             * command's standard output.
             */
            fp = popen(udp->udata.buf, "r");
            if (fp) {
                /*
                 * Send the output of the command back to
                 * the client.
                 */
                while (fgets(udp->udata.buf,
                  udp->udata.maxlen, fp)) {
                    udp->udata.len =
                      strlen(udp->udata.buf);
                    if (t_sndudata(fd, udp) < 0) {
                        tlog("Cannot send data");
                        return;
                    }
                }
                pclose(fp);

                /*
                 * Send final message.  Format is one
                 * byte containing 0.
                 */
                udp->udata.len = 1;
                *udp->udata.buf = '\0';
                if (t_sndudata(fd, udp) < 0) {
                    tlog("Cannot send data");
                    break;
                }
            } else {
                log("Cannot exec command");
            }
```

```
                }
            }
        }
```

The `initserver` routine was given in Example 4.2.2. After a transport end-point has been initialized, we allocate a `t_unitdata` structure to be used for communication. Since we will use the same structure for both sending and receiving, we allocate all valid fields. Note that since this application is acting as a server process, it does not print to standard error on failure. Instead, it records a message in a log file and returns to the caller.

The server blocks in `t_rcvudata`, waiting for work. As in the client case, if a TLOOK error occurs, we call `t_rcvuderr` to clear the error condition, ignoring the error information.

When a request comes in, we execute the command using `popen(3C)`. This routine basically creates a pipe and forks, allowing the parent to read from the standard output of the command (or write to the standard input). We read one line at a time from the output of the command. For each line, we package it up and send it to the client using `t_sndudata`. When there are no data left, we close the pipe to the child and transmit one NULL byte to the client to signal that no more data will be sent. We do not use a zero-length message, because some transport providers do not support transmission of zero-length TSDUs.   □

One might notice that the examples presented so far have carefully avoided the issues of addressing and network selection. These topics will be covered in Chapter 5.

4.4 CONNECTION-ORIENTED SERVICE

As stated before, there are two kinds of connection mode service: plain connection-oriented and connection-oriented with orderly release. Everything covered in this section, except, of course, the orderly release functions, applies to both modes of service.

Connection Establishment

By far, the most complicated aspect of connection-oriented service is connection establishment. Unlike connectionless mode, a transport user does not supply a destination address with each message transmitted. Instead, a destination address is "connected to" before data transfer begins. Then the transport provider associates the destination address with the messages on behalf of the transport user until the connection is released.

The client process connects to the server process using `t_connect(3N)`:

```
#include <tiuser.h>

int t_connect(int fd, struct t_call *sndp,
    struct t_call *rcvp);
```

fd is the file descriptor for the transport endpoint. The caller initializes sndp with information used to determine the address to which the connection is to be made. On successful return, rcvp contains information about the address to which the connection has been made. Both sndp and rcvp point to a t_call structure:

```
struct t_call {
     struct netbuf    addr;
     struct netbuf    opt;
     struct netbuf    udata;
     int              sequence;
};
```

In the sending t_call structure, addr describes the address of the destination transport endpoint, opt describes optional implementation-specific protocol options to be used with the connection, and udata describes optional user data to be transmitted with the connect request. The caller should set the len fields of the netbuf structures to indicate the amount of information to be transmitted in each buffer.

In the receiving t_call structure, on successful return from the t_connect call, addr describes the address of the transport endpoint at the other end of the connection, opt describes any implementation-specific protocol options associated with the connection, and udata describes any user data transmitted with the connect response from the server. For t_connect, sequence is not used in either of the t_call structures.

If the calling application is not interested in the information about the other end of the connection, rcvp can be NULL, and the information will not be returned. If, on the other hand, the application does want the information, rcvp should contain the address of a t_call structure and the maxlen fields of the netbuf structures should be set to the sizes of the buffers. If the application uses t_alloc to allocate the t_call structure, then these details are already taken care of.

A transport endpoint can participate in only one connection at a time. After a connection is released, the transport endpoints can be used in other connections if desired.

By default, t_connect is synchronous: it blocks until either the connection is established or the server rejects the connection request. Applications that do not wish to block (because they can do something useful in the meantime) can change this behavior by placing the file descriptor in nonblocking mode. Then t_connect will return −1 with t_errno set to TNODATA to indicate that the connection is not yet established. The application can poll for the connect confirmation, or it can arrange to be notified via SIGPOLL (see Section 3.4). The response will arrive in a normal-priority protocol message.

When the connect confirmation arrives, it can be retrieved using t_rcvconnect(3N):

```
#include <tiuser.h>

int t_rcvconnect(int fd, struct t_call *rcvp);
```

fd and rcvp are the same as in t_connect. In fact, t_rcvconnect behaves just like `t_connect`. If the file descriptor is still in nonblocking mode, `t_rcvconnect` will return −1 with `t_errno` set to `TNODATA`. If nonblocking mode is turned off, `t_rcvconnect` will block until the connection completes or is rejected. Both `t_connect` and `t_rcvconnect` return 0 if the connection is established, and −1 on error.

If the server rejects the connection, a disconnect indication will arrive, causing `t_connect` and `t_rcvconnect` to fail with `t_errno` set to `TLOOK`. If the client application wants to continue to use the transport endpoint, then it needs to receive notification of the rejection with `t_rcvdis(3N)`:

```
#include <tiuser.h>

t_rcvdis(int fd, struct t_discon *disp);
```

`fd` is the file descriptor for the transport endpoint, and `disp` points to a `t_discon` structure describing the reason for rejection:

```
struct t_discon {
     struct netbuf    udata;
     int              reason;
     int              sequence;
};
```

The `udata` field describes any user data sent by the server along with the disconnect (if the transport provider supports this facility). `reason` identifies an implementation-specific reason for the connection rejection, and `sequence` is unused in this instance. If the caller is not interested in the reason for rejection, then `disp` can be `NULL`, and the disconnect indication will be discarded. Again, since STREAMS queues are FIFOs, the disconnect indication must be dealt with before using the endpoint to receive any more messages.

Because the server's connection queue is finite (recall the `qlen` field in the `t_bind` structure), callers of `t_connect` need to be persistent in their attempts at establishing a connection. If the connection is rejected, a retry is probably in order. Disconnects can occur from two sources. First, the server process might deny the client the connection because of invalid permissions or limited resources. Second, the transport provider might generate the disconnect, thereby denying the connection. The server's transport provider might do this because the server's connection queue is full or the server's transport endpoint is in the wrong state. The client's transport endpoint might even do this because a response has not arrived in a reasonable amount of time.

Since the reason code for the disconnect is implementation-dependent, applications wishing to remain neutral have to assume a retry is needed. Different retry algorithms exist, from simple iterative loops, to iterative loops with random delays inserted between attempts, to iterative loops with exponentially longer delays inserted between attempts.

Example 4.4.1. The following routine exhibits typical client-side connection establishment code, using an exponential backoff algorithm if attempts are rejected.

```
#include <sys/types.h>
#include <tiuser.h>
#include <errno.h>
#include <unistd.h>
#include <stdio.h>

#define MAXSLP    32

int
connect(int fd, char *addr, uint_t alen)
{
    struct t_call *callp;
    int i;
    extern int t_errno;

    /*
     * Allocate a t_call structure for the connect
     * request and point the destination address at
     * the address passed in by the caller.
     */
    callp = (struct t_call *)t_alloc(fd, T_CALL, 0);
    if (callp == NULL) {
        t_error("Cannot allocate call structure");
        return(-1);
    }
    callp->addr.buf = addr;
    callp->addr.len = alen;

    /*
     * Try several times to connect.
     */
    for (i = 1; i <= MAXSLP; i <<= 1) {
        if (t_connect(fd, callp, NULL) == 0) {
            /*
             * Connection accepted.
             */
            callp->addr.buf = NULL;
            t_free(callp, T_CALL);
            return(0);
        }
        if (t_errno == TLOOK) {
            /*
             * Connection rejected.
             */
            t_rcvdis(fd, NULL);
        } else {
            /*
             * Fatal error.
             */
            t_error("Cannot connect");
            callp->addr.buf = NULL;
            t_free(callp, T_CALL);
            return(-1);
        }
```

```
        /*
         * Delay before trying again.
         */
        sleep(i);
    }

    /*
     * We reached the maximum retry count.  Free the
     * t_call structure, print an error message, set
     * the global error codes, and return -1.
     */
    callp->addr.buf = NULL;
    t_free(callp, T_CALL);
    fprintf(stderr, "Connect timed out\n");
    t_errno = TSYSERR;
    errno = ETIME;
    return(-1);
}
```

First, we allocate a t_call structure using t_alloc. We use the address information passed to us instead of allocating a buffer for the address in the t_call structure. Then we try to connect to the server. If we succeed, we return 0. Otherwise, if t_errno is set to TLOOK, we discard the disconnect indication using t_rcvdis. Any other error results in failure, and we return −1.

Actually, if we really wanted to be robust, there is a number of other resource shortage errors that would warrant a retry, such as t_errno set to TSYSERR and errno set to EAGAIN or ENOSR. (EAGAIN is sometimes used for temporary memory shortages and ENOSR is used when STREAMS resources cannot be allocated.)

Each time a connection request is denied, we sleep for an exponentially longer time (1 s, 2 s, 4 s, 8 s, 16 s, and 32 s) and try again. Eventually, we give up, set t_errno to TSYSERR and errno to ETIME, and return −1.   □

So far we have seen how client applications create connections to server applications. Before we see how servers respond to connect requests, a word about terminology. Primitives generated by transport users are called *requests* when they are processed by the local transport provider. When they arrive at the remote transport provider, they are called *indications*. For example, a call to t_connect transmits a connect request to the local transport provider. This results in a message being transmitted to the remote transport provider, which converts it into a connect indication for the server.

The characteristic that identifies a transport endpoint as one willing to accept connect requests is that its qlen is nonzero in the t_bind structure that is used when an address is associated with the endpoint. The qlen is the number of connect indications that an application is willing to receive and process at any given time. The transport provider may or may not choose to queue additional connect indications (this is an implementation detail), but it will restrict the number of connect indications sent to the transport user such that there are never more than qlen indications outstanding at one time. During the binding process, the transport provider may choose to alter the value of qlen based on its ability to queue connect indications. The server can find out the accepted value of qlen by looking at its value in the t_bind structure returned by t_bind(3N).

When a connect indication arrives, a server process can receive it with t_listen(3N):

```
#include <tiuser.h>

int t_listen(int fd, struct t_call *callp);
```

fd is the file descriptor for the transport endpoint, and callp is a pointer to a t_call structure used to identify the transport endpoint originating the connect request. All fields of the t_call structure have the same meaning as they did with t_connect, except sequence is set to a number that uniquely identifies the connect indication. This can be used to differentiate between multiple connect indications with endpoints whose qlen is greater than 1.

On success, t_listen returns 0; on failure it returns −1. By default, t_listen will block until a connect indication arrives, or any other asynchronous event occurs. If the stream is in nonblocking mode, however, t_listen can be used to poll for connect indications. In this mode, t_listen will immediately return −1 with t_errno set to TNODATA if no connect indication is present.

If a transport endpoint's stream is in blocking (default) mode and the transport endpoint is in the idle state with a qlen of zero, an application that calls t_listen will block indefinitely. This is because the library routine will block trying to retrieve a connect indication from the stream, but the transport provider will never send one upstream since the qlen is zero.

Once the connect indication has been received, the server can either accept the connection or reject it. Accepting the connection involves initializing the transport endpoint to be used in the connection (t_open and t_bind) and using t_accept(3N) to notify the transport provider and the client process that the connection has been accepted:

```
#include <tiuser.h>

int t_accept(int fd, int afd, struct t_call *callp);
```

fd is the file descriptor for the transport endpoint on which the connect indication arrived, afd is the file descriptor for the transport endpoint to be used for the connection, and callp is a pointer to a t_call structure used to identify the transport endpoint originating the connect request.

Once the connection has been accepted, the transport endpoint goes from the idle state to the data-transfer state. The server can either accept the connection on the same transport endpoint on which the connect indication arrived (fd == afd), or it can provide a new transport endpoint for the connection (fd != afd). In the former case, no more connect indications can be queued until the endpoint reenters the idle state. In the latter case, the server can continue to listen for connect indications on the original endpoint (fd).

Table 4.3. Server Design Alternatives

Transport Endpoints	qlen
fd == afd	== 1
fd != afd	== 1
fd != afd	> 1

There are three ways to design servers with respect to the combinations of file descriptors that they can use to accept connections. They are summarized in Table 4.3, in increasing order of complexity. (fd is the file descriptor used to listen for connect indications, and afd is the file descriptor designated in the call to t_accept to participate in the connection.) The reason that the fourth possibility (fd == afd, qlen > 1) is not used is that it increases the complexity, yet yields no extra benefit. It is possible for an application to specify a queue length greater than 1 and use the same endpoint in the connection, though additional connect indications that are queued must be dealt with first.

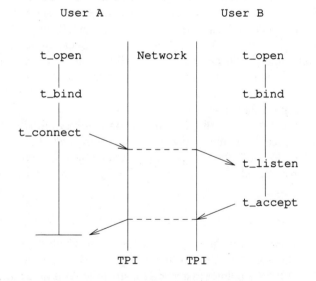

Fig. 4.5. Synchronous Connect Request Accepted

Figure 4.5 shows the sequence of events occurring during a successful connection attempt. Figure 4.6 shows the same thing, but with an asynchronous connection attempt. The server cannot tell if the client is connecting synchronously or asynchronously. The difference between the two figures is that, with a synchronous request, the caller blocks until the request is either accepted or rejected, but with an asynchronous request, the caller returns from t_connect after the connect request has been generated. The server responds the same in both cases, but with the asynchronous connect request, the server's response will be queued on the client side until the client application calls t_rcvconnect.

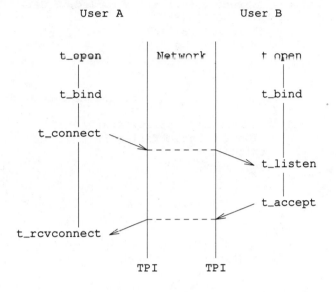

Fig. 4.6. Asynchronous Connect Request Accepted

Example 4.4.2. This example illustrates the server-side connection establishment code for a server with a qlen of 1 and accepting on the same transport endpoint on which the connect indication arrived. Servers designed like this provide their service to one client at a time. Other clients will not connect successfully until the server is done with the current connection.

```
#include <sys/types.h>
#include <stdlib.h>
#include <tiuser.h>

extern int t_errno;
extern char *t_errlist[];

extern void log(const char *, ...);

#define tlog(STR) log("%s: %s", (STR), t_errlist[t_errno])

void
serve(int fd)
{
        struct t_call *callp;
```

```
        /*
         * Allocate a t_call structure to be used when
         * receiving connect indications.
         */
        callp = (struct t_call *)t_alloc(fd, T_CALL, T_ALL);
        if (callp == NULL) {
            tlog("t_alloc failed");
            exit(1);
        }
        for ( ; ; ) {
            /*
             * Block until a connect indication arrives.
             */
            if (t_listen(fd, callp) < 0) {
                tlog("t_listen failed");
                exit(1);
            }

            /*
             * Accept the connection on the same file
             * descriptor used for listening.
             */
            if (t_accept(fd, fd, callp) < 0) {
                if (t_errno == TLOOK) {
                    /*
                     * Someone canceled the connect request.
                     */
                    if (t_rcvdis(fd, NULL) < 0) {
                        tlog("t_rcvdis failed");
                        exit(1);
                    }
                } else {
                    tlog("t_accept failed");
                    exit(1);
                }
            } else {
                /*
                 * Perform the service using fd and release
                 * the connection.
                 */
                    .
                    .
                    .
            }
        }

}
```

We want the server to provide its service more than once, so we place all processing in an infinite loop. We block in t_listen, waiting for a connect indication. When one arrives, we accept the connection on the same file descriptor on which the connect indication arrived. This prevents connect requests from other clients from succeeding until the connection is released.

If t_accept fails with t_errno set to TLOOK, then the caller has canceled the connect request by either requesting a disconnect or closing the transport endpoint. Any other failure of t_accept is treated as a fatal error.

After the connection is made, we perform the service. When we are through, we release the connection and go back to listen for more connect indications.   □

The previous example is simple, but if the service takes too long, users can experience intolerable delays or failures when invoking the client-side command. To solve this problem, the server can accept the connection on a different transport endpoint. This way, the original transport endpoint is used only for listening for connect indications.

This new benefit comes with a cost, however: a new point of failure is introduced when the server attempts to initialize the new transport endpoint. Instead of exiting when the initialization of the new endpoint fails, the server can deny the connection (presumably because of resource shortages) and continue listening for new connect indications. A connect request is rejected using t_snddis(3N):

```
#include <tiuser.h>

int t_snddis(int fd, struct t_call *callp);
```

fd is the file descriptor for the transport endpoint on which the connect indication arrived, and callp is a t_call structure identifying the caller to reject. The addr and opt fields of the t_call structure are ignored. The udata field is for optional user data to be sent with the disconnect request. Not all transport providers support this option, so its use is discouraged for those applications wishing to remain network-independent. The only mandatory field is sequence. It must be set to the sequence number from the t_call structure corresponding to the connect request to be rejected.

On success, t_snddis returns 0; on failure, it returns −1. Figure 4.7 shows the sequence of events when a client tries to create a connection synchronously and the server rejects the request. Figure 4.8 shows the same thing, but with the client attempting to establish the connection asynchronously.

t_snddis can also be used as an abortive release of an existing connection. In this case, the sequence field has no meaning. In fact, if the caller does not have any user data to transmit with the disconnect, then callp can be NULL. Connection release will be discussed more at the end of this section.

Example 4.4.3. This example illustrates the server-side connection establishment code for a server with a qlen of 1 and accepting on a different transport endpoint from the one on which the connect indication arrived. Servers designed like this can handle multiple clients at once by forking a new child process to handle each connection. The parent process is designed only to listen for connect indications and create connections.

We use a routine similar to initclient to obtain the transport endpoint to be used in the connection. This routine, getfd, calls t_open to create a new transport endpoint and then calls t_bind to bind an arbitrary address to the endpoint. getfd returns the file descriptor for the transport endpoint on success, or −1 on failure.

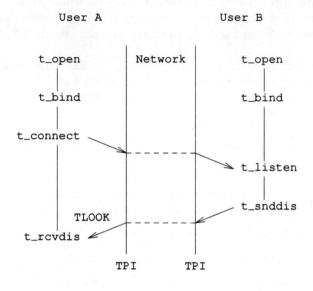

Fig. 4.7. Synchronous Connect Request Rejected

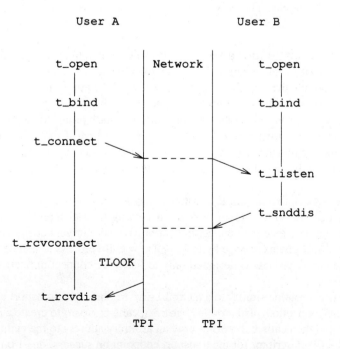

Fig. 4.8. Asynchronous Connect Request Rejected

```c
#include <sys/types.h>
#include <unistd.h>
#include <stdlib.h>
#include <tiuser.h>
#include <fcntl.h>
#include <signal.h>

extern int t_errno;
extern char *t_errlist[];

extern void log(const char *, ...);

#define tlog(STR) log("%s: %s", (STR), t_errlist[t_errno])

int
getfd(char *transport)
{
    int fd;

    /*
     * Open the transport provider.
     */
    if ((fd = t_open(transport, O_RDWR, NULL)) < 0)
        return(-1);

    /*
     * Bind an arbitrary address to the transport
     * endpoint.
     */
    if (t_bind(fd, NULL, NULL) < 0) {
        t_close(fd);
        return(-1);
    }
    return(fd);
}

void
serve(int fd, char *transport)
{
    int afd;
    pid_t pid;
    struct t_call *call;

    /*
     * Allocate a t_call structure to be used when
     * receiving connect indications.
     */
    call = (struct t_call *)t_alloc(fd, T_CALL, T_ALL);
    if (call == NULL) {
        tlog("t_alloc failed");
        exit(1);
    }
    for ( ; ; ) {
        /*
```

```
 * Block until a connect indication arrives.
 */
if (t_listen(fd, call) < 0) {
    tlog("t_listen failed");
    exit(1);
}

/*
 * Get a new transport endpoint to be used in
 * the connection.
 */
if ((afd = getfd(transport)) < 0) {
    /*
     * Can't get a new endpoint -- reject
     * the connect request.
     */
    if (t_snddis(fd, call) < 0) {
        tlog("t_snddis failed");
        exit(1);
    }
    continue;
}

/*
 * Accept the connection on afd instead of fd.
 */
if (t_accept(fd, afd, call) < 0) {
    if (t_errno == TLOOK) {
        /*
         * Someone canceled the connect request.
         */
        if (t_rcvdis(fd, NULL) < 0) {
            tlog("t_rcvdis failed");
            exit(1);
        }
    } else {
        tlog("t_accept failed");
        exit(1);
    }
} else {
    /*
     * Fork and let the child process do the real
     * work.  The parent goes back to listen for
     * more connect indications.
     */
    if ((pid = fork()) < 0) {
        /*
         * Fork failed -- reject
         * the connect request.
         */
        log("fork failed");
        if (t_snddis(afd, NULL) < 0) {
            tlog("t_snddis failed");
            exit(1);
```

```
        }
    } else if (pid == 0) {
        /*
         * Child resumes here.  Don't need
         * the file descriptor used to listen
         * for connect indications.
         */
        t_close(fd);

        /*
         * Perform the service using afd and exit.
         */
        .
        .
        .
    }
}

/*
 * After a successful fork, the parent continues
 * here. Close the file descriptor used in the
 * connection and continue to listen for more
 * connect indications.
 */
t_close(afd);
}
}
```

The server in this example is similar to the one in Example 4.4.2; however, after obtaining the connect indication from t_listen, we create a new transport endpoint (afd) using getfd. If this fails, we use t_snddis to reject the connect request, using the same t_call structure returned from the previous call to t_listen.

If we are able to initialize a new endpoint, we accept the connection, specifying that afd be used as the transport endpoint for this end of the connection. If this succeeds, then we fork a child process to perform the service. The child does not need the file descriptor used to listen for connect requests, so we call t_close to relinquish access to the transport endpoint.

If fork fails, we disconnect the connection. Note that we do not need to specify a t_call structure in this case because the connection is already established, so the disconnect request is unambiguous.

After forking the child process, continuing execution in the context of the parent, we close the newly created transport endpoint and continue to listen for more connect indications.   □

Even though the server in the previous example is able to provide service to more than one client at a time, it might still be common for clients to experience too many failed connection attempts. This is possible if the time to open the transport provider and bind an address for the new endpoint is long enough for too many more connect requests to occur.

One solution to this problem is to use a value for qlen that is greater than 1.

This further complicates the server implementation, however, by requiring that the server retrieve all connect indications and disconnect indications before it can successfully accept a connection.

As can be seen from Figure 4.9, the call to t_accept can fail with t_errno set to TLOOK because of the arrival of another connect indication. The first connect indication cannot be accepted until the second one is retrieved from the stream. Unlike the previous two examples, when t_accept fails with t_errno set to TLOOK, the server cannot assume it knows what the asynchronous event is. The server has to use t_look(3N) to identify the event:

```
#include <tiuser.h>

int t_look(int fd);
```

fd is the file descriptor for the transport endpoint. t_look returns −1 if there is an error, 0 if no event occurred, or one of the codes listed in Table 4.4, depending on the event received.

Table 4.4. t_look Return Codes

Return Code	Event	Service Type
T_LISTEN	Connect indication	T_COTS/T_COTS_ORD
T_CONNECT	Connect confirmation	T_COTS/T_COTS_ORD
T_DATA	Normal data	T_COTS/T_COTS_ORD
T_EXDATA	Expedited data	T_COTS/T_COTS_ORD
T_DISCONNECT	Disconnect indication	T_COTS/T_COTS_ORD
T_UDERR	Datagram error indication	T_CLTS
T_ORDREL	Orderly release indication	T_COTS_ORD

Strangely enough, t_look can also return the value T_ERROR if it cannot peek at the message on the front of the stream head read queue. All other errors result in a return value of −1. There is no useful reason to distinguish this particular error from any other.

Example 4.4.4. This example illustrates the server-side connection establishment code for a server with a qlen greater than 1 and accepting on a different transport endpoint from the one on which the connect indication arrived. Since we have to retrieve all connect indications before accepting any of them, we need some way to remember the outstanding connect indications when we are ready to process them. We will use the following structure for this purpose:

```
#include <sys/types.h>
#include <unistd.h>
#include <stdlib.h>
#include <fcntl.h>
#include <tiuser.h>
#include <signal.h>
```

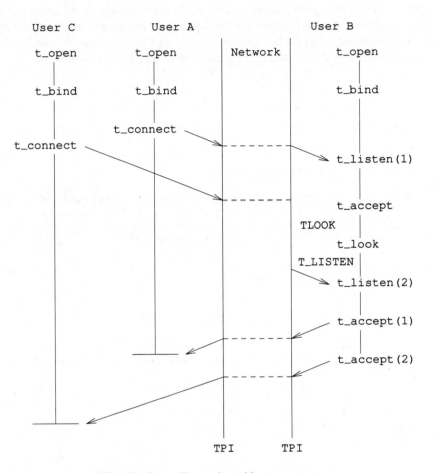

Fig. 4.9. Server Processing with `qlen > 1`

```
typedef struct creq {
     struct creq *next;
     struct creq *prev;
     struct t_call *callp;
     int afd;
} creq_t;

creq_t *cfree;
creq_t *chead;
creq_t *ctail;
```

The `creq` structure represents elements in a doubly linked list containing the
transport endpoint to be used to accept the connection and a pointer to the `t_call`
structure containing the connect information. A freelist containing the `creq` structures is headed by `cfree`. Since we will need to remove and enter elements from
only one end of the list, the freelist will be singly linked, using only the `next`

pointer. We might have to remove an element from the middle of the list of pending connect requests, however, so we will use both `next` and `prev` when an element is on the pending list. This list is represented by `chead` and `ctail`. `chead` points to the first element on the list, and `ctail` points to the last element on the list.

```c
struct t_discon *disp;

void dolook(int fd);

extern int t_errno;
extern char *t_errlist[];

extern void log(const char *, ...);

#define tlog(STR) log("%s: %s", (STR), t_errlist[t_errno])

void
serve(int fd, int qlen, char *transport)
{
    creq_t *creqp;
    struct t_call *callp;
    pid_t pid;
    int i;

    /*
     * Allocate a t_discon structure to be used when
     * retrieving disconnect indications from the stream.
     */
    disp = (struct t_discon *)t_alloc(fd, T_DIS, T_ALL);
    if (disp == NULL) {
        tlog("t_alloc failed");
        exit(1);
    }

    /*
     * Allocate an array of t_call structures.  (qlen
     * specifies the number of structures to allocate.)
     * For each structure, initialize it and then link
     * it onto the freelist.
     */
    creqp = calloc(qlen, sizeof(creq_t));
    if (creqp == NULL) {
        log("calloc failed");
        exit(1);
    }
    for (i = 0; i < qlen; i++, creqp++) {
        callp = (struct t_call *)t_alloc(fd, T_CALL,
            T_ALL);
        if (callp == NULL) {
            tlog("t_alloc failed");
            exit(1);
        }
        creqp->callp = callp;
        creqp->afd = -1;
```

```
        creqp->next = cfree;
        cfree = creqp;
}
creqp = NULL;
for ( ; ; ) {
    /*
     * Use the current connect request structure
     * in processing the next connect indication.
     * If we have no current structure, pull one
     * off of the freelist.
     */
    if (creqp == NULL) {
        creqp = cfree;
        cfree = cfree->next;
    }
    callp = creqp->callp;

    /*
     * Wait for a connect indication to arrive.
     */
    if (t_listen(fd, callp) < 0) {
        tlog("t_listen failed");
        exit(1);
    }

    /*
     * Get a new transport endpoint to be used in
     * the connection.
     */
    if ((creqp->afd = getfd(transport)) < 0) {
        /*
         * Can't get a new endpoint -- reject
         * the connect request.
         */
        if (t_snddis(fd, callp) < 0) {
            tlog("t_snddis failed");
            exit(1);
        }
        continue;
    }
    while (creqp != NULL) {
        /*
         * Accept the connection on creqp->afd.
         */
        if (t_accept(fd, creqp->afd, callp) < 0) {
            if (t_errno != TLOOK) {
                tlog("t_accept failed");
                exit(1);
            }

            /*
             * A pending event is preventing t_accept
             * from succeeding.  Save creqp on the
             * list of pending connections and call
```

```
         * dolook to process the event.
         */
        creqp->next = chead;
        creqp->prev = NULL;
        if (chead != NULL)
            chead->prev = creqp;
        else
            ctail = creqp;
        chead = creqp;
        dolook(fd);
    } else {
        /*
         * Accept succeeded. Fork and let the
         * child process do the real work.  The
         * parent goes back to listen for more
         * connect indications.
         */
        if ((pid = fork()) < 0) {
            /*
             * Fork failed -- reject
             * the connect request.
             */
            log("fork failed");
            if (t_snddis(creqp->afd, NULL) < 0) {
                tlog("t_snddis failed");
                exit(1);
            }
        } else if (pid == 0) {  /* child */
            /*
             * Child resumes here.  Don't need
             * the file descriptor used to listen
             * for connect indications.
             */
            t_close(fd);

            /*
             * Perform the service using
             * creqp->afd and exit.
             */
        }

        /*
         * After a successful fork, the parent
         * continues here. Close the file
         * descriptor used in the connection,
         * place the creq structure back on the
         * freelist, and continue to listen for
         * more connect indications.
         */
        t_close(creqp->afd);
        creqp->afd = -1;
        creqp->next = cfree;
        cfree = creqp;
    }
```

```
                        /*
                         * Process the next creq structure, if there
                         * is one, on the pending list.
                         */
                        creqp = chead;
                        if (creqp != NULL) {
                            callp = creqp->callp;
                            chead = creqp->next;
                            if (chead != NULL)
                                chead->prev = NULL;
                            else
                                ctail = NULL;
                        }
                    }
                }
        }
```

The first thing we do is to allocate all the data structures we will need. This includes a t_discon structure for processing disconnect indications and multiple t_call structures for processing connect indications. We know that we will never have more than qlen outstanding connect indications. So we use calloc(3C) to allocate and clear enough space for qlen creq structures. Then we initialize every creq structure by allocating a t_call structure for it and setting the file descriptor (afd) to an invalid value.

The bulk of the server work is done in an infinite loop. If we do not currently have a creq structure, we get one off the freelist. We block in t_listen, waiting for a connect indication. When one arrives, we create a new transport endpoint for the connection using getfd (see Example 4.4.3). We save the new endpoint in the creq structure. If we were not able to get a new endpoint, we reject the connect request using t_snddis. Then we continue with the loop, but since we have a creq structure this time, we do not need to get one from the freelist, and we go back to waiting for another connect indication.

If we are able to get a new endpoint, we enter a loop to accept the connection. If t_accept fails with t_errno set to TLOOK, then we place creqp on the front of the list of pending connections and call dolook to process the asynchronous event preventing us from accepting the connection. Then we get the first element off the pending connection list, if the list is not empty, and continue in the accept loop.

If t_accept succeeds, we fork a child process to handle the service. If the fork fails, we abort the connection and close the transport endpoint that was allocated for the connection. Otherwise, the child performs the service using creqp->afd. The child does not need the transport endpoint used for listening, so it closes it. The parent continues by closing the transport endpoint for the connection, since the child will hold it open, and placing the creq structure on the freelist. As in the error case, we continue processing the pending connection list until it is empty.

```
    void
    dolook(int fd)
    {
```

```
creq_t *creqp;
struct t_call *callp;
int event;
char buf[64];

switch (event = t_look(fd)) {
case T_LISTEN:
    /*
     * Another connect indication has arrived.
     * Take a creq structure off the freelist and
     * remove the connect indication from the stream.
     */
    creqp = cfree;
    cfree = cfree->next;
    if (t_listen(fd, creqp->callp) < 0) {
        tlog("t_listen failed");
        exit(1);
    }

    /*
     * Put the connect indication on the end of
     * the pending list of connections.
     */
    creqp->next = NULL;
    creqp->prev = ctail;
    if (ctail != NULL)
        ctail->next = creqp;
    else
        chead = creqp;
    ctail = creqp;
    break;

case T_DISCONNECT:
    /*
     * Someone canceled a connect request.  Remove
     * the disconnect indication from the stream and
     * find a pending connection that matches it.
     */
    if (t_rcvdis(fd, disp) < 0) {
        tlog("t_rcvdis failed");
        exit(1);
    }
    for (creqp = chead; creqp; creqp = creqp->next) {
        callp = creqp->callp;
        if (callp->sequence == disp->sequence) {
            /*
             * We found a match.  Close the transport
             * endpoint allocated for the connection,
             * unlink the creq structure from the list
             * of pending connections, and place it on
             * the freelist.
             */
            t_close(creqp->afd);
            if (creqp->prev != NULL)
```

```
                            creqp->prev->next = creqp->next;
                    else
                            chead = creqp->next;
                    if (creqp->next != NULL)
                            creqp->next->prev = creqp->prev;
                    else
                            ctail = creqp->prev;
                    creqp->next = cfree;
                    cfree = creqp;
                    break;
                }
            }
            break;

    case T_ERROR:
    case -1:
        tlog("t_look failed");
        exit(1);

    default:
        /*
         * This shouldn't happen.
         */
        sprintf(buf, "unknown t_look event %d", event);
        log(buf);
        exit(1);
    }
}
```

dolook is used to process the asynchronous event that is preventing the server from accepting a connection. We use t_look to identify the event. Under normal conditions, there are only two possible events: another connect indication arrived or a disconnect indication arrived for a pending connect request.

If the event is a connect indication (case T_LISTEN), we get a creq structure off the freelist and call t_listen to pull the indication off the stream. Then we place the creq structure on the end of the pending connection list and return.

If the event was a disconnect indication (case T_DISCONNECT), we pull the indication off the stream using t_rcvdis. Then we step through the list of pending connections trying to match the sequence number in the t_discon structure with the sequence number in the saved t_call structure. If a match is found, we close the transport endpoint allocated for the connection, remove the creq structure from the pending list, and add it to the freelist.   □

Data Transfer

Now that we have spent considerable effort establishing a connection, we can finally transfer some data. For this, we use t_snd(3N):

```
#include <tiuser.h>

int t_snd(int fd, char *buf, uint_t nbytes, int flags);
```

fd is the file descriptor for the transport endpoint, buf points to the data to be
transmitted, nbytes is the number of bytes to transmit, and flags indicates
characteristics of the transmission. Like write(2), this routine will block if the
stream is flow-controlled. Unlike write, however, if the stream is in nonblocking
mode and is flow-controlled, t_snd will return −1 with t_errno set to TFLOW.
On success, t_snd returns the number of bytes transmitted. On failure, it returns
−1.

Callers of t_snd do not have to worry about the TIDU size of the transport
provider. t_snd will fragment the data, sending multiple messages to the transport
provider, if nbytes is greater than the TIDU size. Protocol-independent applications should avoid calling t_snd when nbytes is zero. Not all transport providers
support zero-length data messages. If an application attempts to send a zero-length
message over a transport provider that does not support it, t_snd will fail with
t_errno set to T_BADDATA.

An application can create logically larger messages from multiple smaller ones
by setting the T_MORE flag in flags. This indicates to the transport provider that
this message will be followed by another that is logically a continuation of the
current message, or TSDU. When a message is transmitted with T_MORE off, this is
viewed as the last portion of the TSDU.

Not all transport providers support logical message boundaries. Those protocols that are byte-stream-oriented do not have a concept of a TSDU and do not support this flag. TCP, for example, has no provision for marking message boundaries.
Note that transport providers that support message boundaries are supposed to support the T_MORE flag. For portable applications, it is best to avoid using the
T_MORE flag.

By default, t_snd generates normal data messages. If the T_EXPEDITED flag
is set in flags, however, expedited data messages are generated. Expedited data
are treated with a higher priority than normal data. This means the protocol usually
tries to deliver the expedited data as quickly as possible, often ahead of normal data
already sent but not yet received by the other transport user. In addition, the transfer
of expedited data is unaffected by the flow-control constraints of the normal data
flow.

Not all protocols support the concept of expedited data. For example, TCP has
the notion of a single byte in the data stream, called the *urgent mark*, that the user
can elect to receive inline with other data, or out-of-band (ahead of other data). This
facility can be viewed as if TCP supports an ETSDU size of 1 byte. On the other
hand, SNA's LU6.2 transport protocol does not support the notion of out-of-band
data at all.

If a user attempts to transmit expedited data over a transport provider that does
not support it, the results are implementation-specific. The transport provider might
choose to treat the expedited data request as if it were a normal data request. On the
other hand, the transport provider might instead choose to place the stream in error

mode, thereby making the stream effectively useless.

The `t_rcv(3N)` function is used to receive data over a connection:

```
#include <tiuser.h>

int t_rcv(int fd, char *buf, uint_t nbytes, int *flagsp);
```

`fd` is the file descriptor for the transport endpoint, `buf` points to the buffer where the data are to be stored, `nbytes` is the size of the buffer in bytes, and `flagsp` points to an integer that indicates the characteristics of the data received. Like `read(2)`, this routine will block if no data are available. Unlike `read`, however, if the stream is in nonblocking mode and no data are immediately available, `t_rcv` will return −1 with `t_errno` set to `TNODATA`. On success, `t_rcv` returns the number of bytes received. On failure, it returns −1.

If `t_rcv` fails with `t_errno` set to `TLOOK`, then an asynchronous event has occurred that will prevent data from being received until the event is acknowledged. If the transport provider is of type `T_COTS`, an application can just assume that a disconnect indication has been received and call `t_rcvdis` to retrieve the indication. After this has been done, however, the transport endpoint is no longer in data-transfer mode. If the transport provider is of type `T_COTS_ORD`, the application should call `t_look` to identify the event. It will be either a disconnect indication or an orderly release indication. We will discuss orderly release shortly.

On return, if the `T_MORE` flag is set in the integer pointed to by `flagsp`, then the current data do not constitute the entire message, or TSDU. The application should perform multiple `t_rcv` calls to obtain the entire TSDU. The last portion of the message is indicated by the absence of the `T_MORE` flag.

If the `T_EXPEDITED` flag is set in the integer pointed to by `flagsp`, then the data are expedited instead of normal.

Applications wishing to remain protocol-independent should not assume that messages will be received in the same sizes in which they are sent. Lower-level protocols might fragment the TSDUs into smaller messages for transmission. Additionally, byte-stream protocols make no attempt to retain message boundaries.

Example 4.4.5. This example shows the data-transfer primitives in action. In it, we rework the remote who command from Example 4.3.1. This time, however, we redesign things such that any noninteractive command can be executed by the server. That is to say, any command that does not require terminal input from the client will be run by the server.

The reason for this restriction lies in the problems we would face when trying to deal with type-ahead. The client side of the command would have to read data from its standard input (usually the user's terminal) and ship it to the server to be used as input to the command. We can never know how much data the command would want to read, so we might be faced with the situation where we have read more data than the command needs. There is no clean way to ''unread'' the data. Thus, data that had been typed ahead, intended to be read by the shell after the command completed, would instead be read by the client command, shipped to the server, and ultimately ignored.

```
#include <sys/types.h>
#include <stdlib.h>
#include <stdio.h>
#include <tiuser.h>
#include <string.h>
#include <signal.h>
#include <unistd.h>

#define CMDSZ    256

void timeout(int);
extern int initclient(char *);
extern int connect(int, char *, uint_t);

void
rcmd(int argc, char *argv[], char *transport, char *addr,
    uint_t alen)
{
    int fd, i, n, flags;
    struct sigaction sa;
    char buf[CMDSZ];

    if (argc < 3) {
        fprintf(stderr,
            "usage: rcmd host command [options]\n");
        exit(1);
    }

    /*
     * Create a client-style transport endpoint.
     */
    if ((fd = initclient(transport)) < 0)
        exit(1);

    /*
     * Create a connection to the server.
     */
    if (connect(fd, addr, alen) < 0)
        exit(1);

    /*
     * Copy the command and its arguments to buf.  The
     * command string is NULL-terminated and buf[0]
     * contains the total number of bytes to be sent.
     */
    strcpy(&buf[1], argv[2]);
    for (i = 3; i < argc; i++) {
        strcat(&buf[1], " ");    /* add a space */
        strcat(&buf[1], argv[i]);
    }
    i = strlen(&buf[1]);
    buf[i+1] = '\0';
    buf[0] = i + 2;
```

```
        /*
         * Set an alarm so we don't block forever.
         */
        sa.sa_handler = timeout;
        sa.sa_flags = 0;
        sigemptyset(&sa.sa_mask);
        sigaction(SIGALRM, &sa, NULL);
        alarm(60);

        /*
         * Send the command string to the server.
         */
        if ((n = t_snd(fd, buf, i, 0)) != i) {
            if (n < 0)
                t_error("rcmd: Cannot send request");
            else
                fprintf(stderr, "rcmd: Partial transmission");
            exit(1);
        }

        /*
         * Receive response messages until we encounter an
         * error or receive the end of the messages (a single
         * byte containing 0).
         */
        while ((n = t_rcv(fd, buf, CMDSZ, &flags)) > 0) {
            if (buf[n-1] == '\0') {
                n--;
                break;
            }
            /*
             * Write the response to the standard output.
             */
            write(1, buf, n);
        }

        /*
         * The final byte might have been appended to the
         * preceding message, so we might have more to write.
         */
        if (n > 0) {
            write(1, buf, n);
        } else if (n < 0) {
            t_error("rcmd: Cannot receive data");
            exit(1);
        }
        exit(0);
}

void
timeout(int sig)
{
        fprintf(stderr, "rcmd: Command timed out\n");
        exit(1);
```

```
}
```

We start out by initializing the transport connection using `initclient` from Example 4.2.1. Then we create a virtual circuit to the server using the `connect` function from Example 4.4.1. We will send a message to the server consisting of one byte containing the size of the message followed by a NULL-terminated command string. This message will be built in `buf`, an array of 256 bytes (characters). Historically, terminal drivers have only accepted a maximum of 256 characters per line, so 256 should be more than enough for the buffer, considering we will not be sending the `rcmd` string or the host name.

We build the message by copying the command name into the buffer starting at the second byte (`buf[1]`). Then we append each command option to the end of the buffer and place a NULL byte at the end. We store the size of the message in the first byte. This is the length of the string plus 1 for the NULL byte and 1 for the length byte.

Before engaging in any network communication, we set an alarm to fire off in 60 seconds. If the server does not complete in this amount of time, we assume an error occurred and execute `timeout`, the signal handler for `SIGALRM`.

Then we send the command message to the server. If this fails, or if we can only send part of the message, we fail and exit. When the server tries to receive a message, `t_rcv` will fail with TLOOK, and the server will exit. If the default for the transport provider is an abortive release, the connection will be taken down when the client exits. If the default is an orderly release, then the connection will be taken down when both the client and the server exit.

If the server produces any output, we will receive it in the `while` loop. We send the output to the standard output using `write`. If the last byte in the message is a NULL, then we do not want to write that byte, so we decrement the number of bytes received by 1. This NULL byte indicates the end of the last message that will be sent by the server. In this case we print the message contents and exit indicating success (an exit code of 0).   □

We now present the server-side of the previous example, in the interest of completeness.

Example 4.4.6. The `doservice` function is designed to be executed from the context of a child process that was forked off by the parent server (see Examples 4.4.3 and 4.4.4). The `doservice` function is passed the file descriptor for the transport endpoint that is the server side of the connection to the client `rcmd` process.

```
#include <sys/types.h>
#include <stdio.h>
#include <stdlib.h>
#include <unistd.h>
#include <tiuser.h>
#include <signal.h>

void timeout(int);
extern int t_errno;
```

```c
extern char *t_errlist[];
extern void log(const char *, ...);

#define tlog(STR) log("%s: %s", (STR), t_errlist[t_errno])
#define CMDSZ     256
#define BUFSZ     1024

void
doservice(int fd)
{
    int i, n, flags;
    char *p;
    FILE *fp;
    struct sigaction sa;
    char cmd[CMDSZ];
    char buf[BUFSZ];

    /*
     * Receive the command string.  Must make multiple
     * calls to t_rcv because the original message
     * might have been fragmented during transmission.
     */
    n = t_rcv(fd, cmd, CMDSZ, &flags);
    if (n < 0) {
        tlog("Cannot receive request");
        exit(1);
    }

    /*
     * p is the current location in the command string
     * and n is the amount remaining to be read.
     */
    p = &cmd[n];
    n = cmd[0] - n;
    while (n > 0) {
        i = t_rcv(fd, p, (int)(CMDSZ + p - cmd), &flags);
        if (i < 0) {
            tlog("Cannot receive request");
            exit(1);
        }
        p += i;
        n -= i;
    }

    /*
     * Execute the command.  fp is open to the
     * command's standard output.
     */
    fp = popen(&cmd[1], "r");
    if (fp) {
        /*
         * Read the output of the command and send it
         * back to the client.
         */
```

```
      while ((n = fread(buf, sizeof(char), BUFSZ,
        fp)) != 0) {
          if ((i = t_snd(fd, buf, n, 0)) != n) {
              if (i < 0)
                  tlog("Cannot send data");
              else
                  log("Partial t_snd");
              exit(0);
          }
      }
      pclose(fp);

      /*
       * Send the terminating message to the client.
       */
      buf[0] = '\0';
      if (t_snd(fd, buf, 1, 0) < 0) {
          tlog("Cannot send data");
          exit(0);
      }
  } else {
      log("Cannot exec command");
      exit(0);
  }

  /*
   * Set an alarm so we don't block forever in t_rcv,
   * awaiting the disconnect or orderly release.
   */
  sa.sa_handler = timeout;
  sa.sa_flags = 0;
  sigemptyset(&sa.sa_mask);
  sigaction(SIGALRM, &sa, NULL);
  alarm(60);
  t_rcv(fd, buf, 1, &flags);
  exit(0);
}

void
timeout(int sig)
{
    log("Never got disconnect");
    exit(0);
}
```

We start by retrieving the command string from the client. The first call to
t_rcv might not retrieve the entire message, so we save a pointer to the next byte in
the buffer and calculate the number of bytes left to be read. If this is zero, then we
do nothing. Otherwise, while it is greater than zero, we try to get the next part of the
message from the transport provider. The amount of space left in the buffer is given
by (CMDSZ + p - cmd). As we fill up the buffer, p increases and this value
decreases proportionally.

When we have received the entire message, we use popen(3C), as in

Example 4.3.2. Then we read from the standard output of the command and send what we read to the client. When the command completes, `fread` will return 0 and we will close the file descriptor (not strictly necessary since we will soon be exiting) and send a message to the client consisting of a single NULL byte. This indicates to the client that there will be no more output from the command.

Finally, we set a timer to fire off in 60 seconds and then block in `t_rcv`. When the client exits, we should be sent either a disconnect indication or an orderly release indication. This will cause us to return from `t_rcv` so we can exit. If the transport provider supported orderly release by default, the trailing NULL byte and final `t_rcv` would not be necessary, but since we want the application to work over all connection-oriented networks, we have to wait for the client to retrieve all the data successfully and initiate the connection release. This prevents data loss when the transport provider supports an abortive release as the default.   □

Connection Release

As we have seen, `t_snddis` can be used to abort an established connection. If not used properly, however, this primitive can cause the loss of data. When the local transport provider receives the disconnect request, it flushes the stream of any data that might be queued. Also, on the remote side, when the transport provider receives the disconnect indication, it flushes its stream of any data queued there. This requires applications to "handshake" before releasing a connection with a disconnect. This is exhibited in the previous example, where even though the server has finished its job, it waits for the client to release the connection to ensure that the client has received all the data.

To relieve the application of this burden, some transport providers support the optional orderly release mechanism. This mechanism employs the handshaking necessary to ensure that all data are received before the connection is taken down. To use this mechanism, the service type of the transport provider must be T_COTS_ORD.

An application can issue an orderly release using `t_sndrel(3N)`:

```
#include <tiuser.h>

int t_sndrel(int fd);
```

`fd` is the file descriptor for the transport endpoint. This function indicates to the transport provider that the transport user is finished transmitting data. After calling `t_sndrel`, the user may not attempt to send data; otherwise the transport provider may put the stream in error mode, making it effectively useless. The user can, however, continue to receive data until an orderly release indication arrives, or the connection is aborted with a disconnect.

If the stream is in nonblocking mode and is flow-controlled, `t_sndrel` can fail, returning −1 with `t_errno` set to TFLOW. On success, `t_sndrel` returns 0.

When an orderly release indication is generated by the transport provider, the indication is enqueued behind any unretrieved data present in the stream. Unlike the reaction to a disconnect, the stream is not flushed. When the user has retrieved all the data from the stream, t_rcv will fail with t_errno set to TLOOK. The user can then use t_look to identify the event. If t_look returns T_ORDREL, then the user should use t_rcvrel(3N) to acknowledge this half of the orderly release:

```
#include <tiuser.h>
```

```
int t_rcvrel(int fd);
```

fd is the file descriptor for the transport endpoint. After calling this function, the user cannot receive any more data. Data can still be transmitted, however, until the user calls t_sndrel. The connection remains intact until both sides issue successful orderly release requests.

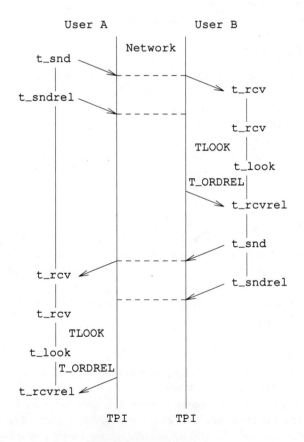

Fig. 4.10. Orderly Release

On success, t_rcvrel returns 0. On failure, it returns −1. Figure 4.10 shows the sequence of events during an orderly release.

Connection-oriented State Machine

Unfortunately, transport users must be aware of the TLI state transitions to avoid calling a TLI routine from the wrong state. While some functions will fail with t_errno set to TOUTSTATE, a nonfatal error, others will place the stream in error mode, making it virtually useless.

The state diagram for connection-oriented service (see Figure 4.11) is much more complex than for connectionless service. The transitions shown assume successful completion of the primitives. The state diagram has been simplified so it is more understandable. For example, the opening and binding primitives are absent. The states are described shortly.

For t_accept, the state transitions for the endpoint used for listening are shown. The transition for the endpoint used for the connection is not shown, but in all cases, it goes from the idle state to the data-transfer state.

To find out what state a transport endpoint is in, an application can use t_getstate(3N):

```
#include <tiuser.h>

int t_getstate(int fd);
```

fd is the file descriptor for the transport endpoint. On error, t_getstate returns −1 and sets the error code in t_errno. On success, t_getstate returns the state. The possible state values returned are listed in Table 4.5.

Table 4.5. State Values Returned by t_getstate

State	Description
T_UNBND	Unbound
T_IDLE	Idle
T_OUTCON	Outgoing connection pending
T_INCON	Incoming connection pending
T_DATAXFER	Data transfer
T_OUTREL	Orderly release sent
T_INREL	Orderly release received

One interesting error return is TSTATECHNG. This is set when the library cannot determine the actual state of the transport endpoint. This is a side effect of the fact that the state of the transport endpoint is maintained by the transport provider, but the library also needs state information to avoid generating TPI primitives that would result in a fatal error for the stream. Since the library data are lost after an exec(2), it is not possible to identify the library state in all cases.

The reconstruction of the library data after an exec can be performed by calling t_sync(3N):

```
#include <tiuser.h>

int t_sync(int fd);
```

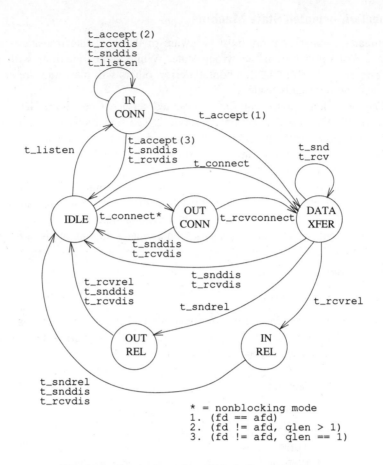

Fig. 4.11. Connection-oriented Mode State Diagram

fd is the file descriptor for the transport endpoint. On success, the current state is returned. On error, −1 is returned. Before SVR4, this function provided the only mechanism for applications to regain the library state after an exec. In SVR4, the TLI library was changed so that the invocation of any TLI routine will automatically result in an internal t_sync being performed. Thus, applications can effectively ignore this issue.

t_sync can still be used to obtain current state information when multiple processes are accessing the same transport endpoint at the same time. However, this situation is very rare.

The state diagram in Figure 4.11 is simplified. It shows the state transitions for the transport endpoint from the perspective of the TLI library. The transport provider's state machine is more complex, including a number of intermediate states. This split of state information between the library and the transport provider is the source of problems with state reporting. The TSTATECHNG error was invented to identify inconsistencies.

For `t_sync`, this error is returned when the transport provider is in an intermediate state for which there is no library equivalent. For `t_getstate`, this error is returned when the transport provider is not in a quiescent state (`T_IDLE` or `T_DATAXFER`) after an `exec`.

4.5 TLI AND READ/WRITE

The two most commonly used system calls are `read(2)` and `write(2)`. Unfortunately, they cannot be used by naive applications with unmodified transport endpoints. This is because `read`, by default, cannot handle `M_PROTO` or `M_PCPROTO` messages. In addition, some transport providers cannot support zero-length messages, and there is nothing to prevent a user from generating a zero-length data message with `write`. Luckily, a special module, TIRDWR, is available to convert the transport provider interface into a read/write interface (see Figure 4.12).

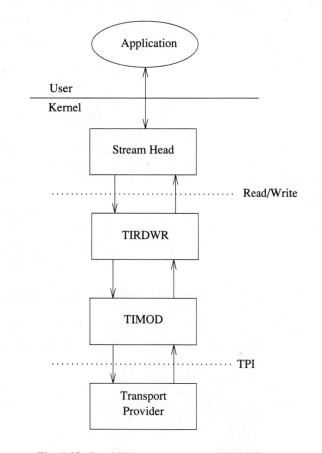

Fig. 4.12. Read/Write Interface with TIRDWR

While a transport provider is in data-transfer phase, TIRDWR can be added to the stream with the following:

```
ioctl(fd, I_PUSH, "tirdwr");
```

Two interesting errors can occur when pushing TIRDWR onto the stream. First, if there is anything on the stream head read queue that TIRDWR would not have let through, such as a message that would have caused read to fail, then TIRDWR will fail the push with errno set to EPROTO. Second, if TIRDWR cannot allocate an unused data structure for the stream, then the push will fail with errno set to ENOSPC. This can be remedied by increasing the tunable number of TIRDWR "devices."

TIRDWR converts the TPI into a read/write interface in the following manner. On the write side, TIRDWR will discard any zero-length M_DATA message, regardless of whether or not the transport provider supports zero-length data messages. Transport providers need to handle plain M_DATA messages as part of the TPI, so TIRDWR does not need much other write-side processing.

On the read side, TIRDWR strips the protocol headers off TPI data indications, resulting in just data messages being sent upstream. If a disconnect indication is received, TIRDWR turns this into a hangup message and forces the stream to act as if the device "hung up." This will cause all further calls to write to fail. In addition, all further calls to read will consume any data on the stream head read queue until no data remain, after which read will return zero.

If an orderly release indication is received, TIRDWR remembers it so when TIRDWR is popped off the stream, it can generate an orderly release request to finish closing the connection. Otherwise, TIRDWR does nothing to release the connection when it is removed from the stream. If neither a disconnect indication nor an orderly release indication has been received before TIRDWR is popped, the transport endpoint is still usable for data transfer.

While TIRDWR is on the stream, TLI routines should not be used, although some will still work. If expedited data arrive, TIRDWR will put the stream in error mode, forcing all system calls using the transport endpoint to fail with errno set to EPROTO.

Example 4.5.1. To show how a read/write interface is useful, we rewrite the server's child process code (doservice) from Example 4.4.6. First, we need to make some changes to the client side in rcmd. Instead of separating the arguments in the command message with spaces, we will separate them with NULL bytes.

```
strcpy(&buf[1], argv[2]);
n = strlen(&buf[1]) + 2;
for (i = 3; i < argc; i++) {
    strcpy(&buf[n], argv[i]);
    n += strlen(argv[i]) + 1;
}
buf[0] = n;
```

Since strcpy inserts a NULL after the end of the string, there is no need to do it ourselves.

In our rewrite, we will have the parent server disconnect the virtual circuit. Thus, the client code that receives the output from the command will change to:

```
while ((n = t_rcv(fd, buf, len, &flags)) > 0)
    write(1, buf, n);
if (n < 0) {
    if (t_errno == TLOOK)
        exit(0);
    t_error("rcmd. Cannot receive data")
    exit(1);
}
exit(0);
```

As long as data can be read, we write it to the standard output. If `t_rcv` fails because of an asynchronous event, we assume the server has released the connection.

The portion of the server that creates the child (Examples 4.4.3 or 4.4.4, for instance) will change as follows:

```
#define MAXACTIVE      1024

struct active {
    pid_t    pid;
    int fd;
} active[MAXACTIVE];

struct sigaction sa;
sigset_t s;

void endconn(int);

    .
    .
    .
    /*
     * Set up SIGCHLD signal handler.
     */
    sa.sa_handler = endconn;
    sigemptyset(&sa.sa_mask);
    sa.sa_flags = SA_NOCLDSTOP;
    sigaction(SIGCHLD, &sa, NULL);
    sigemptyset(&s);
    sigaddset(&s, SIGCHLD);
    .
    .
    .
    /*
     * Critical section: block SIGCHLD.
     */
    sigprocmask(SIG_BLOCK, &s, NULL);
    if ((pid = fork()) < 0) {
        /*
         * Fork failed.  Reject the connect request,
         * unblock SIGCHLD, and continue waiting for
         * more connect indications.
         */
        log("fork failed");
        if (t_snddis(afd, NULL) < 0) {
```

```
                    tlog("t_snddis failed");
                    exit(1);
              }
              sigprocmask(SIG_UNBLOCK, &s, NULL);
              continue;
       } else if (pid == 0) {
              /*
               * The child process handles the service
               * request and then exits.  First restore
               * the default disposition of SIGCHLD.
               */
              sa.sa_handler = SIG_DFL;
              sigemptyset(&sa.sa_mask);
              sa.sa_flags = 0;
              sigaction(SIGCHLD, &sa, NULL);
              sigprocmask(SIG_UNBLOCK, &s, NULL);
              doservice(afd);
       } else {
              /*
               * The parent remembers the process ID
               * of the child so it can disconnect the
               * connection when the child exits.  First
               * find an unused entry.
               */
              for (i = 0; i < MAXACTIVE; i++)
                     if (active[i].fd == -1)
                            break;
              if (i >= MAXACTIVE) {
                     log("Too many active children");
                     exit(1);
              }
              active[i].pid = pid;
              active[i].fd = afd;

              /*
               * End of critical section.  Parent unblocks
               * SIGCHLD and continues to wait for more
               * connect indications.
               */
              sigprocmask(SIG_UNBLOCK, &s, NULL);
       }
       .
       .
       .
```

Here, the child executes `doservice` on behalf of the client. The parent, instead of closing the newly created transport endpoint, will save it in an `active` structure, along with the process ID of the child that is using the endpoint. The parent also has to change to install a signal handler for `SIGCHLD`, used to clean up after the child is done.

The server used `sigprocmask(2)` to manage the critical sections where it is inconvenient for `SIGCHLD` to interrupt it. If the child process exits before the parent has made an entry in the `active` array, then the parent's signal handler will not find the connection and will avoid cleaning it up. To prevent this, the parent blocks

SIGCHLD between the time it calls `fork` and the time it initializes the entry in the `active` array.

Since the server blocks in `t_listen` while there is nothing to do, it will also have to change to treat failure with `t_errno` set to `TSYSERR` and `errno` set to `EINTR` as a nonfatal error. This type of error will occur when the `t_listen` is interrupted by the execution of the `SIGCHLD` signal handler.

Before generating the disconnect, the parent needs to pop TIRDWR off the stream. The following function will be used:

```
/*
 * SIGCHLD signal handler.
 */
void
endconn(int sig)
{
    int i;
    siginfo_t si;

    while (waitid(P_ALL, 0, &si, WEXITED|WNOHANG) == 0) {
        /*
         * Find the entry corresponding to the child
         * process that just terminated.
         */
        for (i = 0; i < MAXACTIVE; i++) {
            if (active[i].pid == si.si_pid) {
                /*
                 * Found it.  Mark the entry as
                 * unused, pop TIRDWR off the
                 * stream, disconnect the client,
                 * and free the transport endpoint.
                 */
                active[i].pid = 0;
                ioctl(active[i].fd, I_POP, 0);
                t_snddis(active[i].fd, NULL);
                t_close(active[i].fd);
                active[i].fd = -1;
                break;
            }
        }
    }
}
```

When a child dies, the parent will be interrupted, and this function will be executed. Of course, the parent server should be modified either to hold `SIGCHLD` when it is inconvenient to be interrupted, or to handle `t_errno` being set to `TSYSERR` and `errno` being set to `EINTR` in all the error paths.

The new version of `doservice` parses the command message differently to set up the arguments to be passed to `execvp`.

```
#define CMDSZ        256
#define MAXARG       128

void
```

```
doservice(int fd)
{
    int i, n, flags, nargs;
    char *p, *cmd;
    char buf[CMDSZ];
    char *args[MAXARG];


    /*
     * Receive the command string.  Must make multiple
     * calls to t_rcv because the original message
     * might have been fragmented during transmission.
     */
    n = t_rcv(fd, buf, CMDSZ, &flags);
    if (n < 0) {
        tlog("Cannot receive request");
        exit(1);
    }

    /*
     * p is the current location in the command string
     * and n is the amount remaining to be read.
     */
    p = &buf[n];
    n = buf[0] - n;
    while (n > 0) {
        i = t_rcv(fd, p, (int)(CMDSZ + p - buf), &flags);
        if (i < 0) {
            tlog("Cannot receive request");
            exit(1);
        }
        p += i;
        n -= i;
    }

    /*
     * Set up the arguments for exec.
     */
    cmd = &buf[1];
    p = strrchr(&buf[1], '/');
    if (p)
        args[0] = p+1;
    else
        args[0] = &buf[1];
    nargs = 1;
    n = buf[0] - 1 - strlen(&buf[1]) - 1;
    p = &buf[strlen(&buf[1])+1];
    while (n > 0) {
        args[nargs++] = p;
        n -= strlen(p) + 1;
        p += strlen(p) + 1;
    }

    /*
```

```
         * Prepare to execute the command by making sure
         * file descriptor 0 is open to /dev/null and file
         * descriptors 1 and 2 are associated with the
         * network connection.
         */
        close(0);
        close(1);
        close(2);
        n = open("/dev/null", O_RDONLY);
        if (n != 0) {
            if (n < 0)
                log("Cannot open /dev/null");
            else
                log("Error setting up stdin");
            exit(0);
        }
        if (dup(fd) != 1) {
            log("Error setting up stdout");
            exit(0);
        }
        if (dup(fd) != 2) {
            log("Error setting up stderr");
            exit(0);
        }

        /*
         * Push TIRDWR on the stream to get a read/write
         * interface.
         */
        if (ioctl(fd, I_PUSH, "tirdwr") < 0) {
            log("Cannot push tirdwr");
            exit(0);
        }

        /*
         * Close the extra file descriptor open to the
         * network connection and execute the command.
         */
        close(fd);
        execvp(cmd, args);
        log("Cannot exec command");
        exit(0);
}
```

The command message is received as before. Then we save a pointer to the command pathname in cmd and initialize args[0] to point to the last component of the pathname. For each argument, we increment nargs and save a pointer to the argument string. We know we are through processing arguments when we reach the end of the command message.

Then we close our standard input, output, and error streams and make the new standard input come from /dev/null. Thus, if the application we are about to exec attempts to read from its standard input, read will return 0. We associate the standard output and standard error with the network connection using dup(2).

Next we push TIRDWR on the stream, converting the transport interface into a read/write interface. We close the file descriptor to the transport endpoint (which stays intact since we still have two references to it, not including the one the parent is holding). Finally, we use `execvp(2)` to execute the command. If the command generates output to its standard output or standard error, then the output will go down the stream to the transport provider and will be sent to the client process. Since `execvp` never returns, we treat the code after the exec as an error case.   □

What advantages does using TIRDWR provide? First, one less process per connection is needed. In Example 4.4.6, one process reads from the pipe and writes to the network while the other executes the command (this is hidden behind the `popen` interface). With TIRDWR, the command writes directly to the network, avoiding the extra process and the intermediate data copying.

Second, Example 4.4.6 loses the error output from the command. With `popen`, the child process created behind the interface will inherit the standard error of the caller. In the server case, this will result in standard error messages from the command going to `/dev/null`. In Example 4.5.1, however, the standard error is attached to the network. Therefore, error messages are transmitted to the client along with the standard output.

When pushing other modules on a transport endpoint's stream, one can pop TIMOD off the stream beforehand if the endpoint will only be used for data transfer. If other TLI routines need to be used, then TIMOD must remain on the stream.

Summary

The transport layer interface library provides applications with a way to access transport-level networking protocols. We have presented the TLI library routines with an emphasis on designing applications to be independent of the protocol and network implementation and options. The TIRDWR module can be pushed on a stream to provide a read/write interface over a transport connection. This is useful in allowing applications to communicate over a network connection without requiring that the application use the TLI library to perform I/O.

Exercises

4.1 Rewrite Example 4.3.2 using larger messages, but break the data after newline boundaries so lost messages will not result in strange output for the client.

4.2 In Figure 4.4, which user is the client and which is the server? Why?

4.3 Rewrite Example 4.4.1 using a random delay in place of the exponential delay.

4.4 What kinds of security holes might there be in Example 4.3.2? How can they be fixed?

4.5 What problems might arise from using a hard-coded timeout value in programs like that from Example 4.4.5? How can you work around these problems?

4.6 In Example 4.5.1, the standard output and standard error streams are merged into one stream. The client command cannot separate the two. How can you modify the example to allow data written to the standard output stream to be distinguished from data written to the standard error stream?

4.7 Modify Example 4.5.1 so that there is no chance that the server parent process will cause the client process to lose data when the connection is broken.

Bibliographic Notes

ISO 8072 defines the OSI Transport Service Definition, the specification on which the TLI was based. The *SVR4 Programmer's Guide: Networking Interfaces* [USL 1990d] contains information on using the TLI library. The TPI is documented in *SVR4.2 STREAMS Modules and Drivers* [USL 1992a].

Current drafts of POSIX P1003.12 [IEEE 1992] include the transport layer interface as one of the proposed standard networking interfaces for portable operating systems. This interface is based on the XTI superset of TLI defined by the X/OPEN consortium.

5

Selecting Networks
and Addresses

So far we have avoided discussing network addresses and how applications can identify the correct ones to use. We have also avoided the issue of how applications select network devices. Instead of hard-coding networks and addresses, we have included them as function parameters and command-line arguments in the previous examples. This chapter will show how applications can select networks and addresses without hard-coding them, while at the same time relieving users from having to provide them explicitly.

5.1 INTRODUCTION

Designing an application to work over only one network is an expensive proposition. Every time a new network or protocol is developed, the application would have to be modified for it to work. If vendors supply similar applications with different networks, users not only have to buy the new applications with each network, but users also have to learn how to operate each application.

Unless they are acting as gateways, host computers are usually connected to a single network. As networks become more popular and less expensive, however, we will find it more common to connect multiple networks to our computers. When this happens, unless one network provides a service unavailable on another, users will not care which network they use. Users will concern themselves only with obtaining the service they require from the proper host computer. In many cases users will not even care which host computer provides the service.

The network-selection mechanism in SVR4 provides solutions to both network independence and network coexistence. First, the network-selection mechanism provides a standard way for applications to identify the proper network to use. Second, it allows administrators and users to specify multiple networks that can be used by applications in whatever ways the applications choose. One use might be to distribute network loads more evenly. Another use might be to increase the reliability of network services by using alternate networks when the default ones are unavailable.

217

The network-selection mechanism can be used with the name-to-address translation facility to identify the address to use when accessing a particular service. Once the network has been identified, the address corresponding to the desired service can be found by using the network's *directory service* library. (A directory service provides applications with a way to find the address of a given host or service, similar to the way a phone directory provides people with a way to find the phone numbers used to contact other people.)

Address formats are sometimes protocol-specific and sometimes implementation-specific. This means some address formats are specified by the protocol definition and some are not. The ones specified by the protocol share the same format across all implementations. The ones that are not specified by the protocol, however, do not necessarily share the same formats.

For example, the Ethernet protocol specification defines the exact format of an Ethernet address. Interfaces to Ethernet drivers will export the same address format as appears in the packets transmitted. The TCP protocol, on the other hand, does not specify an address format. A TCP packet contains only destination and source port numbers in its header. A fully qualified TCP address, however, contains the IP address, as well as the TCP port number. To be compatible, all implementations of TCP must use the same address format. Otherwise, applications that exchange addresses might not work when run on machines with different address representations. Most implementations use an address format that originated with the BSD version of the UNIX system. We shall see this format in an example later in this section.

The name-to-address translation facility provides applications with a way to isolate themselves from address formats. It will not, however, solve the compatibility problems created when applications exchange addresses using protocol implementations with different address formats.

5.2 NETWORK SELECTION

At the heart of the network-selection mechanism is a database file, /etc/netconfig [see netconfig(4)]. It contains at least one entry for every network installed in the system. Each entry is composed of seven fields. The format, with examples, is shown in Figure 5.1.

Net ID	Semantics	Flags	Protocol Family	Protocol Name	Network Device	Directory Lookup Libraries
tcp	tpi_cots_ord	v	inet	tcp	/dev/tcp	/usr/lib/tcpip.so
udp	tpi_clts	v	inet	udp	/dev/udp	/usr/lib/tcpip.so

Fig. 5.1. Format of /etc/netconfig

The system administrator is in charge of maintaining the /etc/netconfig database. The first field is a network identifier that must uniquely identify the network and protocol on the system. The second field, called the network ''semantics,'' defines the type of service provided. Legal values currently include `tpi_clts` for connectionless transport service, `tpi_cots` for connection-oriented transport service, `tpi_cots_ord` for connection-oriented transport service with orderly release, and `tpi_raw` for pseudo-transport interfaces to other protocols, such as transport interfaces to internetworking protocols. In SVR4, the `tpi_raw` interface is used to access ICMP and IP.

The third field contains flags, or if no flags are specified, a dash (–). The only flag defined so far is `v`, indicating the network entry is visible to the NETPATH library routines (described shortly). An administrator can temporarily stop applications from finding a network by replacing this flag with a dash.

The fourth field contains a name for the protocol family. The Internet protocols are grouped under the name `inet`, for example. A dash can be used if no family name exists. Examples of different protocol families can be found in `<sys/netconfig.h>`. The fifth field specifies the name of the protocol supported by the network device. Again, a dash can be used to indicate that no protocol name exists.

The sixth field contains the pathname of the device to use when accessing the network and protocol. For a transport protocol, this is the name the application would pass to `t_open(3N)`. The seventh field is a comma-separated list of dynamic shared libraries that contain the network protocol's name-to-address translation routines. A dash can be used in this field to indicate that no library routines exist.

By requiring that the library routines be implemented as dynamic shared libraries, the routines can be shared by multiple programs and will not be linked with a program until execution time. The deferred linking is made possible through the use of position-independent code (PIC) in the library routines. See `cc(1)` and `ld(1)` for the flags needed to generate PIC and dynamic shared libraries.

Two sets of library routines can be used to access the information in `/etc/netconfig`. The network-configuration library routines access the information line by line, and the NETPATH library routines access the information based on a shell variable. The network-configuration library routines and NETPATH library routines return information from the `netconfig` file through the `netconfig` structure:

```
struct netconfig {
      char      *nc_netid;        /* network identifier */
      ulong_t   nc_semantics;     /* service type */
      ulong_t   nc_flag;          /* flags */
      char      *nc_protofmly;    /* protocol family */
      char      *nc_proto;        /* protocol */
      char      *nc_device;       /* device pathname */
      ulong_t   nc_nlookups;      /* number of libraries */
      char      **nc_lookups;     /* list of library names */
};
```

Each member of the `netconfig` structure corresponds to a field in

/etc/netconfig. The nc_semantics field can take on one of the values NC_TPI_CLTS, NC_TPI_COTS, NC_TPI_COTS_ORD, or NC_TPI_RAW. The nc_flag field is a bitmask with only one flag currently defined, NC_VISIBLE. If no flags are set, the value of this field is NC_NOFLAG.

The last two fields describe the list of directory lookup libraries provided for the protocol and network. nc_nlookups is the number of libraries, and nc_lookups is a pointer to a list of pathnames, one per library. The libraries implement the necessary steps to translate between addresses and services. We will look at them more closely in Section 5.4.

There are actually two independent pieces of information stored in a netconfig entry: the protocol and the network. The same protocol can run over different network devices, and different protocols can be used on the same network. The network device usually selects the physical network to use. Two devices can be on separate networks, or they can be connected to the same network.

For example, suppose a computer was connected to two different networks, accessed through /dev/net1 and /dev/net2. If protocol "proto" is to be used on both networks, the system administrator must have two similar entries in /etc/netconfig, differing only in device name and network ID, as illustrated in Figure 5.2.

| proto1 | tpi_cots | v | – | proto | /dev/net1 | /usr/lib/proto.so |
| proto2 | tpi_cots | v | – | proto | /dev/net2 | /usr/lib/proto.so |

Fig. 5.2. Specifying the Same Protocol Used with Two Networks

The order of entries in the /etc/netconfig database is the order in which applications find networks and protocols to use. System administrators can implicitly specify a default search list for applications by ordering the entries to reflect the preferred order of use. In the previous example, applications looking for protocol "proto" will first try /dev/net1. If this is unsuccessful, applications will find another entry for the same protocol and can try /dev/net2 next.

The Network-Configuration Library Routines

The network services library (linked with the −lnsl option) provides the routines that give applications access to the network-configuration database [see getnetconfig(3N)]. The routines are similar in function to those that access other system databases, such as /etc/passwd and /etc/group.

```
#include <netconfig.h>

void *setnetconfig(void);
int endnetconfig(void *handle);
```

Initially, applications call setnetconfig to gain access to the network-configuration database. Applications can also use it, however, to restart a search from the beginning of the database (this is called "rewinding" the file). `setnetconfig` returns a "typeless" identifier, called a *handle*, that is used with the other `netconfig` routines. A new handle is returned on each call to `setnetconfig`. The handles are used to remember the current location in the file and to prevent library routines that use the `netconfig` routines from interfering with applications that also search the `netconfig` database. If an error occurs, `setnetconfig` returns NULL.

When an application finishes using the network-configuration routines, and is not going to exit, it should call `endnetconfig` with the handle obtained from a previous call to `setnetconfig`. The purpose of `endnetconfig` is to deallocate the data structures allocated by the calls to `setnetconfig`. On success, `endnetconfig` returns 0; on error, it returns −1. Most applications just ignore the return code.

To retrieve the next entry in the database, applications can use `getnetconfig(3N)`:

```
#include <netconfig.h>

struct netconfig *getnetconfig(void *handle);
```

`handle` is the handle returned from a previous call to `setnetconfig`. When the end of the file is reached, `getnetconfig` returns NULL. Otherwise, it returns the next entry in `/etc/netconfig` as a `netconfig` structure.

The first time an application calls `setnetconfig`, the library routine will allocate enough memory to hold the entire network-configuration database and will convert each entry into a `netconfig` structure. Each call to `getnetconfig` will return a pointer to the next structure in this list. Be aware that the structure's underlying memory is freed by `endnetconfig`, so applications must copy the `netconfig` structure and the character strings to which it points if the structure and strings are going to be used after calling `endnetconfig`.

If an application knows the local network identifier of the network and protocol desired, then multiple calls to `getnetconfig` can be avoided by using `getnetconfigent` instead.

```
#include <netconfig.h>

struct netconfig *getnetconfigent(char *netid);
void freenetconfigent(struct netconfig *ncp);
```

`getnetconfigent` will return the `netconfig` structure associated with the network identifier, `netid`. Applications are not required to call `setnetconfig` before using `getnetconfigent`. On error, or if `netid` is an invalid network identifier, `getnetconfigent` will return NULL.

In contrast to `getnetconfig`, the `netconfig` structures returned by `getnetconfigent` are allocated separately. Instead of calling `endnetconfig` to free the memory allocated by `getnetconfigent`, applications should call `freenetconfigent`.

Example 5.2.1. The following program prints all the entries in the
/etc/netconfig database:

```c
/* netconfig.c */
#include <sys/types.h>
#include <stdlib.h>
#include <stdio.h>
#include <netconfig.h>

void
main()
{
    struct netconfig *ncp;
    void *p;
    int i;

    /*
     * Gain access to /etc/netconfig.
     */
    if ((p = setnetconfig()) == NULL) {
        nc_perror("setnetconfig failed");
        exit(1);
    }

    /*
     * Get each entry and print the information.
     */
    while ((ncp = getnetconfig(p)) != NULL) {
        printf("network: %s\n\tsemantics = ",
            ncp->nc_netid);
        switch (ncp->nc_semantics) {
        case NC_TPI_CLTS:
            printf("connectionless transport\n");
            break;

        case NC_TPI_COTS:
            printf("connection-oriented transport\n");
            break;

        case NC_TPI_COTS_ORD:
            printf("connection-oriented transport\n");
            printf("\t\t\twith orderly release\n");
            break;

        case NC_TPI_RAW:
            printf("raw transport\n");
            break;

        default:
            printf("unknown (%d)\n", ncp->nc_semantics);
        }
        printf("\tflags =");
        if (ncp->nc_flag == NC_NOFLAG)
            printf(" none\n");
```

```
            else if (ncp->nc_flag & NC_VISIBLE)
                printf(" visible\n");
            else
                printf(" unknown (0x%x)\n", ncp->nc_flag);
            printf("\tprotocol family = %s\n",
              ncp->nc_protofmly);
            printf("\tprotocol = %s\n", ncp->nc_proto);
            printf("\tdevice = %s\n", ncp->nc_device);
            printf("\tnlookups = %d\n", ncp->nc_nlookups);
            if (ncp->nc_nlookups > 0) {
                printf("\tdirectory lookup libraries:\n");
                for (i = 0; i < ncp->nc_nlookups; i++)
                    printf("\t\t%s\n", ncp->nc_lookups[i]);
            }
        }
    exit(0);
}
```

We start out by calling setnetconfig to allocate and initialize the data structures to be used by getnetconfig. If setnetconfig returns NULL, we have encountered an error and call nc_perror(3N) to print an error message on the standard error stream. nc_perror is like perror(3C), but is customized to understand the network-selection errors.

Another function, nc_sperror, returns a string containing an error message corresponding to the error encountered. The function prototypes are

```
#include <netconfig.h>

void nc_perror(const char *s);
char *nc_sperror(void);
```

The format of the output string is s, followed by a colon, a space, and the message describing the network-selection error. The network-selection error itself is stored in a private (static) variable in the library.

If we are able to obtain a handle, we repeatedly call getnetconfig to obtain each entry in /etc/netconfig. When getnetconfig returns NULL, we know we are done. We do not bother to call endnetconfig since we immediately exit.

When we run this program on an SVR4 system without any networks installed, we get the following output:

```
$ ./netconfig
setnetconfig failed: cannot open /etc/netconfig
$
```

When we run this program on a system containing the SVR4 Internet protocol suite, we get the following output:

```
$ ./netconfig
network: ticlts
      semantics = connectionless transport
      flags = visible
      protocol family = loopback
      protocol = -
```

```
        device = /dev/ticlts
        nlookups = 1
        directory lookup libraries:
            /usr/lib/straddr.so
network: ticots
        semantics = connection-oriented transport
        flags = visible
        protocol family = loopback
        protocol = -
        device = /dev/ticots
        nlookups = 1
        directory lookup libraries:
            /usr/lib/straddr.so
network: ticotsord
        semantics = connection-oriented transport
                         with orderly release
        flags = visible
        protocol family = loopback
        protocol = -
        device = /dev/ticotsord
        nlookups = 1
        directory lookup libraries:
            /usr/lib/straddr.so
network: tcp
        semantics = connection-oriented transport
                         with orderly release
        flags = visible
        protocol family = inet
        protocol = tcp
        device = /dev/tcp
        nlookups = 1
        directory lookup libraries:
            /usr/lib/tcpip.so
network: udp
        semantics = connectionless transport
        flags = visible
        protocol family = inet
        protocol = udp
        device = /dev/udp
        nlookups = 1
        directory lookup libraries:
            /usr/lib/tcpip.so
network: rawip
        semantics = raw transport
        flags = none
        protocol family = inet
        protocol = -
        device = /dev/rawip
        nlookups = 1
        directory lookup libraries:
            /usr/lib/tcpip.so
network: icmp
        semantics = raw transport
        flags = none
```

```
protocol family = inet
protocol = icmp
device = /dev/icmp
nlookups = 1
directory lookup libraries:
    /usr/lib/tcpip.so
$                                                                      □
```

The NETPATH Library Routines

The second set of routines that access the network-configuration database is the NETPATH library [see getnetpath(3N)]. These routines provide users with a way of customizing the network search list by setting the NETPATH environment variable. Its format is similar to the shell's PATH variable: a list of names separated by colons. Unlike PATH, however, the names are network identifiers instead of path-names.

The order of precedence of networks to select is from left to right. If a user included

```
NETPATH=osi_tp4:tcp:udp export NETPATH
```

in his or her .profile, any commands using the NETPATH library routines would use the OSI TP4 protocol and network before trying the Internet TCP or UDP protocol and network.

Note that protocols with different service types can be mixed together in the NETPATH. Applications are responsible for selecting protocols with the required service type by inspecting the nc_semantics field of the netconfig structure.

To enable applications to search /etc/netconfig based on NETPATH, setnetpath must first be called. It is similar to setnetconfig, performing data structure allocation and initialization and returning a handle. Just as endnetconfig should be called to clean up, endnetpath can be used to deallocate the data structures allocated by the call to setnetpath.

```
#include <netconfig.h>

void *setnetpath(void);
int endnetpath(void *handle);
```

Once setnetpath is called, applications can use getnetpath to obtain a netconfig structure for the next entry in the database file.

```
#include <netconfig.h>

struct netconfig *getnetpath(void *handle);
```

handle is the handle returned from a prior call to setnetpath. The next entry returned is determined by two criteria. First, if the caller's NETPATH environment variable includes the network ID for the next entry, then the entry is returned. Second, if the caller's NETPATH environment variable is uninitialized, the next entry is returned if it is visible in /etc/netconfig (that is, if the v flag is present in the third column of the database).

Example 5.2.2. The following program is a rewrite of the one presented in Example 5.2.1, with the `netconfig` library routines replaced by the `NETPATH` routines.

```c
/* netpath.c */
#include <sys/types.h>
#include <stdlib.h>
#include <stdio.h>
#include <netconfig.h>

void
main()
{
    struct netconfig *ncp;
    void *p;
    int i;

    /*
     * Gain access to /etc/netconfig.
     */
    if ((p = setnetpath()) == NULL) {
        nc_perror("setnetpath failed");
        exit(1);
    }

    /*
     * Get each entry as specified by NETPATH,
     * and print the information.
     */
    while ((ncp = getnetpath(p)) != NULL) {
        printf("network: %s\n\tsemantics = ",
          ncp->nc_netid);
        switch (ncp->nc_semantics) {
        case NC_TPI_CLTS:
            printf("connectionless transport\n");
            break;

        case NC_TPI_COTS:
            printf("connection-oriented transport\n");
            break;

        case NC_TPI_COTS_ORD:
            printf("connection-oriented transport\n");
            printf("\t\t\twith orderly release\n");
            break;

        case NC_TPI_RAW:
            printf("raw transport\n");
            break;

        default:
            printf("unknown (%d)\n", ncp->nc_semantics);
        }
```

```
                    printf("\tflags =");
                    if (ncp->nc_flag == NC_NOFLAG)
                        printf(" none\n");
                    else if (ncp->nc_flag & NC_VISIBLE)
                        printf(" visible\n");
                    else
                        printf(" unknown (0x%x)\n", ncp->nc_flag);
                    printf("\tprotocol family = %s\n",
                      ncp->nc_protofmly);
                    printf("\tprotocol = %s\n", ncp->nc_proto);
                    printf("\tdevice = %s\n", ncp->nc_device);
                    printf("\tnlookups = %d\n", ncp->nc_nlookups);
                    if (ncp->nc_nlookups > 0) {
                        printf("\tdirectory lookup libraries:\n");
                        for (i = 0; i < ncp->nc_nlookups; i++)
                            printf("\t\t%s\n", ncp->nc_lookups[i]);
                    }
            }
            exit(0);
    }
```

Although this example is almost the same as the last, its behavior is noticeably different. If the system has the SVR4 Internet protocol suite installed and we run the program without defining NETPATH, we get the following output:

```
$ unset NETPATH
$ ./netpath
network: ticlts
        semantics = connectionless transport
        flags = visible
        protocol family = loopback
        protocol = -
        device = /dev/ticlts
        nlookups = 1
        directory lookup libraries:
            /usr/lib/straddr.so
network: ticots
        semantics = connection-oriented transport
        flags = visible
        protocol family = loopback
        protocol = -
        device = /dev/ticots
        nlookups = 1
        directory lookup libraries:
            /usr/lib/straddr.so
network: ticotsord
        semantics = connection-oriented transport
                        with orderly release
        flags = visible
        protocol family = loopback
        protocol = -
        device = /dev/ticotsord
        nlookups = 1
        directory lookup libraries:
```

```
           /usr/lib/straddr.so
network: tcp
     semantics = connection-oriented transport
                        with orderly release
     flags = visible
     protocol family = inet
     protocol = tcp
     device = /dev/tcp
     nlookups = 1
     directory lookup libraries:
           /usr/lib/tcpip.so
network: udp
     semantics = connectionless transport
     flags = visible
     protocol family = inet
     protocol = udp
     device = /dev/udp
     nlookups = 1
     directory lookup libraries:
           /usr/lib/tcpip.so
$
```

The only networks found were those marked "visible" in /etc/netconfig. The
order found is the order in which they appear in the database file.

If we set our NETPATH to a network that is not installed in the system, we get
the following behavior:

```
$ NETPATH=starlan ./netpath
$
```

The command did not generate any output. This means that it could not find any network identifier equal to starlan. The NETPATH variable overrides the default
network list found in /etc/netconfig. We get the same results if we set
NETPATH to an empty string, as in

```
$ NETPATH=
$ ./netpath
$
```

To illustrate this point further, let's set our NETPATH variable to two network
identifiers from /etc/netconfig, but in the opposite order from that in which
they appear in the file. The output is

```
$ NETPATH=udp:tcp ./netpath
network: udp
     semantics = connectionless transport
     flags = visible
     protocol family = inet
     protocol = udp
     device = /dev/udp
     nlookups = 1
     directory lookup libraries:
           /usr/lib/tcpip.so
network: tcp
     semantics = connection-oriented transport
```

```
                              with orderly release
          flags = visible
          protocol family = inet
          protocol = tcp
          device = /dev/tcp
          nlookups = 1
          directory lookup libraries:
              /usr/lib/tcpip.so
   $
```

Just as we expected, the NETPATH variable overrides the order of networks found in /etc/netconfig. Even though tcp appears before udp in /etc/netconfig, we find udp first, since it appears first in our NETPATH environment variable.

   If we set the NETPATH variable to a network identifier that is in /etc/netconfig but is not marked visible, we get the information for the invisible entry. This behavior might surprise some users, but the absence of the visible flag does not prevent an entry from being returned if the caller's NETPATH variable explicitly includes that network's ID. (Thus, the visible flag is really a ''default'' flag — ''visible'' is a misnomer.) For example, ICMP is marked as being invisible in the database file. Using its network identifier, we get the following output:

```
$ NETPATH=icmp ./netpath
network: icmp
     semantics = raw transport
     flags = none
     protocol family = inet
     protocol = icmp
     device = /dev/icmp
     nlookups = 1
     directory lookup libraries:
          /usr/lib/tcpip.so
   $                                                                    □
```

   The NETPATH library routines are better suited to client-style applications, since this is usually the type of program run by users. Daemons (server-style applications), on the other hand, will probably use the network-configuration library routines because daemons are not usually associated with a particular user, and the NETPATH variable might not be set properly when the daemons are run. There are no fixed rules regarding usage, however. A client-style application that wants to run uninfluenced by a user's NETPATH environment variable could, for example, use the network-configuration routines.

5.3 NAME-TO-ADDRESS TRANSLATION

The name-to-address translation facility, also called *name-to-address mapping*, provides applications with a way to find an address corresponding to a service, and vice versa. The name-to-address translation facility relies on the network-selection library to provide information about the networks and protocols. Specifically, field 7 of /etc/netconfig contains the list of shared libraries that implement the network- and protocol-dependent portions of the generic name-to-address mapping library routines.

With SVR4, two shared libraries are provided. They both use information stored in ASCII files to perform name-to-address translation. The system administrator is responsible for maintaining these files.

/usr/lib/tcpip.so contains the routines that translate between services and addresses for the Internet protocol suite. It assumes that host names and their corresponding addresses are stored in /etc/inet/hosts, and service names and their corresponding port numbers are stored in /etc/inet/services. The addressing information returned is in the format of a sockaddr_in structure, defined in <netinet/in.h>.

The second library is /usr/lib/straddr.so. It can be used with any network whose addresses are character strings. It assumes host names and their corresponding addresses are stored in /etc/net/*transport*/hosts, and service names and their corresponding port numbers are stored in /etc/net/*transport*/services, where *transport* is the name of the transport provider for the network. The addressing information returned is in the form of *hostaddress.serviceport*. The loopback transport providers found in SVR4 use strings for addresses.

Each network product is expected to provide its own shared libraries that handle the translation details if the default two libraries do not suffice. The generic name-to-address translation library routines are provided in the network services library (linked with the −lnsl option). The generic routines provide the glue necessary to link the dynamic shared libraries into the address space of the calling process.

To convert from a host name and service name to an address, applications can use netdir_getbyname(3N) [see netdir(3N)]:

```
#include <netdir.h>

int netdir_getbyname(struct netconfig *ncp,
    struct nd_hostserv *hsp, struct nd_addrlist **alpp);
```

ncp is a pointer to a netconfig structure returned by one of the network-selection library routines. The nd_hostserv structure, which follows, defines the host and service whose address the caller is interested in obtaining.

```
struct nd_hostserv {
    char    *h_host;    /* host name */
    char    *h_serv;    /* service name */
};
```

The h_host field points to the name of the host computer, and the h_serv field points to the name of the service.

If successful, netdir_getbyname will return a list of addresses (through alpp) that can be used to connect to the host computer to obtain the desired service. The nd_addrlist structure is used to represent the addresses:

```
struct nd_addrlist {
    int             n_cnt;      /* # of addresses */
    struct netbuf   *n_addrs;   /* array of addresses */
};
```

Each address is contained in a `netbuf` structure (introduced in Section 4.2). The `n_addrs` field points to an array of `netbuf` structures, one `netbuf` per address. The number of addresses is stored in n_cnt.

On success, `netdir_getbyname` returns 0; otherwise, it returns a nonzero value. If an error occurs, the application can call `netdir_perror` to print an error message on the standard error stream. `netdir_sperror` can be used to obtain the error string. Both functions are similar to their network-selection counterparts. The function prototypes are as follows:

```
#include <netdir.h>

void netdir_perror(const char *s);
char *netdir_sperror(void);
```

`netdir_getbyname` supports three predefined host name aliases, defined in `<netdir.h>`. Applications can use these aliases to request that the network-specific name-to-address mapping routines return the special addresses associated with the aliases, if they exist.

If the host name is set to `HOST_SELF`, then the network-specific name-to-address translation library will return the address to be used by programs that want to access the requested service on the local machine (the machine on which the applications are running).

The special host name `HOST_ANY` is a wildcard, representing any host accessible on the network. It can be used by applications to request a service without specifying the particular host name. The library will select the host for the caller, although this alias is not supported by all network-specific name-to-address translation libraries.

If the host name is set to `HOST_BROADCAST`, then the network-specific translation library will return the address that can be used to broadcast the service request to all hosts on the network. This alias is not supported by all network-specific name-to-address translation libraries since the ability to broadcast messages is not available on all types of networks.

The name-to-address translation library also allows applications to translate a given address into a list of host-service pairs using that address. This is the inverse function of `netdir_getbyname`. The function is `netdir_getbyaddr`:

```
#include <netdir.h>

int netdir_getbyaddr(struct netconfig *ncp,
        struct nd_hostservlist **hslpp, struct netbuf *addrp);
```

`ncp` is a pointer to a `netbuf` structure returned from one of the network-selection routines, `hslpp` is a pointer to a pointer to an `nd_hostservlist` structure containing the list of hosts and services corresponding to the address, and `addrp` is a pointer to a `netbuf` structure containing the address. The `nd_hostservlist` structure follows:

```
struct nd_hostservlist {
        int                     h_cnt;          /* # of entries */
        struct nd_hostserv      *h_hostservs;   /* array of */
                                                /* host-service */
                                                /* pairs */
};
```

The `h_hostservs` field points to the start of an array describing the host and service names. The number of `nd_hostserv` entries in the array is stored in `h_cnt`. On success, a `hostservlist` structure is allocated and returned through `hslpp`, and 0 is returned. `netdir_getbyaddr` returns a nonzero value on failure.

The `netdir_getbyname` and `netdir_getbyaddr` routines are similar. They both return information in structures that describe arrays, and they both allocate the memory for the arrays and structures dynamically. Applications can free this memory using `netdir_free`:

```
#include <netdir.h>

void netdir_free(void *ptr, int type);
```

`ptr` is a ''typeless'' pointer that can be set to the address of the `nd_addrlist` or `nd_hostservlist` structure to free, and `type` indicates the type of the structure. It can be set to either `ND_ADDRLIST` or `ND_HOSTSERVLIST`.

Example 5.3.1. The following function shows how a client can create a connection to a server without worrying about the correct network and address to use. It uses the `initclient` routine from Example 4.2.1 and the `connect` routine from Example 4.4.1.

The caller passes in the name of the host computer and the name of a service to obtain from the host. On success, a file descriptor is returned that represents one end of a transport connection to the process providing the requested service on the requested host computer. On failure, −1 is returned.

```
#include <sys/types.h>
#include <stdio.h>
#include <netconfig.h>
#include <netdir.h>
#include <tiuser.h>

extern int initclient(char *);
extern int connect(int, char *, uint_t);

int
conn(char *host, char *service)
{
        void *p;
        int i, fd;
        struct netconfig *ncp;
```

```
struct nd_hostserv hs;
struct nd_addrlist *alp;
struct netbuf *np;

/*
 * Gain access to /etc/netconfig.
 */
if ((p = setnetpath()) == NULL)
    return( 1);

/*
 * Check all networks using connection-oriented
 * protocols specified by NETPATH.
 */
hs.h_host = host;
hs.h_serv = service;
while ((ncp = getnetpath(p)) != NULL) {
    if ((ncp->nc_semantics != NC_TPI_COTS) &&
        (ncp->nc_semantics != NC_TPI_COTS_ORD))
            continue;

    /*
     * Convert the requested host and service
     * to a list of addresses.
     */
    if (netdir_getbyname(ncp, &hs, &alp) != 0)
        continue;

    /*
     * Get a transport endpoint.  initclient
     * is from Example 4.2.1.
     */
    if ((fd = initclient(ncp->nc_device)) < 0) {
        netdir_free((void *)alp, ND_ADDRLIST);
        continue;
    }

    /*
     * Try to connect to one of the addresses.
     * connect is from Example 4.4.1.
     */
    np = alp->n_addrs;
    for (i = 0; i < alp->n_cnt; i++, np++) {
        if (connect(fd, np->buf, np->len) == 0) {

            /*
             * We've got a connection.  Clean
             * up and return.
             */
            netdir_free((void *)alp, ND_ADDRLIST);
            endnetpath(p);
            return(fd);
        }
    }
}
```

```
            /*
             * Not able to connect to any of the addresses.
             * Clean up and continue checking other networks.
             */
            netdir_free((void *)alp, ND_ADDRLIST);
            t_close(fd);
        }

        /*
         * Not able to connect to the given host and service.
         * Clean up and return.
         */
        endnetpath(p);
        return(-1);
    }
```

The outer loop of the function is similar to the one in Example 5.2.2, where we search the available networks in the network-configuration database based on the value of the NETPATH environment variable. For each network, we first ensure that it provides a transport-level, connection-oriented class of service. If so, we call netdir_getbyname to see if the requested service is configured for the requested host. If it is, we try to open a transport endpoint to the network. If this fails, we free the nd_addrlist structure using netdir_free and continue searching the network-configuration database.

Otherwise, we try to create a connection to the server, trying each address in the list if the prior one does not work. If a connection is created, we free the nd_addrlist structure, call endnetpath to free the memory allocated by setnetpath, and return the file descriptor for the connection.

If we cannot connect to the server using any of the addresses, we simply free the nd_addrlist structure, close the transport endpoint, and continue searching /etc/netconfig. Eventually, if we do not connect, we will exhaust the entries in /etc/netconfig, call endnetpath, and return −1.   □

The previous example illustrated how all the network-related details associated with a client process creating a transport-level connection to a server process can be abstracted away, leaving a clean and simple interface for applications to use. The implementation, however, might not be suitable for several reasons.

First, it assumes all processes have the necessary permissions to access the network devices. This implies that either the network devices are publicly readable and writable, or the programs that access them run as set-ID processes with the necessary permissions. The former alternative provides no security, and the latter alternative presents an administrative nightmare. (Set-ID processes are one of the first places people look for security holes.)

Second, there is no easy way to generate an audit trail of the users that attempt to access particular services. If logging was built into the conn library routine, users could just write their own client application to bypass the logging step. Audit trails are useful because they do not prevent users from accessing services, while providing a way for administrators to track unauthorized attempts to access the services.

These security concerns can be addressed by designing the connection facility into a separate, privileged server process. The network device special files can be given restricted ownership, so that only the connection server and the super-user can access them. By providing a publicly accessible mounted stream pipe in the file system, the server can accept requests from client processes wishing to make network connections. The server can log the requests, make the connection, and pass the connection back to the client through the pipe, similar to Examples 3.6.2 and 3.6.3. The Tenth Edition Research UNIX System implements the connection server in a way similar to this. In addition, SVR4.2 includes a connection server daemon that can be contacted by client applications to create authenticated connections to servers.

The network-selection and name-to-address translation facilities are useful to server-style processes as well as client-style processes. A server can be designed to offer its services on many networks, or it can be designed to offer several instantiations of its services using multiple addresses on any single network.

Example 5.3.2. The following example illustrates how a server process can identify the different networks and addresses for which it should offer its service. The first routine processes the network-configuration database, and the second routine initializes the transport endpoint for use by the server. The transport endpoints are stored in the global `pollfd` array called `pfd`. The number of entries in the array is stored in `nnet`. The size of the array is fixed for simplicity.

```
#include <sys/types.h>
#include <poll.h>
#include <unistd.h>
#include <stdio.h>
#include <fcntl.h>
#include <memory.h>
#include <tiuser.h>
#include <netconfig.h>
#include <netdir.h>

#define MAXNET    32

struct pollfd pfd[MAXNET];
int nnet;

void getnets(char *);
void addnet(struct netconfig *, struct netbuf *);

void
getnets(char *service)
{
        struct nd_hostserv hs;
        struct netconfig *ncp;
        struct nd_addrlist *nalp;
        struct netbuf *np;
        void *handle;
        int i;
```

```
        nnet = 0;
        hs.h_host = HOST_SELF;
        hs.h_serv = service;

        /*
         * Gain access to /etc/netconfig.
         */
        if ((handle = setnetconfig()) == NULL)
            return;

        /*
         * Get all addresses for this host and service.
         */
        while ((ncp = getnetconfig(handle)) != NULL) {
            /*
             * Look for connection-oriented networks only.
             */
            if ((ncp->nc_semantics == NC_TPI_COTS) ||
              (ncp->nc_semantics == NC_TPI_COTS_ORD)) {
                if (netdir_getbyname(ncp, &hs, &nalp) == 0) {
                    /*
                     * Found some matches.  Add as
                     * many entries as will fit.
                     */
                    np = nalp->n_addrs;
                    for (i = 0; i < nalp->n_cnt; i++, np++)
                        if (nnet < MAXNET)
                            addnet(ncp, np);

                    /*
                     * Free the address list.
                     */
                    netdir_free((void *)nalp, ND_ADDRLIST);
                }
            }
        }

        /*
         * Free the memory allocated by setnetconfig.
         */
        endnetconfig(handle);
    }
```

The getnets routine can be called by a server process after initialization to identify the networks and addresses it should use. We search the network-configuration database looking for connection-oriented transport providers. For each one, we call netdir_getbyname to find any addresses to be used for the requested service. Note that the host name we use is the alias for the local machine.

If netdir_getbyname succeeds and we have not yet reached the maximum number of network connections that we can handle, we call addnet to create a transport endpoint and add it to an array of file descriptors used to poll for incoming connection requests. We do this for every address to be used by the daemon for this service. When we are through with the list, we free the nd_addrlist structure

returned by `netdir_getbyname`. When we are through searching
`/etc/netconfig`, we call `endnetconfig` to free the memory associated with
the handle returned by `setnetconfig`.

```
void
addnet(struct netconfig *ncp, struct netbuf *np)
{
    struct t_bind req;
    struct t_bind *retp;
    int fd;

    /*
     * Open the transport endpoint.
     */
    fd = t_open(ncp->nc_device, O_RDWR, NULL);
    if (fd < 0)
        return;

    /*
     * Bind the requested address.
     */
    retp = (struct t_bind *)t_alloc(fd, T_BIND, T_ADDR);
    if (retp == NULL) {
        t_close(fd);
        return;
    }
    req.addr = *np; /* structure assignment */
    req.qlen = 1;
    if (t_bind(fd, &req, retp) < 0) {
        t_close(fd);
        t_free(retp, T_BIND);
        return;
    }

    /*
     * Verify the bound address is what we requested.
     */
    if ((req.addr.len != retp->addr.len) ||
      (memcmp(req.addr.buf, retp->addr.buf,
      req.addr.len) != 0)) {
        t_close(fd);
        t_free(retp, T_BIND);
        return;
    }

    /*
     * Add the transport endpoint to the array of
     * file descriptors and free the t_bind structure
     * previously allocated.
     */
    pfd[nnet].fd = fd;
    pfd[nnet++].events = POLLIN;
    t_free(retp, T_BIND);
}
```

In `addnet`, we open the device special file contained in the `nc_device` field of the `netconfig` structure. Then we bind the address specified by the `netbuf` structure to the transport endpoint. If the requested address is bound, we save the file descriptor in the global array of `pollfd` structures and increment the number of valid network file descriptors to poll.   □

Universal Addresses

Addresses in formats understandable by network drivers are not always suitable for human comprehension. Text strings are easier for people to read than are hexadecimal or binary data. To make addresses easier for people to read, the name-to-address mapping library provides two routines, `taddr2uaddr` and `uaddr2taddr`, that convert between a machine's network address and the human-readable form of the address.

The form understandable by humans is called the *universal address*, which is a machine-independent, textual representation of the network address. Each network-translation library can use its own format for the universal address. For example, a network whose addresses are composed of printable ASCII characters would not need to perform any translation, since strings of ASCII characters can generally be understood by humans.

```
#include <netdir.h>

char *taddr2uaddr(struct netconfig *ncp,
    struct netbuf *addr);
struct netbuf *uaddr2taddr(struct netconfig *ncp,
    char *addr);
```

`taddr2uaddr` translates the address represented by the `netbuf` structure pointed to by `addr` to a universal address character string. `uaddr2taddr` takes a universal address character string and returns the corresponding address in a `netbuf` structure in a format suitable for the network. On error, the routines return NULL.

Example 5.3.3. In SVR4 the TCP and UDP address format is described by a `sockaddr_in` structure (defined in `<netinet/in.h>`). It contains fields for the address family, the port number of the application, and the Internet address. The Internet address, described by an `in_addr` structure, contains four *octets*. (An octet is simply an eight-bit quantity. Network addresses use the term ''octet'' instead of ''byte'' because the size of a byte can vary with machine architecture.) The address structures are as follows:

```
struct in_addr {
    union {
        struct { uchar_t s_b1, s_b2, s_b3, s_b4; } S_un_b;
        struct { ushort_t s_w1, s_w2; } S_un_w;
        ulong_t S_addr;
    } S_un;
```

```
};
#define  s_addr  S_un.S_addr

struct sockaddr_in {
      short           sin_family;
      ushort_t        sin_port;
      struct in_addr  sin_addr;
      char            sin_zero[8];
};
```

The following program illustrates how taddr2uaddr works. We initialize a
sockaddr_in structure and pass it in a netbuf structure to taddr2uaddr,
printing the character string returned. To create the universal address, the network's
address is treated as a sequence of octets. Each octet is separated from the next by a
decimal point.

```
/* praddr.c */
#include <sys/types.h>
#include <sys/socket.h>
#include <netinet/in.h>
#include <stdlib.h>
#include <stdio.h>
#include <string.h>
#include <netconfig.h>
#include <netdir.h>
#include <tiuser.h>

void
main()
{
      int i;
      char *uap;
      struct netconfig *ncp;
      struct netbuf nb;
      struct sockaddr_in sa;

      if ((ncp = getnetconfigent("tcp")) != NULL) {
          /*
           * If tcp is defined in /etc/netconfig, initialize
           * the netbuf structure to represent a TCP address
           * and print the corresponding universal address.
           */
          nb.len = sizeof(struct sockaddr_in);
          nb.maxlen = nb.len;
          nb.buf = (char *)&sa;
          sa.sin_family = AF_INET;
          sa.sin_port = 1025;
          sa.sin_addr.s_addr = 0x01020304;
          for (i = 0; i < sizeof(sa.sin_zero); i++)
              sa.sin_zero[i] = 0;
          uap = taddr2uaddr(ncp, &nb);
          if (uap != NULL)
              printf("universal address is: %s\n", uap);
      }
```

```
        exit(0);
    }
```

When we run the program, we get the following output:

```
$ ./praddr
universal address is: 4.3.2.1.1.4
$
```

As we can see, the address family and filler fields are not included in the universal address. The Internet address portion is contained in the first four octets, from least significant byte to most significant byte. The port number is printed in the same order (1 + 4 * 256 = 1025).   □

The name-to-address translation library provides one last function, mostly for the support of the Internet protocols, that hides some of the protocol-specific details regarding addresses reserved for special purposes. The function prototype is

```
#include <netdir.h>

int netdir_options(struct netconfig *ncp, int option,
    int fd, char *arg);
```

ncp is a pointer to a netconfig structure obtained from one of the network-selection library routines, option is the command option, fd is the file descriptor of the network device, and arg is a pointer to option-specific data. netdir_options returns 0 on success and a nonzero value on failure.

The command options supported are summarized in Table 5.1. With the ND_SET_BROADCAST option, arg is unused.

Table 5.1. netdir_options Command Options

Command	Description
ND_SET_BROADCAST	Enable broadcasts on transport endpoint.
ND_SET_RESERVEDPORT	Bind endpoint to a reserved port.
ND_CHECK_RESERVEDPORT	Check if address is a reserved port.
ND_MERGEADDR	Put local address in remote format.

The ND_SET_RESERVEDPORT option binds the transport endpoint to a reserved port. A reserved port requires special permissions to allow binding. fd must be unbound at the time of the call to netdir_options. If arg is NULL, the transport endpoint will be bound to an unused reserved port. Otherwise, arg points to a netbuf structure that contains the address of the reserved port. Not all transport providers support the concept of a reserved port.

The ND_CHECK_RESERVEDPORT option returns 0 if the address specified by the netbuf structure pointed to by arg is that of a reserved port. Otherwise, a nonzero value is returned. With this option, fd is unused.

The ND_MERGEADDR option is used to transform an address that has significance on the local host to one that has significance on a remote host. This way, if the network supports local aliases, an application can obtain an address that another application on a remote machine can use to create a network connection between the two machines. `fd` is unused, and `arg` points to an `nd_mergearg` structure:

```
struct nd_mergearg {
        char    *s_uaddr;
        char    *c_uaddr;
        char    *m_uaddr;
};
```

where `s_uaddr` points to the server (local machine) universal address, `c_uaddr` points to the client (remote machine) universal address, and `m_uaddr` points to the resulting (merged) universal address.

For example, TCP supports the notion that the universal address 0.0.0.0 represents the IP address of the local machine. This alias, however, is useless to a client application on a remote machine. The ND_MERGEADDR command can be used to convert 0.0.0.0 into the actual IP address of the machine to which the client wants to connect. This might be used by a process to advertise its address to processes that might want to contact it from other machines on the network.

Example 5.3.4. This example illustrates the use of the `netdir_options` ND_MERGEADDR command with the TCP protocol. We bind a default address and print its format to show the alias used for local addresses. Then we convert the address to one that would have significance to an application on another machine and print the results.

```
/* mergeaddr.c */
#include <sys/types.h>
#include <sys/socket.h>
#include <netinet/in.h>
#include <stdlib.h>
#include <stdio.h>
#include <string.h>
#include <netconfig.h>
#include <netdir.h>
#include <tiuser.h>
#include <fcntl.h>

void
main()
{
        int i, fd;
        char *uap, *ruap;
        struct netconfig *ncp;
        struct t_bind *retp;
        struct netbuf nb;
        struct sockaddr_in sa;
        struct nd_mergearg m;

        if ((ncp = getnetconfigent("tcp")) != NULL) {
            /*
             * If tcp is defined in /etc/netconfig, initialize
```

```
 * the netbuf structure to represent a TCP address.
 */
nb.len = sizeof(struct sockaddr_in);
nb.maxlen = nb.len;
nb.buf = (char *)&sa;
sa.sin_family = AF_INET;
sa.sin_port = 1025;
sa.sin_addr.s_addr = 0x01020304;
for (i = 0; i < sizeof(sa.sin_zero); i++)
    sa.sin_zero[i] = 0;

/*
 * Next open a transport endpoint and bind the
 * default address.
 */
fd = t_open(ncp->nc_device, O_RDWR, NULL);
if (fd < 0) {
    t_error("t_open failed");
    exit(1);
}
retp = (struct t_bind *)t_alloc(fd, T_BIND, T_ADDR);
if (retp == NULL) {
    t_error("t_alloc failed");
    exit(1);
}
if (t_bind(fd, NULL, retp) < 0) {
    t_error("t_bind failed");
    exit(1);
}

/*
 * Convert the bound address to a universal address
 * and print it.
 */
uap = taddr2uaddr(ncp, &retp->addr);
if (uap == NULL) {
    netdir_perror("taddr2uaddr failed");
    exit(1);
}
printf("local universal address is: %s\n", uap);

/*
 * Convert the dummy remote address to a universal
 * address and print it.
 */
ruap = taddr2uaddr(ncp, &nb);
if (ruap == NULL) {
    netdir_perror("taddr2uaddr failed");
    exit(1);
}
printf("remote universal address is: %s\n", ruap);

/*
 * Now merge the local address with the remote
```

```
        * address and print the result.
        */
       m.s_uaddr = uap;
       m.c_uaddr = ruap;
       if (netdir_options(ncp, ND_MERGEADDR, fd,
         (char *)&m) != 0) {
          netdir_perror("netdir_options failed");
          exit(1);
       }
       printf("merged address is: %s\n", m.m_uaddr);
   }
   exit(0);
}
```

When we run the command, we get the following output:

```
$ ./mergeaddr
local universal address is: 0.0.0.0.4.2
remote universal address is: 4.3.2.1.1.4
merged address is: 192.102.88.33.4.2
$
```

Note that the local IP address alias is indeed 0.0.0.0. The real IP address of the host happens to be 192.102.88.33. The real IP address is used in creating the merged TCP address.   □

5.4 NAME-TO-ADDRESS LIBRARY DESIGN

Other than `netdir_options`, the name-to-address translation routines have no hardwired knowledge that they are being used to deal with transport-level addresses or transport-level devices. The same goes for the `netconfig` database. The semantics field, for example, could be extended to support network-level connection-less and connection-oriented services by defining the symbols `NC_NPI_CLNS` and `NC_NPI_CONS`.

The name-to-address translation routines export interfaces that hide the details of how addresses and services are specified. The details are relegated to administrative procedures associated with the maintenance of each particular network implementation. For example, the addresses and services could be recorded in database files, or they could be registered with a daemon whose job would be to maintain the lists. This type of daemon is called a *directory server* or a *name server*.

This section provides an example implementation of a network-specific name-to-address translation library. Such a library needs to support the entry points listed in Table 5.2.

The function prototypes for the network-specific library routines are given on the next page. The `netconfig` structure corresponding to the network being used is passed to the routines, so they can access the network device if needed and distinguish between services provided on multiple networks using the same library.

Table 5.2. Network-Specific Name-to-Address Library Functions

Function Name	Description
_netdir_getbyname	Return all the addresses for the given host and service.
_netdir_getbyaddr	Return all the hosts and services using the given address.
_netdir_options	Handle transport-specific options.
_taddr2uaddr	Translate a transport address into a universal address.
_uaddr2taddr	Translate a universal address into a transport address.

```
#include <tiuser.h>
#include <netconfig.h>
#include <netdir.h>

struct nd_addrlist *_netdir_getbyname(struct netconfig *ncp,
    struct nd_hostserv *hsp);

struct nd_hostservlist *_netdir_getbyaddr(
    struct netconfig *ncp, struct netbuf *np);

int _netdir_options(struct netconfig *ncp, int option,
    int fd, void *arg);

char *_taddr2uaddr(struct netconfig *ncp,
    struct netbuf *np);

struct netbuf *_uaddr2taddr(struct netconfig *ncp,
    char *uap);
```

The first routine, _netdir_getbyname, returns a pointer to an nd_addrlist structure on success, or NULL on error. The nd_addrlist structure should be dynamically allocated from the heap (using malloc(3C), for example), so that it can be freed by a later call to netdir_free. The nd_addrlist structure contains the list of addresses corresponding to the host and service given by the nd_hostserv structure.

The second routine, _netdir_getbyaddr, returns a pointer to an nd_hostservlist structure on success, or NULL on error. Like the previous routine, _netdir_getbyaddr should allocate the nd_hostservlist structure from the heap. The nd_hostservlist structure should contain all the host and service names that correspond to the address represented by the given netbuf structure.

The next routine, _netdir_options, is used to implement the optional network addressing features discussed in the previous section. This function returns 0 on success and −1 on failure. Not all options are supported by all network-specific libraries.

The last two routines, _taddr2uaddr and _uaddr2taddr, are used to convert between address formats. _taddr2uaddr returns the character string representing the universal address for the address represented by the given `netbuf` structure. `_uaddr2taddr` returns a netbuf structure containing the network-specific address for the universal address passed to it. Both return NULL on error.

All five routines will set the global integer `_nderror` to indicate the reason for failure.

Example 5.4.1. This longer-than-usual example illustrates how a network-specific name-to-address translation library can be written. It is written assuming 32-bit network addresses and 16-bit port numbers. The network name is `testnet`.

```
#include <sys/types.h>
#include <sys/utsname.h>
#include <stdio.h>
#include <stdlib.h>
#include <string.h>
#include <limits.h>
#include <tiuser.h>
#include <netconfig.h>
#include <netdir.h>

#define HOSTFILE      "/etc/net/testnet/hosts"
#define SERVICEFILE   "/etc/net/testnet/services"
#define TADDRLEN      6   /* total address length */
#define NADDRLEN      4   /* network address length */
#define OCTMAX        255 /* maximum value of an octet */

struct host {
     struct host *h_next;
     char        *h_name;
     ulong_t     h_naddr;
};

struct svc {
     struct svc  *s_next;
     char        *s_name;
     ushort_t    s_port;
};

struct addr {
     ulong_t     a_n;
     ushort_t    a_p;
};

static struct host *hosts;
static struct svc *svcs;

static void clrhosts(void);
static void clrsvcs(void);
static int rdhosts(void);
static int rdsvcs(void);
static int counthosts(char *);
static struct svc *findsvc(char *);
static struct host *findhost(struct host *, char *);
```

```
static struct host *findaddr(struct host *, struct addr *);
```

```
extern int _nderror;
```

The `host` structure describes an entry in `/etc/net/testnet/hosts`. The variable `hosts` is the head of a linked list of `host` structures. The `svc` structure describes an entry in `/etc/net/testnet/services`. The variable `svcs` heads the linked list of `svc` structures from the database. The `addr` structure is used to describe an address. Since the network portion of the address is 32 bits long, we use an `unsigned long` to represent it. Similarly, the port number portion of the address is 16 bits long, so we use an `unsigned short` for it.

The variable `_nderror` is defined by the generic name-to-address translation routines. The network-specific routines set it on failure to indicate the reason for failure. The first routine is `_netdir_getbyname`.

```
struct nd_addrlist *
_netdir_getbyname(struct netconfig *ncp,
    struct nd_hostserv *hsp)
{
    char *hostname;
    struct host *hp;
    struct svc *sp;
    int i, nhosts;
    struct utsname self;
    struct netbuf *np;
    struct nd_addrlist *nalp;
    struct addr *ap;

    _nderror = ND_OK;

    /*
     * Check for special aliases we don't support.
     */
    if ((strcmp(hsp->h_host, HOST_ANY) == 0) ||
        (strcmp(hsp->h_host, HOST_BROADCAST) == 0)) {
        _nderror = ND_NOHOST;
        return(NULL);
    }

    /*
     * If local alias is specified, call uname(2)
     * to get the local host name.  Otherwise use
     * name supplied by caller.
     */
    if (strcmp(hsp->h_host, HOST_SELF) == 0) {
        if (uname(&self) < 0) {
            _nderror = ND_SYSTEM;
            return(NULL);
        }
        hostname = self.nodename;
    } else {
        hostname = hsp->h_host;
    }
```

```
/*
 * Read the hosts database, if we haven't already
 * done so.
 */
if ((hosts == NULL) && (rdhosts() < 0)) {
    _nderror = ND_SYSTEM;
    return(NULL);
}

/*
 * Read the services database, if we haven't already
 * done so.
 */
if ((svcs == NULL) && (rdsvcs() < 0)) {
    _nderror = ND_SYSTEM;
    return(NULL);
}

/*
 * Count the number of host entries matching the
 * given host name.
 */
if ((nhosts = counthosts(hostname)) == 0) {
    _nderror = ND_NOHOST;
    return(NULL);
}

/*
 * See if the requested service is defined.
 */
if ((sp = findsvc(hsp->h_serv)) == NULL) {
    _nderror = ND_NOSERV;
    return(NULL);
}

/*
 * Allocate the address list to be returned.
 */
if ((nalp = malloc(sizeof(struct nd_addrlist))) ==
  NULL) {
    _nderror = ND_NOMEM;
    return(NULL);
}
nalp->n_cnt = nhosts;
nalp->n_addrs = malloc(nhosts*sizeof(struct netbuf));
if (nalp->n_addrs == NULL) {
    free(nalp);
    _nderror = ND_NOMEM;
    return(NULL);
}
hp = hosts;
np = (struct netbuf *)nalp->n_addrs;
for (i = 0; i < nalp->n_cnt; i++, np++) {
```

```
        /*
         * Allocate a netbuf address buffer for each
         * address.
         */
        if ((np->buf = malloc(TADDRLEN)) == NULL) {
            np = (struct netbuf *)nalp->n_addrs;
            for (; i > 0; i--, np++)
                free(np->buf);
            free(nalp->n_addrs);
            free(nalp);
            _nderror = ND_NOMEM;
            return(NULL);
        }
        np->len = TADDRLEN;
        np->maxlen = TADDRLEN;

        /*
         * Find the host and copy the address into
         * the netbuf structure.
         */
        hp = findhost(hp, hostname);
        ap = (struct addr *)np->buf;
        ap->a_n = hp->h_naddr;
        ap->a_p = sp->s_port;
    }
    return(nalp);
}
```

We start off by setting _nderror to ND_OK (defined in <netdir.h>) to indicate that no error has been encountered. Then we check the host name for the aliases HOST_ANY and HOST_BROADCAST. We do not support these aliases, so we set _nderror to ND_NOHOST (also defined in <netdir.h>) and return NULL. We do, however, support the HOST_SELF alias. If this is used, we get our host name by using uname(2). Otherwise, we use the host name provided by the caller.

If the list of hosts is empty, we initialize it by calling rdhosts. Similarly, if the list of services is empty, we call rdsvcs to initialize it. If either function fails, we set _nderror to ND_SYSTEM to indicate a system error has been encountered and then return NULL.

Next we call counthosts to count the number of entries in the list of host names that match the name specified by the caller. If none matches, we set _nderror to ND_NOHOST and return NULL.

Then we search for the service requested by the caller. If it is not found, we set _nderror to ND_NOSERV and return NULL. Otherwise, we assume that only one service matches, and we allocate memory for the nd_addrlist structure and the list of netbuf structures. If malloc fails, we set _nderror to ND_NOMEM and return NULL.

For each address in the entry, we allocate the memory for the address, find the next host that matches, and copy in the host address and port number. Finally, we return the pointer to the nd_addrlist structure.

The next routine is _netdir_getbyaddr.

```
struct nd_hostservlist *
_netdir_getbyaddr(struct netconfig *ncp, struct netbuf *np)
{
    struct host *hp;
    struct svc *sp;
    int i, nhosts;
    struct nd_hostservlist *hslp;
    struct nd_hostserv *hsp;
    struct addr *ap;

    _nderror = ND_OK;

    /*
     * Make sure the address is the proper length.
     */
    if (np->len != TADDRLEN) {
        _nderror = ND_BADARG;
        return(NULL);
    }

    /*
     * Read the hosts database, if we haven't already
     * done so.
     */
    if ((hosts == NULL) && (rdhosts() < 0)) {
        _nderror = ND_SYSTEM;
        return(NULL);
    }

    /*
     * Read the services database, if we haven't already
     * done so.
     */
    if ((svcs == NULL) && (rdsvcs() < 0)) {
        _nderror = ND_SYSTEM;
        return(NULL);
    }

    /*
     * Check if the port number is assigned to a
     * service.
     */
    ap = (struct addr *)np->buf;
    for (sp = svcs; sp; sp = sp->s_next)
        if (sp->s_port == ap->a_p)
            break;
    if (sp == NULL) {
        _nderror = ND_NOSERV;
        return(NULL);
    }

    /*
     * Check for matching hosts based on the network
     * portion of the address.
```

```
    */
    nhosts = 0;
    for (hp = hosts; hp; hp = hp->h_next)
        if (hp->h_naddr == ap->a_n)
            nhosts++;
    if (nhosts == 0) {
        _nderror = ND_NOHOST;
        return(NULL);
    }

    /*
     * Allocate memory for the list of hosts and
     * services that match the given address.
     */
    hslp = malloc(sizeof(struct nd_hostservlist));
    if (hslp == NULL) {
        _nderror = ND_NOMEM;
        return(NULL);
    }
    hsp = malloc(sizeof(struct nd_hostserv) * nhosts);
    if (hsp == NULL) {
        free(hslp);
        _nderror = ND_NOMEM;
        return(NULL);
    }
    hslp->h_cnt = nhosts;
    hslp->h_hostservs = hsp;
    hp = hosts;
    for (i = 0; i < nhosts; i++, hsp++) {
        /*
         * Copy the name of the matching service.
         */
        hsp->h_serv = strdup(sp->s_name);
        if (hsp->h_serv == NULL) {
            hsp = hslp->h_hostservs;
            for (; i > 0; i--, hsp++) {
                free(hsp->h_host);
                free(hsp->h_serv);
            }
            free(hslp->h_hostservs);
            free(hslp);
            _nderror = ND_NOMEM;
            return(NULL);
        }

        /*
         * Find the next matching host and copy
         * its name.
         */
        hp = findaddr(hp, ap);
        hsp->h_host = strdup(hp->h_name);
        if (hsp->h_host == NULL) {
            free(hsp->h_serv);
            hsp = hslp->h_hostservs;
```

```
            for (; i > 0; i--, hsp++) {
                free(hsp->h_host);
                free(hsp->h_serv);
            }
            free(hslp->h_hostservs);
            free(hslp);
            _nderror = ND_NOMEM;
            return(NULL);
        }
    }
    return(hslp);
}
```

_netdir_getbyaddr is similar to _netdir_getbyname. If the length of the address in the caller's netbuf structure is incorrect, we set _nderror to ND_BADARG. Otherwise, we proceed to initialize the host and service lists if necessary.

Then we look for a matching port number. If one is found, we count the number of hosts that use the network portion of the address. If no matches are found in either case, we set the appropriate error number and return NULL. Otherwise, we allocate memory for an nd_hostservlist structure and the array of nd_hostserv structures it contains.

Next we initialize each nd_hostserv structure in the array. We use strdup(3C) to copy the service name. Then we call findaddr to find the next host name that matches the address and duplicate it as well. If a memory allocation fails, we free all previously allocated memory and return NULL. Otherwise, after initializing the entire array, we return a pointer to the nd_hostservlist structure.

The _netdir_options function is next:

```
int
_netdir_options(struct netconfig *ncp, int option, int fd,
  void *arg)
{
    int ret;
    struct nd_mergearg *nmp;

    _nderror = ND_OK;
    ret = 0;
    switch (option) {
    case ND_MERGEADDR:
        /*
         * No local aliases supported.  Just return
         * a copy of the local universal address.
         */
        nmp = (struct nd_mergearg *)arg;
        nmp->m_uaddr = strdup(nmp->s_uaddr);
        if (nmp->m_uaddr == NULL) {
            _nderror = ND_NOMEM;
            ret = -1;
        }
        break;
```

```
        default:
            /*
             * No other commands supported.
             */
            _nderror = ND_NOCTRL;
            ret = -1;
        }
        return(ret);
    }
```

We only support the ND_MERGEADDR command. Since we do not support a local alias for the host, we just duplicate the universal address of the server and set the merged universal address to the result. If this is successful, we return 0. Otherwise, we set _nderror and return −1.

All other option commands are unsupported by our network implementation, so if they are attempted, we set _nderror to ND_NOCTRL to indicate that they are unimplemented, and we return −1.

The address translation routines will be shown next. They convert between a binary address stored in a netbuf structure and a character string of the format

N1.N2.N3.N4.P1.P2

where N1, N2, N3, and N4 are the octets of the 32-bit network address, and P1 and P2 are the octets of the 16-bit port number. N1 is the most significant byte of the network address, and N4 is the least significant byte. Similarly, P1 is the most significant byte of the port number, and P2 is the least significant byte.

The byte order is important because the same universal address on two computers with different byte orders must evaluate to the correct binary address. When we build the universal address, we are careful to do so in a way that is independent of the byte order.

The _taddr2uaddr routine takes an address represented by a netbuf structure and converts it into a universal address.

```
char *
_taddr2uaddr(struct netconfig *ncp, struct netbuf *np)
{
    char *p;
    struct addr *ap;
    char buf[128];

    _nderror = ND_OK;

    /*
     * Make sure the address length is valid.
     */
    if (np->len != TADDRLEN) {
        _nderror = ND_BADARG;
        return(NULL);
    }
    ap = (struct addr *)np->buf;

    /*
```

```
 * Convert the address to ASCII and return a copy.
 */
sprintf(buf, "%d.%d.%d.%d.%d.%d", (ap->a_n>>24),
    ((ap->a_n>>16)&0xff), ((ap->a_n>>8)&0xff),
    (ap->a_n&0xff), ((ap->a_p>>8)&0xff), (ap->a_p&0xff));
if ((p = strdup(buf)) == NULL)
    _nderror = ND_NOMEM;
return(p);
}
```

We build the universal address in a buffer on the stack, duplicate the string using `strdup`, and return the copy of the string to the caller. We use `strdup` so the underlying memory for the string comes from the heap instead of the stack. It would be an error to return a pointer to `buf` because the memory for it resides on the stack, and this memory is reused after we return from the function.

_uaddr2taddr takes a universal address and converts it into a binary address represented by a `netbuf` structure.

```
struct netbuf *
_uaddr2taddr(struct netconfig *ncp, char *uaddr)
{
    uint_t i1, i2, i3, i4, i5, i6;
    struct netbuf *np;
    struct addr *ap;

    _nderror = ND_OK;

    /*
     * Parse the universal address.
     */
    if (sscanf(uaddr, "%d.%d.%d.%d.%d.%d", &i1, &i2, &i3,
      &i4, &i5, &i6) != 6) {
        _nderror = ND_BADARG;
        return(NULL);
    }

    /*
     * Validate each octet.
     */
    if ((i1 > OCTMAX) || (i2 > OCTMAX) || (i3 > OCTMAX) ||
      (i4 > OCTMAX) || (i5 > OCTMAX) || (i6 > OCTMAX)) {
        _nderror = ND_BADARG;
        return(NULL);
    }

    /*
     * Allocate a netbuf structure with a buffer large
     * enough to hold a transport address.
     */
    if ((np = malloc(sizeof(struct netbuf))) == NULL) {
        _nderror = ND_NOMEM;
        return(NULL);
    }
```

```
    if ((np->buf = malloc(TADDRLEN)) == NULL) {
        free(np);
        _nderror = ND_NOMEM;
        return(NULL);
    }

    /*
     * Initialize the netbuf structure with the binary
     * address.
     */
    np->len = TADDRLEN;
    np->maxlen = TADDRLEN;
    ap = (struct addr *)np->buf;
    ap->a_n = (i1<<24)|(i2<<16)|(i3<<8)|i4;
    ap->a_p = (i5<<8)|i6;
    return(np);
}
```

If the universal address is not in the correct format, `sscanf` will not return 6 as the number of matched variables. In this case, we set `_nderror` to `ND_BADARG` and return `NULL`. If the correct number of octets are present, we do a bounds check to make sure none of the numbers is greater than the largest number representable by an octet.

If the universal address is valid, we allocate a `netbuf` structure and a buffer for the address. If either allocation fails, we set `_nderror` to `ND_NOMEM` and return `NULL`. Otherwise, we cast a pointer to an `addr` structure over the buffer and fill in the network address and port number. We take care to use the same byte order as used in the rest of the library.

Since the lifetime of the `netbuf` structure is unknown to the library, and since an application can call the library routine several times, we use dynamically allocated memory from the heap instead of static memory. This provides the additional benefit that the `netbuf` structure can be freed later by associating it with the proper TLI data structure and passing a pointer to the structure to `t_free(3N)`.

The following routines are private support functions used by the library to implement the five previous public library routines. `clrhosts` frees the list of host structures starting at `hosts`. `clrsvcs` frees the list of `svc` structures starting at `svcs`.

```
    /*
     * Free all host information.
     */
    static void
    clrhosts(void)
    {
        struct host *hp, *nhp;

        hp = hosts;
        while (hp != NULL) {
            nhp = hp->h_next;
            free(hp);
            hp = nhp;
```

```
        }
        hosts = NULL;
}

/*
 * Free all service information.
 */
static void
clrsvcs(void)
{
        struct svc *sp, *nsp;

        sp = svcs;
        while (sp != NULL) {
            nsp = sp->s_next;
            free(sp);
            sp = nsp;
        }
        svcs = NULL;
}
```

rdhosts scans the host database file and builds the linked list of host structures.

```
static int
rdhosts(void)
{
        FILE *fp;
        uint_t i1, i2, i3, i4;
        struct host *hp;
        char hname[256];
        char buf[256];

        /*
         * Open the host database.
         */
        if ((fp = fopen(HOSTFILE, "r")) == NULL)
            return(-1);

        /*
         * Check one line at a time.
         */
        while (fgets(buf, sizeof(buf), fp) != NULL) {
            /*
             * Skip comment lines.
             */
            if (buf[0] == '#')
                continue;

            /*
             * Skip lines not in the format of a host name
             * followed by the network address in universal
             * format.
             */
```

```
        if (sscanf(buf, "%s %d.%d.%d.%d", hname, &i1, &i2,
          &i3, &i4) != 5)
            continue;

        /*
         * Validate the octet values.
         */
        if ((i1 > OCTMAX) || (i2 > OCTMAX) ||
          (i3 > OCTMAX) || (i4 > OCTMAX))
            continue;

        /*
         * Allocate a host structure.  If the allocation
         * fails, free the entire host list.
         */
        hp = malloc(sizeof(struct host)+strlen(hname)+1);
        if (hp == NULL) {
            fclose(fp);
            clrhosts();
            return(-1);
        }

        /*
         * Initialize the host structure and put it on
         * the front of the list.
         */
        hp->h_name = (char *)hp + sizeof(struct host);
        strcpy(hp->h_name, hname);
        hp->h_naddr = (i1<<24)|(i2<<16)|(i3<<8)|i4;
        hp->h_next = hosts;
        hosts = hp;
    }

    /*
     * Don't forget to close the file.
     */
    fclose(fp);
    return(0);
}
```

We start by reading the file, one line at a time, treating lines that begin with a pound sign (#) as comments. We ignore any lines that do not follow the format of a host name followed by a four-octet universal network address. For valid lines, we allocate a host structure and initialize it with the data from the line. Then we place the host structure on the linked list headed by hosts.

rdsvcs is similar to rdhosts, but parses the service file instead. The format is a service name followed by a port number.

```
static int
rdsvcs(void)
{
    FILE *fp;
    uint_t port;
```

```
struct svc *sp;
char sname[256];
char buf[256];

/*
 * Open the service database.
 */
if ((fp = fopen(SERVICEFILE, "r")) == NULL)
    return(-1);

/*
 * Check one line at a time.
 */
while (fgets(buf, sizeof(buf), fp) != NULL) {
    /*
     * Skip comment lines.
     */
    if (buf[0] == '#')
        continue;

    /*
     * Skip lines not in the format of a service
     * name followed by a port number.
     */
    if (sscanf(buf, "%s %d", sname, &port) != 2)
        continue;

    /*
     * Validate the port number.
     */
    if (port > USHRT_MAX)
        continue;

    /*
     * Allocate a service structure.  If the
     * allocation fails, free the entire
     * service list.
     */
    sp = malloc(sizeof(struct svc)+strlen(sname)+1);
    if (sp == NULL) {
        fclose(fp);
        clrsvcs();
        return(-1);
    }

    /*
     * Initialize the service structure and put it
     * on the front of the list.
     */
    sp->s_name = (char *)sp + sizeof(struct svc);
    strcpy(sp->s_name, sname);
    sp->s_port = (ushort_t)port;
    sp->s_next = svcs;
    svcs = sp;
```

```
        }

        /*
         * Don't forget to close the file.
         */
        fclose(fp);
        return(0);
}
```

counthosts returns the number of host structures for the given host name. findsvc returns the svc structure corresponding to the given service name, or NULL if the service is not defined by the services file. If a service name appears twice in the database, we only recognize the first occurrence.

```
static int
counthosts(char *name)
{
        struct host *hp;
        int n = 0;

        for (hp = hosts; hp; hp = hp->h_next)
                if (strcmp(hp->h_name, name) == 0)
                        n++;
        return(n);
}

static struct svc *
findsvc(char *name)
{
        struct svc *sp;

        for (sp = svcs; sp; sp = sp->s_next)
                if (strcmp(sp->s_name, name) == 0)
                        return(sp);
        return(NULL);
}
```

findhost returns the next host structure with the given host name. hp is a pointer to a host structure in the list from which the search will begin. NULL is returned if a match is not found. findaddr is like findhost, but matches on network address instead.

```
static struct host *
findhost(struct host *hp, char *name)
{
        if (hp != hosts)
                hp = hp->h_next;
        while (hp != NULL) {
                if (strcmp(hp->h_name, name) == 0)
                        return(hp);
                hp = hp->h_next;
        }
        return(NULL);
}
```

```
static struct host *
findaddr(struct host *hp, struct addr *ap)
{
    if (hp != hosts)
        hp = hp->h_next;
    while (hp != NULL) {
        if (hp->h_naddr == ap->a_n)
            return(hp);
        hp = hp->h_next;
    }
    return(NULL);
}
```

□

Summary

We have seen how applications can use the `netconfig` routines and `NETPATH` routines to select networks and protocols. We have also seen how the name-to-address translation routines can be used to isolate applications from the details of addressing. Both the network-selection library and the name-to-address translation library help developers design their applications to be network-independent. This ultimately enhances application portability and reusability. Finally, we illustrated the entry points to be supplied when designing the network-specific portions of the name-to-address mapping routines.

Exercises

5.1 Rewrite Example 5.3.1 as a separate server process as discussed in the text. Include the suggested logging for an audit trail.

5.2 Example 4.3.1 describes the client-side communication routine for a remote who command. Complete the command by adding the necessary network-selection and name-to-address translation support.

5.3 Just as in Exercise 5.2, finish the server side of the remote who command shown in Example 4.3.2.

Bibliographic Notes

The name-to-address translation routines were based on similar functions found in 4BSD. The network-selection and name-to-address translation libraries were developed jointly by AT&T and Sun Microsystems for UNIX SVR4. These facilities are documented in Chapter 7 of the *SVR4 Programmer's Guide: Networking Interfaces* [USL 1990d] and in Chapter 12 of the *SVR4 System Administrator's Guide* [USL 1990c].

The connection server was originally developed by Dave Presotto at AT&T Bell Laboratories [Presotto and Ritchie 1985, 1990].

6

The Network
Listener Facility

The network listener facility makes it easier to develop server-style applications by handling the details of server-side connection establishment over connection-oriented transport providers. This leaves server applications free to concentrate on providing services. At the center of this facility is the listener process. It is a special kind of server, called a *port monitor*, that executes as part of the *service access facility* to provide clients access to system services over networks. This chapter describes the framework of the service access facility and explains how applications can make use of the network listener facility.

6.1 THE SERVICE ACCESS FACILITY

The service access facility (SAF) is an administrative framework in which server applications can run. The administrative framework is needed to provide consistency both to the users of a computer's services and to the system administrators.

The SAF provides a consistent model of administration by exporting the same command interface used to administer all the servers that provide access to a computer system. Behind the command-line interface, the servers use configuration files that adhere to consistent naming conventions. All of this makes the job of administration easier.

In addition, the SAF provides administrators with the ability to run individual configuration scripts before a service is invoked. This gives administrators the opportunity either to ensure that different servers providing similar services can do so consistently, or to customize the environment of individual servers.

For example, the service of logging into a computer can be provided by a server that monitors terminal lines or by a server that allows logins over a network. Both servers will eventually run `login(1M)`, but the SAF helps administrators ensure that users logging in see the same environment, regardless of how `login` is started.

Any server process that controls a port, or a point of access to a computer, is a port monitor. For example, `ttymon(1M)` is a port monitor that controls access to serial communication lines. Not all server processes are port monitors, however. The line printer scheduling daemon, `lpsched(1M)`, and the batch processing daemon, `cron(1M)`, are two examples of servers that are not port monitors.

A special process, called the service access controller (SAC), has the responsibility of starting and monitoring the individual port monitors [see `sac(1M)`]. The port monitors communicate with the SAC through a pair of FIFOs. The SAC receives messages from all port monitors using one FIFO, and each port monitor has a private FIFO on which it can receive messages from the SAC. A pair of FIFOs is used instead of a single pipe because it insulates the port monitors from the death of the SAC. (Recall from Chapter 3 that when one end of a pipe is closed, the other end is placed in hangup mode. If pipes were used instead, the port monitors would require extra code to reestablish the communication channel. With FIFOs, on the other hand, the communication channel is unaffected by the death of the SAC because a FIFO is really only one "end" of a stream — see Figure 3.6 — and the port monitors also hold that "end" open.)

Besides starting the port monitors, the SAC will optionally make entries for them in `/var/adm/utmp`. This file contains a record of each login session, along with records for special system processes involved in the login process. See `utmp(4)` for more details.

The SAC, `/usr/lib/saf/sac`, runs in its home directory, `/etc/saf`. On starting up, it configures its environment according to the script `/etc/saf/_sysconfig`. The environment is inherited by all the port monitors that the SAC started. If a port monitor fails, the SAC will attempt to restart it, up to a specified maximum number of times.

The SAC itself is started out of `/etc/inittab` by `init(1M)`. It takes one argument: `-t interval`, where `interval` is the number of seconds between attempts to poll port monitors. Polling entails the SAC sending a sanity message to each port monitor and receiving a response to determine the port monitor status. The SAC receives response messages on a FIFO named `/etc/saf/_sacpipe`. During execution, the SAC logs its actions to the file `/var/saf/_log`.

The list of port monitors governed by the SAC is stored in `/etc/saf/_sactab`. Each port monitor is identified by a unique string called a *tag*. The tag is at most 14 characters long, not including the terminating NULL byte. The tag also names the directory in `/etc/saf` containing the port monitor's data files. Each port monitor has a configuration script, similar to the one used by the SAC, called `/etc/saf/`*tag*`/_config`. This can be used to customize the environment of an individual port monitor. The format of the configuration scripts is described shortly.

The `sacadm(1M)` command provides the administrative interface for the SAC. It insulates administrators from the format of `/etc/saf/_sactab`. There are many options to the `sacadm` command to allow administrators to maintain the port monitors and the SAC. These options include adding a port monitor to the SAF, removing a port monitor from the SAF, starting and stopping a port monitor, enabling and disabling a port monitor, and replacing the port monitor and SAC configuration scripts.

Configuration Scripts

The SAC and port monitor configuration scripts are used to customize the environments of the server processes. They have the same format: lines must be shorter than 1024 characters, and those characters following a pound sign (#) are ignored as comments.

Each line can contain one of the following five commands:

`assign` *variable=value*

>   will place the environment variable with the specified value in the environment of the server.

`push` *module₁* [*, module₂ , . . . , moduleₙ*]

>   will push the comma-separated list of modules on the stream associated with the service, in the order specified. In other words, after successful completion, *module_N* will be on top of *module_{N-1}*.

`pop` [*module*]

>   will pop modules off the stream. If no parameter is specified, the topmost module is popped off the stream. Otherwise, modules are popped until the specified module is left on the top of the stream. The special module alias `ALL` will result in all modules being popped off the stream.

`run` *command*

>   will run the specified command in a subshell (i.e., a child process is created and `sh -c` is executed with the specified command). The parent does not wait for the command to complete before returning.

`runwait` *command*

>   will do the same as the `run` command, but the parent will wait for the command to finish execution before returning. If the command fails, then `runwait` will return a failure indication.

Three special shell built-in commands can be executed by `run` and `runwait`. These are `cd`, to change the current working directory; `ulimit`, to change the maximum file size the server can create; and `umask`, to change the server's file creation mask. See `sh(1)` for more details.

Besides being run as part of starting the SAC and the port monitors, configuration scripts can also be run before individual services are started. The `push` and `pop` commands can be used in this case to modify the list of modules present in the stream used to provide the service. In the configuration scripts associated with the SAC and the port monitors, these two commands cannot be used, because there is no stream on which operations can be performed.

Example 6.1.1. Before starting the SAC or a port monitor, typical tasks that might be performed in a configuration script are setting the `TZ` environment variable so that the SAC and the port monitors have the correct notion of the time zone, modifying the `PATH` environment variable, and increasing the limit to the maximum file

creation size. An example of a configuration script that performs these modifications
follows:

```
TZ=EST5EDT                      # east coast
PATH=/usr/ucb:/usr/bin:/sbin # get BSD commands first
runwait ulimit unlimited        # big files are okay
```

For individual services, modules can be pushed on or popped off the stream in
addition to setting environment variables and running commands. A typical case
where an individual service might be customized is the remote login service.

Administrators have the ability to configure line disciplines to be pushed onto
streams automatically with the `autopush(1M)` command. The autopush mechanism is most often used to associate line discipline modules with serial line drivers
so that a line discipline will always be present when a serial line driver is opened.
Network drivers, on the other hand, usually are not configured through the autopush
mechanism because of two reasons. First, network drivers are usually accessed
through the clone interface, and the minor device is not available ahead of time to be
used in the autopush configuration process. Second, network drivers are used in a
wider variety of applications and are not usually dedicated for use with a single
application as serial line drivers are, so few modules are appropriate to be used with
every network connection. (TIMOD is pushed by the TLI library, not by the autopush mechanism.)

For example, assume a system administrator wanted to make sure TTCOMPAT
was present in every terminal stream on the system. In this case, the autopush mechanism can be used to configure the serial communication drivers. The system
administrator can use the following configuration script for the network-based
remote login service:

```
push ttcompat        # support BSD TTY ioctl commands
```
                                                                             □

A special library routine, `doconfig(3N)`, will process the configuration
script. Port monitors can call it to customize the environment of a service before
starting the service.

```
#include <sac.h>

int doconfig(int fd, char *script, long flags);
```

`fd` is the file descriptor associated with the service connection, `script` is the pathname of the configuration script to be used, and `flags` is a bitmask used to restrict
the set of commands that can be executed in the configuration script. Two flags are
defined: NOASSIGN and NORUN. NOASSIGN prevents `assign` commands from
being executed, causing `doconfig` to return an error. Similarly, NORUN prevents
`run` and `runwait` commands from being executed. We shall see how the flags are
used later in this chapter.

6.2 PORT MONITORS

Port monitors provide access to system services through various mechanisms. One example of a port monitor is `ttymon`, which is used to monitor asynchronous communication lines. Another port monitor is `listen`, used to monitor connection-oriented networks at the transport level. The role of a port monitor is to sense service requests and either deny the requests, or satisfy them by executing a service, usually using the port on which the request arrived.

Port monitors are the port-specific components in the framework of the SAF. They isolate all knowledge about the types of ports they monitor. For example, `ttymon` knows how to deal with asynchronous communication devices, handling break detection, terminal mode and baud rate selection, and the printing of prompts. `listen`, on the other hand, is specialized to know only about connection-oriented transport-level network devices. It knows how to initialize transport endpoints, accept incoming connect indications, and perform limited communication.

In addition to monitoring ports and starting services, port monitors also have the responsibility of creating `utmp` entries for individual services. This feature is controlled by an option that can be selected by system administrators on a per-service basis. In the past, system administrators had no control over whether or not the software that gave users access to their computer created `utmp` entries, so it was difficult to get a consistent, accurate view of the users logged in. Now, with the SAF, administrators can decide for themselves which services result in `utmp` entries being created.

A port monitor is allowed to provide only one service per port (although that service can itself start other services), and only one port monitor can be monitoring a given port at a time. The same service, however, can be offered on many ports at the same time. A port monitor can monitor any number of ports it wants.

Each port monitor has two directories associated with it. First, the initial working directory in which it runs is /etc/saf/*pmtag*, where *pmtag* is the port monitor's tag in `_sactab`. This directory contains all the files required by the SAF framework, including the port monitor database file (`_pmtab`), the port monitor process ID lock file (`_pid`), the mounted stream or FIFO used by the port monitor to receive messages from the SAC (`_pmpipe`), the port monitor configuration script (`_config`), and any service-specific configuration scripts. The second directory is a private work area for the port monitor's implementation-dependent files, such as log files. It is named /var/saf/*pmtag*, where *pmtag* is the port monitor's tag in `_sactab`.

When the SAC starts a port monitor, two environment variables are initialized to direct the port monitor as to how it should act. The first of these is `ISTATE`. It contains a string indicating what the initial state of the port monitor should be. If the string is "enabled," then the port monitor should honor service requests. If the string is "disabled," then the port monitor should not honor service requests. In the latter case it can either ignore the requests or print an error message when requests arrive.

As far as the SAC is concerned, a port monitor is in one of six possible states.

In the ENABLED state, a port monitor is running and will accept requests for service. In contrast, in the DISABLED state, the port monitor is running but will not accept service requests. Between the time that the SAC starts a port monitor and the time the port monitor responds with its initial state, the port monitor is said to be in the STARTING state. Similarly, when a port monitor terminates, the time between the start of termination and its completion is called the STOPPING state.

If a port monitor encounters enough fatal errors during its execution to exceed its retry count, then the port monitor is placed in the FAILED state, from the perspective of the SAC. Port monitors that have the x flag in the _sactab are not started by the SAC and are said to be in the NOTRUNNING state. Port monitors that are killed by explicit request from the system administrator are also placed in the NOTRUNNING state. The states are important because port monitors must report their states to the SAC when requested, and they must be sure that no errors will occur from the execution of duplicate port monitors in the STARTING and STOPPING states.

The second environment variable is PMTAG. This contains the port monitor's tag from the _sactab database. The port monitor uses this string to build the pathnames of the directories where it will create its private files.

When a port monitor starts, it creates a file (/etc/saf/*pmtag*/_pid) containing the process ID of the port monitor and places an advisory record lock on the entire file. This prevents multiple port monitors from trying to manage the same ports.

The port monitor's database file is /etc/saf/*pmtag*/_pmtab. Obviously, no administrative framework can foresee the requirements of every user of that framework, so part of the database file is defined by the SAF, and part is defined by the port monitor. Two administrative commands are used to maintain the _pmtab. First, pmadm(1M) is used to administer the SAF-related portions of the file. Second, each port monitor must provide its own port-monitor-specific command to maintain the rest of the file.

Each line in the _pmtab database contains information about a different service supported by the port monitor. The first few fields of the line are defined by the SAF, and the remainder is defined by the port monitor. ttymon's port-monitor-specific command is ttyadm(1M). Like sacadm, the goal of these additional administrative commands is to insulate system administrators from the details of the database files.

Like sacadm, the pmadm command can be used to perform several administrative tasks. It can be used to add a service, remove a service, enable and disable a service, and list information about services. It can also be used to display and replace the configuration script associated with an individual service.

A service is identified by a string known as its *service tag*. Each per-service configuration script is named /etc/saf/*pmtag*/*svctag*, where *pmtag* is the port monitor tag and *svctag* is the tag for the individual service.

6.3 THE LISTENER PROCESS

The listener process implements a networking service available with UNIX System V that removes the burden of transport-level connection establishment from server applications. The listener runs as a port monitor under the SAF framework. The "ports" it monitors are transport endpoints.

When the listener starts, it reads its database file, _pmtab. For each address found, the listener creates a transport endpoint, binds the address to the endpoint, and listens for connect indications. When a connect indication arrives, the listener accepts it on a new transport endpoint and "starts" the service associated with the address. (In some cases the server is already running, so starting the service entails merely passing the network connection to the server.) The services "started" by the listener have two characteristics that determine how the network connection is created and received: the address type and the execution type.

Addresses can be *private* or *shared*. With private addresses, each service is associated with a unique address. The same service can be offered on multiple addresses, but an address can have only one service associated with it. Different services can share a single address, however, by acting as subservices to the NLPS service. (NLPS stands for *network listener protocol service*, so strictly speaking, the phrase "NLPS service" is redundant.) This might seem like a contradiction, but the NLPS service is the actual service associated with the address. The ultimate service invoked is determined by a protocol string received by the NLPS server. This is described in detail in Section 6.6.

The second characteristic is the execution type. A *one-shot* server is a server that is executed by the listener each time a connection is established. A one-shot server runs only as long as necessary to satisfy the service request, then exits. In contrast, a *standing* server runs continuously, and the listener passes it the network connection through a FIFO or mounted stream.

Recall that each port monitor must supply an administrative command to maintain the port-monitor-specific portion of its _pmtab file. For the listener, this command is nlsadmin(1M).

nlsadmin and the listener were introduced in UNIX System V Release 3.0. Because the service access facility was not introduced until SVR4, nlsadmin performed much of the work now done by pmadm. The command options that became redundant in SVR4 have been retained for compatibility. The primary role of nlsadmin in SVR4 is to print the listener-specific strings when adding services to the listener's _pmtab. We will see examples of its use in later sections.

6.4 ONE-SHOT SERVERS

The listener starts a one-shot server in the following manner. After a connection is established, the listener forks a child process to handle the service request. The listener process (the parent) then continues to listen for more connect indications. Meanwhile, the child process sets up its environment and execs the server.

When a server is started, it inherits its environment variables from the listener's environment. The listener explicitly modifies the server's environment in the following ways:

1. If the PATH environment variable does not have a value, the listener sets it to /usr/bin:/sbin:/usr/sbin:/etc. Otherwise, if PATH already has a value, then it is left unmodified. The value for PATH is inherited from the environment of the process that starts the listener (usually the SAC).

2. Places the ASCII hexadecimal representation of the client's address in the environment variable NLSADDR.

3. Places any options received in the connect indication in the environment variable NLSOPT, in ASCII hexadecimal format.

4. Places the transport provider's name in the environment variable NLSPROVIDER. The clone device node for the network is usually named /dev/$NLSPROVIDER.

5. Places the network's device name prefix in the environment variable MPREFIX. This tells servers to use the names /dev/"$MPREFIX"00, /dev/"$MPREFIX"01, etc., for the device nodes to access the network.

6. Places any user data sent with the connect indication in the environment variable NLSUDATA, in ASCII hexadecimal format.

7. Creates a utmp entry if so indicated by the _pmtab database file.

8. Duplicates file descriptors 0, 1, and 2 to the network connection.

9. Pushes any optional modules (specified through nlsadmin) on the network connection's stream. If there are modules to push and TIMOD is on top of the stream, then the listener pops TIMOD off the stream before pushing the modules.

10. Runs the commands listed in the optional per-service configuration file.

11. Sets the user and group IDs of the process based on the login name specified in the _pmtab.

12. Places the home directory associated with the login name in the environment variable HOME.

13. Changes the current working directory of the process to the server's home directory.

Example 6.4.1. The following program illustrates a simple server that depends on the network listener facility for establishing the network connection and initializing the stream to the proper state. The server can be used with cu(1) to provide a network-based remote login facility (see Figure 6.1).

The server depends on the listener to push three modules on the stream: NTE, TIRDWR, and LDTERM. NTE (network terminal emulator) makes the network stream seem like a terminal stream, supporting all the device-controlled portions of the terminal ioctl commands. This module is used as the example in Chapter 11. It is potentially network-specific, thus each network usually has to provide its own implementation of a module with NTE's functionality. TIRDWR, provided with SVR4, turns the TLI interface into a read/write interface. LDTERM is the standard terminal line discipline module provided with SVR4. It handles canonical

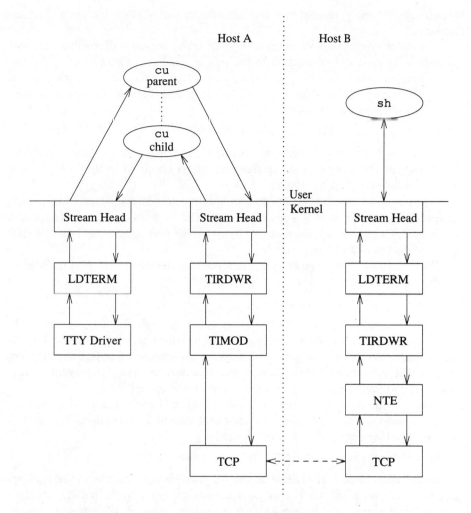

Fig. 6.1. cu over TCP

processing, recognition of special characters, and the device-independent parts of the terminal `ioctl` commands.

The server can be added with the following command:

```
pmadm -a -p <pmtag> -s netty -i root -v `nlsadmin -V` -fu \
    -m `nlsadmin -c/usr/net/netty -pnte,tirdwr,ldterm \
    -A <addr>`
```

where `<pmtag>` is the port monitor's tag, and `<addr>` is the private address the listener will use for the service. The `-s` option specifies the service tag; the `-i` option specifies the identity with which the server will run; the `-fu` option directs the listener to create a `utmp` entry for the service; and the `-m` option specifies the

listener-specific string, created by nlsadmin, to be placed in the listener's _pmtab
database.

On client machines, we need to change the uucp database files so that cu will
know how to go about connecting to the proper machine. First, an entry for the
server machine must be made in /etc/uucp/Systems. If, for example, the
machine's name is *oz*, its address is 192.102.88.4, and the *netty* service is on port
2766, the following entry would be needed:

```
oz Any TCP - \002\000\012\316\300\146\130\004 in:--in: nuucp word: <p>
```

where <p> is the clear text password for the nuucp login on the server machine.
The format of the Systems uucp database file is specified in the *SVR4 System
Administrator's Guide* [USL 1990c].

We can use uucp's octal notation to specify the address. Recall that a TCP
address is in the format of a sockaddr_in. The first two bytes are the address
family (AF_INET == 2), the next two bytes are the port number, and the last four
bytes are the Internet address.

There also needs to be an entry that describes the device to use. This is added to
/etc/uucp/Devices.

```
TCP,e tcp - - TLIS \D
```

This tells uucp that device TCP is accessible through the file system node
/dev/tcp, and that the device supports a TLI interface over STREAMS. The ,e
tells uucp to use its "e" protocol, which assumes a reliable, error-free transmission
channel that delivers data unduplicated and in sequence. The \D prevents uucp
from trying to translate the phone number token, if one is used.

One last file needs to be modified: /etc/uucp/Devconfig. This file tells
uucp how to configure the stream on the client side of a connection. We need to
add the following entry for cu to work properly:

```
service=cu   device=TCP   push=tirdwr
```

We do not need to push LDTERM on the cu side, because cu places the terminal
stream in raw mode and sends characters as they are typed to the remote machine,
where they are processed by the LDTERM module in the shell's network stream.
Thus, echoing is performed by the remote machine. If we were to push LDTERM on
the local side of the connection as well, then both LDTERM modules would attempt
echo processing, resulting in each character being printed twice.

Now that we have seen how to add the server, we will look at what it does.

```
/* netty.c */
#include <sys/types.h>
#include <sys/stat.h>
#include <sys/mkdev.h>
#include <unistd.h>
#include <stdlib.h>
#include <stdio.h>
#include <errno.h>
#include <string.h>
#include <fcntl.h>
```

```
#define DEVMODE   (S_IRUSR|S_IWUSR)
#define FATAL(s) { log((s), strerror(errno)); exit(1); }

extern int initlog(const char *);
extern void log(const char *, ...);

void
main()
{
    char *name;
    char devname[64];
    struct stat sbuf;
    dev_t dev;
    int fd;

    /*
     * Open the log file.
     */
    if (initlog("/var/tmp/netty.log") < 0)
        exit(1);

    /*
     * Find the device number of the standard input,
     * which is connected to the network stream.
     */
    if (fstat(0, &sbuf) < 0)
        FATAL("cannot stat stdin");

    /*
     * Get the transport provider's device name
     * prefix.
     */
    name = getenv("MPREFIX");
    if (name == NULL) {
        log("cannot find provider's device name");
        exit(1);
    }

    /*
     * Create the device filename corresponding to the
     * network connection.
     */
    dev = sbuf.st_rdev;
    sprintf(devname, "/dev/%s%03d", name, minor(dev));

    /*
     * If the device node is not there, try to create
     * it.  Otherwise, change the owner to the super-
     * user and make it accessible only by the owner.
     * login will change this later.
     */
    if (stat(devname, &sbuf) < 0) {
        if (mknod(devname, S_IFCHR|DEVMODE, dev) < 0)
            FATAL("cannot make node: %s");
```

```
      } else {
          if (chown(devname, 0, 0) < 0)
              FATAL("cannot change device ownership: %s");
          if (chmod(devname, DEVMODE) < 0)
              FATAL("cannot change device mode: %s");
      }

      /*
       * Now open the device node.
       */
      if ((fd = open(devname, O_RDWR)) < 0)
          FATAL("cannot open device: %s");

      /*
       * Close file descriptors 0, 1, and 2.  Since
       * we've just reopened the network device, the
       * connection will remain intact.
       */
      close(0);
      close(1);
      close(2);

      /*
       * Now make file descriptors 0, 1, and 2 into
       * copies of the file descriptor of the device node.
       * Then close the original fd open to the node.
       */
      if ((dup(fd) != 0) || (dup(fd) != 1) ||
        (dup(fd) != 2))
          FATAL("cannot set up file descriptors: %s");
      close(fd);

      /*
       * Finally exec login to complete the remote
       * login process.
       */
      execl("/usr/bin/login", "login", "-d", devname, NULL);
      FATAL("cannot exec login: %s");
  }
```

We first need to determine the device special file that can be used to access the same stream for the network connection, so we can tell login which device to open. Transport providers are accessed by the listener through clone device nodes. There might not be a separate node in the file system for each minor device. If so, we will have to create the node ourselves. Without the per-minor device nodes, functions like ttyname(3C) would not work.

We open a log file using the initlog function from Example 2.4.8. Since the server is started from the listener, file descriptors 0, 1, and 2 will refer to the stream for the network connection. We use fstat(2) to obtain the file statistics for the connection.

Next we use getenv(3C) to retrieve the MPREFIX environment variable. This tells us the prefix for the device name to use to access the stream. In this example, we assume the format of a device name is the prefix followed by three decimal digits representing the minor device number.

If we cannot `stat` the device node, we assume the file does not exist and we then attempt to create it using `mknod(2)`. If this does not work, we exit. If the node does exist, we change the ownership and permissions to make the stream inaccessible to unprivileged users. Since the stream is about to be used for password authentication during login, it would be a potential security breach if ordinary users could access the stream.

After verifying the existence of the device node, we open it and close file descriptors 0, 1, and 2. The reference to the stream by `fd` will prevent the device from being closed. Then we duplicate file descriptors 0, 1, and 2 to the newly opened file descriptor. This will enable functions like `ttyname(3C)` to identify the proper device node used for the login session.

There are usually many files under /dev, and `ttyname` will `stat` them all, one at a time, until it finds a node that matches the device number, file system identifier, and inode number of the file descriptor passed to it. File descriptors returned from clone opens are guaranteed to fail the inode number comparison, so `ttyname` will end up checking every file under the /dev subtree. If we make all the possible device nodes ahead of time, `ttyname` will eventually match on a node with only the same device number and file system identifier, but only after having performed a `stat` on every file under /dev.

There is another way to solve this problem: make all the device nodes in advance. Then modify /etc/ttysrch to specify the device nodes to `stat` first and to restrict the search criteria used by `ttyname` to ignore the inode number. See `ttysrch(4)` for details.

In this example, we make sure that an exact match will occur, so we do not have to rely on yet another administrative file. The duplicated file descriptors will have the same inode number, device number, and file system identifier as the device node residing in the file system.

After duplicating `fd`, there is no need to keep it open, so we close it. Finally, we `exec` the /usr/bin/login to complete the login process. We use the −d option to `login` to tell it the device node to use, so it can avoid calling `ttyname`. □

Two utility routines, defined below, are provided in /usr/lib/libnls.a to return connection information to one-shot servers.

```
#include <sys/tiuser.h>

char *nlsprovider(void);
struct t_call *nlsgetcall(int fd);
```

The first function, `nlsprovider`, returns a pointer to a string indicating the name of the transport provider over which the connection has been made. The second function, `nlsgetcall`, returns a pointer to a `t_call` structure (see Section 4.4) containing all the information obtained from the `t_listen` call made by the listener. This function can be used to access any user data or options sent by the client with the connect request. The information is converted from the ASCII hexadecimal representation in which it is stored in the environment back into the binary format in which it was originally received.

If a one-shot server uses a private address, then client processes can connect to the server in the same way as if the server were handling the connection establishment itself. In other words, a client application has no way of knowing whether a given service is listening on its own behalf, or using the listener instead. As it turns out, there is not any need for clients to know if a connection is created by the listener for a server that uses a private address.

Furthermore, the network-selection and name-to-address translation facilities described in Chapter 5 can be used by client applications connecting to servers via the listener process, as long as the servers use private addresses. In Section 6.6, we shall see how servers can share addresses under the NLPS service and how this affects client applications. First, however, we will look at standing servers.

6.5 STANDING SERVERS

A one-shot server executes only as long as is necessary to perform its task, and then it exits. In contrast, standing servers are independent server processes that run for long periods of time, exceeding the length of a single network connection. Standing servers can be designed to use fewer resources than multiple concurrent one-shot servers. Standing servers are useful for applications that require data collection over periods of time, because the server can be designed to handle both the data collection and the network communication.

Standing servers, unlike one-shot servers, are not started by the listener. They are started in implementation-defined ways, such as through /etc/inittab or an initialization script residing in /etc/rc2.d. Instead of prompting the creation of a new instance of a server, each connection is passed through a mounted pipe or FIFO to the server. The server can choose whether to handle the request itself (iteratively) or to fork and let a child process handle it (concurrently).

Because the listener and standing server are unrelated processes, the only way the listener can affect the server's environment is by changing the state of the stream passed to the server. Before passing a file descriptor to the server, the listener performs the following actions:

1. Pushes any optional modules (specified through nlsadmin) on the network connection's stream. If there are modules to push and TIMOD is on top of the stream, then the listener pops TIMOD off the stream before pushing the modules.
2. Runs the commands listed in the optional per-service configuration file. doconfig is called with the NOASSIGN and NORUN flags, so the only operations that can be performed are pushing and popping modules. The assign command is disallowed because, if executed, it would affect the environment of the listener instead of the environment of the server. The run and runwait commands are disallowed because the shell built-in commands that they can execute will change the listener's environment, and the runwait command

could potentially block the listener indefinitely, denying service to other users.

Example 6.5.1. The following is an example of a standing server. The server can be added using the command

```
pmadm -a -p <pmtag> -s mond -i root -v `nlsadmin -V` \
    -m `nlsadmin -o/var/.monpipe -A <addr>`
```

where `<pmtag>` is the port monitor's tag, and `<addr>` is the private address the listener will use for the service. The $-o$ option specifies the name of the mounted pipe or FIFO through which the server will receive file descriptors.

The `mond` service provides clients with information about system performance. Thus clients can monitor remote machines to see what kinds of loads each is incurring. Every 30 seconds the server sends 4 bytes to each client. The data represent the percentages of time spent active at user level, active at system (kernel) level, waiting for disk I/O, and idle, respectively, during the last time interval. Clients can use this information any way they choose.

The example is long, so it is presented in small fragments.

```
/* mond.c */
#include <sys/types.h>
#include <sys/stropts.h>
#include <sys/sysinfo.h>
#include <sys/poll.h>
#include <sys/stat.h>
#include <unistd.h>
#include <stdlib.h>
#include <string.h>
#include <errno.h>
#include <fcntl.h>
#include <nlist.h>
#include <signal.h>

#define DELAY     30   /* delay between samples */
#define NFD       16   /* grow pollfd array in NFD units */
#define PIPENAME  "/var/.monpipe"
#define PIPEMODE  (S_IRUSR|S_IWUSR)
#define ELOG(s)   log((s), strerror(errno))
#define FATAL(s)  { ELOG(s); exit(1); }

static struct pollfd *pfd;
static struct pollfd ppfd;
static int fd, nfd, maxfd, memfd;
static int pipefd[2];
static time_t cpu1[4];
static time_t cpu2[4];
static float tot1, tot2;
static char *kmem = "/dev/kmem";
static char *adotout = "/unix";
static struct nlist list[] = {
    { "sysinfo", 0, 0, 0, 0, 0 },
    { "", 0, 0, 0, 0, 0 }
```

```
};

static void addclient(void), rmvclient(int);
static int moreclients(void);
static void sigpoll(int), sigalrm(int);
static void gettimes(uchar_t *, uchar_t *, uchar_t *,
    uchar_t *);

extern void log(const char *, ...);
extern void daemonize(const char *);
```

The delay time (DELAY) between snapshots of the system performance is defined to be 30 seconds. pfd points to an array of pollfd structures. As client file descriptors are received from the listener, they are added to the pfd array. When the array fills, it is increased by NFD more entries.

We use the file named /var/.monpipe to mount the pipe over which we will receive file descriptors from the listener. The ppfd variable is the pollfd structure for the unmounted end of the pipe.

We use the nlist structure [see nlist(3E)] to define the kernel symbol we will be reading through /dev/kmem, the device special file that gives privileged users access to the kernel's memory image. Thus, the mond daemon must run as the super-user. The symbol sysinfo represents a data structure (defined in <sys/sysinfo.h>) that contains system statistics, including the number of clock ticks spent during each task. No system call provides this information, so we are reduced to reading the kernel's memory image to find it. This is strictly nonportable.

```
void
main()
{
    struct stat sbuf;
    struct sigaction sa;

    /*
     * Become a daemon.
     */
    daemonize("mond");

    /*
     * Find the kernel symbol we need.
     */
    if (nlist(adotout, list) < 0)
        FATAL("cannot get namelist: %s");

    /*
     * Open the kernel memory image and seek to
     * the symbol's address.
     */
    if ((memfd = open(kmem, O_RDONLY)) < 0)
        FATAL("cannot open kernel memory: %s");
    if (lseek(memfd, list[0].n_value, SEEK_SET) == -1)
        FATAL("lseek failed: %s");
```

```
    /*
     * Read only the first four entries in the structure.
     */
    if (read(fd, &cpu1, sizeof(cpu1)) != sizeof(cpu1))
        FATAL("read of kernel memory failed: %s");

    /*
     * Calculate the total CPU time.
     */
    tot1 = cpu1[CPU_USER] + cpu1[CPU_KERNEL] +
      cpu1[CPU_WAIT] + cpu1[CPU_IDLE];

    /*
     * If the rendezvous point doesn't exist, create
     * it.  Otherwise, make sure that another copy of
     * mond isn't already running.
     */
    if (stat(PIPENAME, &sbuf) < 0) {
        close(creat(PIPENAME, PIPEMODE));
    } else {
        if (S_ISFIFO(sbuf.st_mode)) {
            log("mon process already running");
            exit(1);
        }
    }

    /*
     * Allocate the initial pollfd array.
     */
    maxfd = NFD;
    pfd = malloc(maxfd * sizeof(struct pollfd));
    if (pfd == NULL)
        FATAL("cannot allocate pollfd array: %s");
```

The first thing we do is become a daemon. Then we use nlist(3E) to find the address of the symbol sysinfo. If found, we open /dev/kmem for reading, seek to the specified address, and read the first four long integers. According to <sys/sysinfo.h>, these are the counters we are interested in reading. It would waste our time to read the entire structure.

Next we stat the file on which we will mount the pipe. If stat fails, we create the pipe and immediately close the file descriptor returned. We do not need to check if creat(2) fails, because we will find out soon enough and exit then. If the stat succeeds, we know the file exists, so we check its type. If it is a pipe, then we know another occurrence of mond is running, so we exit. Otherwise, the file has been left over from a previous execution of the server.

Then we set the maximum number of file descriptors to its initial value and allocate the memory for the pollfd array.

```
    /*
     * Create the pipe for the rendezvous point.
     */
    if (pipe(pipefd) < 0)
```

```
        FATAL("cannot create pipe: %s");

    /*
     * Save one end of the pipe for receiving poll events
     * and mount the other end in the file system.
     */
    ppfd.fd = pipefd[0];
    ppfd.events = POLLIN;
    if (fattach(pipefd[1], PIPENAME) < 0) {
        log("cannot attach pipe to %s: %s", PIPENAME,
            strerror(errno));
        exit(1);
    }

    /*
     * Install signal handlers for SIGPOLL and SIGALRM.
     * Block each signal inside the handlers.
     */
    sigemptyset(&sa.sa_mask);
    sigaddset(&sa.sa_mask, SIGPOLL);
    sigaddset(&sa.sa_mask, SIGALRM);
    sa.sa_handler = sigalrm;
    sa.sa_flags = 0;
    if (sigaction(SIGALRM, &sa, NULL) < 0)
        FATAL("cannot install handler for SIGALRM: %s");
    sa.sa_handler = sigpoll;
    if (sigaction(SIGPOLL, &sa, NULL) < 0)
        FATAL("cannot install handler for SIGPOLL: %s");

    /*
     * Register to receive SIGPOLL from the pipe.
     */
    if (ioctl(pipefd[0], I_SETSIG, S_INPUT) < 0)
        FATAL("cannot I_SETSIG on pipe: %s");

    /*
     * It's not pretty, but all processing is
     * done in the signal handlers.  This is the
     * only place where SIGPOLL and SIGALRM can
     * interrupt the processing.
     */
    for (;;) {
        pause();
    }
}
```

Continuing with the main procedure, we create the pipe to be used to receive file descriptors from the listener and set up the pollfd structure for the end of the pipe we will be using. The other end (pipefd[1]) is mounted on /var/.monpipe when we call fattach(3C).

Then we set up signal handlers for SIGALRM and SIGPOLL, making sure to block both signals when we are in either handler. We will use SIGPOLL to tell us two things. First, when a file descriptor arrives from the listener, we will have the pipe's stream head notify us with `SIGPOLL`. Second, when a client goes away, we will arrange for the network connection's stream head to inform us by generating `SIGPOLL`. Since we can get `SIGPOLL` from multiple streams, we will have to use `poll(2)` to sort things out.

The last thing we do before entering an infinite loop is to request that the pipe's stream head send us `SIGPOLL` for all input events. The remainder of the processing is done in the signal handlers.

We will use `addclient` to add a file descriptor to the `pollfd` array when the listener passes us a new network connection.

```
static void
addclient(void)
{
        struct strrecvfd recv;
        int fl;

        /*
         * Receive a file descriptor from the listener.
         * If it fails, flush the read side of the pipe.
         */
        if (ioctl(pipefd[0], I_RECVFD, &recv) < 0) {
            ioctl(pipefd[0], I_FLUSH, FLUSHR);
            return;
        }

        /*
         * Register to receive SIGPOLL for input events
         * on the stream.
         */
        if (ioctl(recv.fd, I_SETSIG, S_INPUT) < 0) {
            ELOG("cannot I_SETSIG on fd: %s");
            close(recv.fd);
            return;
        }

        /*
         * Get the file flags and place the stream in
         * nonblocking mode.
         */
        if ((fl = fcntl(recv.fd, F_GETFL, 0)) < 0) {
            ELOG("cannot get file flags on fd: %s");
            close(recv.fd);
            return;
        }
        fl = (fl & ~O_NDELAY) | O_NONBLOCK;
        if (fcntl(recv.fd, F_SETFL, fl) < 0) {
            ELOG("cannot set file flags on fd: %s");
            close(recv.fd);
            return;
        }

        /*
         * If no entries are available in the array, try
```

```
            * to extend the array.
            */
           if ((nfd == maxfd) && (moreclients() < 0)) {
               ELOG("cannot grow pollfd array: %s");
               close(recv.fd);
               return;
           }

           /*
            * Add the file descriptor to the pollfd array and
            * increment the number of array entries.  If this
            * is the only entry in the array, set an alarm.
            */
           pfd[nfd].fd = recv.fd;
           pfd[nfd].events = POLLIN;
           nfd++;
           if (nfd == 1)
               alarm(DELAY);
       }
```

We start by trying to receive the file descriptor over the pipe. If this fails, we flush the read side of the pipe and return. This ensures that unscrupulous users will not be able to prevent us from performing our task if they should manage to write data to the pipe using the mounted end. (Any program that runs as the super-user and produces output could be redirected to write to the pipe.)

If the file descriptor is received successfully, we enable input event notification on it and place it in nonblocking mode. By using nonblocking mode, we can avoid blocking when writing to a client that is not reading its data. The amount of data we are writing is small with respect to the time intervals between which it is written, so the client applications should be able to keep up. We want to protect against a malicious user connecting to the mond service and causing the daemon to block indefinitely.

After we prepare the file descriptor, if we discover there is no room for it in the array, we call moreclients to enlarge the array. If we cannot increase the size of the array, we close the file descriptor just received and return. Otherwise, we add the file descriptor to the next available entry in the pollfd array, set its events field to POLLIN, and increment the number of valid entries in the array. If this number equals 1, then the first client has been received, so we start an alarm to generate SIGALRM in DELAY seconds.

We use moreclients to grow the pollfd array.

```
static int
moreclients(void)
{
       struct pollfd *newpfd;
       int n;

       /*
        * Calculate the new size of the array and
        * try to allocate new memory.
        */
```

```
        n = maxfd + NFD;
        newpfd = realloc(pfd, n*sizeof(struct pollfd));
        if (newpfd == NULL)
            return(-1);

        /*
         * Save the new address of the pollfd array
         * and the new maximum number of entries.
         */
        pfd = newpfd;
        maxfd = n;
        return(0);
}
```

We calculate the new size of the array and call `realloc(3C)` to allocate more memory, copy the contents of the old memory to the new, and free the old memory. If this fails, the old memory remains intact, and we return an indication of failure. Otherwise, we set the pointer to the array to the new memory location, set the maximum number of entries in the array to the new value, and return success.

The `rmvclient` function is called when we receive an event associated with a client's network connection.

```
static void
rmvclient(int idx)
{
        /*
         * Generate a disconnect, just to be sure
         * the connection gets cleaned up.
         */
        t_snddis(pfd[idx].fd, NULL);

        /*
         * Close the network connection.
         */
        t_close(pfd[idx].fd);

        /*
         * Copy the last element in the array into
         * the position of the defunct connection and
         * decrease the count of the number of entries
         * in the array.
         */
        pfd[idx].fd = pfd[nfd-1].fd;
        nfd--;
}
```

We send a disconnect, close the file, and remove the entry from the array. To remove the entry, we copy the last valid entry to the entry being deleted and decrease the number of valid entries in the array.

`sigalrm` is called when we receive `SIGALRM`. In it, we take another snapshot of the system's times and send the data to the clients.

```
static void
```

```
sigalrm(int sig)
{
    int i;
    uchar_t cusr, csys, cwio, cidle;

    /*
     * No clients -- do nothing.
     */
    if (nfd == 0)
        return;

    /*
     * Get the system's time percentages.
     */
    gettimes(&cusr, &csys, &cwio, &cidle);

    /*
     * Send each percentage to the client.
     */
    for (i = 0; i < nfd; i++) {
        write(pfd[i].fd, &cusr, 1);
        write(pfd[i].fd, &csys, 1);
        write(pfd[i].fd, &cwio, 1);
        write(pfd[i].fd, &cidle, 1);
    }

    /*
     * Reinstall the alarm.
     */
    alarm(DELAY);
}
```

If there are no clients, there is nothing to do, so we just return. Otherwise, we call gettimes to calculate the time percentages. Then, for each client, we write the percentages of user, system, wait-I/O, and idle times on the network connection. (As long as a zero-length message is not written, write(2) is a valid operation on a transport endpoint, even if TIRDWR is not present.) Finally, we set the alarm to go off again in another DELAY seconds.

sigpoll is called when one of the streams has an event outstanding and generates SIGPOLL.

```
static void
sigpoll(int sig)
{
    int i;

    /*
     * Service the listener as long as it is sending
     * us file descriptors.
     */
    while (poll(&ppfd, 1, 0) == 1) {
        if (ppfd.revents == POLLIN) {
            addclient();
```

```
        } else {
            log("poll on pipe, revents %d", ppfd.revents);
            exit(1);
        }
    }

    /*
     * Now check if any of the clients have gone away.
     * rmvclient will pack the array by shifting the
     * last valid entry into a deleted slot, so we need
     * to check entry "i" again if we remove an entry.
     */
    while (poll(pfd, nfd, 0) > 0) {
        for (i = 0; i < nfd; i++)
            if (pfd[i].revents != 0)
                rmvclient(i--);
    }
}
```

We can receive SIGPOLL for two reasons: addition and removal of clients. We check the pipe for events first. While there is a pollable read event on the pipe, we call addclient to receive the file descriptor. If an event other than POLLIN is returned, we treat it as an error and exit.

When there are no more events pending on the pipe, we poll the network connections for readable events. We do not expect client applications to write to us, so the only valid readable events should be a disconnect indication or an orderly release indication. Regardless, if an event is found, we call rmvclient to tear down the connection, close the file descriptor, and remove the entry from the array.

The gettimes function is used to calculate the percentages of time spent in the system. We call it with the previous values stored in cpu1[] and tot1.

```
static void
gettimes(uchar_t *up, uchar_t *sp, uchar_t *wp, uchar_t *ip)
{
    float deltat;
    int usr, sys, wio, idle;

    /*
     * Seek to the beginning of the sysinfo structure.
     */
    if (lseek(memfd, list[0].n_value, SEEK_SET) == -1)
        FATAL("lseek failed: %s");

    /*
     * Read only the first four entries in the structure.
     */
    if (read(memfd, &cpu2, sizeof(cpu2)) != sizeof(cpu2))
        FATAL("read of kernel memory failed: %s");

    /*
     * Calculate the new total CPU time.
     */
    tot2 = cpu2[CPU_USER] + cpu2[CPU_KERNEL] +
```

```
        cpu2[CPU_WAIT] + cpu2[CPU_IDLE];

    /*
     * Calculate the difference between the current
     * and previous totals.
     */
    deltat = tot2 - tot1;

    /*
     * Calculate the percentages, rounding up and
     * converting to integers.
     */
    usr = (cpu2[CPU_USER]-cpu1[CPU_USER])/deltat*100.+
        0.5;
    sys = (cpu2[CPU_KERNEL]-cpu1[CPU_KERNEL])/deltat*100.+
        0.5;
    wio = (cpu2[CPU_WAIT]-cpu1[CPU_WAIT])/deltat*100.+
        0.5;
    idle = (cpu2[CPU_IDLE]-cpu1[CPU_IDLE])/deltat*100.+
        0.5;

    /*
     * Save the current values in the previous slots.
     */
    tot1 = tot2;
    cpu1[CPU_USER] = cpu2[CPU_USER];
    cpu1[CPU_KERNEL] = cpu2[CPU_KERNEL];
    cpu1[CPU_WAIT] = cpu2[CPU_WAIT];
    cpu1[CPU_IDLE] = cpu2[CPU_IDLE];

    /*
     * Return the percentages.
     */
    *up = (uchar_t)usr;
    *sp = (uchar_t)sys;
    *wp = (uchar_t)wio;
    *ip = (uchar_t)idle;
}
```

First, we seek to the start of the `sysinfo` structure and read the new values. Then we calculate the total number of clock ticks returned by this snapshot. The difference between `tot2` and `tot1` is the number of clock ticks that occurred between the two snapshots. Each time percentage is calculated as the difference in the number of clock ticks attributed to the type of processing, divided by the total number of clock ticks in the interval, times 100. We round up if the fractional part of the percentage is 0.5 or greater. Note that this type of rounding can lead to the sum of the percentages exceeding 100.

Next we set the `cpu1` and `tot1` values to those obtained during this snapshot, so the next set of percentages can be calculated relative to the current times. Finally, we store the percentages of user time, system time, wait-I/O time, and idle time in the parameters passed to the function and return. Note that we report integer values for simplicity. Since no value will exceed 100, a percentage fits in one byte,

avoiding the need to worry about a network of computers with heterogeneous architectures.   □

Like one-shot servers, if a standing server uses a private address, then client
processes can connect to the server in the same way as if the server were handling the
connection establishment itself. Both the network-selection and name-to-address
translation facilities can be used by client applications to identify and connect to the
server, as long as the server uses a private address. In the next section, we will see
how sharing an address under the NLPS server complicates the coding of client-side
connection establishment.

6.6 THE NLPS SERVER

The NLPS server in a one-shot server that allows multiple services to share the same
address used for connection establishment. Since port monitors only allow one service per port, and a port can only have one address associated with it, the NLPS
server is the service associated with the address and port. Once started, the NLPS
server reads a protocol message from the network connection to determine the actual
service to invoke.

Any service provided through the NLPS server is really a subservice (the NLPS
service is the primary service). As such, subservices do not have addresses associated with their entry in the listener's `_pmtab`. Thus, the `-A` option to `nlsadmin` is
never used when adding a subservice. (Of course, a subservice can also be made
available as a primary service at the same time by using a private address.)

The NLPS server supports both one-shot and standing subservers. The environment of a one-shot subserver is initialized in the same way as the listener does for
one-shot servers. The same goes for standing servers, except that `run` and
`runwait` commands are allowed since the NLPS server simply exits after passing
the file descriptor to the standing server.

The disadvantage of using the NLPS service is that it changes the way client
applications must ask for services. After connecting to the listener, client applications must send a protocol message to the NLPS server to identify the subservice to
invoke. The protocol message has the form

> `NLPS:`*low*`:`*high*`:`*svc_code*`\0`

where *low* is a 3-digit version number representing the lowest version of the protocol
understood by the client, *high* is a 3-digit version number representing the highest
version of the protocol understood by the client, and *svc_code* is a string of at most
14 characters that uniquely identifies the subservice. Legal characters for the service
code are letters (a–z and A–Z), digits (0–9), and the underscore (_).

The protocol message must be `NULL`-terminated. Two protocol versions are
supported. One (version 0) just starts the service after receiving the request. The
other (version 2) does the same thing as version 0, but sends a response message
back to the client in the form

vernum : *msgcode* : *string*

where *vernum* is the protocol version being used, *msgcode* is a code (defined in
`<listen.h>`) that defines the status of the service request, and *string* is a message
suitable for printing that also indicates the status of the service request.

On success, the response message is useless because, after the service is
invoked, something can still go wrong that will result in the service request ultimately failing. On the other hand, if the service code is unknown or if the service is
disabled, the messages provide more information than if the connection were simply
dropped by the NLPS server.

Four strings are defined in `<listen.h>` for applications to use when creating
the NLPS protocol message. They are summarized in Table 6.1.

Table 6.1. NLPS Protocol Strings

String Name	Description
nls_v0_d	Protocol version 0 and decimal service codes
nls_v0_s	Protocol version 0 and string service codes
nls_v2_d	Protocol version 2 and decimal service codes
nls_v2_s	Protocol version 2 and string service codes

One function is provided in `/usr/lib/libnls.a` to send a protocol
version 2 message and receive the response. It is `nlsrequest(3N)`:

```
#include <listen.h>

extern int    _nlslog;
extern char   *_nlsrmsg;

int nlsrequest(int fd, char *svc_code);
```

`fd` is the client's file descriptor for the network connection, and `svc_code` is a
pointer to the string representing the service code. Initially, `_nlslog` is set to zero.
If the caller sets `_nlslog` to a nonzero value, then `nlsrequest` will print error
messages on the standard error. A pointer to the *string* portion of the message
received from the NLPS server is stored in `_nlsrmsg`. The message itself is stored
in a `static` buffer whose contents are overwritten with each call to `nlsrequest`.

If a local error occurs, `nlsrequest` returns −1. Otherwise, the return value
corresponds to the *msgcode* in the NLPS server's response message. Possible values,
defined in `<listen.h>`, are `NLSSTART` to indicate the service was started,
`NLSFORMAT` to indicate the request message format was incorrect, `NLSUNKNOWN` to
indicate the service code was unknown, and `NLSDISABLED` to indicate the service
was disabled.

Example 6.6.1. Assuming we do not care about the response message, the following
function uses protocol version 0 to request a subservice from the NLPS server.

```
#include <sys/types.h>
#include <stdio.h>
```

```
#include <string.h>
#include <errno.h>
#include <tiuser.h>
#include <listen.h>

extern int conn(char *, char *);

int
nlps_conn(char *host, char *service)
{
    int fd, len;
    char buf[64];

    /*
     * Check for invalid service code.
     */
    if (!service ||
      (strlen(service) > (size_t)SVC_CODE_SZ)) {
        errno = EINVAL;
        return(-1);
    }

    /*
     * Connect to the listener (see Example 5.3.1).
     */
    if ((fd = conn(host, "listen")) < 0)
        return(-1);

    /*
     * Create and send the NLPS protocol message.
     * Be sure to transmit the terminating NULL byte.
     */
    len = sprintf(buf, nls_v0_s, service) + 1;
    if (t_snd(fd, buf, len, 0) != len) {
        t_close(fd);
        return(-1);
    }

    /*
     * The service should now be available.
     */
    return(fd);
}
```

This example assumes the listener is registered in the network's name-to-address translation database files as service listen.

First, we validate that the service code is within the proper length limits. If so, we connect to the listener using the conn function from Example 5.3.1. Then we create a protocol version 0 message in buf and send it to the NLPS server using t_snd(3N). Note that the number of bytes sent includes the NULL byte at the end of the message.

On success, we return the file descriptor for the network connection to the requested server. On failure, we return −1.   □

The previous example illustrates the difference between connecting to a primary service using a private address and connecting to a secondary service sharing an address under the NLPS service. The drawback in the latter case is that the client must be aware that the server is operating under the NLPS service to create a connection to the server.

The NLPS server exists primarily to maintain compatibility with previous versions of the network listener facility. It does provide the advantage, however, of making the maximum number of services independent of the number of ports supported by the network.

Summary

The service access facility provides a uniform environment for the execution and administration of servers that give users access to a computer's resources. These servers are called port monitors. The network listener process is a port monitor that can perform connection establishment on behalf of other servers. Two kinds of servers — one-shot servers and standing servers — can be used with the network listener facility. One-shot servers are executed by the listener to handle a single service request. Standing servers are independent of the listener. They receive the network connection from the listener through a mounted pipe or FIFO. The NLPS service can be used to provide a common service through which other services are provided.

Exercises

6.1 Modify Example 6.4.1 to check for the required modules and add them if they are not present. Do the same for the utmp entry. Provide a rationale for performing these tasks in the server instead of relying on the listener to handle them.

6.2 Propose an alternate design for Example 6.5.1 that does away with the reliance on SIGPOLL. What kinds of problems arise with SIGALRM handling?

6.3 Example 4.4.6 illustrates a function that can be used in a server to provide a simple remote execution facility. Integrate that function into a server that can be used with the network listener facility.

6.4 Now take the result from Exercise 6.3 and implement the server as a single shell script. Show the command you would use to add the server to the listener's _pmtab database.

6.5 Example 6.5.1 is not very portable because it reads kernel data structures directly. Explain how you could redesign the server to use sar(1M). What problems are presented by this approach?

Bibliographic Notes

The network listener facility was first included in UNIX System V Release 3.0. It originally consisted of the NLPS server only. Support for standing servers and servers with private addresses was added in UNIX System V Release 4.0.

Sample port monitor code is provided in Chapter 13 of the *SVR4 Programmer's Guide: Networking Interfaces* [USL 1990d].

The *SVR4 System Administrator's Guide* [USL 1990c] contains information on configuring the uucp database files. uucp administration is also discussed by Nowitz [1990] and O'Reilly and Todino [1989].

7

Sockets

The socket interface that originated in the BSD UNIX operating system is also provided in System V Release 4. This allows the many applications written to the socket interface to be ported, relatively easily, to SVR4-based systems. This chapter presents the socket interface, comparing it to the Transport Layer Interface (TLI) and describing the deviations from the BSD implementation.

7.1 INTRODUCTION

The socket mechanism first appeared in the 4.1c release of the BSD UNIX operating system, circa 1982. Sockets became widely used with the 4.2 release shortly thereafter. The socket interface was refined and enhanced in the 4.3BSD release in 1986. The interface was enhanced again in the 4.3BSD Reno release in 1990. In it, the structure of a socket address changed slightly (the two-byte protocol family field was split up into a one-byte length field and a one-byte protocol family field). Several other changes were made to support ISO protocols.

The socket interface proposed as part of the POSIX P1003.12 Protocol Independent Interface standard is based on the 4.3BSD Reno socket implementation. The socket interface provided in SVR4 is based on the original 4.3BSD implementation. Throughout this chapter we use the term 4BSD to refer to the family of 4.xBSD UNIX operating system versions.

Sockets were designed to provide a consistent communication facility for processes, regardless of whether or not the processes are on the same machine. In addition, sockets were designed to hide as much detail as possible about how the underlying communication occurs.

Figure 7.1 shows the architecture of the socket mechanism in 4BSD. Applications make system calls that are handled by the socket layer. The socket layer translates a file descriptor to a socket and invokes a routine in the protocol layer to service the call. The socket data structure is shared between the socket layer and the protocol layer. The protocol layer itself may contain several protocols corresponding to different layers in the OSI reference model. Finally, the protocol layer communicates with the network driver to send and receive packets to and from the network.

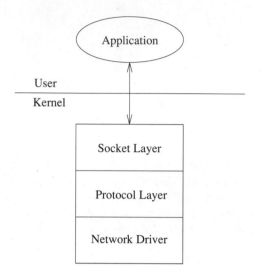

Fig. 7.1. The Socket Architecture in 4BSD

As far as an application program is concerned, the socket mechanism is analogous to the TLI. From the communication protocol's perspective, however, the socket mechanism is similar to STREAMS. In the BSD UNIX operating system, network protocols are implemented in the socket framework, while in the System V UNIX operating system, network protocols are implemented in the framework provided by STREAMS.

To avoid requiring two implementations of each communication protocol in SVR4, the socket mechanism is implemented in the STREAMS framework (see Figure 7.2). A user-level library provides the socket calls, some of which were originally implemented as system calls in 4BSD. Using `read(2)`, `write(2)`, `getmsg(2)`, `putmsg(2)`, and `ioctl(2)`, the library routines interact with a stream that has a module called SOCKMOD on top of it. The role of SOCKMOD is to help provide socket semantics on the stream and convert the Transport Provider Interface (TPI) exported by the communication protocols to an internal service interface between SOCKMOD and the socket library.

As we shall see, in some cases this implementation has the undesirable effect of providing different semantics from those found in the 4BSD implementation. Usually these differences are minor, but we shall point them out as we cover each socket call.

The original implementation of sockets in SVR4 was meant to provide source-code compatibility for applications that used sockets. Since then, other implementations of the socket interface have been designed to support binary compatibility with

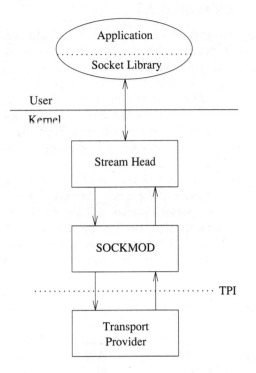

Fig. 7.2. The Socket Architecture in SVR4

existing applications on particular architectures. (For example, System V Release 4 Version 4 for the Intel 80x86 architecture includes an additional socket interface to support binary compatibility with SCO UNIX applications.) These later implementations export an interface based on system calls instead of a user-level library. Since these additional implementations are meant only for binary compatibility and do not replace the library-based implementation, we will discuss only the original library-based one.

To include the socket library in a program, the -lsocket and -lnsl flags must be used. If the program is being ported from 4BSD, the BSD compatibility library should be used to provide the BSD functions. More importantly, the BSD compatibility library contains the BSD-style signal interfaces. Applications using signal(2) in 4BSD will break in subtle ways when ported to SVR4 unless linked with the BSD compatibility library. In summary, if sockprog.c is a System V application that uses sockets and bsd_sockprog.c is a BSD socket application, the two programs can be compiled as follows:

```
cc sockprog.c -lsocket -lnsl
cc bsd_sockprog.c -L/usr/ucblib -lsocket -lnsl -lucb
```

The -L option directs the link editor to look in the specified directory for additional libraries. The BSD compatibility library is located in /usr/ucblib.

7.2 SOCKET MANAGEMENT

A *socket* is an abstraction used as a communication endpoint, similar to the transport endpoint discussed in Chapter 4. It is implemented as a file descriptor with some state information stored in the socket library.

Each socket is associated with a *communication domain* when it is created. Communication domains are logical groupings of protocols based on similar communication and naming conventions. Two common communication domains are implemented: the UNIX domain and the Internet domain. The UNIX domain contains facilities used for interprocess communication within the boundaries of a single machine.

The Internet domain contains the protocols originally developed under the sponsorship of the Defense Advanced Research Projects Agency (DARPA). These include the Transmission Control Protocol (TCP), the User Datagram Protocol (UDP), the Internet Protocol (IP), and the Internet Control Message Protocol (ICMP). Other protocols belong to this family, but these are the only ones available through the socket interface. (The Internet family of protocols is often referred to as simply "TCP/IP.")

Each socket has an associated type that determines the semantics of the communication. Stream sockets (SOCK_STREAM), not to be confused with the standard I/O file streams or the streams found in the STREAMS subsystem, provide connection-oriented byte streams. Data are transmitted in sequence and are delivered reliably without duplication. Because the sockets are byte streams, the underlying protocols do not maintain the concept of message boundaries. Datagram sockets (SOCK_DGRAM), on the other hand, support unreliable, connectionless, message-based communication.

Raw sockets (SOCK_RAW) provide direct access to a protocol for building administrative tools and layered protocols at user level. Sequenced packet sockets (SOCK_SEQPACKET) are like stream sockets, but maintain the notion of message boundaries. Finally, reliably delivered message sockets (SOCK_RDM) provide a reliable, connectionless communication facility.

Stream and datagram sockets are the most commonly used types of sockets. By default in the Internet domain, stream sockets use the TCP protocol and datagram sockets use the UDP protocol. A socket is created using the socket(3N) library routine:

```
#include <sys/types.h>
#include <sys/socket.h>

int socket(int family, int type, int protocol);
```

where family identifies the communication domain, type indicates the type of the socket, and protocol selects the particular protocol to use. On success, socket returns a file descriptor that represents the socket endpoint. On failure, socket returns −1 with errno set to indicate the reason for failure.

The communication domain is characterized by two constants: the address family and the protocol family. The address family groups protocols with similar address formats, and the protocol family groups protocols that share the same network architecture. While logically different, the address family and protocol family are treated identically. The value of the protocol family identifier for the UNIX domain (PF_UNIX) is equal to the value of its address family identifier (AF_UNIX). Similarly, the value of the protocol family identifier for the Internet domain (PF_INET) is equal to the value of the Internet domain's address family identifier (AF_INET). Thus, either family identifier can be used as the family argument.

The only socket types currently implemented in SVR4 are SOCK_STREAM, SOCK_DGRAM, and SOCK_RAW, although adding support for others is simply a matter of adding the correct definitions to <sys/netconfig.h> and recompiling the network services library. (Simple, that is, if you have the source code handy.)

The protocol parameter is usually set to 0 to choose the default protocol for the family and type. The caller can set the protocol parameter to an integer that represents a specific protocol, however. The only values currently supported are IPPROTO_ICMP, IPPROTO_TCP, and IPPROTO_UDP. They are defined in <netinet/in.h>.

To use protocol families other than the ones previously mentioned, two steps must be taken. First, the caller must pass in the family identifier corresponding to the protocol family to be used. Second, the /etc/netconfig database (described in Section 5.2) must be modified to include the protocol family string listed in Table 7.1.

Once a socket is created, an address must be associated with it so that the socket can be used for communication. Usually only a server needs to bind an address explicitly. Most of the time client processes can skip this step because the socket routines will automatically bind an arbitrary (unique) address to an unbound socket when presented with one.

One exception to this is a UNIX domain socket in 4BSD. As we shall see in Section 7.5, a UNIX domain socket's address appears in the file system namespace as a file. Instead of having the kernel choose an unused filename, the designers of UNIX domain sockets decided to leave this up to the application. The SVR4 implementation does not suffer from this limitation, choosing to skip the file creation step if the application binds a UNIX domain socket address implicitly.

The bind(3N) library routine is used to bind an address to a socket:

```
#include <sys/types.h>
#include <sys/socket.h>

int bind(int fd, struct sockaddr *addrp, int alen);
```

fd is the file descriptor for the socket endpoint, addrp is a pointer to the socket address, and alen is the address length in bytes.

The sockaddr structure is really just a placeholder that is cast over the protocol-specific address. Its format is somewhat misleading.

```
struct sockaddr {
    ushort_t    sa_family;
    char        sa_data[14];
};
```

Table 7.1. Protocol Families

Protocol Family ID	netconfig Protocol Family String	Description
PF_UNSPEC	–	Unspecified family
PF_UNIX	loopback	UNIX domain
PF_INET	inet	Internet protocols
PF_IMPLINK	implink	Arpanet IMP addresses
PF_PUP	pup	Old Xerox protocols
PF_CHAOS	chaos	M.I.T. CHAOS protocols
PF_NS	ns	Xerox Network System protocols
PF_NBS	nbs	NBS protocols
PF_ECMA	ecma	European Computer Manufacturers Association
PF_DATAKIT	datakit	DATAKIT protocols
PF_CCITT	ccitt	CCITT protocols
PF_SNA	sna	IBM System Network Architecture
PF_DECnet	decnet	DECnet protocols
PF_DLI	dli	DEC direct data link interface
PF_LAT	lat	LAN terminal interface
PF_HYLINK	hylink	NSC Hyperchannel
PF_APPLETALK	appletalk	AppleTalk protocols
PF_NIT	nit	Network interface tap
PF_802	ieee802	IEEE 802.2 (ISO 8802)
PF_OSI	osi	OSI protocols
PF_X25	x25	CCITT X.25
PF_OSINET	osinet	OSI protocols
PF_GOSIP	gosip	U.S. government OSI protocols

Even though the structure is a fixed size, socket addresses are not limited to 16 bytes in length. The only requirements on the address format are that the first two bytes contain the address family identifier and that the length of the address be no greater than 112 bytes. The address length restriction is only present in 4BSD; SVR4 addresses can be of any length (the restriction is imposed by the transport provider).

Example 7.2.1. In Example 4.2.1 we presented a function that could be used by server processes to initialize their communication endpoints. Below is the socket version of the same routine.

```
#include <sys/types.h>
```

```
#include <sys/socket.h>

extern void fatal(const char *, ...);

int
initserver(int type, struct sockaddr *addrp, uint_t alen,
    uint_t qlen)
{
    int fd;

    /*
     * Create a socket endpoint.
     */
    if ((fd = socket(addrp->sa_family, type, 0)) < 0)
        fatal("cannot create socket");

    /*
     * Bind the specified address.
     */
    if (bind(fd, addrp, alen) < 0)
        fatal("cannot bind address");

    /*
     * If this is a stream socket, inform the transport
     * provider of the queue length (backlog), indicating
     * that the server is willing to accept connections.
     */
    if (type == SOCK_STREAM)
        listen(fd, qlen);

    /*
     * Return the endpoint.
     */
    return(fd);
}
```

A socket is created using the default protocol for the specified socket type and address (protocol) family. Then the address passed in is bound to the socket. If the transport provider binds a different address than requested, bind will unbind the address and return an error.

With the TLI, connection-oriented servers specify the number of outstanding connect indications that they are willing to handle in the qlen field of the t_bind structure. With sockets, the analogous operation is done using listen(3N), which we will cover in Section 7.3. Thus, if the socket is connection-oriented, we call listen to specify the queue length (also called the *backlog*) for outstanding connect indications. Then we return the file descriptor to be used by the server.

Recall the structure of a TCP address, originally presented in Example 5.3.3:

```
struct in_addr {
    union {
        struct { uchar_t s_b1, s_b2, s_b3, s_b4; } S_un_b;
        struct { ushort_t s_w1, s_w2; } S_un_w;
        ulong_t S_addr;
```

```
        } S_un;
};
#define  s_addr   S_un.S_addr

struct sockaddr_in {
        short           sin_family;
        ushort_t        sin_port;
        struct in_addr  sin_addr;
        char            sin_zero[8];
};
```

If we were writing a server that used TCP/IP, we would call `initserver` as shown below.

```
 .
 .
 .
#define QLEN 10

int i, fd;
struct sockaddr_in myaddr;
extern ushort_t myport;
extern ulong_t myipaddr;

myaddr.sin_family = AF_INET;
myaddr.sin_port = myport;
myaddr.sin_addr.s_addr = myipaddr;
for (i = 0; i < sizeof(myaddr.sin_zero); i++)
        myaddr.sin_zero[i] = 0;
fd = initserver(SOCK_STREAM, (struct sockaddr *)&myaddr,
        sizeof(struct sockaddr_in), QLEN);
 .
 .
 .
```

Note how the protocol-specific address structure is cast to a generic `sockaddr` structure. The server's IP address and port number can be obtained using the methods described either in Chapter 5 or in Section 7.8.   □

A process can call `close(2)` to discard a socket it no longer needs. If the transport provider supports orderly release on close, then any data still queued for transmission by the protocol will be retained until either delivery is accomplished or a timer (usually a long one) expires. If the timer expires, the data are discarded. If the transport provider defaults to an abortive release on close, any data still queued for transmission will be discarded.

Finer control over the disabling of a socket is available through `shutdown(3N)`:

```
int shutdown(int fd, int how);
```

`fd` is the file descriptor for the socket endpoint, and `how` determines the action to be taken. If `how` is 0, no more data can be received from the socket. If `how` is 1, no more data can be transmitted using the socket. Neither reception nor transmission can be performed if `how` is 2. `shutdown` is often used to prevent the system from trying to deliver data not yet delivered when an application wishes to abort a connection.

Calling shutdown with how set to 1 or 2 will generate an orderly release request if the transport provider supports the orderly release facility. If the transport provider does not support orderly release, calling shutdown with how set to 2 will generate a disconnect request. On success, shutdown returns 0. On failure, it returns −1 and sets errno to indicate the reason for failing. shutdown can only be used on sockets that have been previously connected (described in Section 7.3).

If how is set to 0, then any data not yet retrieved by the application are discarded. With transport providers that support orderly release, if how is set to 1 or 2, any data sent but not yet delivered to its destination will be given the opportunity to be delivered. This behavior can be changed with the SO_LINGER socket option (see Table 7.2). With TCP, in particular, if the linger time is set to 0, then TCP will discard any queued data not yet transmitted to the peer and reset the connection.

Socket Options

Like the TLI, the socket interface provides functions that allow applications to manage options supported by the underlying protocol. Unlike the TLI, however, some options are supported by the generic socket layer. Thus the socket options are available with all protocols, while other options are protocol-specific.

Several interesting problems exist with getting and setting socket options. The socket interface allows the caller to specify the protocol level controlling the option. Since sockets are implemented on top of STREAMS-based transport-level drivers that support the Transport Provider Interface, some conflicts between the two interfaces occur.

The Transport Provider Interface (TPI) only allows options management between the time an endpoint is bound and the time it is connected. (This corresponds to the idle states shown in Figures 4.3 and 4.11.) The socket interface makes no such restriction. The SVR4 socket implementation gets around this problem by requiring that the transport providers not enforce this restriction if they are to be accessed via the socket interface.

Another problem is that the TPI does not allow consumers direct access to lower-level protocols. This is mainly because the TPI was patterned after the OSI reference model. In the OSI reference model, a consumer at one level only has access to the facilities offered by the provider at the adjacent lower level. For socket options to be accessible at multiple protocol layers, the transport provider must help out by translating and passing requests to other levels down the protocol stack.

Socket options can be set by calling setsockopt(3N):

```
#include <sys/types.h>
#include <sys/socket.h>

int setsockopt(int fd, int level, int cmd, char *arg,
    int len);
```

where fd is the socket file descriptor, level is the protocol level, cmd is the option being modified, arg points to the address of the option value to be set, and len is the length of the option value in bytes.

`level` should be set to `SOL_SOCKET` to modify options at the socket level. Otherwise, it should be set to the protocol number of the protocol controlling the option. (Obtaining the protocol number is described in Section 7.8.) Table 7.2 summarizes the socket-level (generic) options that can be set in SVR4.

Table 7.2. Socket Options

Option	`arg` points to	Description
SO_DEBUG	`int`	Nonzero to enable and zero to disable debugging.
SO_REUSEADDR	`int`	Nonzero to enable and zero to disable local address reuse.
SO_KEEPALIVE	`int`	Nonzero to enable and zero to disable connection keep-alive messages.
SO_DONTROUTE	`int`	Nonzero to enable and zero to disable routing of outgoing messages.
SO_LINGER	`struct linger`	Delay on close if data are present.
SO_BROADCAST	`int`	Nonzero to enable and zero to disable broadcast message transmission.
SO_OOBINLINE	`int`	Nonzero to enable and zero to disable delivery of out-of-band data inline with normal data.
SO_SNDBUF	`int`	Set output buffer size.
SO_RCVBUF	`int`	Set input buffer size.
SO_SNDLOWAT	`int`	Set output low-water mark.
SO_RCVLOWAT	`int`	Set input low-water mark.
SO_SNDTIMEO	`int`	Set output timeout (unused).
SO_RCVTIMEO	`int`	Set input timeout (unused).
SO_USELOOPBACK	`int`	Nonzero to enable and zero to disable hardware bypass (when possible).
SO_PROTOTYPE	`int`	Set protocol type.

Other options defined by the protocol implementations may be supported. Socket options can be retrieved by calling `getsockopt(3N)`:

```
#include <sys/types.h>
#include <sys/socket.h>

int getsockopt(int fd, int level, int cmd, char *arg,
    int *lenp);
```

where `fd` is the socket file descriptor, `level` is the protocol level, `cmd` is the option being queried, `arg` points to a buffer where the option value is to be returned, and lenp initially points to the size of the buffer (in bytes). On return, the integer pointed to by lenp is updated with the length of the value returned (also in bytes).

In addition to those options listed in Table 7.2, two other socket-level options can be used with getsockopt. If cmd is set to SO_TYPE, then the integer pointed to by arg will contain the socket type on return. For example, a TCP socket will return type SOCK_STREAM. If cmd is set to SO_ERROR, then the integer pointed to by arg will be set to an error code associated with the socket. The socket's error code is then cleared.

For those options that take a boolean argument, a zero will be stored in the integer pointed to by arg if the option is disabled. If the option is enabled, a nonzero value will be stored there instead. Usually the nonzero value will be some number other than 1, so applications should only test for equality or inequality to zero.

Both setsockopt and getsockopt return 0 on success and −1 on failure.

7.3 CONNECTION ESTABLISHMENT

Client-side applications can use connect(3N) to create a logical connection between two sockets. For SOCK_STREAM-type sockets, a virtual circuit is created. For SOCK_DGRAM-type sockets, the destination address is cached so that the application does not have to provide the destination address with every packet transmitted. In addition, only datagrams received from the cached address are available to be received. Thus caching allows applications to use data-transfer primitives that would otherwise only be applicable with connection-oriented protocols.

If the client's socket is not bound, connect will bind it to an unused address before proceeding. The synopsis is

```
#include <sys/types.h>
#include <sys/socket.h>

int connect(int fd, struct sockaddr *addrp, int alen);
```

where fd is the socket file descriptor, addrp points to the destination address, and alen is the length of the address in bytes. On success, connect returns 0; on failure, it returns −1. Note that if connect is unable to establish a connection after binding an address to the socket, the address still remains bound upon return.

Example 7.3.1. Example 4.4.1 shows a simple function that attempts several connect requests, using an exponential backoff algorithm if a request fails. The following is the same function coded using sockets.

```
#include <sys/types.h>
#include <sys/socket.h>
#include <unistd.h>
#include <stdio.h>
#include <errno.h>
```

```
#define MAXSLP    32

int
myconnect(int fd, struct sockaddr *addrp, int alen)
{
    int i;

    /*
     * Try several times to connect.
     */
    for (i = 1; i <= MAXSLP; i <<= 1) {
        if (connect(fd, addrp, alen) == 0)
            /*
             * Connection accepted.
             */
            return(0);

        /*
         * Delay before trying again.
         */
        sleep(i);
    }

    /*
     * We reached the maximum retry count.  Print
     * an error message, set the global error code,
     * and return -1.
     */
    fprintf(stderr, "Connect timed out\n");
    errno = ETIME;
    return(-1);
}
```

The most striking difference between this function and the one presented in Example
4.4.1 is the simplicity of using the socket interface for client-side connection establishment.   □

We saw the use of listen(3N) in Example 7.2.1. A server-style application
uses it to mark a socket as willing to receive connect indications. The synopsis is

```
int listen(int fd, int backlog);
```

where fd is the socket file descriptor on which the server wishes to receive connect
indications, and backlog is the number of connect indications the system should
queue up while waiting for the server to accept them. Note the difference between
the qlen field of the t_bind structure and the backlog parameter to listen.
The qlen field specifies the maximum number of connect indications an application
is prepared to receive at any given time. It is not the maximum number of connect
indications that are to be queued by the protocol, but the maximum number of connect indications the protocol is allowed to send to the transport user at any given
time. The transport provider may choose to queue more indications than specified by
the qlen. The backlog parameter, on the other hand, informs the protocol of the

maximum number of connect indications to queue.

In 4BSD, the maximum value of the `qlen` parameter is five (`SOMAXCONN` from `<sys/socket.h>`). In SVR4, however, the maximum value depends on the implementation of the transport provider.

`listen` is only applicable to connection-oriented sockets, such as socket types `SOCK_STREAM` and `SOCK_SEQPACKET`. `listen` return 0 on success and −1 on failure. Once a server calls `listen`, incoming connect indications can be accepted by calling `accept (3N)`:

```
#include <sys/types.h>
#include <sys/socket.h>

int accept(int fd, struct sockaddr *addrp, int *alenp)
```

`fd` is the socket file descriptor, `addrp` is a pointer to a buffer used to hold the client's address, and `alenp` is a pointer to the length of the buffer in bytes. If there are no pending connect indications queued, `accept` will block until one arrives.

On return, the integer referred to by `alenp` is updated to contain the actual length of the client address, and the contents of the memory buffer to which `addrp` points is filled with the address of the client making the connection request. If the server is not interested in the identity of the client, then `addrp` and `alenp` can be set to NULL.

The return value from `accept` is a new socket file descriptor on success and −1 on failure. The new socket file descriptor will be of the same type and refer to the same protocol as `fd`, and it represents the server's side of the connection. In addition, the new file descriptor will inherit the nonblocking and asynchronous I/O settings of `fd`. The socket `fd` refers to does not participate in the connection. It remains available to receive further connect indications. Unlike the TLI, a socket-based server does not have the option of accepting the connection on the same file descriptor that it is using to listen for connect indications.

Another difference between the TLI and the socket mechanism is that a server does not have the ability to reject a connection request using sockets. If a server wants to deny a potential client the service, then the server must first accept the connection and then close the resulting (returned) file descriptor, thus releasing the connection.

Like `listen`, `accept` can only be used with sockets that are connection-oriented. A diagram of the sequence of events that occur during connection establishment is shown in Figure 7.3. In it, the interface that the socket library communicates with, labeled "SSI," is the socket service interface exported by SOCKMOD.

As we can see, the sequence of events is similar to those found in the TLI library. A client process (user A) creates a socket endpoint, binds an address to it (often indirectly by calling `connect`), and attempts to initiate a connection with a server. The server process (user B) initializes its own endpoint in the same way as the client, but then calls `listen` to indicate to the transport provider that the process is willing to accept connect indications on this endpoint. Then the server calls `accept` to wait for connect indications.

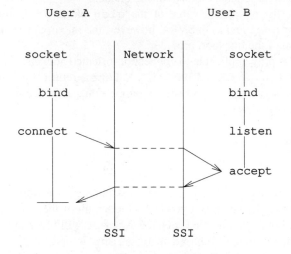

Fig. 7.3. Connection Establishment

Example 7.3.2. This example illustrates the framework for a socket-based, connection-oriented server. Its structure is similar to that of the servers presented in previous chapters. In an infinite loop, a connection is established and a child process is created to handle the service while the parent continues to wait for additional connect indications.

```
#include <sys/types.h>
#include <sys/socket.h>
#include <unistd.h>
#include <stdlib.h>
#include <string.h>
#include <errno.h>

int softerror(int);

extern void log(const char *, ...);

void
serve(int fd)
{
    int nfd, pid;

    for (;;) {
        /*
         * Block until a connect indication arrives;
         * then accept it.
         */
        nfd = accept(fd, NULL, NULL);
        if (nfd < 0) {
            log("cannot accept connection: %s",
                strerror(errno));
```

```
                    /*
                     * If this was a recoverable error,
                     * then try again.
                     */
                    if (softerror(errno))
                        continue;
                    else
                        exit(1);
                }

                /*
                 * Fork off a child process to handle the
                 * service request.
                 */
                if ((pid = fork()) < 0) {
                    log("cannot create child: %s",
                        strerror(errno));
                    if (!softerror(errno))
                        exit(1);
                } else if (pid == 0) {
                    /*
                     * The child doesn't need the file
                     * descriptor used to accept connections.
                     */
                    close(fd);

                    /*
                     * This is where the child would
                     * perform the service.
                     */
                        .
                        .
                        .
                }

                /*
                 * The parent doesn't need the file descriptor
                 * for the newly created connection.
                 */
                close(nfd);
            }
        }

        /*
         * Return 1 if error is recoverable and
         * 0 if unrecoverable.
         */
        int
        softerror(int num)
        {
            switch (num) {
            case EAGAIN:
            case ENOSR:
            case ENODEV:
            case ENOSPC:
```

```
        case ENOMEM:
        case ENXIO:
        case ENOBUFS:
            return(1);

        default:
            return(0);
        }
    }
```

The child closes the socket that its parent is using to listen for connect indications since the child will be handling the connection with the file descriptor returned by accept. Similarly, the parent needs only the socket it is using to receive connect indications, so it closes the socket used for the connection.

Besides illustrating the framework for a socket-based, connection-oriented server, this example introduces a level of robustness not found in previous examples. Not all errors are fatal. Some merely indicate a temporary resource shortage. We have defined the softerror function to return 1 if the error is "soft," i.e., temporary. Permanent errors ("hard" ones) will cause the function to return 0.

Usually, the list of soft errors will vary from system to system, mostly because there are no clear rules that spell out the conditions under which each error can be returned. Often different driver implementations will return different errors for the same condition. For example, memory allocation failures can result in EAGAIN, ENOSR, ENOMEM, or ENOBUFS being returned. When all available devices are in use, drivers can return ENODEV, ENOSPC, or ENXIO.

While some of these error codes are being used for purposes other than originally intended, they have all been observed to be used in various driver implementations.   □

7.4 DATA TRANSFER

Like the TLI, the socket mechanism provides additional interfaces for sending and receiving messages. Unlike the TLI, however, the socket mechanism allows these interfaces to be used on any type of socket.

If a socket is connected (recall that datagram sockets can be "connected" too), data can be sent using write and received using read. These are important capabilities because they allow socket file descriptors to be passed to applications that do not know anything about sockets. The applications can use the file descriptors as if they were open to regular files.

The socket library provides three additional interfaces to transmit data. The first of these is send(3N):

```
int send(int fd, char *buf, int len, int flags);
```

fd is the socket's file descriptor, buf is the address of the buffer containing the data to be transmitted, len is the number of bytes to transmit, and flags is a bitmask of flags that can be used to modify the characteristics of the transmission.

Two flags are defined. If MSG_OOB is set and the protocol supports the notion of out-of-band data, then the data transmitted are treated with a higher priority than the normal data. If MSG_DONTROUTE is set, then the messages generated are sent directly to the destination host in a single hop, if possible.

send can only be used on sockets that are connected. It returns the number of bytes transmitted or −1 if an error occurred.

The second interface is sendto(3N). It is similar to send, but allows the caller to specify the destination.

```
#include <sys/types.h>
#include <sys/socket.h>

int sendto(int fd, char *buf, int len, int flags,
    struct sockaddr *addrp, int alen);
```

addrp points to the destination address, and alen is its length in bytes. The other parameters are the same as in send. Also similar to send, sendto returns the number of bytes transmitted or −1 if an error occurred.

sendto is usually used for connectionless sockets, but it can also be used with connection-oriented ones. With SOCK_STREAM sockets, addrp and alen are ignored.

The third interface, sendmsg(3N), provides more generality and functionality.

```
#include <sys/types.h>
#include <sys/uio.h>
#include <sys/socket.h>

int sendmsg(int fd, struct msghdr *msgp, int flags);
```

fd and flags are the same as in send and sendto. The return values for sendmsg are also the same as those of the other two routines.

With sendmsg, callers specify characteristics of the messages to be transmitted with the msghdr structure. (Note that the msghdr structure was changed in the Reno version of 4.3BSD.)

```
struct msghdr {
    caddr_t msg_name;        /* destination address */
    int     msg_namelen;     /* size of address */
    iovec_t *msg_iov;        /* scatter/gather array */
    int     msg_iovlen;      /* # elements in msg_iov */
    caddr_t msg_accrights;   /* access rights */
    int     msg_accrightslen;
};

typedef struct iovec {
    caddr_t iov_base;
    int     iov_len;
} iovec_t;
```

The msg_name field points to the optional destination address, which is msg_namelen bytes long. The msg_iov field points to an array of iovec structures that describe the data to be sent. Each entry in the array describes one contiguous extent of memory by specifying its starting address (`iov_base`) and its length in bytes (`iov_len`). An application might use more than one entry in the array when it is transmitting data from multiple independent memory locations. For example, one buffer may contain user data and another may contain header or trailer information. The number of `iovec` structures that can be used in the `msg_iov` array is limited to `MSG_MAXIOVLEN`, which is set to 16 in SVR4.

The `msg_accrights` and `msg_accrightslen` fields are used to transmit *access rights* (a fancy name for file descriptors) over UNIX domain sockets. We will see how they are used in Section 7.5.

`SOCK_STREAM` sockets must be connected before data can be transmitted. If transmission is attempted before a connection is established, then `send`, `sendto`, and `sendmsg` will fail with `errno` set to `ENOTCONN`. If `write` is used, the behavior differs depending on whether the application is running on a 4BSD system or on an SVR4 system. With 4BSD, a `write` is just like a `send`. With SVR4, on the other hand, `write` will fail silently, appearing to succeed. The data are discarded and the socket is updated with the error `ENOTCONN`. Applications can get the error using the `SO_ERROR getsockopt` command.

The destination addresses that callers can specify using `sendto` and `sendmsg` are ignored with `SOCK_STREAM`-style sockets. With `SOCK_DGRAM` sockets, however, an address has to be provided, either explicitly with `sendto` or `sendmsg`, or implicitly through a previous call to `connect`. If a datagram socket is not connected and an address is not provided, then the attempt to transmit data will fail with `errno` set to `EDESTADDRREQ`. Again, in 4BSD, `write` behaves like `send`, but in SVR4, `write` will fail silently and the socket error is set to `ENOTCONN`.

If the socket is connected and an address is specified, 4BSD will fail the transmission attempt with `errno` set to `EISCONN`. The behavior in SVR4, however, is different. The datagram will be sent to the specified address, effectively ignoring the one cached by the prior call to `connect`.

The socket library also provides three interfaces for receiving data, symmetric to those used to transmit data. The receive interfaces can be used on all types of sockets. The first is `recv(3N)`:

```
#include <sys/types.h>
#include <sys/socket.h>

int recv(int fd, char *buf, int len, int flags);
```

`fd` is the socket's file descriptor, `buf` is the address of a buffer to which the data are to be copied, `len` is the size of the buffer in bytes, and `flags` is a bitmask of flags that can be set to modify the behavior of `recv`. On success, the number of bytes received is returned. On failure, −1 is returned and `errno` is set to indicate the reason for the failure.

If the `MSG_OOB` flag is set, then the caller will receive any out-of-band data that have not yet been consumed. If the `MSG_PEEK` flag is set, then `recv` is nondestructive. In other words, the data are not freed after they are returned. Instead, the same data will be delivered on the next call to `recv`. This provides applications with a way of peeking at the data on the input queue without actually consuming the data.

Using `recv` with datagram sockets, the reader will not have any idea who sent the data. To obtain the sender's address, the second interface, `recvfrom(3N)`, can be used.

```
#include <sys/types.h>
#include <sys/socket.h>

int recvfrom(int fd, char *buf, int len, int flags,
     struct sockaddr *addrp, int *alenp);
```

The first four parameters are the same as in `recv`. `addrp` points to a buffer to contain the sender's address, and `alenp` points to an integer containing the size of the buffer in bytes. On return, this integer will be updated with the actual size of the address, and the sender's address will be stored in the memory referenced by `addrp`. The return values are the same as for `recv`.

The third interface is `recvmsg(3N)`. Like `sendmsg`, `recvmsg` relies on the `msghdr` structure to specify most of the information. `recvmsg` is like `recvfrom`, with the added functionality of being able to receive access rights and retrieve data into multiple noncontiguous memory buffers. The synopsis is

```
#include <sys/types.h>
#include <sys/socket.h>

int recvmsg(int fd, struct msghdr *msg, int flags);
```

where `msg` points to the `msghdr` structure shown earlier. The return values for `recvmsg` are the same as for `recv` and `recvfrom`.

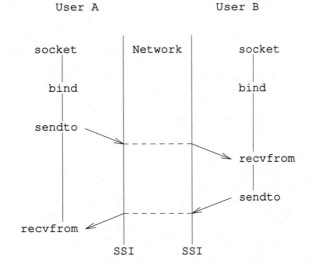

Fig. 7.4. Connectionless Data Transfer

Although any type of socket can be used with the receive interfaces, SOCK_STREAM sockets must be connected before data can be exchanged. On the other hand, any of the three receive interfaces can be used with SOCK_DGRAM sockets, regardless of whether or not the socket is connected.

Figure 7.4 illustrates a two-way data exchange using datagram sockets. As soon as the sockets are bound, data transfer can occur. If the sender transmits a message and the message arrives at its destination before the intended recipient has bound an address to its socket, then the datagram is discarded.

Example 7.4.1. In Example 4.3.1, we present the client side of a datagram-based remote who function. This example is the socket version of the same function. Instead of passing it the pathname of the transport provider, we pass it the address family or protocol family in the socket version.

Rather than just translate the example from TLI to sockets, we have added an extra feature. Datagrams can be received from any source on the network. Since we are only interested in messages from one particular host, we have added the sameaddr function to compare the address of the host from which we want to receive data with the source address contained in the datagram received. This allows us to screen the messages received and ignore any packets from sources trying to interfere (either intentionally or unintentionally) with the operation of the remote who command.

```
#include <sys/types.h>
#include <sys/socket.h>
#include <stdlib.h>
#include <stdio.h>
#include <string.h>
#include <signal.h>
#include <unistd.h>

void timeout(int);
int sameaddr(struct sockaddr *, int, struct sockaddr *,
    int);
extern void fatal(const char *, ...);

void
rwho(int argc, char *argv[], int family,
    struct sockaddr *ap, uint_t alen)
{
    int fd, i, rlen;
    struct sigaction sa;
    char raddr[128];
    char buf[1024];

    if (argc < 2) {
        fprintf(stderr, "usage: rwho host [options]\n");
        exit(1);
    }

    /*
```

```
 * Create a socket endpoint.
 */
if ((fd = socket(family, SOCK_DGRAM, 0)) < 0)
    fatal("rwho: cannot create socket");

/*
 * Build the command string to send to the server.
 */
strcpy(buf, "who");
for (i = 2; i < argc; i++) {
    strcat(buf, " ");
    strcat(buf, argv[i]);
}

/*
 * Set an alarm so we don't block forever.
 */
sa.sa_handler = timeout;
sa.sa_flags = 0;
sigemptyset(&sa.sa_mask);
sigaction(SIGALRM, &sa, NULL);
alarm(20);

/*
 * Send the request.
 */
if (sendto(fd, buf, strlen(buf)+1, 0, ap, alen) < 0)
    fatal("rwho: cannot send request");

/*
 * Receive response messages until we encounter an
 * error or receive the last message (a single byte
 * containing 0).
 */
for ( ; ; ) {
    rlen = sizeof(raddr);
    if ((i = recvfrom(fd, buf, sizeof(buf), 0,
      (struct sockaddr *)raddr, &rlen)) < 0)
        fatal("rwho: cannot receive data");

    /*
     * Only process the message if it is from the
     * server we contacted.
     */
    if (sameaddr(ap, alen, (struct sockaddr *)raddr,
      rlen)) {
        /*
         * If this is the last message, exit.
         */
        if ((i == 1) && (buf[0] == '\0'))
            exit(0);
        /*
         * Write the response on the standard output.
         */
```

```
                    write(1, buf, i);
            }
        }
}

void
timeout(int sig)
{
        fprintf(stderr, "rwho: command timed out\n");
        exit(1);
}

/*
 * Return 0 if the two addresses are different, and
 * 1 if they are the same.
 */
int
sameaddr(struct sockaddr *a1p, int l1, struct sockaddr *a2p,
        int l2)
{
        int i;

        /*
         * If the lengths or address families differ,
         * then the addresses don't match.
         */
        if ((l1 != l2) || (a1p->sa_family != a2p->sa_family))
            return(0);

        /*
         * We already checked the address family.  Now
         * compare the data portion.
         */
        l1 -= sizeof(a1p->sa_family);
        for (i = 0; i < l1; i++)
            if (a1p->sa_data[i] != a2p->sa_data[i])
                    return(0);
        return(1);
}
```

In Example 4.3.1, we use `t_alloc(3N)` to allocate the receive buffer, and its size is stored in the `netbuf` structure returned. The TLI library uses the recommendation of the transport provider in selecting the size. With sockets, we have to select our own buffer size based on the protocol and the needs of the application. (With 4BSD, the `SO_RCVBUF` socket option could be used to obtain the receive buffer size. For datagram sockets, this is the size of the largest packet that can be received. With SVR4, however, the `SO_RCVBUF` socket option returns the high-water mark for the transport provider's read queue, which is not necessarily related to the size of the largest packet that can be received.)

If an error occurs during transmission, the application is not notified, so there is no step in this example that corresponds to the `t_rcvuderr(3N)` call in Example 4.3.1.

The `sameaddr` function compares two addresses, returning 1 if they are the same and 0 if not. We first check the sizes and address families of the two addresses to save time. If either of these is different, then we know the two addresses are different. Finally, we do a byte-by-byte comparison of the remaining portion of the addresses.   □

An example of the use of `sendmsg` and `recvmsg` can be found in Example 7.5.2. The use of `send` and `recv` is illustrated in Example 7.8.1.

7.5 UNIX DOMAIN SOCKETS

Processes running on the same machine can use UNIX domain sockets to communicate with one another. The advantage to using sockets for local IPC is that applications can treat local and remote (i.e., networked) IPC in the same way. This greatly simplifies the way applications are designed. If the interfaces to local and remote IPC differed, then applications would require special-case code to distinguish between the two cases.

UNIX domain sockets are more efficient than Internet domain sockets used in a loopback mode because UNIX domain sockets do not do any protocol processing. There are no headers to add or remove, no checksums to calculate, no acknowledgements to send, and no sequence numbers to generate. In addition, UNIX domain sockets are inherently reliable. Packets cannot be lost, even with UNIX domain datagram sockets. (Actually, in SVR4, the transport provider [TICLTS] used to implement UNIX domain datagram sockets contains a symbol that if defined will cause TICLTS to be compiled so that it does not support flow control. In this case, messages are freed if the receiver's stream is flow-controlled, instead of letting the flow control propagate back to the sender. In 4BSD, a transmit request can fail because of buffer shortages, but messages are not lost.)

The `socketpair(3N)` routine is used to create a pair of unnamed, connected sockets. It is similar to `pipe(2)` in that it returns a bidirectional communication channel. The file descriptors, however, support socket semantics. The synopsis for `socketpair` is

```
#include <sys/types.h>
#include <sys/socket.h>

int socketpair(int family, int type, int protocol,
    int fds[2]);
```

where `family` identifies the communication domain, `type` indicates the socket type, and `protocol` selects the particular protocol to use. For UNIX domain sockets, `protocol` should be set to 0. On success, `socketpair` returns 0, storing one socket file descriptor in `fds[0]` and the other in `fds[1]`. On failure, `socketpair` returns −1 with `errno` set to indicate the reason for failing. `socketpair` is only implemented for the UNIX domain.

The UNIX communication domain supports both SOCK_STREAM and

SOCK_DGRAM sockets. When creating UNIX domain sockets, the socket library will use the netconfig database to identify the underlying transport provider (see Section 5.2). For a transport provider to be a possible candidate for use with UNIX domain sockets, it must belong to the loopback protocol family.

When a UNIX domain SOCK_DGRAM socket is created, a stream is opened to a loopback driver (TICLTS) that exports a transport level interface (the TPI). SOCKMOD is then pushed on the stream to provide socket semantics. Figure 7.5 shows the resulting configuration after calling socketpair to create a pair of connected UNIX domain datagram sockets.

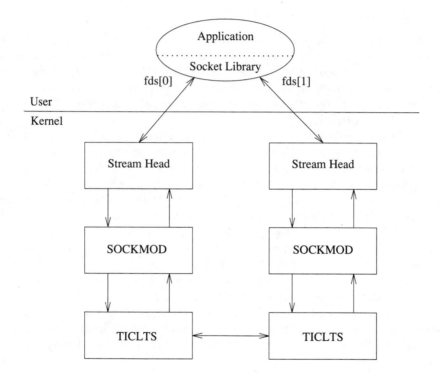

Fig. 7.5. UNIX Domain Datagram Sockets Returned by socketpair(3N)

A similar configuration is established for SOCK_STREAM sockets. In this case, however, a different loopback driver is used, depending on the connection-oriented loopback entry appearing first in /etc/netconfig. If ticots appears before ticotsord, then the TICOTS driver will be used, providing a connection-oriented transport interface that does not support orderly release. If ticotsord appears first, then the TICOTSORD driver will be used instead, resulting in the socket supporting orderly release semantics.

In 4BSD, UNIX domain SOCK_STREAM sockets provide flow control, and UNIX domain SOCK_DGRAM sockets do not. In SVR4, UNIX domain

SOCK_STREAM sockets provide flow control, and UNIX domain SOCK_DGRAM sockets might support flow control, depending on how the TICLTS driver is compiled.

Other differences between 4BSD UNIX domain sockets and SVR4 UNIX domain sockets are related to the side effect of a bind request. The format of a UNIX domain address is defined by the sockaddr_un structure, defined in <sys/un.h>:

```
struct sockaddr_un {
        short   sun_family;           /* AF_UNIX */
        char    sun_path[108];        /* pathname */
};
```

The sun_path field is a UNIX pathname. When a UNIX domain address is bound, the file represented by the pathname is created. In 4BSD, the file is of type S_IFSOCK, but in SVR4 it is of type S_IFIFO. Files of type S_IFSOCK cannot be opened. This characteristic does not hold true for FIFOs. Although the files created by bind can be opened in SVR4, they do not provide access to the sockets they represent.

The 108-character pathname in the address does not include the terminating NULL byte. Recall that all socket interfaces that take an address also take a field specifying the size of the address. A compatibility problem could exist when porting applications from 4BSD to SVR4 because of the size of filenames. In the 4BSD file system (called UFS), the maximum filename is 255 characters. Although SVR4 also supports an implementation of UFS, many systems use the traditional System V file system (called S5), which has a maximum filename length of 14 bytes. If two UNIX domain addresses have the first 14 characters of the filename in common, and the files reside in the same S5 directory, then one of the bind requests will fail with errno set to EEXIST.

When the socket is closed, the file does not magically go away. Applications must explicitly unlink the file before exiting to avoid littering the file system with unnecessary files. Such a file left around from a previous invocation of a command will prevent the command from binding to the proper name on the next execution, unless the command unlinks the pathname before attempting to bind the address.

Because the pathnames need to be unique, 4BSD applications cannot rely on the implicit binding capabilities of sockets when using UNIX domain sockets. If an application wants to bind an address to a UNIX domain socket, it must do so explicitly by calling bind. In an SVR4 environment, however, this is unnecessary. If a socket primitive is used on an unbound socket, the socket library will perform an implicit bind. The transport provider will select an unused address, but no file is created in this case, so there is no chance of name collision.

Example 7.5.1. This example illustrates how one can bind an address to a UNIX domain socket. Because UNIX domain addresses appear in the file system namespace, an application that binds an address needs to be careful that the filename does not already exist.

Functions that choose an unused filename, such as tmpnam(3S) and

tempnam(3S), could be used to select an address for binding, but then it is more
difficult to advertise services without a name server. In the absence of a name
server, client applications often assume services will be available at well-known
addresses.

Assuming a name service is not available, the following function shows a safe
way to bind a UNIX domain socket. We use stat(2) to see if the address to be
bound already exists as a file. If it does and its type indicates it is not a socket, the
bind attempt has to be aborted. If the type indicates the file is a socket, then we can
proceed to unlink the file if we have the appropriate permission.

```
#include <sys/types.h>
#include <sys/socket.h>
#include <sys/un.h>
#include <sys/stat.h>
#include <string.h>
#include <errno.h>
#include <unistd.h>

#ifdef SYSV
#define ISSOCKET(mode)      (((mode)&S_IFMT) == S_IFIFO)
#else /* BSD */
#define ISSOCKET(mode)      (((mode)&S_IFMT) == S_IFSOCK)
#endif

int
mksocket(char *name)
{
    int fd, len;
    struct sockaddr_un addr;
    struct stat sbuf;

    /*
     * If the length of the socket address is
     * too large, fail the request.
     */
    if (strlen(name) > sizeof(addr.sun_path)) {
        errno = ENAMETOOLONG;
        return(-1);
    }
    if (stat(name, &sbuf) < 0) {
        /*
         * If stat fails because the file is missing,
         * ignore the error (we're about to create it).
         */
        if (errno == ENOENT)
            errno = 0;
        else
            return(-1);
    } else {
        /*
         * If the file exists and it is a socket, then
         * unlink it.  Otherwise the name is in use.
         */
```

```
            if (ISSOCKET(sbuf.st_mode)) {
                if (unlink(name) < 0)
                    return(-1);
            } else {
                errno = EBUSY;
                return(-1);
            }
        }

        /*
         * Create a UNIX domain datagram socket.
         */
        if ((fd = socket(AF_UNIX, SOCK_DGRAM, 0)) < 0)
            return(-1);

        /*
         * Create and bind the address.
         */
        addr.sun_family = AF_UNIX;
        strcpy(addr.sun_path, name);
        len = sizeof(addr.sun_family) + strlen(name);
        if (bind(fd, (struct sockaddr *)&addr, len) < 0)
            return(-1);

        /*
         * Return the socket endpoint.
         */
        return(fd);
    }
```

Since the type of a socket file differs between SVR4 and 4BSD, this example relies on the person compiling it to define the SYSV symbol if the application is intended to run on a System V-based computer.   □

Passing File Descriptors

Sockets support the ability for an application to pass access rights to other processes. The only access rights currently implemented are in the form of file descriptors in the UNIX domain. The socket paradigm could be extended in the future to allow access rights to represent other objects, such as shared memory, for example.

Similarly, the ability to pass access rights between processes could be extended across other communication domains if the underlying support was present in the operating system. File descriptors refer to file table entries that only have meaning within a single machine. A distributed operating system, on the other hand, might have a different representation for the handle that represents a file, and this representation could have meaning on different nodes in the network. In this type of environment, it would be possible to extend the Internet communication domain to support the exchange of access rights between processes on different nodes.

For now, however, the socket library only allows passing file descriptors between processes running on the same node. In Chapter 3 we saw some examples of how this might be useful. We could reimplement the examples here, but instead we will look at another way passing file descriptors can be useful.

The following software architecture was originally proposed by Presotto and Ritchie [1985, 1990]. Consider an application that needs to perform device-specific actions to enable a device to be used for communication. Such an application would be difficult to maintain. Every time a piece of hardware is developed that requires different initialization procedures, the application must be modified to add support for the new device. uucp(1) and cu(1) are examples of such applications.

A better way to structure the application is to isolate the device-specific portions in separate a.outs. This way, the main application can remain unchanged when new hardware is to be supported. All that need be done is to modify some configuration file that the application uses to determine the program to run to initialize a given device.

By segmenting an application into a primary device-independent portion and multiple device-dependent portions, the device-independent part of the application can be designed to fork and exec the device-specific program to handle device initialization. A pipe or UNIX domain socket can be used to transfer a file descriptor that refers to the initialized device from the device-specific program back to the main application.

Example 7.5.2. This example illustrates the software architecture just discussed. The main application calls setup with the pathname of the device to be used, the pathname of the program to be used to initialize the device, and the list of arguments to the program.

setup creates two interconnected UNIX domain sockets and forks a child process to exec the requested initialization program. The parent process uses one of the sockets and the child process uses the other. After initializing the device, the program executed by the child will use the socket to send an open file descriptor for the device back to the parent. The parent will then receive the file descriptor and return it to the caller.

```
#include <sys/types.h>
#include <sys/uio.h>
#include <sys/socket.h>
#include <sys/wait.h>
#include <unistd.h>
#include <stdio.h>
#include <stdlib.h>
#include <errno.h>
#include <string.h>

int
setup(char *device, char *initprog, char *args[])
{
        int fds[2];
        int i, nfd, narg, cstat;
        pid_t pid;
        struct iovec iov;
```

```
struct msghdr msg;
char **eargs;

/*
 * Create a pair of interconnected sockets.
 */
if (socketpair(AF_UNIX, SOCK_STREAM, 0, fds) < 0)
    return(-1);

/*
 * Fork off a child process to execute the
 * device-specific initialization program.
 */
if ((pid = fork()) < 0) {
    /*
     * fork failed.  Close the pair of
     * sockets just created.
     */
    close(fds[0]);
    close(fds[1]);
    return(-1);
} else if (pid == 0) {
    /*
     * Child processing.  Close the parent's socket
     * descriptor and file descriptor 0.  Then dup
     * the child's socket to fd 0.  This gives the
     * program a well-known file descriptor to use
     * when sending the device file descriptor.  We
     * don't need fds[1] after it is duplicated.
     */
    close(fds[0]);
    close(0);
    if (dup(fds[1]) != 0)
        exit(1);
    close(fds[1]);

    /*
     * Count the number of arguments and allocate
     * enough space for the pointers plus the command
     * name, the device name, and a terminating NULL
     * pointer.
     */
    for (narg = 0; args[narg] != NULL; narg++)
        ;
    eargs = malloc((narg+3)*sizeof(char *));
    if (eargs == NULL)
        exit(1);

    /*
     * The first argument is the basename of the
     * command to be executed.
     */
    eargs[0] = strrchr(initprog, '/');
    if (eargs[0] == NULL)
```

```
            eargs[0] = initprog;
        else
            eargs[0]++;

        /*
         * Copy the other arguments.
         */
        for (i = 0;  i < narg;  i++)
            eargs[i+1] = args[i];

        /*
         * The last argument is the name of the device.
         * End the array with a NULL pointer.
         */
        eargs[++i] = device;
        eargs[++i] = NULL;

        /*
         * Execute the specified program.
         */
        execvp(initprog, eargs);
        exit(1);
    } else {
        /*
         * The parent has no use for the child's socket
         * descriptor, so close it.
         */
        close(fds[1]);

        /*
         * Wait for the child to terminate.
         */
        if (waitpid(pid, &cstat, 0) < 0) {
            close(fds[0]);
            return(-1);
        }

        /*
         * If the child terminated because of a signal,
         * set errno to EINTR.  Otherwise, if the child
         * terminated on its own with an unsuccessful
         * status, set errno to EPROTO.
         */
        if (WIFSIGNALED(cstat)) {
            close(fds[0]);
            errno = EINTR;
            return(-1);
        } else if (WIFEXITED(cstat)  &&
          (WEXITSTATUS(cstat) != 0)) {
            close(fds[0]);
            errno = EPROTO;
            return(-1);
        }
```

```
/*
 * Prepare to receive the file descriptor.
 */
iov.iov_base = NULL;
iov.iov_len = 0;
msg.msg_iov = &iov;
msg.msg_iovlen = 1;
msg.msg_name = NULL;
msg.msg_accrights = (caddr_t)&nfd;
msg.msg_accrightslen = sizeof(nfd);

/*
 * If recvmsg fails, make sure the file
 * descriptor is invalid.
 */
if (recvmsg(fds[0], &msg, 0) < 0)
    nfd = -1;

/*
 * Close the socket descriptor and return the
 * file descriptor for the device.
 */
close(fds[0]);
return(nfd);
}
}
```

The child process will close file descriptor 0 and dup its end of the socket connection (fds[1]) so the initialization program can access the socket using file descriptor 0. Then the original file descriptor for the socket is closed and the child builds the arguments to execvp and executes the specified program. The command-line format of the initialization program is:

```
program_name  [args]  device_name
```

The parent does not need the end of the socket that the child is using, so the parent can close it. If the child exits abnormally, an error is returned. Otherwise, the parent receives the file descriptor sent by the child, closes the socket, and returns the file descriptor to the device.

The skeleton for a sample initialization program is shown below. It opens the device, does whatever is necessary to prepare the device for communication, and sends the file descriptor over the socket back to the parent. Note that the file descriptor sent does not have to be a socket endpoint; it can be open to any type of file.

```
#include <sys/types.h>
#include <sys/uio.h>
#include <sys/socket.h>
#include <unistd.h>
#include <stdio.h>
#include <stdlib.h>
#include <fcntl.h>

extern void fatal(const char *, ...);
```

```
main(int argc, char *argv[])
{
    int fd;
    struct iovec iov;
    struct msghdr msg;

    if (argc < 2) {
        fprintf(stderr, "usage: %s [args] device\n",
          argv[0]);
        exit(1);
    }

    /*
     * Open the device.
     */
    if ((fd = open(argv[argc-1], O_RDWR)) < 0)
        fatal("%s: cannot open %s", argv[0],
          argv[argc-1]);

    /*
     * Perform device-specific initialization.
     */
        .
        .
        .
    /*
     * Send the file descriptor for the device back to
     * the parent using file descriptor 0.
     */
    iov.iov_base = NULL;
    iov.iov_len = 0;
    msg.msg_iov = &iov;
    msg.msg_iovlen = 1;
    msg.msg_name = NULL;
    msg.msg_accrights = (caddr_t)&fd;
    msg.msg_accrightslen = sizeof(int);
    if (sendmsg(0, &msg, 0) < 0)
        fatal("%s: cannot pass fd", argv[0]);
    exit(0);
}
```

When sending the file descriptor back to the parent, the child sets up the iovec structure to indicate that no data are being sent. The access rights field (msg_accrights) is set to point at the file descriptor, and the msg_accrightslen field is set to the number of bytes making up the access rights (in this case, the size of a file descriptor, an integer). If multiple file descriptors were to be sent, then msg_accrights would point to the start of an array of file descriptors and msg_accrightslen would be set to the number of file descriptors to send multiplied by the size of a file descriptor.   □

7.6 ADVANCED TOPICS

This section covers some of the more advanced aspects of using sockets, including ways to find the address bound to a socket at either end of a connection, out-of-band data, I/O multiplexing, asynchronous I/O, and nonblocking I/O.

Socket Identification

With the ability to pass sockets between processes, it is sometimes necessary to find the local address bound to the socket, since the application using the socket might not be the one that initialized it. More importantly, applications that want to perform limited authentication need to find out who is on the other end of the connection. We say the authentication is limited because it is vulnerable to mischievous or malevolent users masquerading as others.

The `getsockname(3N)` function can be used to find the (local) address bound to a socket:

```
#include <sys/types.h>
#include <sys/socket.h>

int getsockname(int fd, struct sockaddr *addrp,
    int *alenp);
```

`fd` is the socket file descriptor, `addrp` points to a buffer used to store the address on return, and `alenp` points to an integer initially containing the size of the buffer in bytes. On success, `getsockname` stores the address in the buffer referenced by `addrp`, stores the size of the address in the integer referenced by `alenp`, and returns 0. On failure, `getsockname` sets `errno` to indicate the reason for failure and returns −1.

The `getpeername(3N)` function can be used to find the remote address of a socket (i.e., the address of the socket at the other end of the connection):

```
#include <sys/types.h>
#include <sys/socket.h>

int getpeername(int fd, struct sockaddr *addrp,
    int *alenp);
```

All the parameters and return values are the same as for `getsockname`, except that the address returned is that bound at the remote end of the connection.

Using `getsockname` and `getpeername` with *reserved ports* increases the reliability of the authentication, but it still is not entirely effective. Reserved ports are supported by some protocols to restrict the ability of users to bind selected port numbers. Only privileged users (those running as the super-user) can bind these port numbers. For the Internet protocols, ports 0 through 1023 are reserved.

Applications that use `getsockname` and `getpeername` to find the local and remote addresses associated with a connection often assume that if an IP address is from a known (trusted) host and the port number used is within the range of reserved port numbers, the process that bound the address to the socket can be trusted. This assumption is usually good enough, except when unprivileged users illegitimately obtain privileges, either by exploiting a security hole or through carelessness on the part of legitimately privileged users.

Out-of-Band Data

Out-of-band data are treated with a higher priority than normal data. Only some protocols support out-of-band data. The TCP protocol refers to out-of-band data as *urgent data*, since there is a sense of urgency associated with its use.

The socket mechanism allows protocols to support out-of-band data, but does not require it. The facility is managed by the protocol, but the socket mechanism provides a minimal interface for applications to use.

Out-of-band data can be sent by an application by specifying the MSG_OOB flag in the send, sendto, or sendmsg function call. Applications can retrieve the out-of-band data by using the MSG_OOB flag with recv, recvfrom, or recvmsg.

When out-of-band data are received by the protocol, the point where they would go in the normal data stream is marked. This point, called the *urgent mark*, can be sensed with the SIOCATMARK ioctl command:

```
int atmark;

ioctl(fd, SIOCATMARK, &atmark);
```

On return, atmark will be set to 1 if the next byte to be read is where the urgent mark is. Otherwise, it will be set to 0. If more out-of-band data arrive, the urgent mark is updated to the end of the newly arrived data, effectively losing the previous urgent mark.

Normally, SOCKMOD holds onto the out-of-band data so the application can receive them when desired. (This is handled by the protocol in 4BSD.) In addition to receiving the out-of-band data independently from the normal data, applications may elect to receive the out-of-band data inline with the normal data. The S_OOBINLINE socket option can be used to toggle this behavior. When this option is in effect, out-of-band data are duplicated as they are received and then placed with the normal data, in the order received. Applications can either read them with the normal data (without the MSG_OOB flag) or retrieve them ahead of any normal data present (by setting the MSG_OOB flag). Once an application reads past the urgent mark in the normal data stream, the out-of-band data are no longer accessible, even if they were to be delivered out-of-line from the normal data.

If an application has arranged to receive signals from a socket (using the F_SETOWN fcntl command or the FIOSETOWN or SIOCSPGRP ioctl command), then the SIGURG signal is sent to the process when out-of-band data arrive. The default disposition of SIGURG is ignore, so a process will not notice it unless a signal handler has been installed to catch it.

I/O Multiplexing

Although, strictly speaking, select(3N) is not part of the socket interface (it works with all file types), it is probably used most often with sockets. It is similar to poll(2) in that it allows applications to wait for I/O-related events on multiple file descriptors at one time. This interface is different, however.

```
#include <sys/time.h>
#include <sys/types.h>

int select(int nfds, fd_set *readsetp, fd_set *writesetp,
    fd_set *exceptsetp, struct timeval *timeout);
void FD_SET(int fd, fd_set *setp);
void FD_CLR(int fd, fd_set *setp);
int FD_ISSET(int fd, fd_set *setp);
void FD_ZERO(fd_set *setp);
```

A set of file descriptors is represented by an fd_set structure, where there is one bit for each file descriptor. The fd_set structure is big enough to select 1024 file descriptors, but the size can be changed by defining the symbol FD_SETSIZE before including <sys/types.h>.

Four macros are defined to manage fd_set structures. FD_ZERO can be used to clear all the bits in the structure. A single bit corresponding to a file descriptor can be set to 1 with FD_SET. Similarly, a single bit can be cleared with FD_CLR. The FD_ISSET macro will return a nonzero value if the bit for the given file descriptor is set to 1 in the given set. It returns 0 otherwise.

There are three sets representing three conditions that select will check. readsetp points to an fd_set structure initially representing all the file descriptors to be checked for data ready to read. writesetp is like readsetp, but is used for file descriptors to which data can be written. exceptsetp is used to represent the file descriptors to check for exceptional conditions. Currently, the only exceptional condition is the availability of out-of-band data for reading. (4BSD systems also support an additional exceptional condition: the arrival of status information on the master side of a pseudo-terminal in packet mode. See Stevens [1990] for details.)

As far as sockets are concerned, select will treat a file descriptor as being readable when a connect indication arrives. Thus servers can use select to wait for connect indications on multiple sockets, instead of blocking inside accept on one of the sockets. Client applications can also use select. If a socket is in non-blocking mode and a process calls connect, a connection attempt will be started and connect will return −1 with errno set to EINPROGRESS. The application can call select to wait for the file descriptor to be marked as writable. When it is, the connection will have been completed and data transfer may begin.

The caller sets the bits corresponding to the file descriptors that are to be checked. On return, only those file descriptors with the events satisfied will still have their corresponding bits turned on in the sets. If the caller is not interested in some of the conditions, the corresponding fd_set pointer can be set to NULL. The nfds parameter is the maximum number of file descriptors to check in the sets.

(This is a different kind of maximum than used in `poll`.) `select` starts at file descriptor 0 and checks all the consecutive file descriptors up to, but not including, `nfds`. For example, if an application wants to check file descriptors 0, 1, 2, and 5 for input, then `nfds` should be set to 6. This will result in `select` checking file descriptors 0, 1, 2, 3, 4, and 5.

The `timeout` parameter specifies an optional period of time after which `select` will return if no conditions have been satisfied. If `timeout` is `NULL`, `select` will block until an event is satisfied or until it is interrupted by a signal. Otherwise, `timeout` points to a `timeval` structure that describes the length of the waiting period in seconds and microseconds. The `timeval` structure can be set to zeros to use `select` for polling. The `timeval` structure is defined in `<sys/time.h>` as containing two fields: one that represents seconds and another than represents microseconds.

```
struct timeval {
    long    tv_sec;      /* seconds */
    long    tv_usec;     /* and microseconds */
};
```

On success, `select` returns the number of file descriptors that have events pending. If the same file descriptor is being checked for more than one type of event, it can be counted more than once in the return value if more than one event is satisfied. In this sense, the return value can be thought of as the total number of bits set on return instead of the number of file descriptors with pending events. If the time limit expires, `select` returns 0. On return, the file descriptor sets and the `timeval` structure might be modified, so applications have to reinitialize them if the applications intend to call `select` again. Use of `select` is illustrated in Example 7.8.1.

Nonblocking and Asynchronous I/O

Nonblocking I/O techniques like those described in Section 3.4 can also be applied to sockets. When a socket file descriptor is ready for I/O, the socket mechanism provides a way to notify the process with a signal. In socket terminology, this technique is called *asynchronous I/O*. We have deliberately avoided this term in the past because it is easily confused with more elaborate asynchronous I/O mechanisms, such as those proposed by the IEEE's P1003.4 draft standard.

The BSD signal used to notify processes of asynchronous I/O events is `SIGIO`. In SVR4, `SIGIO` is defined to be `SIGPOLL`. This is transparent to applications, except for one detail. In 4BSD, the default disposition for `SIGIO` is ignore. In SVR4, the default disposition for `SIGPOLL` is to kill the process. For this reason, applications must establish their signal handlers for `SIGIO` before enabling its generation.

Asynchronous I/O is most useful when performing nonblocking I/O. It can, however, be used with normal (blocking) I/O to avoid blocking while trying to receive data from a socket file descriptor. In this manner, an application would only try to read from a socket when data are present and `SIGIO` is generated.

Nonblocking I/O simplifies this task by allowing an application to use the read error to indicate that no data are present. Without nonblocking I/O, an application has to employ other methods to figure out that the socket has no data available (such as the FIONREAD ioctl command).

Applications can use either fcntl(2) or ioctl(2) to enable asynchronous I/O or nonblocking I/O on a socket file descriptor. With fcntl, nonblocking I/O for a socket is enabled by setting the FNDELAY flag with the F_SETFL command. With ioctl, nonblocking I/O on a socket can be enabled with the FIONBIO command. In this case, if the argument points to a nonzero integer, nonblocking I/O is enabled. Otherwise, if the integer is zero, nonblocking I/O is disabled.

Note the difference between the flags used with the F_SETFL fcntl command in SVR4 and those used in 4BSD. In SVR4, the flags are defined by the same symbols used with open(2). For example, to set no-delay mode, an application uses the O_NDELAY flag. In 4BSD, however, the flag symbols are the same as those used in the kernel's file table (FNDELAY, for example). The open flags have the same values as the file table flags, so they are interchangeable. (More recent versions of 4BSD have moved to using the open flags instead of the file table flags, but the file table flag symbols remain defined for source-level compatibility.)

Example 7.6.1. This example shows two different implementations of a pair of functions that enable and disable nonblocking I/O on a socket. The first pair uses fcntl and the second pair uses ioctl.

```
#include <sys/types.h>
#include <sys/file.h>
#include <fcntl.h>

int
setsocknoblock(int fd)
{
        int flags;

        /*
         * Enable nonblocking mode:
         * get the file flags and
         * set the FNDELAY flag.
         */
        flags = fcntl(fd, F_GETFL, 0);
        if (flags != -1)
            return(fcntl(fd, F_SETFL, (flags|FNDELAY)));
        return(-1);
}

int
setsockblock(int fd)
{
        int flags;

        /*
         * Disable nonblocking mode:
```

```
 * get the file flags and
 * clear the FNDELAY flag.
 */
flags = fcntl(fd, F_GETFL, 0);
if (flags != -1)
    return(fcntl(fd, F_SETFL, (flags&~FNDELAY)));
return(-1);
}
```

fcntl is somewhat inconvenient to use because the current file flags must be obtained before setting or clearing the FNDELAY flag. The ioctl-based implementation is simpler.

```
#include <sys/filio.h>
#include <unistd.h>

int
setsocknoblock(int fd)
{
    int flag = 1;

    /*
     * Enable nonblocking mode.
     */
    return(ioctl(fd, FIONBIO, &flag));
}

int
setsockblock(int fd)
{
    int flag = 0;

    /*
     * Disable nonblocking mode.
     */
    return(ioctl(fd, FIONBIO, &flag));
}
```

                                                                                                                            □

Nonblocking I/O will cause most socket calls to fail with errno set to EWOULDBLOCK instead of blocking. One exception to this is connect: it sets errno to EINPROGRESS. In SVR4, EWOULDBLOCK is defined to be EAGAIN.

After the signal handler is installed, enabling asynchronous I/O is a two-step process. First, the application needs to register its process ID with the socket so signals can be sent to the right place. Second, signal generation needs to be enabled.

With fcntl, the first step uses the F_SETOWN command and the second step uses the F_SETFL command to turn on the FASYNC file flag. With ioctl, the first step is accomplished by using either the FIOSETOWN or SIOCSPGRP command. The second step is accomplished by using the FIOASYNC command.

The 4BSD implementation allows a process to register its process ID or its process group ID with the socket. In the former case, signals are sent to the calling process. In the latter case, signals are sent to the calling process's process group. The argument is interpreted as a process group if it is negative. The process group ID is derived by taking the absolute value of the argument. Applications cannot set process IDs for any process other than their own. Similarly, applications cannot set process group IDs for any process group other than the one to which they belong.

The SVR4 socket implementation only supports sending signals to the process, not the entire process group. In practice, this has not presented any compatibility problems.

Example 7.6.2. The following functions can be used to enable and disable asynchronous I/O on a socket file descriptor. As in the previous example, implementations using both fcntl and ioctl are presented.

```
#include <sys/types.h>
#include <sys/file.h>
#include <unistd.h>
#include <fcntl.h>

int
setasync(int fd)
{
        int flags;

        /*
         * Enable asynchronous mode:
         * register this process to receive signals
         * from the socket, get the file flags, and
         * set the FASYNC flag.
         */
        if (fcntl(fd, F_SETOWN, getpid()) != -1) {
            flags = fcntl(fd, F_GETFL, 0);
            if (flags != -1)
                return(fcntl(fd, F_SETFL, (flags|FASYNC)));
        }
        return(-1);
}

int
setsync(int fd)
{
        int flags;

        /*
         * Disable asynchronous mode:
         * get the file flags, and
         * clear the FASYNC flag.
         */
        flags = fcntl(fd, F_GETFL, 0);
        if (flags != -1)
            return(fcntl(fd, F_SETFL, (flags&~FASYNC)));
        return(-1);
}
```

The examples use getpid(2) to obtain the process ID of the calling process.

The `ioctl`-based versions follow:

```
#include <sys/filio.h>
#include <unistd.h>

int
setasync(int fd)
{
    int flag = 1;
    pid_t pid = getpid();

    /*
     * Register this process to receive signals
     * from the socket and enable asynchronous
     * mode.
     */
    if (ioctl(fd, FIOSETOWN, &pid) != -1)
        return(ioctl(fd, FIOASYNC, &flag));
    return(-1);
}

int
setsync(int fd)
{
    int flag = 0;

    /*
     * Disable asynchronous mode.
     */
    return(ioctl(fd, FIOASYNC, &flag));
}
```
□

7.7 COMPARISON WITH THE TLI

Given the job of developing software that uses network communication facilities, which interface should a person use: the TLI or sockets? The answer lies more with taste than technical superiority.

Developers used to the 4BSD interfaces will undoubtedly want to continue to use sockets for their communication needs. Similarly, people more comfortable with the System V world will want to use the TLI. Both interfaces provide adequate functionality to allow a developer to write programs that communicate over a network. People concerned with developing applications that run under both SVR4 and 4BSD will want to use the socket interface since an implementation exists for both environments.

The socket interface exports a simpler model for interprocess communication than does the TLI. On the other hand, the TLI is more flexible than sockets. One example of this is server-side connection establishment. The TLI provides three choices for designing the way a server accepts a connection, depending on the queue length (analogous to the backlog) and whether the file descriptor used for the connection is the same endpoint used to listen for connect indications (see Table 4.3). The socket mechanism provides only two choices, not allowing the server to accept the connection on the same endpoint used for listening. With the socket mechanism, however, the design of the server is unaffected by the choice of the connection establishment method.

The socket model comes closest to the TLI model in the case where the connection is accepted on a different endpoint and the queue length is one, regardless of the queue length in the socket model. The reason for the independence of the queue length is that the socket model does not allow multiple connect requests to interfere with the process of a server accepting a connection. Recall from Section 4.4 that t_accept(3N) can fail with a TLOOK error if another connect indication arrives before the current one is accepted.

The socket mechanism was designed as an interprocess communication interface, as well as a transport-level network communication interface. The TLI, on the other hand, was designed as an interface to the OSI transport level. While the socket mechanism was designed to support naive applications (ones that use read and write and are ignorant of the network), the TLI was designed with the belief that network transport semantics are inherently different from UNIX file semantics. Nonetheless, the TLI does allow naive applications to use transport endpoints as long as TIRDWR is pushed on the stream. The main difference is that with a socket, either the socket calls or read and write can be used with the endpoint. With the TLI, once TIRDWR is on the stream, most of the TLI calls cannot be used. If TIRDWR is absent, other than the TLI calls, only write can be used (and only with connection-oriented endpoints).

One convenient thing about the TLI is that applications use filenames to identify transport providers. The socket interface uses manifest constants to identify address families and protocol families. It is easier to add a new driver and device file to a system than it is to add a manifest constant to a public header file.

Endpoint Management

A transport endpoint is created by calling t_open. A socket endpoint is created by calling socket. With the TLI, all endpoints must be bound using t_bind before they can participate in any communication. With sockets, applications do not have to call bind explicitly. Most socket primitives, when presented with an unbound socket, will perform an implicit bind automatically (except for UNIX domain sockets in 4BSD).

Another difference is that servers declare their intention to accept connection requests on a particular endpoint when they call t_bind, but using sockets, servers accomplish this by calling listen.

The TLI allows an address to be disassociated from a transport endpoint by calling t_unbind. The socket mechanism provides no such facility. Instead, addresses are automatically unbound when a socket is closed. (This happens with the TLI too.)

With the TLI, applications can find out various characteristics of the transport provider by calling `t_getinfo`. There is not an equivalent socket interface, although some information is available via `getsockopt`.

The TLI allows callers to allocate data structures based on the limits determined by the transport provider. `t_alloc` and `t_free` are provided to allocate and free the memory, respectively. They are most often used when allocating space for addresses. Address formats are protocol- and implementation-dependent.

The socket interface handles the specification of addresses differently. It defines a structure to overlay addresses that forces socket addresses to follow a format that guarantees an address will identify its own communication domain. The first two bytes of every socket address must contain the value of a manifest constant that identifies the domain of the address. The rest of the address is treated as a variable-length byte string whose format is protocol- and implementation-dependent. Whenever an address appears as a parameter in an interface, the address length also appears.

If a socket routine fails, applications can call `perror(3C)` to print an error message corresponding to the reason for failure. TLI-based applications call `t_error` instead, because the TLI library maintains its own error code in addition to the system's `errno`.

A transport endpoint follows a set of state transitions throughout its use. `t_getstate` is used to query the current state. With a socket endpoint, the state transitions are more or less hidden from the application. They only show through in some of the error returns (`ENOTCONN`, for example).

`t_look` is used when a transport library function fails because an asynchronous event has occurred that requires some response from an application. An example is the arrival of a disconnect indication. In contrast, the socket model does not require that applications respond to asynchronous events.

Both interfaces provide for options management. The TLI library provides `t_optmgmt`, and the socket library provides `setsockopt` and `getsockopt`. One way the two facilities differ is the socket model allows applications to get and set options at different protocol levels, while the TLI model restricts applications to transport-level options only. Another way they differ is that the socket routines can be used at any time during the life of a socket endpoint. The TLI, however, restricts the use of `t_optmgmt` to the time between when a transport endpoint is bound and when it is connected (i.e., when it is in the idle state).

Connection Establishment

Socket applications can call `connect` to create a virtual circuit over a connection-oriented protocol, or to cache the destination address using a connectionless protocol. TLI applications use `t_connect` to create virtual circuits, but `t_connect` can only be used with connection-oriented protocols. The TLI allows applications to send user data and protocol options with a connect request if the transport provider supports it. The socket mechanism has no such facility.

In the TLI, server-side connection establishment is a two-step process: receive the connect indication and either accept or reject it. The socket model reduces this to a one-step process where the connect indication is received and accepted all at once. TLI applications use `t_listen` to retrieve a connect indication, blocking if one is not immediately available. The connection can be accepted by calling `t_accept` or rejected by calling `t_snddis`. Since `accept` completes the connection before returning to the application, socket-based server applications can only close the connection immediately if they do not wish to satisfy the request for service.

As discussed earlier, `accept` always returns a new file descriptor to be used with the connection. The TLI gives applications control over whether or not the connection is to be established using a new endpoint.

If a connect request is made with an endpoint in nonblocking mode, the socket model ensures that applications can send and receive data when `select` indicates that the socket is writable. With the TLI, on the other hand, applications can be notified of the arrival of the connect confirmation message (by polling for the `POLLIN` or `POLLRDNORM` event), which they then have to retrieve by calling `t_rcvconnect`.

Data Transfer

When it comes to transferring data, the main difference between sockets and the TLI is that all the I/O interfaces can be used with any socket, regardless of its type (as long as the socket is "connected"). The TLI restricts the use of I/O primitives based on whether an endpoint is connectionless or connection-oriented. `t_snd` and `t_rcv` can only be used with connection-oriented endpoints. Similarly, `read` and `write` can only be used with connection-oriented endpoints, but TIRDWR must be pushed on the stream first. Once on the stream, however, TIRDWR will not allow `t_snd` to be used.

The socket mechanism does not make any of these restrictions. Applications can use `send`, `sendmsg`, `sendto`, or `write` to transmit data as long as a connection has been established. For datagram sockets, the only requirement is that the destination address be cached in the socket by calling `connect` before using a primitive that does not provide an explicit destination address. Data can be received from a socket using `recv`, `recvfrom`, `recvmsg`, or `read`.

With connectionless TLI endpoints, `t_sndudata` and `t_rcvudata` are the only I/O primitives allowed to be used. `t_rcvuderr` must be used to retrieve error notifications. No such rule exists with the socket interface, although asynchronously generated errors are retrievable using the `SO_ERROR` option to `getsockopt`. (Under some conditions in 4BSD, asynchronous errors cause the next socket call to fail, but this semantic is not maintained in SVR4.)

If a connection-oriented protocol supports logical message boundaries, the TLI allows applications to use a "more" flag to control when a message represents a logical continuation of a previous message. No such mechanism exists with `SOCK_SEQPACKET` sockets in the original 4.3BSD socket interface, but recent versions of 4BSD have added a new flag (`MSG_EOR`) to allow applications to mark the logical end of a message.

Connection Release

When a socket is closed down and the underlying protocol is reliable, the socket mechanism will try to deliver any data transmitted but not yet delivered. This can be avoided by using shutdown before closing the socket.

The TLI makes a distinction between abortive release and orderly release, providing different primitives for each. Orderly releases are initiated with t_sndrel and completed by the peer with t_rcvrel. Similarly, abortive releases are made with t_snddis. Peer processes obtain notification of the abortive connection release by calling t_rcvdis. The socket mechanism, on the other hand, leaves the type of connection release up to the protocol.

Socket applications call close to dismantle a socket endpoint, while TLI applications call t_close. This difference is an implementation side effect since the socket mechanism was originally developed as a system call interface and the TLI was developed as a library interface.

7.8 NAME-TO-ADDRESS TRANSLATION

The name-to-address translation library routines introduced in Chapter 5 were derived from the 4BSD library routines that provided similar functionality. The 4BSD routines, however, are implemented for the Internet domain only.

There are four sets of routines, each providing access to a different database file. One file is /etc/hosts, which maps host names to Internet addresses. Another is /etc/networks, which maps network names to network numbers. A third file, /etc/protocols, maps protocol names to protocol numbers. Finally, /etc/services maps service names to port numbers.

The functions return entries from the files as pointers to data structures stored in statically allocated memory. The memory is overwritten on every function call. If an application needs to save the data, the data should be copied to a private buffer before the next call that will overwrite them.

The gethostent(3N) routines provide access to /etc/hosts. Information about each entry is returned in a hostent structure:

```
struct hostent {
    char    *h_name;        /* official name of host */
    char    **h_aliases;    /* alias list */
    int     h_addrtype;     /* address type */
    int     h_length;       /* length of address */
    char    **h_addr_list;  /* list of addresses */
};
```

The h_name field points to the name of the host. Each host can optionally have a set of name aliases, pointed to by h_aliases. The list is terminated by a NULL pointer. The h_addrtype field is provided to allow for extending the routines to handle other domains in the future. Currently, it only takes on the value AF_INET. The h_length field is also for future extension, and is currently only set to 4, the length of an Internet address. The h_addr_list field points to a list of binary addresses (in network byte order) for the host with the name h_name. Multiple addresses are possible because a host can have multiple network interfaces.

The hostent structure is defined in <netdb.h>. The function prototypes for the gethostent routines are shown below.

```
#include <sys/types.h>
#include <sys/socket.h>
#include <netdb.h>

struct hostent *gethostent(void);
struct hostent *gethostbyaddr(char *addrp, int len,
    int type);
struct hostent *gethostbyname(char *name);
void sethostent(int stayopen);
void endhostent(void);

extern int h_errno;
```

gethostent will open /etc/hosts the first time called. It returns the next entry in the file as a hostent structure. When the end of the file is reached, or if an error is encountered, gethostent returns NULL. endhostent is used to close the file when processing is complete.

Given an address, its length, and the address type, gethostbyaddr will return a pointer to the corresponding hostent structure, or NULL if a match cannot be found. In the latter case, the external integer h_errno will be set to indicate the reason for failure. The only reason currently used is HOST_NOT_FOUND when no host matches the given address.

The Internet protocol suite includes a domain name service facility as specified by RFC 1034 and RFC 1035. It enlists the use of name server daemons to provide name-to-address translation and is enabled by adding the resolv.so library to the list of directory lookup libraries found in /etc/netconfig. If the domain name service is being used, other errors that can be returned are TRY_AGAIN for temporary resource outages, NO_RECOVERY for fatal errors, and NO_DATA for no corresponding data or address.

The gethostbyname function will return a hostent structure for the given host name. The name parameter can match either the host name or one of the host's aliases. Like gethostbyaddr, gethostbyname returns NULL and sets h_errno if a match cannot be made. sethostent can be used to rewind the file if it is open and optionally cause it to remain open after calls to gethostbyaddr and gethostbyname. If stayopen is nonzero, the database file remains open until endhostent is called. Otherwise, gethostbyaddr and gethostbyname will close it before returning.

The getnetent(3N) routines provide access to /etc/networks. Information about each entry is returned in a netent structure:

```
struct netent {
     char     *n_name;          /* official name of net */
     char     **n_aliases;      /* alias list */
     int      n_addrtype;       /* net number type */
     long     n_net;            /* net number */
};
```

The n_name field is the name of the network (for example, "arpanet" is a network name). If the network name has any aliases, the n_aliases field will point to a NULL-terminated list of name aliases. The n_addrtype field contains the domain to which the network belongs. Currently, it is only set to AF_INET. The n_net field contains the network number.

The netent structure is defined in <netdb.h>. The function prototypes for the getnetent routines are shown below.

```
#include <netdb.h>

struct netent *getnetent(void);
struct netent *getnetbyname(char *name);
struct netent *getnetbyaddr(long net, int type);
void setnetent(int stayopen);
void endnetent(void);
```

The getnetent function will open /etc/networks if it is not already open and return the next entry in the file as a netent structure. endnetent can be used to close the file. getnetbyname will return the netent structure corresponding to the given network name, or NULL if a match cannot be found. A match will be found if the name is the same as either the network name or one of its aliases.

getnetbyaddr will return the netent structure for the given network number and type. setnetent can be used to rewind the database file and optionally keep it open after invocations of getnetbyname and getnetbyaddr.

The getprotoent(3N) routines provide access to /etc/protocols. Information about each entry is returned in a protoent structure:

```
struct protoent {
     char     *p_name;          /* official protocol name */
     char     **p_aliases;      /* alias list */
     int      p_proto;          /* protocol number */
};
```

The p_name field points to the name of the protocol. The p_aliases field points to an array of alias names, if they exist. The array is terminated with a NULL. The p_proto field contains the protocol number.

The protoent structure is defined in <netdb.h>. The function prototypes for the getprotoent routines are

```
#include <netdb.h>

struct protoent *getprotoent(void);
struct protoent *getprotobyname(char *name);
struct protoent *getprotobynumber(int proto);
void setprotoent(int stayopen);
void endprotoent(void);
```

The getprotoent function opens /etc/protocols if it is not already open and returns the next entry in the file as a protoent structure. If an error occurs, or if the end of file is reached, getprotoent returns NULL. endprotoent can be called to close the file. getprotobyname returns the protoent structure corresponding to the specified protocol name, or NULL if a match cannot be made. getprotobyname will return a match if the specified name is the same as either the protocol name or one of its aliases.

getprotobynumber returns the protoent structure corresponding to the specified protocol number. The setprotoent function can be used to rewind the file and, if stayopen is nonzero, cause the file to remain open after calls to getprotobyname and getprotobynumber.

The getservent(3N) routines provide access to /etc/services. Information about each entry is returned in a servent structure:

```
struct servent {
     char    *s_name;        /* official service name */
     char    **s_aliases;    /* alias list */
     int     s_port;         /* port service resides at */
     char    *s_proto;       /* protocol to use */
};
```

The s_name field points to the name of the service. The s_aliases field points to a NULL-terminated list of alias names for the service, if any exist. The s_port field contains the port number associated with the service, in network byte order. The s_proto field points to the name of the protocol to use to access the service.

The servent structure is defined in <netdb.h>. The function prototypes for the getservent routines are shown below.

```
#include <netdb.h>

struct servent *getservent(void);
struct servent *getservbyname(char *name, char *proto);
struct servent *getservbyport(int port, char *proto);
void setservent(int stayopen);
void endservent(void);
```

The getservent function opens /etc/services if it is not already open and returns the next entry in the file as a servent structure. If the end of file is reached, or if an error occurs, getservent returns NULL. endservent can be called to close the file. The getservbyname function will return the servent structure that corresponds to the given service name and protocol name. The protocol name can be NULL, in which case the function only matches on service name. Like the other name-based functions, if an alias matches the specified name, the servent structure is returned for that entry.

The getservbyport function will return the servent structure that corresponds to the specified port number and protocol name. The protocol name can be NULL to force a match on port number alone. As with the other functions, setservent can be called to rewind the file and, if stayopen is nonzero, cause the file to remain open after calls to getservbyname and getservbyport.

For all the database files, if stayopen is set to 0 in the call to the set*ent routines, the file offset is set to 0, but this will not undo the effect of a prior call with stayopen set to a nonzero value. In other words, if the file was marked to be kept open, this cannot be changed until the file is closed using the end*ent routines.

The major difference between the library routines summarized in this section and the name-to-address mapping routines discussed in Chapter 5 is that the BSD routines provide a simple mapping of the information stored in configuration files. A different set of routines is used to access the information stored in each file. The SVR4 routines, on the other hand, supply a level of abstraction, providing mappings between host–service pairs and network addresses. Ultimately, both sets of routines provide the same functionality.

Example 7.8.1. This is an extended example, combining some of the information presented in the last three sections. In it, we use send and recv to communicate over a SOCK_STREAM socket connection. We use the BSD name-to-address mapping routines to identify the application's port number and the Internet addresses of other machines on the network. Also, we use select to identify when a connect indication has arrived.

By convention, files placed in /var/news are treated as containing system news. The news(1) program can be used to print only those news items that have been changed or added since the last time a user has read news.

The following program illustrates a simple news server. It looks for newly created or modified files in /var/news and distributes them to other machines on the network. One copy of the daemon should be running on each machine. The daemon acts as both a client and a server, depending on whether it is transmitting or receiving a file. Instead of containing system-only news, this server extends /var/news to contain networkwide news.

This example is limited to work in the Internet domain only. Assume the daemon is registered as the service named "newsd" in /etc/services. Because of the length of the example, it will be presented in small pieces, function by function. The main flow of control is as follows:

1. Become a daemon.
2. Create a list of all hosts in /etc/hosts.
3. Initialize a socket to accept connections from news daemons on other machines.
4. Wait for connection indications.
5. If 30 seconds have passed without a connect indication, check /var/news for new or modified files.
6. If any are found, send them to the other systems on the network.

7.   When a connection indication arrives, accept it, read the file, and store it in
      `/var/news`.

We start out by looking at the definitions and global variables.

```
#include <sys/types.h>
#include <sys/socket.h>
#include <sys/param.h>
#include <sys/stat.h>
#include <sys/utsname.h>
#include <netinet/in.h>
#include <netdb.h>
#include <utime.h>
#include <dirent.h>
#include <errno.h>
#include <fcntl.h>
#include <unistd.h>
#include <stdlib.h>
#include <string.h>

#define NEWSTIME "/var/.newstime"
#define NEWSPERM (S_IRUSR|S_IWUSR|S_IRGRP|S_IROTH)
#define NETBUFSZ 8192

struct newshost {
      struct newshost     *nh_next;
      char                *nh_name;
      struct in_addr      nh_addr;
};

char *service = "newsd";
struct newshost *hostlist;
char lastrecv[MAXNAMELEN];
ushort_t newsport;
time_t scantime;
struct utsname u;
```

The file `/var/.newstime` will be used to identify the last time the daemon
scanned `/var/news` for changes or additions. The news files will be created with
permissions that will allow everyone to read them, but only the daemon can modify
or delete them. `NETBUFSZ` specifies the size of the buffers used to transmit and
receive file data over the network connection.

When we scan `/etc/hosts` for all the machines on the network, we will use
the `newshost` structure to remember the host addresses. For each host we come
across, we will allocate another `newshost` structure and link it onto a list headed by
`hostlist`.

The name of the last file received is kept in `lastrecv` so that it will not be
mistaken as a file originating from the current host. Every time we receive a file
from another host, we will scan `/var/news` for new files created on the local host,
skipping the last one received from the network. This prevents a second file arriving
from the network from overwriting the name of the last received file before we have
had a chance to scan `/var/news`. It also prevents the server from being kept so

busy receiving files from the network that the server is unable to check for files created on the local host.

The `service` variable points to the daemon's service name. The port number for the service is stored in `newsport`. `scantime` contains the time that the last scan of `/var/news` was done. The name of the host on which the daemon is running is stored in the `u` variable. We will use the `log` and `daemonize` routines presented in Chapter 2.

The daemon is partitioned into five functions, in addition to the `main` procedure. The list of addresses for hosts on the network is built by `gethosts`. A news file is transmitted to all the machines on the network by calling `broadcast`. A news file is received from another machine by calling `recvnews`. The `newstime` function records the modification time for `/var/.newstime`, optionally setting it to the current time. The files in `/var/news` are checked for changes and additions by calling `doscan`.

```
void gethosts(void);
void broadcast(char *, struct stat *);
void recvnews(int);
void newstime(int);
void doscan(void);

extern void daemonize(const char *);
extern void log(const char *, ...);

void
main(void)
{
    struct stat sbuf;
    struct sockaddr_in addr;
    int fd, nfd, i;
    struct timeval t;
    fd_set rset;
    struct servent *sp;

    /*
     * Become a daemon.
     */
    daemonize(service);

    /*
     * Change the current working directory to
     * the location where news items are stored.
     */
    if (chdir("/var/news") < 0) {
        log("cannot cd to /var/news: %s",
            strerror(errno));
        exit(1);
    }

    /*
     * Get the local host name.
     */
```

```
if (uname(&u) < 0) {
    log("uname failed: %s", strerror(errno));
    exit(1);
}

/*
 * Check the last time /var/news was scanned.
 */
if (stat(NEWSTIME, &sbuf) < 0) {
    if (errno == ENOENT) {
        /*
         * /var/.newstime doesn't exist --
         * create it.
         */
        if ((fd = creat(NEWSTIME, NEWSPERM)) < 0) {
            log("cannot create %s: %s", NEWSTIME,
                strerror(errno));
            exit(1);
        }
        close(fd);
    } else {
        /*
         * stat failed for an unexpected reason.
         */
        log("cannot stat %s: %s", NEWSTIME,
            strerror(errno));
        exit(1);
    }
}
```

After becoming a daemon process, we change the current working directory to /var/news since that is the place where we will be scanning for modified files and placing the new ones we receive. Then we get the system name by calling uname(2). (BSD applications would call gethostname instead.)

If /var/.newstime does not exist, we have a problem: we have no reference point from which we can determine the new files in /var/news. Two possible solutions are to retransmit all the files or to do nothing, thereby creating the possibility that some files never get transmitted. The first choice will cause files to appear as if they are changed on all the systems whenever one system restarts the daemon if /var/.newstime is missing. This will lead to people rereading news items. The second choice will probably result in fewer complaints from the user population, and administrators can check every now and then to make sure no files miss getting propagated to the other machines. An administrator can force redistribution of a file by changing its modification time with touch(1).

If /var/.newstime does not exist, stat will fail with errno set to ENOENT, and we will create the file. Note that fatal errors cause the daemon to write a message to the log file and exit.

```
/*
 * Create a list of hosts and addresses
 * from /etc/hosts.
```

```
 */
gethosts();

/*
 * Create a socket to use when sending and
 * receiving news files.
 */
if ((fd = socket(AF_INET, SOCK_STREAM, 0)) < 0) {
    log("cannot create socket: %s", strerror(errno));
    exit(1);
}

/*
 * Identify the port number to use for the
 * news service.
 */
sp = getservbyname(service, NULL);
if (!sp) {
    log("cannot find service for %s", service);
    exit(1);
}

/*
 * Create the address and bind it to the socket.
 */
newsport = sp->s_port;
addr.sin_family = AF_INET;
addr.sin_port = newsport;
addr.sin_addr.s_addr = INADDR_ANY;
for (i = 0; i < sizeof(addr.sin_zero); i++)
    addr.sin_zero[i] = 0;
if (bind(fd, &addr, sizeof(struct sockaddr_in)) < 0) {
    log("cannot bind address: %s", strerror(errno));
    exit(1);
}

/*
 * Enable the socket to be used to receive
 * connect indications.
 */
if (listen(fd, 10) < 0) {
    log("cannot listen: %s", strerror(errno));
    exit(1);
}

/*
 * Read the time of the last scan of /var/news.
 */
newstime(0);

/*
 * Scan /var/news for news items to transmit.
 */
doscan();
```

The next steps are to create the list of host addresses and open a socket for receiving files from other machines. We use `getservbyname` to find the port number for the `newsd` service and store it in `newsport`. Then we initialize the `sockaddr_in` address we will be using to listen for connect indications. The Internet address is set to the special value `INADDR_ANY`. This is treated like a wildcard by the protocol, enabling all TCP/IP network interfaces on the host to deliver messages to the daemon.

Once the address is bound to the socket, we call `listen` to mark the socket as willing to receive connect indications. We request a backlog of 10, which is greater than the maximum (`SOMAXCONN`) that can be used on a BSD system, because there is no such restriction in SVR4 and there is a good chance we might queue up that many connect indications given the structure of the daemon.

Before starting the main service loop, we obtain the time of the last scan by calling `newstime`. The 0 parameter prevents `newstime` from updating the modification time of `/var/.newstime`. Then we check all the files in `/var/news` to see if any have been changed or added since the last scan. If so, `doscan` will call `broadcast` to send the new files to the other systems, as we shall see.

```
/*
 * This is the main processing loop.  Wait
 * for connect indications for 30 seconds.
 * If none arrive, scan /var/news for files
 * to transmit.
 */
for (;;) {
    /*
     * Use select to avoid blocking indefinitely.
     */
    t.tv_sec = 30;
    t.tv_usec = 0;
    FD_ZERO(&rset);
    FD_SET(fd, &rset);
    i = select(fd+1, &rset, NULL, NULL, &t);
    if (i < 0) {
        log("select failed: %s", strerror(errno));
        exit(1);
    } else if (i == 0) {
        /*
         * No network traffic -- scan /var/news.
         */
        doscan();
        continue;
    } else if ((i != 1) || !FD_ISSET(fd, &rset)) {
        /*
         * This shouldn't happen.
         */
        log("select ret %d, isset %d; unknown error",
            i, FD_ISSET(fd, &rset));
        exit(1);
    }
```

```
       /*
        * We know fd is now readable, meaning that
        * a connect indication has arrived.  Accept it.
        */
       nfd = accept(fd, NULL, NULL);
       if (nfd < 0) {
           log("cannot accept connection: %s",
             strerror(errno));
           exit(1);
       }

       /*
        * Receive the news file and store it in
        * /var/news.  Then close the newly created
        * network connection.
        */
       recvnews(nfd);
       close(nfd);

       /*
        * Before waiting for more connect indications,
        * check /var/news for newly created news items.
        */
       doscan();
    }
} /* end of main */
```

We start out our infinite service loop by initializing the `timeval` structure to 30 seconds and 0 microseconds. Then we zero an `fd_set` to be used in the call to `select` and set one bit in the `fd_set` structure. The bit corresponds to the file descriptor we are using for the socket that will receive connect indications. We call `select` to see if there are any data to be read on the socket. It will return with the bit representing the file descriptor set to 1 when a connect indication arrives. Instead of using `select` for I/O multiplexing, we use it as a timed wait.

If the 30-second time limit expires, `select` will return 0. We scan the directory for new or changed files and continue waiting for connect indications. If a connect indication arrives in under 30 seconds, `select` will return 1. In this case we accept the connection and call `recvnews` to receive and save the new news file. Then we discard the socket for the connection, scan /var/news for news items to transmit, and continue waiting for more connect indications.

The `gethosts` function reads /etc/hosts and builds a list of addresses for all the hosts on the network.

```
void
gethosts(void)
{
    struct hostent *hp;
    struct newshost *nhp;
    struct in_addr *ip;

    /*
     * Read /etc/hosts one line at a time.
```

```
        */
        while ((hp = gethostent()) != NULL) {
            /*
             * Skip any entries that represent the
             * local host.
             */
            if ((strcmp(hp->h_name, "localhost") == 0) ||
                (strcmp(hp->h_name, "anyhost") == 0) ||
                (strcmp(hp->h_name, u.nodename) == 0))
                    continue;

            /*
             * Allocate a newshost structure to represent
             * this entry.
             */
            nhp = malloc(sizeof(struct newshost));
            if (nhp == NULL) {
                log("cannot allocate memory for host list");
                exit(1);
            }

            /*
             * Initialize the newshost structure with the
             * address and name of the host.  Then put the
             * structure on the front of the list of hosts.
             */
            ip = (struct in_addr *)hp->h_addr;
            nhp->nh_addr.s_addr = ip->s_addr;
            nhp->nh_name = strdup(hp->h_name);
            nhp->nh_next = hostlist;
            hostlist = nhp;
        }

        /*
         * Close /etc/hosts and clean up.
         */
        endhostent();
    }
```

For each host entry, we allocate a newshost structure, save the Internet address, and place the newshost structure on the front of the list (hostlist). We skip the entries for the host the daemon is running on (u.nodename) and the special entries localhost and anyhost. (localhost is a name that can be used to access loopback facilities of the current host. It can be used to connect to services on the machine on which an application is currently running. anyhost is a name that can be used to access the wildcard address defined to receive packets from all network interfaces on the current host.) When we reach the end of /etc/hosts, we call endhostent to close the file.

The doscan function searches /var/news for files added or modified since the last time the daemon checked. It starts out by saving the time we last scanned the directory in lastscan. We need to save the time because we are going to change it with the call to newstime. We cannot defer the call to newstime until after we search the directory, because there is a window between the time we start the search and the time we change the modification time where files that we have already scanned can change. By setting the time before the search, we avoid this possibility altogether.

```c
void
doscan(void)
{
      DIR *dp;
      struct dirent *dep;
      struct stat sbuf;
      time_t lastscan;

      /*
       * Remember the last time we scanned /var/news.
       */
      lastscan = scantime;

      /*
       * Update /var/news with the current time.
       */
      newstime(1);

      /*
       * Open the current directory (/var/news).
       */
      dp = opendir(".");
      if (dp == NULL) {
          log("cannot open directory: %s",
            strerror(errno));
          exit(1);
      }

      /*
       * Use readdir to read one directory entry at a time.
       */
      while ((dep = readdir(dp)) != NULL) {
          /*
           * Skip the directory entries for dot and
           * dot-dot.  Also skip the entry for the
           * last file received from the network.
           */
          if ((strcmp(dep->d_name, ".") == 0) ||
            (strcmp(dep->d_name, "..") == 0) ||
            (strcmp(dep->d_name, lastrecv) == 0))
              continue;

          /*
           * Get the file attributes.  If this fails,
           * just skip the file.
           */
          if (stat(dep->d_name, &sbuf) < 0)
              continue;
```

```
                        /*
                         * If the file has been modified since the last
                         * scan of /var/news, and if it is a regular
                         * file, transmit it to the other hosts.
                         */
                        if ((sbuf.st_mtime > lastscan) &&
                          S_ISREG(sbuf.st_mode))
                            broadcast(dep->d_name, &sbuf);
                }

                /*
                 * Close /var/news.
                 */
                closedir(dp);
        }
```

After calling `newstime`, we open the current directory (`/var/news`) and read each entry with `readdir(3C)` [see `directory(3C)`]. `readdir` returns a pointer to a `dirent` structure containing the filename, among other things. We can skip the dot and dot-dot entries in the directory, as well as the last file we received. For all other files, we call `stat` to retrieve the file attributes.

If the modification time of the file is newer than the time we last scanned and the file is a regular file, we send a copy of it to all the machines in our list by calling `broadcast`. After we check every entry, we close the directory and return.

We have now seen the two types of calls to `newstime`: one at the beginning of execution with a parameter of 0 and one before scanning the directory with a parameter of 1. The parameter controls whether or not the modification time of `/var/.newstime` is set to the current time.

```
        void
        newstime(int touchit)
        {
                struct stat sbuf;

                /*
                 * If touchit is nonzero, update the modification
                 * time on /var/.newstime.
                 */
                if (touchit && (utime(NEWSTIME, NULL) < 0)) {
                    log("cannot change mod time on %s: %s", NEWSTIME,
                      strerror(errno));
                    exit(1);
                }

                /*
                 * Get the modification time of /var/.newstime and
                 * save it in scantime.
                 */
                if (stat(NEWSTIME, &sbuf) < 0) {
                    log("cannot stat %s: %s", NEWSTIME,
                      strerror(errno));
                    exit(1);
```

```
        }
        scantime = sbuf.st_mtime;
}
```

If the `touchit` flag is nonzero, we call `utime(2)` to set the modification and access times of `/var/.newstime` to the current time. Then we call `stat` to read the time. We save it in the global variable `scantime` and return.

The `broadcast` function is used to send a file to all the other hosts on the network. It takes two parameters: the filename and the `stat` structure describing the file. We open the file and initialize the constant parts of the destination address (the address family and the port number). Since we will be communicating with the other `newsd` daemons, we already know the port number.

```
void
broadcast(char *filename, struct stat *stp)
{
        int fd, nfd, len, ret;
        struct newshost *nhp;
        struct sockaddr_in dest;
        char buf[NETBUFSZ];

        /*
         * Open the file to be transmitted.
         */
        if ((fd = open(filename, O_RDONLY)) < 0) {
            log("cannot open %s for broadcast: %s", filename,
              strerror(errno));
            return;
        }

        /*
         * Create most of the destination address.
         */
        dest.sin_family = AF_INET;
        dest.sin_port = newsport;
        for (len = 0; len < sizeof(dest.sin_zero); len++)
            dest.sin_zero[len] = 0;

        /*
         * Step through the list of hosts and transmit the
         * file to each one.
         */
        for (nhp = hostlist; nhp; nhp = nhp->nh_next) {

            /*
             * Seek to the beginning of the file.
             */
            lseek(fd, 0, SEEK_SET);

            /*
             * Finish initializing the destination
             * address.
             */
```

```
    dest.sin_addr.s_addr = nhp->nh_addr.s_addr;

    /*
     * Create a socket.
     */
    if ((nfd = socket(AF_INET, SOCK_STREAM, 0)) < 0) {
        log("cannot create socket: %s",
          strerror(errno));
        continue;
    }

    /*
     * Connect to the host.
     */
    if (connect(nfd, (struct sockaddr *)&dest,
      sizeof(struct sockaddr_in)) < 0) {
        log("cannot connect to %s: %s", nhp->nh_name,
          strerror(errno));
        close(nfd);
        continue;
    }
```

For each host in the list, we need to send the file. We seek to the beginning of the file, save the destination Internet address in the `sockaddr_in` structure, and create a socket to communicate with the other host. If we cannot connect to the host, we close the socket and continue down the list.

After a connection is made, the first thing we want to send to the other host is the name of the file we are about to send. We include the trailing NULL byte so the other host can determine where the filename ends. If the transmission fails, we close the socket and continue processing the list.

```
    /*
     * Calculate the length of the filename and
     * send it to the remote host.
     */
    len = strlen(filename)+1;
    ret = send(nfd, filename, len, 0);
    if (len != ret) {
        if (ret < 0)
            log("send failed: %s", strerror(errno));
        else
            log("sent less than requested (%d/%d)",
              ret, len);
        close(nfd);
        continue;
    }

    /*
     * Now read the file in NETBUFSZ chunks
     * and transmit each chunk to the host.
     */
    while (stp->st_size > 0) {
        len = read(fd, buf, NETBUFSZ);
```

```
                if (len < 0) {
                    log("cannot read file: %s",
                      strerror(errno));
                    break;
                }
                ret = send(nfd, buf, len, 0);
                if (len != ret) {
                    if (ret < 0)
                        log("send failed: %s",
                          strerror(errno));
                    else
                        log("sent less than requested (%d/%d)",
                          ret, len);
                    break;
                }
                stp->st_size -= len;
            }

            /*
             * Close the connection.
             */
            close(nfd);
        }

        /*
         * Close the news file.
         */
        close(fd);
    } /* end of broadcast */
```

We read the file into a buffer, NETBUFSZ bytes at a time, and transmit it using send. When we have transmitted the entire file, we close the socket and continue with the rest of the addresses in the list. When we reach the end of the list, we close the news file and return.

The recvnews function is called by the other side of the connection to receive a news file to be placed in /var/news. The single parameter is the socket file descriptor returned from the accept call in the main processing loop.

We need to get the filename first, but we do not want to consume too much of the data sent and have to handle the case where we have read part of the file contents along with the filename. Since SOCK_STREAM-type sockets are byte streams, there are no guarantees that we will receive exactly what was sent in the first call to send. In fact, most efficient protocols would probably combine the filename with the file data since the filename probably is not too long.

```
void
recvnews(int nfd)
{
    int fd, n, ret;
    char *p;
    char buf[NETBUFSZ];

    /*
```

```
 * Read the name of the file to be received.
 */
p = lastrecv;
for (;;) {
    /*
     * Don't consume the data; just peek at it.
     */
    ret = recv(nfd, buf, NETBUFSZ, MSG_PEEK);
    if (ret < 0) {
        log("recv failed: %s", strerror(errno));
        return;
    }

    /*
     * Copy the filename to lastrecv.
     */
    for (n = 0; n < ret; n++)
        if (buf[n] == '\0')
            break;
    n++;
    strncpy(p, buf, n);
    p += n;

    /*
     * Now consume the filename.
     */
    if ((ret = recv(nfd, buf, n, 0)) != n) {
        if (ret < 0)
            log("recv failed: %s", strerror(errno));
        else
            log("recv expected %d, returned %d", n,
                ret);
        lastrecv[0] = '\0';
        return;
    }

    /*
     * If we've reached the end of the filename,
     * break out of the loop and receive the file.
     */
    if (*(p - 1) == '\0')
        break;
}

/*
 * Create the file, making it publicly readable.
 */
if ((fd = creat(lastrecv, NEWSPERM)) < 0) {
    log("cannot create /var/news/%s: %s", lastrecv,
        strerror(errno));
    lastrecv[0] = '\0';
    return;
}
```

```
    /*
     * Read the contents of the file from the network
     * and save it on disk.
     */
    while ((n = recv(nfd, buf, NETBUFSZ, 0)) > 0)
        write(fd, buf, n);

    /*
     * Close the file.
     */
    close(fd);
}
```

To solve this problem, we use the MSG_PEEK flag with recv to read the data, but not really consume it. The next time we read from the socket, we will get the same data again. We search through the data we have peeked at, looking for the terminating NULL. If we do not find it, then the entire filename has not arrived yet, so we copy what we have read to lastrecv, and we call recv without any flags to really consume the data this time. Note we only ask for as many bytes as we were able to peek at.

If we find the NULL, we end our search and consume only as many bytes as the filename uses. If the last byte we have copied into the lastrecv array is the NULL byte, we know we have gotten the entire filename, so we break out of the loop. Otherwise, we make another trip around to peek at more of the data.

After we have the filename, we create a file in /var/news with the same name as the filename sent to us. Then, while we can still receive data from the socket, we write what we receive to the file. Finally, we close the file and return to the main processing loop, where we close the network connection and call doscan to rescan the directory for new files.   □

Summary

The socket mechanism provides a common set of primitives for applications to use for interprocess communication, regardless of the location of peer processes. It contains functionality similar to the TLI library presented in Chapter 4. We have compared and contrasted both mechanisms, each having its own strengths and weaknesses. In SVR4, the socket mechanism is implemented in the STREAMS framework.

Exercises

7.1 Assume you are developing a new network communication protocol. How can you use socket(3N) to create a socket to communicate over the new protocol without changing header files and recompiling the socket library?

7.2 Modify Example 7.5.1 to prevent two instances of the same server from running at the same time.

7.3 What kind of problems can arise from an application designed like Example 7.8.1, where it is both a client and a server, and the service is iterative instead of concurrent? What can be done to retain the structure but alleviate the problems?

7.4 What information would have to be exchanged between the parent and child processes if Example 7.8.1 were redesigned as a concurrent server instead of an iterative one? Would there be any synchronization issues to deal with?

7.5 Modify Example 7.8.1 to maintain the original ownership of the news files. What permissions does the daemon need? How do you overcome the problems of users who do not have logins on all the machines? How do you overcome the problems associated with the same user having different user IDs on different machines?

Bibliographic Notes

Stevens [1990] discusses socket programming and provides many real-life examples illustrating the use of sockets. The topic of converting socket-based applications to the TLI is addressed in the *SVR4 Programmer's Guide: Networking Interfaces* [USL 1990d].

Leffler et al. [1989] cover the socket implementation in the 4.3BSD operating system. Vessey and Skinner [1990] discuss the socket implementation in UNIX SVR4, along with some of the problems presented by the STREAMS framework and the TPI.

Presotto and Ritchie [1985, 1990] suggest ways in which file-descriptor passing can be used to architect communications software in a more extensible manner.

RFC 1034 [Mockapetris 1987a] and RFC 1035 [Mockapetris 1987b] specify the Internet domain name service facility.

8

Remote
Procedure Calls

System V Release 4 includes a remote procedure call (RPC) interface derived from the one created and made popular by Sun Microsystems. Remote procedure calls are useful because they allow programmers to develop applications that ignore the details of communication but still make use of communication facilities. This chapter describes the RPC components and how programmers can use them to develop network-independent applications.

8.1 INTRODUCTION

Ordinary (local) procedure calls transfer the control flow of a program from one procedure to another within the same process on a single machine. Consider the following code fragment:

```
main()
{
    struct inargs inargs;
    struct outargs outargs;
    int retval;
    .
    .
    .
    retval = function(&inargs, &outargs);
    .
    .
    .
}
```

The `main` procedure calls the `function` procedure, passing it the address of a structure containing input arguments (ones set by the caller) and the address of a structure containing output arguments (ones set by the callee). The return value indicates whether the procedure succeeded or failed. This is the general structure of an ordinary procedure call.

Figure 8.1 illustrates the time-ordered flow of control that occurs when the program is executed. The computer executes the `main` procedure until the `function` procedure is invoked. Then control is transferred to `function`, and the computer

355

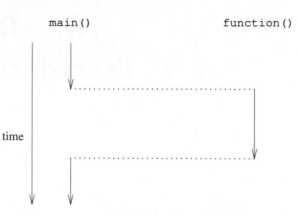

Fig. 8.1. Control Flow of Local Procedure Call

executes its statements. When `function` completes its task, control is returned to the `main` procedure, where the computer can continue executing the statements after the call to `function`.

Now consider what would happen if `function` were to be executed in the context of another process. That other process could be running on the same machine, but we would have more flexibility if we could design our application with the process running on a different machine, connected to the local one by some sort of communication mechanism. This is called a *remote* procedure call (as opposed to an ordinary, or local, one).

Figure 8.2 illustrates the flow of control during a remote procedure call. The call to `function` results in a different sequence of events. The input arguments are packaged up and transmitted to the remote process. The remote process unpackages the arguments and executes the procedure specified by the message. When the procedure completes, the output arguments and return value are packaged up and sent back to the calling process. Then the calling process unpackages the results and continues just as if the procedure call had been executed within its own context.

As far as the `main` procedure is concerned, there is no noticeable difference between `function` implemented as a local procedure call or as a remote one. (The term ''remote'' can sometimes be misleading because there is no requirement that the process providing the service reside on a different computer.) This is the major benefit of using the RPC paradigm. Applications can be developed that are ignorant of the details of connection establishment, message transmission and reception, and of the differences between data representations on different computer architectures.

As you might expect, there is a cost for insulating applications in this way: they give up control of the communication characteristics. Since all the details are hidden, applications are not able to customize the way the communication occurs if they want to remain ignorant of a procedure's context of execution. That is not to say that customization is impossible. The lower-layer functions of the RPC library that

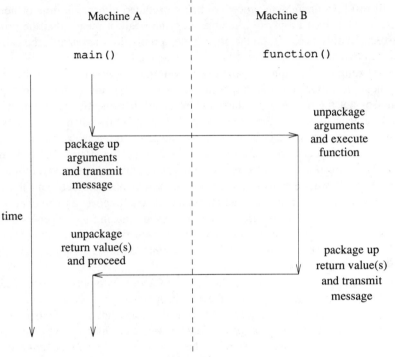

	Machine A		Machine B

main()   function()

Fig. 8.2. Control Flow of Remote Procedure Call

expose some characteristics of the communication are available for applications that want to sacrifice the insulation.

As we shall see, the SVR4 RPC library allows an application to use any transport it desires to communicate with the server process that implements the remote procedure. The transport provider can be connectionless or connection-oriented, but the type of transport used will affect the kind of procedures that can be implemented remotely.

Because the steps involved with packaging parameters and communicating with other processes introduce additional points of failure, applications can only take advantage of remote procedure calls when the remote procedure's behavior is compatible with the execution semantics. There are no restrictions on local procedures, because they present *exactly-once* execution semantics. This means that when a local procedure is invoked, the caller knows on return that the procedure was executed exactly one time.

With remote procedures, execution delays, dropped packets, and retransmissions make *exactly-once* semantics difficult to obtain. Instead, remote procedures are usually designed to operate under either *at-most-once* semantics or *at-least-once* semantics.

At-most-once semantics mean that the caller is assured that a remote procedure call will result in the remote procedure being executed either one time or not at all. If the caller receives a reply to a remote procedure call, it means that the procedure was executed only once. If, on the other hand, a reply does not arrive, the caller cannot be sure whether or not the procedure was executed.

For example, if a request is sent to a server and the server successfully executes the remote procedure but the response message is lost, the caller cannot be sure whether or not the remote procedure was executed, because the caller cannot tell if the failure occurred before the request was delivered. Only when the response message is received can the caller be sure the remote procedure was executed.

If the caller decides to retransmit the request message after a certain amount of time without a response, then the remote procedure could be executed multiple times. For example, if we were using a connectionless transport protocol and the request message were routed through an intermediate node that happened to be overloaded at the time, the delay might be greater than expected, causing us to generate another request. If both requests eventually made it to the server machine, the remote procedure would be executed twice for the one call made on the local machine. This is known as at-least-once semantics.

Remote procedures that can be designed to avoid state changes can work with all of the call semantics discussed above. Such procedures are called *idempotent*. They can be executed any number of times without any adverse effects (other than, perhaps, increasing the network load). Some examples of idempotent procedures are returning portions of a file and returning the time of day. *Nonidempotent* procedures cause a change to take effect, such as writing to a file or setting the time of day.

The RPC protocol does not impose the execution semantics. These are determined by the client and the server and depend on the type of transport protocol, what the remote procedure does, and whether the client retransmits unanswered requests. If a connection-oriented transport provider is used and a reply is received, then the caller knows the procedure was executed once; but if no reply is received, the caller does not know if the procedure was executed. These are at-most-once semantics. At-most-once semantics are also provided if a connectionless transport protocol is used and the application does not retransmit requests. If, however, the application retransmits requests, at-least-once semantics are provided. Retransmissions are only necessary with unreliable connectionless protocols. Connection-oriented protocols are reliable, and a response will only be lost when a host crashes or the network medium fails.

By default, the RPC library will attempt retransmissions when a connectionless protocol is used, so at-least-once semantics are provided. The library provides a function (presented in Section 8.4) that servers can call to simulate at-most-once semantics. The function causes the server to cache reply messages so that if a retransmitted request arrives, the function is not executed again. Instead, the reply from the original remote procedure call is copied from the cache and sent to the client. A transaction ID in the request message allows the server to identify a duplicate request. The reason at-most-once semantics are only simulated is because this method is not reliable. The server's cache size is fixed, so if a duplicate request arrives after its reply has been replaced in the cache, the server cannot identify the request as a duplicate, and thus calls the remote procedure again.

Client applications identify a remote procedure with three numbers: the program number, the version number, and the procedure number. The program number identifies a set of related procedures. The version number identifies the version of the program containing the procedure. It allows for compatibility to be maintained with older versions of a program when its procedures are modified. The procedure number identifies the particular procedure within a program to be executed. The programmer selects the server's version and procedure numbers. The program numbers, which are summarized in Table 8.1, are administered in blocks of 0x20000000.

Table 8.1. RPC Program Number Ranges

Program Number Range	Description
0x00000000 - 0x1FFFFFFF	Defined by Sun Microsystems for programs of general interest.
0x20000000 - 0x3FFFFFFF	Defined by programmers for local services and debugging.
0x40000000 - 0x5FFFFFFF	Transient numbers used for short time periods, such as with callback RPC.
0x60000000 - 0x7FFFFFFF	Reserved.
0x80000000 - 0x9FFFFFFF	Reserved.
0xA0000000 - 0xBFFFFFFF	Reserved.
0xC0000000 - 0xDFFFFFFF	Reserved.
0xE0000000 - 0xFFFFFFFF	Reserved.

Developers can register program numbers in the first range listed in Table 8.1 with Sun Microsystems. Instructions are provided in the materials referenced at the end of this chapter.

The RPC facility included in SVR4 contains four components: the RPC library, the XDR library, the `rpcgen` translator, and the `rpcbind` server. The RPC library provides the functions necessary to implement the RPC protocol, enabling client and server processes to use remote procedure calls. The XDR library provides the routines used to convert data to be transmitted into a machine-independent format. The `rpcgen` translator converts program specifications written in the RPC language into the client and server routines that communicate with each other. The `rpcbind` server provides a service-to-port number mapping facility.

8.2 XDR

Packaging and unpackaging arguments involves more than just copying the arguments to and from a buffer. It also involves the conversion of data from one machine architecture's representation to another's. Examples of differences include byte order, integer size, floating-point representation, and string representation. RPC uses a standard eXternal Data Representation (XDR) to describe data in a format that is independent of the computer architecture, programming language, and compiler conventions.

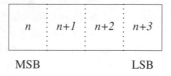

MSB   LSB

Fig. 8.3. Big-endian Byte Order

Byte order is probably the most common architectural computer difference that programmers encounter. When a 32-bit number is viewed as a sequence of bytes, the numbering of those bytes can be different. Two byte orders are used: *big-endian* or *little-endian*. With big-endian byte order, shown in Figure 8.3, the bytes are numbered consecutively from left to right in the word. (We will refer to a 32-bit quantity as a ''word,'' although terminology differs from architecture to architecture.) With little-endian byte order, shown in Figure 8.4, the byte numbering is reversed, increasing as you go from right to left.

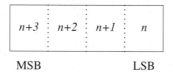

MSB   LSB

Fig. 8.4. Little-endian Byte Order

Regardless of the byte order, the left-most byte is the most significant byte (MSB) as far as the word is concerned. Similarly, the right-most byte is the least significant byte (LSB). Assuming the number represented by the word is unsigned, its value can be calculated as:

$$16777216(a) + 65536(b) + 256(c) + (d)$$

where a is the value of the left-most byte, b is the value of the next byte, c is the value of the byte to the left of the least significant byte, and d is the value of the right-most, least significant, byte.

An easy way to remember the difference between the two byte orders is to look for the lowest-numbered byte in the word. If this is the most significant byte of the word, then the architecture is big-endian. If, on the other hand, the lowest-numbered byte in the word is the least significant byte, the architecture is little-endian. For example, the Intel 80x86 processor line uses little-endian byte ordering, and the Sun SPARC processor line uses big-endian byte ordering.

Besides differences in computer architectures, different programming languages can define different representations for similar data objects. For example, a string in PASCAL is stored as a fixed-length packed array of characters, but a string in C is stored as a variable-length, NULL-terminated sequence of bytes. Even within the same programming language, different implementations can represent data structures in different ways. Consider the following data structure:

```
struct foo {
      short   a;
      long    b;
};
```

If a short is two bytes and a long is four bytes on a given architecture, depending on how the compiler pads structure elements, struct foo might take up six bytes when compiled with one C compiler and eight bytes when compiled with another. It depends on whether the compilers insert two pad bytes between a and b, effectively aligning b on a word boundary (assuming structures are aligned on word boundaries, also).

The XDR library helps to hide these kinds of differences in data representation by selecting a standard representation for each data type. For example, XDR uses big-endian byte order and IEEE floating-point representation. All data types are multiples of four bytes. If the length of a host-dependent type is not a four-byte multiple, then enough pad bytes are added until it is. The pad bytes are always set to 0.

XDR assumes that bytes themselves are portable between architectures. This is usually a safe assumption because the data link layer protocol specification for each particular communication medium should contain information specifying the bit order in which each byte is transmitted on the medium. For example, the Ethernet protocol specifies that when transmitting a byte, the least significant bit is transmitted first and the most significant bit is transmitted last.

The data encoded in XDR format are implicitly typed, in contrast to other data description standards (like X.409). This means that XDR makes no provision for including any information about the data type represented by a sequence of bytes. Thus, the sender of data encoded in XDR format must agree with the receiver on the format of the data so that the receiver can successfully decode the data. Figure 8.5 shows this relationship. A sending process uses XDR library routines to encode data in a machine-independent format. This process is known as *serializing* the data. The receiving process uses the same XDR library routines to decode the data in a machine-dependent format understandable by the receiver. This process is known as *deserializing* the data.

The XDR library supports the notion of XDR data streams. These are byte streams to and from which encoded and decoded data are copied. Serialization involves converting machine-dependent data into the machine-independent XDR format and then copying the encoded data to the XDR stream. Deserialization involves removing XDR data from the XDR stream and then decoding them into the machine-dependent representation.

There are three types of XDR streams supported by the XDR library. Developers can add others if one of the basic three is not appropriate. The first is a standard

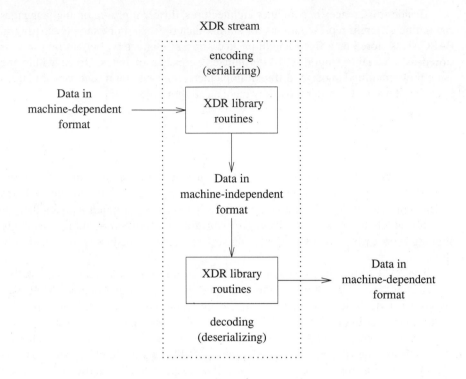

Fig. 8.5. An XDR Stream

I/O stream. With it, data encoded in XDR format can be written to and read from any file using the `stdio` routines found in the C library. The second is a memory stream. Instead of writing and reading XDR-encoded data to and from a file, a memory stream allows a buffer in memory to be used. The third is a record stream. It allows variable-size records to be written to and read from an XDR stream. Each record contains a 32-bit header that stores the size of the record and a flag denoting the last record.

XDR streams are represented by XDR *handles*. The XDR `typedef` is used to declare an XDR handle. It is described in `rpc(3N)`, but most applications should treat the structure as opaque (i.e., its structure members should not be used) unless some nonstandard behavior is desired. `xdr_create(3N)` describes each routine used to create XDR streams. Each initializes an XDR handle as part of its operation. We will only discuss standard I/O streams in this text.

Once an XDR stream is created, there are three operations that can be applied to it: `XDR_ENCODE`, `XDR_DECODE`, and `XDR_FREE`. The `XDR_ENCODE` operation can be used to encode data onto the stream. The `XDR_DECODE` operation can be used to decode data from the stream. The `XDR_FREE` operation can be used to free any space that was allocated during a decode operation. A field in the XDR handle contains the operation to be performed.

A standard I/O stream is used to either encode or decode data, but usually not both. Thus, the XDR_ENCODE and XDR_DECODE operations are determined when the XDR stream is created and associated with the standard I/O stream. A standard I/O stream is created with xdrstdio_create(3N):

```
#include <stdio.h>
#include <rpc/xdr.h>
```

```
void xdrstdio_create(XDR *handle, FILE *fp, enum xdr_op op);
```

handle is a pointer to the XDR handle, fp is a pointer to the FILE structure representing the stdio stream, and op is either XDR_ENCODE or XDR_DECODE. Space for the XDR handle must be allocated prior to calling xdrstdio_create.

An XDR stream can be disassociated from its handle by calling xdr_destroy(3N). The synopsis is

```
#include <rpc/xdr.h>
```

```
void xdr_destroy(XDR *handle);
```

where handle is a pointer to the XDR handle. For a standard I/O stream, xdr_destroy flushes the data in the standard I/O stream by calling fflush(3S). The standard I/O stream remains open after calling xdr_destroy, so programmers need to call fclose(3S) themselves. If the program is about to exit, neither routine need be called.

The XDR library routines that encode and decode data are called *filters*. Filters are provided for simple data types [described in xdr_simple(3N)] and for complex data types [described in xdr_complex(3N)]. Each native data type is mapped into a corresponding XDR data type. Table 8.2 lists the XDR data types, along with pictures describing the data representations, and sample declarations.

XDR filters have several things in common. They all return type bool_t (TRUE if they succeed and FALSE if they fail). They will encode or decode data, depending on the operation field in the XDR handle. The simple filters all take the same two arguments: a pointer to the XDR handle and a pointer to the object to encode or decode. The synopses for the simple filters follow:

```
#include <rpc/xdr.h>
```

```
bool_t xdr_bool(XDR *handle, bool_t *p);
bool_t xdr_char(XDR *handle, char *p);
bool_t xdr_u_char(XDR *handle, uchar_t *p);
bool_t xdr_short(XDR *handle, short *p);
bool_t xdr_u_short(XDR *handle, ushort_t *p);
bool_t xdr_int(XDR *handle, int *p);
bool_t xdr_u_int(XDR *handle, uint_t *p);
bool_t xdr_long(XDR *handle, long *p);
bool_t xdr_u_long(XDR *handle, ulong_t *p);
bool_t xdr_enum(XDR *handle, enum_t *p);
bool_t xdr_double(XDR *handle, double *p);
bool_t xdr_float(XDR *handle, float *p);
```

Table 8.2. XDR Data Types

Type	Representation	Sample Declaration
Integer	0 1 2 3 — MSB ... LSB	`int x;`
Unsigned integer	0 1 2 3 — MSB ... LSB	`unsigned int x;`
Enumeration	0 1 2 3 — MSB ... LSB	`enum { a=1, b=2 } x;`
Boolean	0 1 2 3 — MSB ... LSB	`bool x;`
Hyper integer and unsigned hyper integer	0 1 2 3 4 5 6 7 — MSB ... LSB	`hyper int x;` `unsigned hyper int y;`
Floating point	0 1 2 3 — 1-bit sign, 8-bit exponent, 23-bit fraction	`float x;`
Double precision Floating point	0 1 2 3 4 5 6 7 — 1-bit sign, 11-bit exponent, 52-bit fraction	`double x;`
Fixed-length opaque data	0 1 ... $n-1$ pad — n bytes	`opaque x[n];`
Variable-length opaque data	0 1 2 3 0 1 ... $n-1$ pad — size, n bytes	`opaque x<>;`

Table 8.2. XDR Data Types (cont.)

Type	Representation	Sample Declaration
String	0 1 2 3 0 1 ... n-1 pad — size — n bytes	`string x<>;`
Fixed-length array	el. 0 el. 1 ... el. n-1 (each element can be a different size, but all are multiples of 4 bytes.)	*type-name* `x[n];`
Variable-length array	0 1 2 3 el. 0 ... el. n-1 — size —	*type-name* `x<>;`

Structure	comp. A comp. B ... (each component is a multiple of 4 bytes)	`struct {`
		    component A;
		    component B;
		    `...`
		`};`

Discriminated union	0 1 2 3 implied arm discriminant 4-byte multiple	`union switch(` *disc.-decl.* `) {`
		    `case` *discriminant-value-A*:
		        arm-declaration-A;
		    `case` *discriminant-value-B*:
		        arm-declaration-B;
		    `...`
		    `default:`
		        default-declaration;
		`} x;`

Void	0 bytes (no data)	`void;`
Constant	(doesn't declare data)	`const x = 1;`

Typedef	(doesn't declare data)	`typedef enum {`
		    `FALSE=0,`
		    `TRUE=1`
		`} bool;`

Optional data	(special type of union used for recursive data structures)	*type-name* `*x;`

In addition, the filter xdr_void(3N) takes no parameters and always returns TRUE. It is used to describe the XDR processing for functions with no arguments or no return value. The function prototype is

```
#include <rpc/xdr.h>

bool_t xdr_void(void);
```

The filters provided by the XDR library for complex data types all have different arguments, depending on the data type. The first argument, however, is always a pointer to the XDR handle for the XDR stream.

The function used to translate strings between the local and XDR representations is xdr_string(3N):

```
#include <rpc/xdr.h>

bool_t xdr_string(XDR *handle, char **pp, uint_t maxsize);
```

maxsize is the maximum length of the string. During encoding, pp is a pointer to a pointer to the string. During decoding, pp is a pointer to a pointer to the memory location where the string is to be placed. If *pp is NULL and the operation is XDR_DECODE, xdr_string will allocate space for the string and store the address in the memory location referred to by pp.

For copying a fixed array of bytes uninterpreted through an XDR stream, xdr_opaque(3N) can be used:

```
#include <rpc/xdr.h>

bool_t xdr_opaque(XDR *handle, char *p, uint_t size);
```

where p is a pointer to the array of bytes, and size is the number of bytes in the array. If, on the other hand, the array is of variable length, xdr_bytes(3N) can be used:

```
#include <rpc/xdr.h>

bool_t xdr_bytes(XDR *handle, char **pp, uint_t *sizep,
    uint_t maxsize);
```

pp is a pointer to a pointer to the array, sizep is a pointer to the size of the array, and maxsize is the maximum size of the array in bytes. If the operation is to decode the array and *pp (the pointer to the array) is NULL, xdr_bytes will allocate space for the array and store its address in the memory location referenced by pp. The size of the array is stored in the integer pointed to by sizep. If the operation is to encode the array, then pp should point to a pointer to the array and sizep should point to the size of the array in bytes before calling xdr_bytes. Just as xdr_opaque does not interpret the contents of the array, xdr_bytes copies the contents of the array without interpreting them.

xdr_vector(3N) can be used to translate a fixed-size array of an object other than a byte:

```
#include <rpc/xdr.h>

bool_t xdr_vector(XDR *handle, char *p, uint_t size,
      uint_t elsize, xdrproc_t fn);
```

With this function, p points to the array, `size` is the number of elements in the array, `elsize` is the size of an element in bytes, and `fn` is the address of an XDR filter to be used to encode and decode each element.

An XDR filter of type `xdrproc_t` returns a type `bool_t`: TRUE if the translation succeeds and FALSE otherwise. An example of why translation might fail is because memory cannot be allocated. XDR filters of this type take only two arguments. The first is a pointer to the XDR handle and the second is a pointer to the object to be encoded or decoded.

Example 8.2.1. To encode or decode a fixed-length array of integers, we could use `xdr_vector`. We would not need to write a function to encode and decode each element because the XDR library already provides us with `xdr_int`. An array of 10 integers could be encoded or decoded as follows:

```
#include <rpc/types.h>
#include <rpc/xdr.h>
    .
    .
    int a[10];
    bool_t ret;
    XDR *handle;
    .
    .
    ret = xdr_vector(handle, (char *)a, 10, sizeof(int),
        xdr_int);
```
                                                                        □

When the size of an array is not known ahead of time, `xdr_array(3N)` can be used to translate it. The synopsis is

```
#include <rpc/xdr.h>

bool_t xdr_array(XDR *handle, char **pp, uint_t *sizep,
      uint_t maxsize, uint_t elsize, xdrproc_t fn);
```

where pp is a pointer to a pointer to the array, `sizep` is a pointer to the number of elements in the array, `maxsize` is the maximum number of elements in the array, `elsize` is the size of an individual element of the array in bytes, and `fn` is the address of an XDR filter that can be used to encode and decode an array element. If the operation is to decode the array and the pointer (`*pp`) to the array is NULL, `xdr_array` will allocate space for the array and store its address in the memory location referenced by pp. The size of the array is stored in the integer pointed to by `sizep`. If the operation is to encode the array, then pp should point to a pointer to the array and `sizep` should point to the size of the array in bytes before calling `xdr_array`.

When encoding text, be careful to use `xdr_string` or `xdr_vector` (with xdr_char) instead of xdr_opaque or xdr_bytes. Although most computers represent text with ASCII data, some computers still use alternate representations, such as EBCDIC. xdr_string and xdr_vector will handle these data conversions, but xdr_opaque and xdr_bytes will not.

The XDR library supports a compound data type called a *discriminated union*. Its ultimate type is derived from one element in its set of data types. The element is selected by a key, called a *discriminant*. The discriminant can take on a range of values, each one with a different data type associated with it. The actual data in the XDR stream will include the discriminant, followed by the data whose type is described by the discriminant. A discriminated union is declared as:

```
union switch (discriminant_declaration) {
case discriminant_value_A:
     arm_declaration_A;
case discriminant_value_B:
     arm_declaration_B;
.
.
.
default:
     default_declaration;
} identifier;
```

Each discriminant is declared in a separate *arm* of the declaration. The default arm is optional. The xdr_union(3N) function can be used to translate a discriminated union:

```
#include <rpc/xdr.h>

bool_t xdr_union(XDR *handle, enum_t *dscrp, char *p,
     struct xdr_discrim *armp,
     bool_t (*defaultarm)(const XDR *, const char *, int));
```

For encoding, dscrp points to a memory location containing the value of the discriminant and p points to the memory location containing the object whose type is determined by the discriminant. For decoding, xdr_union places the value of the discriminant in the memory location pointed to by dscrp and its corresponding object in the memory location referred to by p. The type enum_t is defined to be an integer in <rpc/types.h>.

The armp parameter points to an array of xdr_discrim structures that describe each arm of the discriminated union. It is defined as:

```
struct xdr_discrim {
     int          value;  /* discriminant value */
     xdrproc_t    proc;   /* XDR filter for object */
};
```

where value is the discriminant value, and proc is the address of an XDR filter to be used to encode and decode the object. The array is terminated with an entry whose proc is set to NULL. The value of the discriminant is compared with the value elements in the array of xdr_discrim structures. If a match is found, the corresponding function is called to encode or decode the data object.

The XDR library also includes two functions for translating pointers. They work by encoding the object to which the pointer refers instead of encoding the pointer itself. Since the process encoding the data will usually be different than the process decoding the data, the address spaces are different and pointers from one address space have no meaning in the other. The first function is `xdr_reference(3N)`, used to handle a reference to an object.

```
#include <rpc/xdr.h>

bool_t xdr_reference(XDR *handle, char **pp, uint_t size,
    xdrproc_t fn);
```

pp is a pointer to a pointer to the memory containing the object, `size` is the size of the object in bytes, and `fn` is an XDR filter that can be used to encode and decode the object. When decoding, if the pointer referenced by `*pp` is NULL, memory is allocated to hold the object and the address of the memory extent is placed in `*pp`.

The one problem with `xdr_reference` is that it does not handle NULL pointers. This is solved with `xdr_pointer(3N)` by encoding a boolean with each object to indicate whether or not an additional object follows (i.e., whether or not the pointer is non-NULL). With `xdr_pointer`, data structures like linked lists and trees can be encoded and decoded. The synopsis is

```
#include <rpc/xdr.h>

bool_t xdr_pointer(XDR *handle, char **pp, uint_t size,
    xdrproc_t fn);
```

where the parameters are the same as for `xdr_reference`.

One final filter is provided by the XDR library to ease the restriction of only passing two parameters to functions of type `xdrproc_t`. Since strings are commonly used and `xdr_string` takes three parameters, `xdr_wrapstring(3N)` is provided. It assumes the maximum length of the string to be the maximum size of an unsigned integer. The synopsis is

```
#include <rpc/xdr.h>

bool_t xdr_wrapstring(XDR *handle, char **pp);
```

where pp is a pointer to a pointer to the memory location containing the string. For decoding, if the contents of the pointer is NULL, enough memory is allocated to store the string and `*pp` is set to the address of the memory.

Since some of the complex XDR filters can allocate memory, programs need a way to free the memory that has been allocated. `xdr_free(3N)` can be used for this purpose:

```
#include <rpc/xdr.h>

void xdr_free(xdrproc_t fn, char *p);
```

The address of the XDR filter used to encode and decode the object is passed as `fn`, and a pointer to the object is passed as p. This is where the XDR_FREE operation is used. `xdr free` will call the filter, passing it the pointer to the object to be freed and the operation XDR_FREE. The memory to which p refers is freed recursively.

Now that we have covered the XDR filters, we will look at how they are used. In particular, the XDR routines can be used independently of the RPC facility, as the following example illustrates.

Example 8.2.2. Assume you are in charge of monitoring a network of computers composed of several different hardware architectures, and periodically you want to check who is logging in to each system. A record of each login session is kept in `/var/adm/utmp`. This is a binary file made up of records with a format defined in `<utmp.h>`.

Instead of logging into each machine and checking the file, you would prefer to work on a single machine, so you use `rcp(1)` to copy all the `utmp` files to your current machine. The files that came from machines with the same byte order, integer size, etc., are usable, but the others are not. You could convert the files to the current machine's format, but that would require that you write a program that understands all the different types of computer architectures with which the files were created.

A better solution is to convert the files to XDR format before copying them to your home machine. Then all the files would be in the same format and you could decode them into a format that your home machine could understand. You could use `rsh(1)` to run the conversion programs, and then use `rcp(1)` to copy the machine-independent files to your home machine. The format of a `utmp` entry is defined as:

```
struct utmp {
    char                  ut_user[8];  /* login name */
    char                  ut_id[4];    /* inittab ID */
    char                  ut_line[12]; /* device name */
    short                 ut_pid;      /* process ID */
    short                 ut_type;     /* type of entry */
    struct exit_status    ut_exit;     /* exit status */
    time_t                ut_time;     /* time entry made */
};

struct exit_status {
    short   e_termination;        /* termination status */
    short   e_exit;               /* exit status */
};
```

Note that the process ID is a `short` (it should be a `pid_t`). The `utmp` file is maintained for compatibility with pre-SVR4 programs that accessed it. Most of the fields have grown and are now stored in the extended `utmp` file, `/var/adm/utmpx`. Processing the extended format is left for an exercise at the end of the chapter.

The following program takes two parameters: the name of a file to encode in XDR format (usually `/var/adm/utmp`) and the name of the file to contain the encoded structures. Common sense would suggest including the machine name as part of the output filename so it is easy to remember from which machine each file came.

The program is fairly simple. We call utmpname to tell the utmp library routines which file we want to process, in case it is a different one than /var/adm/utmp. Then we create the output file and attach it to an XDR stream using xdrstdio_create. The rest of the program just iterates, reading an entry at a time and calling the appropriate XDR filters to encode the fields.

One interesting thing to note is the use of xdr_vector to encode the fixed-length strings. xdr_string is inappropriate in this case because the strings might not be terminated by a NULL byte.

To compile the program, you need to include the XDR library routines, found in the network services library (/usr/lib/libnsl.so). Use the -lnsl option when creating the a.out.

```c
#include <sys/types.h>
#include <rpc/types.h>
#include <rpc/xdr.h>
#include <stdio.h>
#include <stdlib.h>
#include <utmp.h>

extern void fatal(const char *, ...);

void
main(int argc, char *argv[])
{
    FILE *fp;
    XDR xh;
    struct utmp *up;
    int err = 0;

    if (argc != 3) {
        fprintf(stderr, "usage: mkut infile outfile\n");
        exit(1);
    }

    /*
     * Open the utmp file.
     */
    if (utmpname(argv[1]) != 1)
        fatal("mkut: input filename too long");

    /*
     * Create the output file.
     */
    if ((fp = fopen(argv[2], "w")) == NULL)
        fatal("mkut: cannot create %s", argv[2]);

    /*
     * Create the XDR stream.
     */
    xdrstdio_create(&xh, fp, XDR_ENCODE);
```

```
        /*
         * Encode each utmp entry.
         */
        while ((up = getutent()) != NULL) {
            if (xdr_vector(&xh, up->ut_user,
                sizeof(up->ut_user), sizeof(char),
                xdr_char) == FALSE) {
                    err = 1;
                    break;
            }
            if (xdr_vector(&xh, up->ut_id, sizeof(up->ut_id),
                sizeof(char), xdr_char) == FALSE) {
                    err = 2;
                    break;
            }
            if (xdr_vector(&xh, up->ut_line,
                sizeof(up->ut_line), sizeof(char),
                xdr_char) == FALSE) {
                    err = 3;
                    break;
            }
            if (xdr_short(&xh, &up->ut_pid) == FALSE) {
                    err = 4;
                    break;
            }
            if (xdr_short(&xh, &up->ut_type) == FALSE) {
                    err = 5;
                    break;
            }
            if (xdr_short(&xh, &up->ut_exit.e_termination) ==
                FALSE) {
                    err = 6;
                    break;
            }
            if (xdr_short(&xh, &up->ut_exit.e_exit) ==
                FALSE) {
                    err = 7;
                    break;
            }
            if (xdr_long(&xh, &up->ut_time) == FALSE) {
                    err = 8;
                    break;
            }
        }
        if (err != 0)
            fatal("mkut: XDR error %d converting data", err);
        exit(0);
    }
```

Note that the time_t type is defined to be a long in <sys/types.h>.   □

When using RPC, you might be faced with the need to build a *composite* filter.
A composite filter is just an XDR filter that uses other XDR filters to encode and

decode a data structure. The next example shows how to build a composite filter for `struct utmp`.

Example 8.2.3. If we had to pass the address of an XDR filter to one of the functions that requires a filter of type `xdrproc_t`, we would be restricted to only two parameters. This would force us to write a composite filter with the first parameter being the XDR handle and the second parameter being a pointer to the object to be encoded and decoded (the `utmp` structure). The following procedure is such a filter. It follows all the conventions required, including returning FALSE on error and TRUE on success.

```
#include <rpc/types.h>
#include <rpc/xdr.h>
#include <utmp.h>

bool_t
xdr_utmp(XDR *handle, struct utmp *up)
{
    if (xdr_vector(handle, up->ut_user,
      sizeof(up->ut_user), sizeof(char),
      xdr_char) == FALSE)
        return(FALSE);
    if (xdr_vector(handle, up->ut_id, sizeof(up->ut_id),
      sizeof(char), xdr_char) == FALSE)
        return(FALSE);
    if (xdr_vector(handle, up->ut_line,
      sizeof(up->ut_line), sizeof(char),
      xdr_char) == FALSE)
        return(FALSE);
    if (xdr_short(handle, &up->ut_pid) == FALSE)
        return(FALSE);
    if (xdr_short(handle, &up->ut_type) == FALSE)
        return(FALSE);
    if (xdr_short(handle, &up->ut_exit.e_termination) ==
      FALSE)
        return(FALSE);
    if (xdr_short(handle, &up->ut_exit.e_exit) == FALSE)
        return(FALSE);
    if (xdr_long(handle, &up->ut_time) == FALSE)
        return(FALSE);
    return(TRUE);
}
```

□

8.3 HIGH-LEVEL RPC PROGRAMMING

The RPC library routines can be partitioned into two broad categories other than the obvious client-side and server-side classifications. The two categories, high-level routines and low-level routines, determine how much of the network is exposed to applications. The high-level routines hide the details of the network protocols, trading off control and efficiency for insulation and ease of use. The low-level routines provide applications with more control over the communication characteristics at the expense of exposing details of the underlying network.

The client-side RPC library routines provide applications with the ability to make remote procedure calls. The server-side routines provide applications the functionality needed to execute functions in response to remote procedure call requests. This section will cover the high-level routines used by client and server applications. The low-level routines are discussed in the next section.

The RPC library routines provided in SVR4 are independent of the underlying transport protocols. Unlike their predecessors, the routines are not restricted to use with only TCP or UDP. The RPC library routines interact with the network selection and name-to-address translation facilities (see Chapter 5) to allow any transport protocol to be used. Some low-level routines allow the caller to specify the exact transport to use. Other routines, including the high-level ones, require the caller to specify the type of transport, such as datagram or virtual circuit.

The type of transport is specified as a character string whose value limits the set of transport protocols and networks to use. The set is further influenced by the order of entries in /etc/netconfig and by the contents of the NETPATH environment variable. Table 8.3 summarizes the possible values for the string and the way they influence the set of networks and protocols.

Table 8.3. Transport Selection Strings

String	Description
netpath	Choose from network IDs specified in NETPATH. If NETPATH is unset or NULL, acts as visible.
visible	Choose from network IDs with visible flag set in /etc/netconfig.
circuit_v	Same as visible, but restricts set to only connection-oriented protocols.
datagram_v	Same as visible, but restricts set to only connectionless protocols.
circuit_n	Same as netpath, but restricts set to only connection-oriented protocols.
datagram_n	Same as netpath, but restricts set to only connectionless protocols.
udp	Use UDP only.
tcp	Use TCP only.
raw	Use memory-based RPC (used during performance analysis and debugging).
NULL	Same as netpath.

Recall that a remote procedure is uniquely identified by a program number, a version number, and a procedure number. Client applications use these three numbers when requesting a particular service from a host computer. The problem with this scheme is that a client cannot figure out how to contact a server unless the server is using an agreed-upon address to accept requests. If each service were to reserve an address for every protocol over which the service is to be offered, the required administration would be a nightmare.

The RPC mechanism solves this problem with the *rpcbind facility* by providing a place for server processes to register their numbers and addresses. A daemon, called the *rpcbinder*, waits for messages using transport endpoints bound to well-known addresses. (Previously, the rpcbinder was known as the *portmapper*.) Clients contact the rpcbinder to find the address corresponding to the program and version numbers. The client then uses the address to contact the process offering the service.

With the rpcbind facility, a server application can let the transport provider choose its address to use, in much the same way as a client application can. This limits the proliferation of reserved addresses to the ones used by the rpcbinder. Thus, administration is reduced to managing a set of network-independent, protocol-independent, {program, version, procedure}-number 3-tuples.

An instance of the rpcbinder runs on each machine that is to offer services through the remote procedure call mechanism. A server contacts the rpcbinder running on the machine where the server is running. A client contacts the rpcbinder running on the machine from which the service is to be obtained. Before the rpcbinder transmits the address of the server to the client, it converts the address to its universal address format (discussed in Chapter 5). This avoids problems associated with machine dependencies when the client tries to interpret the address. The client will convert the address from its universal representation to its local representation before trying to use it.

RPC Conventions

For a function to be made available through the RPC framework, it must follow several conventions. First, a remote function can only accept one input argument. If a function needs multiple arguments, they must be packed in a single structure, with the address of the structure used as the input argument.

For example, consider a function that adds two integers:

```
sum = add(a, b);      /* local function */
```

To make this function available as a remote procedure, we would have to define the input argument and function as:

```
struct addarg {
    int a;
    int b;
};
int *add(struct addarg *arg);    /* remote function */
```

Note that the return value is a pointer to an integer instead of an integer. Remote procedure arguments and return values are always declared as pointers to the input and output objects. These conventions allow the RPC functions to treat all remote procedures uniformly, regardless of the number and types of their arguments and return values.

If a function had multiple return values (through output arguments, for example), then the return values would need to be defined and passed in a single structure, similar to the arguments. Consider the `stat` system call. If we were to implement a remote procedure that performs the `stat` system call, the remote procedure and its return values would be declared similar to:

```
struct rstatret {
      int            errno;  /* error number or 0 on success */
      struct stat sbuf;   /* contains file statistics */
};
struct rstatret *rstat(char *filename);
```

Even though it appears as if the argument and return value are passed by reference, they are actually passed by value. Since the calling process and the process executing the remote procedure have different address spaces, an address from one process does not have the same significance to the other process.

Other conventions concern the input and output arguments for remote procedures. If a remote procedure has no input arguments or no output arguments, then the pointers to the nonexistent input or output arguments, as specified in the RPC functions called by the client, are set to NULL. Since the return values from remote procedures are pointers, the variables to which they point must be declared as either static or global. The contents of the memory will be accessed when packaging up the reply to the client, so the memory must remain unaltered after the function returns. Variables declared on the stack (*automatic* variables) have undefined values once the scope of the procedure is left.

Every remote program can support several procedures, and every procedure can be implemented in several versions of a program. Procedure number 0, however, is reserved for the *null procedure*. This procedure takes no arguments and has no return value. All remote programs must define this procedure and return a reply when its execution is requested. It can be used to "ping" a host to see if a particular RPC service is currently available.

There are many RPC library header files. Applications can include them all simply by including `<rpc/rpc.h>`. Instead of containing declarations, `<rpc/rpc.h>` contains #include directives that include all the RPC header files.

RPC Library Client Functions

The primary high-level, client-side RPC library routine is `rpc_call(3N)` [see `rpc_clnt_calls(3N)`]. It is used to make a remote procedure call.

```
#include <rpc/rpc.h>

enum clnt_stat rpc_call(const char *host, ulong_t prognum,
      ulong_t versnum, ulong_t procnum,
      const xdrproc_t inproc, const char *inarg,
      const xdrproc_t outproc, char *outarg,
      const char *nettype);
```

`host` is the name of the host computer providing the service, `prognum` is the RPC program number, `versnum` is the version number of the program, `procnum` identifies the procedure to invoke, `inproc` is the address of an XDR filter used to encode the input argument, `inarg` is a pointer to the input argument, `outproc` is the address of an XDR filter used to decode the output argument (the result), `outarg` is the address of the output argument, and `nettype` is a character string (as described in Table 8.3) that influences the network and protocol used to make the remote procedure call.

`rpc_call` will use the first network ID with the characteristics that match `nettype` when making the remote procedure call. The only way a user can influence the selection of the network and protocol used by a compiled application is if the application uses a `nettype` that consults the `NETPATH` environment variable and the variable is set in the user's environment. If the call succeeds, 0 is returned; otherwise, an error code is returned that describes the reason for failure. The return code only applies to the status of the remote procedure call itself; it has no relation to the return value of the remote function. Even if the remote procedure call succeeds, the remote function can still fail (because of insufficient privileges, for example). The return value (`outarg`) from the remote procedure call will usually contain an indication of success or failure of the function itself.

Once `rpc_call` makes a remote procedure call, if the transport provider is connection-oriented and a response is not received in 25 seconds, an error is returned. If the transport provider is connectionless and a response is not received in 5 seconds, then the request is retransmitted. If a response to this second request is not received in 10 seconds, then the request is transmitted a third time. If no response to the third request is received in 20 seconds, then an error is returned. The library does not need to retransmit with connection-oriented protocols, because the transport providers handle the retransmission themselves.

Note that, other than retransmission, the RPC library makes no other attempt at providing a reliable data-transfer mechanism. If a connectionless protocol is being used, it is up to the application to provide whatever is necessary to ensure reliability. With the low-level RPC library routines, applications can customize parameters like the initial retransmission period, the total timeout period, and the authentication type. (The high-level routines do not employ any authentication mechanism.)

On success, `rpc_call` returns the value `RPC_SUCCESS`. Other return codes indicate different reasons for failing. Applications can convert the return code into an error message with `clnt_sperrno(3N)`, or print the message on the standard error stream with `clnt_perrno(3N)`:

```
#include <rpc/rpc.h>

void clnt_perrno(enum clnt_stat stat);
char *clnt_sperrno(enum clnt_stat stat);
```

`stat` is the value returned from `rpc_call`. `clnt_perrno` will append a newline to the end of the string before printing it on the standard error stream.

Example 8.3.1. Assume you had to administer heterogeneous computers on a network. If there were so many that you could not remember what the type of each machine was, or if they were upgraded so quickly that keeping track of the types was difficult, then an application that helped you to identify the type would be useful.

This example illustrates the client side of such an application. The following are the definitions for the RPC numbers and XDR filter, stored in a header file (machtype.h):

```
#define MACH_PROG    0x22222222  /* program # */
#define MACH_VER     1           /* current version # */
#define MACH_PROC    1           /* returns machine type */

extern bool_t xdr_machtype(XDR *, char **);
```

The program number is selected from the range reserved for local services. The initial version number for the program is 1. Procedure number 0 is reserved for the null procedure, so the first number available for applications is 1.

The XDR filter is stored in a separate file so it can be shared between the client and server.

```
#include <sys/utsname.h>
#include <rpc/types.h>
#include <rpc/xdr.h>

bool_t
xdr_machtype(XDR *handle, char **spp)
{
        return(xdr_string(handle, spp, SYS_NMLN));
}
```

The client program merely validates the number of arguments, calls rpc_call to make the remote procedure call, and prints the results. The remote function takes no arguments and returns a string that indicates the machine type.

```
#include <rpc/rpc.h>
#include <stdio.h>
#include <stdlib.h>
#include "machtype.h"

void
main(int argc, char *argv[])
{
        enum clnt_stat status;
        char *machtype;

        if (argc != 2) {
            fprintf(stderr, "usage: %s hostname\n", argv[0]);
            exit(1);
        }
        machtype = NULL;

        /*
         * Make the remote procedure call.
         */
        status = rpc_call(argv[1], MACH_PROG, MACH_VER,
          MACH_PROC, xdr_void, NULL, xdr_machtype, &machtype,
```

```
        NULL);
    if (status == RPC_SUCCESS) {
        /*
         * RPC succeeded.  Print the string returned.
         */
        printf("machine type is %s\n", machtype);
        exit(0);
    } else {
        /*
         * RPC failed.  Print an error message.
         */
        fprintf(stderr, "%s: rpc failed: %s\n", argv[0],
          clnt_sperrno(status));
        exit(1);
    }
}
```

Since the remote function takes no input arguments, the `inproc` parameter to `rpc_call` is set to `xdr_void`, and the `inarg` parameter is set to NULL. The output parameter is a string, so `outproc` is set to the address of a function that calls `xdr_string`. We cannot use `xdr_string` directly, because it expects three arguments and RPC library routines call XDR filters with only two arguments: a pointer to the XDR handle and a pointer to the object to be encoded or decoded.

`outarg` is set to the address of a character pointer, `machtype`, which will be used to refer to the machine name returned by the remote procedure. Note that we set `machtype` to NULL before making the remote procedure call. This is an indication to `xdr_string` that it should allocate memory for the string (in other words, the caller is not providing the memory).

The `nettype` parameter to `rpc_call` is set to NULL so that the user's NETPATH environment variable (or /etc/netconfig, if NETPATH is unset) will determine the network and protocol to use. The server side of this application is shown in the next example.   □

RPC Library Server Functions

Before a server can accept requests from a client for remote procedure calls, the server must first register itself with the rpcbinder on the machine where the server is to run. The high-level function `rpc_reg(3N)` [see `rpc_svc_calls(3N)`] informs the rpcbinder that a given service is available.

```
#include <rpc/rpc.h>

int rpc_reg(ulong_t prognum, ulong_t versnum,
        ulong_t procnum, const char *(*procname)(),
        const xdrproc_t inproc, const xdrproc_t outproc,
        const char *nettype);
```

`prognum` is the program number, `versnum` is the version number, `procnum` is the procedure number, `procname` is the address of the server procedure, `inproc` is the address of an XDR filter used to decode the input argument, `outproc` is the address of an XDR filter used to encode the output argument, and `nettype` is a character string that specifies the set of networks and protocols over which the service is to be offered.

The `nettype` parameter influences the set of network IDs chosen to provide the service. Unlike the client side, where only the first network ID specified by the `nettype` is used, the `nettype` here results in an endpoint being created for each network ID. The server provides the service over all the networks and protocols that match the `nettype`.

`rpc_reg` performs several tasks. First, it creates the network endpoints necessary to serve all the networks specified. Then it registers the program numbers, version numbers, and network addresses with the rpcbinder. Finally, it associates a server procedure with the {program, version, procedure}-number 3-tuple.

When a request arrives that matches the program number, version number, and procedure number, then the `procname` procedure is invoked. It is passed a pointer to its single input parameter and must return a pointer to its single result.

If successful, `rpc_reg` returns 0; otherwise, it returns −1. If it encounters an error, a message is logged using `syslog(3)`. (`syslog` is a BSD facility that allows system error messages to be directed to a system daemon and, from there, redirected to log files, or mailed to administrators, or printed on the system console.)

Once a server has registered all its procedures with the rpcbinder (it is unnecessary to register the null procedure), the server can begin accepting requests for remote procedure calls to be executed. The `svc_run(3N)` routine can be used to process client requests:

```
#include <rpc/rpc.h>

void svc_run(void);
```

`svc_run` never returns control to the caller. It waits for incoming requests in an infinite loop. When a request arrives, the client's argument is decoded, and the server procedure corresponding to the procedure number sent by the client is called with the argument. Then the result is encoded and sent to the client in the reply message.

Example 8.3.2. This example shows the server side of Example 8.3.1. The server becomes a daemon and calls `rpc_reg` to create its endpoints and register itself with the rpcbinder. Then it calls `svc_run` to process requests for service. Since `svc_run` should never return, the server logs an error message if it does return.

```
#include <sys/utsname.h>
#include <rpc/rpc.h>
#include <stdio.h>
#include <stdlib.h>
#include "machtype.h"

static char **mach_type_1(void);
extern void daemonize(const char *);
extern void log(const char *, ...);
```

```
void
main()
{
      /*
       * Become a daemon.
       */
      daemonize("mtyped");

      /*
       * Register with the rpcbinder.
       */
      if (rpc_reg(MACH_PROG, MACH_VER, MACH_PROC,
        mach_type_1, xdr_void, xdr_machtype,
        "visible") < 0) {
           log("error: cannot start service");
           exit(1);
      }

      /*
       * Wait for requests and service them.
       */
      svc_run();

      /*
       * svc_run should never return.
       */
      log("error: unexpected return from svc_run");
      exit(1);
}

static char **
mach_type_1(void)
{
      static struct utsname u;
      static char *p;

      /*
       * If uname fails, return the address of
       * a NULL pointer.
       */
      p = NULL;
      if (uname(&u) >= 0)
          p = u.machine;
      return(&p);
}
```

The function mach_type_1 is registered as the procedure to invoke when procedure number 1 is requested. It has no input argument, so xdr_void is specified
as the inproc argument to rpc_reg. The output argument is a string (a pointer to
a NULL-terminated sequence of characters), but we cannot use xdr_string, so we
use the xdr_machtype wrapper for the outproc parameter, just like the client
side does.

By passing ''visible'' for the nettype, this service will be offered over all networks and protocols that are marked as visible in /etc/netconfig. It makes little sense to use the NETPATH for servers, because they are sometimes started by hand and can accidentally pick up the NETPATH from the environment of the user starting them.

The mach_type_1 routine calls uname(2) to get the host's names. The utsname structure returned by uname contains a field that describes the computer's machine type, the machine field shown below.

```
struct utsname {
      char sysname[SYS_NMLN];  /* system name (local) */
      char nodename[SYS_NMLN]; /* network name (global) */
      char release[SYS_NMLN];  /* operating system release */
      char version[SYS_NMLN];  /* operating system version */
      char machine[SYS_NMLN];  /* machine type */
};
```

After calling uname, the mach_type_1 function sets the character pointer p to point at the machine type field. If uname fails, the pointer is NULL. In either case, the address of the character pointer is returned. Note that both the utsname structure and the character pointer are declared as static. This ensures they will still contain valid data after mach_type_1 returns.

If we were to return NULL if uname failed, then the server would not send a reply to the client. Eventually the client would time out and return an error. By returning a pointer to a NULL string, we enable the server to send a message back to the client. After the client decodes the return value, the client will be left with a zero-length string.   □

8.4 LOW-LEVEL RPC PROGRAMMING

While the high-level routines are fairly simple to use, they do present a rather restrictive interface. Applications have limited control over the selection of a network and transport protocol to use. The default timeout values and lack of authentication must be acceptable to the application.

The low-level routines, on the other hand, allow applications to control more details of the communication at the expense of exposing more of the underlying mechanism.

RPC Library Client Functions

A client-side application making a remote procedure call with the low-level functions does so in three steps. First, a *client handle* must be created. The client handle is a data structure that represents the client side of the communication about to take place. Second, the application must make the remote procedure call. Finally, the client handle must be destroyed if the application is not about to exit.

The client handle is defined as type CLIENT. In most cases, applications do not need to know the structure of the handle. One exception to this is when an application wants to use an alternate form of authentication. This is discussed in Section 8.6. When a client handle is created, it is initialized to do no authentication during the remote procedure call.

Applications can choose from five different interfaces to create client handles [see `rpc_clnt_create(3N)`]. The interfaces vary based on how much work the client has to do to initialize the transport endpoint beforehand. They are summarized in Table 8.4.

Table 8.4. Low-level RPC Client Handle Creation Routines

Library Routine	Description
`clnt_create`	Uses `nettype` (`NETPATH` and `/etc/netconfig`) to choose transport provider.
`clnt_tp_create`	Uses caller-supplied `netconfig` structure indicating desired transport provider.
`clnt_tli_create`	Uses caller-supplied `netconfig` structure or pre-existing transport endpoint.
`clnt_dg_create`	Uses bound connectionless transport endpoint.
`clnt_vc_create`	Uses bound and optionally connected (connection-oriented) transport endpoint.

The first interface, `clnt_create`, is similar to `rpc_call` in its use of the `nettype` parameter: the set of network IDs is determined by the `nettype`, and the first one that works is used for the client handle. The other interfaces depend on the caller providing either the `netconfig` entry or the bound file descriptor representing the transport endpoint. The synopses for the functions used to create client handles are

```
#include <rpc/rpc.h>

CLIENT *clnt_create(const char *host, ulong_t prognum,
     ulong_t versnum, const char *nettype);
CLIENT *clnt_tp_create(const char *host, ulong_t prognum,
     ulong_t versnum, const struct netconfig *ncp);
CLIENT *clnt_tli_create(int fd, const struct netconfig *ncp,
     const struct netbuf *svcaddr, ulong_t prognum,
     ulong_t versnum, uint_t sendsz, uint_t recvsz);
CLIENT *clnt_dg_create(int fd, const struct netbuf *svcaddr,
     ulong_t prognum, ulong_t versnum, uint_t sendsz,
     uint_t recvsz);
CLIENT *clnt_vc_create(int fd, const struct netbuf *svcaddr,
     ulong_t prognum, ulong_t versnum, uint_t sendsz,
     uint_t recvsz);
```

In all functions, `prognum` is the program number and `versnum` is the version number. `clnt_create` and `clnt_tp_create` specify the location of the service as a machine name (`host`) and contact the rpcbinder on that host to find the address of the server. The other functions rely on the caller supplying the network address of the server (svcaddr).

For clnt_tp_create and clnt_tli_create, ncp is a pointer to the netconfig entry corresponding to the network and protocol to use for communication. With clnt_tp_create, the transport endpoint is created for the caller. With clnt_tli_create, the caller can supply the transport endpoint (fd), in which case ncp is optional. If, however, fd is set to RPC_ANYFD, clnt_tli_create will use ncp to identify the transport device to open. If the endpoint is not bound, clnt_tli_create will take care of binding it.

For clnt_dg_create and clnt_vc_create, the transport endpoint must be both opened and bound. For clnt_vc_create, if the endpoint is not already connected to the server, an attempt to connect to the address specified by svcaddr is made. Otherwise, if the endpoint is already connected, svcaddr can be NULL. For clnt_dg_create, however, svcaddr must always be supplied.

The sendsz and recvsz parameters specify the sizes of the transmit and receive buffers, respectively, used by the RPC library. A size of zero indicates that the library should consult the transport provider for the appropriate size.

On success, the client-create functions return an initialized client handle. On failure, they return NULL. The client handle is initialized to the defaults pertaining to the type of transport service. For datagram service, the retry interval is set to 15 seconds. For virtual circuit service, there is no retry interval because the communication is reliable.

If creation of a client handle is unsuccessful, two routines are provided to help the application report the error:

```
#include <rpc/rpc.h>

void clnt_pcreateerror(const char *s);
char *clnt_spcreateerror(const char *s);
```

clnt_pcreateerror prints the string referred to by s followed by a colon, a space, a string describing the error, and a newline on the standard error stream. clnt_spcreateerror performs the same formatting, but does not append a newline to the end of the string, and returns the string to the caller instead of printing it. In both cases, the colon and space are included, regardless of whether or not s points to an empty string.

To use the functions that provide the address of the server as an argument, the application must first obtain the proper address for the given host, program number, version number, and network. This can be done with rpc_getaddr(3N) [see rpcbind(3N)]:

```
#include <rpc/rpc.h>

bool_t rpcb_getaddr(ulong_t prognum, ulong_t versnum,
        const struct netconfig *ncp, struct netbuf *svcaddr,
        const char *host);
```

prognum is the program number, versnum is the version number, ncp is a pointer to the netconfig structure that describes the network and protocol to be used, svcaddr points to a preallocated netbuf structure where the address is stored on return, and `host` is the name of the host machine where the service resides. The `netbuf` structure, introduced in Chapter 4, is as follows:

```
struct netbuf {
      uint_t  maxlen; /* buffer size */
      uint_t  len;    /* amount of data stored in buffer */
      char    *buf;   /* data buffer */
};
```

`rpcb_getaddr` will contact the rpcbinder on the given host to map the program and version numbers to a network address. The network address is stored in the caller's machine format on return. Before calling `rpcb_getaddr`, the caller must make sure enough space exists in the `netbuf` data buffer for the address and then set the `maxlen` field to the size of the buffer in bytes. On return, the `len` field is updated to contain the actual length in bytes of the address.

On success, `rpcb_getaddr` returns TRUE; on failure, it returns FALSE. Applications can use `clnt_spcreateerror` or `clnt_pcreateerror` to report the reason for the failure.

The default characteristics of a client handle can be changed after the handle is created. Applications can call `clnt_control(3N)` to modify client handle attributes:

```
#include <rpc/rpc.h>

bool_t clnt_control(CLIENT *handle, uint_t cmd, char *arg);
```

`handle` is a pointer to the client handle, `cmd` identifies the operation, and `arg` is a "typeless" pointer to the information. Table 8.5 summarizes the commands and the type of data to which `arg` refers for each command.

Table 8.5. `clnt_control` Commands

Option	arg points to	Description
CLSET_TIMEOUT	struct timeval	Set total timeout.
CLGET_TIMEOUT	struct timeval	Get total timeout.
CLGET_FD	int	Get the file descriptor associated with the handle.
CLGET_SVC_ADDR	struct netbuf	Get the address of the server.
CLSET_FD_CLOSE	unused	Close the file descriptor when destroying the handle.
CLSET_FD_NCLOSE	unused	Do not close the file descriptor when destroying the handle.
CLSET_RETRY_TIMEOUT	struct timeval	Set retry timeout (connectionless protocols only).
CLGET_RETRY_TIMEOUT	struct timeval	Get retry timeout (connectionless protocols only).

If an application uses the `CLSET_TIMEOUT` command, then the `timeout` parameter used in `clnt_call` (described below) is ignored. `clnt_control` returns 1 on success and 0 on failure. Timeouts are specified using a `timeval` structure:

```
struct timeval {
        long    tv_sec;     /* number of seconds */
        long    tv_usec;    /* and microseconds */
};
```

After the client handle has been created and any desired parameters have been modified, a remote procedure call can be made using `clnt_call(3N)` [see `rpc_clnt_calls(3N)`]:

```
#include <rpc/rpc.h>

enum clnt_stat clnt_call(CLIENT *handle, ulong_t procnum,
        const xdrproc_t inproc, char *inarg,
        const xdrproc_t outproc, char *outarg,
        struct timeval timeout);
```

`handle` is a pointer to the client handle, `procnum` is the procedure number representing the procedure to invoke, `inproc` is the address of an XDR filter used to encode the input argument, `inarg` is the address of the input argument, `outproc` is the address of the XDR filter used to decode the output argument, `outarg` is a pointer to the output argument, and `timeout` specifies the maximum amount of time to wait for a reply before returning an error. Note that `timeout` is a `timeval` structure, *not* a pointer to the structure.

If the remote procedure call succeeds, `RPC_SUCCESS` is returned. Otherwise, an appropriate error code is returned. Errors can be reported using `clnt_perrno` or `clnt_sperrno`, but applications can be more informative by using one of two other routines, `clnt_perror` or `clnt_sperror`. The function prototypes are

```
#include <rpc/rpc.h>

void clnt_perror(const CLIENT *handle, const char *s);
char *clnt_sperror(const CLIENT *handle, const char *s);
```

where `handle` is a pointer to the client handle, and `s` is a pointer to a character string to be prepended to the error message.

`clnt_perror` is similar to `clnt_perrno`, except that the error message printed on the standard error stream is obtained from an error code stored in the client handle. More error information is stored in the handle than just the return from `clnt_call`. Additional information includes the TLI error and the value of `errno`. `clnt_sperror` is like `clnt_sperrno` except that the error information is obtained from the client handle, and the string returned is stored in a statically allocated buffer that is overwritten on each call.

When a client application makes multiple remote procedure calls, it can consume additional memory with each call if the XDR filter for the output argument allocates memory to decode the results. A client application that runs for an extended period of time will experience degraded performance, ultimately resulting in failures, if allowed to allocate memory continually without freeing any.

The RPC library provides a function to free any memory allocated by a client's output filter. Once used, the output arguments can no longer be referenced. The function is `clnt_freeres(3N)`:

```
#include <rpc/rpc.h>

int clnt_freeres(CLIENT *handle, const xdrproc_t outproc,
     char *outarg);
```

`handle` is a pointer to the client handle, `outproc` is the address of the XDR filter used to decode the output arguments from `clnt_call`, and `outarg` is a pointer to the output arguments.

`clnt_freeres` returns 1 if it successfully freed memory, and 0 otherwise. The XDR routines were discussed in Section 8.2. Only the complex filters that take the address of a character pointer will allocate memory when decoding arguments, and only if the character pointer is `NULL`.

Example 8.4.1. In the previous section, we illustrated a simple RPC-based application that returned the machine type of a given host. In this section we extend the example to return the entire `utsname` structure. The client side is shown here and the server side will be shown in the next example. We start with the header file, `runame.h`:

```
/*
 * Program number.
 */
#define UNAME_PROG    0x22222223

/*
 * Current version number.
 */
#define UNAME_VER 1

/*
 * Procedure returns struct utsname.
 */
#define UNAME_PROC    1

/*
 * XDR filter for struct utsname.
 */
extern bool_t xdr_utsname(XDR *, struct utsname *);
```

We begin the client side by validating the command-line arguments and creating a client handle with `clnt_create`. If this fails, we print an error message using `clnt_spcreateerror` and exit. Otherwise, we set the call timeout to 10 seconds and use `clnt_call` to make the remote procedure call.

```
#include <sys/utsname.h>
#include <rpc/rpc.h>
#include <stdio.h>
#include <stdlib.h>
```

```c
#include "runame.h"

void
main(int argc, char *argv[])
{
    enum clnt_stat status;
    struct utsname u;
    CLIENT *handle;
    struct timeval t;
    char buf[64];

    if (argc != 2) {
        fprintf(stderr, "usage: %s hostname\n", argv[0]);
        exit(1);
    }

    /*
     * Create the client handle.
     */
    handle = clnt_create(argv[1], UNAME_PROG, UNAME_VER,
        "netpath");
    if (handle == NULL) {
        fprintf(stderr,
            "%s: can't create client handle: %s\n",
            argv[0], clnt_spcreateerror(""));
        exit(1);
    }

    /*
     * Use a 10-second timeout.
     */
    t.tv_sec = 10;
    t.tv_usec = 0;

    /*
     * Make the remote procedure call.
     */
    status = clnt_call(handle, UNAME_PROC, xdr_void, NULL,
        xdr_utsname, (char *)&u, t);
    if (status == RPC_SUCCESS) {
        /*
         * RPC succeeded.  Print the strings returned.
         */
        printf("sysname is %s\n", u.sysname);
        printf("nodename is %s\n", u.nodename);
        printf("release is %s\n", u.release);
        printf("version is %s\n", u.version);
        printf("machine type is %s\n", u.machine);
        exit(0);
    } else {
        /*
         * RPC failed.  Print an error message.
         */
        sprintf(buf, "%s: rpc failed", argv[0]);
```

```
        clnt_perror(handle, buf);
        exit(1);
    }
}
```

Since there is no input argument, `inarg` is NULL and `inproc` is set to `xdr_void`.

If the remote procedure call succeeds, then the results will have been run through the output filter `xdr_utsname` to decode the architecture-independent data into the system-dependent format and will be stored in the `utsname` structure. If the call fails, then we print an error message using `clnt_perror`.

The XDR filter, `xdr_utsname`, is shown below. We use `xdr_vector` to encode and decode each element of the structure. Recall that `xdr_vector` is used with fixed-size arrays. We tell `xdr_vector` to process each array element using `xdr_char`.

```
#include <sys/utsname.h>
#include <rpc/rpc.h>

bool_t
xdr_utsname(XDR *handle, struct utsname *up)
{
    if (!xdr_vector(handle, up->sysname, SYS_NMLN,
        sizeof(char), xdr_char))
          return(FALSE);
    if (!xdr_vector(handle, up->nodename, SYS_NMLN,
        sizeof(char), xdr_char))
          return(FALSE);
    if (!xdr_vector(handle, up->release, SYS_NMLN,
        sizeof(char), xdr_char))
          return(FALSE);
    if (!xdr_vector(handle, up->version, SYS_NMLN,
        sizeof(char), xdr_char))
          return(FALSE);
    if (!xdr_vector(handle, up->machine, SYS_NMLN,
        sizeof(char), xdr_char))
          return(FALSE);
    return(TRUE);
}
```
                                                                    □

RPC Library Server Functions

A server-side RPC application needs to do four things to support remote procedure calls with the low-level functions. First, a *server handle* must be created. The server handle is similar to the client handle, but contains information about the server end of the communication. Second, the server must register its RPC numbers and addresses with the rpcbinder. The third step is for the server to wait for requests. The last step involves determining the procedure to execute on behalf of the request (this process is called *dispatching*).

Functions similar to those used to create client handles exist to create server handles. They are summarized in Table 8.6.

Table 8.6. Low-level RPC Server Handle Creation Routines

Library Routine	Description
svc_create	Uses `nettype` (`NETPATH` and `/etc/netconfig`) to choose transport providers.
svc_tp_create	Uses caller-supplied `netconfig` structure indicating desired transport provider.
svc_tli_create	Uses caller-supplied `netconfig` structure or pre-existing transport endpoint.
svc_fd_create	Uses bound and connected connection-oriented transport endpoint.
svc_dg_create	Uses bound connectionless transport endpoint.
svc_vc_create	Uses bound connection-oriented transport endpoint.

svc_create is the only interface that creates multiple server handles. The other interfaces create a single handle. svc_create allows the caller to influence the set of transport providers and networks used through the nettype parameter. svc_tp_create and svc_tli_create allow the caller to select the transport provider and network by passing in a pointer to the corresponding netconfig structure. The other functions expect the caller to pass in a file descriptor corresponding to the transport endpoint to use for communication. Like clnt_tli_create, svc_tli_create gives the caller the option of whether or not to provide a file descriptor. The synopses for the functions are

```
#include <rpc/rpc.h>

int svc_create(const void (*dispatch)(), ulong_t prognum,
    ulong_t versnum, const char *nettype);
SVCXPRT *svc_tp_create(const void (*dispatch)(),
    ulong_t prognum, ulong_t versnum,
    const struct netconfig *ncp);
SVCXPRT *svc_tli_create(int fd, const struct netconfig *ncp,
    const struct t_bind *bindaddr, uint_t sendsz,
    uint_t recvsz);
SVCXPRT *svc_dg_create(int fd, uint_t sendsz,
    uint_t recvsz);
SVCXPRT *svc_fd_create(int fd, uint_t sendsz,
    uint_t recvsz);
SVCXPRT *svc_vc_create(int fd, uint_t sendsz,
    uint_t recvsz);
```

Both svc_create and svc_tp_create contact the rpcbinder to register the service program number, prognum, and version number, versnum. The other interfaces assume the server will register itself with the rpcbinder some other way. The dispatch parameter is the address of the function to be called when a request is received. Its job is to dispatch the request to the appropriate server procedure. It is declared as:

```
void (*dispatch)(const struct svc_req *req,
    const SVCXPRT *handle);
```

where `req` describes the request for service, and `handle` is the server handle. We will look at dispatch functions in more detail shortly.

For `svc_tp_create` and `svc_tli_create`, `ncp` is a pointer to the `netconfig` entry corresponding to the network and protocol to use for communication. With `svc_tp_create`, the transport endpoint is created for the server. With `svc_tli_create`, the server can supply the transport endpoint (`fd`), in which case `ncp` is optional. If, however, `fd` is set to `RPC_ANYFD`, `svc_tli_create` will use `ncp` to identify the transport device to open. If the endpoint is not bound, `svc_tli_create` will bind it to the address specified by `bindaddr`. If `bindaddr` is NULL, then the transport provider selects an unused address. When `svc_tli_create` binds the address, it uses a hard-coded queue length of 8 for the maximum number of outstanding connections that the transport provider should enqueue while waiting for a connection to be established.

For `svc_dg_create` and `svc_vc_create`, the transport endpoint must be both opened and bound. For `svc_fd_create`, the transport endpoint must also be connected to the client. `svc_fd_create` is used when the server is spawned from a port monitor, such as `inetd` or `listen`.

As with the client-side interfaces, the `sendsz` and `recvsz` parameters specify the sizes of the transmit and receive buffers, respectively, used by the RPC library. A size of zero indicates that the library should consult the transport provider for the appropriate size.

On success, `svc_create` returns the number of server handles created (one per network ID specified by `nettype`). On failure, it returns zero. The other functions return a pointer to the server handle on success, or NULL on failure. When an error occurs, a message is logged by calling `syslog`.

The server handle is defined by the type SVCXPRT. There is usually no need for a server to know the structure of a server handle. Servers merely pass pointers to server handles to RPC library routines.

After creating the server handle, the server needs to register itself with the rpcbinder and associate its dispatching routine with its program and version numbers. These are two separate actions. The rpcbinder maps program and version numbers to network addresses, but the server maps these numbers to its dispatching function itself. Both `svc_create` and `svc_tp_create` take care of these additional steps for the caller. If any of the other routines are used to create server handles, the server must handle registration itself.

Servers can call `svc_reg(3N)` [see `rpc_svc_calls(3N)`] to handle registration. It will associate the server's dispatching routine with its program and version numbers and optionally register the server with the rpcbinder. The synopsis is

```
#include <rpc/rpc.h>

int svc_reg(const SVCXPRT *handle, ulong_t prognum,
    ulong_t versnum, const void (*dispatch)(),
    const struct netconfig *ncp);
```

where handle is the server handle, prognum is the program number, versnum is the version number, dispatch is the address of the server's dispatching routine, and ncp is a pointer to the netconfig structure that represents the protocol and network over which communication will occur. If ncp is NULL, no attempt is made to register with the rpcbinder. svc_reg returns 1 if it succeeds and 0 if it fails.

To undo the work done by svc_reg, a server can call svc_unreg(3N). It unregisters the service with the rpcbinder for all networks and protocols, and breaks the association between the dispatching function and the server's program and version numbers. The synopsis is

```
#include <rpc/rpc.h>

void svc_unreg(ulong_t prognum, ulong_t versnum);
```

where prognum is the program number and versnum is the version number.

If a server is starting up, it does not yet have an association between its dispatching function and its program and version numbers. But if another instance of the server is running, or if a prior instance of the server terminated abnormally, the rpcbinder might still have an association between the program and version numbers and some other network address. Thus, it is usually a good idea for the server to unregister the program and version numbers with the rpcbinder before calling svc_reg.

The server can call svc_unreg first, or it can contact the rpcbinder directly by calling rpcb_unset(3N) [see rpcbind(3N)]:

```
#include <rpc/rpc.h>

bool_t rpcb_unset(ulong_t prognum, ulong_t versnum,
    const struct netconfig *ncp);
```

prognum is the program number, versnum is the version number, and ncp points to a netconfig structure that describes the network and protocol that were previously registered. rpcb_unset will contact the rpcbinder and arrange for the mapping between prognum, versnum, and any network address using the same network and protocol as specified by ncp to be destroyed. If ncp is NULL, all mappings of prognum and versnum are removed. rpcb_unset returns TRUE on success and FALSE on failure.

The mapping between a server's program and version numbers and its network address exists independently of the server itself. If a server exits without first unregistering itself with the rpcbinder, then the mapping will remain in effect, even though the service is unavailable. Thus, it is usually a good idea for servers to call rpcb_unset before exiting.

After creating a server handle and registering itself with the rpcbinder, a server usually calls `svc_run` to wait for requests. `svc_run` will call RPC library routines that will invoke the server's dispatching function associated with the program and version numbers in the client's request.

The server dispatching routine is called with two parameters: a pointer to a structure that describes the client RPC request, and a pointer to the server handle. The client request is represented by a `svc_req` structure:

```
struct svc_req {
      ulong_t                rq_prog;     /* program number */
      ulong_t                rq_vers;     /* protocol version */
      ulong_t                rq_proc;     /* procedure number */
      struct opaque_auth     rq_cred;     /* raw creds */
      caddr_t                rq_clntcred; /* cooked creds */
      SVCXPRT                *rq_xprt;    /* server handle */
};
```

The `rq_cred` and the `rq_clntcred` fields will be discussed when we cover authentication in Section 8.6.

The primary role of the server's dispatching function is to call the proper server procedure that corresponds to the RPC numbers requested by the client. The dispatching routine performs the following steps:

1.   Optionally validates the caller's credentials.
2.   Gets the caller's input arguments.
3.   Calls the server function corresponding to the procedure number in the request.
4.   Sends a reply back to the client.
5.   Frees any memory that might have been allocated when decoding the input arguments.

Input arguments are extracted from the client request and converted into the local machine representation by `svc_getargs(3N)` [see `rpc_svc_reg(3N)`]:

```
#include <rpc/rpc.h>

int svc_getargs(const SVCXPRT *handle,
      const xdrproc_t inproc, char *inarg);
```

`handle` is a pointer to the server handle, `inproc` is the address of the XDR filter used to decode the arguments, and `inarg` is a pointer to the memory location where the arguments are to be stored. `svc_getargs` returns 1 if decoding succeeds and 0 if it fails.

Since the decoding process can cause memory to be allocated, servers need to free the memory after having replied to the client. `svc_freeargs(3N)` can be used for this purpose:

```
#include <rpc/rpc.h>

int svc_freeargs(const SVCXPRT *handle,
      const xdrproc_t inproc, char *inarg);
```

The arguments are the same as in `svc_getargs`. If `svc_freeargs` successfully frees memory, it returns 1; otherwise, it returns 0.

Replies are sent back to the client using `svc_sendreply`(3N):

```
#include <rpc/rpc.h>

int svc_sendreply(const SVCXPRT *handle,
    const xdrproc_t outproc, const char *outarg);
```

`handle` is a pointer to the server handle, `outproc` is the address of the XDR filter used to encode the output arguments, and `outarg` is a pointer to the output arguments. `svc_sendreply` will call the XDR filter to encode the results and transmit them in a message back to the client. On success, `svc_sendreply` returns 1; on failure, it returns 0.

If the server encounters an error while trying to service an RPC request, it should send a message back to the client informing the client that the request failed. (If the server never responds to a client's request, then the client will eventually timeout and possibly retry the request.) Several functions are provided by the RPC library to generate failure responses. They are summarized in Table 8.7.

Table 8.7. Server Error Response Functions

Library Routine	Description
`svcerr_auth`	Authentication failed.
`svcerr_decode`	Cannot decode the input parameters.
`svcerr_noproc`	Invalid procedure number.
`svcerr_systemerr`	System error.
`svcerr_weakauth`	Correct, but insufficient, authentication parameters.

`svcerr_auth` takes two parameters: a pointer to the server handle, and a code indicating the type of authentication error. All of the other functions take a pointer to the server handle as their only argument.

If a server should ever need to destroy a handle, it can use `svc_destroy`(3N):

```
void svc_destroy(SVCXPRT *handle);
```

The handle cannot be used after `svc_destroy` is called. Destruction involves closing the transport endpoint associated with the handle and freeing any memory allocated by the handle.

Now that we have seen the primary RPC server functions, we will take a look at the server side of the previous example.

Example 8.4.2. In Example 8.4.1, we presented the client side of an application that obtained and printed the `utsname` structure from machines on a network. The server uses the same header file and shares the same implementation of the XDR filter.

The server creates (possibly multiple) server handles with `svc_create` after becoming a daemon. If handle creation fails, it logs an error and exits. Otherwise, it calls `svc_run` to wait for RPC requests.

```c
#include <sys/utsname.h>
#include <rpc/rpc.h>
#include <stdio.h>
#include <stdlib.h>
#include <string.h>
#include "runame.h"

extern void daemonize(const char *);
extern void log(const char *, ...);
static void uname_prog(struct svc_req *, SVCXPRT *);

void
main()
{
    /*
     * Become a daemon.
     */
    daemonize("runamed");

    /*
     * Create the server handle(s).  svc_create will
     * unregister UNAME_PROG and UNAME_VER if they are
     * currently registered with the rpcbinder.
     */
    if (svc_create(uname_prog, UNAME_PROG, UNAME_VER,
      "visible") == 0) {
        log("runamed: cannot start service");
        exit(1);
    }

    /*
     * Wait for requests and service them.
     */
    svc_run();

    /*
     * svc_run should never return.
     */
    log("error: unexpected return from svc_run");

    /*
     * Unregister this program and version
     * before exiting.
     */
    rpcb_unset(UNAME_PROG, UNAME_VER, NULL);
    exit(1);
}

static void
uname_prog(struct svc_req *req, SVCXPRT *handle)
{
    static struct utsname u;
```

```
switch (req->rq_proc) {
case NULLPROC:              /* null procedure */
    svc_sendreply(handle, xdr_void, NULL);
    return;

case UNAME_PROC:            /* return utsname */
    break;

default:                    /* unknown procedure */
    svcerr_noproc(handle);
    return;
}

/*
 * Copy dummy names to utsname structure elements.
 * Then call uname.  If uname fails, we send dummy
 * names back to the client.
 */
strcpy(u.sysname, "unknown");
strcpy(u.nodename, "unknown");
strcpy(u.release, "unknown");
strcpy(u.version, "unknown");
strcpy(u.machine, "unknown");
uname(&u);

/*
 * Send reply to client.
 */
if (!svc_sendreply(handle, xdr_utsname, (char *)&u))
    svcerr_systemerr(handle);
}
```

The server's dispatching function is `uname_prog`. This example does no authentication and has no input arguments, so we skip these steps. We begin identifying the procedure to be executed using the procedure number field (`rq_proc`) in the `svc_req` structure. If the procedure number is 0 (NULLPROC, the null procedure number, defined in the RPC header files), then we use `svc_sendreply` to send a successful reply back to the client. Note that the `outproc` argument is set to `xdr_void`, and the `outarg` argument is set to NULL. This is because the null procedure has no input arguments or output arguments.

If the procedure number is 1 (UNAME_PROC), then we call `uname` and send a reply back to the client, using `xdr_utsname` as the XDR filter to encode the output argument. If `svc_sendreply` fails, we call `svc_systemerr` to notify the client of the error.

Any other value for the procedure number will result in a call to `svcerr_noproc` to inform the client that the procedure number is invalid.   □

It is often necessary to modify programs after they have been distributed. Two common reasons for this are to apply bug fixes and to add enhancements. In a networked environment, however, it is difficult to synchronize the software updates such that the new version of a program replaces the current version on all the machines at the same time.

The version number in XDR helps to solve this problem by giving RPC servers the flexibility to offer old versions of programs and by allowing RPC clients to request an older version of a service as a means of recovering from a version mismatch error. Thus, applications can be designed so as modifications are made, older clients work with newer servers and older servers work with newer clients.

The following example illustrates the remote uname client and server dealing with multiple versions of the same procedure.

Example 8.4.3. Assume, for the purposes of this example, that your network load has increased significantly because many users are running the remote uname application you installed last month (an unlikely possibility). After closer scrutiny, you realize that you can make the communication more efficient by reducing the size of the encoded data. The xdr_vector filter was overkill because each field in the utsname structure is NULL-terminated, allowing you to encode each field as a string instead of a fixed-length array of characters.

In addition to the space savings that result in going from a fixed-length representation to a variable-length representation, additional space savings can be obtained because xdr_char pads a single byte to a four-byte quantity, while xdr_string does not. What originally took 5140 bytes to represent now takes 20 bytes plus the sum of the lengths of each string rounded to a multiple of 4 bytes. (On my machine, the size went from 5140 bytes to 48 bytes.)

The change in XDR representation will result in a new protocol that is incompatible with the old programs because the amount and type of data in the messages will have changed. Since it will be difficult to replace all the client and server programs at the same time, you decide to support the old version as well.

The header file now defines two version numbers and declares two XDR filters.

```
/*
 * Program number.
 */
#define UNAME_PROG    0x22222223

/*
 * Current version number.
 */
#define UNAME_VER_2   2
#define UNAME_VER     UNAME_VER_2

/*
 * Old version numbers.
 */
#define UNAME_VER_1   1

/*
 * Procedure returns struct utsname.
 */
#define UNAME_PROC    1
```

```
/*
 * XDR filters for struct utsname.
 * Version 1 uses xdr_vector.
 * Version 2 uses xdr_string.
 */
extern bool_t xdr_utsname_1(XDR *, struct utsname *);
extern bool_t xdr_utsname_2(XDR *, struct utsname *);
```

The server main procedure is the same as before, with the addition of the second call to svc_create. The two calls differ only in the version number registered.

```
#include <sys/utsname.h>
#include <rpc/rpc.h>
#include <stdio.h>
#include <stdlib.h>
#include <string.h>
#include "runame.h"

extern void daemonize(const char *);
extern void log(const char *, ...);
static void uname_prog(struct svc_req *, SVCXPRT *);

void
main()
{
    /*
     * Become a daemon.
     */
    daemonize("runamed");

    /*
     * Create the server handle(s).  svc_create will
     * unregister UNAME_PROG and UNAME_VER_[12] if they
     * are currently registered with the rpcbinder.
     */
    if (svc_create(uname_prog, UNAME_PROG, UNAME_VER_1,
      "visible") == 0) {
        log("runamed: cannot start service");
        exit(1);
    }
    if (svc_create(uname_prog, UNAME_PROG, UNAME_VER_2,
      "visible") == 0) {
        log("runamed: cannot start service");
        rpcb_unset(UNAME_PROG, UNAME_VER_1, NULL);
        exit(1);
    }

    /*
     * Wait for requests and service them.
     */
    svc_run();

    /*
```

```
            * svc_run should never return.
            */
           log("error: unexpected return from svc_run");

           /*
            * Unregister this program and versions
            * before exiting.
            */
           rpcb_unset(UNAME_PROG, UNAME_VER_1, NULL);
           rpcb_unset(UNAME_PROG, UNAME_VER_2, NULL);
           exit(1);
   }
```

The only modification we need to make to the dispatching function is to check the version number in the `svc_req` structure and call `svc_sendreply` with the corresponding XDR filter. There is no need to check for a version mismatch here, because the rpcbinder would have already made that check and failed any attempt at creating a client handle with an unsupported version number.

```
   static void
   uname_prog(struct svc_req *req, SVCXPRT *handle)
   {
           static struct utsname u;
           int ret;

           switch (req->rq_proc) {
           case NULLPROC:                  /* null procedure */
               svc_sendreply(handle, xdr_void, NULL);
               return;

           case UNAME_PROC:                /* return utsname */
               break;

           default:                        /* unknown procedure */
               svcerr_noproc(handle);
               return;
           }

           /*
            * Copy dummy names to utsname structure elements.
            * Then call uname.  If uname fails, we send dummy
            * names back to the client.
            */
           strcpy(u.sysname, "unknown");
           strcpy(u.nodename, "unknown");
           strcpy(u.release, "unknown");
           strcpy(u.version, "unknown");
           strcpy(u.machine, "unknown");
           uname(&u);


           /*
            * Send reply to client.  If version 1, use
            * xdr_utsname_1; else use xdr_utsname_2.
```

```
        */
    if (req->rq_vers == UNAME_VER_1)
        ret = svc_sendreply(handle, xdr_utsname_1,
            (char *)&u);
    else
        ret = svc_sendreply(handle, xdr_utsname_2,
            (char *)&u);
    if (ret == 0)
        svcerr_systemerr(handle);
}
```

We renamed the `xdr_utsname` filter from Example 8.4.1 to `xdr_utsname_1`. The new filter using `xdr_string` is called `xdr_utsname_2`:

```
#include <sys/utsname.h>
#include <rpc/rpc.h>

bool_t
xdr_utsname_2(XDR *handle, struct utsname *up)
{
    char *p;

    p = up->sysname;
    if (!xdr_string(handle, &p, SYS_NMLN))
        return(FALSE);
    p = up->nodename;
    if (!xdr_string(handle, &p, SYS_NMLN))
        return(FALSE);
    p = up->release;
    if (!xdr_string(handle, &p, SYS_NMLN))
        return(FALSE);
    p = up->version;
    if (!xdr_string(handle, &p, SYS_NMLN))
        return(FALSE);
    p = up->machine;
    if (!xdr_string(handle, &p, SYS_NMLN))
        return(FALSE);
    return(TRUE);
}
```

The reason we need to use the temporary variable p is that each element in the `utsname` structure is an array. Since an array name in C is an alias for the address of the initial element in the array, the array name will always evaluate to the same value as the array name prefixed by the & operator. In other words, up->sysname is the same as &up->sysname. `xdr_string` will dereference its second parameter to find the address of the string, so we need to provide a pointer for it to dereference.

To the client program, we add an extra variable, `xdr_outproc`, to hold the address of the XDR filter to use. Initially, we try the most recent version number. If `clnt_create` fails with a status of `RPC_VERSMISMATCH`, then we know to try an older version.

```
#include <sys/utsname.h>
#include <rpc/rpc.h>
#include <stdio.h>
#include <stdlib.h>
#include "runame.h"

void
main(int argc, char *argv[])
{
    enum clnt_stat status;
    struct utsname u;
    CLIENT *handle;
    struct timeval t;
    bool_t (*xdr_outproc)();

    if (argc != 2) {
        fprintf(stderr, "usage: %s hostname\n", argv[0]);
        exit(1);
    }

    /*
     * Assume version 2 to start.
     */
    xdr_outproc = xdr_utsname_2;

    /*
     * Create the client handle.
     */
    handle = clnt_create(argv[1], UNAME_PROG, UNAME_VER_2,
      "visible");
    if (handle == NULL) {
        /*
         * If we received a version mismatch error, try
         * an older version of the program.  Note that
         * rpc_createerr.cf_stat is undocumented.
         */
        if (rpc_createerr.cf_stat == RPC_VERSMISMATCH) {
            handle = clnt_create(argv[1], UNAME_PROG,
              UNAME_VER_1, "visible");
            if (handle == NULL)
                goto errout;
            xdr_outproc = xdr_utsname_1;
        } else {
errout:
            fprintf(stderr,
              "%s: can't create client handle: %s\n",
              argv[0], clnt_spcreateerror(""));
            exit(1);
        }
    }

    /*
     * Use a 10-second timeout.
     */
```

```
    t.tv_sec = 10;
    t.tv_usec = 0;

    /*
     * Make the remote procedure call.
     */
    status = clnt_call(handle, UNAME_PROC, xdr_void, NULL,
      xdr_outproc, (char *)&u, t);
    if (status == RPC_SUCCESS) {
        /*
         * RPC succeeded.  Print the strings returned.
         */
        printf("sysname is %s\n", u.sysname);
        printf("nodename is %s\n", u.nodename);
        printf("release is %s\n", u.release);
        printf("version is %s\n", u.version);
        printf("machine type is %s\n", u.machine);
        exit(0);
    } else {
        /*
         * RPC failed.  Print an error message.
         */
        fprintf(stderr, "rpc failed: %s\n",
          clnt_sperrno(status));
        exit(1);
    }
}
```

Since `clnt_create` does not return the status of the attempt to create the client handle, we need to reach into the RPC library and pick out the status. `rpc_createerr` is defined in `<rpc/clnt.h>` to include a return status and error code. There is no official interface to get this value, so we just reference it, noting that it might result in a future compatibility problem. If we had used `rpc_call` in the client program, we could have avoided the reference to `rpc_createerr.cf_stat` because this is the value returned from `rpc_call`. □

When a server is using a connectionless transport and wants to simulate at-most-once execution semantics, it can enable caching of response messages (as discussed in Section 8.1) by calling `svc_dg_enablecache`:

```
#include <rpc/rpc.h>

int svc_dg_enablecache(SVCXPRT *handle, ulong_t size);
```

`handle` is a pointer to the server handle, and `size` is the number of hash buckets in the cache.

`svc_dg_enablecache` enables caching, as the name implies. It returns 1 on success and 0 on failure. Once a server enables caching, it cannot be disabled, except by destroying the server handle and recreating it.

8.5 RPCGEN

The `rpcgen` command can ease the task of developing RPC-based applications by removing the need for the programmer to write any communication-oriented code. This allows the programmer to concentrate on designing the application to perform its intended function, instead of concentrating on the communication between the client and the server.

`rpcgen` is a translator that takes as its input a file containing the RPC specifications for an application. By default, `rpcgen` creates four output files: a file containing client-side stub routines, a file containing server-side stub routines, a header file to be included by the client and server programs, and a file containing the XDR filters used to process any data structures defined in the input file.

The `rpcgen` input file is called the "remote program interface specification" because it specifies the interfaces to a given RPC service. It is often referred to as the "protocol specification" for the service since the data structures exchanged affect the resulting protocol between the client and server. Developers often make this file available, similar to the way header files are made available, so that others can develop client and server programs that use the same interface.

By convention, the protocol specification file ends with a `.x` suffix to distinguish it from other files. `rpcgen` uses the rest of the filename to create names for the output files, as shown below:

```
$ ls
abc.x
$ rpcgen abc.x
$ ls
abc.h          abc.x          abc_clnt.c  abc_svc.c    abc_xdr.c
$
```

After `abc.x` is processed by `rpcgen`, a header file (`abc.h`) is created containing all the constants and data structures defined in `abc.x`. `abc_clnt.c` contains the client stub functions that make the remote procedure calls. `abc_svc.c` contains the framework for the server process. If `abc.x` contains any data structure definitions, then `rpcgen` will create an XDR filter for each one and store them in `abc_xdr.c`.

All that needs to be done to finish the application is to write the `main` procedure for the client side and the remote procedures for the server side. The client `main` procedure will create a client handle and invoke the necessary client stub functions to make the remote procedure calls. Figure 8.6 illustrates the process of using `rpcgen` to create an RPC-based application.

If the `-T` option is used with `rpcgen`, then `rpcgen` creates a fifth file containing a table of the server's dispatching functions. The table can be used to help the server check authorizations before executing a remote procedure. If the input filename were `abc.x`, then the file containing the server dispatch table would be named `abc_tbl.i`.

Identifiers in `rpcgen`-related files follow naming conventions, too. One such convention is to code the program, version, and procedure names in capital letters in the specification file. An RPC program is declared using the `program` keyword,

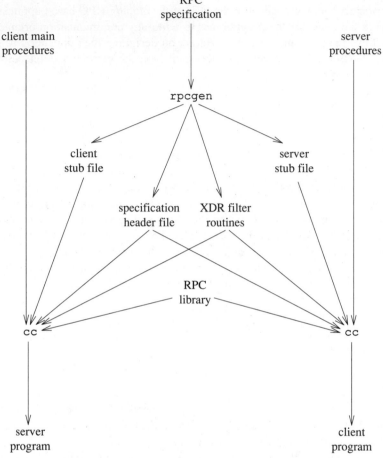

Fig. 8.6. Using `rpcgen` to Build an RPC Application

and a version is declared using the `version` keyword, with the following format:

```
program PROGNAME {
    version VERSNUM {
        outtype PROCNAME (intype) = procedure_number;
    } = version_number;
} = program_number;
```

where *outtype* specifies the type of the output parameter, and *intype* specifies the type of the input parameter.

From this specification, `rpcgen` will generate a header file with definitions for the program, version, and procedure numbers. In addition, a declaration for the procedure will appear with it returning a pointer to type *outtype*. `rpcgen` creates the procedure name by translating it to lower case and appending an underscore and the version number to the end of the name.

XDR filters generated by `rpcgen` follow another naming convention. The name of each filter is composed of the string `xdr_` followed by the name of the data type it encodes and decodes. For example, `rpcgen` would create a filter called `xdr_account` to encode and decode a structure named `account`.

Example 8.5.1. If we were to reimplement Example 8.3.1 using `rpcgen`, we would need a protocol specification similar to the one shown below. It defines version 1 (MACH_VERS) of program MACH_PROG to consist of one procedure (number 1) called MACH_PROG. The procedure has no input argument and returns a string as its result.

```
/* mtype.x */

program MACH_PROG {
    version MACH_VERS {
        string MACH_PROC(void) = 1;
    } = 1;
} = 0x22222222;
```

From this specification, `rpcgen` will create the following header file, converting the RPC numbers into constants and adding a declaration for every version of each function.

```
/*
 * Please do not edit this file.
 * It was generated using rpcgen.
 */
#include <rpc/types.h>

#define MACH_PROG ((u_long)0x22222222)
#define MACH_VERS ((u_long)1)
#define MACH_PROC ((u_long)1)
extern char **mach_proc_1();
```

The file containing the client stub for the procedure is shown below, as it was created by `rpcgen`. The first argument to the client stub is a pointer to the input argument to the remote function. The second argument is a pointer to the client handle. The return value is a pointer to the string (itself a character pointer).

```
/*
 * Please do not edit this file.
 * It was generated using rpcgen.
 */
#include <rpc/rpc.h>
#include "mtype.h"

/* Default timeout can be changed using clnt_control() */
static struct timeval TIMEOUT = { 25, 0 };

char **
mach_proc_1(argp, clnt)
    void *argp;
```

```
        CLIENT *clnt;
    {
        static char *res;

        (void) memset((char *)&res, 0, sizeof(res));
        if (clnt_call(clnt, MACH_PROC, xdr_void, argp,
          xdr_wrapstring, &res, TIMEOUT) != RPC_SUCCESS) {
            return (NULL);
        }
        return (&res);
    }
```

The portion of the client-side command to be provided by the programmer is shown below. We still have to validate the command-line arguments and print the results, but if we want to use the mach_proc_1 function generated for us by rpcgen, we cannot use the high-level RPC interfaces. Instead, we have to create our own client handle to pass to mach_proc_1. This also affects how we print errors.

```
#include <rpc/rpc.h>
#include <stdio.h>
#include <stdlib.h>
#include "mtype.h"

void
main(int argc, char *argv[])
{
    char **machtype;
    CLIENT *handle;

    if (argc != 2) {
        fprintf(stderr, "usage: %s hostname\n", argv[0]);
        exit(1);
    }
    machtype = NULL;

    /*
     * Create a client handle.
     */
    handle = clnt_create(argv[1], MACH_PROG, MACH_VERS,
      "netpath");
    if (handle == NULL) {
        fprintf(stderr,
          "%s: can't create client handle: %s\n",
          argv[0], clnt_spcreateerror(""));
        exit(1);
    }

    /*
     * Make the remote procedure call.
     */
    machtype = mach_proc_1(NULL, handle);
    if (machtype == NULL) {
        /*
```

```
            * RPC failed.   Print an error message.
            */
           fprintf(stderr, "%s: %s\n", argv[0],
             clnt_sperror(handle, "rpc failed"));
           exit(1);
    } else {
           /*
            * RPC succeeded.   Print the string returned.
            */
           printf("machine type is %s\n", *machtype);
           exit(0);
    }
}
```

On the server side, all we need to do is provide an implementation of mach_proc_1 whose first argument is a pointer to the input argument of the remote function (NULL in this example), and whose second argument is a pointer to the svc_req structure. The return value is a pointer to the string.

```
char **
mach_proc_1(void *inarg, struct svc_req *req)
{
       static struct utsname u;
       static char *p;

       p = NULL;
       if (uname(&u) >= 0)
           p = u.machine;
       return(&p);
}
```

Finally, the file containing the framework for the server is shown below. Again, this portion was generated by rpcgen.

```
/*
 * Please do not edit this file.
 * It was generated using rpcgen.
 */
#include <stdio.h>
#include <signal.h>
#include <rpc/rpc.h>
#include <memory.h>
#include <stropts.h>
#include <netconfig.h>
#include <stropts.h>
#include <sys/resource.h>
#ifdef SYSLOG
#include <syslog.h>
#else
#define LOG_ERR 1
#define openlog(a, b, c)
#endif
#include "mtype.h"

#ifdef DEBUG
```

```
#define RPC_SVC_FG
#endif

#define _RPCSVC_CLOSEDOWN 120

static void mach_prog_1();
static void msgout();
static void closedown();

static int _rpcpmstart;    /* Started by a port monitor ? */
static int _rpcfdtype;     /* Whether Stream or Datagram ? */
static int _rpcsvcdirty;   /* Still serving ? */

main()
{
    pid_t pid;
    int i;
    char mname[FMNAMESZ + 1];

    if (!ioctl(0, I_LOOK, mname) &&
      (!strcmp(mname, "sockmod") ||
      !strcmp(mname, "timod"))) {
        char *netid;
        struct netconfig *nconf = NULL;
        SVCXPRT *transp;
        int pmclose;
        extern char *getenv();

        _rpcpmstart = 1;
        if ((netid = getenv("NLSPROVIDER")) == NULL) {
            msgout("cannot get transport name");
        } else if ((nconf = getnetconfigent(netid)) ==
          NULL) {
            msgout("cannot get transport info");
        }
        if (strcmp(mname, "sockmod") == 0) {
            if (ioctl(0, I_POP, 0) ||
              ioctl(0, I_PUSH, "timod")) {
                msgout("could not get the right module");
                exit(1);
            }
        }
        pmclose = (t_getstate(0) != T_DATAXFER);
        if ((transp = svc_tli_create(0, nconf, NULL, 0,
          0)) == NULL) {
            msgout("cannot create server handle");
            exit(1);
        }
        if (nconf)
            freenetconfigent(nconf);
        if (!svc_reg(transp, MACH_PROG, MACH_VERS,
          mach_prog_1, 0)) {
            msgout("unable to register (MACH_PROG, \
MACH_VERS).");
```

```
                        exit(1);
                }
            if (pmclose) {
                (void) signal(SIGALRM, closedown);
                (void) alarm(_RPCSVC_CLOSEDOWN);
            }
            svc_run();
            exit(1);
            /* NOTREACHED */
    }
#ifndef RPC_SVC_FG
    pid = fork();
    if (pid < 0) {
        perror("cannot fork");
        exit(1);
    }
    if (pid)
        exit(0);
    for (i = 0; i < 20; i++)
        (void) close(i);
    setsid();
    openlog("mtype", LOG_PID, LOG_DAEMON);
#endif
    if (!svc_create(mach_prog_1, MACH_PROG, MACH_VERS,
        "netpath")) {
            msgout("unable to create (MACH_PROG, MACH_VERS) \
for netpath.");
            exit(1);
    }

    svc_run();
    msgout("svc_run returned");
    exit(1);
    /* NOTREACHED */
}

static void
mach_prog_1(rqstp, transp)
    struct svc_req *rqstp;
    register SVCXPRT *transp;
{
    union {
        int fill;
    } argument;
    char *result;
    bool_t (*xdr_argument)(), (*xdr_result)();
    char *(*local)();

    _rpcsvcdirty = 1;
    switch (rqstp->rq_proc) {
    case NULLPROC:
        (void) svc_sendreply(transp, xdr_void,
            (char *)NULL);
        _rpcsvcdirty = 0;
```

```
                    return;

          case MACH_PROC:
              xdr_argument = xdr_void;
              xdr_result = xdr_wrapstring;
              local = (char *(*)()) mach_proc_1;
              break;

          default:
              svcerr_noproc(transp);
              _rpcsvcdirty = 0;
              return;
          }
          (void) memset((char *)&argument, 0,
            sizeof (argument));
          if (!svc_getargs(transp, xdr_argument, &argument)) {
              svcerr_decode(transp);
              _rpcsvcdirty = 0;
              return;
          }
          result = (*local)(&argument, rqstp);
          if (result != NULL && !svc_sendreply(transp,
            xdr_result, result)) {
              svcerr_systemerr(transp);
          }
          if (!svc_freeargs(transp, xdr_argument, &argument)) {
              msgout("unable to free arguments");
              exit(1);
          }
          _rpcsvcdirty = 0;
          return;
}

static void
msgout(msg)
      char *msg;
{
#ifdef RPC_SVC_FG
      if (_rpcpmstart)
          syslog(LOG_ERR, msg);
      else
          (void) fprintf(stderr, "%s\n", msg);
#else
      syslog(LOG_ERR, msg);
#endif
}

static void
closedown()
{
      if (_rpcsvcdirty == 0) {
          extern fd_set svc_fdset;
          static int size;
          int i, openfd;
```

```
            struct t_info tinfo;

            if (!t_getinfo(0, &tinfo) &&
               (tinfo.servtype == T_CLTS))
                   exit(0);
            if (size == 0) {
                struct rlimit rl;

                rl.rlim_max = 0;
                getrlimit(RLIMIT_NOFILE, &rl);
                if ((size = rl.rlim_max) == 0)
                    return;
            }
            for (i = 0, openfd = 0; i < size && openfd < 2;
               i++)
                   if (FD_ISSET(i, &svc_fdset))
                       openfd++;
            if (openfd <= 1)
                exit(0);
        }
        (void) alarm(_RPCSVC_CLOSEDOWN);
    }
```

Before a protocol specification file is translated, rpcgen runs it through the C preprocessor, so any valid C preprocessor directive (#if, for example) can be used in a protocol specification file. rpcgen defines one of five symbols, depending on which output file it is generating. When it is generating the header file, the symbol RPC_HDR is defined. rpcgen defines the symbol RPC_XDR when it is creating the file containing the XDR filters. While the server skeleton is being created, the symbol RPC_SVC is defined. Similarly, RPC_CLNT is defined during the generation of the client stub file. Finally, RPC_TBL is defined when rpcgen is creating the file containing the server dispatch table.

These symbols can be used to include statements in the protocol specification file that will only be included in particular output files. For example, to include a declaration in the client stub file only, one might bracket it with:

```
#if defined(RPC_CLNT)
    .
    .
    .
#endif
```

rpcgen also supports a pass-through mode of operation: any lines beginning with a percent sign (%) in column 1 are passed unchanged (except for the removal of the percent sign) to the output files. These lines, however, might not retain their original positions with respect to other portions of the input file.

C-style comments are also supported by rpcgen. Characters that occur between matching pairs of /* and */ are treated as comments. The RPC language specification is a superset of the XDR language specification. The protocol specification files are written in the RPC language and translated into the C language by rpcgen. For example, the type bool in the RPC language is translated into the bool_t typedef in the C language. (bool_t is defined in <rpc/types.h> as type int.)

8.6 ADVANCED RPC FEATURES

This section discusses some of the more complicated aspects of RPC-based applications, including how to authenticate clients, how to design asynchronous applications, how to broadcast RPC requests, and how to use RPC servers with port monitors.

Authentication

The RPC mechanism provides for authentication: a way to help servers verify that clients are who they claim to be. When a client makes a remote procedure call, credentials identifying the client are placed in the request message. In addition to the credentials, the request message also contains a verifier. The credentials identify the caller, and the verifier ensures that the credentials are valid.

The server response message contains a verifier, but no credentials. It is assumed that since the client has initiated the connection, the client knows who the server is. The RPC library handles authenticating the credentials on the server side and authenticating the reply on the client side. It is up to the client to select the authentication mechanism and the server to use the credentials to decide whether to deny the service request.

Three types (called *flavors*) of authentication are provided with the RPC library: null, UNIX-style, and DES (Data Encryption Standard, also known as "secure RPC"). The default flavor of authentication is null (AUTH_NONE). This means no authentication is done unless the client explicitly arranges for it. Shorthand system authentication (AUTH_SHORT), available in older versions of RPC, is not supported in SVR4.

When a client handle is first created, the authentication information for the AUTH_NONE flavor is associated with the handle. If the client wishes to change the authentication flavor, then this information needs to be discarded. auth_destroy(3N) [see rpc_clnt_auth(3N)] can be used for this purpose:

```
#include <rpc/rpc.h>

void auth_destroy(AUTH *auth);
```

auth points to the authentication information being discarded. The authentication information is stored in the cl_auth field of the client handle.

Once the old authentication information has been discarded, the client can create new authentication information and point the handle's cl_auth field at it. Authentication information for the AUTH_NONE flavor can be allocated with authnone_create(3N):

```
#include <rpc/rpc.h>

AUTH *authnone_create(void);
```

`authnone_create` returns a pointer to the null credentials on success and returns NULL on failure.

Slightly more secure is the UNIX-style authentication (the AUTH_SYS flavor). It identifies a client by its numeric UNIX user and group IDs. (It assumes the client has the same numeric IDs on both the client machine and the server machine.) UNIX-style authentication is only slightly more secure than AUTH_NONE because the credentials can be forged easily. Thus, no verifier is used with AUTH_SYS authentication. Applications using this flavor of authentication trust the users on the network.

To create AUTH_SYS credentials, the client can call either `authsys_create(3N)` or `authsys_create_default(3N)`. The former allows the caller to specify the credentials and the latter obtains them from the caller's process state. The synopses are

```
#include <rpc/rpc.h>

AUTH *authsys_create(const char *host, uid_t uid,
        gid_t gid, int len, const gid_t *supgids);
AUTH *authsys_create_default(void);
```

where `host` is a pointer to the name of the host computer on which the client is running, `uid` is the client's user ID, `gid` is the client's group ID, `len` is the number of supplementary group IDs to which the client belongs, and `supgids` is the address of the array of supplementary group IDs. Both functions return a pointer to the credentials on success, and NULL on failure.

Example 8.6.1. This example shows how a client program can employ UNIX-style authentication. We free any memory underlying the old authentication information by calling `auth_destroy`. Then we allocate new AUTH_SYS authentication information by calling `authsys_create_default`.

```
#include <rpc/rpc.h>
#include <stdio.h>
#include <stdlib.h>

void
main(int argc, char *argv[])
{
      enum clnt_stat status;
      CLIENT *handle;
      struct timeval t;

      if (argc != 2) {
          fprintf(stderr, "usage: %s hostname\n", argv[0]);
          exit(1);
      }

      /*
       * Create a client handle.
       */
      handle = clnt_create(argv[1], PROGNUM, VERSNUM,
```

```
        "netpath");
    if (handle == NULL) {
        fprintf(stderr,
          "%s: can't create client handle: %s\n",
          argv[0], clnt_spcreateerror(""));
        exit(1);
    }

    /*
     * Get rid of the default authentication info.
     */
    auth_destroy(handle->cl_auth);

    /*
     * Allocate AUTH_SYS credentials using the
     * current process context.
     */
    handle->cl_auth = authsys_create_default();
    if (handle->cl_auth == NULL) {
        fprintf(stderr,
          "%s: can't create client handle\n", argv[0]);
        exit(1);
    }

    /*
     * Set the timeout and make the remote procedure call.
     */
    t.tv_sec = 10;
    t.tv_usec = 0;
    status = clnt_call(...);
       .
       .
       .

}
```

□

Recall that the server has two authentication-related fields in the `svc_req` structure passed to it. The `rq_cred` field points to a data structure of type `opaque_auth`:

```
struct opaque_auth {
    enum_t  oa_flavor;   /* authentication flavor */
    caddr_t oa_base;     /* address of more auth info */
    u_int   oa_length;   /* length of auth info */
};
```

This structure should not be used by the server, except for the `oa_flavor` field. The server can use it to identify the authentication flavor.

The second field in the `svc_req` structure is the cooked credentials, `rq_clntcred`. They are called "cooked" because they are decoded into the server's machine architecture representation. (Actually, fields in the `opaque_auth` structure are also decoded. Only the memory to which `oa_base` points is untouched.) For `AUTH_SYS` style authentication, `rq_clntcred` points to a `authsys_parms` structure:

```
struct authsys_parms {
     ulong_t  aup_time;        /* when created */
     char     *aup_machname;   /* where created */
     uid_t    aup_uid;         /* user ID */
     gid_t    aup_gid;         /* group ID */
     uint_t   aup_len;         /* # of supplementary IDs */
     gid_t    *aup_gids;       /* supplementary IDs */
},
```

If a server decides to deny a request for service, it can call `svcerr_auth` with a code describing the reason for denial. The reason codes are defined in `<rpc/auth.h>`.

Example 8.6.2. This example illustrates how a server can use the `AUTH_SYS` flavor of authentication. Only the dispatching function is shown. Notice that no authentication is performed for the null procedure.

```
#include <rpc/rpc.h>

static void
dispatcher(struct svc_req *req, SVCXPRT *handle)
{
     struct authsys_parms *ap;

     /*
      * Don't authenticate client for the null
      * procedure.
      */
     if (req->rq_proc == NULLPROC) {
         svc_sendreply(handle, xdr_void, NULL);
         return;
     }

     /*
      * If the client isn't using AUTH_SYS style
      * authentication, deny the service request.
      */
     if (req->rq_cred.oa_flavor != AUTH_SYS) {
         svcerr_weakauth(handle);
         return;
     }

     /*
      * Deny service for all users with user IDs
      * greater than 200.
      */
     ap = (struct authsys_parms *)req->rq_clntcred;
     if (ap->aup_uid > 200) {
         svcerr_weakauth(handle);
         return;
     }

     /*
```

```
 * Service is allowed.
 */
switch (req->rq_proc) {
    .
    .
    .
}
```

In this example, we check that the flavor of authentication is AUTH_SYS. Alternatively, we could have chosen to support AUTH_DES as well. If the user ID is greater than 200, we choose to deny service.   □

The AUTH_DES flavor of authentication attempts to solve several of the shortcomings found with other flavors. First, AUTH_DES authentication includes a verifier, so it is very difficult to forge credentials. Second, the UNIX-specific parameters constituting the AUTH_SYS credentials are replaced by system-independent, globally unique, printable strings, called *netnames*. Netnames can be mapped to user IDs and host names using functions provided by the RPC library.

Both the request and the reply messages contain verifiers. The client credentials contain an encrypted timestamp. When the server receives a request, it decrypts the timestamp and, if the timestamp is close to the real time on the server's machine, the server assumes the credentials are valid, since only the real client is supposed to know the key used to encrypt the credentials. This implies that the client and server machines must maintain the same notion of time. This can be accomplished using a network time protocol, such as NTP.

The client verifies the response from the server by decrypting a timestamp generated by the server. If the server's timestamp equals the one the caller sent minus one second, then the client knows the message came from the correct server.

After the first request, the server returns an integer *nickname* in its verifier that the client can use in successive transactions instead of passing the netname, DES key, and window (discussed below) in every request. The server keeps a cache mapping nickname to the actual credentials. When the cache fills and an entry needs to be removed from the cache, a client's request using the corresponding nickname will fail with a status of RPC_AUTHERROR and a reason of AUTH_REJECTEDCRED.

Timestamps expire after a certain amount of time, called the client's *window*. The window is included in the client's first message sent to the server. After expiration, additional requests will fail with a status of RPC_AUTHERROR and a reason of AUTH_REJECTEDVERF. The same error occurs when the clocks on the two machines drift so far apart that verification fails.

Whenever a remote procedure call fails, the RPC library will refresh its credentials and attempt the call again. In this way, applications are isolated from authentication errors that arise from temporary conditions such as cache misses and window expirations.

Since the client and server processes are encrypting and decrypting the same fields, they need to use the same key (a DES key). The client sends its DES key to the server in the first RPC call, but only after encrypting it with a public key scheme (Diffie-Hellman encryption). The public key scheme requires that a keyserv(1M) daemon run on both the client and the server machines and that each user be assigned a pair of keys: one public and one private. The user provides a password that is used to encrypt the private key.

The Diffie-Hellman encryption algorithm allows a common key to be derived from the client's private key and the server's public key. The same common key can be calculated from the server's private key and the client's public key. Thus, the client and the server can encode and decode the client's DES key while remaining ignorant of each other's private key. This double encryption reduces the probability that someone will be able to decrypt the messages, find the key, and masquerade as either the client or the server.

A client can create AUTH_DES credentials by calling `authdes_seccreate(3N)` [see `secure_rpc(3N)`]:

```
#include <rpc/rpc.h>

AUTH *authdes_seccreate(const char *netname, uint_t window,
        const char *timehost, const des_block *key);
```

netname points to the netname of the host or user corresponding to the server process, `window` is the number of seconds the credentials will remain valid, `timehost` points to the name of a host to contact when attempting to resynchronize clocks, and `key` is a pointer to the DES key to be used to encrypt the credentials.

If `timehost` is NULL, then time resynchronizations are disabled. If `key` is NULL, a random one is obtained from the `keyserv` daemon. On success, `authdes_seccreate` returns a pointer to the DES credentials; otherwise, it returns NULL.

On the server side, the `rq_clntcred` field in the `svc_req` structure points to an `authdes_cred` structure. This structure can be converted to the corresponding UNIX credentials by using `authdes_getucred(3N)`:

```
#include <rpc/rpc.h>

int authdes_getucred(const struct authdes_cred *ap,
        uid_t *uidp, gid_t *gidp, short *lenp, gid_t *supgids);
```

ap points to the DES credentials, `uidp` points to the memory location where the client's user ID is to be stored, `gidp` points to the memory location where the client's group ID is to be stored, `lenp` points to a `short` where the size of the client's supplementary group list is to be stored, and `supgids` points to the buffer where the array of supplementary group IDs is to be stored. If `authdes_seccreate` succeeds, it returns 1; otherwise, it returns 0.

Other routines are provided that convert between netnames and host names or user IDs. See `secure_rpc(3N)` for more details.

Nonblocking RPC

If a client application does not need a response from the server, then nonblocking RPC can be used. Nonblocking RPC does not mean the RPC library uses the non-blocking mode of operation with the system calls used for data transfer. Instead, no attempt is made to receive the response message from the server.

By setting the `timeout` parameter's fields to zeros, a client application informs the RPC library that it wishes to return immediately after transmitting the request. In this case, `clnt_call` will return `RPC_TIMEDOUT` without attempting to receive a response. No retransmissions are made when RPC is used this way, so it can only be used with connectionless transports if the application can tolerate lost requests.

If the server knows a response is not needed, it need not generate one. With the low-level interfaces, the programmer controls this by not calling `svc_sendreply`. If `rpcgen` is used in creating the server, the generation of a response message can be suppressed by coding the remote procedure to return `NULL` instead of a pointer to the results. (Look at the server skeleton in Example 8.5.1. If the procedure returns `NULL`, no reply is made.)

Callback RPC

If a client application wants to use nonblocking RPC, but needs the response from the server, then *callback* RPC can be used. This might be the case when a client has other tasks it can accomplish instead of waiting for the response message. Callback RPC allows an application to be both a client and a server.

The application generating the original request is the client and uses nonblocking RPC. The request includes the program number that the server should use to contact the client. The server processes the request, but sends no response. Instead, the server acts like a client and makes a callback RPC call to the original client using the program number stored in the request message. The original client then processes the request as if it were a server.

For callbacks to occur, the client must create a server handle, as well as a client handle. (The same goes for the server, if it uses the low-level library routines.) The client then has to register with the rpcbinder running on its machine. A program number from the transient range ($0x40000000 - 0x5FFFFFFF$) is usually used. No interface exists to have the rpcbinder return an unused program number, so the client is reduced to attempting to register program numbers iteratively until one succeeds. `rpcb_set (3N)` can be used in this case:

```
#include <rpc/rpc.h>

bool_t rpcb_set(ulong_t prognum, ulong_t versnum,
    const struct netconfig *ncp,
    const struct netbuf *svcaddr);
```

`prognum` is the program number, `versnum` is the version number, `ncp` points to a `netconfig` structure describing the network and protocol over which the service is to be offered, and `svcaddr` points to a `netbuf` structure describing the address to contact to obtain the service.

After an unused program number is reserved, the client should call `svc_reg` to map its dispatching routine to the program and version numbers. Recall that if `svc_reg` is presented with a `NULL` `netconfig` pointer, it will avoid contacting the rpcbinder. This is desired in this case because `rpcb_set` just took care of that.

Example 8.6.3. The following function can be used by client-side RPC applications to establish the necessary mappings to support callbacks. The client passes it a pointer to the `netconfig` structure describing the network and protocol to use, the address of the client's function to be invoked during the callback (the equivalent of the server's dispatch routine), the version number, and the address of an unsigned long where the function will store the program number before returning. On success, a pointer to the server handle is returned; on failure, NULL is returned.

```
#include <rpc/rpc.h>
#include <netconfig.h>

SVCXPRT *
init_callback(const struct netconfig *ncp,
    void (*callback) (struct svc_req *, SVCXPRT *),
    ulong_t versnum, ulong_t *prognump)
{
    SVCXPRT *handle;
    int prognum;

    /*
     * Create a server handle.
     */
    handle = svc_tli_create(RPC_ANYFD, ncp, NULL, 0, 0);
    if (handle == NULL)
        return(NULL);

    /*
     * Find an unused transient program number.
     */
    for (prognum = 0x40000000; prognum < 0x60000000;
      prognum++)
        if (rpcb_set(prognum, versnum, ncp,
          &handle->xp_ltaddr))
            break;

    /*
     * None found.  Get rid of the handle and return.
     */
    if (prognum >= 0x60000000) {
        svc_destroy(handle);
        return(NULL);
    }

    /*
     * Map the dispatching routine to the program and
     * version numbers.
     */
    if (!svc_reg(handle, prognum, versnum, callback,
      NULL)) {
        svc_destroy(handle);
        rpcb_unset(prognum, versnum, ncp);
        return(NULL);
    }
```

```
        /*
         * Return the program number and the handle.
         */
        *prognump = prognum;
        return(handle);
}
```

We use `svc_tli_create` to create a server handle, letting the transport provider choose the address. Then we call `rpcb_set`, starting with `0x40000000` for the program number, incrementing the program number each time, until it either succeeds, or the program number reaches the end of the transient range, `0x60000000`. Note that the address bound by `svc_tli_create` is stored in a `netbuf` structure in the service handle field named `xp_ltaddr`. The `SVCXPRT` data structure is described in `rpc(3N)`.

If all transient numbers are in use (unlikely), we destroy the handle and return `NULL`. Otherwise, we call `svc_reg` to associate the program and version number with the client's callback handler, `callback`. If this fails, we destroy the server handle and contact the rpcbinder to break the association between the program and version numbers and the network address. If `svc_reg` succeeds, we store the program number in the memory location referred to by `prognump` and return a pointer to the server handle.   □

After making the initial remote procedure call, the client can call `svc_run` to wait for the callback. `svc_run` will cause the client to block indefinitely, until a message is received. If this is inappropriate for the application, then the client can always fork a child process to wait for the callback.

Broadcast RPC

With the help of the rpcbinder, client applications can broadcast remote procedure calls to multiple servers, as long as the underlying transport provider is connectionless and supports broadcast packets. Then clients receive a response message from each server answering the request. Only successful replies are delivered to the client.

The `rpc_broadcast(3N)` function [see `rpc_clnt_calls(3N)`] broadcasts a remote procedure call request to the rpcbinders on the network. The rpcbinder on each machine forwards the request to the server implementing the remote procedure. The server responds to the rpcbinder, which then transmits the reply back to the client. The synopsis for `rpc_broadcast` is

```
#include <rpc/rpc.h>

enum clnt_stat rpc_broadcast(ulong_t prognum,
        ulong_t versnum, ulong_t procnum,
        const xdrproc_t inproc, char *inarg,
        const xdrproc_t outproc, char *outarg,
        const bool_t (*resfn)(), const char *nettype);
```

where `prognum` is the program number of the remote procedure, `versnum` is its version number, `procnum` is the procedure number, `inproc` is the address of an

XDR filter used to encode the input argument, `inarg` is a pointer to the input argument, `outproc` is the address of an XDR filter used to decode the output argument, `outarg` is a pointer to the output argument, `resfn` is the address of a function to be called for each response message received, and `nettype` is used to influence the class of networks and protocols used.

The only valid choices for `nettype` are `datagram_v`, `datagram_n`, and `NULL`. If `nettype` is `NULL`, it defaults to `datagram_n`. For each response received, the function identified by `resfn` is called. `resfn` is declared as:

```
bool_t resfn(const char *outarg, const struct netbuf *addr,
        struct netconfig *ncp);
```

where `outarg` is a pointer to the output argument (the same one passed to `rpc_broadcast`) where the decoded results are placed, `addr` is a pointer to a `netbuf` structure containing the address of the server answering the request, and `ncp` points to a `netconfig` structure corresponding to the network and protocol over which the reply was received.

As long as `resfn` returns `FALSE`, `rpc_broadcast` will wait for more replies. When `resfn` returns `TRUE`, `rpc_broadcast` will return a status value indicating the result of the broadcast request. If `resfn` never returns `TRUE`, `rpc_broadcast` will eventually time out and return `RPC_TIMEDOUT`.

`rpc_broadcast` cannot receive more replies until `resfn` returns, so developers should try to minimize the amount of processing done in `resfn`, lest packets be lost. The broadcast request and corresponding responses each must fit in one packet, the size of which depends on the network and protocol used.

With broadcast RPC, the default authentication style is `AUTH_SYS`.

Port Monitor Interfaces

RPC servers can be spawned from port monitors, like `inetd` and `listen`. These servers are already connected to the client and can use either `svc_tli_create` or `svc_fd_create` to create a server handle. Next, they should call `svc_reg` with a `NULL` `netconfig` pointer to associate the dispatching routine with the program and version numbers. Finally, servers call `svc_run` to process the request.

When a server is started from the listener, file descriptor 0 is used to access the transport endpoint. With a standing server, the transport endpoint is passed to the server over a mounted pipe or FIFO. The port monitors handle the registration of the service with the rpcbinder. Chapter 6 discusses port monitors and the network listener service in more detail.

Summary

The RPC library provides programmers with a way to write networked and distributed applications without having to use low-level communication interfaces such as sockets or the TLI. The details of how communication occurs are hidden at the cost of having less control over the communication. The RPC library supports several

levels of interfaces that expose varying amounts of detail about the underlying communication. Most interfaces can be avoided through the use of `rpcgen`, a translator
that converts an RPC protocol specification into the client stub functions and server
skeleton needed to build an application. Finally, the XDR functions provide a way to
represent data in an architecture-independent manner.

Exercises

8.1 Write a program similar to that in Exercise 8.2.2 but for `/etc/utmpx`, the
extended `utmp` file, instead.

8.2 The filter shown in Example 8.2.3 has a flaw in it. If any of the XDR
library routines should fail, only a partial `utmp` record is written to (or read
from) the file. Modify the routine to avoid this pitfall.

8.3 Write an `rpcgen` protocol specification for a program supporting two
remote procedures: one that returns the list of jobs queued for printing [see
`lpstat(1)`] and one that cancels the job corresponding to the given job
ID.

8.4 Add UNIX-style authentication to Examples 8.4.1 and 8.4.2 so only you can
execute the remote procedure. Then write a program to subvert the authentication mechanism.

8.5 Add DES-style authentication to Examples 8.4.1 and 8.4.2 so only you can
execute the remote procedure. (You will need help from your system
administrator in setting up the public keys.)

Bibliographic Notes

Sun [1987] describes the XDR language developed by Sun Microsystems, and Sun
[1988] contains the Sun Microsystems RPC protocol specification. These standards
provide the bases for the XDR and RPC implementations supported in SVR4.
Corbin [1991] provides considerable detail on using Sun Microsystem's RPC to
create distributed applications. Except for function name changes, most of the information still applies to the transport-independent RPC found in SVR4.

Stevens [1990] provides an overview of several different RPC and XDR implementations.

The *SVR4 Programmer's Guide: Networking Interfaces* [USL 1990d] contains other
examples of RPC client and server applications.

The Data Encryption Standard is described in NBS [1977]. Diffie and Hellman
[1976] describe Diffie-Hellman encryption. The NTP protocol can be found in
RFC 1305 [Mills 1992].

Part 3
Kernel-level Network Programming

9

The STREAMS
Subsystem

In Chapter 3, we presented an overview of the STREAMS mechanism found in UNIX System V Release 4. Chapter 3 is oriented toward the programmer who develops applications at user level. This chapter provides the other half of the picture; it presents the STREAMS mechanism from the perspective of a programmer writing kernel-level software. Therefore, we discuss the kernel environment and internals of the STREAMS mechanism. (We only deal with the uniprocessor implementations, since the dust has not settled yet in the battle among the numerous multiprocessor implementations.)

This chapter, and the three chapters that follow, differ from the preceding ones in several ways. First, this chapter does not include any examples. Second, Chapters 10 through 12 are each structured around one large example that provides the central focus for each chapter. These later chapters provide ample opportunity to observe the concepts and functions discussed in this chapter.

9.1 THE KERNEL ENVIRONMENT

Since the STREAMS mechanism is a subsystem of the UNIX kernel, it is important to understand the environment provided by the kernel. STREAMS drivers and modules have to abide by the constraints imposed by both the STREAMS subsystem and the rest of the kernel. This section describes the kernel environment and how it affects STREAMS drivers and modules.

Kernel-level Programming

Kernel-level programming is like user-level programming, except that the kernel environment is much more constrained than the user-level environment. It does not take a guru to write kernel code—merely someone who understands these constraints. Developers should not hesitate to consider kernel-level solutions, such as using STREAMS drivers and modules in their designs.

When you encounter a bug in a user-level program, the program might end

425

abnormally, possibly leaving a core image in its current working directory. Or it might produce the wrong output. No matter how the bug manifests itself, its effect is usually restricted to the processes and files associated with the program's execution.

When a bug occurs in kernel-level software, however, the effects are vastly different. Such a bug could crash the entire computer system, making it unavailable until rebooted, and possibly even resulting in the loss of data in files that were modified shortly before the crash. If the computer is connected to a network, a bug in the networking software could even cause other systems on the same network to crash. Such potentially severe results require not only that communication software be designed to tolerate badly formed messages, but that programmers writing kernel-level software be extremely careful and program defensively.

Drivers and modules are the most common kernel-level components written. Even though they are not part of the kernel proper, they execute within the environment of the kernel, so bugs in them are often as serious as bugs in the core kernel.

Some of the constraints imposed by the kernel environment have to do with resources. For example, memory (RAM) is a limited resource. Unlike user level, where a process can have some of its data paged out to the swap device, the kernel is generally not paged (except for the user area, a per-process data structure defined to be pageable and always mapped at the same virtual address regardless of which process is running). Because memory is a limited resource and often in demand, kernel software must use it sparingly.

As systems are built with more and more physical memory, this problem becomes somewhat less of an issue. Even so, driver developers must remain frugal in their memory usage, since the UNIX system runs on a wide variety of computer systems and portability to smaller machines is often required.

One effect that limited memory has had on the system design is that the memory allocated for the kernel stack is limited. When a process executes a system call, it executes a special instruction to "trap" into kernel mode. At this point, the stack is switched to one stored in the user area. Since the kernel stack size is fixed, kernel programmers have to guard against using too many layers in their software designs. In addition, the space needed for automatic variables (allocated from the stack) needs to be minimized.

Proper process context is another constraint that must be followed. Some kernel functions manipulate data associated with the currently running process and thus may not be called under all circumstances. For example, when an interrupt occurs, the currently running process is preempted and the driver's interrupt service routine is called. (Interrupts are described shortly.) The interrupt service routine cannot access any data associated with a process, because it can never know if the currently running process is the correct one. This limits the set of kernel utility routines that can be called from interrupt level.

Additionally, interrupt service routines cannot block (sleep) to await a pending event. Besides not being associated with a process to put to sleep, there is usually only one interrupt stack, and all interrupt service routines share it. If an interrupt service routine were to suspend execution and another interrupt arrived, the suspended routine's information on the interrupt stack would likely be overwritten. Thus, if an interrupt service routine had slept, the likelihood will be high that the system will crash when the routine resumes.

Not so much a constraint as it is a fringe benefit, execution in the kernel is nonpreemptable (except for interrupts). The only time a process executing in kernel mode goes to sleep is if it explicitly does so on its own. This means that kernel-level programmers must keep in mind that kernel software can consume as much time as it wants during execution. The UNIX system is still a time-sharing system, and the kernel must not monopolize the processor if it is to provide an acceptable response time to its users.

The kernel programmer's equivalent of the *Programmer's Reference Manual* is called the *Device Driver Interface/Driver-Kernel Interface Reference Manual* (DDI/DKI, for short). It defines all the data structures and interface routines provided by the kernel for use by drivers and modules, as well as the entry points drivers and modules must define to operate in the kernel.

The DKI portion refers to implementation-independent interfaces. It promotes portability for the same version of the operating system across different hardware architectures. The DDI portion refers to processor-specific and platform-specific interfaces. It promotes (*not* guarantees) compatibility from release to release for a particular hardware architecture. Interfaces can belong to the DDI, the DKI, or both. Table 9.1 summarizes the sections of the DDI/DKI.

Table 9.1. DDI/DKI Sections

Section	Description
D1	Global data symbols defined by drivers
D2	Driver entry point functions
D3	Kernel utility routines used by drivers
D4	Kernel data structures accessed by drivers
D5	Kernel #defines used by drivers

DDI/DKI manual pages follow a naming convention similar to other manual pages. They begin with the function or symbol name followed by a code in parentheses. The code is made by concatenating the section name (D1 – D5) with a string describing whether the entry belongs to the DDI, the DKI, or both. For the DDI, a "D" is appended. Similarly, a "K" is appended for the DKI. If the entry is in both the DDI and the DKI, a "DK" is appended. Finally, if the entry is in the DDI but is specific to a particular platform or series of computer systems, then an "X" is appended. For example, bcopy (D3DK) is in Section 3 of the DDI/DKI, but vtop (D3D) is in Section 3 of the DDI only.

Each system implementation includes its own version of the DDI/DKI. All systems share the same DKI. All systems using the same processor type have the same DDI, except possibly for platform-specific interfaces. Each system implementation also includes a separate manual describing how to add kernel object files, such as drivers and modules, to the system, how to build a new UNIX image, and any other implementation-specific configuration information. For the Intel 80x86 processor line, for example, this manual is the *Integrated Software Development Guide* [USL 1990e].

By convention, kernel-level header files are stored under `/usr/include/sys`, although this convention is slowly being replaced by one that groups the header files in separate directories by functional area. For example, the header files pertaining to the virtual memory system can be found in `/usr/include/vm`. Table 9.2 lists some of the commonly used system header files with a short summary of their contents.

Table 9.2. Common Kernel Header Files

Header File	Contents
`<sys/cmn_err.h>`	Kernel `printf` definitions
`<sys/cred.h>`	User credentials structure
`<sys/ddi.h>`	DDI/DKI declarations
`<sys/debug.h>`	Debugging declarations
`<sys/errno.h>`	Error numbers
`<sys/file.h>`	File flags for open and close routines
`<sys/kmem.h>`	Dynamic kernel memory allocator flags
`<sys/param.h>`	System parameters
`<sys/signal.h>`	Signal numbers
`<sys/stream.h>`	Public STREAMS data structures
`<sys/strlog.h>`	STREAMS logging declarations
`<sys/stropts.h>`	STREAMS options and `ioctl` commands
`<sys/systm.h>`	Kernel function prototypes
`<sys/types.h>`	System `typedef`s

Table 9.3 summarizes some of the common `typedef` definitions you will see in the next few chapters. Most types come from `<sys/types.h>`, although the STREAMS-related ones are defined in `<sys/stream.h>`.

Addressing

Two kinds of addresses are visible in the kernel. The *physical address* is the sequence of bits representing a memory location that is presented to the system's address bus. The *virtual address* is an alias for the physical address that is translated by a memory management unit (MMU). There may be many virtual addresses for a single physical address but for any given process, a virtual address will map to one and only one physical address.

The virtual address mode is used in the kernel so that it may take advantage of the large, sparse address space that would otherwise be unavailable on systems with limited physical (real) memory. Early in the boot process, the kernel switches from physical mode to virtual mode.

Drivers usually deal only with virtual addresses. They may need to use physical addresses, however, when presenting an address to a direct memory access (DMA)

Table 9.3. Common `typedef`s

typedef	Definition
ulong_t	unsigned long
uint_t	unsigned int
ushort_t	unsigned short
uchar_t	unsigned char
caddr_t	Virtual (core) memory address
paddr_t	Physical address
dev_t	Device number
major_t	Major device number
minor_t	Minor device number
size_t	Size of an object
clock_t	Clock tick
mblk_t	STREAMS message block
dblk_t	STREAMS data block
queue_t	STREAMS queue

controller. Although some DMA controllers can use virtual addresses, it is more common for them to use physical addresses.

The `vtop(D3D)` function can be used to convert a virtual address to a physical one:

```
#include <sys/types.h>
#include <sys/proc.h>

paddr_t vtop(caddr_t vaddr, struct proc *p);
```

`vaddr` is the virtual address, and `p` is a pointer to a process structure. If the caller does not have user context, then the process pointer should be NULL. On success, `vtop` returns the physical address corresponding to `vaddr`. If an invalid user virtual address is provided, `vtop` returns 0. If an invalid kernel virtual address is provided, `vtop` will cause a system panic (an intentional system crash).

STREAMS drivers never access user virtual addresses. If the drivers perform DMA, it is only to and from STREAMS message buffers which are allocated within the kernel's virtual address space. Therefore, a STREAMS driver should always call `vtop` with the process pointer set to NULL.

Device Numbers

Devices are identified by *device numbers*. Device numbers are composed of *major numbers* and *minor numbers*. Major numbers select the device and associated driver. Minor numbers select the subdevices of the device. *External* device numbers are those device numbers visible to the user. For example, the device number stored in the `stat` structure by the `stat` and `fstat` system calls is an external device number. The major number namespace may be large and sparse. To save space in the kernel tables, the external major numbers are mapped into *internal* major numbers. The internal major device numbers are used as indices into kernel tables.

Similarly, external minor numbers are mapped into internal minor numbers, but not to save space. The mapping is done so that drivers can use internal minor numbers to index private tables. When multiple I/O boards of the same type are installed in a system, there is usually a different external major device number for each I/O board. For each of these major device numbers, a range of minor device numbers is available for use. The minor device mapping allows each of these external ranges to be the same while the internal ranges are consecutive. For example, consider an RS-232 I/O board with four ports. If there are two such boards on a system, the device mapping numbers might be as shown in Table 9.4.

Table 9.4. Possible Device Number Mapping for Multiple I/O Boards

Board	Port	External Major	External Minor	Internal Major	Internal Minor
1	1	17	0	6	0
1	2	17	1	6	1
1	3	17	2	6	2
1	4	17	3	6	3
2	1	31	0	6	4
2	2	31	1	6	5
2	3	31	2	6	6
2	4	31	3	6	7

External major devices 17 and 31 are mapped to internal major device 6. Each board has four ports, numbered 1 through 4. The corresponding external minor numbers are numbered 0 through 3. The second board's internal minor device numbers are offset so that the entire range of internal minor device numbers from both boards can index a private table with one entry per port.

Some implementations may choose to rely on their configuration software to select major device numbers, packing device numbers tightly and making no distinction between external and internal device numbers. Nonetheless, to remain portable, drivers need to behave as if the two number types are not equivalent.

Several functions exist to extract the major and minor numbers from a device number. The synopses are as follows:

```
#include <sys/types.h>
#include <sys/ddi.h>

major_t getmajor(dev_t dev);
major_t getemajor(dev_t dev);
minor_t getminor(dev_t dev);
minor_t geteminor(dev_t dev);
```

where dev is an external device number. getmajor(D3DK) returns the internal major number, getemajor(D3DK) returns the external major number, getminor(D3DK) returns the internal minor number, and geteminor(D3DK) returns the external minor number. None of the functions validates `dev`, so the caller must be careful to pass only valid device numbers.

Drivers can use `makedevice(D3DK)` to create a device number from a major number and minor number. This is useful during a clone open, when a driver needs to select a device number to be returned to the caller. It does not matter whether the numbers are internal or external, as long as they are both the same classification. The synopsis for `makedevice` is

```
#include <sys/types.h>
#include <sys/ddi.h>

dev_t makedevice(major_t major, minor_t minor);
```

where `major` is the major number, and `minor` is the minor number. As with the other functions, no validation is done on either `major` or `minor`.

There are also two routines that convert between internal and external major numbers. `etoimajor(D3DK)` converts an external major number to an internal one. `itoemajor(D3DK)` converts an internal major number to an external one. The synopses are

```
#include <sys/types.h>
#include <sys/ddi.h>

major_t etoimajor(major_t emaj);
major_t itoemajor(major_t imaj, major_t lastemaj);
```

where `emaj` is an external major number, `imaj` is an internal major number, and `lastemaj` is the major number returned from the previous call to `itoemajor`. If `emaj` is invalid, `etoimajor` returns NODEV.

An external major number can map to only one internal major number. An internal major number, on the other hand, can map to several external major numbers, as illustrated by Table 9.4. Thus, `itoemajor` might have to return multiple external major numbers. It does this by returning one at a time. The caller provides the previous return value as the `lastemaj` parameter, and `itoemajor` returns the next one. If `lastemaj` is set to NODEV, then `itoemajor` will start at the beginning of its tables to look for a match. When `lastemaj` is set to the final external number mapped to `imaj`, `itoemajor` will return NODEV.

Interrupts

Drivers have two ways of figuring out that they have to interact with their I/O hardware: *polling* and *interrupts*. Polling is a technique where the driver checks the hardware at intervals to see if events have occurred, such as data arrival, transmission completion, or a hardware state change. This technique is used with simple devices that are unable to interrupt the host computer.

Interrupts are just what their name implies—interruptions in the normal execution of the system. An interrupt occurs when an I/O device needs to be serviced or wants to notify the host of a particular event and asserts an electrical signal that causes the processor to execute an *interrupt service routine* (also called an *interrupt handler*) associated with the signal. Interrupts are more efficient than polling because the driver is notified by the hardware when something needs to be done and is thus relieved of the responsibility of having to check for itself. Many of the checks in polling are wasteful because the driver is busy when it need not be, because there is usually no activity.

In the UNIX kernel, each I/O board that supports interrupts is assigned a priority with which it will interrupt the host processor. Most priority levels are shared among devices. The devices that share priority levels are usually of the same type. For example, all controllers for disk-like devices typically use the same priority level. To distinguish between devices that share common interrupt priorities, each I/O device is assigned an *interrupt vector number*. The interrupt vector is essentially a table that identifies the interrupt service routines. The interrupt vector number is an index into this table.

When an interrupt occurs, normal processing stops, the current state (e.g., register set) is saved, and the interrupt handler that corresponds to the given interrupt vector is executed. The interrupt handler is passed a value that can be used to identify which I/O board caused the interrupt so that the handler can distinguish between interrupts from multiple boards of the same type. The value depends on the implementation of the operating system. Some implementations pass a sequential board number, some pass a device number, and others pass the interrupt vector number. The operating system provides the facilities necessary to allow a driver to map the value to an index into its private data structures associated with the interrupting device.

Before an interrupt handler is called, the system will block all interrupts from devices that interrupt the system at the same level and any lower level. Higher-priority interrupts, however, can interrupt a handler running at a lower priority. When the handler is done, the interrupted state is restored and processing resumes from the place it left off. At this time, if devices had attempted to interrupt the host but were blocked, the highest priority one is serviced. In other words, when an interrupt is blocked, it is not lost; it is deferred until it can be processed.

Because interrupts can preempt the code currently executing on the host processor, access to data shared between the currently executing code and the interrupt handler must be serialized; otherwise, the data can be corrupted. Thus, *critical regions* exist when data are manipulated in sections of code that can be interrupted by interrupt handlers that manipulate the same data. (Note the similarity between interrupt handlers and signal handlers.) The critical regions can be protected by raising the computer's *interrupt priority mask* (also called the *processor priority level*) to a level that is high enough to block out the interrupts competing for access to the same data. When the critical section is complete, the mask is reset to its previous value. If an event that would have generated an interrupt occurs during the critical section, the corresponding interrupt is deferred until the processor priority level is lowered.

Noninterrupt code, called *base-level* code, can block interrupts during critical sections using the `spl(D3D)` functions. One function, `splhi`, is defined to block all interrupts on the system. Others are available to block only those interrupts at or below a certain level. The `splx` function can be used to restore the priority level to its previous value. The synopses are

```
int splhi(void);
void splx(int oldspl);
```

where `oldspl` is the return value from one of the previous functions called to set the processor priority level.

The processor priority level is an abstraction that is mapped to the interrupt priority level in an implementation-specific way. Not all processors support priority levels. For example, the Intel 80x86 only supports the notion of enabling and disabling interrupts, leaving the arbitration of priority levels to external circuitry.

Historically, there have been eight processor priority levels, numbered 0 to 7. Priority level 0 allows all interrupts, priority level 1 only blocks out the lowest priority interrupts, and so on, up to priority level 7, which is equivalent to `splhi`. Traditionally, interrupts from terminal-like devices (except the system console) are blocked by level 5, and interrupts from disk-like devices are blocked by level 6. Each level has an associated `spl` function named `spln`, where *n* is the processor level. The current trend is to move away from using these numeric names in favor of more informative symbolic ones. For example, `spltty` is preferred over `spl5`.

Blocking interrupts for long periods of time can have a negative effect on system performance. For example, if a network interface is prevented from interrupting the host, its buffers will fill up and it will have to stop accepting packets from the network. Then the senders will have to start retransmitting their packets. The retransmissions will increase the network load, lowering overall throughput.

The System Clock

To aid system accounting and process scheduling, the kernel maintains a system clock that interrupts the system `HZ` times per second. `HZ` is defined in `<sys/param.h>`. The two most common values are 60 and 100.

Each clock interrupt is called a *tick*. The number of ticks since the system started is maintained in a variable called `lbolt`. It is now considered nonportable to reference global kernel data symbols, so `drv_getparm(D3DK)` can be used to read the values of several of them.

```
#include <sys/types.h>
#include <sys/ddi.h>

int drv_getparm(ulong_t parm, ulong_t *valuep);
```

`parm` is a value indicating the kernel symbol to be returned, and `valuep` is a pointer to the memory location where the symbol's value is to be stored. On success, `drv_getparm` returns 0; on failure, it returns −1. Table 9.5 summarizes the possible values for `parm`.

Many other system timing services are built around the system clock interrupt scheme. One such service is the ability to schedule a function for execution at some time in the future. These functions are called *timeout* routines, after the name of the function used to schedule them. The functions are not called directly from the clock

Table 9.5. `drv_getparam` Parameters

parm	Description
LBOLT	Number of clock ticks since system boot
TIME	Current time in seconds
UPROCP	Pointer to the current process
UCRED	Pointer to the credentials (permissions) of the current process

interrupt handler. Instead, the system arranges to have them run shortly after the clock interrupt handler returns.

Some implementations use software interrupts to execute `timeout` routines. Systems without this capability use ad hoc techniques, such as checking for pending timeout routines before returning to processor priority level 0 from an interrupt. Although implementation-dependent, a driver can usually defer the execution of timeout routines by raising the processor priority level to block out the lowest priority interrupt level. The synopsis for `timeout`(D3DK) is

```
#include <sys/types.h>

int timeout(void (*fn)(caddr_t), caddr_t arg, long ticks);
```

where `fn` is the address of a function to execute in at least `ticks` clock ticks from the current time. The function `fn` takes a single argument, `arg`. When `fn` runs, it will not have user context and all interrupts will be blocked, so `fn` should not spend too much time accomplishing its task.

`timeout` returns an identifier that represents the scheduling request. If `timeout` runs out of data structures to store requests, the system will panic; therefore there is no return value that represents an error. The identifier can be used as a parameter to `untimeout`(D3DK) to cancel the request:

```
void untimeout(int id);
```

`id` is an identifier returned from a prior call to `timeout`.

Since the frequency of clock ticks can vary from implementation to implementation, the following two functions are available to convert between clock ticks and microseconds. Microseconds are portable; clock ticks are not. The synopses are

```
#include <sys/types.h>

clock_t drv_hztousec(clock_t ticks);
clock_t drv_usectohz(clock_t usecs);
```

where `ticks` is the number of clock ticks, and `usecs` is the number of microseconds. `drv_hztousec`(D3DK) converts clock ticks to microseconds, and `drv_usectohz`(D3DK) converts microseconds to clock ticks. Both functions will return the maximum value for a variable of type `clock_t` if an overflow occurs.

The system clock interrupts the system at the highest maskable interrupt level. The clock interrupt can be blocked by calling `splhi`. This should be done sparingly; otherwise, your computer's clock might lose time.

I/O

The transfer of data between a driver and its I/O hardware can be implemented in a number of ways. With very simple hardware, I/O can occur by writing the data to I/O board registers that are mapped into the kernel address space. If the CPU supports special I/O instructions, these may be used instead of load and store instructions. (When load and store instructions are used, the I/O is said to be *memory-mapped*. When special I/O instructions are used, the I/O is said to be *I/O mapped* because a different namespace [the I/O namespace] is used to identify the location to and from which data are transferred.)

More advanced ways of transferring data between the host computer and the I/O board include using dual-ported RAM and DMA. Dual-ported RAM is memory that exists on the I/O card and is accessible to two buses: the CPU's bus and the I/O board's internal bus. The memory is mapped into the kernel's address space so it looks just like any other memory on the system, except that it can be read and written directly by both the host CPU and the I/O board (see Figure 9.1).

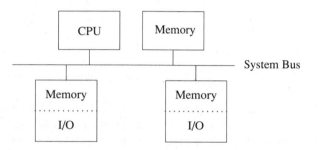

Fig. 9.1. Memory-mapped I/O Architecture

DMA is used when the I/O board's memory is on a separate bus and is isolated from the host's memory. Here, a DMA controller (DMAC) is used to transfer data between the host memory and the I/O board memory (see Figure 9.2). There are two kinds of DMA controllers: physical and virtual. Physical DMA controllers use physical addresses. Virtual DMA controllers use virtual addresses by doing their own address translation.

With physical DMA, the largest amount of memory that can be copied at one time is the system page size because it is the largest unit of memory that is guaranteed to be physically contiguous. If a driver wants to transmit or receive a buffer larger than the system page size, the driver will have to DMA each page separately. Some devices support scatter–gather I/O, allowing a list of address-length pairs to be presented for copying as a single logical operation.

The easiest way for a driver to discover the system page size is to use a global system constant defined in a system header file. This is not portable, however, because several conventional processors support a configurable page size. An alternate way to identify the system page size at run time is to use ptob (D3DK):

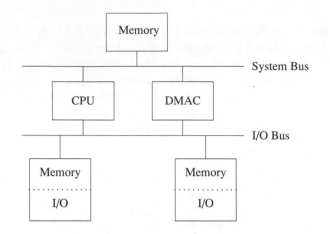

Fig. 9.2. DMA I/O Architecture

```
#include <sys/types.h>

ulong_t ptob(ulong_t npg);
```

npg is the number of pages. ptob returns the number of bytes in the specified number of pages.

Converting from bytes to pages is slightly harder. Two functions are provided, depending on whether you want to truncate or round up when an amount is not an integral multiple of the system page size. btop(D3DK) converts from bytes to pages, truncating any remainder, and btopr(D3DK) converts from bytes to pages, rounding up any remainder.

```
#include <sys/types.h>

ulong_t btop(ulong_t nb);
ulong_t btopr(ulong_t nb);
```

nb is the number of bytes to convert.

Process Context

Some driver entry points are called from the context of the currently running process. These entry points can cause the process to suspend its execution to await a particular event, thus enabling other processes to run. The sleep(D3K) function can be used in this case:

```
#include <sys/types.h>
#include <sys/param.h>

int sleep(caddr_t chan, int pri);
```

chan is an address associated with the event, such as the address of a data structure, and `pri` represents the relative priority that the process should be assigned when it is awakened. Lower numerical values have higher priorities.

As a side effect, `pri` also indicates whether or not the sleep may be interrupted by signals. If `pri` is less than or equal to `PZERO` (defined in `<sys/param.h>`), then signals are ignored. Otherwise, if the priority is greater than `PZERO` and the `PCATCH` flag is set in `pri` [for example, if `pri` equals `(PCATCH|(PZERO+1))`], then the signal is caught, allowing cleanup to be performed. In this case, `sleep` will return 1. If `pri` is greater than `PZERO` and `PCATCH` is not set, `sleep` will execute a longjump on receipt of a signal. If the sleep is not interrupted and a `wakeup` for the event occurs, `sleep` will return 0.

A sleeping process can be awakened by a call to `wakeup` (D3K):

```
#include <sys/types.h>

void wakeup(caddr_t chan);
```

`chan` is the address on which a process is sleeping. `wakeup` will awaken all processes waiting for the event represented by `chan`. Which one runs first depends on their scheduling priorities and scheduling classes. The processes do not run immediately; they become runable and then execute only after the current context either goes to sleep or exits.

If a driver does not have an explicit event to wait for, but just wants to block for a specified amount of time, it can use `delay` (D3DK):

```
void delay(long ticks);
```

`ticks` is the number of clock ticks to sleep. Drivers can use `drv_usectohz` to convert microseconds to clock ticks so that they can use `delay` in a portable manner.

If a driver does not have the necessary process context needed to sleep, then it can *busy-wait* until the desired event occurs. A busy-wait is essentially a finite loop that wastes CPU time. The `drv_usecwait` (D3DK) routine provides this capability:

```
void drv_usecwait(clock_t usecs);
```

`usecs` is the number of microseconds to busy-wait.

Each process has a set of credentials that identify it, including a user ID and a group ID. The `drv_priv` (D3DK) function can be used to test if a set of credentials is privileged (in other words, represents the super-user):

```
#include <sys/cred.h>

int drv_priv(cred_t *crp);
```

`crp` is a pointer to the process credentials. `drv_priv` returns 0 if the caller has permission for privileged operations, or the error `EPERM` otherwise. This routine is intended to replace checks that compare the user ID with 0.

Memory Allocation and Manipulation

The SVR4 kernel contains a dynamic kernel memory allocator that can be used to allocate buffers at run time instead of at compile time. This results in more efficient use of kernel memory, since different subsystems only use as much memory as they need instead of preallocating the maximum amount that they might use.

An indirect benefit of using dynamic allocation over static allocation is the removal of tunable parameters that need to be administered. Usually, if a driver uses a statically allocated table for its data structures, the developer invents a new tunable parameter to control the size of the table. If a system administrator is expected to increase or decrease the size of the table, recommended bounds need to be documented.

By replacing the table with a linked list (or some other data structure) whose elements are dynamically allocated, the capacity of the driver can grow and shrink with system demand. kmem_alloc(D3DK) and kmem_zalloc(D3DK) can be used to allocate memory, and kmem_free(D3DK) can be used to release memory back to the system. Their synopses are

```
#include <sys/types.h>
#include <sys/kmem.h>

void *kmem_alloc(size_t size, int flags);
void *kmem_zalloc(size_t size, int flags);
void kmem_free(void *p, size_t size);
```

where size is the size of the buffer (in bytes) to be allocated or freed, flags indicates whether the caller is willing to sleep if memory is not immediately available, and p is a pointer to the memory extent to be freed.

kmem_alloc and kmem_zalloc are the same, except that kmem_zalloc will set the contents of the buffer to zeros before returning the buffer to the caller. If flags is set to KM_NOSLEEP and no memory is available, NULL is returned. If flags is set to KM_SLEEP, kmem_alloc will not return until the memory is available. kmem_alloc will sleep at an uninterruptible priority. On success, a pointer to the start of the allocated memory range is returned.

kmem_free frees memory previously allocated by kmem_alloc or kmem_zalloc. The size parameter must be the same as the size passed to the routine that allocated the memory.

A driver can clear a buffer itself, setting it to all zeros, by calling bzero(D3DK):

```
int bzero(caddr_t addr, int nbytes);
```

addr is the starting address of the extent to clear, and nbytes is the number of bytes to set to zero. The address must be in kernel space. If an error occurs, −1 is returned. On success, 0 is returned. Callers usually ignore the return value.

Drivers can copy data from one buffer to another by using bcopy(D3DK):

```
int bcopy(caddr_t from, caddr_t to, long nbytes);
```

from is the address from which data are to be copied, to is the address to which data are to be copied, and `nbytes` is the number of bytes to copy. If the addresses overlap, the result is undefined. Both addresses must be in kernel space. The return value is always 0, so callers do not need to check it.

Error Reporting

When a driver detects an error of some sort, it usually tries to notify the user by failing the system call associated with the error. Often, however, it is difficult or inconvenient to associate an error with a particular system call. If, for example, one port on an I/O board stopped functioning properly, the driver could fail all system calls associated with the minor device. But if no processes were using the port when it failed, there would be no pending system call to fail.

In this situation, drivers usually log errors to the system console. `cmn_err`(D3DK) can be used for this purpose:

```
void cmn_err(int level, char *fmt, .../* args */);
```

`level` indicates the type of message to print, and `fmt` points to a `printf`-like string. The only conversion specifiers supported are `%s`, `%u`, `%d`, `%o`, and `%x` [see `printf`(3S) for a discussion of the conversion specifiers]. Each conversion specifier in the format string will correspond to an additional argument passed to `cmn_err`. No length modifiers are supported.

By default, the message goes to both the system console and `putbuf`, a circular kernel buffer used for debugging. If the first character in the format string is an exclamation point ("`!`"), the message is only stored in `putbuf`. If the first character in the format string is a caret ("`^`"), the message is only displayed on the console.

Four values of `level` are supported: `CE_CONT`, `CE_NOTE`, `CE_WARN`, and `CE_PANIC`. `CE_CONT` is used to continue a previous message or to print a message on the console during debugging. `CE_NOTE` will cause `cmn_err` to print the string `NOTICE:` , followed by the message and a newline. It is used to print messages about system events that may be of interest to system administrators. `CE_WARN` prints the string `WARNING:` , followed by the message and a newline. It is used to print messages that require immediate attention. `CE_PANIC` prints the string `PANIC:` , followed by the message and a newline, and then halts the system. It is used in only the most severe cases, when the system cannot continue to function properly.

9.2 THE STREAMS ENVIRONMENT

The architecture of a stream was discussed briefly in Section 3.2. Recall that the topmost processing element in every stream is the stream head. Below the stream head are any intermediate processing elements (modules) that have been pushed onto the stream. The device driver is the processing element located at the tail of the stream. Figure 9.3 shows the structure of a typical stream with one module pushed on it.

Drivers usually control I/O hardware. Software drivers, often called pseudo-drivers, are not associated with hardware. Instead, they provide services to processes, such as administrative interfaces or hardware emulation. Either type can be a STREAMS driver.

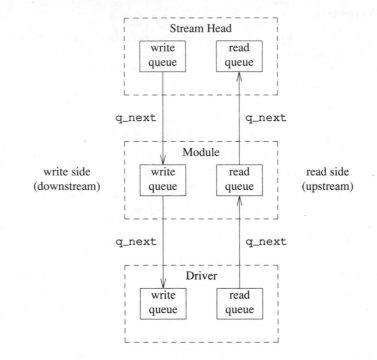

Fig. 9.3. Structure of a Typical Stream

The STREAMS mechanism supports a special kind of software driver, called a multiplexing driver (multiplexor, for short). Generic multiplexors are not provided by the STREAMS mechanism. Instead, drivers can be implemented as multiplexing drivers by supporting the proper `ioctl` commands and partitioning their processing into an upper half and a lower half. The upper half deals with the stream above the multiplexor, and the lower half deals with the stream below the multiplexor. Multiplexors are discussed in detail in Chapter 12.

Each processing element in a stream has a pair of queues: one for the read side of the stream and one for the write side. Each queue contains a pointer to the next processing element in the stream. Besides being the basic building blocks that form a stream, queues provide the interfaces between processing elements. A processing element uses its neighboring processing element's queue to identify the function to call to pass a message to the neighbor.

In addition to the queue pair, drivers and modules consist of a set of processing routines and private, per-stream data structures. Two kinds of processing, immediate and deferred, are available to give developers the flexibility to partition driver and module processing into high-priority and low-priority procedures.

Driver and module *put procedures* are used for immediate processing. They are invoked when a message is passed to the processing element. Drivers and modules can process the messages when received, or they can enqueue the messages for later processing by their *service procedures*. Messages are the sole means of communication within a stream. Pointers to messages are passed from one processing element to another to avoid the overhead of copying the contents of the message.

When a message is placed on a queue, if the queue's service procedure is not already scheduled to run, the queue is placed on a list of queues whose service procedures are to be run. The STREAMS scheduler will run the service procedures of these queues at implementation-dependent times during the operation of the kernel.

The STREAMS scheduler is distinct from the process and memory schedulers. The STREAMS scheduler is composed of one function that calls the service procedure of every queue on the list of queues to be serviced, plus several hooks throughout the system to call the function. For example, before the system goes idle, it checks if any service procedures need to be run and if so calls the function that runs them.

Service procedures are intended for lower-priority processing than put procedures. Thus, service procedures are run with most interrupts enabled and are run sometime after their associated put procedure processing. Consider what happens when a user writes to the stream shown in Figure 9.3. The stream head allocates a message, copies the user's data into it, and passes the message to the module's write put procedure. The module can either process the message in the put procedure or place it on the write queue for later processing by the queue's service procedure. In either case, the module will eventually pass the message to the driver's write put procedure. The driver can choose to handle the message in its put procedure or place the message on its write queue for its write service procedure to handle. Either way, the driver will transmit the data in the message to the I/O device and then free the message.

Now consider what happens when the I/O device receives data and interrupts the computer system. The driver interrupt routine allocates a message, copies the data received into it, and passes the message to the module's read put procedure. The read put procedure is still running in the context of the interrupt, so all other interrupts of equal and lower priority are blocked. To avoid blocking these interrupts for too long, it is a good idea to minimize read-side put procedure processing and use service procedures on the read side.

If no processing elements have read-side service procedures, then each read-side put procedure will call the put procedure of the neighboring processing element in the stream above it, one by one, until the stream head read put procedure is called. Since the interrupt stack is fixed in size, this can create many function call frames on the stack, eventually extending beyond the end of the interrupt stack and leading to a system panic.

If a message traveling up the read side of a stream is placed on a queue to be processed by that queue's service procedure, there is less chance that the interrupt stack will overflow. This is because processing of the message will continue in the service procedure from the context of the STREAMS scheduler after the interrupt handler returns. Thus, fewer frames will be needed on the interrupt stack.

Assume that the module in Figure 9.3 has a service procedure on the read side and the read put procedure enqueues the message. After calling the module's read put procedure, the driver interrupt handler returns, and interrupts that had been blocked are now enabled. Sometime later the STREAMS scheduler calls the module's read service procedure. The read service procedure will process the message and pass it to the stream head's read put procedure, which will place the message on the stream head read queue until a process retrieves it.

Since read-side put procedures of modules can be called from interrupt level, modules have to protect the critical regions of code where their read put procedures manipulate the same data structures as their base-level routines. Similarly, drivers need to protect their data structures from conflicting access between their base-level routines and their interrupt routines, but this is straightforward because drivers know what interrupt priority levels they are using and can use the appropriate spl routines for those levels. Modules, however, have no idea at what interrupt level they are being called, and do not know the proper spl (D3D) routine to use. To solve this problem, the splstr function is defined to block out interrupts from all STREAMS devices:

```
int splstr(void);
```

The return value is the previous processor priority level so that it can be restored by calling splx after the critical section.

Note that the read side of a driver is not the only place where synchronization might be needed. If an I/O board generates interrupts to notify its driver that data can be transmitted, the driver's interrupt routine will have to be serialized with portions of the driver's write-side processing.

Put and service procedures do not have user context, so they cannot call any functions that sleep. That means they need to employ other methods to wait for events to occur. This usually involves using a queue to hold messages and arranging for the service procedure to run when the events occur. One such example is buffer availability. If a put or service procedure needs to allocate a message and no memory is available, it usually puts the current message back on the queue and arranges for the service procedure to be called again when message allocation is more likely to succeed.

Lack of user context means that it is hard to fail a system call from a put or service procedure. Drivers and modules have the option of making the stream unusable by placing it in an error mode, but this is rather drastic. For nonfatal errors, the best that drivers and modules can do is log the failure. cmn_err can be used, but the STREAMS subsystem provides an alternate function that enables processes to obtain the logged messages and store them in a file or print them on a terminal. The function is strlog (D3DK):

```
#include <sys/types.h>
#include <sys/stream.h>
#include <sys/strlog.h>
#include <sys/log.h>

int strlog(short mid, short sid, char level, ushort_t flags,
    char *fmt, ... /* args */);
```

mid identifies the calling module or driver, sid is a sub-ID that can be used to further identify the caller, level is a number that indicates the intended recipients of the message, flags indicates the purpose of the message, and fmt is a printf-like string. (The conversion specifiers %s, %e, %g, and %G are not supported.) Up to three arguments to be interpreted according to fmt may be supplied.

The flags parameter allows callers to send log messages to any of three classes of processes. If SL_ERROR is set, the message goes to all processes logging error messages. If SL_TRACE is set, the message goes to all processes logging trace messages. Trace messages are used for debugging. If SL_CONSOLE is set, the message goes to all processes logging console messages.

Four additional flags can be used as modifiers to the previous three. If SL_NOTIFY is set in conjunction with SL_ERROR, then the message is mailed to the super-user. SL_FATAL can be set to indicate a fatal error. SL_WARN can be set to indicate the message is just a warning. SL_NOTE can be set to indicate the message is providing notice to a system administrator.

strlog returns 0 if an error occurs, or 1 if it was able to send a copy of the message to all logging processes. Log messages can be lost if memory is unavailable or if the consumers of the log messages do not keep up with the producers.

Flow Control

A stream is said to be *flow-controlled* when its queues become full. When the number of bytes of data in the messages on a queue becomes greater than the queue's *high-water mark*, the queue is considered full. Flow control is an advisory state where the processing element passing messages to the full queue stops sending messages and places them on its own queue. This way, flow control can propagate from one end of the stream to the other.

At the stream head, when a process tries to write to a stream whose topmost write queue with a service procedure is full, the process goes to sleep until the number of bytes of data stored in the queue reaches the queue's *low-water mark*. At this point, the queue is no longer flow-controlled. Note the distinction between the queue being full and being flow-controlled. The queue is only full as long as the amount of data it contains is over its high-water mark, but the queue remains flow-controlled after the amount of data falls below the high-water mark. Of course, if the high and low-water marks are set to the same value, then there is no such distinction.

The flow control is lifted when the number of bytes of data in messages on the queue becomes less than the queue's low-water mark. When this happens, the sender's service procedure is *backenabled*. This involves rescheduling the sender's service procedure so it can start sending messages again.

The flow control provided by the STREAMS mechanism is not intended to be used by communication protocols to implement flow control as defined by the protocol. Instead, STREAMS flow control protects the host computer from any one stream using up too much kernel memory. STREAMS drivers and modules usually employ other mechanisms to implement protocol flow control.

Required Data Structures

There are three data structures that every STREAMS driver and module must define. The first, the `module_info` structure [see `module_info(D4DK)`], provides global information about the driver or module and its queues.

```
struct module_info {
      ushort_t    mi_idnum;     /* module ID */
      char        *mi_idname;   /* module name */
      long        mi_minpsz;    /* min packet size */
      long        mi_maxpsz;    /* max packet size */
      ulong_t     mi_hiwat;     /* high-water mark */
      ulong_t     mi_lowat;     /* low-water mark */
};
```

The first field, `mi_idnum`, is a unique number used to identify the module or driver. It is selected by the programmer, but USL maintains a database of in-use module IDs (among other things) to avoid duplication. The module ID is used in STREAMS logging.

The second field, `mi_idname`, is the address of a unique string representing the module's name, used when a module is pushed onto a stream. Although drivers do not need module names, they usually are given names for consistency and to simplify administration (see the `I_LIST ioctl` command in Section 3.3). Note that the configuration software for a particular implementation of System V might have a different convention for identifying the module name, such as requiring that the module name be specified in a configuration file. In this case, programmers need to make sure that the names match.

The next two fields are the minimum and maximum packet sizes, respectively, accepted by the driver or module. These fields refer only to the size of the data portion of messages. Between drivers and modules, these values are merely advisory. The stream head, however, will honor the values on the write side of the topmost processing element in the stream. Large `writes` are fragmented, if possible, and attempts to send oversized messages with `putmsg` are denied.

The last two fields are the high and low water marks, respectively, of the queue. They represent the initial values and are duplicated in the queue so that drivers and modules can modify the defaults on a queue-by-queue basis if necessary.

The `module_info` structure may be shared by the read and write queues of a driver or module, or there may be separate `module_info` structures for each queue.

The second data structure is the `qinit` structure [see `qinit(D4DK)`]. It defines the characteristics and processing routines associated with a queue.

```
struct qinit {
    int                    (*qi_putp)();    /* put */
    int                    (*qi_srvp)();    /* service */
    int                    (*qi_qopen)();   /* open */
    int                    (*qi_qclose)();  /* close */
    int                    (*qi_qadmin)();  /* reserved */
    struct module_info     *qi_minfo;       /* module info */
    struct module_stat     *qi_mstat;       /* statistics */
};
```

The first five fields in the `qinit` structure are the addresses of the processing routines associated with the driver or module. `qi_putp` is the address of the queue's put procedure, and `qi_srvp` is the address of the queue's service procedure. Although the open and close routines are not associated with a queue, they are included in the `qinit` structure so that all processing routines are defined in the same place. `qi_qopen` is the address of the open routine and `qi_qclose` is the address of the close routine. They can be NULL for the `qinit` structure on the write side; the STREAMS subsystem only uses the ones from the read-side `qinit` structure. `qi_qadmin` is the address of the administrative procedure, which is currently unused and should be set to NULL.

`qi_minfo` is a pointer to the queue's `module_info` structure. `qi_mstat` is a pointer to a structure (defined in `<sys/strstat.h>`) that can be used to hold statistics about the driver or module. Most drivers and modules do not use it and set `qi_mstat` to NULL.

Just as with the `module_info` structure, one `qinit` structure can be shared by the read and write queues, or each queue can have its own `qinit` structure.

The final data structure, the `streamtab` structure [see `streamtab(D4DK)`], provides the operating system with a handle into the driver or module.

```
struct streamtab {
    struct qinit *st_rdinit;      /* (upper) read side */
    struct qinit *st_wrinit;      /* (upper) write side */
    struct qinit *st_muxrinit;    /* lower read side */
    struct qinit *st_muxwinit;    /* lower write side */
};
```

The first two entries in the `streamtab` are the addresses of the read-side and write-side `qinit` structures. The next two entries are only used for multiplexing drivers. They contain the addresses of the read-side and write-side `qinit` structures for the lower half of the multiplexor. These will be NULL for modules and nonmultiplexing drivers. For a multiplexing driver, the first two entries pertain to the upper half of the multiplexor.

The `streamtab` is the only STREAMS data structure required to be globally accessible in the module or driver (i.e., it should not be declared `static`). The configuration software expects it to be named *xxx*`info`, where *xxx* is a character string (whose length is implementation-dependent), called the *module prefix*, that uniquely identifies the module or driver in the system. Like the module ID and module name, the module prefix is chosen by the programmer and can be registered with USL to improve the likelihood that it will be unique.

9.3 STREAMS MESSAGES

STREAMS messages are described by triplets consisting of a message block header, a data block header, and a data buffer. The message block header describes the message, the data block header describes the data buffer, and the data buffer contains the actual data.

The message block is represented by an `msgb` structure [see `msgb (D4DK)`]:

```
struct msgb {
        struct msgb  *b_next;    /* next on queue */
        struct msgb  *b_prev;    /* previous on queue */
        struct msgb  *b_cont;    /* next in message */
        uchar_t      *b_rptr;    /* first byte to read */
        uchar_t      *b_wptr;    /* next byte to write */
        struct datab *b_datap;   /* describes data buffer */
        uchar_t      b_band;     /* priority band */
        ushort_t     b_flag;     /* flags */
};
```

The `b_next` and `b_prev` fields are used when the message is linked on a queue's message list. The `b_cont` field is used to create one complex message from two or more simple messages. The `b_rptr` field points to the first byte to be read in the data buffer. The `b_wptr` field points to the next byte to be written in the data buffer. The `b_datap` field contains the address of the data block header associated with the message. The `b_band` field contains the priority band to which the message belongs (priority bands are discussed in Section 9.4).

The `b_flag` field contains a bitmask of flags interpreted by the stream head. The only two of interest to drivers and modules are `MSGMARK` and `MSGDELIM`. The `MSGMARK` flag provides a way to "mark" a given message. An application can use the `I_ATMARK` ioctl command to determine if the message about to be read is marked or not. The `MSGDELIM` flag marks the message as being delimited as the logical end of a `read` request. If the stream is in the proper mode (set by an `M_SETOPTS` option, discussed in Section 9.6), a `read` of the stream will only return data in messages up to and including the delimited message. Successive `read`s will return any data in additional messages on the queue. This provides the ability to maintain message boundaries while using calls that are oriented toward byte streams.

For example, assume there are two messages on the stream head read queue and the stream is in byte stream mode (recall the discussion of read modes from Section 3.7). The first message contains 100 bytes of data and the second message has 50 bytes of data. A read of 150 bytes will retrieve the contents of both messages. If, however, the first message has the `MSGDELIM` flag set, then a `read` of 150 bytes will return only the 100 bytes from the first message.

The data block header is represented by a `datab` structure [see `datab (D4DK)`]:

```
struct datab {
    .
    .
    uchar_t *db_base;     /* start of data buffer */
    uchar_t *db_lim;      /* end of data buffer */
    uchar_t db_ref;       /* reference count */
    uchar_t db_type;      /* message type */
    .
    .
};
```

The vertical ellipses indicate that there are other fields in the structure, but drivers and modules are not allowed to reference them. They are internal to the STREAMS mechanism and subject to change.

The db_base field points to the start of the data buffer. The db_lim field points one byte past the end of the data buffer. Together, they define the minimum and maximum values, respectively, for the read and write pointers (b_rptr and b_wptr).

The db_ref field contains a reference count of the number of message blocks sharing the data block. If this number is greater than 1, drivers and modules must be aware that any changes made to the data buffer might affect other processing elements in the stream.

The db_type field contains the message type, which dictates in two ways how the processing elements in a stream will treat the message. First, the message type indicates the intended use of the message. Messages can be used for tasks such as data transfer, device control operations, changing the behavior of the stream head, and signaling applications. Second, the type of a message has an implicit priority associated with it, independent of the b_band field in the message block. The message types are partitioned into two priority classes: high-priority and normal-priority. By convention, the high-priority types are unaffected by flow control.

When placed on a queue, high-priority messages are always placed at the front of the queue, after any other high-priority messages already enqueued. Placing a high-priority message on a queue unconditionally schedules that queue's service procedure to run. This helps to move high-priority messages through a stream in a timely manner.

Table 9.6 lists the normal-priority message types and their uses. Table 9.7 lists the high-priority messages. The different message types are described in Section 9.6.

A simple STREAMS message consists of a single message block header, data block header, and data buffer (see Figure 9.4). The valid range of data in the message is bounded by [b_rptr, b_wptr). In other words, the first valid byte of data in the message begins at the location represented by b_rptr, and the b_wptr field points one byte past the last valid byte of data in the message. Since a message block header describes a simple message, the phrase "message block" is often used in place of the phrase "simple message." Throughout this text, the word "message" used without qualifiers means "simple or complex message."

From Figure 9.4, a simple message appears to be composed of three separate elements. While this is true conceptually, the actual implementation may choose to allocate several of the elements in one contiguous chunk of memory and then divide

Table 9.6. Normal-Priority Messages

Message Type	Use
M_DATA	User data.
M_PROTO	Control portion of service interface primitives.
M_IOCTL	User `ioctl` request.
M_PASSFP	Pass file descriptor between processes.
M_SIG	Send a signal to a process.
M_SETOPTS	Set stream head options.
M_BREAK	Request transmission of line break.
M_DELAY	Request real-time delay.
M_CTL	Implementation-dependent communication.
M_RSE	Reserved for Remote STREAMS Environment.

Table 9.7. High-Priority Messages

Message Type	Use
M_PCPROTO	High-priority version of M_PROTO.
M_IOCACK	`ioctl` positive acknowledgement.
M_IOCNAK	`ioctl` negative acknowledgement.
M_COPYIN	Copy from user buffer during transparent `ioctl`.
M_COPYOUT	Copy to user buffer during transparent `ioctl`.
M_IOCDATA	Response to M_COPYIN or M_COPYOUT.
M_PCSIG	High-priority version of M_SIG.
M_READ	Someone is reading from the stream.
M_FLUSH	Flush messages from the stream.
M_STOP	Stop output immediately.
M_START	Restart output.
M_STOPI	Stop input immediately.
M_STARTI	Restart input.
M_HANGUP	Mark stream as disconnected from device.
M_ERROR	Mark stream in error.
M_PCRSE	Reserved for Remote STREAMS Environment.

the memory up into the individual elements.

A simple message is allocated with `allocb(D3DK)`:

```
#include <sys/types.h>
#include <sys/stream.h>

mblk_t *allocb(int size, uint_t pri);
```

`size` is the size in bytes of the message to be allocated, and `pri` indicates how badly the message is needed. Possible values for `pri` are BPRI_LO, BPRI_MED, or

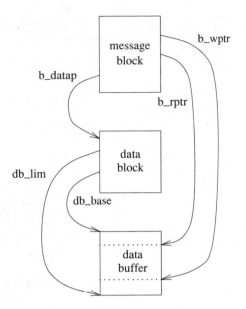

Fig. 9.4. A Simple Message

BPRI_HI. On success, allocb returns a pointer to the message; on failure, it returns NULL.

The message returned will have a type of M_DATA. Its b_rptr and b_wptr fields will be set to the beginning of the data buffer, b_datap->db_base. The b_band field will be set to 0, and the reference count will be set to 1. The contents of the data buffer are undefined (i.e., the data buffer is not initialized).

To free a simple message, drivers and modules can use freeb (D3DK):

```
#include <sys/stream.h>
```

```
void freeb(mblk_t *bp);
```

bp is a pointer to the message to be freed. freeb will first decrement the message's reference count. If it goes to zero, the message block, data block, and data buffer are freed. Otherwise, just the message block is freed.

A complex message consists of two or more simple messages linked via their b_cont pointers (see Figure 9.5). Here, the data in one buffer are viewed as logically contiguous to the data in the next buffer. The type of the message is determined by the db_type field in the first message block in the message.

Drivers and modules cannot use freeb to free a complex message, because freeb will only free the first message block, and any additional messages blocks linked to it via the b_cont pointer will be lost. Instead of freeb, freemsg (D3DK) can be used to free either a simple or a complex message:

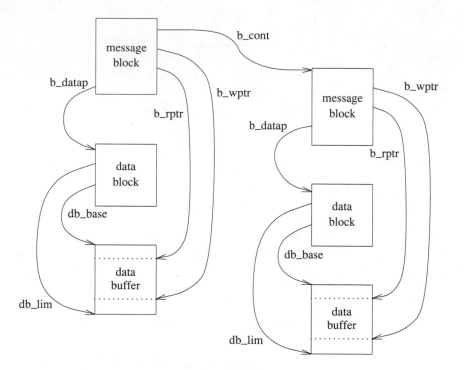

Fig. 9.5. A Complex Message

```
#include <sys/stream.h>

void freemsg(mblk_t *mp);
```

mp is a pointer to the message to be freed. freemsg operates by calling freeb for each message block in the message.

The reason for the separation between the message block and the data block is so that the data block can be shared by multiple message blocks. This allows copies of messages to be made without actually copying the data in the message. Instead, an additional message block is allocated, its b_datap field is set to the address of the data block from the original message, and the data block's reference count is incremented. This process is known as *duplicating* the message, to distinguish it from copying the message.

A duplicated message is shown in Figure 9.6. Duplicated messages are useful when drivers or modules need to retain a copy of the message after forwarding it to the neighboring processing element in the stream. For example, a protocol module might retain a copy of a message for later retransmission.

A simple message can be duplicated with dupb (D3DK):

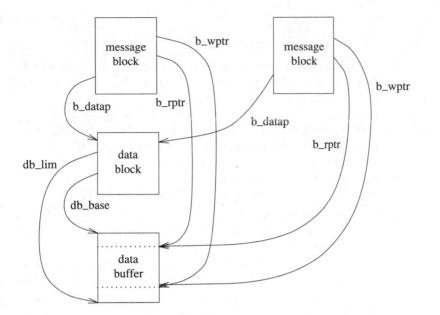

Fig. 9.6. A Duplicated Message

```
#include <sys/stream.h>
```

```
mblk_t *dupb(mblk_t *bp);
```

bp is a pointer to the simple message to be duplicated. If successful, dupb returns a pointer to the new message. Otherwise, it returns NULL. The new message block will have its b_rptr, b_wptr, b_flag, and b_band fields copied from bp.

Either a simple or a complex message can be duplicated with dupmsg (D3DK):

```
#include <sys/stream.h>
```

```
mblk_t *dupmsg(mblk_t *mp);
```

mp points to the message to be duplicated. dupmsg duplicates a message by calling dupb for each message block in the message. Each new message block is then linked via its b_cont pointer. On success, dupmsg returns a pointer to the new message. On failure, dupmsg returns NULL.

Sometimes, however, message duplication is inappropriate. The contents of a duplicated message can be changed by any processing element that has been passed either of the messages. When a driver or module wants to ensure that the original contents of the message are retained, a copy has to be made instead.

A simple message can be copied with copyb (D3DK):

```
#include <sys/stream.h>

mblk_t *copyb(mblk_t *bp);
```

bp is a pointer to the simple message to be copied. `copyb` will call `allocb` to allocate the new message and then copy the contents of the data buffer associated with bp to the data buffer in the new message.

The new message will have the same type, priority band, and flags as bp. Also, the read and write pointers in the new message will be at the same relative positions as those in bp, except they will be pointing to their own data buffer. The reference count in the new message will be 1. `copyb` returns a pointer to the new message on success. If the allocation fails, `copyb` returns NULL.

Simple and complex messages can be copied with `copymsg(D3DK)`:

```
#include <sys/stream.h>

mblk_t *copymsg(mblk_t *mp);
```

mp is a pointer to the message to be copied. `copymsg` copies a message by calling `copyb` for each message block in the message. The new message blocks are then linked together via their `b_cont` pointers. On success, `copymsg` returns a pointer to the new message. On failure, `copymsg` returns NULL.

A consequence of using multiblock messages is that sometimes concatenation is necessary. For example, suppose a data structure is stored in the data buffers. To access all members of the structure, the members need to be stored in one contiguous extent of memory. In addition, some architectures make requirements on data structure alignment. Drivers and modules can use `pullupmsg(D3DK)` to concatenate and align the data stored in a complex message:

```
#include <sys/stream.h>

int pullupmsg(mblk_t *mp, int len);
```

mp is a pointer to the message to be pulled up, and `len` indicates the number of bytes to concatenate.

When `pullupmsg` concatenates the messages, it will allocate a new data block and data buffer for the new message, but it will reuse the old message header. The reason for the new data block is that the old one might be shared, and the allocation mechanism sometimes allocates the data block header and data buffer as one contiguous chunk of memory.

Figure 9.7 shows what happens when a complex message is pulled up. The original message was composed of two message blocks: one containing 100 bytes of data and another containing 50 bytes of data. After calling `pullupmsg`, the data in both buffers have been concatenated in a new data buffer.

If `len` is less than the number of bytes in the message, then the remaining bytes will be placed in their original message blocks and linked to mp via their `b_cont` pointers. If `len` is −1, then `pullupmsg` will attempt to concatenate and align the contents of the entire message into a single data buffer. As `pullupmsg` copies data into the new data buffer, the message block from which the data are copied is freed if

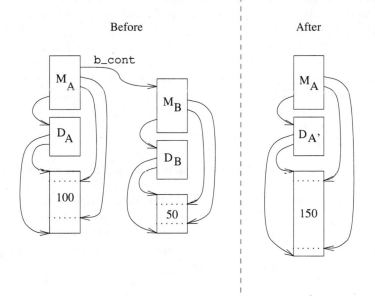

Before   After

b_cont

Fig. 9.7. Pulling Up a Complex Message

it is no longer needed.

On success, `pullupmsg` returns 1; on failure, it returns 0. `pullupmsg` can fail if there are less than `len` bytes in the message or if a big enough data buffer cannot be allocated. The concatenation only applies to message blocks of the same type. For example, the contents of an `M_PROTO` message block will never be concatenated with the contents of an `M_DATA` message block.

Since STREAMS drivers and modules do not have user context in their put and service procedures, they have to be prepared for functions to fail if memory is unavailable to allocate messages. In this case, the only course of action they can take is to save their processing state and try again later. The `bufcall`(D3DK) function can be used in this situation:

```
#include <sys/types.h>
#include <sys/stream.h>

int bufcall(uint_t size, int pri, void (*fn)(long),
     long arg);
```

`size` is the size of the allocation request that failed, `pri` is the priority at which the request failed (BPRI_HI, BPRI_MED, or BPRI_LO), `fn` is the address of a function to be called when there is a good chance that the allocation request will succeed, and `arg` is the single parameter to the function.

When `fn` is called, it is not guaranteed that the requested memory is available, since someone else could have allocated it between the time the memory became available and the time that `fn` tries to allocate it again. `fn` will be called without user context, so it cannot call any functions that sleep. All interrupts from STREAMS devices will be blocked when `fn` runs.

If `bufcall` successfully arranges to have the function called, it returns an identifier, called a *bufcall ID*, that represents the registration of the function. If `bufcall` itself runs out of memory, it cannot register any more functions, so it returns 0, an invalid bufcall ID.

The bufcall ID can be passed to `unbufcall` (D3DK) to cancel the request that the function be called:

```
void unbufcall(int id);
```

`id` is a bufcall ID. If `id` does not match an outstanding request, then `unbufcall` has no effect.

Besides duplicating messages, the STREAMS mechanism supports another method to avoid copying data. It allows drivers to use private buffers for the data buffers associated with messages. These externally supplied buffers can reside in memory that is shared between an I/O card and the host computer, so that no copying is needed when the driver receives a message.

Instead of calling `allocb`, a driver can call `esballoc` (D3DK) to "wrap" a STREAMS message around an externally supplied buffer. The synopsis is

```
#include <sys/types.h>
#include <sys/stream.h>

mblk_t *esballoc(uchar_t *base, int size, int pri,
    frtn_t *frtnp);
```

where `base` is a pointer to the beginning of the data buffer, `size` is the size of the buffer in bytes, `pri` is the allocation priority and can take on the same values as with `allocb`, and `frtnp` is a pointer to a `free_rtn` structure [see `free_rtn` (D4DK)] defined as:

```
typedef struct free_rtn {
    void (*free_func)(char *);
    char *free_arg;
} frtn_t;
```

where `free_func` is the address of a function to be called when the message is freed, and `free_arg` is the single argument to the function. When `free_func` is called, the data buffer is no longer in use and the driver can reuse it. The function runs without user context. Since the `free_rtn` structure is associated with the message created, the structure must be remain intact until `free_func` is called.

`esballoc` will attempt to allocate a message block and data block, and associate the caller's buffer with it. On success, a pointer to the message is returned. On failure, `NULL` is returned.

If `esballoc` fails, drivers cannot use `bufcall` to recover, since `bufcall` assumes the caller wants to allocate a normal message. Instead, `esbbcall` (D3DK) can be used:

```
#include <sys/stream.h>

int esbbcall(int pri, void (*func)(long), long arg);
```

where `pri` is the same as for `bufcall`, `func` is the address of a function to call when there is a good chance that `esballoc` will succeed, and `arg` is the single argument to the function.

If successful, `esbbcall` returns a `bufcall` ID that may be used with `unbufcall`. Otherwise, `esbbcall` returns 0.

9.4 STREAMS QUEUES

The STREAMS queue is the basic building block in a stream. Each processing element has a pair of queues, one for the read side of the stream and one for the write side. The `queue` structure [see `queue (D4DK)`] represents a STREAMS queue:

```
struct queue {
        .
        .
        .
        struct qinit *q_qinfo;   /* queue functions */
        struct msgb  *q_first;   /* head of message list */
        struct msgb  *q_last;    /* tail of message list */
        struct queue *q_next;    /* next queue in the stream */
        void         *q_ptr;     /* module private data */
        ulong_t      q_count;    /* # band 0 + hipri bytes */
        ulong_t      q_flag;     /* flags */
        long         q_minpsz;   /* min packet size */
        long         q_maxpsz;   /* max packet size */
        ulong_t      q_hiwat;    /* high-water mark */
        ulong_t      q_lowat;    /* low-water mark */
        .
        .
        .
};
```

The `q_qinfo` field points to the driver or module `qinit` structure so that the procedures and parameters associated with the queue can be identified. The `q_first` field points to the first message on the queue, and the `q_last` field points to the last message on the queue. The `q_next` field points to the next queue in the stream.

The `q_ptr` field is a typeless pointer that can be used by the driver or module to point to a private data structure associated with the queue. The `q_flag` field contains a bitmask of flags providing information about the queue. They are defined in `<sys/stream.h>`. The only ones of interest to drivers and modules are QREADR, set in all the read queues so that they can be distinguished from the write queues, and QFULL, set when a queue is full.

The `q_minpsz` and `q_maxpsz` fields are the minimum and maximum packet sizes, respectively, accepted by the driver or module. They are initialized with values from the `module_info` structure when the queue is created. The reason they are duplicated is that the `q_minpsz` and `q_maxpsz` fields may be modified throughout the course of the queue's use. Similarly, the `q_hiwat` and `q_lowat` fields are initialized from the `mi_hiwat` and `mi_lowat` fields, respectively, in the `module_info` structure. The `q_count` field contains the number of bytes in messages with normal and high priorities on the queue. This is discussed further in the next subsection, ''Message Queueing.''

As mentioned, queues are allocated in pairs, one for the read side and one for the write side. Often a driver or module needs to access the read queue during write-side processing, and vice versa. Three functions are provided to convert between queues: `OTHERQ(D3DK)`, `RD(D3DK)`, and `WR(D3DK)`. Their synopses are

```
#include <sys/stream.h>

queue_t *OTHERQ(queue_t *q);
queue_t *RD(queue_t *q);
queue_t *WR(queue_t *q);
```

where `q` is a pointer to a queue. If `q` is a read queue, then `OTHERQ` and `WR` each return a pointer to its mate write queue, while the return value from `RD` is indeterminate. If `q` is a write queue, then `OTHERQ` and `RD` each return a pointer to its mate read queue, and the return value from `WR` is indeterminate.

Message Queueing

The priority of a message affects its placement in a queue. High-priority messages are always placed at the front of the queue but after any other high-priority messages already on the queue. Normal-priority messages, also known as *ordinary* messages, are always placed at the end of the queue. Normally, drivers and modules only need to deal with these two priority types. Some special applications, however, require a finer-grained priority mechanism. The priority band field (`b_band`) in the message block provides this capability.

Normal-priority messages have their `b_band` field set to 0. The `b_band` field in high-priority messages is ignored, but should be set to 0 as well. Up to 255 additional priority bands are available for use, although one additional band is usually sufficient for most applications.

Priority bands were added to the STREAMS mechanism to support networking protocols that define out-of-band operations. In OSI terms, these are called *expedited* operations. They have a higher precedence than most other operations defined by the protocol.

Even though today's networking protocols only define one out-of-band channel, the changes made to the STREAMS subsystem were generalized to support up to 255 out-of-band channels. This was done to avoid changing the STREAMS mechanism every time another protocol was invented that defined a new out-of-band channel. Although the support is present, the cost for its use is proportional to the priority band number, so extra priority bands should not be defined unless absolutely necessary.

Messages are placed on a queue by linking their `b_next` and `b_prev` pointers together to form a doubly linked list (see Figure 9.8). A message's priority

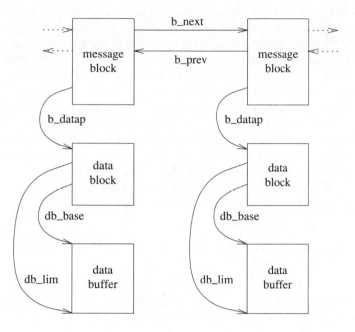

Fig. 9.8. Message Linkage on a Queue

determines the ordering of the message on a queue. Between the normal-priority and high-priority messages are the messages with nonzero priority band fields (called *priority band messages*). Any normal-priority message can be changed into a priority band message by assigning it a nonzero b_band value. Figure 9.9 illustrates the relative ordering of messages on a queue.

head	high-priority messages	priority band 255 messages	...	priority band 2 messages	priority band 1 messages	normal messages (band 0)	tail

Fig. 9.9. Message Ordering on a Queue

The queue maintains a linked list of auxiliary data structures, one per priority band. The list is built in a lazy fashion to conserve memory. The first time a priority band message is enqueued and there is no associated data structure to represent it, a data structure is allocated and placed on the list.

Each priority band is viewed as a separate flow of messages, as far as flow control is concerned. Each priority band has separate high-water and low-water marks, initially the same values as those found in the queue structure. These can be changed later. Each priority band also has a separate count of the number of bytes in messages in that band on the queue. Thus, each band can flow-control separately.

Since each band of message flow in a stream contains its own flow-control parameters, the flow-control information contained in the `queue` structure pertains to normal messages alone (those in priority band 0). Note that the test `(q->q_count > 0)` is not sufficient to determine if a message is on the queue. The message may be in a nonzero priority band, so `q_count` may be unaffected. The correct way to test for a nonempty queue is `(q->q_first != NULL)`.

To insulate modules and drivers from needing to distinguish between parameters contained in the `queue` structure and the corresponding parameters contained in the auxiliary per-band structures, two utility routines, `strqget (D3DK)` and `strqset (D3DK)`, can be used to access the necessary fields.

`strqget` returns information about a queue. The synopsis is

```
#include <sys/types.h>
#include <sys/stream.h>

int strqget(queue_t *q, qfields_t what, uchar_t pri,
    long *valp);
```

where `q` is a pointer to the queue, `what` defines the field of interest, `pri` specifies the priority band of interest, and `valp` is a pointer to the memory location where the value is to be stored. Possible values for `what` are summarized in Table 9.8.

Table 9.8. `qfields_t` Values

`what` Value	Description
QHIWAT	High-water mark for specified band
QLOWAT	Low-water mark for specified band
QMAXPSZ	Maximum packet size for queue
QMINPSZ	Minimum packet size for queue
QCOUNT	Number of bytes of data in specified band
QFIRST	Pointer to first message in specified band
QLAST	Pointer to last message in specified band
QFLAG	Flags for the specified band

If `pri` is nonzero and there is no auxiliary data structure for the corresponding band, the necessary structures will be allocated. For QMAXPSZ and QMINPSZ, `pri` must be set to zero because the auxiliary structures do not have separate packet size parameters.

Except for QREADR when `pri` is zero, none of the queue flags is included in the DDI/DKI, so drivers and modules that use them risk being nonportable. `strqget` returns 0 on success or an error number on failure.

`strqset` allows a driver or module to change some of the queue parameters:

```
#include <sys/types.h>
#include <sys/stream.h>

int strqset(queue_t *q, qfields_t what, uchar_t pri,
    long val);
```

q is a pointer to the queue, what defines the field to be changed, pri specifies the priority band of interest, and val is the new value of the field.

Possible values for what are QHIWAT to change the high-water mark of the specified band, QLOWAT to change the low-water mark of the specified band, QMAXPSZ to change the queue's maximum packet size, and QMINPSZ to change the queue's minimum packet size. Like strqget, pri must be zero when changing the queue's packet sizes. Also, if pri is nonzero and there is no auxiliary data structure for the corresponding band, the necessary structures will be allocated. strqset returns 0 on success or an error number on failure.

Enqueueing Messages

Three functions are available to place messages on a queue. Drivers and modules should never link messages onto a queue by directly manipulating the pointers themselves, because these functions do more than just enqueue messages. They also perform the work needed to support flow control within a stream.

The most commonly used function to put a message on a queue is putq(D3DK):

```
#include <sys/stream.h>

int putq(queue_t *q, mblk_t *mp);
```

q is a pointer to the queue, and mp is a pointer to the message to be enqueued. The message is enqueued based on its priority. If messages of the same priority are already on the queue, then mp is placed after them.

Placing a message on a queue will cause that queue's service procedure to be scheduled to run if it has not been disabled (disabling a queue's service procedure is discussed shortly). Placing a high-priority message on a queue will unconditionally schedule that queue's service procedure to run.

If the message belongs to a priority band for which there is no existing auxiliary band structure, an attempt is made to allocate all nonexistent auxiliary band structures for band numbers up to and including the one needed to describe the message. If the allocation fails, the message is not enqueued and 0 is returned. On success, 1 is returned and flow-control parameters are updated. Even though putq can fail, most callers ignore its return value because the auxiliary structures are small, and if they cannot be allocated, the system is probably in a lot more trouble than the problems resulting from being unable to enqueue a message and losing it.

Sometimes a driver or module may need to put a message back on a queue after taking it off. In this case, putbq(D3DK) can be called:

```
#include <sys/stream.h>

int putbq(queue_t *q, mblk_t *mp);
```

q is a pointer to the queue, and mp is a pointer to the message to be put back on the
queue. The message is placed on the queue *before* any other messages of the same
priority. In all other ways, putbq is just like putq.

On success, putbq updates the queue's flow-control parameters and returns 1.
On failure, putbq returns 0. Like putq, callers rarely check the return value from
putbq. If a message is being placed back on a queue and the band of the message
has not changed, then the auxiliary structures should already be in place. Callers can,
however, use putbq the first time a message is placed on a queue, thereby forcing
the message ahead of other messages in its band.

When putq and putbq do not provide the functionality needed by a driver or
module, insq(D3DK) can be used:

```
#include <sys/stream.h>

int insq(queue_t *q, mblk_t *emp, mblk_t *mp);
```

q is a pointer to a queue, emp is a pointer to a message already in the queue's list of
messages, and mp is a pointer to a new message to be placed directly before emp in
the queue. If emp is NULL, then insq places mp at the end of the queue. insq follows rules similar to those followed by putq and putbq concerning auxiliary band
structure allocation and service procedure scheduling.

When drivers and modules use insq, they must maintain the proper ordering of
messages in the queue based on the priorities of the messages. If the caller attempts
to insert a message out of order in the queue, insq will print a warning message on
the console and will return 0 without enqueueing the message. On success, insq
updates the queue's flow-control parameters and returns 1. Otherwise, insq returns
0 without enqueueing the message.

Dequeueing Messages

Two functions are available to retrieve a message from a queue. In addition, two
functions are provided to flush (i.e., discard) messages from a queue. Drivers and
modules should never unlink messages from a queue by directly manipulating the
pointers themselves, because these functions do the bookkeeping necessary to support flow control within a stream.

Drivers and modules can use getq(D3DK) to retrieve the first message on a
queue:

```
#include <sys/stream.h>

mblk_t *getq(queue_t *q);
```

q is a pointer to the queue from which a message is to be obtained. If the queue is
empty, getq returns NULL. Otherwise, getq removes the first message from the
queue, updates the queue's flow-control parameters, and returns a pointer to the

message. If, after removing the message, the number of bytes in messages on the queue falls below the queue's low-water mark and someone is waiting to pass messages to the queue, then `getq` will search back through the stream to find the first queue with a service procedure and *backenable* it. Backenabling is the process of removing the state information associated with one queue that has previously been prevented from sending messages to another queue, and enabling the originating queue so it can begin sending messages again.

Occasionally, a driver or module might want to remove a particular message from a queue. Instead of removing them one at a time with `getq` until the desired message is removed and then putting all the others back on the queue, `rmvq (D3DK)` can be used to remove any message from the queue:

```
#include <sys/stream.h>

void rmvq(queue_t *q, mblk_t *mp);
```

q is a pointer to the queue, and `mp` is a pointer to the message to be removed from the queue. No checking is done to verify that `mp` is actually enqueued on q, so the caller must be sure that this condition is met. Like `getq`, `rmvq` will update flow-control parameters and possibly backenable a blocked writer.

When a driver or module wants to remove and discard messages from the queue, `flushq (D3DK)` can be used:

```
#include <sys/stream.h>

void flushq(queue_t *q, int flag);
```

q is a pointer to the queue to be flushed, and `flag` indicates the type of messages to discard. If `flag` is FLUSHALL, all messages are freed. If `flag` is FLUSHDATA, only data messages are freed [see `datamsg (D3DK)`]. `flushq` will recalculate flow-control parameters after the queue is flushed. Blocked writers are backenabled if the number of bytes left on the queue is below the low-water mark.

With the introduction of multiple bands of data flow, the `flushband (D3DK)` function was added to give drivers and modules the flexibility to flush messages in a single priority band. The synopsis is

```
#include <sys/types.h>
#include <sys/stream.h>

void flushband(queue_t *q, uchar_t pri, int flag);
```

where q is a pointer to the queue, `pri` is the priority band to flush, and `flag` indicates the type of messages to flush. Other than operating on a single band, `flush-band` performs the same operations as `flushq`.

Queue Scheduling

Several flags in the queue control whether or not the service procedure is scheduled when a message is enqueued. One of these prevents scheduling while the service procedure is still running. The flag is usually on, enabling the service procedure to be scheduled. When the service procedure runs, the first call to `getq` shuts the flag off, disabling scheduling. The last call to `getq`, where `getq` returns `NULL` because the queue is empty, will turn the flag back on. (Note that this process is not implemented by `rmvq`.)

When a queue's service procedure has been scheduled to run, we say that the queue has been *enabled*. A queue is normally enabled when a message is placed on it. The STREAMS subsystem also provides a way for drivers and modules to schedule their service procedures directly. The `qenable(D3DK)` function can be used to schedule a queue's service procedure to run:

```
#include <sys/stream.h>

void qenable(queue_t *q);
```

q is a pointer to the queue to be enabled. If the queue does not have a service procedure, or if the service procedure is already scheduled to run, then `qenable` does nothing. Otherwise, `qenable` places the queue on a list of queues whose service procedures are ready to be run. This is done regardless of whether the queue has been disabled via `noenable` (see below).

When a driver or module wants more control over its service procedure scheduling, it can disable the implicit scheduling that occurs when `putq`, `putbq`, and `insq` are used. This is done with `noenable(D3DK)`:

```
#include <sys/stream.h>

void noenable(queue_t *q);
```

q is a pointer to the queue. Note, however, that `noenable` does not stop the queue from being enabled when a high-priority message is placed on the queue. Also, `noenable` does not prevent backenabling when flow-control restrictions are lifted.

Drivers and modules can use `enableok(D3DK)` to restore the implicit scheduling that occurs when `putq`, `putbq`, and `insq` are used. The synopsis is

```
#include <sys/stream.h>

void enableok(queue_t *q);
```

where q is a pointer to the queue.

9.5 COMMUNICATING WITH MESSAGES

By convention, high-priority messages can be passed to the next processing element in a stream at any time. With all other messages, though, drivers and modules must check if a message can be sent before sending it. While flow control is asserted, messages in the affected bands cannot be sent.

Drivers and modules can call `canput(D3DK)` to see if the stream can accept more messages:

```
#include <sys/stream.h>

int canput(queue_t *q);
```

q is a pointer to the queue intended to receive the message. If a message can be passed along in the stream in the direction indicated by q, then canput returns 1. Otherwise, it returns 0.

canput assumes that a message will eventually be enqueued. Thus, canput traverses the stream, starting at q, until it reaches a queue with a service procedure. If one is found and its band 0 is full, then band 0 of the stream is flow-controlled at that point, and canput returns 0. If canput reaches the end of the stream without finding a service procedure, it assumes the message can be sent, so it returns 1. canput helps to implement STREAMS flow control by informing queues of the caller's desire to transmit messages. This is how the functions described in the previous section know when to backenable a service procedure.

To prevent all of kernel memory from being consumed when priority bands are used with modules that do not support the notion of priority bands, canput will also return 0 if any nonzero priority band is flow-controlled. If this were not the case, then someone sending priority band messages to a module that uses canput would never be flow-controlled.

Since a single band can become flow-controlled, bcanput (D3DK) is provided to test if a message can be sent in a particular band. The synopsis is

```
#include <sys/stream.h>

int bcanput(queue_t *q, uchar_t pri);
```

where q is a pointer to the queue, and pri is the priority band in which the caller desires to send a message. Other than the pri parameter, bcanput is like canput, except that it does not consider the state of any band other than pri.

The primary function used to pass a message along in a stream is putnext (D3DK):

```
#include <sys/stream.h>

int putnext(queue_t *q, mblk_t *mp);
```

q is a pointer to the queue from which the message is being sent, and mp is a pointer to the message. putnext will pass mp to the put procedure of the next queue in the stream. putnext returns the put procedure's return value, but no meaning can usually be associated with it.

Two functions can be used to send control messages in a stream. (Control messages are discussed in Section 9.6.) putctl (D3DK) can be used to send a control message without data, and putctl1 (D3DK) can be used to send a control message with one byte of data. Their synopses are

```
#include <sys/stream.h>

int putctl(queue_t *q, int type);
int putctl1(queue_t *q, int type, int param);
```

where q is a pointer to the queue to which the message is to be sent, type is the type
of the message, and param is the one-byte parameter to store in the message's data
buffer. param should really be defined as an unsigned char.

Both routines create a control message, initialize the type to type, and pass the
message to q's put procedure. The type must not be a data message [see
datamsg(D3DK)], except M_DELAY messages are allowed (see Section 9.6 for a
discussion of the M_DELAY message type). If the message cannot be allocated,
putctl and putctl1 fail and return 0. Otherwise, they return 1.

One final function is provided to ease the task of sending a message in the opposite direction in a stream. Drivers and modules can call qreply(D3DK) as a shorthand way of saying putnext(OTHERQ(q), mp). The synopsis is

```
#include <sys/stream.h>

void qreply(queue_t *q, mblk_t *mp);
```

where q is a pointer to the queue from which the message is to be sent, and mp is a
pointer to the message.

Note the differences in the queue parameters for the functions used to send messages in a stream. putnext and qreply take a pointer to the sender's queue as a
parameter, while putctl and putctl1 take a pointer to the receiver's queue.
canput and bcanput also take a pointer to the receiver's queue.

9.6 MESSAGE TYPES

We presented two tables (Tables 9.6 and 9.7) summarizing the various STREAMS
message types in Section 9.3. In this section, we will discuss the structure and use of
each message type.

Recall that the message type also indicates whether or not the message is high-
priority. High-priority messages have db_type >= QPCTL.

Besides their priority, STREAMS message types can be divided into two broad
categories: data messages and control messages. Data messages are used to
exchange data between a process and a device or another process. Control messages
are used to change the state of the stream and perform device-specific actions.

Data Transfer

There are three message types used for data transfer: M_DATA, M_PROTO, and
M_PCPROTO. All other message types are control messages.

M_DATA messages are used to hold ordinary data. They can be composed of
any number of message blocks. Alone, M_DATA messages represent data from system calls and devices. In complex messages they are used to hold the data portions

of service interface primitives and `ioctl` commands. An `M_DATA` message is usually normal-priority, but can be associated with a higher-priority band by altering the `b_band` field in the message block.

`M_PROTO` messages are used to hold the control portion of service interface primitives (see Section 3.5). They usually contain data structures interpreted by the service consumer and service provider. The format for service interface primitives is one `M_PROTO` message block linked to zero or more `M_DATA` message blocks. Since data structures are usually contained in the data buffer associated with `M_PROTO` message blocks, the structures should be aligned according to the requirements of the system. Like `M_DATA` messages, `M_PROTO` messages are usually normal-priority unless their priority bands are changed.

`M_PCPROTO` messages are high-priority versions of `M_PROTO` messages. They are used for service interface primitives that should take precedence over other primitives, like interface acknowledgements, for example. Their use, however, should be limited because there can be at most one `M_PCPROTO` message on the stream head read queue at one time. This restriction prevents the system from running out of memory if a driver or module continually sends `M_PCPROTO` messages upstream but the user process is not retrieving them. Since `M_PCPROTO` messages are not affected by flow control, the driver or module will not stop when the stream head's read queue becomes full. Thus, to prevent excess memory consumption, if the stream head receives an `M_PCPROTO` message when there already is one on the read queue, the new message is freed.

`ioctl` Processing

When the `ioctl` system call is applied to a stream, the corresponding command can be processed in one of two ways. If the command is one of the generic stream head commands described in `streamio(7)`, then processing is done entirely by the stream head. All other commands result in the stream head creating an `M_IOCTL` message and sending it downstream for the modules and driver to process.

When an application makes one of these `ioctl` calls, it will block until the `ioctl` processing is complete or when a signal interrupts the sleep. Other applications attempting to perform `ioctl`s on the same stream will block until the current one is complete. Thus, drivers and modules usually process only one `ioctl` command at a time.

The message generated by an `ioctl` call is composed of one `M_IOCTL` message block linked to zero or more `M_DATA` message blocks. The `M_IOCTL` message block contains an `iocblk` structure [see `iocblk(D4DK)`]:

```
struct iocblk {
      int      ioc_cmd;      /* ioctl command */
      cred_t   *ioc_cr;      /* user credentials */
      uint_t   ioc_id;       /* sequence ID */
      uint_t   ioc_count;    /* amount of data */
      int      ioc_error;    /* error value */
      int      ioc_rval;     /* return value */
};
#define ioc_uid ioc_cr->cr_uid          /* user ID */
#define ioc_gid ioc_cr->cr_gid          /* group ID */
```

The command parameter from the `ioctl` system call is stored in the `ioc_cmd` field of the `iocblk` structure. This is what drivers and modules use to identify the control operation. The `ioc_cr` field points to a credentials structure that identifies the process making the `ioctl` system call. The credentials structure is defined in `<sys/cred.h>`.

The `ioc_id` field is a unique identifier used by the stream head to match the `ioctl` request message with the `ioctl` response message. The `ioc_count` field indicates the amount of data associated with the `ioctl` request. If the field is nonzero, then there will be one or more `M_DATA` message blocks linked to the `M_IOCTL` message block containing `ioc_count` bytes of data. If `ioc_count` is equal to the special value `TRANSPARENT`, then there is one `M_DATA` message block linked that contains four bytes constituting the third parameter (`arg`) of the `ioctl` system call. The `ioc_error` and `ioc_rval` fields are not used in the `M_IOCTL` message. They are only used in `ioctl` response messages.

When an `M_IOCTL` message is sent downstream, it is acted on by the first processing element that recognizes the `ioc_cmd` field. If a module does not support the command, it passes the message downstream. Otherwise the module will perform the requested action, then convert the message into an `ioctl` response message and send it back upstream.

There are two kinds of response messages: positive acknowledgements and negative acknowledgements. If an `M_IOCTL` message reaches a driver, it usually means no module on the stream understood the command. If the driver does not support it either, it will convert the message into a negative acknowledgement message and send it back upstream.

The `M_IOCACK` message is the positive acknowledgement. It is usually used to indicate the success of an `ioctl` operation. `M_IOCACK` messages are high-priority messages consisting of an `M_IOCACK` message block linked to zero or more `M_DATA` blocks. Like the `M_IOCTL` message, the `M_IOCACK` message contains an `iocblk` structure.

Drivers and modules usually do not create an `M_IOCACK` message from scratch. Instead, they convert the `M_IOCTL` message into an `M_IOCACK` message by changing the type of the message. The stream head depends on matching the `ioc_id` field in the `iocblk` structure to complete the `ioctl` system call. By converting the `M_IOCTL` message into an `M_IOCACK` message, drivers and modules are relieved of having to worry about details like this.

Drivers and modules can control the return value from the `ioctl` system call by setting `ioc_rval`. If `ioc_error` is set to a nonzero value, however, the system call will fail, returning −1 and setting `errno` to the specified error number. If there is no error, `ioc_count` is nonzero, and if this is not a transparent `ioctl`, the M_IOCACK message block must be linked to one or more M_DATA message blocks containing `ioc_count` bytes of data. The data will be copied out to the user's buffer specified in the `ioctl` system call.

Recall the way an I_STR `ioctl` works (see Section 3.3). An application provides a data buffer containing the information needed to perform the `ioctl` command. If the driver or module needs to return information, the information is placed in this same data buffer. Transparent `ioctl` commands, on the other hand, do not transfer data with M_IOCACK messages, as we shall see shortly.

M_IOCNAK messages are sent upstream by drivers and modules to indicate the failure of an `ioctl` request. They are high-priority messages made up of one M_IOCNAK message block containing an `iocblk` structure. As with the M_IOCACK message, drivers and modules just convert the M_IOCTL message into an M_IOCNAK message by changing the message's type. If `ioc_error` is set to zero, the `ioctl` system call will fail with `errno` set to EINVAL. Otherwise, the system call will fail with `errno` set to the value specified by `ioc_error`. No data are copied to the user's buffer.

When the STREAMS mechanism was first introduced into System V, the only way applications could perform driver-specific or module-specific `ioctl` operations was with the I_STR `ioctl` command. This was fine until a prototype of the terminal subsystem was reimplemented using the STREAMS framework. Then it became apparent that many applications would have to be rewritten to use I_STR instead of the traditional terminal `ioctl` commands. At the time, people felt that it was more important to provide compatibility with existing applications. Any solution that required an application to change or be recompiled was deemed unsatisfactory. Thus, the transparent `ioctl` mechanism was born. The example in Chapter 11 illustrates how a module can support transparent `ioctl` commands.

With transparent `ioctls`, the stream head does not expect an application to use only the I_STR command to perform device-specific or module-specific control operations. Instead of returning an error in response to unrecognized commands, the stream head assumes they are transparent `ioctls` intended for a driver or module downstream. Thus, the stream head creates a partial M_IOCTL message and sends it downstream. The message is identified as being transparent by the `ioc_count` field in the `iocblk` structure being set to the constant TRANSPARENT.

In this case, the M_IOCTL message is linked to a single M_DATA block containing the four bytes making up the third argument to the `ioctl` system call. If this argument is a pointer to a user's buffer, then drivers and modules can use the M_COPYIN message to get a copy of the buffer and the M_COPYOUT message to modify the contents of the buffer. M_COPYIN and M_COPYOUT messages are high-priority messages because they represent communication between the driver or module and the stream head. No modules between the two usually need to process the messages.

The format of an M_COPYIN message is one message block of type M_COPYIN whose data buffer contains a `copyreq` structure [see `copyreq(D4DK)`]:

```
struct copyreq {
        int     cq_cmd;     /* ioctl command */
        cred_t  *cq_cr;     /* user credentials */
        uint_t  cq_id;      /* sequence ID */
        caddr_t cq_addr;    /* user buffer address */
        uint_t  cq_size;    /* amount of data */
        int     cq_flag;    /* reserved */
        mblk_t  *cq_private;/* module/driver private data */
};
#define cq_uid cq_cr->cr_uid     /* user ID */
#define cq_gid cq_cr->cr_gid     /* group ID */
```

Drivers and modules should create the M_COPYIN message from the M_IOCTL message by changing the type of the message and reusing the data buffer. The first three fields require no processing and correspond to the first three fields in the `iocblk` structure. The `cq_addr` field contains the address of a user buffer from which data will be copied. The `cq_size` field contains the number of bytes to be copied. The `cq_flag` field should be set to zero. It is reserved for future use.

The `cq_private` field can be used to hold state information needed by drivers and modules so they can continue with `ioctl` processing when the response from the stream head is received. This allows the message to be self-describing and frees drivers and modules from having to retain information about the state of their `ioctl` processing. The reason that the type of this field is a pointer to a message block is that the transparent `ioctl` mechanism predates both the ANSI C (`void *`) type and the dynamic kernel memory allocator. Before SVR4, the only way a STREAMS driver or module could allocate memory dynamically was by using `allocb`.

The format of an M_COPYOUT message is one message block of type M_COPYOUT linked to one or more M_DATA blocks containing the data to copy to the user's buffer. The data buffer in the M_COPYOUT message contains a `copyreq` structure. All fields are the same as with the M_COPYIN message, except the `cq_addr` field contains the address of the user's buffer to which data will be copied.

M_COPYIN and M_COPYOUT messages are needed because drivers and modules do not have the necessary context to access user-level addresses. The stream head, on the other hand, does have the needed context, so it does the work on behalf of drivers and modules. When the stream head receives an M_COPYIN or M_COPYOUT message, it copies the requested data and responds by sending an M_IOCDATA message downstream.

The M_IOCDATA message is a high-priority message. Its format is one message block of type M_IOCDATA linked to zero or more M_DATA message blocks. In response to an M_COPYIN message, the M_DATA portion of the M_IOCDATA message contains the data copied in from the user's buffer. In response to an M_COPYOUT message, there are no M_DATA blocks present, but the M_IOCDATA message block contains an indication of whether or not the copy succeeded. The data buffer of the M_IOCDATA block contains a `copyresp` structure [see `copyresp(D4DK)`]:

```
struct copyresp {
        int      cp_cmd;       /* ioctl command */
        cred_t   *cp_cr;       /* user credentials */
        uint_t   cp_id;        /* sequence ID */
        caddr_t  cp_rval;      /* status of copy request */
        uint_t   cp_pad1;      /* reserved */
        int      cp_pad2;      /* reserved */
        mblk_t   *cp_private;  /* module/driver private data */
};
#define cp_uid cp_cr->cr_uid      /* user ID */
#define cp_gid cp_cr->cr_gid      /* group ID */
```

The stream head converts M_COPYIN and M_COPYOUT messages into M_IOCDATA messages by changing the type of the message, so it is absolutely necessary that the copyreq structure be properly formed and initialized. The iocblk, copyreq, and copyresp structures all overlay one another. In the copyresp structure, the first three fields are the same as in the other two structures. The cp_rval field is set to zero if the copy was successful, or to an error number if the copy failed. The cp_private field has the same value as it did in the copyreq structure, so drivers and modules can recover their saved state information.

With an I_STR ioctl, data are transferred between a single user buffer and STREAMS messages. Note that this constraint is not present with transparent ioctls. Any number of user buffers can be used, allowing arbitrarily complex data structures to be copied into and out of the kernel.

The user's transparent ioctl call will not return until the stream head receives either an M_IOCACK or M_IOCNAK message. Thus, drivers and modules terminate transparent ioctl processing by sending one of these messages upstream. The messages are used to indicate the return value and error status of the system call. During a transparent ioctl, no data can be copied to the user's buffer with the M_IOCACK message, as this is accomplished with the M_COPYOUT message.

Stream Head Control

Several messages are available to control the operation of the stream head. They isolate drivers and modules from the details of stream head processing, thereby enhancing portability. The messages only affect the stream in which they are sent, so each stream head in the system can be customized to meet the needs of its modules and driver.

Unfortunately, there is no way for drivers or modules to query the state of the stream head to identify the current set of options in effect. This detracts from the ability to mix and match arbitrary sets of modules and drivers, because one processing element might use an option that conflicts with another processing element.

The M_SETOPTS message is a normal-priority message that can be sent upstream to change some of the characteristics of the stream head. The format of the M_SETOPTS message is one message block of type M_SETOPTS with its data buffer containing an stroptions structure [see stroptions (D4DK)]:

```
struct stroptions {
       ulong_t     so_flags;    /* flags */
       short       so_readopt;  /* read modes */
       ushort_t    so_wroff;    /* write offset */
       long        so_minpsz;   /* min packet size */
       long        so_maxpsz;   /* max packet size */
       ulong_t     so_hiwat;    /* high-water mark */
       ulong_t     so_lowat;    /* low-water mark */
       uchar_t     so_band;     /* priority band */
};
```

The so_flags field indicates the options to set, as summarized in Table 9.9. The
other fields in the structure are ignored unless the corresponding flag is set in the
so_flags field.

Table 9.9. stroptions Flags

Flag	Description
SO_READOPT	Set read option (so_readopt).
SO_WROFF	Set write offset (so_wroff).
SO_MINPSZ	Set minimum read packet size (so_minpsz).
SO_MAXPSZ	Set maximum read packet size (so_maxpsz).
SO_HIWAT	Set read queue high-water mark (so_hiwat).
SO_LOWAT	Set read queue low-water mark (so_lowat).
SO_ALL	Set all above options.
SO_BAND	Change water marks of specified band (so_band).
SO_MREADON	Turn read notification on.
SO_MREADOFF	Turn read notification off.
SO_NDELON	Use old TTY semantics for O_NDELAY reads & writes.
SO_NDELOFF	Use STREAMS semantics for O_NDELAY reads & writes.
SO_ISTTY	The stream is acting as a terminal.
SO_ISNTTY	The stream is no longer acting as a terminal.
SO_TOSTOP	Stop on background writes to this stream.
SO_TONSTOP	Do not stop on background writes to this stream.
SO_DELIM	Turn on M_DATA delimiters.
SO_NODELIM	Turn off M_DATA delimiters.
SO_STRHOLD	Enable write message coalescing.

The SO_READOPT flag is used to set read options. There are six different read
options that can be set. The options are discussed in Section 3.7 since they can also
be set by an application with the I_SRDOPT ioctl command, but we will review
them here. Three affect how the stream head treats M_DATA messages read by an
application, and three affect how the stream head treats M_PROTO and M_PCPROTO
messages read by an application. None of the options affects the behavior of
getmsg(2).

RNORM, RMSGD, and RMSGN are mutually exclusive flags that affect the way
M_DATA messages are read. RNORM mode causes the stream head to treat M_DATA

messages as a byte stream. A single read can consume data from multiple messages. If a read only consumes part of the data in a message, however, the remaining portion is put back on the stream head read queue for the next read to retrieve. This is the default treatment of M_DATA messages.

RMSGD (message-discard) mode causes the stream head to read only one message at a time, and if only part of a message is read, the stream head discards the remainder. RMSGN (message-nondiscard) mode is like RMSGD in that it causes the stream head to read only one message at a time. It differs from RMSGD, however, because a message that is only partially read is put back on the stream head read queue to be retrieved by the next read.

RPROTNORM, RPROTDIS, and RPROTDAT are mutually exclusive flags that affect the way M_PROTO and M_PCPROTO messages are treated by the read system call. RPROTNORM mode, the default treatment of protocol messages, causes read to fail with errno set to EBADMSG when an M_PROTO or M_PCPROTO message is at the front of the stream head read queue.

RPROTDIS (protocol-discard) mode causes the stream head to discard an M_PROTO or M_PCPROTO message block but retain any M_DATA blocks that were linked to the protocol blocks when an application calls read. The contents of the M_DATA blocks are available to the application to be read.

RPROTDAT (protocol-data) mode causes the stream head to convert M_PROTO and M_PCPROTO message blocks to type M_DATA when an application reads from the stream. With both RPROTDIS and RPROTDAT modes, any resulting M_DATA blocks are read according to the read modes for M_DATA blocks.

When the SO_WROFF flag is set, the so_wroff field specifies a write offset that is to be used in the beginning of the first M_DATA message block in every data message (M_DATA, M_PROTO, and M_PCPROTO) generated by the stream head. The data are placed starting so_wroff bytes from the beginning of the message. This is useful for drivers and modules that want to add headers as part of the data in a message. If this option is enabled, however, the requesting driver or module cannot assume every data message received on the write side will contain the requested offset. If a data message originates from a module upstream instead of from the stream head, then the message probably will not have the requested offset. This can be detected by checking if the read pointer in the message is offset from the beginning of the data buffer by the expected amount.

When the SO_MINPSZ flag is set, the so_minpsz field contains the value to be set in the minimum packet size field (q_minpsz) of the stream head's read queue. Similarly, when the SO_MAXPSZ flag is set, the so_maxpsz field contains the new value for the maximum packet size field (q_maxpsz) of the stream head's read queue. These fields are advisory information for modules and drivers downstream from the stream head. The stream head write queue values cannot be modified, because they are not used for anything. On the write, the stream head uses the minimum and maximum packet sizes of the topmost driver or module in the stream.

If the SO_HIWAT flag is set, the so_hiwat field contains the new value for the high-water mark field (q_hiwat) of the stream head's read queue. If the SO_LOWAT flag is set, the so_lowat field contains the new value for the low-water mark field (q_lowat). Like the packet size parameters, the high-water and low-water marks for the stream head's write queue cannot be changed, because they are not used. If the SO_BAND flag is set in the so_flags field, then the water mark values apply to the band specified in the so_band field. If the SO_BAND flag is not set, then the change affects the normal message flow (band 0).

If the SO_MREADON flag is set, then the stream head will generate M_READ messages (described later in this section). The SO_MREADOFF flag will disable this feature. By default, M_READ generation is off.

If the SO_NDELON flag is set, then the stream head will support non-STREAMS semantics for no-delay reads and writes. If a stream is in no-delay mode [set in open (2) or fcntl (2) with the O_NDELAY flag], but not in non-blocking mode (set with the O_NONBLOCK flag), then a read will return zero if no data are available, and a write will block if the stream is flow-controlled. The SO_NDELOFF flag will disable this feature, causing the stream head to use default STREAMS semantics for no-delay reads and writes. These are the same as the nonblocking semantics for a stream. Nonblocking I/O is discussed in Section 3.4.

The SO_ISTTY flag enables the stream to act as a controlling terminal stream. If the process opening the device is a session leader without a controlling terminal, and the device is not yet allocated as a controlling terminal for another session, then the stream will act as the controlling terminal stream for the session. Drivers and modules can send an M_SETOPTS message with the SO_ISTTY flag set upstream from their open (D2DK) routine to enable controlling terminal allocation.

Once a stream is allocated as a session's controlling terminal stream, then signals generated from the stream can be sent to processes in the session's foreground process group. (To learn more about sessions, process groups, and job control, refer to Stevens [1992].) The SO_ISNTTY flag disables the stream from allocating a controlling terminal, which is the default.

The SO_TOSTOP flag will cause the stream head to stop any process that attempts to write to the stream from the background. If the SO_TONSTOP flag is set, the stream head will allow processes in the background to write to the stream. This is the default behavior.

If the SO_DELIM flag is set, then the stream will generate message delimiters, similar to Research UNIX Version 10 streams [Ritchie 1990]. The SO_NODELIM flag will shut off delimiters. (They are off by default.) When delimiters are on, the last message block generated by a write to a stream will be marked as delimited (the b_flag field will have the MSGDELIM flag set). Also, reads will fragment around delimited messages (see Section 9.3).

If the SO_STRHOLD flag is set, then the stream head will attempt to coalesce multiple writes into the same message block to improve performance. This is mainly used with terminal lines, where small writes are common. This option is off by default. Once turned on, there is no way to shut it off.

The way message coalescing works is that the stream head holds onto the message created when a process writes to a stream if enough free space remains in the message to hold the data from another write of the same size. Typically, this condition will be satisfied only by very small writes. If another write does not occur within a reasonable amount of time, the held message is sent downstream as is. Otherwise, if the next write is for an amount that will fit in the held message, the data are copied to the message instead of creating a new one. If the data will not fit, the held message is sent downstream and a new message is allocated for the current request.

A driver or module can place the stream in *hangup mode* by sending an M_HANGUP message upstream. The M_HANGUP message is a high-priority control message without any data. In hangup mode, processes can still read data from the stream, but when no more data are available, read returns zero. write, on the other hand, will fail with errno set to EIO when the stream is in hangup mode. ioctl and putmsg will fail with errno set to ENXIO. getmsg will return with zero-length control and data buffers.

The event that initiates hangup mode is up to the driver, but it usually has something to do with the device no longer being logically connected to the transmission medium. Terminal drivers, for example, will generate M_HANGUP messages when they sense loss of carrier.

If the stream is acting as a controlling terminal, the stream head will send a SIGHUP signal to the session leader and a SIGTSTP signal to the foreground process group when an M_HANGUP message is received. A process can clear the hangup state by reopening the device.

M_ERROR messages are high-priority messages used to put the stream into *error mode*. The M_ERROR message has two formats: a one-byte version and a two-byte version. If there is only one byte in the data buffer, then both the read and write errors at the stream head are set to the error number specified in the message. A value of zero is ignored. Other values are defined in <sys/errno.h>. All system calls except close(2) will fail with the specified error number.

If the data buffer contains two bytes, then the first byte contains the read error and the second byte contains the write error. This allows different error numbers to be set on the read and write sides, having the effect that read and getmsg will fail with the error specified by the read side and write and putmsg will fail with the error specified by the write side. The ioctl system call will fail if either error is set, giving precedence to the write-side error if both are set. So that one side can have its error number set without affecting the other side, the special value NOERROR may be substituted for the error number of the side that is to remain unchanged. A value of zero will clear the error for the specified side.

Regardless of whether the one-byte or two-byte format is used, when the stream head receives an M_ERROR message, it generates an M_FLUSH message to flush whichever sides are in error.

Drivers and modules can use M_SIG messages to send signals to processes in the foreground process group that has the stream as its controlling terminal stream. The format of an M_SIG message is one message block of type M_SIG containing one byte of data representing the signal to generate. Signal numbers are defined in <sys/signal.h>.

If the stream is not a controlling terminal stream, then the M_SIG message is ignored, except for the SIGPOLL signal. Recall from Section 3.4 that applications must register with the stream head to receive SIGPOLL. If a process uses the S_MSG flag with the I_SETSIG ioctl command, then when an M_SIG message containing SIGPOLL is received at the stream head, SIGPOLL is sent to the process, regardless of the controlling terminal status.

The M_SIG message is a normal-priority message. This means it is enqueued along with data messages and retains its relative position as it travels throughout the stream. When it reaches the stream head, the signal is not generated immediately if there are other messages already on the queue. The signal is generated only when the M_SIG message reaches the front of the queue.

The M_PCSIG message is a high-priority version of the M_SIG message. It can be used to send a signal ahead of any data already in the stream. When it arrives at the stream head, the signal is generated immediately; the message is not enqueued.

Device Control

There are six STREAMS messages that can be used to perform device control operations. The M_BREAK message is a normal-priority message (without data) that can be used to request a line break to be transmitted on a terminal line.

The M_DELAY message is used to request real-time delays on output devices. The format is one message block of type M_DELAY whose data buffer contains an integer indicating the length of the delay in clock ticks. Even though the M_DELAY message is a control message, it is treated as if it were a data message because it is usually closely associated with M_DATA messages.

For example, if a device is known to be slow, a module might follow a data message sent to the driver with an M_DELAY message. If the driver places all messages on its write queue before transmission and happens to flush its queue with the FLUSHDATA flag, it would be undesirable for the M_DELAY messages to be left on the queue, resulting in an unnecessary delay. For this reason, the FLUSHDATA flag also causes M_DELAY messages to be flushed.

The M_STOP message is a high-priority message (without data) that can be sent to a driver to request that output be suspended immediately. To restart output, an M_START message can be sent to the driver. The M_START message is also a high-priority message without any data.

The M_STOPI and M_STARTI messages are high-priority messages similar to the previous two, but they affect input instead of output.

Other Messages

The M_FLUSH message is a high-priority message used to clear messages from the queues in a stream. These messages can be generated either by the user as a result of an I_FLUSH or I_FLUSHBAND ioctl call, or by a driver or module in the stream. The format of the M_FLUSH message is one message block of type M_FLUSH with a data buffer of either one or two bytes.

The first byte in the data buffer contains flags indicating which queues to flush. The flags are FLUSHR for the read queues, FLUSHW for the write queues, FLUSHRW (the logical OR of FLUSHR and FLUSHW) for both queues, and FLUSHBAND for flushing a specific band. If FLUSHBAND is not set, the whole queue is flushed. If FLUSHBAND is set, then the data buffer contains a second byte that indicates the band to flush.

We briefly discuss how M_FLUSH messages work in a pipe in Section 3.6. Here, we will discuss how they are used in a device stream. When the stream head receives an M_FLUSH message, if FLUSHR is set, the stream head flushes its read queue and turns off the FLUSHR flag. If FLUSHW is set, the stream head sends the message down the write side of the stream. It is unnecessary for the stream head to flush its write queue, because it never enqueues messages there. If FLUSHW is not set, the stream head frees the message.

Drivers follow similar, but reversed, processing rules. When an M_FLUSH message is received by a driver, if FLUSHW is set, the driver will flush its write queue and turn FLUSHW off in the message. If FLUSHR is set, the driver will flush its read queue and send the message back up the read side of the stream. If FLUSHR is not set, the driver frees the message instead.

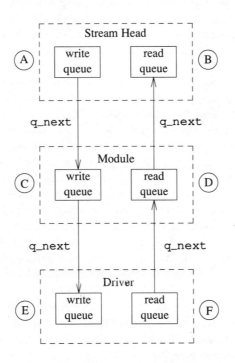

Fig. 9.10. Flushing in a Stream

Consider the stream shown in Figure 9.10. If the driver wanted to flush the read side of the stream, it would need to allocate an M_FLUSH message, set the FLUSHR flag in the first byte of the data buffer, and send the message up the read side of the stream. The order of queue flushing would be F, D, B.

If the driver wanted to flush the entire stream instead, it would set the first byte of the M_FLUSH message to FLUSHRW. Assuming that the driver and module flush their read queues before their write queues, the order of queue flushing would then be F, E, D, C, B, C, E. The reason for the duplicated queue flushing is that drivers and modules flush their queues independently of the side of the stream on which they received the M_FLUSH message. The first time the module sees the message, it flushes both of its queues. When the message arrives at the stream head, the stream head shuts off the FLUSHR flag and sends the message downstream, so the module and driver see it a second time, but only with the FLUSHW flag set this time.

Now consider how the module would flush the read side of the stream. The module would have to create an M_FLUSH message, set the first byte in the data buffer to FLUSHR, and send it down the write side of the stream. The driver will receive the message, flush its read queue, and send the message up the read side of the stream. Thus, the order of queue flushing is F, D, B.

Similarly, to flush only the write side of the stream, the module will send an M_FLUSH message with FLUSHW set upstream. The stream head will send the message back downstream. The order of queue flushing will be C, E. The module cannot just send the message down the write side of the stream, because the module cannot make any assumptions about its position in the stream. Nor can the module look upstream at its neighboring queue and try to infer its owner.

When drivers and modules need to communicate among themselves, they can use M_CTL messages. An M_CTL message is a normal-priority message whose format is undefined. It is up to the drivers and modules using the message to agree on its content. The TTY line discipline module (LDTERM), for example, exchanges M_CTL messages with the stream's driver to negotiate the amount of canonical processing LDTERM needs to perform on the data passing through it.

M_READ messages are generated by the stream head if requested by a previous M_SETOPTS message. M_READ messages are generated when there are no data on the stream head read queue and a process issues a read system call. The format of the message is one message block of type M_READ whose data buffer contains a long that indicates the number of bytes that the process is trying to read. M_READ messages are used in the implementation of raw mode with STREAMS-based terminals [see termio(7)]. M_READ messages are not generated by getmsg system calls.

M_PASSFP messages are sent between stream heads for the purpose of passing file descriptors between processes. They are generated by the I_SENDFD ioctl and received by the I_RECVFD ioctl. These messages do not pass through the stream, although in future releases they might. Regardless, drivers and modules should ignore this message type.

M_PASSFP messages can only be sent on streams that have stream heads at both ends, as in the case of pipes and loopback drivers. The format of the M_PASSFP message is one message block of type M_PASSFP with a data buffer containing an strrecvfd structure, defined in <sys/stropts.h>.

Finally, the M_RSE and M_PCRSE messages are used by an AT&T product called the Remote STREAMS Environment (RSE). The RSE product supports a STREAMS environment on peripheral boards, allowing drivers and modules to be migrated from the host computer to peripheral hardware. A compromise was made to minimize the impact of the RSE product on the STREAMS mechanism, so special messages were defined solely for its use. The M_PCRSE message type is a high-priority version of the M_RSE message type. Drivers and modules should ignore these messages, too.

Summary

We have introduced the kernel environment, and the STREAMS environment in particular, in preparation for studying the next three chapters. The major DDI/DKI routines and data structures necessary for writing STREAMS drivers and modules have been described. The two most important data structures in the STREAMS subsystem are the STREAMS queue and the STREAMS message. The queue provides an interface between a driver or module and the rest of the stream. Since all communication within a stream occurs through message passing, we also summarized the use of each STREAMS message type.

Exercises

9.1 Should the type of a message be stored in the message block or the data block? Explain why.

9.2 Explain why flow control still works when modules that do not recognize priority bands are mixed with those that do.

9.3 What could happen if a service procedure places a high-priority message back on its own queue?

9.4 Explain how you would flush the entire stream from within a module.

Bibliographic Notes

Ritchie and Thompson [1974] present the original description of the UNIX system. Thompson [1978] describes the early implementation of the UNIX system. These two papers deal with the research version of the UNIX system. Bach [1986] discusses the algorithms and data structures constituting the System V Release 2 version of the UNIX system, with some information from SVR3.

Ritchie [1984, 1990] describes the research version of STREAMS. More details about the System V STREAMS mechanism can be found in the *UNIX System V Release 4 Programmer's Guide: STREAMS* [USL 1990b].

Rago [1989] describes the changes made to the STREAMS subsystem to support multiple bands of data flow. Williams [1989] describes the implementation of

POSIX job control within the STREAMS TTY subsystem.

10
STREAMS
Drivers

This chapter describes how to write STREAMS drivers. It assumes the reader is familiar with the material presented in Chapter 9. After discussing the system entry points into drivers, we introduce the Data Link Provider Interface (DLPI), a service interface for drivers implementing data link layer services. The remainder of the chapter focuses on the design of a simple Ethernet driver.

10.1 INTRODUCTION

The primary task of a hardware driver is to copy data between the kernel and an I/O device. A software driver is like a hardware driver, but instead of interacting with an I/O device, a software driver provides a service to applications. Some examples include a pseudo-terminal driver that enables one process to present a terminal-like interface to another process, a loopback driver that makes the same data written to it available for reading, and an administrative driver that provides an interface for processes to obtain information about, and control the operation of, hardware and other software.

System V Release 4 contains many software drivers. The PTS and PTM drivers provide pseudo-terminal functionality. The LLCLOOP driver is a link-level loopback driver, and the TICLTS, TICOTS, and TICOTSORD drivers are transport-level loopback drivers. The LOG driver is an administrative driver that allows processes to obtain log messages. The SAD driver is an administrative driver that provides an administrative interface to the STREAMS subsystem.

In the UNIX operating system, drivers are accessed as files. They have nodes in the file system that are either of type *block special* or of type *character special*. STREAMS drivers are always accessed through character-special files. For example, access to a TCP network might be through the file /dev/tcp:

```
$ ls -l /dev/tcp
crw-rw-rw-   1 root    sys      9, 48 Mar  1 23:47 /dev/tcp
$
```

Access to a driver is gained by opening its device-special file. When a STREAMS driver is opened, a stream is created (see Figure 10.1) and processes can access the stream through file descriptors. During the `open(2)` system call, the driver is assigned a pair of queues, placed at the end (tail) of the stream, and is notified of the `open` through the invocation of the driver's `open(D2DK)` routine. There is one stream per minor device, so if the driver is already open, another stream is not created when the same minor device is opened again.

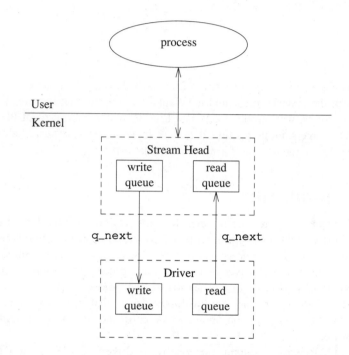

Fig. 10.1. Opening a STREAMS Driver

Once a driver is open, processes can write data to the device by writing to the stream (using its file descriptor). The stream head will copy data from the user's buffer into STREAMS messages and pass them to the driver. The driver will process the messages and transmit data destined for the device to its I/O board. If the device generates input, the driver will copy data from the device into STREAMS messages and send the messages upstream, where they can be obtained by users reading from the stream.

When the last process closes its file descriptor referring to a stream, the driver's `close(D2DK)` routine is called and the stream is dismantled. Thus, the driver's close routine is only called when the last reference to the stream is given up.

Every driver in the system has a prefix [see `prefix(D1DK)`] that is used to create unique text and data symbols. By convention, driver entry points and global variables include this prefix at the beginning of their names. This helps simplify the process of configuring drivers into the operating system.

10.2 DRIVER ENTRY POINTS

The driver entry points are defined by the DDI/DKI and are called at well-defined points during the execution of the operating system. Seven of these interfaces are of interest to STREAMS drivers and will be discussed in this section. The first two deal with driver initialization. They are the `init(D2D)` and `start(D2DK)` entry points:

```
void prefixinit(void);
void prefixstart(void);
```

The init routine is called at system initialization time, before system services are available. Interrupts are disabled during its execution. Drivers use init routines to allocate memory (one of the few services available at this point) and to initialize the I/O devices they control. The init routines run without user context, so they cannot call any routines that sleep.

The start entry point is also used for driver initialization, but is called after system services are available, and with interrupts enabled. Like the init routine, the start routine runs without user context. Both entry points are optional.

Note that the init routine is in the DDI, but the start routine is in both the DDI and the DKI. This means that drivers that use the init entry point might have to perform initialization another way on different architectures. If drivers confine their initialization to the start routine, then fewer changes will be needed. In reality, however, changes will almost always be needed when porting drivers to computers with different architectures. Characteristics that might differ across architectures include I/O bus protocols, data-transfer methods, I/O board identification methods, and interrupt priority levels.

As one might expect, the entry point for the driver's interrupt handler is only governed by the DDI [see `intr(D2D)`]. In fact, the naming convention can be different across architectures. For example, in the AT&T 3B2 architecture, the interrupt handler suffix is `int`, but in the Intel 80x86 architecture, the suffix is `intr`.

The synopsis for the interrupt handler is

```
void prefixintr(int ivec);
```

where `ivec` is an *implementation-dependent* integer used to identify the source of the interrupt. `ivec` is usually used (either directly or indirectly) to index a driver's table of data structures that describe the hardware.

In SVR4 on the Intel 80x86 architecture, the configuration software defines symbols consisting of the driver's prefix, followed by an underscore, the board unit number, and the string `_VECT`. The board unit number is a sequential identifier, starting at 0, for each board of the same type in the system. The value of the symbol is the index into the interrupt vector, but drivers can only use it to match up interrupts with private data structures. Therefore, each driver defines a table of data structures that represents its I/O hardware, one entry per I/O board, and stores the interrupt vector number for each board in the corresponding table entry. See the *Integrated Software Development Guide* [AT&T 1990e] for more details.

There are three steps every interrupt handler takes:

1. Determine the reason for the interrupt. This is usually done by reading a register or memory location on the I/O board causing the interrupt.
2. Service the interrupt. This can involve anything from copying data and acknowledging the interrupt to merely incrementing a counter to record the event.
3. Wake up any processes sleeping on the event that just occurred.

Interrupt handlers do not run in the context of user processes, so they cannot access any state information associated with a particular process. Because interrupt handlers are called with the processor priority level elevated, they prevent interrupts of the same or lower priority from interrupting the CPU. Interrupt handlers should never lower the processor priority level below that corresponding to their interrupt priority level. Since interrupts are blocked, interrupt-handler processing should be minimal to decrease the performance degradation that can occur from deferring other interrupts.

When a process opens a character-special file, the driver identified by the file's major device number is notified by a call to its open entry point:

```
#include <sys/types.h>
#include <sys/file.h>
#include <sys/stream.h>
#include <sys/errno.h>
#include <sys/cred.h>
#include <sys/ddi.h>

int prefixopen(queue_t *q, dev_t *devp, int oflag, int sflag,
    cred_t *crp);
```

q is a pointer to the driver's read queue, devp is a pointer to the device number, oflag is a bitmask of flags associated with the open, sflag provides an indication of the type of STREAMS open to perform, and crp is a pointer to the process's credentials (user ID, group ID, etc.). On success, the driver open routine returns 0. On failure, it returns an error number.

The driver open flags, which are summarized in Table 10.1, are derived from the flags used by the application in the open system call. If the device is opened for both reading and writing, then FREAD and FWRITE will be set in oflag. If an application opening the device wants to use System V no-delay semantics, FNDELAY will be set. On the other hand, if the application wants the more recent POSIX nonblocking semantics, FNONBLOCK will be set. For most streams except terminals and pipes the sematics are identical (see Sections 3.4 and 3.6).

FEXCL is a flag originally intended only for use with the creation of regular files, but it has been usurped by driver writers for so long that it found its way into the DDI/DKI. Drivers can interpret it any way they want. Most just ignore it, but those that use it typically interpret it to mean the application wants exclusive access to the device.

Table 10.1. Driver Open Flags

Flag	Description
FREAD	Open the device for reading.
FWRITE	Open the device for writing.
FNONBLOCK	Open the device without blocking (POSIX).
FNDELAY	Open the device without blocking (System V).
FEXCL	Driver-dependent flag.

The STREAMS flag, sflag, can take on one of three values. It is usually zero for a normal device open. If a STREAMS module is being opened, it will be set to MODOPEN. Drivers should never be called with sflag set to MODOPEN. (Note that a driver can also be configured as a module, in which case sflag will normally be 0 when the driver is being called as a driver. When the driver is being called as a module, however, sflag will be set to MODOPEN. Chapter 13 illustrates a driver that is also a module.) The third value, CLONEOPEN, is used to request that the driver select an unused minor device. Clone opens are discussed shortly.

Opens of the same minor device are serialized. If more than one process attempts to open the same device at the same time, one will proceed while the others wait until the first one completes. When the driver's open routine is called, all interrupts from STREAMS devices are blocked. The open routine has user context, so drivers can sleep, but they must either do so at an uninterruptible priority or set PCATCH in the call to sleep.

Driver open routines usually allocate and initialize private data structures associated with the minor device being opened. Since the minor device number is obtained from the file node, which is administered independently from the driver's data structures, drivers should always validate the minor device number before using it. An administrator could make a node with a minor device number that, when used by a driver to index a table of data structures, references a memory location past the end of the table.

When a driver's open routine is called for a minor device that is already open, the driver usually has very little to do since its data structures were initialized during the first open. Most implementations of STREAMS neglect to block interrupts from STREAMS devices on these successive opens. Thus, driver writers need to raise the processor priority level themselves if they need to serialize access to data structures between interrupt-level code and successive opens.

When no more references to the device exist, the driver's close routine is called:

```
#include <sys/types.h>
#include <sys/file.h>
#include <sys/stream.h>
#include <sys/cred.h>
#include <sys/ddi.h>

int prefixclose(queue_t *q, int flag, cred_t *crp);
```

q is a pointer to the driver's read queue, `flag` is a bitmask of flags indicating the file status, and `crp` is a pointer to the process's credentials.

The flags that can be present are listed in Table 10.1. As with the open entry point, if `FNDELAY` or `FNONBLOCK` is set, then the driver should avoid blocking, if possible, when closing the device. Note that the flags present when the driver is closed might be different than those present when the driver was opened. This is because of the many-to-one relationship of file table entries to the device (see Bach [1986] or Stevens [1992] for more details), as well as the ability of processes to toggle nonblocking mode on and off through `fcntl(2)`.

Closing the device involves undoing the work done in the open routine. Examples include cleaning up data structures, freeing memory, and canceling pending `timeout` and `bufcall` routines. It is easier to cancel pending `timeout` and `bufcall` routines in the close routine than to let them run and try to determine for themselves if the device is still active.

Like the open routine, the close routine is called with interrupts from all STREAMS devices blocked. If messages remain on the driver's queues when the close routine returns, the system will free the messages (any messages that the driver had placed on private lists must be freed by the driver). After a close routine returns, the queues associated with the minor device closed can no longer be accessed by the driver. Chances are that the memory used for the queues will be reused for some other system data structure since the STREAMS subsystem allocates its queues from the dynamic kernel memory allocator.

The close routine has user context and can sleep, but should do so only at an uninterruptible priority or with the `PCATCH` flag set to avoid longjumps. The close routine should return zero on success or an error number on failure, even though the STREAMS subsystem currently ignores the return value.

The last two driver interfaces are the ones used to transfer data. They are the put procedure [see `put(D2DK)`] and the service procedure [see `srv(D2DK)`]. The synopsis for the put procedure is

```
#include <sys/types.h>
#include <sys/stream.h>
#include <sys/stropts.h>

int prefixput(queue_t *q, mblk_t *mp);
```

where q is a pointer to the driver's queue, and mp is a pointer to the message being passed to the driver. On the write side, the put procedure is mandatory. On the read side, it is optional because there is no processing element passing the message to the driver—the driver is generating the message itself, usually from its interrupt handler.

When a message is passed to a driver, the driver can either process it or not. In either case, the driver can do one of three things with it:

1. Free the message.
2. Route the message back upstream (as with an `M_FLUSH` message).
3. Enqueue the message for processing by the driver's service procedure.

Put procedures do not have user context, so they cannot call routines that sleep.

If a driver writer wants to perform all write-side message processing in the service procedure, then `putq`(D2DK) can be specified as the put procedure in the driver's write-side `qinit` structure. Usually, however, flush processing is done in the put procedure to minimize the time needed to flush a stream.

The canonical flushing algorithm for a driver that does not distinguish individual message bands is shown below. Assume q is a pointer to the write queue and mp is a pointer to the `M_FLUSH` message.

```
if (*mp->b_rptr & FLUSHW) {
    flushq(q, FLUSHDATA);
    *mp->b_rptr &= ~FLUSHW;
}
if (*mp->b_rptr & FLUSHR) {
    flushq(RD(q), FLUSHDATA);
    qreply(q, mp);
} else {
    freemsg(mp);
}
```

Recall the way drivers help in flushing the entire stream. If the FLUSHR flag is on, then the message is sent back up the read side of the stream instead of being freed. If the driver does not ensure that FLUSHW is shut off before sending the message upstream, then the `M_FLUSH` message will loop through the stream infinitely.

If a driver maintains the notion of different bands of data flow, then the flushing algorithm needs to change to honor the FLUSHBAND flag. The new algorithm becomes

```
if (*mp->b_rptr & FLUSHW) {
    if (*mp->b_rptr & FLUSHBAND)
        flushband(q, FLUSHDATA, *(mp->b_rptr + 1));
    else
        flushq(q, FLUSHDATA);
    *mp->b_rptr &= ~FLUSHW;
}
if (*mp->b_rptr & FLUSHR) {
    if (*mp->b_rptr & FLUSHBAND)
        flushband(RD(q), FLUSHDATA, *(mp->b_rptr + 1));
    else
        flushq(RD(q), FLUSHDATA);
    qreply(q, mp);
} else {
    freemsg(mp);
}
```

In this case, the priority band to be flushed is contained in the second byte of the `M_FLUSH` message's data buffer.

There are some special rules drivers must follow to operate properly in the STREAMS framework. First, any unrecognized messages must be freed by the driver. This prevents memory from being lost if a message is passed to a driver that never intended to process that message. It also allows for new message types to be added to the STREAMS mechanism without breaking existing drivers.

`M_IOCTL` messages are an exception to this rule. They must always be

answered. If a driver receives an M_IOCTL message and the ioctl command is
not supported by the driver, then the driver must convert the message into an
M_IOCNAK message and send it back upstream. This ensures that processes do not
block infinitely while waiting for the ioctl to complete.

The return value from the put procedure is an integer, but it is ignored. This is
an artifact of the original implementation. The synopsis for the service procedure is

```
#include <sys/types.h>
#include <sys/stream.h>
#include <sys/stropts.h>

int prefixsrv(queue_t *q);
```

where q is a pointer to the queue associated with the service procedure. Service procedures are optional. They are useful for recovering from buffer allocation failures,
for implementing flow control, and for getting off the interrupt stack as discussed in
Section 9.2.

When a service procedure runs, it normally processes all the messages on its
queue until the queue is empty. A service procedure is scheduled to run by placing a
message on its queue. If a service procedure returns without emptying its queue, the
remaining messages will be stranded until another message is enqueued. Thus, if a
service procedure needs to return with messages still on the queue, the service procedure needs to ensure it will be rescheduled somehow.

STREAMS flow control is one mechanism that provides this rescheduling. By
using canput or bcanput, a service procedure will cause itself to be scheduled for
backenabling if the queue to which it is sending messages becomes full. In this case,
canput or bcanput will fail and the service procedure can put the message back
on its queue and return without having to worry about rescheduling itself.

The canonical service procedure algorithm for a driver's read side is shown
below.

```
int
prefixrsrv(queue_t *q)
{
        mblk_t *mp;

        while ((mp = getq(q)) != NULL) {
            if ((mp->b_datap->db_type >= QPCTL) ||
              canput(q->q_next)) {
                /* process message */
                :
                :
                putnext(q, mp);
            } else {
                putbq(q, mp);
                break;
            }
        }
        return(0);
}
```

Note the test for flow control is preceded by the test

```
(mp->b_datap->db_type >= QPCTL).
```

This supports the convention that high-priority messages are unaffected by flow control. Drivers and modules help maintain this convention by ignoring flow control
when passing high-priority messages along in a stream.

If the driver supports priority bands, then the above algorithm becomes

```
int
prefixrsrv(queue_t *q)
{
        mblk_t *mp;

        while ((mp = getq(q)) != NULL) {
            if ((mp->b_datap->db_type >= QPCTL) ||
              bcanput(q->q_next, mp->b_band)) {
                /* process message */
                   :
                   :
                putnext(q, mp);
            } else {
                putbq(q, mp);
                break;
            }
        }
        return(0);
}
```

Note that the only difference is the replacement of `canput` with `bcanput`.

Each priority band has independent flow-control parameters. Even though one
band is technically unaffected by another's flow control, the structure of the canonical service procedure algorithm causes flow control in a given band to block lower
bands as well. Consider what happens when band n flow-controls: `bcanput` will
fail, the service procedure will place the message back on the front of the queue, and
the service procedure will return. If any messages with priority bands less than n are
on the queue, they will not be processed by the service procedure until all of the messages from band n have been removed. Applications trying to send messages in band
n to the queue will be blocked, but because the flow-control parameters are independent, applications can still pass messages in other bands to the queue. The messages
will remain on the queue, however, if a higher-priority band is flow-controlled.

For the write side, the driver's service procedure will be entirely different, doing
whatever is necessary to interact with the I/O hardware instead. Obviously, the
write-side routines will not call `putnext` with a pointer to the write queue, because
the driver is at the end of the stream.

There are other reasons besides flow control that a service procedure might have
to return prematurely. For example, if a service procedure encounters a buffer allocation failure or some other kind of transient error, `bufcall` or `timeout` can be
used to schedule a function to run later on to enable the queue, thereby allowing the
current invocation of the service procedure to return with messages still on its queue.

Like put procedures, service procedures run without user context, so they cannot
call any functions that sleep. The same rules about unknown message types and

unknown `ioctl` commands that apply to put procedures also apply to service procedures. In addition, service procedures must never place high-priority messages back on their queues. This will result in an infinite loop because a high-priority message placed on a queue always causes the queue's service procedure to be scheduled to run.

Clone Opens

The clone open facility is an optional feature a driver can provide to remove the need for applications to search for unused devices. The driver does the work for the application, removing race conditions and simplifying user-level code.

There are two ways clone opens can be implemented. The first way is with the help of a special driver, called the *clone driver*. Applications can open the clone driver, which will call the real driver with `sflag` set to `CLONEOPEN`. This tells the driver to select an unused minor device. Before returning, the driver updates the device number pointed to by `devp` to contain the newly selected device, as in

```
*devp = makedevice(getemajor(*devp), selected_minor);
```

The clone driver identifies the real driver to call by looking at the clone's minor device number. A clone node's major number is equal to the clone driver's major number and its minor number is equal to the real driver's major number. For example, if the major device number for the clone driver is 9 and the major device number for TCP is 48, typical nodes might look like:

```
$ ls -l /dev/tcp /dev/tcp00[0-2]
crw-rw-rw-  1 root    sys     9, 48 Mar   1 23:47 /dev/tcp
crw-rw-rw-  1 root    sys    48,  0 Mar   1 23:47 /dev/tcp000
crw-rw-rw-  1 root    sys    48,  1 Mar   1 23:47 /dev/tcp001
crw-rw-rw-  1 root    sys    48,  2 Mar   1 23:47 /dev/tcp002
$
```

Here, /dev/tcp000, /dev/tcp001, and /dev/tcp002 are normal TCP device nodes used for applications like cu (1) (see Example 6.4.1), and /dev/tcp is the clone device node that provides access to the TCP driver.

The second way a driver can implement clone opens is to reserve a special minor device such as 0, for example, as the driver's clone entry point. The driver can then check if the minor device being opened matches its minor number used for cloning. If so, the driver knows to select an unused minor device. In this case, the clone node appears with a major device number equal to that of the real driver.

The `CLONEOPEN` flag is not used in this type of clone open, because the driver knows which minor number it is using for cloning. The previous method, however, does not require the driver to reserve a special minor device number.

Drivers were given the ability to change the entire device number so that systems that retained small device numbers could support more than 256 minor devices per driver by extending the minor devices across more than one major device number. These systems could be built to retain binary compatibility with older releases, while drivers could take advantage of the clone facility to support large numbers of minor devices.

10.3 THE DATA LINK PROVIDER INTERFACE

The Ethernet driver examined in the next section provides connectionless data link service and conforms to the Data Link Provider Interface (DLPI). The DLPI specification is a STREAMS service interface designed by AT&T to implement the OSI data link layer interface. The DLPI provides protocol-independent access to the data link layer. Available directly from Unix International, the DLPI specification is also documented in *STREAMS Modules and Drivers* [USL 1992a].

The DLPI is not a protocol specification. It is an interface to the service provided by the data link layer. The interface consists of a set of primitives and a set of rules for using the primitives. The primitives are implemented as STREAMS messages.

The advantage of using the DLPI is that data link providers can be replaced without replacing the applications using the data link service, as long as both the consumer and the provider conform to the DLPI. Consumers can be user-level applications, or they can be kernel-level STREAMS modules or multiplexors.

The DLPI defines support for plain connectionless data link service, acknowledged connectionless data link service (for in-sequence delivery of datagrams), and connection-oriented data link service. Although the current version of the DLPI (Version 2.0.0) was published in 1991, most data link provider implementations use older versions. We describe only Version 2.0.0 in this chapter.

Recall from Section 3.5 that consumers of a service interface can generate request primitives, while providers can generate both response primitives and event primitives. These three types of primitives are further classified according to their uses.

There are six classes of primitives in the DLPI. Local management primitives enable the consumer to query and control the provider. Connection-establishment primitives enable the consumer to create a virtual circuit. Data-transfer primitives enable the consumer to communicate with a peer DLPI consumer. Reset primitives allow a data link connection to be resynchronized. Connection-release primitives allow the consumer to tear down a virtual circuit. Test primitives allow the consumer to test the operation of the provider. Table 10.2 summarizes the subset of DLPI primitives we will be dealing with in this chapter.

To use a DLPI-conforming driver, an application must first open the driver and *attach* the stream to the physical medium. Two styles of drivers are supported. The first assigns the physical point of attachment (PPA) implicitly when the device is opened. The second requires explicit use of service interface attach primitives to select the PPA. This is often used when there is more than one physical communication channel supported by the device and an application is required to choose the

Table 10.2. Subset of DLPI Primitives

Primitive	Type	Class	Description
DL_INFO_REQ	Request	Local Mgmt.	Get information.
DL_INFO_ACK	Response	Local Mgmt.	Return information.
DL_ERROR_ACK	Response	Local Mgmt.	Request failed.
DL_BIND_REQ	Request	Local Mgmt.	Bind an address.
DL_BIND_ACK	Response	Local Mgmt.	Bind successful.
DL_UNBIND_REQ	Request	Local Mgmt.	Unbind an address.
DL_OK_ACK	Response	Local Mgmt.	Operation successful.
DL_UNITDATA_REQ	Request	Data Transfer	Transmit data.
DL_UNITDATA_IND	Event	Data Transfer	Data received.
DL_UDERROR_IND	Event	Data Transfer	Transmission failed.

channel explicitly through service interface primitives. The driver described in this chapter supports the implicit style of PPA assignment because there is only one physical channel of communication in an Ethernet.

Each consumer of the DLPI is assigned an abstraction called a *data link service access point* (DLSAP) to represent the consumer's point of communication with the data link provider. The DLSAP represents a communication endpoint, except that the DLPI allows providers to map a DLSAP to several communication endpoints (streams).

A consumer identifies its DLSAP by a *DLSAP address*. Each communication endpoint has its own DLSAP address. The address format depends on the protocol used, but the DLSAP address is composed of two parts: a SAP identifier and the physical address associated with the PPA.

The connectionless DLPI service only supports local management primitives, test primitives, and data-transfer primitives. Each primitive is implemented as a STREAMS message. Normal primitives are implemented as M_PROTO messages. High-priority interface acknowledgement primitives are implemented as M_PCPROTO messages. The first four bytes in each message's data buffer identify the interface primitive it represents.

The first local management primitive is the information request (see Figure 10.2). The consumer generates a DL_INFO_REQ message, and the provider responds with a DL_INFO_ACK message. The response includes information about the provider such as state, address, and service parameters. The DL_INFO_REQ message is implemented as an M_PCPROTO message containing a dl_info_req_t structure:

```
typedef struct {
    ulong_t dl_primitive;          /* DL_INFO_REQ */
} dl_info_req_t;
```

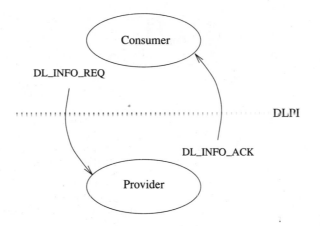

Fig. 10.2. Information Request

The `DL_INFO_ACK` message is implemented as an `M_PCPROTO` message containing a `dl_info_ack_t` structure:

```
typedef struct {
    ulong_t dl_primitive;          /* DL_INFO_ACK */
    ulong_t dl_max_sdu;            /* maximum service  */
                                   /* data unit size */
    ulong_t dl_min_sdu;            /* minimum service */
                                   /* data unit size */
    ulong_t dl_addr_length;        /* total DLSAP */
                                   /* address length */
    ulong_t dl_mac_type;           /* type of medium */
    ulong_t dl_reserved;           /* for future use */
    ulong_t dl_current_state;      /* DLPI state */
    long    dl_sap_length;         /* length of SAP */
                                   /* address component */
    ulong_t dl_service_mode;       /* type of service */
    ulong_t dl_qos_length;         /* quality-of-service */
                                   /* parameters length*/
    ulong_t dl_qos_offset;         /* offset in message */
    ulong_t dl_qos_range_length;   /* size of QOS param */
                                   /* ranges supported */
    ulong_t dl_qos_range_offset;   /* offset in message */
    ulong_t dl_provider_style;     /* PPA type supported */
    ulong_t dl_addr_offset;        /* offset of address */
    ulong_t dl_version;            /* current version */
                                   /* of DLPI */
    ulong_t dl_brdcst_addr_length; /* broadcast address */
                                   /* length */
    ulong_t dl_brdcst_addr_offset; /* offset in message */
    ulong_t dl_growth;             /* for future use */
} dl_info_ack_t;
```

The next local management primitive is the bind request (see Figure 10.3). The

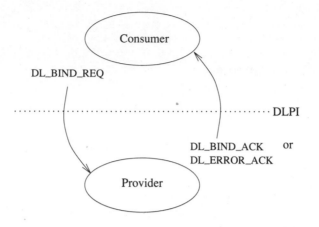

Fig. 10.3. Bind Request

consumer generates a DL_BIND_REQ message. The bind request associates a
DLSAP with a communication endpoint and assigns a DLSAP address to the mapping. The DL_BIND_REQ is implemented as an M_PROTO message containing a
dl_bind_req_t structure:

```
typedef struct {
    ulong_t  dl_primitive;       /* DL_BIND_REQ */
    ulong_t  dl_sap;             /* DLSAP identifier */
    ulong_t  dl_max_conind;      /* maximum connect */
                                 /* queue size */
    ushort_t dl_service_mode;    /* connectionless or */
                                 /* connection-oriented */
    ushort_t dl_conn_mgmt;       /* DLSAP to receive */
                                 /* connect requests */
    ulong_t  dl_xidtest_flg;     /* XID and TEST */
                                 /* handling requested */
} dl_bind_req_t;
```

If the bind request is successful, the provider responds with a DL_BIND_ACK
message. It is implemented as an M_PCPROTO message containing a
dl_bind_ack_t structure:

```
typedef struct {
    ulong_t dl_primitive;        /* DL_BIND_ACK */
    ulong_t dl_sap;              /* DLSAP identifier */
    ulong_t dl_addr_length;      /* total address length */
    ulong_t dl_addr_offset;      /* address location */
                                 /* in message */
    ulong_t dl_max_conind;       /* maximum connect */
                                 /* queue size */
    ulong_t dl_xidtest_flg;      /* XID and TEST */
                                 /* handling supported */
} dl_bind_ack_t;
```

If unsuccessful, the provider responds with a DL_ERROR_ACK message. It is made up of an M_PCPROTO message containing a dl_error_ack_t structure:

```
typedef struct {
    ulong_t dl_primitive;          /* DL_ERROR_ACK */
    ulong_t dl_error_primitive;    /* primitive that */
                                   /* failed */
    ulong_t dl_errno;              /* DLPI error */
    ulong_t dl_unix_errno;         /* UNIX error */
} dl_error_ack_t;
```

The last local management primitive supported by the driver is the unbind request (see Figure 10.4). The consumer generates a DL_UNBIND_REQ message and, if successful, the provider responds with a DL_OK_ACK message. If unsuccessful, the provider responds with a DL_ERROR_ACK message. The unbind request breaks the association between a DLSAP, the communication endpoint, and the DLSAP address.

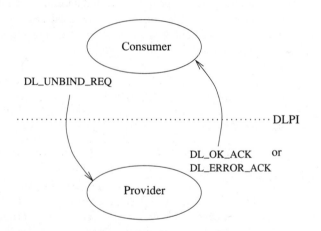

Fig. 10.4. Unbind Request

The format of a DL_UNBIND_REQ message is an M_PROTO message containing a dl_unbind_req_t structure:

```
typedef struct {
    ulong_t dl_primitive;          /* DL_UNBIND_REQ */
} dl_unbind_req_t;
```

The format of the DL_OK_ACK acknowledgement is an M_PCPROTO message containing a dl_ok_ack_t structure:

```
typedef struct {
    ulong_t dl_primitive;             /* DL_OK_ACK */
    ulong_t dl_correct_primitive;     /* primitive */
                                      /* acknowledged */
} dl_ok_ack_t;
```

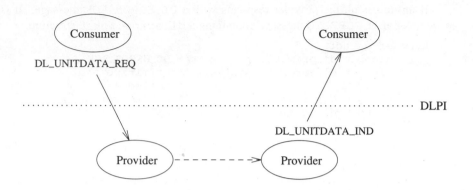

Fig. 10.5. Unitdata Request

There is one data-transfer request primitive, called a unitdata request (see Figure 10.5). It is used to transmit a packet (called a data link service data unit—DLSDU). The unitdata request is implemented as an M_PROTO message containing a dl_unitdata_req_t structure:

```
typedef struct {
     ulong_t dl_primitive;        /* DL_UNITDATA_REQ */
     ulong_t dl_dest_addr_length; /* destination address */
                                  /* length */
     ulong_t dl_dest_addr_offset; /* address location */
                                  /* in message */
     dl_priority_t dl_priority;   /* priority range */
                                  /* of DLSDU */
} dl_unitdata_req_t;
```

The consumer generates a DL_UNITDATA_REQ message. This results in the provider transmitting a packet to its peer. The peer provider sends a DL_UNITDATA_IND message to its consumer. The format of a unitdata indication is an M_PROTO message containing a dl_unitdata_ind_t structure:

```
typedef struct {
     ulong_t dl_primitive;        /* DL_UNITDATA_IND */
     ulong_t dl_dest_addr_length; /* destination address */
                                  /* length */
     ulong_t dl_dest_addr_offset; /* location in message */
     ulong_t dl_src_addr_length;  /* source address length */
     ulong_t dl_src_addr_offset;  /* location in message */
     ulong_t dl_group_address;    /* destination is */
                                  /* multicast */
} dl_unitdata_ind_t;
```

If the packet transmission fails, the provider might send a DL_UDERROR_IND message to the consumer sending the packet (see Figure 10.6), although this is not guaranteed. The error indication is implemented as either an M_PROTO message or an M_PCPROTO message containing a dl_uderror_ind_t structure:

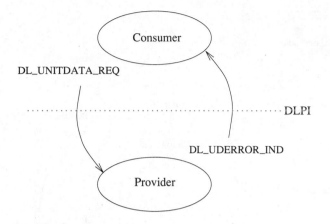

Fig. 10.6. Unitdata Error Indication

```
typedef struct {
    ulong_t dl_primitive;        /* DL_UDERROR_IND */
    ulong_t dl_dest_addr_length; /* destination address */
                                 /* length */
    ulong_t dl_dest_addr_offset; /* location in message */
    ulong_t dl_unix_errno;       /* UNIX error */
    ulong_t dl_errno;            /* DLPI error */
} dl_uderror_ind_t;
```

Recall that a service interface specification not only includes a description of the primitives that pass across the interface, but also includes information about when each primitive may be generated. The state diagram describing the DLPI connectionless service is shown in Figure 10.7. Given that the sample driver in this chapter implicitly assigns a PPA when the driver is opened, the initial state of the DLSAP is `DL_UNBOUND`.

The sample driver actually implements a simpler version of the state diagram by compressing four states into two. This is possible because the driver does not need to delay to perform bind or unbind operations, effectively making the state transitions immediate. The simplified state diagram, showing only requests and successful transitions, is shown in Figure 10.8.

The DLPI specification defines many more primitives and associated states, most of which are used with the connection-oriented mode of service.

10.4 ETHERNET DRIVER EXAMPLE

In this section we study the design of a simple STREAMS Ethernet driver. Using this driver as an example, we will learn the details involved in writing STREAMS drivers. To ease this task, we define a simple, hypothetical hardware interface for the Ethernet I/O board. We start with a short overview of the Ethernet.

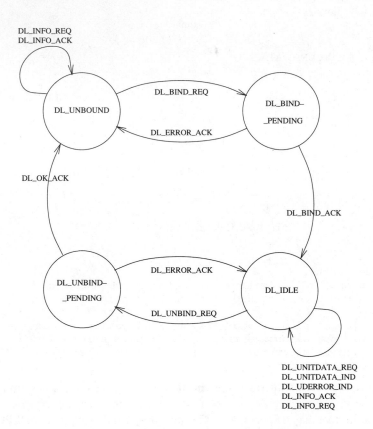

Fig. 10.7. DLPI Connectionless State Diagram

The Ethernet

The Ethernet is a simple local area network that uses a bus topology. Shielded coaxial cabling is used as the transmission medium. Data can be transmitted at 10 megabits per second and are broadcast to all stations on the network at once. At most, 1024 stations can be connected to the network. The access discipline is CSMA/CD—Carrier Sense Multiple Access with Collision Detection. Each station listens to the wire, detects when the signal is present (senses carrier), and detects collisions.

The Ethernet comprises two layers in the OSI model: the physical layer and the data link layer. Recall that the physical layer translates the bits to electrical form, adds and remove preambles, transmits and receives signals, senses the bus for carrier, and detects collisions. The data link layer handles framing (delimiting packets), addressing, error detection, collision avoidance, and collision recovery.

When a collision is detected, the data link layer will wait a random amount of time and then attempt a retransmission (this is usually handled by the I/O hardware).

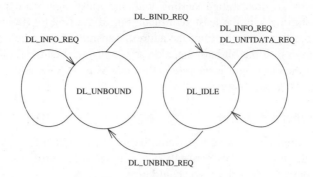

Fig. 10.8. Simplified State Diagram

The amount of time to wait is calculated using a binary exponential backoff algorithm plus a random component. This decreases the probability that two stations that have collided will collide again during their retransmissions.

Framing is the process of creating a *frame*, also called a *packet*. A packet is a sequence of related bytes transmitted as one logical unit, and the packet's format specifies the framework used to transmit data on the network. The format of an Ethernet packet is shown in Figure 10.9.

Preamble	Destination Address	Source Address	Protocol Type	User Data	Checksum
8 bytes	6 bytes	6 bytes	2 bytes	46 – 1500 bytes	4 bytes

Fig. 10.9. Ethernet Packet Format

The preamble is generated by the physical layer and is used to mark the start of a frame and to synchronize the receivers. The destination address is the address of the station(s) to which the packet is being sent. The source address is the address of the station sending the packet. The type field indicates the client layer protocol associated with the packet. The packet may contain between 46 and 1500 bytes of data, inclusive. The end of the packet contains a cyclic redundancy checksum value. Including the preamble and the checksum, the minimum packet size is 72 bytes and the maximum packet size is 1526 bytes.

An Ethernet address is six bytes (octets) long. There are two types of addresses: *physical* and *multicast*. The physical address is a unique address associated with each station on the network. The multicast address represents more than one destination. While destination addresses can be either multicast or physical, source addresses are always physical addresses.

There are two kinds of multicast addresses. The *multicast-group* address represents a particular group of stations. The *broadcast* address represents all stations on the network. The Ethernet broadcast address is 0xFFFFFFFFFFFF.

Addresses are transmitted starting with the most significant byte. Bytes are transmitted starting with the least significant bit. If the first bit (the least significant bit of the most significant byte) of the address transmitted is 1, then the address is a multicast address. If the bit is 0, the address is a physical address. Therefore, if the upper half of the most significant byte in the address is odd, the address is considered to be a multicast group address.

Example Ethernet Driver

When compiling kernel-level software, define the _KERNEL symbol to obtain kernel-only definitions. This convention is supported by most system header files. To compile the Ethernet driver, you could type

```
cc -c -D_KERNEL enet.c
```

You could then link the resultant object file, enet.o, with the other kernel object files to create a new /unix executable image. The details of configuring a driver into the kernel vary among implementations. For the Intel 80x86 architecture, the procedure is documented in the *Integrated Software Development Guide* [AT&T 1990e].

Figure 10.10 summarizes the functions constituting the Ethernet driver. Arrows indicate which routines are called by other driver routines. The driver's write put procedure handles ioctl and flush processing, but places all other messages on its queue to be processed by the write service procedure. The write service procedure interprets the messages as DLPI service primitives and calls the appropriate routine to process each one.

If an allocation error occurs during processing, the routines return a value to indicate that the primitive was unable to be processed. In this case, the write service procedure places the message back on its queue, schedules the service procedure to be reenabled when message allocation might have a better chance of succeeding, and returns.

There is no read-side put procedure. Instead, the driver's interrupt handler receives notification of the arrival of a packet, creates a message, and places it on the read queue. The read service procedure merely forwards the message upstream. In this case, the read service procedure serves to decouple the stream's read-side message processing from interrupt-level processing.

The header file for the Ethernet driver is shown first, followed by the driver itself. Note that comments are used sparingly throughout the driver to decrease the example's length.

```
enetinit
enetopen
enetclose

enetwput
```

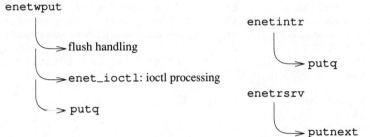

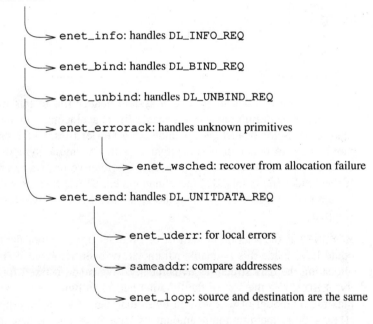

Fig. 10.10. Ethernet Driver Function Diagram

```
 1 #ifndef _SYS_ENET_H
 2 #define _SYS_ENET_H

 3 #define MAXENET        16        /* max # of minor devices */
 4 #define EHDRSZ         14        /* size of ethernet header */
 5 #define MAXDATA        1500      /* max user data per packet */
 6 #define MINDATA        46        /* min user data per packet */
 7 #define MACSZ          6         /* size of ethernet address */
 8 #define SAPSZ          2         /* size of SAP identifier */
 9 #define TOTADDRSZ (MACSZ+SAPSZ)  /* total address size */

10 union protocol {
11    uchar_t     b[2];
12    ushort_t    s;
13 };

14 struct enethdr {
15    uchar_t          dest[MACSZ];
16    uchar_t          src[MACSZ];
17    union protocol   prot;
18 };
```

[1–2]   It is common practice to start each system header file in this manner to avoid multiple definitions when a header file is accidentally included more than once. Some header files include other header files, so the problem is more likely to occur than you might expect. A unique symbol name is created from the pathname of the header file relative to /usr/include. If the header file is included more than once, _SYS_ENET_H will already be defined in successive occurrences, so the body of the file will be skipped.

[3–9]   MAXENET is the maximum number of Ethernet driver minor devices. We could have made this a tunable parameter, or even removed it entirely by allocating the data structures dynamically. We made it fixed for simplicity. EHDRSZ is the size of the Ethernet header in bytes. MAXDATA is the maximum amount of user data in bytes that can fit in an Ethernet packet. MINDATA is the minimum amount of data in bytes needed to send a packet. MACSZ is the size of the physical portion of the driver's DLSAP address. SAPSZ is the size of the service access point identifier portion of the DLSAP address. The sum of these two address components yields the total length of a DLSAP address.

[10–13] The protocol union is defined to manage byte-ordering differences between the host computer and that defined by the Ethernet specification.

[14–18] The enethdr structure defines the Ethernet header, which is composed of a destination address, a source address, and a protocol type. The protocol type identifies the protocol that the sender and the receiver are using.

```
19 #define ENETIOC    ('E'<<8)
20 #define SETADDR    (ENETIOC|1)
21 #define GETADDR    (ENETIOC|2)

22 #ifdef _KERNEL

23 #define CMD_REG_ADDR   0x1000
24 #define SIZE_REG_ADDR  0x1004
25 #define STAT_REG_ADDR  0x1008
26 #define ENET_ADDR      0x100c
27 #define RECV_BUF_ADDR  0x2000
28 #define SEND_BUF_ADDR  0x3000

29 #define CMD_REG        (*(long *)CMD_REG_ADDR)
30 #define SIZE_REG       (*(long *)SIZE_REG_ADDR)
31 #define STAT_REG       (*(long *)STAT_REG_ADDR)
```

[19–21] The driver supports two `ioctl` commands: one to set the Ethernet address and one to get the Ethernet address. The command values need to be unique on the stream because the first processing element in the stream that recognizes the command will act on it. We try to make the commands unique by taking a character representing the driver ('E'), shifting it left eight bits, and OR-ing in different values for each command. Using the letter 'S' should be avoided; it is used in defining the `ioctl` commands recognized by the stream head.

[22]   We group the kernel-only definitions inside the _KERNEL `ifdef` so that both user-level and kernel-level software can include the header file, but user-level applications will not ordinarily gain access to the definitions intended only for kernel-level software.

[23–31] To keep the driver understandable, we will assume a simple hardware interface. The hardware will have three registers and three buffers mapped into the kernel's memory address space. The addresses at which they are mapped are defined as manifest constants for simplicity. In actuality, they will be selected in system configuration files.

One buffer is used for transmitting a packet, one is used for receiving a packet, and the third is used to hold the Ethernet board's address. Most hardware is more complex than this. Multiple buffers, for example, are usually provided to increase I/O throughput.

One register is available for sending commands to the I/O board, one is available for retrieving the status of the I/O board, and the third is used to identify the size of an incoming packet.

```
32 /* command register values */
33 #define SEND_PKT   0x01     /* send a packet */
34 #define RECV_OFF   0x02     /* shut off receiver */
35 #define RECV_ON    0x03     /* turn on receiver */
36 #define SET_ADDR   0x04     /* set ethernet address */

37 /* status register values */
38 #define RECV_PKT   0x01     /* packet has arrived */
39 #define SEND_DONE  0x02     /* packet has been sent */

40 #undef STATIC
41 #ifdef DEBUG
42 #define STATIC
43 #else
44 #define STATIC static
45 #endif

46 #endif /* _KERNEL */
47 #endif /* _SYS_ENET_H */
```

[32–36] The command register accepts four commands. The first is used to transmit a packet. The second command is used to disable the receiver. While the receiver is disabled, the I/O board will not accept any packets from the network. The third command is used to enable the receiver. Finally, the fourth command is used to change the address of the I/O board.

[37–39] The status register provides information about the hardware. Two events are defined. The first indicates that a packet has been received. The second indicates the end of a transmission. The driver uses this to tell when it can transmit the next packet.

[40–47] The <sys/debug.h> header file contains an incorrect definition for the symbol STATIC (this bug has been fixed in SVR4.2). It assumes that any file including <sys/debug.h> will unconditionally want STATIC to evaluate to an empty string. Not only is this assumption wrong, but it ignores the setting of the DEBUG symbol normally used to control debugging options. We define STATIC correctly so that we can still include <sys/debug.h>, but STATIC will evaluate to static when DEBUG is undefined, or to the empty string when DEBUG is defined. This is similar to the way the ASSERT macro is defined. Thus, driver symbols will be defined globally when DEBUG is defined, allowing us to find them with a debugger more easily.

This completes the Ethernet driver's header file. Now we will look at the source code for the driver.

```
 1 #include <sys/types.h>
 2 #include <sys/stream.h>
 3 #include <sys/stropts.h>
 4 #include <sys/cred.h>
 5 #include <sys/dlpi.h>
 6 #include <sys/param.h>
 7 #include <sys/errno.h>
 8 #include <sys/debug.h>
 9 #include <sys/cmn_err.h>
10 #include <sys/ddi.h>
11 #include <sys/enet.h>

12 struct enet {
13    queue_t      *e_rq;        /* read queue */
14    ulong_t      e_dlstate;    /* data link provider state */
15    ushort_t     e_prot;       /* protocol type */
16    ushort_t     e_idtype;     /* ID type (bufcall or timeout) */
17    ulong_t      e_id;         /* ID for bufcalls & timeouts */
18 };

19 #define NO_ID        0
20 #define BUF_ID       1
21 #define TIME_ID      2

22 #define ONESEC       1000000      /* in microseconds */
```

[1–11]   The driver begins by including the header files it needs. `<sys/dlpi.h>` contains the definitions for the Data Link Provider Interface. `<sys/enet.h>` is the driver's header file. The other header files should be familiar (see Table 9.2).

[12–21]   The `enet` structure is the private data structure that the driver uses for each minor device. We define it in the driver source file instead of the header file because no other software needs to know its structure.

The `e_rq` field points to the read queue associated with the minor device. The `e_dlstate` field maintains the data link provider state, as required by the DLPI. The `e_prot` field is the protocol type associated with the minor device. The `e_idtype` field describes the `e_id` field, indicating whether the identifier saved in `e_id` is from a call to `bufcall` or a call to `timeout`.

If `e_idtype` is set to `BUF_ID`, then `e_id` contains a `bufcall` ID. If `e_idtype` is set to `TIME_ID`, then `e_id` contains a `timeout` ID. Since there are no restrictions on the value of `timeout` IDs, a special type, `NO_ID`, indicates that the `e_id` field is not in use.

[22]   `ONESEC` defines the number of microseconds in a second, used during recovery from buffer allocation failures.

```
23 typedef enum retval { DONE, RETRY, ERR } retval_t;

24 STATIC int enetopen(queue_t *, dev_t *, int, int,
25    cred_t *);
26 STATIC int enetclose(queue_t *, int, cred_t *);
27 STATIC int enetrsrv(queue_t *);
28 STATIC int enetwput(queue_t *, mblk_t *);
29 STATIC int enetwsrv(queue_t *);
30 STATIC retval_t enet_info(struct enet *);
31 STATIC retval_t enet_bind(struct enet *, mblk_t *);
32 STATIC retval_t enet_unbind(struct enet *, mblk_t *);
33 STATIC retval_t enet_errorack(struct enet *, ulong_t,
34    ulong_t, ulong_t);
35 STATIC int sameaddr(uchar_t *, uchar_t *);
36 STATIC int isgroupaddr(uchar_t *);
37 STATIC void enet_send(struct enet *, mblk_t *);
38 STATIC void enet_wsched(struct enet *, int);
39 STATIC void enet_wcont(struct enet *);
40 STATIC void enet_uderr(struct enet *, uchar_t *, ulong_t,
41    ulong_t, ulong_t);
42 STATIC void enet_free(char *);
43 STATIC void enet_ioctl(queue_t *, mblk_t *);
44 STATIC void enet_loop(mblk_t *, struct enethdr *, ushort_t);
45 void enetinit(void);
46 void enetintr(int);

47 STATIC uchar_t enet_addr[MACSZ];
48 STATIC uchar_t bcast_addr[MACSZ] = {
49    0xff, 0xff, 0xff, 0xff, 0xff, 0xff
50 };
51 STATIC int enetsndbusy = 0, enetrcvbusy = 0;
```

[23–46]   The `retval_t typedef` defines the type of the return value from func-
         tions that can fail when called from the write service procedure. Figure
         10.10 shows the interrelationships between most of the functions.
         `enetinit` and `enetintr` must be global so that the configuration
         software can identify them. The others are global only if the driver is com-
         piled with the DEBUG flag defined. Otherwise, they remain private to the
         driver.

[47–51]   The `enet_addr` array is used to contain the Ethernet address for the I/O
         board. (This driver only supports one I/O board.) The address is dupli-
         cated in kernel memory for convenience. The `bcast_addr` array con-
         tains the broadcast address, the special address that indicates a packet
         should be sent to all machines on the network. The `enetsndbusy` flag is
         set to 1 when the I/O board is transmitting a packet, and 0 otherwise. The
         `enetrcvbusy` flag is set to 1 when the I/O board's receive buffer is
         busy, and 0 otherwise.

```
52 STATIC int enetnext = 0;
53 STATIC frtn_t enetfrtn = {enet_free, 0};
54 STATIC struct enet enet[MAXENET];

55 STATIC struct module_info enet_minfo = {
56    0x656e, "enet", MINDATA, MAXDATA, 10*MAXDATA, MAXDATA
57 };
58 STATIC struct qinit enet_rinit = {
59    NULL, enetrsrv, enetopen, enetclose, NULL, &enet_minfo,
60    NULL
61 };
```

[52–54]   The enetnext variable is an index into the array of minor devices used to implement a round-robin policy for selecting the next minor device to transmit a packet to the board. The enetfrtn variable is a free-routine specification used with calls to esballoc.

The enet array contains the per-minor private data structure associated with the device. MAXENET could be made a tunable parameter so that the number of minor devices supported by the driver could be changed later. Another alternative is to allocate the per-minor private data structures dynamically, thereby avoiding most configuration issues. Usually, a different minor device will be used by each protocol directly accessing the Ethernet driver. Since the number of protocols using it at the same time will probably be small, it is reasonable to limit the number of minor devices.

[55–57]   The module_info structure is shared between the read and write sides of the driver. The module number, 0x656e, is the hexadecimal ASCII representation of the first two characters of the module name, ''enet.'' This does not guarantee uniqueness, but it provides a convenient approximation. The minimum packet size is the amount of data needed to make the smallest Ethernet packet allowed. The maximum packet size is the maximum amount of data in an Ethernet packet, since the driver does not fragment messages into multiple packets. Fragmentation is handled at a higher layer. The high-water mark is set to the size of 10 full Ethernet packets. The low-water mark is set to the size of one full Ethernet packet. These numbers need to be chosen so that the number of packets received on average is such that the read service procedure gets a chance to run before its queue is filled.

[58–61]   The read-side qinit structure does not specify a put procedure, because the interrupt handler will do the equivalent processing. There is a read-side service procedure, however, so that the interrupt processing is decoupled from the rest of the stream. This reduces both the amount of time interrupts will be blocked and the chance of overrunning the interrupt stack.

```
62 STATIC struct qinit enet_winit = {
63   enetwput, enetwsrv, NULL, NULL, NULL, &enet_minfo, NULL
64 };

65 struct streamtab enetinfo = {
66   &enet_rinit, &enet_winit, NULL, NULL
67 };

68 int enetdevflag = 0;   /* required by config */
69 int enetspurint = 0;   /* spurious interrupts */
70 int enetrcvlost = 0;   /* input packets dropped */

71 void
72 enetinit()
73 {
74   CMD_REG = RECV_OFF;
75 }
```

[62–64] The write side has a put procedure and a service procedure. Any driver
that has to wait for an interrupt to indicate that a transfer is complete will
need a write service procedure so messages can queue up while the driver
is waiting for the completion interrupt.

[65–67] The `streamtab` structure is named `enetinfo`, according to the naming
conventions outlined at the end of Section 9.2. Thus, the driver prefix is
`enet`. The `streamtab` structure contains pointers to the read and write
`qinit` structures. Since the Ethernet driver is not a multiplexing driver,
the other pointers in the `streamtab` structure are NULL.

[68–70] Besides the `streamtab` structure, the only other global data symbol
required in the driver is a driver flag. It must be named *xxx*devflag,
where *xxx* is the driver prefix. We initialize the driver flag to 0 because
there are no flag values that apply to this driver (the flags are defined in
`<sys/conf.h>`).

The next variable, `enetspurint`, is a counter used to keep track of
spurious interrupts. An interrupt is considered spurious if it occurs without
an event to be reported. This can sometimes occur with faulty hardware.
`enetrcvlost` is a counter that keeps track of packets received but
dropped because of insufficient memory. The values of `enetspurint`
and `enetrcvlost` can be printed by a privileged user using
`crash(1M)`.

[71–75] When the system boots up and the driver's init routine is called, we turn
off the receiver on the Ethernet board. This prevents the Ethernet board
from interrupting the host computer when no processes are using the board.

```
76 STATIC int
77 enetopen(queue_t *q, dev_t *devp, int flag, int sflag,
78   cred_t *crp)
79 {
80   int i;

81   if (sflag == MODOPEN)
82       return(EINVAL);
83   if (q->q_ptr != NULL)
84       return(0);

85   if (sflag == CLONEOPEN) {
86       for (i = 0; i < MAXENET; i++)
87           if (enet[i].e_rq == NULL)
88               break;
89       if (i >= MAXENET)
90           return(ENXIO);
91       *devp = makedevice(getemajor(*devp), i);
92   } else {
93       if ((i = getminor(*devp)) >= MAXENET)
94           return(ENXIO);
95   }

96   enet[i].e_rq = q;
97   enet[i].e_idtype = NO_ID;
98   enet[i].e_dlstate = DL_UNBOUND;
```

[76–84] When opening the driver, we want to make sure the system administrator did not mistakenly configure it as a STREAMS module, so we verify that sflag is not equal to MODOPEN. If the value is valid, we check if this minor device is already open and, if so, return success. We use the convention that the driver's private pointer in the queue is nonzero for minor devices that are already open.

[85–91] This driver uses the clone driver to support clone opens. We perform the typical clone open processing, searching the minor device array for an unused entry, indicated by a NULL queue pointer in the enet structure. If one is not found, we fail the open with ENXIO. Otherwise, we set the device number referred to by devp to the unused device number, which is composed of the current major number and the unused minor number.

[92–95] If it is not a clone open, we get the minor device number and validate it so we can use it as an index into the enet array. If the minor device is invalid, we return ENXIO.

[96–98] Since the minor device is not already in use, we initialize its corresponding enet structure. We save the address of the read queue, set the ID type to unused, and set the data link provider state to unbound.

```
 99  q->q_ptr = (caddr_t)&enet[i];
100  WR(q)->q_ptr = (caddr_t)&enet[i];
101  return(0);
102  }

103  STATIC int
104  enetclose(queue_t *q, int flag, cred_t *crp)
105  {
106    struct enet *ep;

107    ep = (struct enet *)q->q_ptr;
108    if (ep->e_idtype == TIME_ID)
109        untimeout(ep->e_id);
110    else if (ep->e_idtype == BUF_ID)
111        unbufcall(ep->e_id);
112    ep->e_dlstate = DL_UNBOUND;
113    ep->e_rq = NULL;
114    q->q_ptr = NULL;
115    WR(q)->q_ptr = NULL;
116    return(0);
117  }
```

[99–102]   By setting the private pointers in the read and write queues to the address of the minor device's private data structure, we enable other functions, such as the put and service procedures, to find the enet structure from the queue pointer. Finally, we indicate a successful open by returning 0.

[103–111]   When closing the minor device, we obtain a pointer to the enet structure from the queue's private pointer. If there is an outstanding timeout or bufcall request, we cancel it.

[112–117]   We change the provider state to indicate that the minor device is no longer bound. This prevents the interrupt routine from using an invalid e_rq pointer, which we set to NULL to indicate that the minor device is now free. We also clear the private pointer in the queues, so if the system decides to reuse the queues, they are not mistakenly interpreted to be associated with a device that is already open.

One enhancement we could make is to sleep in the close routine until any data remaining on the write queue have been transmitted if neither FNDELAY nor FNONBLOCK was specified in the flag parameter. Since the driver implements a datagram interface, it is reasonable that we do not wait for the data to drain. This would not be the case if we were implementing a line printer driver, for example.

```
118 STATIC int
119 enetwput(queue_t *q, mblk_t *mp)
120 {
121   switch (mp->b_datap->db_type) {

122   case M_FLUSH:
123       if (*mp->b_rptr & FLUSHW) {
124           flushq(q, FLUSHALL);
125           *mp->b_rptr &= ~FLUSHW;
126       }
127       if (*mp->b_rptr & FLUSHR) {
128           flushq(RD(q), FLUSHALL);
129           qreply(q, mp);
130       } else {
131           freemsg(mp);
132       }
133       break;

134   case M_IOCTL:
135       enet_ioctl(q, mp);
136       break;

137   case M_PROTO:
138   case M_PCPROTO:
139       putq(q, mp);
140       break;

141   default:
142       freemsg(mp);
143       break;
144   }

145   return(0);
146 }
```

[118–121] The write-side put procedure is just a case statement that switches on the message type.

[122–133] We perform queue flushing in the put procedure to minimize flush latency. If FLUSHW is set, we flush the write queue and shut FLUSHW off. If FLUSHR is set, we flush the read queue and send the message back upstream. Otherwise, we free the message. This is the canonical queue-flushing algorithm.

[134–146] We handle M_IOCTL messages immediately by calling enet_ioctl. (enet_ioctl is described later.) M_PROTO and M_PCPROTO messages are enqueued for processing by the write service procedure. All other message types are simply freed.

```
147 STATIC int
148 enetwsrv(queue_t *q)
149 {
150   mblk_t *mp;
151   struct enet *ep;
152   int s;
153   ulong_t err, prim;
154   union DL_primitives *dlp;

155   ep = (struct enet *)q->q_ptr;
156   if (ep == NULL)
157       return(0);

158   while ((mp = getq(q)) != NULL) {

159       ASSERT((mp->b_datap->db_type == M_PROTO) ||
160         (mp->b_datap->db_type == M_PCPROTO));

161       err = 0;
162       dlp = (union DL_primitives *)mp->b_rptr;
163       prim = dlp->dl_primitive;

164       switch (prim) {
```

[147–154] The write service procedure handles all M_PROTO and M_PCPROTO messages.

[155–157] Since we are only passed a pointer to the queue, we obtain a pointer to the associated enet structure from the private pointer in the queue. If this is NULL, the service procedure returns. This protects against the service procedure running during a close of a driver that sleeps after clearing the private queue pointer. It also protects against programming errors that result in the service procedure running after the minor device has been closed, such as from an outstanding timeout request that has not been canceled.

[158–160] While there are messages left on the queue, we take them off one by one and process them until either a function that we call fails or we process a data message. Since only M_PROTO and M_PCPROTO messages are placed on the queue, we assert that no other message type has been removed. ASSERT is a macro defined in <sys/debug.h> that will print a message and force a system panic when the assertion is false. When DEBUG is not defined, the ASSERT macro has no effect.

[161–164] We cast a pointer to a DL_primitives union over the read pointer in the message so the data link primitive can be determined. The primitive is the first field in every DLPI message. Based on the value of the primitive, different actions are taken.

```
165        case DL_UNITDATA_REQ:
166            s = splstr();
167            if (enetsndbusy)
168                putbq(q, mp);
169            else
170                enet_send(ep, mp);
171            splx(s);
172            return(0);   /* interrupt will reschedule us */

173        case DL_INFO_REQ:
174            if (enet_info(ep) != DONE)
175                cmn_err(CE_WARN,
176                    "enet: can't respond to DL_INFO_REQ");
177            freemsg(mp);
178            break;
```

[165–172] Because several queues can be feeding data to the Ethernet board, the interrupt handler uses a round-robin algorithm to select the next queue to transmit. If we retrieve a DL_UNITDATA_REQ message from the queue, we need to raise the interrupt priority level to block interrupts from the I/O device so we will not miss the qenable from the interrupt handler. When we take the last message off the queue and find that the board is busy, an interrupt could come in before we put the message back on the queue if we do not block interrupts. In that case, the interrupt handler would not pick this queue for enabling because it would be empty. Then this minor would miss its turn. Blocking interrupts prevents this from happening.

If the I/O board is in the process of transmitting a packet, enetsndbusy will be set to 1 and we put the message back on the queue. Before returning, we restore the previous processor priority level. We do not continue processing messages after transmitting a packet, because the completion interrupt will reschedule the service procedure.

[173–178] If the message is a DL_INFO_REQ message, we call enet_info to send a message containing service parameters upstream. If this fails because of an inability to allocate a message, we print a warning on the console. We cannot put the message back on the queue, because the DL_INFO_REQ primitive is implemented as a high-priority (M_PCPROTO) message, so regardless of the return value, we free the message and continue processing other messages on the queue.

```
179        case DL_BIND_REQ:
180            if (enet_bind(ep, mp) == RETRY) {
181                putbq(q, mp);
182                return(0);
183            }
184            break;

185        case DL_UNBIND_REQ:
186            if (enet_unbind(ep, mp) == RETRY) {
187                putbq(q, mp);
188                return(0);
189            }
190            break;

191        case DL_ATTACH_REQ:
192        case DL_DETACH_REQ:
193        case DL_SUBS_BIND_REQ:
194        case DL_ENABMULTI_REQ:
195        case DL_DISABMULTI_REQ:
196        case DL_PROMISCON_REQ:
197        case DL_PROMISCOFF_REQ:
198        case DL_UDQOS_REQ:
199        case DL_CONNECT_REQ:
200        case DL_CONNECT_RES:
201        case DL_TOKEN_REQ:
202        case DL_DISCONNECT_REQ:
203        case DL_RESET_REQ:
204        case DL_RESET_RES:
205        case DL_DATA_ACK_REQ:
206        case DL_REPLY_REQ:
207        case DL_REPLY_UPDATE_REQ:
208        case DL_XID_REQ:
209        case DL_TEST_REQ:
210            err = DL_NOTSUPPORTED;   /* fall through */
```

[179–190] If the message we get off the queue is a DL_BIND_REQ, we call
enet_bind to handle the bind request. If enet_bind is unable to do
its job because of allocation failures, we put the message back on the
queue and return. enet_bind will arrange for the service procedure to
be rescheduled in this case. If, on the other hand, enet_bind is successful, we continue processing messages on the queue. Requests to
unbind an address are handled in a similar manner.

[191–210] Any valid but unsupported DLPI request is denied by sending an error
acknowledgement upstream (see the next page). We use the DLPI error
DL_NOTSUPPORTED to distinguish this case from others. Note that
DL_NOTSUPPORTED is different than the similarly named error,
DL_UNSUPPORTED, which is to be used for valid primitives requesting
unsupported features of supported services.

```
211        default:
212            if (err == 0)
213                err = DL_BADPRIM;

214            if (enet_errorack(ep, prim, err, 0) == RETRY) {
215                if (mp->b_datap->db_type < QPCTL) {
216                    putbq(q, mp);
217                    return(0);
218                }
219                cmn_err(CE_WARN,
220                    "enet: can't generate DL_ERROR_ACK (%d)",
221                    prim);
222            }

223            freemsg(mp);
224            break;
225        }
226   }   /* while */
227   return(0);
228 }

229 STATIC int
230 enetrsrv(queue_t *q)
231 {
232  mblk_t *mp;
```

[211–228] For any M_PROTO or M_PCPROTO message we do not recognize, we send a DL_ERROR_ACK message upstream. If the value of the primitive is valid but the primitive is unsupported, we use the error DL_NOTSUPPORTED. For all other values, we specify the error code to be DL_BADPRIM, to indicate that the primitive is invalid.

After we send the error acknowledgement upstream, we free the unrecognized message and continue processing the messages on the queue until the queue is empty. If we are unable to allocate an error-acknowledgement message and the invalid primitive is not implemented as a high-priority message, we put the message back on the queue and return. If the primitive is implemented as an M_PCPROTO message, on the other hand, we can only print a warning on the console and free the message since we cannot put the message back on the queue.

When the queue finally becomes empty, getq will return NULL, and we will fall out of the while loop and return 0.

[229–232] The read-side service procedure is called as a result of the interrupt handler placing messages on the read queue. It implements an algorithm similar to the canonical service procedure algorithm described in Section 10.2.

```
233  while ((mp = getq(q)) != NULL) {
234      ASSERT(mp->b_datap->db_type == M_PROTO);
235      if (canput(q->q_next)) {
236          putnext(q, mp);
237      } else {
238          putbq(q, mp);
239          return(0);
240      }
241  }
242  return(0);
243  }

244  STATIC retval_t
245  enet_info(struct enet *ep)
246  {
247  dl_info_ack_t *ackp;
248  mblk_t *mp;
249  int i;

250  i = DL_INFO_ACK_SIZE+TOTADDRSZ+MACSZ;
251  if ((mp = allocb(i, BPRI_HI)) == NULL)
252      return(ERR);
253  mp->b_datap->db_type = M_PCPROTO;
```

[233–243]   We process all the messages on the queue unless flow-controlled by a queue upstream. Since the interrupt handler is the only thing placing messages on the read queue, we assert that the message type is appropriate. Then we check if we can send a message upstream. If so, we call putnext to pass the message to the next processing element in the stream. Otherwise, we put the message back on the queue and return.

Note that we are able to simplify the canonical service procedure algorithm by removing the check for high-priority messages. The only type of message placed on the read queue is a unitdata indication, implemented as an M_PROTO message.

[244–249]   enet_info is called in response to receiving a DL_INFO_REQ message from the consumer.

[250–253]   We allocate a DL_INFO_ACK message to hold the operational parameters about the data link provider. These include service parameters, the currently bound DLSAP address, and the broadcast address, if supported. If the allocation fails, we return a failure indication. If the allocation succeeds, we set the type of the message to M_PCPROTO.

```
254    ackp = (dl_info_ack_t *)mp->b_wptr;
255    ackp->dl_primitive = DL_INFO_ACK;
256    ackp->dl_max_sdu = MAXDATA;
257    ackp->dl_min_sdu = MINDATA;
258    ackp->dl_addr_length = TOTADDRSZ;
259    ackp->dl_mac_type = DL_ETHER;
260    ackp->dl_reserved = 0;
261    ackp->dl_current_state = ep->e_dlstate;
262    ackp->dl_sap_length = -SAPSZ;
263    ackp->dl_service_mode = DL_CLDLS;
264    ackp->dl_qos_length = 0;
265    ackp->dl_qos_offset = 0;
266    ackp->dl_qos_range_length = 0;
267    ackp->dl_qos_range_offset = 0;
268    ackp->dl_provider_style = DL_STYLE1;
```

[254–258] We set the `dl_primitive` field to `DL_INFO_ACK` to identify the
message. The `dl_max_sdu` field is the maximum service data unit
size, the maximum amount of data that will fit in one packet, so we set it
to `MAXDATA`. The `dl_min_sdu` field is the minimum service data unit
size, the minimum amount of data needed to send a packet. We set this
to `MINDATA`. The `dl_addr_length` field is the total length of the
DLSAP address in bytes. We set it to `TOTADDRSZ`, the sum of the
lengths of the physical network address and the SAP identifier.

[259–262] The `dl_mac_type` field identifies the type of medium access control.
We set it to `DL_ETHER` to indicate that the media supported is an Ethernet. The `dl_reserved` field is intended for future use, so we initialize
it to 0. The `dl_current_state` field is the current state of the
DLSAP as defined by the DLPI. We set it to the value of the DLPI state
field in the `enet` structure. The absolute value of the
`dl_sap_length` field is the length in bytes of the SAP portion of the
address. Its sign indicates the order in which the separate components
appear in the DLSAP address: positive means the SAP identifier is followed by the physical network address, and negative means the physical
network address appears first, followed by the SAP identifier. In the
example driver, we use the latter format.

[263–268] We set the `dl_service_mode` field to `DL_CLDLS` to indicate that the
driver supports a connectionless data link service. Since the example
driver does not support any quality-of-service (qos) parameters, such as
throughput, transit delay, priority, protection, residual error rate, or resil-
ience, we set all of the quality-of-service fields to 0. We set the
`dl_provider_style` field to `DL_STYLE1`, indicating that the physical device is implicitly attached when the device is opened, instead of
being selected through the use of explicit attach primitives.

```
269  ackp->dl_version = DL_VERSION_2;
270  ackp->dl_brdcst_addr_length = MACSZ;
271  ackp->dl_growth = 0;
272  mp->b_wptr += DL_INFO_ACK_SIZE;
273  if (ep->e_dlstate == DL_IDLE) {
274      ackp->dl_addr_offset = DL_INFO_ACK_SIZE;
275      for (i = 0; i < MACSZ; i++)
276          *mp->b_wptr++ = enet_addr[i];
277      *mp->b_wptr++ = (ep->e_prot>>8) & 0xff;
278      *mp->b_wptr++ = ep->e_prot & 0xff;
279      ackp->dl_brdcst_addr_offset = DL_INFO_ACK_SIZE +
280          TOTADDRSZ;
281  } else {
282      ackp->dl_addr_offset = 0;
283      ackp->dl_brdcst_addr_offset = DL_INFO_ACK_SIZE;
284  }
```

[269–271] The driver adheres to Version 2.0.0 of the DLPI, so we set the dl_version field to the value that represents this version. The length of the broadcast address is the same as the length of a physical network address, so we set the dl_brdcst_addr_length field to MACSZ. The dl_growth field is intended for future use, so we set it to 0.

[272–280] After initializing most of the dl_info_ack_t structure, we advance the write pointer in the message to point one byte past the end of the structure. The read pointer remains at the beginning of the structure. If the endpoint is bound, we set the dl_addr_offset field in the dl_info_ack_t structure to the size of the dl_info_ack_t structure. This is the offset in the message where we will store the address bound to the endpoint. Then we copy the physical network address into the message following the dl_info_ack_t structure. Note that we advance the write pointer as we copy the address. Then we add the SAP identifier (the protocol type) to the end of the address in the byte order specified by the Ethernet standard. The dl_brdcst_addr_offset field is the offset in the message where the broadcast address is found. We set it to the location immediately after the end of the DLSAP address.

[281–284] If the endpoint was not bound, we set the dl_addr_offset field to 0 to indicate that the message will not contain the local address. Then we set the dl_brdcst_addr_offset field to the location in the message immediately following the dl_info_ack_t structure. Even though the endpoint is not bound, we return as much information that we can to the caller. Since the broadcast address is fixed, we can always return it, regardless of the state of the DLSAP.

```
285  for (i = 0; i < MACSZ; i++)
286      *mp->b_wptr++ = bcast_addr[i];
287  putnext(ep->e_rq, mp);
288  return(DONE);
289  }

290  STATIC retval_t
291  enet_bind(struct enet *ep, mblk_t *mp)
292  {
293  int i;
294  dl_bind_req_t *reqp;
295  dl_bind_ack_t *ackp;
296  mblk_t *bp;
297  ushort_t prot;

298  if (ep->e_dlstate != DL_UNBOUND) {
299      if (enet_errorack(ep, DL_BIND_REQ, DL_OUTSTATE,
300        0) == RETRY)
301          return(RETRY);
302      freemsg(mp);
303      return(ERR);
304  }
305  reqp = (dl_bind_req_t *)mp->b_rptr;
```

[285–289] Finally, we copy the broadcast address into the message, send the
DL_INFO_ACK message upstream, and return DONE to indicate success.

[290–297] enet_bind is called in response to receiving a DL_BIND_REQ message from the consumer. It is used to associate a DLSAP address with
the minor device. The DLSAP address is composed of the physical network address and a SAP identifier. The Ethernet driver uses the protocol type (an unsigned short) for the SAP identifier.

[298–305] If the state is not unbound, we call enet_errorack to send a
DL_ERROR_ACK message upstream, failing the bind attempt with an
indication that the minor device is not in the correct state
(DL_OUTSTATE). If we cannot allocate the message, we return an indi-
cation to the caller to try again later. Otherwise, we free the
DL_BIND_REQ message and return ERR to indicate that we are done
processing the message. If we return RETRY, the caller (the write ser-
vice procedure) will put the message back on the queue and return.
Otherwise, it will continue processing messages on the queue. The
DL_BIND_REQ message contains a dl_bind_req_t structure.

```
306   if (reqp->dl_service_mode != DL_CLDLS) {
307         if (enet_errorack(ep, DL_BIND_REQ, DL_UNSUPPORTED,
308           0) == RETRY)
309               return(RETRY);
310         freemsg(mp);
311         return(ERR);
312   }

313   if (reqp->dl_xidtest_flg != 0) {
314         if (enet_errorack(ep, DL_BIND_REQ, DL_NOAUTO,
315           0) == RETRY)
316               return(RETRY);
317         freemsg(mp);
318         return(ERR);
319   }

320   prot = reqp->dl_sap;
321   for (i = 0; i < MAXENET; i++)
322         if ((enet[i].e_prot == prot) &&
323           (enet[i].e_dlstate == DL_IDLE)) {
324               if (enet_errorack(ep, DL_BIND_REQ, DL_NOADDR,
325                 0) == RETRY)
326                     return(RETRY);
327               freemsg(mp);
328               return(ERR);
329         }
```

[306–312] We check the bind request to make sure that the consumer wants connectionless service. If not, we send a DL_ERROR_ACK message
upstream to fail the bind attempt, setting the data link error to
DL_UNSUPPORTED. If this fails, we return RETRY. Otherwise, we
free the DL_BIND_REQ message and return ERR.

[313–319] If the consumer wants the driver to respond to TEST or XID messages
automatically, the dl_xidtest_flg field will have flags set in it
corresponding to the messages to which we should reply. We do not
support this service, so we fail the bind request in a manner similar to
before, but with an error that indicates that automatic responses are not
supported (DL_NOAUTO). XID messages are used to exchange identification information between peer data link providers, and TEST messages are used to ''ping'' peer data link providers to test the data-transfer
paths.

[320–329] We search through the array of minor devices, checking if the same
DLSAP address is already bound on another minor device. If it is, we
send a DL_ERROR_ACK message upstream indicating that we could not
(or more precisely, do not) allocate an alternate address.

```
330   if ((bp = allocb(DL_BIND_ACK_SIZE+TOTADDRSZ, BPRI_HI)) ==
331     NULL) {
332        enet_wsched(ep, DL_BIND_ACK_SIZE+TOTADDRSZ);
333        return(RETRY);
334   }
335   freemsg(mp);
336   bp->b_datap->db_type = M_PCPROTO;
337   ackp = (dl_bind_ack_t *)bp->b_wptr;
338   ackp->dl_primitive = DL_BIND_ACK;
339   ackp->dl_sap = prot;
340   ackp->dl_addr_length = TOTADDRSZ;
341   ackp->dl_addr_offset = DL_BIND_ACK_SIZE;
342   ackp->dl_max_conind = 0;
343   ackp->dl_xidtest_flg = 0;
344   bp->b_wptr += DL_BIND_ACK_SIZE;
345   for (i = 0; i < MACSZ; i++)
346        *bp->b_wptr++ = enet_addr[i];
347   *bp->b_wptr++ = (prot>>8) & 0xff;
348   *bp->b_wptr++ = prot & 0xff;
349   ep->e_dlstate = DL_IDLE;
350   ep->e_prot = prot;
```

[330–335]   We know that no other minor device is bound to the DLSAP address requested, so we allocate a message large enough to hold a dl_bind_ack_t structure plus one DLSAP address. If this allocation fails, we arrange to have the write service procedure scheduled by calling enet_wsched and return RETRY. Otherwise, we free the DL_BIND_REQ message.

[336–343]   The DL_BIND_ACK message is made up of one M_PCPROTO message block. We set the dl_primitive field to indicate that the message represents a bind acknowledgement. Then we set the dl_sap field to the protocol type saved from the bind request message and set the dl_addr_length field to the size of the DLSAP address in bytes. We set the dl_addr_offset field to the size of the dl_bind_ack_t structure since the address will follow this structure in the message. The driver does not provide connection-oriented service, so we set the dl_max_conind field to 0. Nor does the driver respond automatically to TEST or XID messages, so we set the dl_xidtest_flg flag to 0.

[344–350]   We increment the write pointer by the size of the dl_bind_ack_t structure and copy the local address into the message, one byte at a time, incrementing the write pointer as we go. Then we add the SAP identifier to the message using the Ethernet byte ordering. We set the data link state to DL_IDLE for the corresponding enet structure, indicating data transfer is now possible. Then we save the protocol type.

```
351   putnext(ep->e_rq, bp);
352   if (!enetrcvbusy)
353       CMD_REG = RECV_ON;
354   return(DONE);
355 }

356 STATIC retval_t
357 enet_unbind(struct enet *ep, mblk_t *mp)
358 {
359   mblk_t *bp;
360   dl_ok_ack_t *ackp;

361   if (ep->e_dlstate != DL_IDLE) {
362       if (enet_errorack(ep, DL_UNBIND_REQ, DL_OUTSTATE,
363         0) == RETRY)
364           return(RETRY);
365       freemsg(mp);
366       return(ERR);
367   }

368   if ((bp = allocb(DL_OK_ACK_SIZE, BPRI_HI)) == NULL) {
369       enet_wsched(ep, DL_OK_ACK_SIZE);
370       return(RETRY);
371   }
372   freemsg(mp);
```

[351–355] We send the DL_BIND_ACK message upstream. Before returning, we
send a command to the I/O board to enable the receiver if the I/O
board's receive buffer is not in use.

[356–360] enet_unbind is called in response to receiving a DL_UNBIND_REQ
message from the consumer. It is used to disassociate a DLSAP address
from a minor device.

[361–367] If the state is not idle, then the minor device is already unbound. If this
is the case, we call enet_errorack to send a DL_ERROR_ACK mes-
sage upstream. If enet_errorack fails to allocate the needed message, we return RETRY and the caller (the write service procedure) will
put the DL_UNBIND_REQ message back on the queue and return.
Otherwise, we free the message and return ERR to tell the service procedure to continue processing messages on the queue.

[368–372] If the state is idle, we allocate a message large enough to hold a
dl_ok_ack_t structure. If the allocation fails, we call enet_wsched
to schedule the write service procedure to run when a message might be
available. Then we return RETRY. Once we have alloced the message
for the acknowledgement, we free the DL_UNBIND_REQ message, since
we no longer need it.

```
373  if (putctl1(ep->e_rq->q_next, M_FLUSH, FLUSHRW) == 0)
374      cmn_err(CE_WARN,
375          "enet: can't flush stream on unbind");
376  bp->b_datap->db_type = M_PCPROTO;
377  ackp = (dl_ok_ack_t *)bp->b_wptr;
378  ackp->dl_primitive = DL_OK_ACK;
379  ackp->dl_correct_primitive = DL_UNBIND_REQ;
380  bp->b_wptr += DL_OK_ACK_SIZE;
381  ep->e_dlstate = DL_UNBOUND;
382  ep->e_prot = 0;
383  putnext(ep->e_rq, bp);
384  return(DONE);
385  }

386  STATIC void
387  enet_send(struct enet *ep, mblk_t *mp)
388  {
389      int i;
390      uchar_t *p, *dest;
391      dl_unitdata_req_t *reqp;
392      struct enethdr e;
393      mblk_t *bp;
394      long destlen;
```

[373–375] We call putctl1 to send an M_FLUSH message upstream to flush the read and write queues in the stream. The DLPI specification requires that the stream be flushed whenever an address is unbound from it. If putctl1 fails, we print a warning on the console but proceed to unbind the address from the stream. Realistically, putctl1 will not fail, because we just freed a message immediately preceding the call to putctl1, and the probability is high that the message will still be available to be reused for the M_FLUSH message.

[376–379] Next we initialize the DL_OK_ACK response. It is made up of one message block of type M_PCPROTO. Its data buffer contains a dl_ok_ack_t structure made up of two fields. We set the dl_primitive field to DL_OK_ACK. Then we set the dl_correct_primitive to DL_UNBIND_REQ to identify the primitive we are acknowledging.

[380–385] We increment the write pointer by the size of the dl_ok_ack_t structure, set the data link state field in the enet structure to DL_UNBOUND, and clear the protocol type field. Finally, we send the DL_OK_ACK message upstream and return.

[386–394] enet_send is called in response to receiving a DL_UNITDATA_REQ message from the consumer. It is used to transmit a packet on the network.

```
395  reqp = (dl_unitdata_req_t *)mp->b_rptr;
396  p = mp->b_rptr + reqp->dl_dest_addr_offset;
397  dest = p;
398  destlen = reqp->dl_dest_addr_length;
399  if (ep->e_dlstate != DL_IDLE) {
400      enet_uderr(ep, dest, destlen, DL_OUTSTATE, 0);
401      freemsg(mp);
402      return;
403  }
404  if (reqp->dl_dest_addr_length != TOTADDRSZ) {
405      enet_uderr(ep, dest, destlen, DL_BADADDR, 0);
406      freemsg(mp);
407      return;
408  }
409  for (i = 0; i < MACSZ; i++) {
410      e.dest[i] = *p++;
411      e.src[i] = enet_addr[i];
412  }
413  e.prot.s = *(ushort_t *)p;
414  bp = mp;
415  mp = mp->b_cont;
416  i = msgdsize(mp);
```

[395–403] We cast a pointer to a `dl_unitdata_req_t` structure over the read
pointer in the message and calculate the location of the destination
address in the message. If the state is not idle, we send a unitdata error
indication upstream by calling `enet_uderr`. The message will indicate that the provider is in the wrong state for sending data. Then we
free the `DL_UNITDATA_REQ` message and return. If `enet_uderr` is
unable to allocate a message for the error indication, no message is sent
upstream. This is acceptable since the data link provider is not required
to deliver error indications reliably with plain connectionless service.

[404–408] If the provider's state is idle, we validate the length of the address. If it
is incorrect, we send a `DL_UDERROR_IND` message upstream, free
the `DL_UNITDATA_REQ` message, and return. This time, the
`DL_UDERROR_IND` message indicates that the address format is invalid.

[409–413] We save copies of the destination physical address and the local physical
address in an Ethernet header structure (`e`) stored on the stack. Then we
copy the SAP portion of the destination DLSAP address to the protocol
field in the Ethernet header on the stack.

[414–416] We use `bp` to save a pointer to the message block containing the unitdata request. Then we calculate the amount of user data to be transmitted. The user data are contained in `M_DATA` message blocks linked to
the initial `M_PROTO` block.

```
417   if ((i > MAXDATA) || (i < MINDATA)) {
418       freemsg(bp);
419       enet_uderr(ep, dest, destlen, DL_BADDATA, 0);
420       return;
421   }
422   freeb(bp);   /* done with dest */
423   if (sameaddr(e.dest, enet_addr)) {
424       enet_loop(mp, &e, ep->e_prot);
425       return;
426   }
427   p = (uchar_t *)SEND_BUF_ADDR;    /* copy to board memory */
428   bcopy((caddr_t)&e, (caddr_t)p, EHDRSZ);
429   p += EHDRSZ;
430   for (bp = mp; bp; bp = bp->b_cont) {
431       i = bp->b_wptr - bp->b_rptr;
432       bcopy((caddr_t)bp->b_rptr, (caddr_t)p, i);
433       p += i;
434   }
```

[417–421]   If the amount of data in the message is either greater than the maximum packet size or less than the minimum packet size, we free the message (recall from line 414 that bp now points to the first message block in the unitdata request message), send a unitdata error indication upstream to indicate that the consumer sent an invalid amount of data, and return.

[422–426]   When we no longer have to worry about sending unitdata error indications upstream, there is no need to keep the M_PROTO message from the unitdata request around, so we call freeb. Even though the message block is linked to others, freeb only frees the first one. The message to which mp refers still contains the user data.

We call sameaddr to see if the destination address and the source address are the same. If so, we call enet_loop to convert the data into a DL_UNITDATA_IND message and enqueue the message on the proper read queue. Then we return.

[427–434]   We assign the address of the I/O board's transmit buffer to a pointer, p, copy the Ethernet header that we constructed in e to the transmit buffer, and increment p by the size of the header. Then we iterate over every message block in the message to be transmitted, copying the contents of the data buffers to the transmit buffer. Note that we call bcopy to copy the data from the message to the I/O board memory that is mapped into the kernel address space. Some I/O boards place restrictions on the way data are to be stored in their memory (such as 16 bits at a time aligned on even address boundaries), and bcopy might not work with these boards because it is optimized to use several different methods to copy data.

```
435  enetsndbusy = 1;
436  CMD_REG = SEND_PKT;
437  if (sameaddr(e.dest, bcast_addr)) {
438      enet_loop(mp, &e, ep->e_prot);
439      return;
440  }
441  freemsg(mp);
442  }

443  STATIC void
444  enet_wsched(struct enet *ep, int size)
445  {
446  ep->e_id = bufcall(size, BPRI_HI, enet_wcont, (long)ep);
447  if (ep->e_id == 0) {
448      ep->e_id = timeout(enet_wcont, (caddr_t)ep,
449          drv_usectohz(ONESEC));
450      ep->e_idtype = TIME_ID;
451  } else {
452      ep->e_idtype = BUF_ID;
453  }
454  }
```

[435–436] We mark the Ethernet board's transmitter as being busy and then send
the command to the board to tell it to transmit the packet contained in
the transmit buffer. The board will compute and assign the CRC checksum and then transmit the packet.

[437–442] If the destination address is equal to the broadcast address, we try to
send the message upstream. This assumes that the I/O board cannot
listen to its own broadcast messages. If this were not true, the call to
enet_loop would be unnecessary because the message would be
delivered by the board through the driver's interrupt handler. If the destination address is not the broadcast address, we free the message since
we no longer need it.

[443–454] enet_wsched is used to recover from a message allocation failure. It
schedules the write service procedure to be run when the allocation will
have a better chance of succeeding. We first use bufcall to schedule
enet_wcont to be run when a message of size bytes can be allocated. If bufcall fails, it will return 0. In this case, we fall back to
using timeout to run enet_wcont in one second. When the write
service procedure runs, the allocation still might not succeed, but we can
just keep waiting and trying until it does. The amount of time to wait
needs to be chosen so that the delay is not too long, but also so that we
do not waste too much time retrying unsuccessfully. Before returning,
we mark the e_idtype field with an indication of which recovery
mechanism we used.

```
455 STATIC void
456 enet_wcont(struct enet *ep)
457 {
458  if (ep->e_rq != NULL) {
459       ep->e_idtype = NO_ID;
460       qenable(WR(ep->e_rq));
461  }
462 }

463 STATIC retval_t
464 enet_errorack(struct enet *ep, ulong_t prim, ulong_t err,
465  ulong_t uerr)
466 {
467  dl_error_ack_t *errp;
468  mblk_t *bp;

469  if ((bp = allocb(DL_ERROR_ACK_SIZE, BPRI_HI)) == NULL) {
470       enet_wsched(ep, DL_ERROR_ACK_SIZE);
471       return(RETRY);
472  }
473  bp->b_datap->db_type = M_PCPROTO;
474  errp = (dl_error_ack_t *)bp->b_wptr;
475  errp->dl_primitive = DL_ERROR_ACK;
476  errp->dl_error_primitive = prim;
```

[455–462]   enet_wcont is run as a result of a previous call to either bufcall or
            timeout. If the read queue pointer in the enet structure is nonzero,
            then the minor device is still in use. In this case, we set the e_idtype
            field to NO_ID and enable the write service procedure. If the write ser-
            vice procedure encounters another allocation failure when it runs, it will
            be rescheduled by this same mechanism.

[463–468]   enet_errorack is used to send a DL_ERROR_ACK message
            upstream when an error occurs at the data link provider interface. It is
            passed a pointer to the enet structure, the primitive (prim) that
            incurred the error, the data link error number (err), and the UNIX error
            number (uerr). The data link error number comes from
            <sys/dlpi.h>, while the UNIX error number is selected from
            <sys/errno.h>.

[469–476]   We try to allocate a message large enough to hold a dl_error_ack_t
            structure. If this fails, we schedule the write service procedure by call-
            ing enet_wsched and return RETRY. The caller will end up placing
            the message being processed back on the write queue in this case. If the
            allocation succeeds, we set the message type to M_PCPROTO and cast a
            pointer to a dl_error_ack_t structure over the write pointer. Then
            we set the dl_primitive field to DL_ERROR_ACK and set the
            dl_error_primitive field to prim.

```
477  errp->dl_errno = err;
478  errp->dl_unix_errno = uerr;
479  bp->b_wptr += DL_ERROR_ACK_SIZE;
480  putnext(ep->e_rq, bp);
481  return(DONE);
482  }

483  STATIC void
484  enet_uderr(struct enet *ep, uchar_t *dest, ulong_t destlen,
485  ulong_t err, ulong_t uerr)
486  {
487  dl_uderror_ind_t *errp;
488  mblk_t *bp;
489  int i;

490  i = DL_UDERROR_IND_SIZE+destlen;
491  if ((bp = allocb(i, BPRI_HI)) == NULL)
492      return;
493  bp->b_datap->db_type = M_PROTO;
494  errp = (dl_uderror_ind_t *)bp->b_wptr;
495  errp->dl_primitive = DL_UDERROR_IND;
496  errp->dl_errno = err;
497  errp->dl_unix_errno = uerr;
498  errp->dl_dest_addr_length = destlen;
499  errp->dl_dest_addr_offset = DL_UDERROR_IND_SIZE;
```

[477–482] We set the `dl_errno` field to `err` and the `dl_unix_errno` field to `uerr`. Then we increment the write pointer by the size of the `dl_error_ack_t` structure, send the message upstream, and return success.

[483–489] `enet_uderr` is used to send a unitdata error indication upstream when an error occurs while trying to transmit a packet. It is passed a pointer to the `enet` structure, a pointer to the destination address, the length of the address, a data link error number, and a UNIX error number.

[490–494] We try to allocate a message large enough to hold a `dl_uderror_ind_t` structure plus the destination address. If the allocation fails, we just return because delivery of unitdata error indications is not guaranteed. Otherwise, we set the message type to `M_PROTO` and initialize the `dl_uderror_ind_t` structure.

[495–499] We set the `dl_primitive` field to `DL_UDERROR_IND`, the `dl_errno` field to `err`, and the `dl_unix_errno` field to `uerr`. Next we set the `dl_dest_addr_length` field to the length of the destination address. The address will be placed in the message after the `dl_uderror_ind_t` structure, so we set the `dl_dest_addr_offset` field to the size of the structure.

```
500   bp->b_wptr += DL_UDERROR_IND_SIZE;
501   bcopy((caddr_t)dest, (caddr_t)bp->b_wptr, destlen);
502   bp->b_wptr += destlen;
503   putnext(ep->e_rq, bp);
504 }

505 void
506 enetintr(int vec)
507 {
508   dl_unitdata_ind_t *dp;
509   uchar_t *p, *protp;
510   int i, stat, size;
511   mblk_t *mp, *bp;
512   ushort_t prot;

513   stat = STAT_REG;
514   switch (stat) {
515   case SEND_DONE:
516       enetsndbusy = 0;
517       for (i = enetnext; i < MAXENET; i++)
518           if ((enet[i].e_dlstate == DL_IDLE) &&
519               (WR(enet[i].e_rq)->q_first != NULL)) {
520               qenable(WR(enet[i].e_rq));
521               enetnext = i+1;
522               return;
523           }
```

[500–504] Then we increment the write pointer by the size of the dl_uderror_ind_t structure and copy the address into the message. Finally, we increment the write pointer by the size of the address and send the message upstream.

[505–514] The Ethernet driver's interrupt routine is called when the I/O board has an event to report, such as receipt of a packet. The vec parameter is used to distinguish between interrupts from multiple boards controlled by the same driver. In our example, we only support one I/O board, so we can ignore vec. We begin by obtaining the status of the I/O board by reading the contents of its status register.

[515–523] If this is an interrupt designating the completion of a transmission, we mark the board's transmitter as no longer busy and search through the array of minor devices, starting where we left off last time (enetnext), looking for one that is bound and has messages on its write queue. If we find one, we enable the write queue's service procedure, save the value of the next minor to check, and return. If we hit the end of the array, we end this half of the search.

```
524        for (i = 0; i < enetnext; i++)
525            if ((enet[i].e_dlstate == DL_IDLE) &&
526              (WR(enet[i].e_rq)->q_first != NULL)) {
527                qenable(WR(enet[i].e_rq));
528                enetnext = i+1;
529                return;
530            }
531        break;

532  case RECV_PKT:
533        CMD_REG = RECV_OFF;
534        size = DL_UNITDATA_IND_SIZE+TOTADDRSZ+TOTADDRSZ;
535        if ((mp = allocb(size, BPRI_MED)) == NULL) {
536            CMD_REG = RECV_ON;
537            enetrcvlost++;
538            return;      /* drop packet on floor */
539        }
540        size = SIZE_REG;
541        if ((bp = esballoc(RECV_BUF_ADDR, size, BPRI_MED,
542          &enetfrtn)) == NULL) {
543            freeb(mp);
544            CMD_REG = RECV_ON;
545            enetrcvlost++;
546            return;      /* drop packet on floor */
547        }
```

[524–531] We start the second half of the search from the beginning of the array. We look for a write queue to enable as before, until we reach the place where we originally started the search. If we find a nonempty write queue, we enable its service procedure, save the value of the next minor to check, and return. Otherwise, we break out of this case and return from the interrupt handler.

[532–540] The next type of interrupt is the reception of a packet. First we shut the receiver off. Then we try to allocate a message large enough to hold a dl_unitdata_ind_t structure plus the source and destination addresses. If this fails, we turn the receiver back on and return, leaving the packet in the receive buffer, where it will eventually be overwritten. In this case, we increment a counter to keep track of the number of packets lost. If the allocation succeeds, we read the size register to find out the number of bytes in the received packet.

[541–547] Instead of allocating a STREAMS message and copying the data from the board memory to the buffer, we use esballoc to allocate just the message headers to describe the area of memory containing the received data. If this fails, we free the first message we allocated, turn the receiver on, increment the lost-packet counter, and return.

```
548        mp->b_datap->db_type = M_PROTO;
549        dp = (dl_unitdata_ind_t *)mp->b_wptr;
550        dp->dl_primitive = DL_UNITDATA_IND;
551        dp->dl_dest_addr_length = TOTADDRSZ;
552        dp->dl_dest_addr_offset = DL_UNITDATA_IND_SIZE;
553        dp->dl_src_addr_length = TOTADDRSZ;
554        dp->dl_src_addr_offset = DL_UNITDATA_IND_SIZE +
555            TOTADDRSZ;
556        p = bp->b_rptr;
557        dp->dl_group_address = isgroupaddr(p);
558        mp->b_wptr += DL_UNITDATA_IND_SIZE;
559        for (i = 0; i < MACSZ; i++)
560            *mp->b_wptr++ = *p++;
561        protp = mp->b_wptr;
562        mp->b_wptr += SAPSZ;
563        for (i = 0; i < MACSZ; i++)
564            *mp->b_wptr++ = *p++;
565        prot = *p << 8;
566        *mp->b_wptr++ = *p;
567        *protp++ = *p++;
568        prot |= *p;
569        *mp->b_wptr++ = *p;
570        *protp = *p++;
```

[548–557] We initialize the unitdata indication by setting the message type to M_PROTO and storing a dl_unitdata_ind_t structure in the data buffer. We set the dl_primitive field to DL_UNITDATA_IND and initialize the address fields. The destination address will be stored in the message immediately following the dl_unitdata_ind_t structure. The source address will be placed in the message after the destination address. The dl_group_address field is nonzero if the destination address refers to more than one location. We call isgroupaddr (described shortly) to determine if the destination address is multicast.

[558–570] We increment the write pointer by the size of a dl_unitdata_ind_t structure and copy the physical destination and source addresses from the Ethernet header in the receive buffer to the M_PROTO message. Note that we leave room in the message for the SAP identifier. We copy the protocol type to the prot variable and to the SAP identifiers in the destination and source DLSAP addresses.

Note that the Ethernet packet format only contains one protocol field, assuming that the source and the destination are using the same protocol. Since we are using the protocol field as the SAP identifier, we must make the assumption that the sender and the receiver have the same SAP identifier. Even so, the driver allows an endpoint to transmit a packet to a peer with a different SAP identifier.

```
571        bp->b_rptr = p;
572        mp->b_cont = bp;
573        for (i = 0; i < MAXENET; i++)
574            if ((enet[i].e_prot == prot) &&
575               (enet[i].e_dlstate == DL_IDLE)) {
576                if (canput(enet[i].e_rq)) {
577                    putq(enet[i].e_rq, mp);
578                    enetrcvbusy = 1;
579                    return;
580                } else {
581                    freemsg(mp);
582                    enetrcvlost++;
583                }
584                break;
585            }
586        if (i >= MAXENET)
587            freemsg(mp);
588        CMD_REG = RECV_ON;
589        break;

590  default:
591        enetspurint++;
592        break;
593  }
594 }
```

[571–572] We set the read pointer in the message we allocated via `esballoc` to point to the first byte after the Ethernet header in the board's receive buffer. To complete the unitdata indication, we link this message block to the `M_PROTO` message containing the `DL_UNITDATA_IND` header using the `b_cont` field in the `M_PROTO` message.

[573–589] Now we need to find out which stream, if any, should receive the packet. For every minor device in the idle state, we check if the protocol type matches that of the received packet. If so, we have found the correct stream. If that stream's read queue is not flow-controlled, we enqueue the message, mark the receive buffer as busy, and return. Otherwise, we free the message and increment the lost-packet counter. If we exit the loop without finding a match, we free the message. Then we reenable the receiver and return. We do not increment the lost-packet counter in this case, because we do not consider a packet to be lost if a valid destination does not exist.

[590–594] The default case for the `switch` statement represents unidentified interrupts (called "spurious" interrupts). If any interrupts occur without a reason, we remember the event by incrementing a counter. The counter can be queried by a kernel debugger or a special `ioctl` command. Too many spurious interrupts could be an indication of hardware problems.

```
595 STATIC void
596 enet_ioctl(queue_t *q, mblk_t *mp)
597 {
598  int i;
599  uchar_t *p;
600  struct iocblk *iocp;
601  struct enet *ep;

602  iocp = (struct iocblk *)mp->b_rptr;
603  ep = (struct enet *)q->q_ptr;
604  if (iocp->ioc_count == TRANSPARENT)
605      goto nak;
606  switch (iocp->ioc_cmd) {
607  case SETADDR:
608      if (iocp->ioc_count != MACSZ)
609          goto nak;
610      if (ep->e_dlstate != DL_UNBOUND) {
611          iocp->ioc_error = EBUSY;
612          goto nak;
613      }
614      iocp->ioc_error = drv_priv(iocp->ioc_cr);
615      if (iocp->ioc_error != 0)
616          goto nak;
617      p = (uchar_t *)ENET_ADDR;
618      for (i = 0; i < MACSZ; i++) {
619          enet_addr[i] = *mp->b_cont->b_rptr++;
620          *p++ = enet_addr[i];
621      }
622      CMD_REG = SET_ADDR;
```

[595–606] enet_ioctl handles the ioctl requests supported by the Ethernet driver. We start by casting a pointer to an iocblk structure over the read pointer in the M_IOCTL message. Then we get the pointer to the enet structure associated with the queue. If the ioctl command is a transparent ioctl, we fail the request by jumping to the location labeled nak (see the next page).

[607–616] The SETADDR command can be used by administrative commands to set the Ethernet board address. First, we make sure the address is the correct size. If the data link provider is bound, then we fail the request, setting ioc_error to EBUSY. Our final validity check is to see if the user has permission to change the board address. If not, we fail the request.

[617–622] We copy the physical address specified by the user into both enet_addr and the I/O board's address buffer and send a command to the board to tell it to set the address.

```
623        mp->b_datap->db_type = M_IOCACK;
624        iocp->ioc_count = 0;
625        break;

626   case GETADDR:
627        if (iocp->ioc_count != MACSZ)
628            goto nak;
629        mp->b_cont->b_wptr = mp->b_cont->b_rptr;
630        for (i = 0; i < MACSZ; i++)
631            *mp->b_cont->b_wptr++ = enet_addr[i];
632        mp->b_datap->db_type = M_IOCACK;
633        break;

634   default:
635   nak:
636        mp->b_datap->db_type = M_IOCNAK;
637   }
638   qreply(q, mp);
639 }
```

[623–625] To complete the command and indicate its success, we convert the
M_IOCTL message into an M_IOCACK message, set the ioc_count
field to 0 since there is nothing to copy back to the user's buffer, and
send the message upstream.

[626–633] The second ioctl command supported by the driver is GETADDR. It
returns the board's address to the user. If the user's buffer is not the
proper size, we fail the request. Otherwise, we set the write pointer in
the M_DATA block of the message to its read pointer and then copy the
address of the board into the M_DATA message, one byte at a time, incrementing the write pointer as we go. Since ioc_count already equals
MACSZ, there is no need for us to set it. We change the type of the message to M_IOCACK and send the message upstream.

[634–639] The default case is the same as the label nak, where previous code
jumps when a negative acknowledgement is to be generated. An
unknown ioctl command is failed by changing the message type to
M_IOCNAK and sending the message upstream. This will cause the
request to fail with errno set to the value of the ioc_error field in
the iocblk structure stored in the message. If we do not set
ioc_error, then errno defaults to EINVAL.

```
640 STATIC void
641 enet_loop(mblk_t *mp, struct enethdr *ehp, ushort_t srcsap)
642 {
643   dl_unitdata_ind_t *dp;
644   struct enet *ep;
645   mblk_t *bp;
646   ushort_t prot;
647   int i;

648   prot = (ehp->prot.b[0]<<8)|ehp->prot.b[1];
649   ep = NULL;
650   for (i = 0; i < MAXENET; i++)
651       if ((enet[i].e_prot == prot) &&
652         (enet[i].e_dlstate == DL_IDLE)) {
653           if (canput(enet[i].e_rq))
654               ep = &enet[i];
655           break;
656       }

657   if (ep == NULL) {
658       freemsg(mp);
659       return;
660   }
661   i = DL_UNITDATA_IND_SIZE+TOTADDRSZ+TOTADDRSZ;
662   if ((bp = allocb(i, BPRI_MED)) == NULL) {
663       freemsg(mp);
664       return;
665   }
```

[640–647] enet_loop is used to convert the data from a DL_UNITDATA_REQ message sent downstream into a DL_UNITDATA_IND message, then send it back upstream. It is passed a pointer to the data message, a pointer to the Ethernet header, and the source SAP identifier.

[648–656] We start by converting the protocol field contained in the Ethernet header into the proper byte order so the host can interpret it. Then we search through the array of minor devices to find an entry with the same protocol type in the idle state. If we find a match, we call canput to see if its read queue can accept any more messages. If it can, we set ep to point at the minor device's enet entry. Otherwise, ep remains NULL. In either case, we stop the search when a match is found.

[657–665] If ep is still NULL after the search, we free the message and return. Otherwise, we calculate the size of the message we need to allocate. A DL_UNITDATA_IND message contains a dl_unitdata_ind_t structure and two DLSAP addresses. If the allocation fails, we free the data message and return.

```
666  bp->b_datap->db_type = M_PROTO;
667  dp = (dl_unitdata_ind_t *)bp->b_wptr;
668  dp->dl_primitive = DL_UNITDATA_IND;
669  dp->dl_dest_addr_length = TOTADDRSZ;
670  dp->dl_dest_addr_offset = DL_UNITDATA_IND_SIZE;
671  dp->dl_src_addr_length = TOTADDRSZ;
672  dp->dl_src_addr_offset = DL_UNITDATA_IND_SIZE +
673    TOTADDRSZ;

674  bp->b_wptr += DL_UNITDATA_IND_SIZE;
675  for (i = 0; i < MACSZ; i++)
676      *bp->b_wptr++ = ehp->dest[i];
677  *(ushort_t *)bp->b_wptr = ehp->prot.s;
678  bp->b_wptr += SAPSZ;
679  for (i = 0; i < MACSZ; i++)
680      *bp->b_wptr++ = ehp->src[i];
681  *bp->b_wptr++ = (srcsap>>8) & 0xff;
682  *bp->b_wptr++ = srcsap & 0xff;
683  bp->b_cont = mp;
684  putq(ep->e_rq, bp);
685  }

686  STATIC void
687  enet_free(char *dummy)
688  {
689   enetrcvbusy = 0;
690   CMD_REG = RECV_ON;
691  }
```

[666–673] We set the type of the message we just allocated to M_PROTO and store a dl_unitdata_ind_t structure in its data buffer. Just as in enetintr, we set the dl_primitive field to DL_UNITDATA_IND and initialize the destination and source address information to indicate the offsets and lengths of the DLSAP addresses stored in the message.

[674–685] We increment the write pointer by the size of the dl_unitdata_ind_t structure and copy the physical destination address and the SAP identifier (protocol type) from the Ethernet header. Then we copy the physical source address from the header, but we copy the SAP identifier from the srcsap parameter. Finally, we link the M_DATA message on the end of the M_PROTO message and place the resulting message on the recipient's read queue.

[686–691] enet_free is called as a result of the esballoced message's being freed, indicating that the receive buffer is no longer in use. Since this space is now available, we enable the receiver on the I/O board and mark the buffer as no longer in use.

```
692 STATIC int
693 sameaddr(uchar_t *a, uchar_t *b)
694 {
695   int i;

696   for (i = 0; i < MACSZ; i++)
697       if (*a++ != *b++)
698             return(0);
699   return(1);
700 }

701 STATIC int
702 isgroupaddr(uchar_t *dest)
703 {
704   return(*dest & 0x01);
705 }
```

[692–700] `sameaddr` is used to compare two Ethernet addresses. If they match, we return 1. Otherwise, we return 0.

[701–705] `isgroupaddr` is called to determine if an Ethernet address is multicast. It returns 1 if the address is multicast, and 0 otherwise. Recall from the Ethernet overview at the beginning of this section that the low-order bit in the highest-order byte of an Ethernet address is set if the address is multicast.

Drivers that use physical DMA to transfer data between the host computer and an I/O board need to handle the special case where the data in a STREAMS message cross a page boundary. Since a STREAMS data buffer can span several pages, the data might be contained in pages that are not physically contiguous. In this case, the driver will have to DMA each page separately, or if the hardware supports scatter–gather DMA, the driver will specify a new base-length pair for each page.

There are several different conditions under which the data buffer in a STREAMS message will cross a page boundary. First, the buffer size could be larger than the page size of the host computer. Buffers smaller than the page size usually will not cross a page boundary, but this is only a side effect of the STREAMS implementation. Because the implementation can change in the future, driver writers should not rely on this. Second, if the message was allocated via `esballoc`, then the buffer could occupy an arbitrary location in memory.

For these reasons, drivers using physical DMA should never assume that any buffer (with a length greater than one byte) lies entirely within a page. The following code fragment shows how a driver doing physical DMA would transmit data to the I/O device. The details regarding the DMA interface are hardware-dependent.

```
paddr_t addr;      /* physical address */
mblk_t *mp, *bp;
size_t size, off, len;
size_t pagesz, pagemask;

/*
 * Calculate the page size and mask at run time
 * for portability.
 */
pagesz = ptob(1);
pagemask = pagesz - 1;
for (bp = mp; bp; bp = bp->b_cont) {
    size = bp->b_wptr - bp->b_rptr;
    if (size == 0)
        continue;
    off = (size_t)bp->b_rptr & pagemask;
    if ((off + size) > pagesz) {
        /*
         * The data cross a page boundary.
         */
        while (size != 0) {
            /*
             * Convert the virtual address to a
             * physical one.
             */
            addr = vtop((caddr_t)bp->b_rptr, NULL);
            len = min((pagesz - off), size);
            /*
             * Issue a DMA job of (addr, len).
             */
            :
            :
            bp->b_rptr += len;
            size -= len;
            off = (size_t)bp->b_rptr & pagemask;
        }
    } else {
        /*
         * The data lie entirely within a single
         * page.  Convert the virtual address to
         * a physical one.
         */
        addr = vtop((caddr_t)bp->b_rptr, NULL);
        /*
         * Issue a DMA job of (addr, size).
         */
        :
        :
    }
}
```

Summary

We have summarized the entry points that STREAMS drivers can provide and have illustrated common techniques used by drivers to operate in the STREAMS subsystem. As an aid to understanding how to design STREAMS drivers, we have studied a simple Ethernet driver. Even though the hardware interface is oversimplified, this Ethernet driver exhibits techniques used in more realistic network drivers. The DLPI specification it supports enables the Ethernet driver to be used with protocol stacks that rely on the services provided by a DLPI-based network driver.

Exercises

10.1 Modify the Ethernet driver to allow multiple minor devices to be bound to the same protocol type.

10.2 Modify the Ethernet driver to support multiple transmit and receive buffers.

10.3 Replace the `ioctl` commands that get and set the Ethernet board address with the optional primitives described in Appendix A of the DLPI specification.

10.4 On line 521 in the Ethernet driver, `enetnext` is used to save the array index where the search will begin on the next transmission-completion interrupt. Explain what happens when `i` is equal to `MAXENET-1`. Is this a bug?

Bibliographic Notes

The Ethernet was developed at Xerox PARC [Metcalfe and Boggs 1976]. The second version specification was published by Digital Equipment Corporation, Intel Corporation, and Xerox Corporation [Xerox et al. 1982]. The IEEE 802.3 standard specifying the physical layer and the MAC portion of the data link layer for CSMA/CD local area networks is based on the Ethernet specification.

The DLPI specification was developed by AT&T. It is documented in *STREAMS Modules and Drivers* [USL 1992a].

More information about writing STREAMS drivers can be found in *STREAMS Modules and Drivers* [USL 1992a] and *UNIX System V Release 4 Programmer's Guide: STREAMS* [USL 1990b].

The *UNIX System V/386 Release 4 Integrated Software Development Guide* [USL 1990e] describes how to configure drivers in an Intel 80x86-based UNIX SVR4 system. For SVR4.2, configuration information can be found in *Device Driver Programming* [USL 1992b].

11
STREAMS
Modules

STREAMS modules are similar to STREAMS drivers, so many of the techniques described in the last chapter are also applicable to writing STREAMS modules. This chapter describes how to write STREAMS modules and contrasts them with drivers. The terminal interface is also discussed as a prelude to the major example in the chapter: a terminal emulation module for networks.

11.1 INTRODUCTION

STREAMS modules are similar to drivers, but instead of copying data between the host computer and peripheral devices, modules usually only perform intermediate transformations on the messages passing through a stream. Some modules modify the data in the messages they are passed, while other modules only perform translations between one service interface and another.

For example, in System V Release 4, the LDTERM module performs canonical line discipline processing on data traveling in a stream acting as a terminal. LDTERM performs tasks such as erase and kill processing, character echoing, and special character interpretation. As another example, the TIRDWR module can be pushed on a stream connected to a transport-level driver to convert between the transport provider service interface and a read/write byte-stream interface.

Modules are "pushed" onto a stream using either the I_PUSH ioctl command or the autopush mechanism [see autopush(1M)]. This terminology is somewhat misleading because, when a module is pushed on a stream, it is really *inserted* in the stream immediately below the stream head.

Figure 11.1 shows what a stream looks like after a module is pushed on it. (Consider the "before" picture to be the same as Figure 10.1.) Once pushed, the stream head passes messages to the module instead of the driver. The module will optionally process the messages it is passed and then forward them on to the driver. Similarly, the driver will pass messages to the module instead of the stream head.

Modules can be removed from a stream as easily as they are added. The I_POP

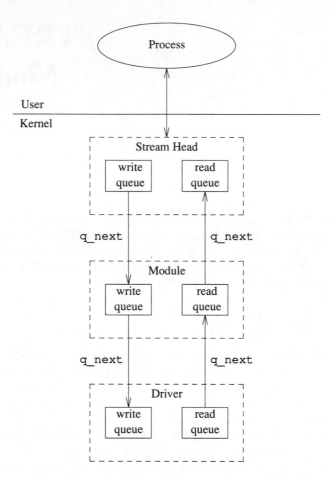

Fig. 11.1. A Module in a Stream

ioctl command removes the topmost module in a stream. No special permissions are usually needed to push and pop modules. As long as a process has a valid file descriptor that refers to a stream, and the modules do not enforce any privilege requirement themselves, that process can push and pop modules. There is a configurable limit (NSTRPUSH) to the number of modules that can be pushed on a given stream, however. Its default value is usually around eight or nine, high enough for most applications.

One of the advantages of the STREAMS framework is the ability to combine several modules in a stream to perform more than one kind of intermediate processing. Figure 11.2 depicts two modules on a stream. In it, the module labeled A was pushed before the module named B.

The advantage to isolating intermediate processing functions in separate modules and then combining modules in a stream is that processing functions only

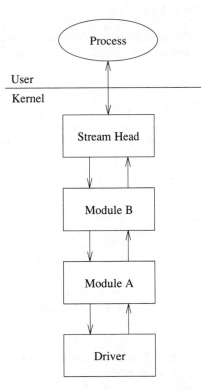

Fig. 11.2. Two Modules in a Stream

need to be implemented once, and then they can be reused wherever needed. For example, the LDTERM module contains all the terminal-related line discipline processing needed in the system. While it is normally pushed on streams connected to terminal devices, it can also be pushed on streams connected to pseudo-terminal drivers and networks. Then, if a terminal stream needs to support XENIX or BSD-style `ioctl` operations, the TTCOMPAT module can be pushed on top of LDTERM in the stream.

Unlike drivers, modules are not accessed through the file system namespace. Instead of being identified by device numbers, they are identified by their module names. Most implementations, however, do not use the module name stored in the `mi_idname` field of the `module_info` structure for the name identifying the module.

Instead of searching a module's object file for the name (which is not that complicated to do), the configuration software usually relies on some other mechanism to associate a name with a module. For the Intel 80x86 architecture, the configuration software uses the first field in the module's `mdevice` file [see `mdevice(4)`]. For consistency, the name used by the configuration software should match the name stored in the `module_info` structure.

11.2 MODULE ENTRY POINTS

With the exception of the interrupt routine, modules have the same entry points as drivers. The `init` (D2D) and `start` (D2DK) routines can be used to initialize the module:

```
void prefixinit(void);
void prefixstart(void);
```

where *prefix* is the module prefix [see `prefix` (D1DK].

When a module is pushed on a stream, the module's `open` (D2DK) routine is called:

```
#include <sys/types.h>
#include <sys/stream.h>
#include <sys/errno.h>
#include <sys/cred.h>
#include <sys/ddi.h>

int prefixopen(queue_t *q, dev_t *devp, int oflag, int sflag,
    cred_t *crp);
```

Although the syntax is the same as the driver open routine, some of the parameters have different meanings. The `q` parameter is a pointer to the module's read queue. The `devp` parameter points to the device number associated with the driver at the end of the stream. Cloning does not apply to modules, so changes to the device number have no effect. The `oflag` argument has no meaning for modules and is set to 0. The `sflag` argument is set to `MODOPEN` to indicate that the processing element is being opened as a module. `crp` is a pointer to the credentials of the process pushing the module on the stream.

The STREAMS subsystem will serialize all processes opening and pushing modules on the same stream. If one process is in the middle of opening a stream, another process trying to push a module on the same stream will block until the open is complete. Similarly, if two processes try to push modules on the same stream at the same time, one will proceed and the other will block until the first one is finished.

Module open routines have user context and can sleep, but need to do so either at an uninterruptible priority or with `PCATCH` set [see `sleep` (D3K)]. When a module open routine runs as a result of the module being pushed onto a stream, interrupts from all STREAMS devices are blocked. Some versions of SVR4 contain a bug dealing with successive opens of a stream. These versions neglect to raise the processor priority level before calling the driver and module open routines. Thus, in their open routines, drivers and modules need to protect any data structures that might change as a result of interrupts occurring during the processing of successive opens.

Since modules are not associated with device numbers, it is difficult for them to use the device number to identify their private data structures associated with the stream. Modules that maintain arrays of private data structures usually just look for unused array entries to use for new instantiations of the module. Alternatively, modules can dynamically allocate the data structures to be used with the stream.

Consider how the stream in Figure 11.2 is built. The driver is opened first. Then module A is pushed and its open routine is called. Finally, module B's open routine is called when module B is pushed on the stream. Now consider what happens when another process opens the driver. The stream is already constructed, so the system will notify the modules and driver by calling their open routines. Thus modules and drivers can tell the number of times the stream is opened.

This information is of limited value, however, because of two things. First, closes and opens are not matched. That is, close routines are only called when no more references to the stream exist, or in the case of modules, when they are popped off the stream. Second, no notification is made when file descriptors are duplicated (via dup(2), for example), so drivers and modules can never be sure exactly how many references to the stream exist.

Successive opens of a stream result in the open routines of the processing elements in the stream being called in the opposite order from which they were called when the stream was first constructed. Consider Figure 11.2 again. If another process opens the driver while the stream is still in use, then module B's open routine will be called, followed by module A's open routine and, finally, the driver's open routine. This usually is not a problem because drivers and modules rarely do any significant processing during successive opens. Still, developers have to make sure that they do not introduce any hidden dependencies on this ordering difference.

Besides the I_PUSH ioctl command, modules can be pushed on the stream when a driver is first opened. The autopush(1M) command provides a way for administrators to configure lists of modules to be pushed automatically by the STREAMS subsystem when a driver is opened.

There are two circumstances under which the module close(D2DK) routine is called. The first is when the last close of the stream occurs. As part of the process of dismantling the stream, each module's close routine is called before the module is removed from the stream. The second circumstance is when a module is on top of a stream and a process issues the I_POP ioctl command. The module close routine has the same syntax as the driver close routine:

```
#include <sys/types.h>
#include <sys/file.h>
#include <sys/stream.h>
#include <sys/errno.h>
#include <sys/cred.h>
#include <sys/ddi.h>

int prefixclose(queue_t *q, int flag, cred_t *crp);
```

Unlike the oflag parameter in the module open routine, the close routine's flag parameter contains the current contents of the file flags. The only ones useful to modules are FNONBLOCK and FNDELAY. If either is set, the module should try to avoid sleeping during close processing.

Module close routines have user context and can sleep, but if they do so, they must sleep so that signals do not cause a longjump. Interrupts from STREAMS devices are blocked during the execution of the module close routine.

Module put procedures are the same as driver put procedures, except that modules are required to provide put (D2DK) procedures for both the read and write sides.

```
#include <sys/types.h>
#include <sys/stream.h>
#include <sys/stropts.h>

int prefixput(queue_t *q, mblk_t *mp);
```

When a message is passed to a module, the module can choose to process it or not. Regardless of the choice, the module can then do one of three things:

1. Free the message.
2. Pass the message on to the next processing element in the stream.
3. Enqueue the message.

Module put procedures do not have user context and cannot call any functions that sleep. All unrecognized messages should be passed on to the next processing element in the stream. If a module recognizes a particular command in an M_IOCTL message, it should usually act on the command instead of forwarding the message. One exception to this is when a module works in concert with other processing elements in the stream. In this situation, the module can pass the message downstream and wait for the response message before taking action. The terminal line discipline module, LDTERM, performs some of its ioctl processing this way.

Module flush processing is similar to that of a driver, except M_FLUSH messages are passed along in the stream instead of being freed or sent back upstream. Assuming q is a pointer to the module's write queue, the canonical flushing algorithm for modules is

```
if (*mp->b_rptr & FLUSHW)
    flushq(q, FLUSHDATA);
if (*mp->b_rptr & FLUSHR) {
    flushq(RD(q), FLUSHDATA);
putnext(q, mp);
```

For the read side of the stream, the flushing algorithm is similar (here, q is a pointer to the module's read queue):

```
if (*mp->b_rptr & FLUSHR)
    flushq(q, FLUSHDATA);
if (*mp->b_rptr & FLUSHW)
    flushq(WR(q), FLUSHDATA);
putnext(q, mp);
```

If a module maintains the notion of different bands of data flow, then the flushing algorithms change to honor the FLUSHBAND flag. For example, the algorithm for the read side is

```
if (*mp->b_rptr & FLUSHR) {
    if (*mp->b_rptr & FLUSHBAND)
        flushband(q, FLUSHDATA, *(mp->b_rptr + 1));
    else
        flushq(q, FLUSHDATA);
}
if (*mp->b_rptr & FLUSHW) {
    if (*mp->b_rptr & FLUSHBAND)
        flushband(WR(q), FLUSHDATA, *(mp->b_rptr + 1));
    else
        flushq(WR(q), FLUSHDATA);
}
putnext(q, mp);
```

In Section 3.6, we discussed the problem of flushing data in a pipe. Since the read and write sides of a stream pipe cross, the flags in an M_FLUSH message need to be switched. PIPEMOD can be pushed on one side of the pipe to do this job.

If you are already pushing modules on a pipe, it is a shame to have to push PIPEMOD, too, just to make sure flushing occurs properly. Thus, when developing a module that you expect to be pushed on a stream pipe, you should add the necessary code to switch the flush flags. Before calling putnext, the flags can be switched with the following algorithm:

```
if (!SAMESTR(q)) {
    switch (*mp->b_rptr & FLUSHRW) {
    case FLUSHR:
        *mp->b_rptr = (*mp->b_rptr & ~FLUSHR) | FLUSHW;
        break;

    case FLUSHW:
        *mp->b_rptr = (*mp->b_rptr & ~FLUSHW) | FLUSHR;
        break;
    }
}
```

where q is a pointer to the module's queue, and mp is a pointer to the M_FLUSH message. SAMESTR will return a nonzero value if q is at the midpoint of a pipe, and 0 otherwise.

Module service procedures [see srv (D2DK)] have the same interface as driver service procedures:

```
#include <sys/types.h>
#include <sys/stream.h>
#include <sys/stropts.h>

int prefixsrv(queue_t *q);
```

Like driver service procedures, module service procedures run without user context, so they cannot call any functions that sleep. Module service procedures honor flow control by using the same canonical algorithm presented in Section 10.2.

11.3 THE TERMINAL INTERFACE

The terminal (TTY for short, a historical mnemonic standing for TeleTYpewriter, an early typewriter-like terminal) interface in SVR4 provides processes with access to devices that support asynchronous serial communications. This interface is the primary one through which users interact with the computer.

Each terminal device is associated with a *line discipline* that processes special characters written to and read from the terminal. In SVR4, the line discipline is implemented as a STREAMS module called LDTERM (see Figure 11.3). The line discipline has two modes of operation. In *raw* mode, characters are passed unprocessed through the stream. In *cooked* mode (also known as *canonical* mode), the line discipline delivers data to the stream head in single-line units and performs special character processing, such as erase and kill processing and echoing characters received.

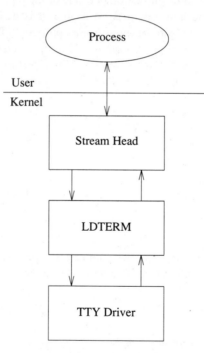

Fig. 11.3. A Terminal Stream

The communication characteristics, special characters, and special character processing can all be manipulated with the ioctl system call. POSIX has created an implementation-independent, higher-level interface to control many of the options [see termios(2)]. The options are described by a termios structure:

```
struct termios {
    tcflag_t     c_iflag;      /* input modes */
    tcflag_t     c_oflag;      /* output modes */
    tcflag_t     c_cflag;      /* control modes */
    tcflag_t     c_lflag;      /* local modes */
    cc_t         c_cc[NCCS];   /* control chars */
};
```

The c_iflag field contains flags that control the input character processing.
The c_oflag field contains flags that control the output processing. The c_cflag
field contains the hardware-related flags. The c_lflag field contains flags that
affect the line discipline processing. The c_cc array contains all the special characters, such as erase and line kill.

In the example module described in the next section, we will only concern ourselves with the c_cflag flags because the module is intended to emulate terminal
hardware. More sophisticated I/O devices might perform some of the line discipline
processing for the host, but since LDTERM is capable of handling the other fields,
we are free to simplify the hardware emulation module. Table 11.1 summarizes the
flags defined for c_cflag.

Table 11.1. c_cflag Flags

Flag	Description
CBAUD	Defines the bits that control the baud rate.
CSIZE	Defines the bits that control the number of bits per character.
CSTOPB	2 stop bits if on, 1 stop bit if off.
CREAD	Enables the receiver.
PARENB	Enables parity checking.
PARODD	Odd parity if on, even parity if off.
HUPCL	Hang up the device on last close.
CLOCAL	Ignore modem status signals (do not generate a hangup if the line drops).
CIBAUD	Defines the bits that control the input baud rate if different than the output baud rate.
PAREXT	Extended parity (mark and space).

The CBAUD flag is actually a mask that defines the set of flags that make up the
possible baud rates that can be set. Each baud rate is defined by a separate flag, as
shown in Table 11.2. B0 is not really a baud rate. It is a flag used to tell the driver
to hang up the device. The CSIZE flag is also a mask. It defines the set of flags that
make up the possible character sizes (number of bits per character) that are to be
used. These flags are summarized in Table 11.3.

Table 11.2. Baud Rate Flags

Flag	Baud Rate	Flag	Baud Rate
B0	Hang up	B600	600
B50	50	B1200	1200
B75	75	B1800	1800
B110	110	B2400	2400
B134	134.5	B4800	4800
B150	150	B9600	9600
B200	200	B19200	19200
B300	300	B38400	38400

Table 11.3. Character Size Flags

Flag	Character Size
CS5	5 bits
CS6	6 bits
CS7	7 bits
CS8	8 bits

The POSIX `termios` structure was derived from the earlier System V `termio` structure:

```
struct termio {
     ushort_t    c_iflag;      /* input modes */
     ushort_t    c_oflag;      /* output modes */
     ushort_t    c_cflag;      /* control modes */
     ushort_t    c_lflag;      /* local modes */
     char        c_line;       /* line discipline */
     uchar_t     c_cc[NCC];    /* control chars */
};
```

All fields are similar to the `termios` structure, except for the `c_line` field. It is obsolete with a STREAMS-based TTY subsystem. The `termios` flag fields are larger than their `termio` counterparts (type `tcflag_t` is an `unsigned long`), and `termios` defines more control characters than `termio`.

Underneath the POSIX interfaces, the terminal options are manipulated with several `ioctl` commands. Most terminal options can be set with commands that use either the `termios` structure or the `termio` structure. Other commands get and set terminal parameters using ad hoc argument formats. Most are described in `termio(7)`. Table 11.4 summarizes the `ioctl` commands supported by the terminal emulator module presented in the next section.

The `TCSETA`, `TCSETAF`, `TCSETAW`, and `TCGETA` commands all use the `termio` structure, while the `TCSETS`, `TCSETSF`, `TCSETSW`, and `TCGETS` commands use the `termios` structure. These `ioctl` commands are processed by the modules and drivers in an atypical manner. LDTERM is usually the first module in

Table 11.4. Terminal Emulator `ioctl` Commands

Command	Description
TCSETA	Set the `termio` terminal parameters immediately.
TCSETAF	Set the `termio` terminal parameters after output has drained, and discard any unread input.
TCSETAW	Set the `termio` terminal parameters after output has drained.
TCGETA	Get the current `termio` terminal parameters.
TCSETS	Set the `termios` terminal parameters immediately.
TCSETSF	Set the `termios` terminal parameters after output has drained, and discard any unread input.
TCSETSW	Set the `termios` terminal parameters after output has drained.
TCGETS	Get the current `termios` terminal parameters.
TCSBRK	Send a break after output drains.
TIOCSTI	Simulate terminal input.
TIOCSWINSZ	Set the terminal's notion of the screen size.
TIOCGWINSZ	Get the terminal's notion of the screen size.
EUC_MSAVE	Save current codeset mode and switch to ASCII.
EUC_MREST	Restore saved codeset mode.
EUC_IXLOFF	Turn off input conversion.
EUC_IXLON	Restore input conversion.
EUC_OXLOFF	Turn off output conversion.
EUC_OXLON	Restore output conversion.

the stream that recognizes them, but since they affect parameters controlled by both the terminal driver and the line discipline, LDTERM does what work it can and then forwards the M_IOCTL message to the driver. The driver processes the c_cflag field and sends either an M_IOCACK or M_IOCNAK message upstream. Thus, instead of one processing element handling the `ioctl` command, several work together to support it.

The TCSBRK command will cause the terminal to generate a *break* after allowing any output to drain. A break is a condition where the device transmits a sequence of zero-valued bits for an amount of time longer than that needed to transmit a single byte.

The TIOCSTI command is used to simulate a user typing characters at a terminal's keyboard. The command can be used to "unread" data read from the terminal stream. Few applications use this facility, but those that do (csh, ttymon, and mailx) are important enough to warrant our supporting it in the emulation module.

To support windowing-based applications, the emulation module maintains the notion of a window size (screen size). The TIOCSWINSZ command changes the window size, and the TIOCGWINSZ command returns the window size. Both commands represent the window size information with the `winsize` structure:

```
struct winsize {
    ushort_t ws_row;      /* # of rows in characters*/
    ushort_t ws_col;      /* # of columns in characters */
    ushort_t ws_xpixel;   /* horizontal size in pixels */
    ushort_t ws_ypixel;   /* vertical size in pixels */
};
```

The EUC `ioctl` commands are used with multibyte (international) character sets. (EUC stands for Extended Unix Code.) These `ioctl` commands are processed by LDTERM and special-purpose, language-dependent modules sold in add-on packages.

The EUC `ioctl` commands are processed in a nonstandard way, too. Modules must forward them downstream so that every module and driver in the stream has a chance to see them, thus being notified of any changes in character processing. Drivers must acknowledge these commands with an `M_IOCACK` message, even if the drivers don't do any multibyte processing. The only reasons a driver should respond with an `M_IOCNAK` message are if the driver supports multibyte processing and the request is invalid, or if the driver encounters an error. This special handling allows internationalized applications to run using standard terminal drivers and line disciplines, augmented with special-purpose modules that handle the particular language processing.

11.4 NETWORK TTY EMULATOR EXAMPLE

Figure 11.4 shows the architecture of the streams involved when using `cu(1)` over a network. For simplicity, we have deliberately omitted the network layer, choosing to have the transport provider communicate directly with the data link provider. In particular, note the position of the network terminal emulator module (NTE). It sits directly above the transport provider. The service interface between the transport provider and NTE is the Transport Provider Interface (TPI). (The TPI is discussed in detail in Chapter 12.) Also note that TIMOD has been popped off the stream. Since the stream will be acting as a terminal stream, TIMOD is not needed.

Above the network terminal emulator module sits TIRDWR, providing a read/write interface to the application. TIRDWR cannot be placed below NTE because, if `HUPCL` has been set, NTE needs to send a TPI disconnect message downstream when the module is popped from the stream. LDTERM sits on top of the stream to complete the emulation of a terminal.

If NTE were not present in the stream, then most terminal-related `ioctl` commands would fail. Functions like `isatty(3C)` [see `ttyname(3C)`] would not recognize the stream as being connected to a terminal. This, in turn, would lead to other problems, such as the standard I/O library using the wrong kind of buffering.

Since the network terminal emulator module needs to interact with the transport provider, we need to introduce the few primitives used. NTE assumes it is being used over a connection-oriented transport protocol so that data are delivered reliably and in sequence.

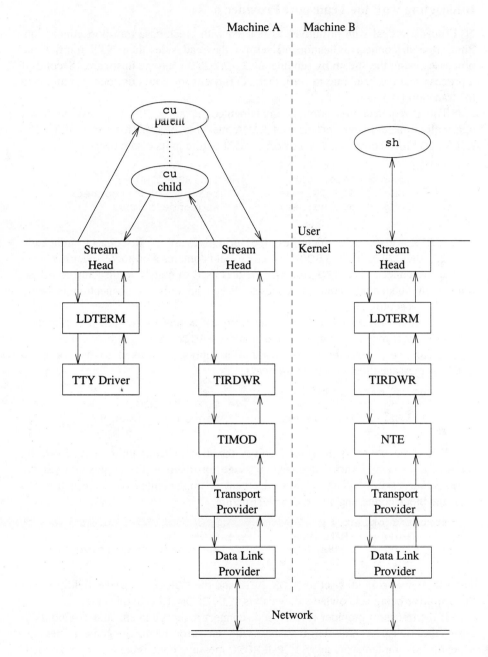

Fig. 11.4. cu over a Network

Interacting with the Transport Provider

NTE needs to deal with primitives associated with breaking a transport connection. First, if a disconnect indication arrives on the read side, then NTE notifies the processes using the stream by sending an M_HANGUP message upstream. Second, if a process sets the baud rate to zero, then NTE needs to send a disconnect request to the transport provider.

The disconnect indication is implemented as an M_PROTO message block optionally linked to one or more M_DATA message blocks (for user data). The M_PROTO block contains a T_discon_ind structure in its data buffer.

```
struct T_discon_ind {
    long    PRIM_type;      /* T_DISCON_IND */
    long    DISCON_reason;  /* reason for disconnect */
    long    SEQ_number;     /* sequence number */
};
```

The PRIM_type field identifies the primitive as a disconnect indication (T_DISCON_IND). The DISCON_reason field contains a protocol-specific reason for the disconnect. The SEQ_number field is used to match up disconnect indications with outstanding connect requests. When an existing connection is being aborted, it is set to −1.

To initiate a disconnect, a disconnect request is sent to the transport provider. The disconnect request is implemented as an M_PROTO message block containing a T_discon_req structure in its data buffer, optionally linked to one or more M_DATA message blocks used for user data.

```
struct T_discon_req {
    long    PRIM_type;      /* T_DISCON_REQ */
    long    SEQ_number;     /* sequence number */
};
```

When the transport provider receives the disconnect request, it responds by sending a success acknowledgement message upstream if the connection can be released successfully. The acknowledgement is implemented as an M_PCPROTO message block containing a T_ok_ack structure.

```
struct T_ok_ack {
    long    PRIM_type;      /* T_OK_ACK */
    long    CORRECT_prim;   /* successful primitive */
};
```

The PRIM_type field is set to T_OK_ACK, and the CORRECT_prim field is set to the primitive being acknowledged, which is T_DISCON_REQ in this case.

If the transport provider receives a disconnect request and encounters a nonfatal error, the transport provider responds with an error-acknowledgement message instead. It is implemented as an M_PCPROTO message containing a T_error_ack message in its data buffer.

```
struct T_error_ack {
        long    PRIM_type;          /* T_ERROR_ACK */
        long    ERROR_prim;         /* failed primitive */
        long    TLI_error;          /* transport error code */
        long    UNIX_error;         /* UNIX error code */
};
```

The PRIM_type field identifies the primitive as a T_ERROR_ACK. The primitive that failed is stored in the ERROR_prim field. TLI_error contains the transport error number. If it has the value TSYSERR, then the UNIX_error field will contain the UNIX error number.

Example Network Terminal Emulator Module

Figure 11.5 shows the module functions, with arrows indicating the module routines called by each function.

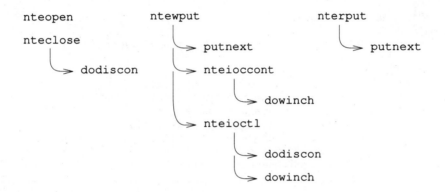

Fig. 11.5. Network Terminal Emulator Module Functions

No init or start entry point is needed because the module has nothing to initialize at system boot time. The module's write put procedure handles ioctl processing, and the module's read put procedure simply passes most messages upstream without processing them. Note that the module does not use service procedures, so flow control will bypass the module entirely.

The NTE module does not have any header files, so we will start with the module source itself. As with the driver in Chapter 10, comments are used sparingly to decrease the length of the example.

```
 1 #include <sys/types.h>
 2 #include <sys/param.h>
 3 #include <sys/systm.h>
 4 #include <sys/signal.h>
 5 #include <sys/stream.h>
 6 #include <sys/termio.h>
 7 #include <sys/termios.h>
 8 #include <sys/eucioctl.h>
 9 #include <sys/strtty.h>
10 #include <sys/errno.h>
11 #include <sys/kmem.h>
12 #include <sys/cred.h>
13 #include <sys/tihdr.h>
14 #include <sys/ddi.h>

15 #ifdef DEBUG
16 #define STATIC
17 #else
18 #define STATIC static
19 #endif
20 #define ONESEC     1000000      /* in microseconds */

21 STATIC int nteopen(queue_t *, dev_t *, int, int, cred_t *);
22 STATIC int nteclose(queue_t *, int, cred_t *);
23 STATIC int ntewput(queue_t *, mblk_t *);
24 STATIC int nterput(queue_t *, mblk_t *);
25 STATIC void nteioctl(queue_t *, mblk_t *);
26 STATIC void nteioccont(queue_t *, mblk_t *);
27 STATIC int dodiscon(queue_t *);
28 STATIC void dowinch(queue_t *, mblk_t *);
```

[1–14] Several familiar header files are used by the NTE module. The new ones
have to do with the terminal and transport interfaces. `<sys/termio.h>`
contains the definitions needed by the `termio` `ioctl` commands. Similarly, `<sys/termios.h>` contains the definitions needed to support
`termios`. `<sys/strtty.h>` contains constants needed by
STREAMS-based TTY drivers, including sleep priorities and M_CTL command values. `<sys/eucioctl.h>` contains the definitions needed for
the EUC `ioctl` commands. Finally, `<sys/tihdr.h>` contains the
declarations for the TPI.

[15–20] If the module is compiled with the DEBUG flag defined, the symbol
STATIC will evaluate to the empty string, and the module's symbols will
be defined globally, making it easier to access them with a kernel
debugger. If DEBUG is undefined, STATIC evaluates to `static`.
ONESEC, used in calls to `timeout`, is defined to be the number of
microseconds in a second.

[21–28] The functions provided by the module are declared next.

```
29 typedef struct nte {
30   ulong_t         nt_cflag;    /* hardware TTY settings */
31   mblk_t          *nt_iocmp;   /* ioctl pending */
32   struct winsize  nt_win;      /* window size */
33 } nte_t;
34 int ntedevflag = 0;

35 STATIC struct module_info nte_minfo = {
36   0x6e74, "nte", 0, 256, 0, 0
37 };
38 STATIC struct qinit nte_rinit = {
39   nterput, NULL, nteopen, nteclose, NULL, &nte_minfo, NULL
40 };
41 STATIC struct qinit nte_winit = {
42   ntewput, NULL, NULL, NULL, NULL, &nte_minfo, NULL
43 };
44 struct streamtab nteinfo = {
45   &nte_rinit, &nte_winit, NULL, NULL
46 };
```

[29–34] The `nte` structure is the module's private data structure. A different
instance of it is used each time the NTE module is pushed on a stream.
The `nt_cflag` field contains the `termio` and `termios` flags managed
by terminal drivers. The `nt_iocmp` field is used to hold M_IOCTL messages during disconnect processing. The `nt_win` field is a `winsize`
structure describing the size of the terminal screen or window.
`ntedevflag` is the "driver" flag required by the configuration software.
Although no flags apply to this module, the symbol still needs to be
defined and set to zero.

[35–46] The minimum and maximum packet sizes were chosen to reflect the range
of data sizes typically written to terminal devices. The maximum number
of characters per line that terminal drivers and line disciplines historically
have supported is 256. This limit used to be known as TTYHOG (check
`<sys/tty.h>`, if your system still includes a `clist`-based terminal
header file). For drivers and modules that have no limit to the size of messages they can process, the STREAMS subsystem defines the symbol
INFPSZ (in `<sys/stream.h>`) to represent an infinite maximum
packet size. Since the NTE module has no service procedures, high and
low water marks are meaningless. Accordingly, they are set to zero.

The module has put procedures, but is without service procedures because
it does not need to recover from buffer allocation failures during message
processing. Note that only the first two members of the `streamtab`
structure pertain to modules. Also note that, like drivers, the only data
symbols that need be global are the `streamtab` structure and the driver
flag. The naming conventions are the same as for drivers.

```
47 STATIC int
48 nteopen(queue_t *q, dev_t *devp, int flag, int sflag,
49   cred_t *crp)
50 {
51   nte_t *np;
52   mblk_t *mp;
53   struct stroptions *sp;
54   long id;
55   int isbcall;

56   if (sflag != MODOPEN)    /* configuration error */
57       return(EINVAL);
58   if (q->q_ptr != NULL)    /* not first open */
59       return(0);

60   while ((np = (nte_t *)kmem_zalloc(sizeof(nte_t),
61     KM_NOSLEEP)) == NULL) {
62       id = timeout(wakeup, (caddr_t)q,
63         drv_usectohz(ONESEC));
64       if (sleep((caddr_t)q, TTIPRI|PCATCH)) {
65           untimeout(id);
66           return(EINTR);
67       }
68   }
```

[47–55] The module's open routine is called when the module is pushed on the stream. It is also called on successive opens of the device to which the stream is attached.

[56–59] If sflag is not set to MODOPEN, then the module has been configured improperly and we return EINVAL. If the queue's private pointer is non-NULL, then this is a successive open and there is no work to do, so we return success (0).

[60–68] On first opens, we allocate an nte structure to represent this instance of the module. If kmem_zalloc fails, we call timeout to schedule wakeup to be run in one second, and we go to sleep. TTIPRI is a constant defined in <sys/strtty.h> that represents the priority of a process waiting for input from a terminal device. Although this situation is different, using TTIPRI ensures we sleep with a priority similar to that of other terminal-related activities. (There is no sleep priority defined for waiting to open a terminal device.)

If the sleep is interrupted (by receipt of a signal or by the user hitting the interrupt key), sleep will return 1, and we cancel the timeout and return failure (EINTR).

```
69    while ((mp = allocb(sizeof(struct stroptions),
70      BPRI_HI)) == NULL) {
71        isbcall = 1;
72        id = bufcall(sizeof(struct stroptions), BPRI_HI,
73          wakeup, (long)q);
74        if (id == 0) {
75            isbcall = 0;
76            id = timeout(wakeup, (caddr_t)q,
77              drv_usectohz(ONESEC));
78        }
79        if (sleep((caddr_t)q, TTIPRI|PCATCH)) {
80            if (isbcall)
81                unbufcall(id);
82            else
83                untimeout(id);
84            kmem_free(np, sizeof(nte_t));
85            return(EINTR);
86        }
87    }

88    mp->b_datap->db_type = M_SETOPTS;
89    mp->b_wptr += sizeof(struct stroptions);
90    sp = (struct stroptions *)mp->b_rptr;
91    sp->so_flags = SO_HIWAT|SO_LOWAT|SO_ISTTY;
```

[69–87] Next we will send an M_SETOPTS message upstream to give the stream characteristics associated with terminal streams. We attempt to allocate a message large enough to hold a stroptions structure. If this fails, we use bufcall to schedule wakeup to be run when memory is available. If bufcall fails, we resort to using timeout. In either case, isbcall tells us which recovery mechanism is being used.

If the sleep is interrupted, we cancel the wakeup, free the memory previously allocated to hold the nte structure, and return EINTR. Otherwise, when sleep returns because of the wakeup, we retry the message allocation.

[88–91] After we successfully allocate the message, we set the type to M_SETOPTS, increase the write pointer by the size of the stroptions structure, and cast a pointer to a stroptions structure over the read pointer in the message. We set three flags in the so_flags field: SO_HIWAT indicates we want to change the high-water mark of the stream head read queue; SO_LOWAT indicates we want to change the low-water mark; SO_ISTTY indicates the stream will act as a terminal, enabling the stream head to allocate the stream as the controlling terminal if conditions permit.

```
 92   sp->so_hiwat = 512;
 93   sp->so_lowat = 128;
 94   putnext(q, mp);
 95   q->q_ptr = (caddr_t)np;
 96   WR(q)->q_ptr = (caddr_t)np;
 97   np->nt_cflag = B9600|CREAD|HUPCL|CS8;
 98   return(0);
 99   }

100   STATIC int
101   nteclose(queue_t *q, int flag, cred_t *crp)
102   {
103   nte_t *np;
104   long id;

105   np = (nte_t *)q->q_ptr;
106   if (np->nt_cflag & HUPCL) {
107       while (dodiscon(WR(q)) == EAGAIN) {
108           id = bufcall(sizeof(struct T_discon_req), BPRI_HI,
109             wakeup, (long)q);
110           if (id == 0)
111               timeout(wakeup, (caddr_t)q,
112                 drv_usectohz(ONESEC));
113           sleep((caddr_t)q, PZERO);
114       }
115   }
116   q->q_ptr = NULL;
117   WR(q)->q_ptr = NULL;
```

[92–94]   We set the high-water mark to 512 and the low-water mark to 128 to reflect the line-at-a-time processing typical with terminals. Then we send the message upstream.

[95–99]   Finally, we store a pointer to the nte structure in the read and write queues and initialize the terminal flags. We choose the default settings to be 9600 baud (B9600), receiver-enabled (CREAD), hang up on close (HUPCL), and eight bits per character (CS8).

[100–115]   nteclose is called when the module is popped off the stream, either by an I_POP ioctl call or by the last close of the stream. We pick up a pointer to the nte structure stored in the queue. If the HUPCL flag is still set, we call dodiscon to send a disconnect request downstream. If dodiscon returns EAGAIN, then it could not allocate a message, so we schedule a wakeup to be run, and go to sleep at an uninterruptible priority level (PZERO).

[116–117]   We clear the private pointers in the queues to mark them as no longer in use (remember, we do not want to assume too much knowledge about how they are allocated).

```
118   if (np->nt_iocmp != NULL)
119        freemsg(np->nt_iocmp);
120   kmem_free(np, sizeof(nte_t));
121   return(0);
122 }

123 STATIC int
124 ntewput(queue_t *q, mblk_t *mp)
125 {
126   struct iocblk *iocp;

127   switch (mp->b_datap->db_type) {
128   case M_IOCTL:
129        nteioctl(q, mp);
130        break;

131   case M_IOCDATA:
132        nteioccont(q, mp);
133        break;

134   case M_START:
135   case M_STOP:
136   case M_STARTI:
137   case M_STOPI:    /* See exercise 11.1. */
138        freemsg(mp);
139        break;
```

[118–122] If an M_IOCTL message is still saved in the nt_iocmp field, then we free it. Finally, we free the nte structure associated with this instance of the module and return success.

[123–126] Besides messages generated from user level, ntewput has to handle messages originating in LDTERM and TIRDWR. (See ldterm(7) and tirdwr(7) for more details.) The NTE module's job is to act as a terminal driver would when passed messages from these sources.

[127–133] M_IOCTL messages are passed to ntcioctl for processing. Any transparent ioctls that are partially processed by nteioctl are completed by passing the M_IOCDATA message to nteioccont.

[134–139] LDTERM will generate M_START, M_STOP, M_STARTI, and M_STOPI messages to control the output and input of the driver. For example, when the user types the STOP character (usually CTRL–S), LDTERM sends an M_STOP message downstream to inform the driver that it should suspend output. Implementing these operations across a network requires more work than we can go into right now, so it is left as an exercise at the end of the chapter. For now, we just free these messages if they are passed to the module.

```
140  case M_CTL:
141      if ((mp->b_wptr - mp->b_rptr) !=
142        sizeof(struct iocblk)) {
143          freemsg(mp);
144          break;
145      }
146      iocp = (struct iocblk *)mp->b_rptr;
147      if (iocp->ioc_cmd != MC_CANONQUERY) {
148          freemsg(mp);
149          break;
150      }
151      /*
152       * Tell line discipline to do all
153       * canonical processing.
154       */
155      iocp->ioc_cmd = MC_DO_CANON;
156      qreply(q, mp);
157      break;
```

[140–157] An M_CTL message is generated by LDTERM when it is pushed on the stream. The message is used to negotiate which termios flags are processed by the driver (or peripheral hardware) and which are processed by LDTERM. By default, LDTERM assumes it will have to process everything except c_cflag.

The format of the M_CTL message is unspecified by the system, but LDTERM places an iocblk structure in the data buffer. The ioc_cmd field is set to MC_CANONQUERY, defined in <sys/strtty.h>. LDTERM expects the driver to respond by sending an M_CTL message back upstream containing the same structure.

The ioc_cmd field in the response message can be set to one of three values. If the driver sets it to MC_NO_CANON, then all processing is handled by the driver or I/O hardware. If ioc_cmd is set to MC_DO_CANON, the driver depends on LDTERM to do all processing, except for c_cflag. Finally, if ioc_cmd is set to MC_PART_CANON, then the driver links an M_DATA message containing a termios structure to the M_CTL. All flags turned on in the termios structure's c_iflag, c_oflag, and c_lflag fields correspond to the flags processed by the driver or peripheral hardware. LDTERM handles the processing of any flags not set in these fields.

We free any invalid M_CTL messages because they are intended for intermodule communication and nothing upstream should need to communicate with the transport provider directly, except TIRDWR, which does not generate M_CTL messages. Then we tell LDTERM to process all fields except c_cflag.

```
158  case M_DELAY:
159      freemsg(mp);
160      break;

161  default:
162      putnext(q, mp);
163  }
164  return(0);
165  }

166  STATIC void
167  nteioctl(queue_t *q, mblk_t *mp)
168  {
169   int error, s;
170   nte_t *np;
171   struct iocblk *iocp;
172   struct termio *tp;
173   struct termios *tsp;
174   mblk_t *bp;
175   struct copyreq *reqp;
176   struct winsize *wp;

177   np = (nte_t *)q->q_ptr;
178   iocp = (struct iocblk *)mp->b_rptr;
179   switch(iocp->ioc_cmd) {
180   case TCSETS:      /* set terminal parameters */
181   case TCSETSF:
182   case TCSETSW:
```

[158–160]   We free M_DELAY messages because there is no terminal on which we can delay displaying characters. We could delay transmission of the characters across the network, but that is both inefficient and pointless because the purpose of M_DELAY messages in this context is to give the terminal time to move its cursor.

[161–165]   We pass all other messages on to the transport provider. Then we return from the write put procedure.

[166–182]   nteioctl processes all M_IOCTL messages. Since we do not queue data to be displayed in the NTE module, we can treat TCSETS, TCSETSF, and TCSETSW equivalently. Besides the stream head ioctl commands defined in <sys/stropts.h>, the stream head also has embedded in it knowledge of how to handle most terminal-related ioctl commands. These include TCGETA, TCGETS, TCSETA, TCSETAF, TCSETAW, TCSETS, TCSETSF, TCSETSW, TCDSET, TCFLSH, TCSBRK, TCXONC, TIOCGETP, TIOCSETP, TIOCSTI, LDGETT, and LDSETT. Thus, these commands will never appear as transparent ioctls.

```
183          if (mp->b_cont == NULL) {
184              mp->b_datap->db_type = M_IOCNAK;
185              qreply(q, mp);
186              break;
187          }
188          tsp = (struct termios *)mp->b_cont->b_rptr;
189          if (((tsp->c_cflag&CBAUD) == B0) &&
190            ((np->nt_cflag&CBAUD) != B0)) {
191              s = splstr();
192              if (np->nt_iocmp != NULL)
193                  freemsg(np->nt_iocmp);
194              np->nt_iocmp = mp;
195              splx(s);
196              error = dodiscon(q);
197              if (error != 0) {
198                  mp->b_datap->db_type = M_IOCNAK;
199                  iocp->ioc_error = error;
200                  qreply(q, mp);
201              }
202              break;  /* ack sent by nterput */
203          }
```

[183–187] A TCSETS-class ioctl command appears as an M_IOCTL message linked to an M_DATA block containing a termios structure. If the message is improperly formed, we convert it into an M_IOCNAK message and fail the ioctl.

[188–195] The first time the baud rate is set to 0, we attempt to break the transport connection. We raise the processor priority and free any message that might be saved from a previous disconnect attempt. Although the stream head serializes all ioctls to the same stream, a user can get impatient and interrupt the system call. This can lead to another ioctl proceeding before the processing elements in the stream have finished handling the first one. (The stream head uses sequence numbers to avoid mixing up ioctl response messages.)

We use splstr to block the read put procedure from running as a result of an interrupt. If we did not, an interrupt could occur between lines 193 and 194, leading the read put procedure to use the nt_iocmp field after we have freed the message. Once we have saved the new message pointer, it is safe to restore the previous processor priority.

[196–203] We call dodiscon to send a disconnect request to the transport provider. If it fails, we fail the ioctl system call with the error number returned by dodiscon. If dodiscon succeeds, we break without sending an ioctl acknowledgement upstream. This will be done by nterput when the transport provider responds to the disconnect request.

```
204          np->nt_cflag = tsp->c_cflag;
205          mp->b_datap->db_type = M_IOCACK;
206          iocp->ioc_count = 0;
207          qreply(q, mp);
208          break;

209   case TCSETA:       /* set terminal parameters */
210   case TCSETAF:
211   case TCSETAW:
212          if (mp->b_cont == NULL) {
213              mp->b_datap->db_type = M_IOCNAK;
214              qreply(q, mp);
215              break;
216          }
217          tp = (struct termio *)mp->b_cont->b_rptr;
218          if (((tp->c_cflag&CBAUD) == B0) &&
219            ((np->nt_cflag&CBAUD) != B0)) {
220              s = splstr();
221              if (np->nt_iocmp != NULL)
222                  freemsg(np->nt_iocmp);
223              np->nt_iocmp = mp;
224              splx(s);
225              error = dodiscon(q);
226              if (error != 0) {
227                  mp->b_datap->db_type = M_IOCNAK;
228                  iocp->ioc_error = error;
229                  qreply(q, mp);
230              }
231              break;   /* ack sent by nterput */
232          }
233          np->nt_cflag = (np->nt_cflag&0xffff0000)|tp->c_cflag;
234          mp->b_datap->db_type = M_IOCACK;
235          iocp->ioc_count = 0;
236          qreply(q, mp);
237          break;
```

[204–208] If the baud rate is not being set to 0, we copy the c_cflag field from the termios structure to the nte structure. Then we convert the message into an M_IOCACK message and set the ioc_count field to prevent copying any data to the user's buffer. We send the message upstream, causing the ioctl system call to succeed.

[209–237] We treat the TCSETA, TCSETAF, and TCSETAW commands similar to their termios equivalents. Note, however, that the c_cflag field in the termio structure is an unsigned short, whereas the corresponding termios field is an unsigned long. Thus, we only set the lower 16 bits in the nt_cflag field of the nte structure. The termio and termios structures are implemented such that they share these flags in common.

```
238   case TCGETA:     /* get terminal parameters */
239       if (mp->b_cont != NULL) {
240           freemsg(mp->b_cont);
241           mp->b_cont = NULL;
242       }
243       if ((bp = allocb(sizeof(struct termio), BPRI_MED)) ==
244         NULL) {
245           mp->b_datap->db_type = M_IOCNAK;
246           iocp->ioc_error = EAGAIN;
247           qreply(q, mp);
248           break;
249       }

250       bp->b_wptr += sizeof(struct termio);
251       bzero((caddr_t)bp->b_rptr, sizeof(struct termio));
252       tp = (struct termio *)bp->b_rptr;
253       tp->c_cflag = (ushort_t)np->nt_cflag;
254       mp->b_cont = bp;
255       mp->b_datap->db_type = M_IOCACK;
256       iocp->ioc_count = sizeof(struct termio);
257       qreply(q, mp);
258       break;
```

[238–242] For TCGETA, we need to return a termio structure in an M_DATA
block linked to the M_IOCACK message. The M_DATA block is not allocated by the stream head, so we need to do it ourselves. First, we
include a little paranoia check because we are about to overwrite the
b_cont field. If it is non-NULL, we free the message linked to the
M_IOCTL message. This is not necessary if the stream head generated
the message, but if it was generated from within another module on the
stream, we want to be sure we do not create a memory leak if the message is not formed properly.

[243–249] We allocate a message large enough to hold a termio structure. If
allocb fails, we fail the ioctl by setting the ioc_error field to
EAGAIN, converting the M_IOCTL message into an M_IOCNAK message, and sending it back upstream. Since we do not have a write service procedure, recovery from allocation failures is not easily implemented, so we fail the ioctl instead.

[250–258] We increment the write pointer in the message by the size of the
termio structure, clear the contents of the data buffer, and copy the
hardware flags from the nte structure to the termio structure. Then
we link the M_DATA message on the end of the M_IOCTL message, convert the M_IOCTL message to an M_IOCACK message, set the
ioc_count field to the number of bytes to copy to the user's buffer,
and send the message upstream.

```
259  case TCGETS:      /* get terminal parameters */
260      if (mp->b_cont != NULL) {
261          freemsg(mp->b_cont);
262          mp->b_cont = NULL;
263      }
264      if ((bp = allocb(sizeof(struct termios), BPRI_MED)) ==
265        NULL) {
266          mp->b_datap->db_type = M_IOCNAK;
267          iocp->ioc_error = EAGAIN;
268          qreply(q, mp);
269          break;
270      }
271      bp->b_wptr += sizeof(struct termios);
272      bzero((caddr_t)bp->b_rptr, sizeof(struct termios));
273      tsp = (struct termios *)bp->b_rptr;
274      tsp->c_cflag = np->nt_cflag;
275      mp->b_cont = bp;
276      mp->b_datap->db_type = M_IOCACK;
277      iocp->ioc_count = sizeof(struct termios);
278      qreply(q, mp);
279      break;

280  case TIOCSTI:     /* simulate input */
281      bp = mp->b_cont;
282      if ((bp == NULL) || (bp->b_wptr != (bp->b_rptr+1))) {
283          mp->b_datap->db_type = M_IOCNAK;
284          qreply(q, mp);
285          break;
286      }
287      if (!canput(RD(q)->q_next)) {
288          iocp->ioc_error = EAGAIN;
289          mp->b_datap->db_type = M_IOCNAK;
290          qreply(q, mp);
291          break;
292      }
```

[259–279]   The TCGETS processing is handled in a manner similar to that for the TCGETA command. Note that the only difference between TCGETS processing and TCGETA processing is the structure stored in the M_DATA block.

[280–292]   The TIOCSTI M_IOCTL message has an M_DATA message linked to it containing a single byte of data representing the character to be sent upstream as if typed by the user at the terminal. If the message is formatted improperly, we convert it into an M_IOCNAK message and send it upstream. This will cause ioctl to fail with the default error number, EINVAL. If the stream is flow-controlled on the read side, we fail the ioctl by setting ioc_error to EAGAIN, converting the M_IOCTL message to an M_IOCNAK message, and sending it upstream.

```
293        mp->b_cont = NULL;
294        qreply(q, bp);
295        mp->b_datap->db_type = M_IOCACK;
296        iocp->ioc_count = 0;
297        qreply(q, mp);
298        break;

299  case TCSBRK:     /* transmit a break */
300  case EUC_MSAVE:  /* extended unix codes */
301  case EUC_MREST:
302  case EUC_IXLON:
303  case EUC_IXLOFF:
304  case EUC_OXLON:
305  case EUC_OXLOFF:
306        mp->b_datap->db_type = M_IOCACK;
307        iocp->ioc_count = 0;
308        qreply(q, mp);
309        break;

310  case TIOCGWINSZ:     /* get window size */
311        if ((np->nt_win.ws_row == 0) &&
312          (np->nt_win.ws_col == 0) &&
313          (np->nt_win.ws_xpixel == 0) &&
314          (np->nt_win.ws_ypixel == 0)) {
315           mp->b_datap->db_type = M_IOCNAK;
316           qreply(q, mp);
317           break;
318        }
```

[293–298] We unlink the M_DATA message block from the M_IOCTL message and send the M_DATA block upstream. Then we cause the ioctl to succeed by converting the M_IOCTL message into an M_IOCACK message and sending it upstream.

[299–309] We assume the network does not support the transmission of breaks, so we simply acknowledge the TCSBRK ioctl. We also acknowledge the EUC ioctl commands, even though the module does not take any special action to support multibyte functionality. This allows other modules that implement multibyte character sets to be pushed on the stream so that applications can use them over the network.

[310–318] TIOCGWINSZ is one ioctl command not embedded in the stream head. This means it will come down the stream as a result of either a transparent ioctl or an I_STR ioctl. Regardless, if an application has not previously set the window size by using the TIOCSWINSZ ioctl command, then we fail the attempt to get the window size, assuming the terminal does not support windowing.

```
319        if (iocp->ioc_count == TRANSPARENT) {
320            if ((bp = allocb(sizeof(struct winsize),
321              BPRI_MED)) == NULL) {
322                mp->b_datap->db_type = M_IOCNAK;
323                iocp->ioc_error = EAGAIN;
324                qreply(q, mp);
325                break;
326            }
327            wp = (struct winsize *)bp->b_rptr;
328            *wp = np->nt_win;    /* structure assignment */
329            bp->b_wptr += sizeof(struct winsize);
330            reqp = (struct copyreq *)mp->b_rptr;
331            reqp->cq_private = NULL;
332            reqp->cq_flag = 0;
333            reqp->cq_size = sizeof(struct winsize);
334            reqp->cq_addr =
335               (caddr_t)(*(long *)(mp->b_cont->b_rptr));
336            freeb(mp->b_cont);
337            mp->b_cont = bp;
338            mp->b_datap->db_type = M_COPYOUT;
339            mp->b_wptr = mp->b_rptr + sizeof(struct copyreq);
340            qreply(q, mp);
```

[319–332] If TIOCGWINSZ is performed as a transparent ioctl, then ioc_count will be equal to TRANSPARENT. In this case, we need to allocate a message large enough to hold a winsize structure. If allocb fails, we fail the ioctl, setting ioc_error to EAGAIN to indicate that the user should try again later. If allocb succeeds, we copy the winsize structure into the message and cast a copyreq structure on top of the iocblk structure. We need no private state since we only need to perform one copy operation, so we set the cq_private field to NULL. The cq_flag field is intended for future use and is thus set to 0.

[333–340] We set the cq_size field to the size of the winsize structure and set the cq_addr field to the address of the user's buffer to which the structure is to be copied. Once we initialize the address, we have no need for the M_DATA message block originally attached to the M_IOCTL message block, so we free it. Then we link the M_DATA block we just allocated to the M_IOCTL message and change the M_IOCTL message into an M_COPYOUT message. Since the copyreq structure is a different size than the iocblk structure, we need to set the write pointer to the proper offset. Then we send the message upstream. The stream head will copy the data in the M_DATA block to the user's buffer, convert the M_COPYOUT message into an M_IOCDATA message, and send it back downstream. We will finish processing this ioctl command when we pass the M_IOCDATA message to nteioccont.

```
341         } else {
342             if ((mp->b_cont == NULL) ||
343               (iocp->ioc_count != sizeof(struct winsize))) {
344                 mp->b_datap->db_type = M_IOCNAK;
345                 qreply(q, mp);
346                 break;
347             }
348             wp = (struct winsize *)mp->b_cont->b_rptr;
349             *wp = np->nt_win;    /* structure assignment */
350             mp->b_datap->db_type = M_IOCACK;
351             qreply(q, mp);
352         }
353     break;

354 case TIOCSWINSZ:     /* set window size */
355     if (iocp->ioc_count == TRANSPARENT) {
356         reqp = (struct copyreq *)mp->b_rptr;
357         reqp->cq_private = NULL;
358         reqp->cq_flag = 0;
359         reqp->cq_size = sizeof(struct winsize);
360         reqp->cq_addr =
361             (caddr_t)(*(long *)(mp->b_cont->b_rptr));
362         freeb(mp->b_cont);
363         mp->b_cont = NULL;
364         mp->b_datap->db_type = M_COPYIN;
365         mp->b_wptr = mp->b_rptr + sizeof(struct copyreq);
366         qreply(q, mp);
```

[341–347] If the user performs TIOCGWINSZ as an I_STR ioctl, then the
M_IOCTL message block should be linked to an M_DATA message block
large enough to hold a winsize structure. With an I_STR ioctl, the
stream head copies the initial contents of the user's buffer into the
M_DATA message. We are uninterested in what is stored in the data
buffer, however, since all TIOCGWINSZ does is return information to
the user. Checking the value of ioc_count verifies that there is
enough space in the M_DATA block's data buffer and that the user's
buffer is the proper size.

[348–353] We copy the saved winsize structure to the message, change the type
of the message to M_IOCACK, and send the message upstream.

[354–366] TIOCSWINSZ processing is like TIOCGWINSZ processing, but we
need to copy data in from the user's buffer instead. We convert the
M_IOCTL message into an M_COPYIN message and send it upstream.
The stream head will copy data from the user's buffer to an M_DATA
message, link the message to the M_COPYIN message block, convert the
M_COPYIN message to an M_IOCDATA message, and send it downstream. The processing will be completed by nteioccont.

```
367        } else {
368            if ((mp->b_cont == NULL) ||
369               (iocp->ioc_count != sizeof(struct winsize))) {
370                  mp->b_datap->db_type = M_IOCNAK;
371                  qreply(q, mp);
372                  break;
373            }
374            dowinch(q, mp);
375        }
376        break;

377  default:
378        putnext(q, mp);
379        break;
380  }
381  }

382  STATIC void
383  nteioccont(queue_t *q, mblk_t *mp)
384  {
385   struct copyresp *resp;
386   struct iocblk *iocp;

387   resp = (struct copyresp *)mp->b_rptr;
388   switch(resp->cp_cmd) {
389   case TIOCGWINSZ:
390        if (resp->cp_rval != 0) {    /* it failed */
391             freemsg(mp);
```

[367–376] If the user performs TIOCSWINSZ as an I_STR ioctl command, we validate the buffer size in the M_DATA block linked to the M_IOCTL message block. Then we call dowinch to process the change to the winsize structure associated with this instance of the NTE module.

[377–381] All other M_IOCTL messages are passed downstream to the transport provider.

[382–388] nteioccont is called to finish the processing of transparent ioctls. It is always passed a pointer to an M_IOCDATA message.

[389–391] For TIOCGWINSZ, the M_IOCDATA message contains no M_DATA message linked to it. Since it was sent in reply to an M_COPYOUT message, the M_IOCDATA message only contains the status of the copy request. If the cp_rval field is nonzero, then the copy failed and there is no more processing to do, so we free the message. Otherwise, we need to send an M_IOCACK message upstream to complete the ioctl processing.

```
392          } else {
393              iocp = (struct iocblk *)mp->b_rptr;
394              iocp->ioc_count = 0;
395    .         iocp->ioc_error = 0;
396              iocp->ioc_rval = 0;
397              mp->b_datap->db_type = M_IOCACK;
398              mp->b_wptr = mp->b_rptr + sizeof(struct iocblk);
399              qreply(q, mp);
400          }
401          break;

402      case TIOCSWINSZ:
403          if (resp->cp_rval != 0)          /* it failed */
404              freemsg(mp);
405          else
406              dowinch(q, mp);
407          break;

408      default:
409          putnext(q, mp);
410          break;
411      }
412  }
```

[392–401] If the copy succeeded, we need to acknowledge the TIOCGWINSZ
ioctl. We have to be careful when converting the M_IOCDATA message into an M_IOCACK message because several of the fields in the
copyresp structure do *not* correspond to fields in the iocblk structure. We need to initialize the ioc_count, ioc_error, and
ioc_rval fields to 0. Also, we need to reset the write pointer in the
message to reflect the size of the iocblk structure.

[402–407] For TIOCSWINSZ, the M_IOCDATA message is linked to an M_DATA
message block containing the winsize structure copied from the user's
buffer. If the cp_rval field is nonzero, the copy failed, so we have
nothing left to do but free the message. Otherwise, we call dowinch to
update the module's copy of the winsize structure.

[408–412] All other M_IOCDATA messages are passed downstream.

```
413 STATIC void
414 dowinch(queue_t *q, mblk_t *mp)
415 {
416  nte_t *np;
417  struct winsize *wp;
418  struct iocblk *iocp;

419  np = (nte_t *)q->q_ptr;
420  wp = (struct winsize *)mp->b_cont->b_rptr;
421  if ((np->nt_win.ws_row != wp->ws_row) ||
422     (np->nt_win.ws_col != wp->ws_col) ||
423     (np->nt_win.ws_xpixel != wp->ws_xpixel) ||
424     (np->nt_win.ws_ypixel != wp->ws_ypixel)) {
425        putctl1(RD(q)->q_next, M_SIG, SIGWINCH);
426        np->nt_win = *wp;    /* structure assignment */
427  }

428  iocp = (struct iocblk *)mp->b_rptr;
429  iocp->ioc_count = 0;
430  if (mp->b_datap->db_type == M_IOCDATA) {
431        mp->b_wptr = mp->b_rptr + sizeof(struct iocblk);
432        iocp->ioc_error = 0;
433        iocp->ioc_rval = 0;
434  }
435  mp->b_datap->db_type = M_IOCACK;
436  qreply(q, mp);
437 }
```

[413–418]   dowinch is called to change the module's copy of the winsize structure associated with the terminal being emulated. The message passed to it is either an M_IOCTL message or an M_IOCDATA message. Regardless of the type, the message is linked to an M_DATA message block containing the winsize structure.

[419–437]   If the winsize structure is identical to the one already stored, then we simply acknowledge the ioctl. Otherwise, we send an M_SIG message upstream to post SIGWINCH to the process group, indicating that the window size has changed. We use an M_SIG message instead of an M_PCSIG message so that signaling the window size change is synchronized with displaying data in the window. Then we save the changes and acknowledge the ioctl. Note that if the message is an M_IOCDATA message, we reset the fields necessary to convert the copyresp structure into an iocblk structure.

```
438 STATIC int
439 dodiscon(queue_t *q)
440 {
441  mblk_t *mp;
442  struct T_discon_req *reqp;

443  mp = allocb(sizeof(struct T_discon_req), BPRI_HI);
444  if (mp == NULL)
445      return(EAGAIN);
446  mp->b_datap->db_type = M_PROTO;
447  mp->b_wptr += sizeof(struct T_discon_req);
448  reqp = (struct T_discon_req *)mp->b_rptr;
449  reqp->PRIM_type = T_DISCON_REQ;
450  reqp->SEQ_number = -1;
451  putnext(q, mp);
452  return(0);
453 }

454 STATIC int
455 nterput(queue_t *q, mblk_t *mp)
456 {
457  nte_t *np;
458  union T_primitives *p;
459  struct iocblk *iocp;
460  struct T_ok_ack *ackp;
461  struct T_error_ack *errp;
462  struct termio *tp;
463  struct termios *tsp;

464  np = (nte_t *)q->q_ptr;
465  switch (mp->b_datap->db_type) {
466  default:
467      putnext(q, mp);
468      break;
```

[438–453] dodiscon is called to break the transport connection. We try to allocate a message large enough to hold a disconnect request. If allocb
fails, we return EAGAIN. Otherwise, we set the type of the message to
M_PROTO, increment the write pointer by the size of a T_discon_req
structure, and initialize the disconnect request. Note that since we are
not using the primitive to deny a connect request, we set the sequence
number to −1. Then we send the message to the transport provider.

[454–465] nterput is called when messages are passed to the NTE module from
downstream. Its main jobs are to process the transport provider's
response to a disconnect request and to look for disconnect indications.

[466–468] Any nonprotocol messages sent to the read put procedure are passed
upstream.

```
469   case M_PCPROTO:
470       p = (union T_primitives *)mp->b_rptr;
471       switch (p->type) {
472       default:
473           putnext(q, mp);
474           break;

475       case T_OK_ACK:
476           ackp = (struct T_ok_ack *)mp->b_rptr;
477           if ((np->nt_iocmp != NULL) &&
478             (ackp->CORRECT_prim == T_DISCON_REQ)) {
479               freemsg(mp);
480               iocp = (struct iocblk *)np->nt_iocmp->b_rptr;
481               if ((iocp->ioc_cmd == TCSETA) ||
482                 (iocp->ioc_cmd == TCSETAF) ||
483                 (iocp->ioc_cmd == TCSETAW)) {
484                   tp = (struct termio *)
485                     np->nt_iocmp->b_cont->b_rptr;
486                   np->nt_cflag =
487                     (np->nt_cflag&0xffff0000)|tp->c_cflag;
488               } else {
489                   tsp = (struct termios *)
490                     np->nt_iocmp->b_cont->b_rptr;
491                   np->nt_cflag = tsp->c_cflag;
492               }
493               freemsg(np->nt_iocmp->b_cont);
494               np->nt_iocmp->b_cont = NULL;
495               np->nt_iocmp->b_datap->db_type = M_IOCACK;
496               iocp = (struct iocblk *)np->nt_iocmp->b_rptr;
497               iocp->ioc_error = 0;
498               iocp->ioc_count = 0;
499               putnext(q, np->nt_iocmp);
500               np->nt_iocmp = NULL;
501           } else {
502               putnext(q, mp);
503           }
504           break;
```

[469–474] We pass M_PCPROTO messages in which we are not interested upstream.

[475–504] If we receive a T_OK_ACK primitive, we check if we had a disconnect request pending (the only reason nt_iocmp would be non-NULL) and if the T_OK_ACK is a response to a disconnect request. If not, we pass the message upstream. Otherwise, we free the message and commit the changes to the nt_cflag field that were requested when the M_IOCTL message was first received. Then we free the M_DATA message linked to the M_IOCTL message, turn the M_IOCTL message into an M_IOCACK message, and send it upstream. Finally, we clear the nt_iocmp field to indicate that there is no longer an ioctl pending.

```
505    case T_ERROR_ACK:
506        errp = (struct T_error_ack *)mp->b_rptr;
507        if ((np->nt_iocmp != NULL) &&
508           (errp->ERROR_prim == T_DISCON_REQ)) {
509            np->nt_iocmp->b_datap->db_type = M_IOCNAK;
510            iocp = (struct iocblk *)np->nt_iocmp->b_rptr;
511            if (errp->UNIX_error != 0)
512                iocp->ioc_error = errp->UNIX_error;
513            else
514                iocp->ioc_error = EPROTO;
515            freemsg(mp);
516            putnext(q, np->nt_iocmp);
517            np->nt_iocmp = NULL;
518        } else {
519            putnext(q, mp);
520        }
521        break;
522    }
523    break;

524    case M_PROTO:
525        p = (union T_primitives *)mp->b_rptr;
526        if (p->type == T_DISCON_IND) {
527            mp->b_datap->db_type = M_HANGUP;
528            mp->b_wptr = mp->b_rptr;
529        }
530        putnext(q, mp);
531        break;
532    }
533    return(0);
534 }
```

[505–523] If the transport provider responds with an error acknowledgement, we
           again make sure it applies to a disconnect request that we have gen-
           erated. If not, we pass the message upstream. Otherwise, we convert
           the saved M_IOCTL message into an M_IOCNAK message. If the
           T_ERROR_ACK primitive contains a nonzero UNIX_error, then we
           use it as the error code for the M_IOCNAK message. Otherwise, we use
           EPROTO to indicate a protocol error has occurred. Then we free the
           error acknowledgement and send the M_IOCNAK message upstream to
           complete the ioctl. Finally, we clear the nt_iocmp field to indicate
           no disconnect request is pending.

[524–534] If we receive a disconnect indication, then we convert the message into
           an M_HANGUP message and send it upstream. All other M_PROTO mes-
           sages are sent upstream unchanged.

If you want to use cu over a connection-oriented transport-level network, compile the NTE module on your system and configure it into your kernel. You can then use the program from Example 6.4.1, along with the network listener service, to provide remote login services between machines on the network.

Summary

Because STREAMS modules closely resemble STREAMS drivers, many of the techniques they use are similar. We have highlighted differences where they occur. We have studied a simple STREAMS module that emulates a typical terminal device and interacts with the Transport Provider Interface. We have also seen how modules can support transparent ioctl commands.

Exercises

11.1 One drawback of the NTE module is its lack of end-to-end flow control. If a user sitting at a terminal types CTRL-S to stop the output, the character gets transmitted as regular data between the hosts—and it can take quite some time before data stop printing out on the terminal. What can you do to improve this situation? Does your solution require any special facilities from the underlying transport protocol?

11.2 Network protocols usually do not support M_BREAK messages because the networks do not support the notion of a break condition. Modify the NTE module to allow breaks to be transmitted across the network.

11.3 Explain how you might recover from an allocation failure during the processing of an M_IOCTL message when the module does not have service procedures.

11.4 In the NTE module, could we have used the queue instead of the nt_iocmp field to store the M_IOCTL message during disconnect processing? Explain.

11.5 Modify the NTE module to support the termiox(7) hardware flow control ioctl commands.

Bibliographic Notes

Kogure and McGowan [1987] describe changes made to the STREAMS-based TTY subsystem to support multibyte (international) character sets.

More information about writing STREAMS modules can be found in *STREAMS*

Modules and Drivers [USL 1992a] and *UNIX System V Release 4 Programmer's Guide: STREAMS* [USL 1990b].

The Transport Provider Interface specification is available from Unix International and is also documented in *STREAMS Modules and Drivers* [USL 1992a].

The *UNIX System V/386 Release 4 Integrated Software Development Guide* [AT&T 1990e] describes how to configure modules in an Intel 80x86-based UNIX SVR4 system. For SVR4.2, configuration information can be found in *Device Driver Programming* [USL 1992b].

12
STREAMS
Multiplexors

STREAMS multiplexors provide a way to route messages between different streams. Also known as a multiplexing driver, a STREAMS multiplexor (hereafter referred to simply as a ''multiplexor'') is just a special-purpose software driver. This chapter describes how to use and write multiplexors. The bulk of the chapter is a program description of a multiplexor supporting the Transport Provider Interface. Such a driver is known as a *transport provider*.

12.1 INTRODUCTION

Strictly speaking, most ordinary STREAMS drivers do some sort of multiplexing. The Ethernet driver presented in Chapter 10, for example, multiplexes packets between multiple streams and a single I/O device. STREAMS multiplexing drivers, however, are distinguished from these ordinary drivers in several ways.

First, a multiplexor is always a software driver. Since streams are linked under multiplexors, the multiplexor is forced to manage the interface to the streams instead of an interface to hardware devices. Second, a multiplexor routes messages between multiple streams, instead of between an I/O device and streams connected to the device.

Multiplexors are useful in several applications. They are an obvious choice for internetworking protocols, whose primary purpose is to route messages (see Figure 12.1). Multiplexors are also ideal for use in windowing applications (see Figure 12.2), routing messages between a terminal stream and the streams attached to each window.

Multiplexors are also useful for less obvious applications. Consider Figure 12.1 again. The TCP and UDP transport protocols are implemented as multiplexors. This is more for convenience and the ability to isolate the transport connection's stream from the network connection's stream than for the ability to multiplex messages. While IP is a many-to-many multiplexor, TCP and UDP are many-to-one multiplexors.

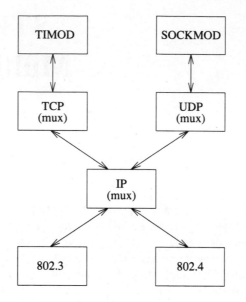

Fig. 12.1. Multiplexors Used in Internetworking

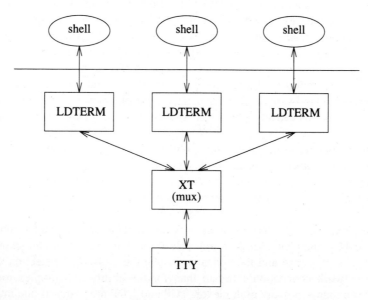

Fig. 12.2. Multiplexors Used in Windowing

Another less obvious reason to use a multiplexor is that it isolates one stream from another. The session TTY driver [Bellovin 1988] provides an added degree of security, among other features, by isolating the processes using a terminal from the real terminal stream. In this example, the multiplexor does not multiplex messages. It merely routes them using a one-to-one mapping between streams open to the multiplexor and streams linked under the multiplexor.

12.2 HOW MULTIPLEXORS WORK

A multiplexor is partitioned into an upper half and a lower half. The upper half deals with the streams opened to the multiplexor and the lower half deals with the streams linked under the multiplexor.

The upper half of a multiplexor acts like a software driver. It follows the same rules as drivers do regarding unrecognized messages, flushing, and M_IOCTL processing. The lower half of a multiplexor, on the other hand, has to act more like the stream head would when processing messages. In particular, flushing is the same as the stream head. Recall the canonical flushing algorithms for drivers presented in Section 10.2.

While the upper half of a multiplexor still needs to handle M_FLUSH messages received from upstream, the lower half of the multiplexor must also be able to receive them from any stream linked under it. The canonical flushing algorithm becomes:

```
if (*mp->b_rptr & FLUSHR) {
    flushq(q, FLUSHDATA);
    *mp->b_rptr &= ~FLUSHR;
}
if (*mp->b_rptr & FLUSHW) {
    flushq(WR(q), FLUSHDATA);
    qreply(q, mp);
} else {
    freemsg(mp);
}
```

In this case, q is the read queue associated with the lower half of the multiplexor.

Multiplexing configurations can be built using the I_LINK ioctl command, whose format is

```
ioctl(muxfd, I_LINK, strfd);
```

where muxfd is a file descriptor open to the multiplexor, and strfd is a file descriptor of the stream to link under the multiplexor. Figure 12.3 shows the state of the two streams before the link is made.

When an I_LINK command is made, the queues from the stream head of the stream to be linked under the multiplexor are borrowed for use by the lower half of the multiplexor. The state of the two streams after the link is made is shown in Figure 12.4.

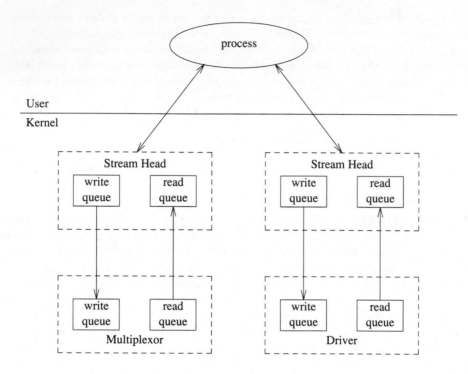

Fig. 12.3. Two Streams before Creating a Link

When an `I_LINK` command is performed, the stream head creates an `M_IOCTL` message and sends it downstream to the multiplexor. The `M_IOCTL` message is linked to one `M_DATA` block containing a `linkblk` structure:

```
struct linkblk {
    queue_t *l_qtop;      /* lowest write queue */
                          /* of upper stream */
    queue_t *l_qbot;      /* highest write queue */
                          /* of lower stream */
    int      l_index;     /* multiplexor link ID */
};
```

The `l_qtop` field contains a pointer to the upper write queue of the multiplexor. The `l_qbot` field is a pointer to the queue to be used as the multiplexor's lower write queue.

The `l_index` field, also known as the *multiplexor ID*, is an integer that uniquely identifies the multiplexor link in the system. Multiplexors can use it in routing messages, if other routing information is lacking. The multiplexor ID is also returned as the return value from the `ioctl` system call. Processes can use it later to dismantle the link.

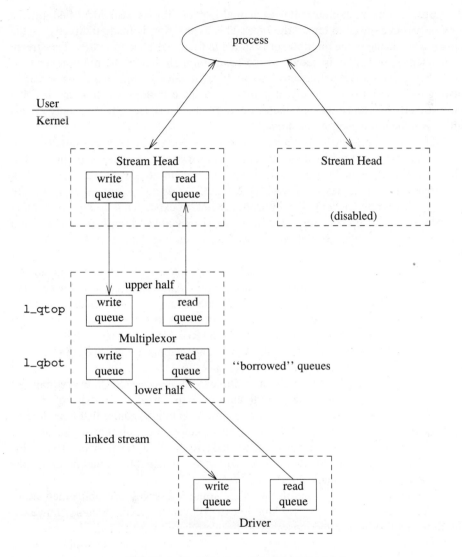

Fig. 12.4. Two Streams after Creating a Link

To unlink a stream from underneath a multiplexor, processes can use the
I_UNLINK ioctl command:

```
ioctl(muxfd, I_UNLINK, muxid);
```

where muxfd is the file descriptor that refers to the same stream used to create the
link, and muxid is the multiplexor ID returned from the I_LINK ioctl command.
The special value MUXID_ALL (defined in <sys/stropts.h>) can be used to
unlink all streams that have been linked under the multiplexor using the stream
represented by muxfd.

Besides the multiplexor ID, each multiplexor link is also identified by the stream (muxfd) used to create the link. This association is made indirectly — the upper write queue of the multiplexor is stored in the linkblk structure. The stream associated with muxfd is known as the *controlling stream* of the multiplexor link. (This has nothing to do with controlling terminal streams.) The controlling stream is distinguished from others in that it is used to create a multiplexor link and it is the only stream that can be used to dismantle that link. Thus, MUXID_ALL only affects links with the same controlling stream.

The controlling stream has another special property with respect to multiplexor links. When the last reference to the controlling stream goes away (i.e., on the last close), all multiplexor links associated with the stream are destroyed. Thus, when processes create multiplexor links with the I_LINK ioctl command, the processes have to stick around as long as they want the link to exist. This usually means that the processes end up becoming daemons. Persistent links, described shortly, are a variation of the multiplexor link that allow links to survive the closing of the controlling stream.

Once a stream has been linked under a multiplexor, the stream is no longer accessible to anything other than the multiplexor. All system calls that access the stream, except open and close, will fail with errno set to EINVAL. Once a stream is linked under a multiplexor, the process making the link can close the stream's file descriptor (strfd) because the STREAMS subsystem retains a reference to the stream by virtue of the link. When the stream is unlinked, the STREAMS subsystem will close it down if no other references to it remain.

Because a stream linked under a multiplexor is inaccessible to everything but the multiplexor, applications that need to customize the stream should do so before it is linked. For example, in Figure 12.3, an application might require that a module be pushed on the driver's stream before it is linked under the multiplexor. As another example, suppose the multiplexor implemented a network-layer protocol. The multiplexor might require that the data link stream linked under it be bound by the application before the link is made.

The criteria used by multiplexors to route messages are implementation-dependent. As we have said, the multiplexor ID can be used. Usually, however, multiplexors use data in the messages to decide where to send them. For example, on the write side, the IP multiplexor uses the IP address to decide which network interface will receive a message. In contrast, the TCP multiplexor only expects to have one stream linked underneath it, connected to IP, so there is no routing decision to make. On the read side, IP uses the protocol type in the IP header of the packet to decide which transport provider gets the message. TCP, on the other hand, uses the port number stored in the TCP header to decide which stream will receive the message.

Unlike the rest of the stream, the lower and upper queues in a multiplexor are not linked together via their q_next pointers. Since there is potentially a many-to-one relationship between them, they cannot be linked. It is up to the multiplexor to make up for this by passing messages properly.

Figure 12.5 illustrates how this can be done. The upper write-side processing of

the multiplexor uses `putq(lower_write_queue, mp)` to enqueue messages
on the lower queues, letting the lower write service procedure send the messages
down the linked stream.

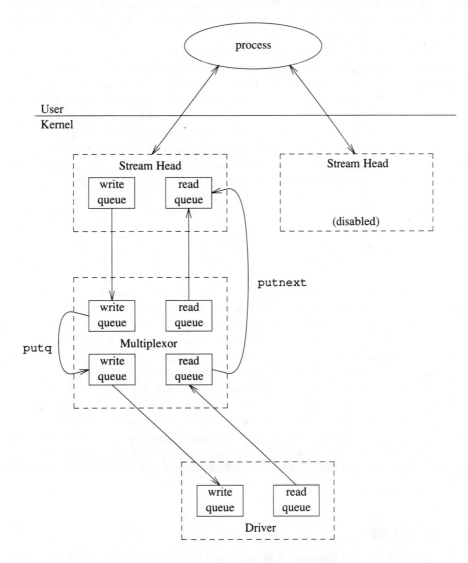

Fig. 12.5. Data Transfer through a Multiplexor

On the read side, the lower processing routines of the multiplexor use
`putnext(upper_read_queue, mp)` to pass messages to the processing element above the multiplexor, thereby bypassing the multiplexor's upper read-side routines. These are just two examples of how messages can pass through a multiplexor.

Recall from Section 9.2 the way flow control works between a transmitting queue and a receiving queue. The transmitting queue can pass messages to the receiving queue until the receiver becomes full. At this point, flow control prevents the transmitter from proceeding. When the amount of data stored in the receiving queue reaches the queue's low-water mark, the transmitter is backenabled, allowing messages to be sent again.

Because of the separation between the upper and lower queues, multiplexors must handle backenabling themselves when flow control subsides. For this reason, multiplexors must always have a lower write service procedure and an upper read service procedure. When the write side of a stream linked under a multiplexor has its flow-control restrictions lifted, the multiplexor's lower write service procedure is backenabled. The lower write service procedure must then backenable all upper write queues that were prevented from forwarding messages downstream while the lower stream was flow-controlled. Similarly, on the read side, the multiplexor's upper service procedure is backenabled when the read side of the multiplexor stream is no longer flow-controlled. The upper read service procedure must enable all lower read service procedures that were prevented from sending messages to the upper stream while it was flow-controlled.

The need for a multiplexor to propagate the backenabling process across the multiplexor's upper and lower queues can lead to two problems if not handled properly. First, consider the situation where one stream is being fed messages by several other streams. If the receiving stream flow-controls, then more than one sending queue might have to be backenabled. In this case, the receiving queue's service procedure usually backenables all of the feeding queues that are holding onto messages when the flow control is relieved. If this is not done properly, the feeding queues will be blocked indefinitely.

Second, consider the opposite scenario, where one stream is sending messages to several other streams. If one of the receiving streams flow-controls, the sending stream should not penalize the other receiving streams by holding all messages on its own queue until the flow control is removed. Selectively forwarding messages, however, will result in the loss of the relative time ordering of the messages as they are delivered to the different streams. Multiplexors can only forward messages in this case if timing does not matter. Most multiplexors ignore this problem and allow the flow control of one receiving stream to prevent message delivery to other receiving streams.

Persistent Links

The persistent link mechanism is a variation of the multiplexor link mechanism that does away with the need to have a process keep the controlling stream open during the duration of the link. Originally conceived and implemented by Guy Harris and Glenn Skinner at Sun Microsystems, the persistent link mechanism was added to System V because developers felt it was unnecessary to require that a process be used to keep a link active and because they were worried that the original multiplexor link mechanism would unduly complicate the process of building a protocol stack to boot a diskless workstation over a network.

The I_PLINK ioctl command is used to create a persistent multiplexor link, and the I_PUNLINK ioctl command is used to destroy a persistent link. Their syntax is the same as the original link mechanisms, but the two sets of commands cannot be intermixed. (In other words, you cannot unlink a persistent link with I_UNLINK nor unlink a regular link with I_PUNLINK.)

With persistent links, the controlling stream has no significance and can be closed after the link is made. To dismantle the multiplexor link, a process needs to open a stream to the multiplexor and use the corresponding multiplexor ID with the I_PUNLINK ioctl command. The stream need not be the same stream used to create the persistent link. The special value MUXID_ALL can be used in place of the multiplexor ID, but this will cause the multiplexor to dismantle *all* streams linked underneath it with persistent links.

As far as STREAMS multiplexing drivers are concerned, the major difference between regular links and persistent links is that the linkblk structure's l_qtop field is NULL for a persistent link. Its value is meaningless since the controlling stream can be closed, thus causing the queue to be deallocated.

12.3 THE TRANSPORT PROVIDER INTERFACE

The Transport Provider Interface (TPI) is a STREAMS service interface designed by AT&T to implement the OSI transport layer interface. Available from Unix International, the TPI is also documented in *STREAMS Modules and Drivers* [USL 1992a].

The TPI is very similar to the data link provider interface presented in Chapter 10. The TPI provides the same advantages as the DLPI: protocol portability and protocol interchangeability. The TPI is arguably more important than the DLPI, however, because the TLI library is implemented using TPI primitives. (Similarly, the socket library works with SOCKMOD to communicate with transport providers using the TPI.) Since we concentrated on the connectionless DLPI primitives in Chapter 10, we will concentrate on the connection-oriented TPI primitives in this chapter.

There are four kinds of primitives defined by the TPI: local management primitives, connection-establishment primitives, data-transfer primitives, and connection-release primitives. Table 12.1 summarizes the primitives we cover. The TPI actually includes additional primitives for options management, expedited data, orderly connection release, and connectionless service, but our sample transport provider does not use them.

The primitives are implemented as M_PROTO and M_PCPROTO messages with the first four bytes in the data buffer indicating the primitive. In addition, if a transport endpoint is in the data-transfer state, the TPI specifies that the transport provider should treat M_DATA messages as if they were associated with T_DATA_REQ primitives. This enables a process to send data over a transport connection using write(2) as well as t_snd(3N).

Table 12.1. TPI Primitives Used in Example

Primitive	Type	Class	Description
T_INFO_REQ	Request	Local Mgmt.	Get information.
T_INFO_ACK	Response	Local Mgmt.	Return information.
T_BIND_REQ	Request	Local Mgmt.	Bind an address.
T_BIND_ACK	Response	Local Mgmt.	Bind successful.
T_ERROR_ACK	Response	Local Mgmt.	Request failed.
T_UNBIND_REQ	Request	Local Mgmt.	Unbind an address.
T_OK_ACK	Response	Local Mgmt.	Operation successful.
T_CONN_REQ	Request	Conn. Setup	Request a connection.
T_CONN_RES	Request	Conn. Setup	Accept a connection.
T_CONN_IND	Event	Conn. Setup	Connect request received.
T_CONN_CON	Event	Conn. Setup	Connect confirmation.
T_DISCON_REQ	Request	Conn. Release	Break a connection.
T_DISCON_IND	Event	Conn. Release	Connection broken.
T_DATA_REQ	Request	Data Transfer	Transmit data.
T_DATA_IND	Event	Data Transfer	Data received.

Local Management Primitives

Figure 12.6 shows the exchange between the transport consumer and provider for the local management primitives. In all cases, the transport consumer generates a request primitive and the transport provider replies with a response primitive.

The T_INFO_REQ primitive is generated by the transport consumer to obtain service information about the transport provider. The transport provider responds with a T_INFO_ACK primitive. The T_INFO_REQ primitive is an M_PCPROTO message containing a T_info_req structure in its data buffer. The T_INFO_ACK primitive is also implemented as an M_PCPROTO message, but its data buffer contains a T_info_ack structure. The definition of these structures follows:

```
struct T_info_req {
    long PRIM_type;         /* T_INFO_REQ */
};

struct T_info_ack {
    long PRIM_type;         /* T_INFO_ACK */
    long TSDU_size;         /* max service data unit size */
    long ETSDU_size;        /* max expedited TSDU size */
    long CDATA_size;        /* max data sent with connect */
    long DDATA_size;        /* max data sent with disconnect */
    long ADDR_size;         /* max protocol address size */
    long OPT_size;          /* max options size */
    long TIDU_size;         /* max interface data unit size */
    long SERV_type;         /* service type */
    long CURRENT_state;     /* TPI state */
    long PROVIDER_flag;     /* special features supported */
};
```

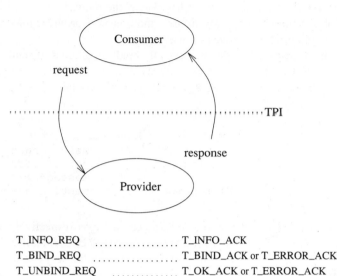

Fig. 12.6. Local Management Primitives

Each field in the `T_info_ack` structure is discussed in the context of the example in the next section.

When a transport provider is first opened, the state of the transport endpoint is unbound. Recall from Chapter 4 that a transport endpoint is an abstraction representing an instance of a use of the transport provider. To make the transport endpoint active, the transport user has to bind an address to it. This is done with the `T_BIND_REQ` primitive. The bind request primitive is implemented as an `M_PROTO` message whose data buffer contains a `T_bind_req` structure.

```
struct T_bind_req {
     long    PRIM_type;        /* T_BIND_REQ */
     long    ADDR_length;      /* address length */
     long    ADDR_offset;      /* offset of address */
                               /* in message */
     ulong_t CONIND_number;    /* connection queue length */
};
```

The `T_bind_req` structure is followed in the message by the address to be bound. The `ADDR_offset` field contains the location of the start of the address in the message. The `CONIND_number` field is set to a nonzero value for endpoints that will be used to receive connection requests. Its value is the number of connect indications that the transport consumer is willing to handle at any given time. Thus, it is the maximum number of outstanding connect indications that the transport provider will deliver to the transport consumer. This field is usually set to zero for endpoints that are used to initiate connections.

If the `ADDR_length` field is zero, then the transport provider should choose an address for the transport user. Otherwise, if the requested address cannot be bound (possibly because it is already in use), the transport provider may optionally bind a different address for the transport user.

If the transport provider successfully binds an address, it sends a T_BIND_ACK primitive upstream containing the address ultimately bound. The bind acknowledgement is implemented as an M_PCPROTO message containing a T_bind_ack structure in its data buffer.

```
struct T_bind_ack {
     long    PRIM_type;       /* T_BIND_ACK */
     long    ADDR_length;     /* address length */
     long    ADDR_offset;     /* offset of address */
                              /* in message */
     ulong_t CONIND_number;   /* connection queue length */
};
```

The ADDR_length and ADDR_offset fields respectively describe the size and location of the address in the buffer. The CONIND_number field contains the queue length chosen by the transport provider. It will always be less than or equal to the number requested by the transport consumer. Although the same address can be bound to different transport endpoints, the transport provider will only allow one instance of a given address to be bound with a nonzero CONIND_number.

If the transport provider cannot bind an address to the endpoint, it sends a T_ERROR_ACK primitive upstream. The error acknowledgement is implemented as an M_PCPROTO message whose data buffer contains a T_error_ack structure.

```
struct T_error_ack {
     long    PRIM_type;   /* T_ERROR_ACK */
     long    ERROR_prim;  /* primitive that failed */
     long    TLI_error;   /* TLI error code */
     long    UNIX_error;  /* UNIX error code */
};
```

When used to fail a bind request, the T_error_ack structure's ERROR_prim field will be set to T_BIND_REQ. Possible values for the TLI_error field are found in <sys/tiuser.h>. Examples include TOUTSTATE, when the request would place the interface in an invalid state, and TSYSERR, when a system error occurs. When TLI_error is set to TSYSERR, the UNIX_error field contains an error code (from <sys/errno.h>) defining the reason that the request failed.

An address can be unbound from a transport endpoint with the T_UNBIND_REQ primitive. It is implemented as an M_PROTO message containing a T_unbind_req structure in its data buffer.

```
struct T_unbind_req {
     long    PRIM_type;   /* T_UNBIND_REQ */
};
```

If the transport provider encounters an error, it responds with a T_ERROR_ACK primitive. If, on the other hand, the transport provider can successfully unbind the address from the transport endpoint, it sends a T_OK_ACK primitive upstream. The

T_OK_ACK is implemented as an M_PCPROTO message containing a T_ok_ack structure.

```
struct T_ok_ack {
        long    PRIM_type;      /* T_OK_ACK */
        long    CORRECT_prim;   /* primitive that succeeded */
};
```

When the transport provider receives a T_UNBIND_REQ, it must flush both the read and write sides of the stream before responding with the T_OK_ACK. This prevents any data queued in the stream from being presented to the transport consumer after the endpoint is unbound. An endpoint in the unbound state cannot be used to transfer data.

Connection-Establishment Primitives

Figure 12.7 shows the primitives involved in the first part of establishing a connection, where the client transport consumer sends a connect request to the transport provider, which acknowledges the request and sends a connect message to its peer transport provider. On the server side, the transport provider receives the connect message, converts it into a connection-indication primitive, and delivers it to the transport consumer (the server).

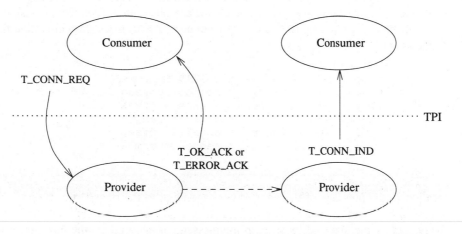

Fig. 12.7. Primitives Used in First Half of Connection Setup

The T_CONN_REQ primitive is implemented as an M_PROTO message containing a T_conn_req structure in its data buffer. The M_PROTO message block can be linked to one or more M_DATA message blocks if the protocol supports transmission of user data with the connect message and the transport consumer elects to use this option.

```
struct T_conn_req {
    long PRIM_type;        /* T_CONN_REQ */
    long DEST_length;      /* destination address length */
    long DEST_offset;      /* destination address offset */
    long OPT_length;       /* options length */
    long OPT_offset;       /* options offset */
};
```

The `DEST_length` field identifies the length in bytes of the destination address, and the `DEST_offset` field is the byte offset of the address in the `M_PROTO` message. If the transport consumer wants to negotiate options with the connect request, then `OPT_length` specifies the length of the options in bytes, and `OPT_offset` is the byte offset in the message where the options data begin. They are used to specify the desired characteristics of the transport connection. The format of the options is implementation-dependent.

If the transport provider encounters an error, it sends a `T_ERROR_ACK` primitive upstream. Otherwise, it responds to the transport user with a `T_OK_ACK` primitive. This does not mean that the connection has been established; it means merely that the transport provider has transitioned the transport endpoint into a state where it is waiting for the confirmation of the connect request.

On the server side, the client's connect request is delivered to the transport consumer as a `T_CONN_IND` primitive. It is implemented as an `M_PROTO` message containing a `T_conn_ind` structure. If the client sent data with the connect request, the `M_PROTO` message will be linked to one or more `M_DATA` messages containing the client's data.

```
struct T_conn_ind {
    long    PRIM_type;  /* T_CONN_IND */
    long    SRC_length; /* source address length */
    long    SRC_offset; /* source address offset */
    long    OPT_length; /* options length */
    long    OPT_offset; /* options offset */
    long    SEQ_number; /* sequence number */
};
```

The `SRC_length` and `SRC_offset` fields respectively specify the size and location in the message of the address corresponding to the transport endpoint generating the connect request. The `OPT_length` and `OPT_offset` fields respectively specify the size and location in the message of any options the transport provider wants to take effect for the connection. The options are ultimately selected by the transport provider, but the selection can be influenced by the transport consumer with the connection request primitive.

The `SEQ_number` field contains a unique identifier that the transport provider uses to match with the response from the transport consumer on the server machine. When the transport provider has multiple connect requests pending, each transport consumer response contains the sequence number corresponding to the request to which it applies. The value −1 is reserved to indicate that the sequence number is unused.

The second half of the connection setup process is shown in Figure 12.8. In it,

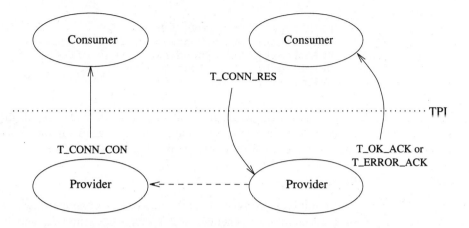

Fig. 12.8. Primitives Used in Second Half of Connection Setup

the transport consumer on the server machine responds to the request initiated by the transport consumer on the client machine.

If the transport consumer wishes to reject the connection request, it will respond with a disconnect request. (Disconnect requests are discussed shortly.) If, on the other hand, the transport consumer wishes to accept the connection request, it sends a connect response primitive (T_CONN_RES) to the transport provider. The connect response primitive is implemented as an M_PROTO message whose data buffer contains a T_conn_res structure.

```
struct T_conn_res {
      long     PRIM_type;   /* T_CONN_RES */
      queue_t *QUEUE_ptr;   /* queue to use for connection */
      long     OPT_length;  /* options length */
      long     OPT_offset;  /* options offset */
      long     SEQ_number;  /* sequence number */
};
```

The QUEUE_ptr field contains a pointer to the transport provider's read queue associated with the stream to be used in the connection. The OPT_length and OPT_offset fields specify the options that will ultimately be used with the connection. The SEQ_number field identifies the connect indication to which the connect response applies.

When the transport provider receives the connect response primitive, it sends a message back to the client machine where its peer transport provider will send a connect confirmation primitive (T_CONN_CON) upstream to the transport consumer. The connect confirmation is implemented as an M_PROTO message with a T_conn_con structure in its data buffer. If the responding transport consumer sent data with the response, then the M_PROTO message will be linked to one or more M_DATA messages containing the data.

```
struct T_conn_con {
    long    PRIM_type;   /* T_CONN_CON */
    long    RES_length;  /* responding address length */
    long    RES_offset;  /* responding address offset */
    long    OPT_length;  /* options length */
    long    OPT_offset;  /* options offset */
};
```

The `RES_length` and `RES_offset` fields describe the address of the server's transport endpoint participating in the connection. Once again, options associated with the connection are described by `OPT_length` and `OPT_offset`.

Data-Transfer Primitives

Figure 12.9 shows the primitives involved in transferring data over an existing connection. The sending transport user generates a `T_DATA_REQ` primitive, and its transport provider converts this into a message and transmits it to the peer transport provider. The receiving transport provider converts the message into a `T_DATA_IND` primitive and delivers it to the receiving transport user.

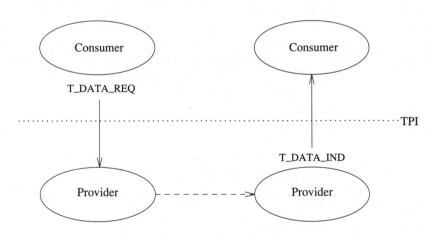

Fig. 12.9. Data-Transfer Primitives

The data request primitive is implemented as an `M_PROTO` message linked to zero or more `M_DATA` message blocks. (Some transport providers support zero-length TSDUs.) The data buffer of the `M_PROTO` message contains a `T_data_req` structure.

```
struct T_data_req {
    long    PRIM_type;   /* T_DATA_REQ */
    long    MORE_flag;   /* more data coming */
};
```

The data request primitive describes a transport interface data unit. There might be several transport interface data units per transport service data unit. (TIDUs and

TSDUs are discussed in Section 4.2.) MORE_flag is nonzero when the data request is part of a larger, logical TSDU. When MORE_flag is zero, then the TIDU is the last portion of the TSDU. Of course, some protocols (e.g., TCP) do not support the notion of message boundaries, so the use of MORE_flag has no effect with these protocols.

M_DATA messages are also accepted by transport providers. Each M_DATA message is treated as if it were a single data request. This enables applications to use write to send data over a transport connection.

The data indication primitive has a format similar to the data request primitive: one M_PROTO message linked to zero or more M_DATA messages, with the data buffer of the M_PROTO message containing a T_data_ind structure. Except for the type of primitive, the T_data_ind structure is the same as the T_data_req structure.

```
struct T_data_ind {
      long    PRIM_type;   /* T_DATA_IND */
      long    MORE_flag;   /* more data coming */
};
```

Connection-Release Primitives

The primitives used to release a connection are shown in Figure 12.10. The transport consumer aborting the connection generates a T_DISCON_REQ primitive. On receipt, the transport provider acknowledges the request by responding with either a T_OK_ACK if the request does not encounter any errors, or a T_ERROR_ACK otherwise. The transport provider then sends a message to its peer, which in turn notifies its transport consumer by sending a T_DISCON_IND primitive upstream.

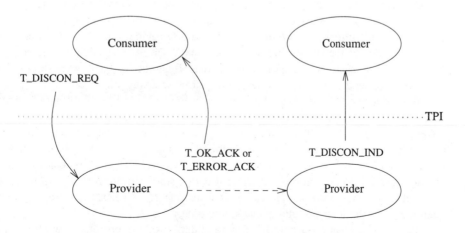

Fig. 12.10. Connection-Release Primitives

The format of a disconnect request is an M_PROTO message containing a

`T_discon_req` structure in its data buffer. The `M_PROTO` message can be linked to one or more `M_DATA` messages if the transport consumer wishes to send data along with the disconnect request.

```
struct T_discon_req {
      long     PRIM_type;    /* T_DISCON_RES */
      long     SEQ_number;   /* sequence number */
};
```

The disconnect request can also be used to deny a connect request. In this case, the `SEQ_number` field is used to match the disconnect request with the connect request being denied. When disconnecting an existing connection, `SEQ_number` is set to −1.

The `T_DISCON_IND` primitive is also implemented as an `M_PROTO` message. If the transport consumer initiating the disconnect sent data along with the disconnect request, then the disconnect indication message will be linked to one or more `M_DATA` messages containing the data. The data buffer in the `M_PROTO` message contains a `T_discon_ind` structure.

```
struct T_discon_ind {
      long     PRIM_type;       /* T_DISCON_IND */
      long     DISCON_reason;   /* reason for disconnect */
      long     SEQ_number;      /* sequence number */
};
```

The `DISCON_reason` field is an implementation-specific code describing the reason for the disconnect. The `SEQ_number` field is used to identify the connect request denied, just as in the `T_discon_req` structure.

Disconnects are abortive releases. They do not guarantee delivery of data that might be queued in a stream. Optional orderly release primitives are available for this purpose. Accordingly, the transport provider must flush the stream when a connection is broken with a disconnect primitive.

On the side initiating the request, the transport provider must flush both the read and write sides of the stream before sending the `T_OK_ACK` upstream. On the side receiving the request, the transport provider must flush the read and write sides of the stream before sending the `T_DISCON_IND` primitive upstream.

Now that we have seen all the transport primitives used by our example transport provider, we can consider the states during which each primitive can be generated. The `T_INFO_REQ` primitive can be generated in almost any state and does not affect the state of the transport endpoint. Since the `T_INFO_ACK` is implemented as an `M_PCPROTO` message, the transport provider has to be careful not to respond to the information request while it is in a state waiting for an acknowledgement of any other request. (Recall that only one `M_PCPROTO` message can be queued on the stream head read queue at one time.)

Figure 12.11 shows a simplified state diagram of the primitives we have discussed. The information request and acknowledgement primitives are omitted for simplicity. Another simplification is the glossing over of the difference between the transport endpoint used to listen for connection requests and the transport endpoint used to participate in the newly accepted connection. Here, the new transport end-point transitions from the bound state directly to the data-transfer state.

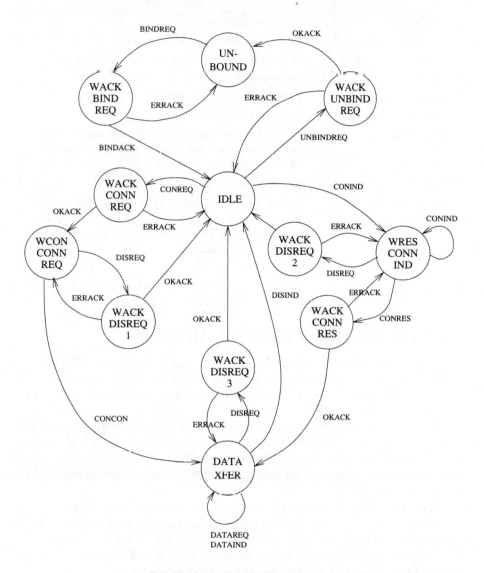

Fig. 12.11. Partial TPI State Diagram

Transport primitives have been abbreviated in the figure to reduce the noise. Similarly, different states have been abbreviated. They are explained in Table 12.2.

Table 12.2. Transport Provider States

State	Description
UNBOUND	Not bound (initial state)
WACK BIND REQ	Waiting for acknowledgement of a bind request
WACK UNBIND REQ	Waiting for acknowledgement of an unbind request
IDLE	Idle (bound, but inactive)
WACK CONN REQ	Waiting for acknowledgement of a connect request
WCON CONN REQ	Waiting for confirmation of a connect request
WACK DISREQ 1	Waiting for acknowledgement of a disconnect request after requesting a connection but before the connection was established
WRES CONN IND	Waiting for response to a connect indication
WACK CONN RES	Waiting for acknowledgement of a connect response
WACK DISREQ 2	Waiting for acknowledgement of a disconnect request after receiving a connect indication and denying the request with a disconnect
DATA XFER	Data transfer
WACK DISREQ 3	Waiting for acknowledgement of a disconnect request (when breaking an existing connection)

12.4 TRANSPORT PROVIDER EXAMPLE

The example in this chapter illustrates issues involved in the design of STREAMS multiplexors. It is a simple connection-oriented transport provider conforming to the TPI service interface. As usual, several simplifications are made to improve the example's understandability.

The first simplification is that the multiplexor talks directly with a data link provider linked underneath it, leaving any network-layer software unused. By restricting the design of the multiplexor to allow it to work only with a single, unsegmented local area network, we remove the need to introduce yet another service interface, the Network Provider Interface (NPI).

The second simplification is the protocol implemented by the multiplexor. The example uses a simple positive acknowledgement protocol with sequence numbers to detect out-of-order packets. While it may not be practical for use as a transport protocol, the simple protocol used in the example does give us a chance to study how protocol-related issues are handled in a STREAMS multiplexor.

Every packet generated by the transport provider starts with the packet header shown in Figure 12.12. Several different packet types are supported, including connect request messages, connect acceptance messages, data messages, disconnect messages, flow-control messages, and positive acknowledgement messages.

Every packet sent is assigned a sequence number. The receiver responds with an acknowledgement packet whose sequence number matches that of the packet

Protocol Version 1 byte	Packet Type 1 byte	Flags 1 byte	Disconnect Reason 1 byte	Source Port 2 bytes	Destination Port 2 bytes	Packet Size 2 bytes	Pad 2 bytes	Sequence Number 4 bytes

Fig. 12.12. Protocol Packet Header Format

being acknowledged. (Acknowledgements themselves are not acknowledged.) After a packet is sent, if an acknowledgement is not received in a fixed amount of time, the original packet is retransmitted. Eventually, if the maximum number of retransmit attempts has been reached, the virtual circuit will be marked as being disconnected.

The protocol version can be used to help different versions of the communication protocol interoperate. The first message received from any host will be a connect request. If the protocol versions do not match, the corresponding acknowledgement message can specify the latest protocol version that both hosts understand. In the first version of the transport provider, there is no need for any special version checks because only one version of the protocol is in use.

Another simplification is the choice of the transport address format. An arbitrary format could be supported if some form of name service was available. Instead, a transport address is built using the data link provider's address. This is similar to the way TCP addresses contain IP addresses. Also similar to TCP, an individual endpoint is distinguished by a port number.

The protocol processing is divided between the upper and lower halves of the multiplexor, as shown in Figure 12.13. Most of the interpretation of protocol messages is performed by the upper half of the multiplexor, although the lower half does handle the validation of sequence numbers and the generation of acknowledgements.

write side	read side	
convert TPI primitives into DLPI primitives	convert DLPI primitives into TPI primitives and propagate flow control to lower half of multiplexor	top half
propagate flow control to upper half of multiplexor	demultiplex and acknowledge messages received	lower half

Fig. 12.13. Partitioning the Work in the Multiplexor

Figure 12.14 summarizes the major functions in the example multiplexing driver. Before we discuss them, we will look at the transport provider's header file, `stp.h`. Because the example is so long, most of the comments have been removed.

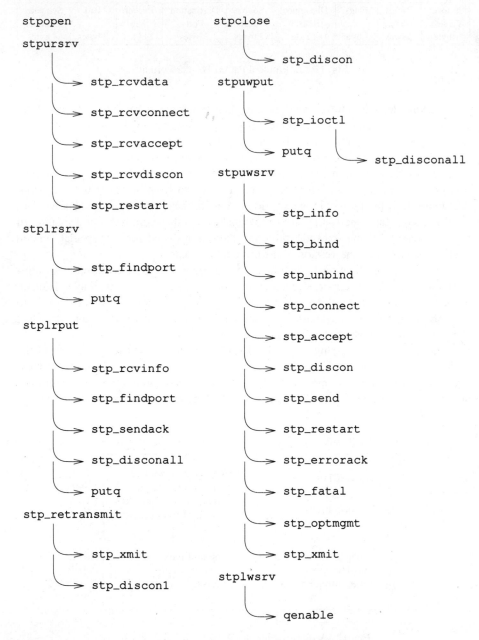

Fig. 12.14. Transport Provider Function Diagram

```
 1 #ifndef _SYS_STP_H
 2 #define _SYS_STP_H

 3 /*
 4  * STP header format.
 5  */
 6 typedef struct stphdr {
 7    uchar_t      h_version;   /* protocol version */
 8    uchar_t      h_type;      /* packet type */
 9    uchar_t      h_flags;     /* see below */
10    uchar_t      h_reason;    /* disconnect reason */
11    ushort_t     h_sport;     /* source port */
12    ushort_t     h_dport;     /* destination port */
13    ushort_t     h_size;      /* number of bytes in packet */
14    ushort_t     h_pad;       /* reserved */
15    ulong_t      h_seqno;     /* sequence number */
16 } hdr_t;

17 /* packet types */
18 #define DATA      0
19 #define ACK       1
20 #define CONNECT   2
21 #define ACCEPT    3
22 #define DISCON    4
23 #define RESTART   5

24 /* flags */
25 #define STOP  0x01    /* if ACK, stop transmitting */
26 #define MORE  0x02    /* if DATA, consumer's T_MORE flag */
27 #define EOM   0x04    /* End Of Message */
```

[1–23]   The stphdr structure defines the transport protocol's packet header. There are six different packet types: data messages, acknowledgements, connection requests, connection acceptances, disconnect messages, and restart messages. The h_size field contains the size of the packet in bytes, including the packet header. The h_reason field is used only in disconnect messages. It describes the cause of the disconnect.

[24–27]   The h_flags field in the packet header conveys special information about particular packet types. If the packet is an acknowledgement, then the presence of the STOP flag tells the host receiving the acknowledgement to stop transmitting. If the packet contains user data, then the MORE flag will be set if the present TSDU is part of a larger logical TSDU. The EOM flag is always set, except when a packet needs to be split up into multiple smaller packets to conform to the data link provider's maximum DLSDU size. In this case, only the last of the segmented packets contains the EOM flag.

```
28 /* disconnect reasons */
29 #define DIS_USER      1     /* user-initiated disconnect */
30 #define DIS_TIMEOUT   2     /* acknowledgement timed out */
31 #define DIS_NOLINK    3     /* mux unlinked */
32 #define DIS_NETERR    4     /* fatal network error */

33 /* address format */
34 #define NETADDRSZ     6          /* size of network address */
35 #define MAXNETSAPSZ   4          /* max net SAP size */
36 #define STPADDRSZ (2+NETADDRSZ)  /* size of stp address */
37 struct stpaddr {
38   ushort_t   a_port;                 /* port number */
39   uchar_t    a_net[NETADDRSZ];   /* network address */
40 };

41 #define MAXCREQ       10     /* max # of connreqs queued */
42 #define MAXPORT       65535  /* maximum port number */
43 #define STPVERS       1      /* protocol version 1 */

44 #ifdef _KERNEL
45 #define MAXTIDUSZ 8192     /* maximum TIDU size */
46 #define RETRTIME  300000   /* retransmit time in usec */
47 #define MAXRETR   4        /* max number of retransmits */
```

[28–32] There are several reasons why a virtual circuit might be disconnected: a
         user can explicitly request a disconnect, an acknowledgement might not
         arrive in time, the data link provider can be unlinked from the multiplexor,
         or the data link provider might encounter an unrecoverable error.

[33–40] The size of the data link provider's address is hard-coded for simplicity.
         The transport provider's address is composed of a port number and the data
         link provider's network address. MAXNETSAPSZ is the maximum size of
         the DLSAP identifier; it is not included in the transport provider address.

[41–43] MAXCREQ is the maximum number of connect requests queued by the
         transport provider. This is independent from the number of connect indica-
         tions specified in the bind request, but we will use MAXCREQ to limit the
         queue length for simplicity. MAXPORT is the largest valid port number.
         STPVERS is the current protocol version.

[44–47] The header file is split into user-level and kernel-level portions so it can be
         shared by both the the driver and any user-level applications that need it. If
         _KERNEL is defined, the kernel-level definitions become accessible.

         MAXTIDUSZ is the maximum transport interface data unit size supported
         by the transport provider. RETRTIME is the time (in microseconds) after
         which an unacknowledged message is retransmitted. MAXRETR is the
         maximum number of times we will retransmit a message before giving up.

```
48 /* transport endpoint definition */
49 typedef struct stp_endpoint {
50    queue_t      *s_rdq;        /* read queue */
51    ulong_t       s_tpstate;    /* TPI state */
52    ulong_t       s_seqno;      /* next sequence number to use */
53    ulong_t       s_ackno;      /* last seqno ack sent */
54    ulong_t       s_rcvack;     /* last seqno ack received */
55    ushort_t      s_lport;      /* local port */
56    ushort_t      s_flag;       /* see below */
57    ushort_t      s_nretr;      /* number of retransmits */
58    ushort_t      s_msgxmitsz;  /* message transmission size */
59    ushort_t      s_totxmitsz;  /* total transmitted so far */
60    mblk_t       *s_rxmp;       /* message to retransmit */
61    mblk_t       *s_rcvmp;      /* message being received */
62    ulong_t       s_txtime;     /* time message transmitted */
63    ulong_t       s_rrecid;     /* read-side allocb failures */
64    ulong_t       s_wrecid;     /* write-side allocb failures */
65    ushort_t      s_maxqlen;    /* max # of conninds for user */
66    ushort_t      s_qlen;       /* # of conninds queued */
67    ulong_t       s_conseq;     /* connect sequence counter */
68    struct stpaddr s_faddr;     /* foreign address */
69    mblk_t       *s_cmp[MAXCREQ];/* connect request array */
70 } stp_t;

71 /* flags */
72 #define RRECBCALL  0x01     /* s_rrecid is a bufcall ID */
73 #define RRECTOUT   0x02     /* s_rrecid is a timeout ID */
74 #define WRECBCALL  0x04     /* s_wrecid is a bufcall ID */
75 #define WRECTOUT   0x08     /* s_wrecid is a timeout ID */
76 #define NOXMIT     0x10     /* other end flow-controlled */
77 #define FLOWCTL    0x20     /* we were flow-controlled */
78 #define DORESTART  0x40     /* restart other transmitter */
79 #endif /* _KERNEL */
80 #endif /* _SYS_STP_H */
```

[48–70]   A transport endpoint (minor device) in this driver is represented by a structure of type stp_t. The s_rxmp field retains a copy of the last message transmitted until either an acknowledgement is received or the retransmit limit has been reached. The s_txtime field records the time a message is sent so that we can tell when the message requires retransmission. The s_rcvmp field holds any message fragments that are being reassembled.

[71–80]   The read and write sides of the multiplexor have separate recovery mechanisms. RRECBCALL and RRECTOUT identify the mechanism being used for read-side recovery. Similarly, WRECBCALL and WRECTOUT identify the write-side recovery mechanism. NOXMIT is set when the other end of the connection tells us to stop transmitting. FLOWCTL is set when the read side of the stream flow-controls. DORESTART is set when a restart message should be sent to the peer transport provider.

Now that the header file has been described, we will look at the example multiplexing driver.

```
 1 #include <sys/types.h>
 2 #include <sys/param.h>
 3 #include <sys/systm.h>
 4 #include <sys/stream.h>
 5 #include <sys/stropts.h>
 6 #include <sys/errno.h>
 7 #include <sys/cred.h>
 8 #include <sys/byteorder.h>
 9 #include <sys/cmn_err.h>
10 #include <sys/tihdr.h>
11 #include <sys/tiuser.h>
12 #include <sys/dlpi.h>
13 #include <sys/ddi.h>
14 #include <sys/stp.h>

15 #ifdef DEBUG
16 #define STATIC
17 #else
18 #define STATIC static
19 #endif

20 #define HALFSEC    500000        /* in microseconds */

21 #define HDRSIZE    ((sizeof(hdr_t) < net.n_minsdu) ? \
22    net.n_minsdu : sizeof(hdr_t))

23 int stpdevflag = 0;
```

[1–14] Most header files are familiar from previous examples. <sys/tihdr.h> contains the definitions that make up the TPI service interface. <sys/tiuser.h> contains definitions used by both the user-level TLI library and the kernel-level transport providers. <sys/byteorder.h> contains the definitions of macros and functions that convert between host and Internet network byte ordering. The STP driver uses the same network byte ordering as the Internet.

[15–23] We define STATIC so that symbols are global when we are debugging the driver, and private otherwise. HALFSEC is the number of microseconds in one half second, the time delay used during recovery from allocation failures. HDRSIZE evaluates to the minimum packet size needed to transmit a packet header. It is used whenever we need to allocate a message to send a packet to the data link provider. stpdevflag is the driver flag required by the system [see devflag(D1D)].

```
24 /*
25  * structure representing underlying network.
26  */
27 enum netstate { DOWN, STATECHG, UP };

28 struct network {
29    queue_t       *n_wrq;        /* upper write queue of network */
30                                 /* (lower write queue of mux) */
31    mblk_t        *n_mp;         /* ioctl message used */
32                                 /* during link and unlink */
33    enum netstate n_state;       /* state of network */
34    int           n_linkid;      /* link ID */
35    uint_t        n_nextsend;    /* next minor to send a message */
36    ulong_t       n_maxsdu;      /* max data unit size */
37    ulong_t       n_minsdu;      /* min data unit size */
38    char          n_saplen;      /* length of sap component of */
39                                 /* network address */
40    uchar_t       n_addrlen;     /* length of complete network */
41                                 /* address */
42    uchar_t       n_addr[NETADDRSZ+MAXNETSAPSZ];   /* network */
43                                 /* (DLSAP) address */
44 };

45 STATIC struct network net;

46 STATIC dl_priority_t stpnopri = { 0, 0 };
```

[24–27] netstate is an enumeration of the possible states of the underlying network. The state is UP while there is an active stream linked under the multiplexor. The state is DOWN when no network stream is linked under the multiplexor, as well as when the stream is linked but is in error mode. STATECHG is an intermediate state used between the time that a link request is initiated and the time that it completes.

[28–44] The network structure is used to represent the network stream linked underneath the multiplexor. Only one such stream is supported (again, for simplicity). The n_linkid field contains the link ID from the linkblk structure used to set up the multiplexing configuration. The n_minsdu and n_maxsdu fields describe the range of message sizes that the data link provider can accept. The n_addrlen field specifies the length of the total DLSAP address. The n_addr field contains the entire data link provider address, composed of the physical address and a SAP identifier.

[45–46] net is the sole instance of the network structure that represents the underlying data link provider. stpnopri is used to initialize the dl_priority field in the data link unitdata request messages. Refer to Section 10.3 for more information about the DLPI primitives.

```
47 /*
48  * TPI state transition definitions.
49  */
50 extern char ti_statetbl[TE_NOEVENTS][TS_NOSTATES];

51 #define NEXTSTATE1(CS, EV)  ti_statetbl[(EV)][(CS)]

52 #define NEXTSTATE2(CS, EV1, EV2) \
53   ti_statetbl[(EV2)][ti_statetbl[(EV1)][(CS)]]

54 #define BADSTATE(CS, EV) \
55   (ti_statetbl[(EV)][(CS)]==127)

56 /*
57  * The following are defined in the driver
58  * configuration file.
59  */
60 extern int nstp;          /* number of endpoints */
61 extern stp_t stpendpt[];  /* array of endpoints */

62 typedef enum retval {
63   DONE,       /* function completed its job */
64   RETRY,      /* temporary failure; try again later */
65   ERR         /* permanent error */
66 } retval_t;
```

[47–55] The operating system defines a two-dimensional table (ti_statetbl) that maps the event associated with a transport primitive and the current state of the transport endpoint to the new state entered when the event occurs. Invalid state transitions lead to cells in the array containing 127, an invalid state number. We will use this table instead of encoding the state transitions ourselves.

We define three macros to process TPI states. NEXTSTATE1 returns the next state entered when a single TPI primitive is received. NEXTSTATE2 is like NEXTSTATE1, but combines two state transitions into one, used when we process request primitives "atomically" with the reception of a request and an immediate response. BADSTATE returns an indication of whether an event will lead us into an invalid state.

[56–61] nstp is the number of transport endpoints, or minor devices, configured. stpendpt is an array of endpoints. Both are allocated via the system's configuration mechanism.

[62–66] Functions for which recovery can occur return a value of type retval_t. Recovery involves placing the message being processed back on a queue and scheduling the queue to be serviced at some future time.

```
 67 STATIC int stpopen(queue_t *, dev_t *, int, int, cred_t *);
 68 STATIC int stpclose(queue_t *, int, cred_t *);
 69 STATIC int stpuwput(queue_t *, mblk_t *);
 70 STATIC int stpuwsrv(queue_t *);
 71 STATIC int stpursrv(queue_t *);
 72 STATIC int stplwsrv(queue_t *);
 73 STATIC int stplrput(queue_t *, mblk_t *);
 74 STATIC int stplrsrv(queue_t *);
 75 STATIC void stp_ioctl(queue_t *, mblk_t *);
 76 STATIC void stp_wsched(stp_t *, int);
 77 STATIC void stp_wcont(stp_t *);
 78 STATIC retval_t stp_info(queue_t *, mblk_t *);
 79 STATIC retval_t stp_bind(queue_t *, mblk_t *);
 80 STATIC retval_t stp_unbind(queue_t *, mblk_t *);
 81 STATIC retval_t stp_connect(queue_t *, mblk_t *);
 82 STATIC retval_t stp_accept(queue_t *, mblk_t *);
 83 STATIC retval_t stp_send(queue_t *, mblk_t *);
 84 STATIC retval_t stp_discon(queue_t *, mblk_t *);
 85 STATIC retval_t stp_optmgmt(queue_t *, mblk_t *);
 86 STATIC retval_t stp_errorack(queue_t *, long, long, long);
 87 STATIC retval_t stp_restart(stp_t *);
 88 STATIC void stp_rsched(stp_t *, int);
 89 STATIC void stp_rcont(stp_t *);
 90 STATIC void stp_fatal(queue_t *, mblk_t *);
 91 STATIC stp_t *stp_findport(ushort_t);
 92 STATIC ushort_t stp_getuport(void);
 93 STATIC void stp_xmit(stp_t *, mblk_t *, int);
 94 STATIC void stp_retransmit(void);
 95 STATIC void stp_disconall(uchar_t);
 96 STATIC void stp_rcvinfo(mblk_t *);
 97 STATIC retval_t stp_rcvdata(queue_t *, mblk_t *);
 98 STATIC retval_t stp_rcvconnect(queue_t *, mblk_t *);
 99 STATIC retval_t stp_rcvaccept(queue_t *, mblk_t *);
100 STATIC retval_t stp_rcvdiscon(queue_t *, mblk_t *);
101 STATIC void stp_buildokack(mblk_t *, ulong_t);
102 STATIC void stp_buildunitdata(mblk_t *, struct stpaddr *);
103 STATIC void stp_buildheader(stp_t *, mblk_t *, uchar_t,
104  uchar_t, uchar_t, ushort_t, ushort_t, int);
105 STATIC void stp_buildaddr(struct stpaddr *, caddr_t,
106  ushort_t);
107 STATIC void stp_discon1(stp_t *, uchar_t);
108 STATIC int stp_sendack(stp_t *, mblk_t *, uchar_t);
109 STATIC int stp_sameaddr(struct stpaddr *,
110  struct stpaddr *);
111 STATIC int stp_samenetaddr(uchar_t *, uchar_t *);
112 STATIC int stp_qinuse(queue_t *);
```

[67–112]   Function prototypes for the simple transport provider are declared next. Figure 12.14, which precedes the example, illustrates the calling sequences of the major driver functions.

```
113 STATIC struct module_info stp_minfo = {
114  0x5354, "stp", 0, MAXTIDUSZ, 10*MAXTIDUSZ, 2*MAXTIDUSZ
115 };
116 STATIC struct qinit stp_urinit = {    /* upper read side */
117  NULL, stpursrv, stpopen, stpclose, NULL, &stp_minfo, NULL
118 };
119 STATIC struct qinit stp_uwinit = {    /* upper write side */
120  stpuwput, stpuwsrv, NULL, NULL, NULL, &stp_minfo, NULL
121 };
122 STATIC struct qinit stp_lrinit = {    /* lower read size */
123  stplrput, stplrsrv, NULL, NULL, NULL, &stp_minfo, NULL
124 };
125 STATIC struct qinit stp_lwinit = {    /* lower write side */
126  NULL, stplwsrv, NULL, NULL, NULL, &stp_minfo, NULL
127 };
128 struct streamtab stpinfo = {
129  &stp_urinit, &stp_uwinit, &stp_lrinit, &stp_lwinit
130 };

131 void
132 stpinit()
133 {
134  net.n_state = DOWN;
135 }
```

[113–130] We initialize the module ID of the transport provider to the hexadecimal ASCII equivalent of the first two characters in the driver's name. The minimum packet size is zero. The maximum packet size is set to the maximum transport interface data unit size. The high-water mark is set to the size of 10 full packets. The low-water mark is set to the size of 2 full packets.

The upper read side of the multiplexor does not have a put procedure because the lower half will place messages directly on the upper read side's queue. The lower write side of the multiplexor does not have a put procedure either. But unlike the read side, the upper write side does not place messages on the lower write queue. The lower write service procedure only exists to propagate the flow control to the upper half of the multiplexor. To transmit packets to the network, the upper write side of the multiplexor will pass messages directly to the processing element linked under it.

Note that this is the only example shown so far where all four members of the streamtab structure point to valid qinit structures.

[131–135] stpinit is called at system boot time. It initializes the state of the network to DOWN, indicating the network is inactive.

```
136 STATIC int
137 stpopen(queue_t *q, dev_t *devp, int flag, int sflag,
138   cred_t *crp)
139 {
140   stp_t *stp;
141   int i;
142   mblk_t *mp;
143   struct stroptions *sp;

144   if (sflag == MODOPEN)    /* configuration error */
145       return(EINVAL);
146   if (q->q_ptr != NULL)    /* not first open */
147       return(0);

148   if (sflag == CLONEOPEN) {
149       for (i = 0; i < nstp; i++)
150           if (stpendpt[i].s_rdq == NULL)
151               break;
152   } else {
153       i = geteminor(*devp);
154   }
155   if (i >= nstp)
156       return(ENXIO);

157   mp = allocb(sizeof(struct stroptions), BPRI_HI);
158   if (mp == NULL)
159       return(EAGAIN);
160   stp = &stpendpt[i];
```

[136–147] If the STREAMS flag is set to MODOPEN, then the multiplexor has been configured incorrectly, so we return an error. If the private pointer in the queue is non-NULL, then this is not the first open of the minor device, so there is nothing to initialize, and we return success.

[148–156] For a clone open, we search the array of transport endpoints for an unused minor device. If the s_rdq field is NULL, then the transport endpoint is not currently in use. For a regular open, we extract the external minor device number from the device number. In both cases, if the minor device number is greater than the number of configured endpoints, we return failure (ENXIO).

[157–160] Next we allocate a message large enough to hold a stroptions structure so we can change the stream head's water marks. If the allocation fails, we return EAGAIN instead of sleeping until memory is available. Either alternative is fine for this driver, but before we sleep during a clone open, we need to reserve the minor device we just found so no other opens select it while we are asleep.

```
161  mp->b_datap->db_type = M_SETOPTS;
162  mp->b_wptr += sizeof(struct stroptions);
163  sp = (struct stroptions *)mp->b_rptr;
164  sp->so_flags = SO_HIWAT|SO_LOWAT;
165  sp->so_hiwat = stp_minfo.mi_hiwat;
166  sp->so_lowat = stp_minfo.mi_lowat;
167  putnext(q, mp);
168  bzero((caddr_t)stp, sizeof(stp_t));
169  stp->s_rdq = q;
170  stp->s_tpstate = TS_UNBND;
171  q->q_ptr = (caddr_t)stp;
172  WR(q)->q_ptr = (caddr_t)stp;
173  if (sflag == CLONEOPEN)
174      *devp = makedevice(getemajor(*devp), i);
175  return(0);
176  }

177  STATIC int
178  stpclose(queue_t *q, int flag, cred_t *crp)
179  {
180   stp_t *stp;
181   int i;

182   stp = (stp_t *)q->q_ptr;
183   if (stp->s_rxmp != NULL) {
184       freemsg(stp->s_rxmp);
185       stp->s_rxmp = NULL;
186   }
```

[161–167] Now that we know the minor device number is valid, we initialize the
          M_SETOPTS message, setting the high and low water marks to match
          those of the multiplexor. This will prevent the read sides of streams
          open to the multiplexor from flow-controlling too often. We do not set
          the stream head's packet sizes, although it would not hurt, because very
          few modules use them. Then we send the message upstream.

[168–176] We initialize the stp_t structure by setting it to zeros, storing the read
          queue pointer in the s_rdq field, and setting the initial state of the
          transport endpoint to TS_UNBND, indicating it is unbound. We store
          pointers to the stp_t structure in the read and write queues to enable
          the put and service procedures to locate the structure given the queue.
          For a clone open, we create a new device number using the initial major
          number and the selected minor number, and we store the new device
          number in the memory location referred to by devp. Finally, we return
          0 to indicate the open completed successfully.

[177–186] stpclose is called when a stream opened to the multiplexor is closed.
          If a message is being held for retransmission, we free it.

```
187  if ((stp->s_tpstate == TS_DATA_XFER) &&
188      (net.n_state == UP)) {
189          stp_discon(WR(q), NULL);
190          if (stp->s_rxmp != NULL) {
191              freemsg(stp->s_rxmp);
192              stp->s_rxmp = NULL;
193          }
194  }
195  if (stp->s_rcvmp != NULL) {
196      freemsg(stp->s_rcvmp);
197      stp->s_rcvmp = NULL;
198  }
199  if (stp->s_flag & RRECBCALL)
200      unbufcall(stp->s_rrecid);
201  else if (stp->s_flag & RRECTOUT)
202      untimeout(stp->s_rrecid);
203  if (stp->s_flag & WRECBCALL)
204      unbufcall(stp->s_wrecid);
205  else if (stp->s_flag & WRECTOUT)
206      untimeout(stp->s_wrecid);
207  for (i = 0; i < MAXCREQ; i++) {
208      if (stp->s_cmp[i] != NULL) {
209          freeb(stp->s_cmp[i]);
210          stp->s_cmp[i] = NULL;
211      }
212  }
213  q->q_ptr = NULL;
214  WR(q)->q_ptr = NULL;
215  stp->s_rdq = NULL;
216  return(0);
217 }
```

[187–194]   If the transport endpoint is in the data-transfer state and the network is
            still up, we call stp_discon to send a disconnect request to the peer.
            Then, if the disconnect request has queued a message for retransmission,
            we free it as before. We do not have to wait for the disconnect message
            to be acknowledged, because if either message is lost the peer will time
            out if it attempts to communicate with us.

[195–212]   If a message is being held for reassembly, we free it. If a bufcall or
            timeout event is pending on the read side, we cancel the event. We
            do the same for the write side. Next we step through the array of con-
            nect indication messages, freeing any that are left over.

[213–217]   Finally, we clear the private pointers in the queues, set the s_rdq field
            to NULL, indicating that this minor device is free to be reallocated, and
            return 0 for success.

```
218 STATIC int
219 stpuwput(queue_t *q, mblk_t *mp)
220 {
221   mblk_t *bp, *nbp;
222   union T_primitives *tp;

223   switch (mp->b_datap->db_type) {
224   case M_PROTO:
225   case M_PCPROTO:
226       tp = (union T_primitives *)mp->b_rptr;
227       if (tp->type == T_DISCON_REQ) {
228           bp = q->q_first;
229           while (bp != NULL) {
230               nbp = bp->b_next;
231               if (bp->b_datap->db_type == M_DATA) {
232                   rmvq(q, bp);
233                   freemsg(bp);
234                   bp = nbp;
235                   continue;
236               }
237               tp = (union T_primitives *)bp->b_rptr;
238               switch (tp->type) {
239               case T_DATA_REQ:
240               case T_CONN_RES:
241                   rmvq(q, bp);
242                   freemsg(bp);
243                   break;
```

[218–225]   The upper write put procedure accepts messages conforming to the TPI service interface. Any messages implementing service interface primitives must be handled according to the precedence rules specified by the TPI, if the messages are to be enqueued.

[226–243]   A disconnect request takes precedence over data requests, connect requests, and connect responses. When a disconnect request is received, we need to remove any enqueued primitives of lower precedence. If a connect request is on the queue, then the disconnect request is to be discarded since there is no need to send a disconnect message to the peer transport provider, because no virtual circuit is present. If no connect request is present, the disconnect request will be enqueued.

If the message is a disconnect request, we search the queue looking for primitives of lower precedence. If we find one, we use rmvq to remove it from the queue and then call freemsg to free it.

```
244                       case T_CONN_REQ:
245                           rmvq(q, bp);
246                           freemsg(bp);
247                           freemsg(mp);
248                           mp = NULL;
249                           break;
250                       }
251                   bp = nbp;
252               }
253           }
254       if (mp == NULL)
255           break;
256       /* FALLTHRU */

257   case M_DATA:
258       putq(q, mp);
259       break;

260   case M_IOCTL:
261       stp_ioctl(q, mp);
262       break;

263   case M_FLUSH:
264       if (*mp->b_rptr & FLUSHW) {
265           flushq(q, FLUSHALL);
266           *mp->b_rptr &= ~FLUSHW;
267       }
268       if (*mp->b_rptr & FLUSHR) {
269           flushq(RD(q), FLUSHALL);
270           qreply(q, mp);
271       } else {
272           freemsg(mp);
273       }
274       break;

275   default:
276       freemsg(mp);
277   }
278   return(0);
279 }
```

[244–259] If we find a connect request, we free both it and the disconnect request message. When we are done searching the queue, we enqueue the disconnect message if it has not been freed. All primitives other than disconnect requests are enqueued for handling by the upper write service procedure. This includes M_DATA messages.

[260–279] We pass all M_IOCTL messages to stp_ioctl for immediate processing. We handle M_FLUSH messages in the same way that a driver does. All other message types are freed.

```
280 STATIC void
281 stp_ioctl(queue_t *q, mblk_t *mp)
282 {
283   struct iocblk *iocp;
284   struct linkblk *lp;
285   dl_info_req_t *dp;
286   mblk_t *bp;

287   iocp = (struct iocblk *)mp->b_rptr;
288   switch (iocp->ioc_cmd) {
289   case I_LINK:
290   case I_PLINK:
291       bp = mp->b_cont;
292       if ((bp == NULL) || ((bp->b_wptr - bp->b_rptr) !=
293         sizeof(struct linkblk)))
294           goto nak;
295       lp = (struct linkblk *)bp->b_rptr;
296       if (net.n_state != DOWN) {
297           iocp->ioc_error = EBUSY;
298           goto nak;
299       }
300       bp = allocb(DL_INFO_REQ_SIZE, BPRI_HI);
301       if (bp == NULL) {
302           iocp->ioc_error = EAGAIN;
303           goto nak;
304       }
```

[280–294] The multiplexor does not support any ioctl commands other than
those used to set up and take down multiplexing configurations. For
link creation, the M_IOCTL message will be linked to one M_DATA
block containing a linkblk structure. If no data block is linked to the
M_IOCTL block, or if the amount of data in the M_DATA block is not
enough to hold a linkblk structure, we fail the ioctl by converting
the M_IOCTL message into an M_IOCNAK message and sending it
upstream (see the label, nak, in the default branch). We can check for
strict equality instead of checking if the message size is less than we
need because the linkblk structure contains sufficient padding to
allow the driver to continue to work even if new fields are added to the
structure in the future.

[295–304] If the network is not down, then it is either already up or in the process
of being set up, so we set the ioc_error field in the iocblk structure to indicate the network is busy and we fail the ioctl request. If
the network is down, we allocate a message large enough to hold a
dl_info_req_t structure. If we cannot allocate the message, we fail
the ioctl request with an indication that the application might have
better luck later.

```
305        if (iocp->ioc_cmd == I_PLINK)
306            lp->l_qtop = q;
307        net.n_mp = mp;
308        net.n_wrq = lp->l_qbot;
309        net.n_linkid = lp->l_index;
310        net.n_state = STATECHG;
311        bp->b_datap->db_type = M_PCPROTO;
312        bp->b_wptr += DL_INFO_REQ_SIZE;
313        dp = (dl_info_req_t *)bp->b_rptr;
314        dp->dl_primitive = DL_INFO_REQ;
315        putnext(net.n_wrq, bp);
316        break;

317   case I_UNLINK:
318   case I_PUNLINK:
319        bp = mp->b_cont;
320        if ((bp == NULL) || ((bp->b_wptr - bp->b_rptr) !=
321          sizeof(struct linkblk)))
322            goto nak;
323        lp = (struct linkblk *)bp->b_rptr;
```

[305–306]   We intend to find out the service parameters of the data link provider by sending it a DL_INFO_REQ primitive. When the data link provider receives the DL_INFO_REQ primitive, it will respond with a DL_INFO_ACK primitive. The multiplexor's lower read put procedure will be passed the message containing the information acknowledgement.

Recall that persistent link requests have a NULL l_qtop value because the link survives past the lifetime of the queue used to create the link. In this case, we store the value of the driver's write queue in l_qtop so that the lower read put procedure can complete the ioctl processing.

[307–316]   We save the M_IOCTL message in the network structure, along with the uppermost write queue of the lower stream and the link ID. Then we set the state of the network to STATECHG to indicate that it is in the middle of being initialized. We finish constructing the DL_INFO_REQ message and send it down the stream being linked under the multiplexor. We will see the end of this ioctl command's processing when we reach stplrput.

[317–323]   When a process dismantles the multiplexor, we are passed either an I_UNLINK or an I_PUNLINK M_IOCTL message. Just as with the link case, we validate that the M_IOCTL message is linked to another message block and that the message block contains the correct amount of data for a linkblk structure.

```
324        if (net.n_state != UP) {
325             iocp->ioc_error = ENONET;
326             goto nak;
327        }
328        if (lp->l_index != net.n_linkid)
329             goto nak;
330        net.n_wrq = NULL;
331        net.n_state = DOWN;
332        mp->b_cont = NULL;
333        freeb(bp);
334        stp_disconall(DIS_NOLINK);
335        mp->b_datap->db_type = M_IOCACK;
336        iocp->ioc_count = 0;
337        qreply(q, mp);
338        break;

339  default:
340 nak:
341        mp->b_datap->db_type = M_IOCNAK;
342        qreply(q, mp);
343   }
344 }

345 STATIC int
346 stpuwsrv(queue_t *q)
347 {
348   mblk_t *mp;
349   stp_t *stp;
350   union T_primitives *tp;
351   retval_t ret;
352   int again;

353   stp = (stp_t *)q->q_ptr;
```

[324–329] If the network is not up, we fail the ioctl request, setting ioc_error
to ENONET. If the link ID from the message does not match the link ID
used to create the link, we fail the request, relying on the default error
code (EINVAL) for M_IOCNAK messages.

[330–338] We mark the network as being down, free the message block linked to
the M_IOCTL block, and call stp_disconall to send disconnect
messages to all the transport endpoints to which connections exist.
Finally, we convert the M_IOCTL message into an M_IOCACK message
and send it upstream, causing the ioctl to return successfully.

[339–344] Any other ioctl command is rejected by converting the M_IOCTL
message into an M_IOCNAK message and sending it upstream.

[345–353] stpuwsrv is the upper write service procedure. Its job is to process
TPI request primitives.

```
354  if (net.n_state != UP) {
355      flushq(q, FLUSHALL);
356      return(0);
357  }
358  if (stp->s_rxmp != NULL) {
359      if ((stp->s_totxmitsz != stp->s_msgxmitsz) &&
360         (stp->s_rcvack == (stp->s_seqno - 1)))
361             stp_xmit(stp, NULL, 0);
362      return(0);
363  }
364  if (stp->s_flag & DORESTART) {
365      stp_restart(stp);
366      return(0);
367  }
368  while ((mp = getq(q)) != NULL) {
369      again = 0;
370      if (mp->b_datap->db_type == M_DATA) {
371          ret = stp_send(q, mp);
372      } else {
373          tp = (union T_primitives *)mp->b_rptr;
374          switch (tp->type) {
375          case T_DATA_REQ:
376              ret = stp_send(q, mp);
377              break;
```

[354–363] If the network is down, we just flush the queues and return. If s_rxmp is non-NULL, then there is a message being held for retransmission. The message will be held until either the entire message is transmitted and acknowledged or the maximum retransmit count is reached. If a message is held and the total amount sent does not equal the amount in the original TSDU, and if the previous segment sent was acknowledged, we call stp_xmit to transmit the next segment. We return in either case. When an acknowledgement arrives, stpuwsrv will be reenabled.

[364–367] If the DORESTART flag is set, we call stp_restart to transmit a RESTART message to the peer. This will occur if we told the peer to stop transmitting when we flow-controlled on the read side, but then when flow-control restrictions were lifted, we were unable to transmit the RESTART message because another message was being held pending reception of an acknowledgement. We cannot transmit a message requiring an acknowledgement until the acknowledgement for the previous one has been received.

[368–377] We pull one message at a time off the queue, until we transmit a message, the queue is empty, or we encounter a temporary failure. Only M_DATA, M_PROTO, and M_PCPROTO messages are placed on the queue. To transmit user data with either an M_DATA message or an M_PROTO T_DATA_REQ primitive, we call stp_send.

```
378            case T_INFO_REQ:
379                again = 1;
380                ret = stp_info(q, mp);
381                break;

382            case T_BIND_REQ:
383                again = 1;
384                ret = stp_bind(q, mp);
385                break;

386            case T_UNBIND_REQ:
387                again = 1;
388                ret = stp_unbind(q, mp);
389                break;

390            case T_CONN_REQ:
391                ret = stp_connect(q, mp);
392                break;

393            case T_CONN_RES:
394                again = 1;
395                ret = stp_accept(q, mp);
396                break;

397            case T_DISCON_REQ:
398                ret = stp_discon(q, mp);
399                break;

400            case T_OPTMGMT_REQ:
401                again = 1;
402                ret = stp_optmgmt(q, mp);
403                break;
```

[378–399] Each TPI primitive is handled by a separate function. We set `again` to 1 in all the cases that do not transmit network messages, so that we continue processing messages on the queue after the function returns. For primitives that generate network messages, we return after the function completes and rely on the acknowledgement returned by the peer to reenable `stpuwsrv`. The connect response primitive is an exception, because it is likely that a connection will be accepted on a different stream, and the acknowledgement will enable the other queue instead of this one. Thus, we set `again` to 1 for connect responses.

[400–403] We cannot use an error acknowledgement with the `TNOTSUPPORTED` error to fail an options management request. The TPI assumes that since options are provider-specific, an application will only attempt to negotiate options with a transport provider that is known to support them. Even though we do not support any options, we must act as if we do.

```
404            default:
405                stp_fatal(q, mp);
406                return(0);
407            }
408        } /* else */
409        if (ret == RETRY) {
410            putbq(q, mp);
411            return(0);
412        } else if ((ret == DONE) && !again) {
413            return(0);
414        }
415    } /* while */
416    return(0);
417 }

418 STATIC retval_t
419 stp_info(queue_t *q, mblk_t *mp)
420 {
421    mblk_t *bp;
422    stp_t *stp;
423    struct T_info_ack *ackp;

424    freemsg(mp);
425    stp = (stp_t *)q->q_ptr;
426    bp = allocb(sizeof(struct T_info_ack), BPRI_HI);
427    if (bp == NULL) {
428        cmn_err(CE_WARN, "TCP: can't respond to T_INFO_REQ");
429        return(DONE);
430    }
```

[404–407] Any unknown primitives will cause us to call stp_fatal, placing the stream in error mode.

[408–417] If the function called to handle the primitive returned RETRY, we place the message back on the queue and return. If the primitive completed successfully and we transmitted a network message, we return since we can only transmit one message at a time. Otherwise, we continue processing the messages on the queue.

[418–430] stp_info is called to respond to a T_INFO_REQ primitive. We free the T_INFO_REQ message since we have no need for it. If we cannot allocate a message large enough to hold a T_info_ack structure, we print a warning message on the system console and return DONE. We could not have returned RETRY because the information request primitive is implemented as an M_PCPROTO message and the upper write service procedure could not have put the message back on its queue.

```
431  bp->b_datap->db_type = M_PCPROTO;
432  bp->b_wptr += sizeof(struct T_info_ack);
433  ackp = (struct T_info_ack *)bp->b_rptr;
434  ackp->PRIM_type = T_INFO_ACK;
435  ackp->TSDU_size = -1;      /* infinite */
436  ackp->ETSDU_size = -2;     /* unsupported */
437  ackp->CDATA_size = -2;     /* no data on connect */
438  ackp->DDATA_size = -2;     /* no data on disconnect */
439  ackp->ADDR_size = STPADDRSZ;
440  ackp->OPT_size = -2;       /* no user-settable options */
```

[431–434] We initialize the type of the message just allocated to M_PCPROTO, because interface acknowledgements are implemented as high-priority messages. Then we increment the write pointer by the size of the T_info_ack structure and cast a pointer to the structure over the read pointer in the message. The response primitive is T_INFO_ACK.

The T_info_ack structure contains parameters that describe the transport provider. Most parameters that describe sizes support two special values. A value of −1 means that the parameter is unlimited in size. A value of −2 means that the parameter is not supported.

[435–436] The TSDU size is the maximum transport service data unit size. This is the maximum amount of data that can be transmitted while retaining its original message boundaries. A value of zero means that the data transmission is a byte stream; no message boundaries are preserved. We set the TSDU_size field to −1 to indicate that the TSDU size is unlimited.

The ETSDU_size field is the expedited TSDU size. The transport provider treats expedited data with a higher priority than normal data. Another name for expedited data is out-of-band data. Since we do not support expedited TSDUs, we set this field to −2.

[437–440] The CDATA_size field is the maximum amount of data a user can transmit with a connect request or connect response. The DDATA_size field is the maximum amount of data a user can transmit with a disconnect request. We do not support these features, so we set the corresponding fields to −2. The ADDR_size field is the maximum size of the transport provider's address. The OPT_size field is the maximum number of bytes of options that the user can specify with primitives that support options. The options themselves are implementation-dependent. Since we do not support options, we set this field to −2.

```
441  ackp->TIDU_size = MAXTIDUSZ;
442  ackp->SERV_type = T_COTS;
443  ackp->CURRENT_state = stp->s_tpstate;
444  ackp->PROVIDER_flag = TP_SNDZERO;
445  qreply(q, mp);
446  return(DONE);
447  }

448  STATIC void
449  stp_wsched(stp_t *stp, int size)
450  {
451  ulong_t id;
452  int s;

453  if (stp->s_flag & (WRECBCALL|WRECTOUT))
454      return;
455  id = bufcall(size, BPRI_HI, stp_wcont, stp);
```

[441–447]   The TIDU size is the transport interface data unit size, the maximum
            message size that can be passed across the transport interface to the
            transport provider. We set it to MAXTIDUSZ, the same as the maximum
            packet size in the module_info structure. t_snd uses the TIDU size
            to limit the size of messages it passes to the transport provider. Simi-
            larly, write uses the maximum packet size to limit the size of mes-
            sages it generates.

            The SERV_type field specifies the type of service the transport pro-
            vider supports. Currently defined services are T_COTS (connection-
            oriented service), T_COTS_ORD (connection-oriented with orderly
            release), and T_CLTS (connectionless service). The CURRENT_state
            field is the current TPI state of the endpoint.

            The PROVIDER_flag field specifies different capabilities of the trans-
            port provider. Two flags are defined. TP_SNDZERO indicates the trans-
            port provider supports the transmission of zero-length TSDUs. The
            TP_EXPINLINE flag indicates that the transport provider wants
            expedited data requests sent to it inline with normal data. (This is used
            by TCP, for example.)

            After populating the T_info_ack structure, we send it upstream and
            return DONE.

[448–455]   stp_wsched is called to recover from buffer allocation failures while
            processing messages from the upper write service procedure. If
            recovery is already scheduled, we just return. Otherwise, we use
            bufcall to schedule stp_wcont to be run when a message of the
            specified size can be allocated.

```
456   s = splstr();
457   if (id == 0) {
458       id = timeout(stp_wcont, (caddr_t)stp,
459         drv_usectohz(HALFSEC));
460       stp->s_flag |= WRECTOUT;
461   } else {
462       stp->s_flag |= WRECBCALL;
463   }
464   splx(s);
465   stp->s_wrecid = id;
466 }

467 STATIC void
468 stp_wcont(stp_t *stp)
469 {
470   if (stp->s_rdq != NULL) {
471       qenable(WR(stp->s_rdq));
472       stp->s_flag &= ~(WRECBCALL|WRECTOUT);
473   }
474 }

475 STATIC retval_t
476 stp_bind(queue_t *q, mblk_t *mp)
477 {
478   stp_t *stp;
479   mblk_t *bp;
480   ushort_t port;
481   struct T_bind_req *reqp;
482   struct T_bind_ack *ackp;
483   struct stpaddr *ap;
484   long terr;
485   int i;
```

[456–466]   We then raise the processor priority to block interrupts from STREAMS
devices. The s_flag field of the stp_t structure can be manipulated
from interrupt level, so we need to protect all modifications to the field
by blocking interrupts. If bufcall fails, we use timeout to schedule
stp_wcont to run in half a second. In either case, we set a flag in
s_flag to indicate the recovery method used.

[467–474]   When stp_wcont runs, we first make sure that the minor device is still
in use. If so, we enable the upper write queue's service procedure. Then
we shut off the flags identifying the recovery method. No explicit
mutual exclusion is necessary because all interrupts are blocked when
stp_wcont is called via a timeout. Similarly, when stp_wcont is
called as a result of a bufcall request, all interrupts from STREAMS
devices are blocked.

[475–485]   stp_bind is called to bind an address to a transport endpoint.

```
486  stp = (stp_t *)q->q_ptr;
487  bp = NULL;
488  if (BADSTATE(stp->s_tpstate, TE_BIND_REQ)) {
489      terr = TOUTSTATE;
490      goto err;
491  }

492  reqp = (struct T_bind_req *)mp->b_rptr;
493  if (((reqp->ADDR_offset != 0) &&
494    ((reqp->ADDR_offset < sizeof(struct T_bind_req)) ||
495    (reqp->ADDR_length != STPADDRSZ))) ||
496    ((mp->b_wptr - mp->b_rptr) < (reqp->ADDR_offset +
497    reqp->ADDR_length))) {
498      terr = TBADADDR;
499      goto err;
500  }
501  bp = allocb(sizeof(struct T_bind_ack)+STPADDRSZ,
502    BPRI_HI);
503  if (bp == NULL) {
504      stp_wsched(stp, sizeof(struct T_bind_ack)+STPADDRSZ);
505      return(RETRY);
506  }

507  if (reqp->CONIND_number > MAXCREQ)
508      reqp->CONIND_number = MAXCREQ;
```

[486–491]   We start by checking the state to see if a bind request is legal. The event associated with the reception of a T_BIND_REQ primitive is TE_BIND_REQ. If this event would cause the transport endpoint to enter an invalid state, we set `terr` to TOUTSTATE and jump to `err`, where we respond to the user with a T_ERROR_ACK primitive.

[492–506]   If either the ADDR_offset or the ADDR_length field is invalid, we fail the bind request with the TLI error TBADADDR. Otherwise, we allocate a message large enough to hold a T_bind_ack structure plus a transport address. If the allocation fails, we call `stp wsched` to arrange to have the service procedure scheduled when the allocation might succeed. Then we return RETRY.

[507–508]   The CONIND_number field in the request contains the maximum number of connect indications that the user wants the transport provider to send upstream while waiting for connect responses from the user. If the number is greater than the maximum supported by the transport provider, we reset it to the maximum.

```
509  if (reqp->ADDR_length == 0) {
510      if ((port = stp_getuport()) == 0) {
511          terr = TNOADDR; /* all ports in use */
512          goto err;
513      }
514  } else {
515      ap = (struct stpaddr *)(mp->b_rptr+reqp->ADDR_offset);
516      port = ntohs(ap->a_port);
517      if (port == 0) {
518          terr = TBADADDR;
519          goto err;
520      }
521      for (i = 0; i < NETADDRSZ; i++)
522          if (ap->a_net[i] != net.n_addr[i])
523              break;
524      if (i < NETADDRSZ) {
525          terr = TBADADDR;
526          goto err;
527      }
528      if (stp_findport(port) != NULL) {
529          terr = TNOADDR;
530          goto err;
531      }
532  }
```

[509–513] If the address length is zero, the user wants the transport provider to select the address to bind, so we call stp_getuport to find an unused port number. If stp_getuport returns 0, all port numbers are in use (very unlikely), so we fail the bind request with the TLI error T_NOADDR to indicate no addresses are available.

[514–532] If the user specified an address to be bound, we have to make sure the address is valid. Recall that port 0 is reserved and that the transport address contains the physical network address. The TPI allows the same address to be bound to multiple endpoints on the same machine, as long as at most one of the endpoints is bound with a nonzero queue length. In our simple transport provider, it is easier to disallow this, so we call stp_findport to see if the requested port number is already in use. If it is, we set terr to TNOADDR and jump to err, where we respond with an error acknowledgement.

Note that the address as specified by the user must be stored in the network's byte order. We use ntohs to convert the two-byte port number from the network's byte order to the host's byte order.

```
533  bp->b_datap->db_type = M_PCPROTO;
534  ackp = (struct T_bind_ack *)bp->b_wptr;
535  ackp->PRIM_type = T_BIND_ACK;
536  ackp->ADDR_length = STPADDRSZ;
537  ackp->ADDR_offset = sizeof(struct T_bind_ack);
538  ackp->CONIND_number = reqp->CONIND_number;
539  bp->b_wptr += sizeof(struct T_bind_ack);
540  *(ushort_t *)bp->b_wptr = htons(port);
541  bp->b_wptr += 2;
542  bcopy((caddr_t)net.n_addr, (caddr_t)bp->b_wptr, NETADDRSZ);
543  bp->b_wptr += NETADDRSZ;
544  stp->s_lport = port;
545  stp->s_maxqlen = reqp->CONIND_number;
546  stp->s_tpstate = NEXTSTATE2(stp->s_tpstate, TE_BIND_REQ,
547      TE_BIND_ACK);
548  freemsg(mp);
549  qreply(q, bp);
550  return(DONE);
551 err:
552  if (bp != NULL)
553      freeb(bp);
554  if (stp_errorack(q, T_BIND_REQ, terr, 0) == RETRY)
555      return(RETRY);
556  freemsg(mp);
557  return(ERR);
558 }
```

[533–543] We create the bind acknowledgement message by initializing the `T_bind_ack` structure and copying the locally bound address after the structure in the message. Note that since `port` contains the port number in the host's byte order, we need to use `htons` to convert it back to the network's byte order.

[544–550] We complete the address binding by storing the port number in the `s_lport` field in the transport endpoint `stp_t` structure. We also store the maximum queue length and place the endpoint in the appropriate state. We free the message that contained the bind request, send the bind acknowledgement message upstream, and return DONE.

[551–558] On error, we jump to `err`, free the bind acknowledgement message if it was allocated, and attempt to send a `T_ERROR_ACK` primitive upstream. If we cannot allocate the error-acknowledgement message, `stp_errorack` will return RETRY, which we return to the upper write service procedure. If we were able to send the error acknowledgement upstream, we free the bind request message and return ERR. Note that we do not free the message if we return RETRY, because the upper write service procedure will put it back on the queue in that case.

```
559 STATIC retval_t
560 stp_unbind(queue_t *q, mblk_t *mp)
561 {
562   stp_t *stp;
563   mblk_t *bp;
564   int s;

565   stp = (stp_t *)q->q_ptr;
566   if (BADSTATE(stp->s_tpstate, TE_UNBIND_REQ)) {
567       if (stp_errorack(q, T_UNBIND_REQ, TOUTSTATE, 0) ==
568         RETRY)
569           return(RETRY);
570       freemsg(mp);
571       return(ERR);
572   }
573   bp = allocb(sizeof(struct T_ok_ack), BPRI_HI);
574   if (bp == NULL) {
575       stp_wsched(stp, sizeof(struct T_ok_ack));
576       return(RETRY);
577   }
578   if (putctl1(RD(q)->q_next, M_FLUSH, FLUSHRW) == 0) {
579       freeb(bp);
580       if (!(stp->s_flag&(WRECBCALL|WRECTOUT))) {
581           stp->s_wrecid = timeout(stp_wcont, (caddr_t)stp,
582             drv_usectohz(HALFSEC));
583           s = splstr();
584           stp->s_flag |= WRECTOUT;
585           splx(s);
586       }
587       return(RETRY);
588   }
```

[559–572] stp_unbind is called to disassociate an address from a transport endpoint. If the unbind request is invalid in the current state, we attempt to
send an error acknowledgement upstream. If this fails, we return
RETRY. Otherwise, we free the unbind request message and return ERR.

[573–588] If an unbind request is valid in the current state, we allocate a message
large enough to hold a T_ok_ack structure. If the allocation fails, we
enable recovery and return RETRY. If the allocation succeeds, we send
an M_FLUSH message upstream to flush the read and write queues, as
required by the TPI. If putctl1 fails, we free the message we just
allocated and, if recovery is not already enabled, call timeout to
schedule stp_wcont to run in half a second. We cannot call
stp_wsched because bufcall might result in an unsuccessful call to
stp_wcont since the message we just freed could satisfy the
bufcall allocation request.

```
589  freemsg(mp);
590  stp_buildokack(bp, T_UNBIND_REQ);
591  stp->s_lport = 0;
592  stp->s_maxqlen = 0;
593  s = splstr();
594  if (stp->s_rxmp != NULL) {
595      freemsg(stp->s_rxmp);
596      stp->s_rxmp = NULL;
597  }
598  splx(s);
599  if (stp->s_rcvmp != NULL) {
600      freemsg(stp->s_rcvmp);
601      stp->s_rcvmp = NULL;
602  }
603  stp->s_tpstate = NEXTSTATE2(stp->s_tpstate, TE_UNBIND_REQ,
604    TE_OK_ACK1);
605  qreply(q, bp);
606  return(DONE);
607  }

608  STATIC void
609  stp_buildokack(mblk_t *bp, ulong_t prim)
610  {
611    struct T_ok_ack *ackp;

612    bp->b_datap->db_type = M_PCPROTO;
613    ackp = (struct T_ok_ack *)bp->b_wptr;
614    ackp->PRIM_type = T_OK_ACK;
615    ackp->CORRECT_prim = prim;
616    bp->b_wptr += sizeof(struct T_ok_ack);
617  }
```

[589–607] If we were able to flush the stream, we free the message containing the unbind request and proceed to unbind the address from the transport endpoint. We initialize the T_OK_ACK primitive by calling stp_buildokack, and then clear the local port number and the maximum queue length in the stp_t structure. If a message is queued for retransmission, we free it. Similarly, if a message was currently being reassembled, we free it as well. Then we change the transport provider state and send the T_OK_ACK upstream.

[608–617] stp_buildokack builds a T_OK_ACK primitive given a message and the primitive to be acknowledged. Since acknowledgement is a high-priority message, we set the message type to M_PCPROTO. We initialize the T_ok_ack structure and increment the write pointer by the size of the structure.

```
618 STATIC retval_t
619 stp_connect(queue_t *q, mblk_t *mp)
620 {
621   stp_t *stp;
622   mblk_t *bp, *hbp, *dbp;
623   struct T_conn_req *reqp;
624   struct stpaddr *ap;
625   int size;
626   long terr, uerr;

627   stp = (stp_t *)q->q_ptr;
628   uerr = 0;
629   bp = hbp = dbp = NULL;
630   if (BADSTATE(stp->s_tpstate, TE_CONN_REQ)) {
631       terr = TOUTSTATE;
632       goto err;
633   }
634   reqp = (struct T_conn_req *)mp->b_rptr;
635   if ((reqp->DEST_offset < sizeof(struct T_conn_req)) ||
636     (reqp->DEST_length != STPADDRSZ) ||
637     ((mp->b_wptr - mp->b_rptr) < (reqp->DEST_offset +
638     reqp->DEST_length))) {
639       terr = TBADADDR;
640       goto err;
641   }

642   if (reqp->OPT_length != 0) {
643       terr = TBADOPT;
644       goto err;
645   }
646   if (mp->b_cont != NULL) {
647       terr = TBADDATA;
648       goto err;
649   }
```

[618–626] `stp_connect` is called to initiate the construction of a virtual circuit.

[627–641] If a connect request is invalid in the current state, we fail the request with the TOUTSTATE TLI error. If the destination address contained in the connect request is the wrong length or the message is not large enough to hold the address, we fail the request with the TBADADDR TLI error.

[642–649] If the connect request contains options, we set the TLI error to TBADOPT and fail the request. If the connect request message has a non-NULL b_cont pointer, then user data was sent with the connect request. Since we do not support this feature, we set the TLI error to TBADDATA and fail the request.

```
650   if (!canput(net.n_wrq->q_next))
651       return(RETRY);
652   bp = allocb(sizeof(struct T_ok_ack), BPRI_HI);
653   if (bp == NULL) {
654       stp_wsched(stp, sizeof(struct T_ok_ack));
655       return(RETRY);
656   }
657   size = HDRSIZE;
658   hbp = allocb(size, BPRI_HI);
659   dbp = allocb(DL_UNITDATA_REQ_SIZE+net.n_addrlen,
660     BPRI_HI);
661   if ((hbp == NULL) || (dbp == NULL)) {
662       terr = TSYSERR;
663       uerr = EAGAIN;
664       goto err;
665   }
666   ap = (struct stpaddr *)(mp->b_rptr + reqp->DEST_offset);
667   stp_buildunitdata(dbp, ap);
668   stp_buildheader(stp, hbp, CONNECT, EOM, 0, sizeof(hdr_t),
669     ap->a_port, size);
670   dbp->b_cont = hbp;
671   stp_xmit(stp, dbp, 0);
672   stp_buildokack(bp, T_CONN_REQ);
673   stp->s_faddr = *ap; /* structure assignment */
674   freemsg(mp);
```

[650–656]   If the stream linked under the multiplexor is flow-controlled, we return
RETRY. If we cannot allocate a message for the T_OK_ACK primitive,
we enable recovery by calling stp_wsched, then return RETRY.

[657–665]   We are about to transmit a message containing a protocol header to the
peer transport endpoint. We set size to a value large enough to hold
the protocol header while satisfying the minimum data link service data
unit size requirement. If we cannot allocate a message containing size
bytes in the data buffer, or if we cannot allocate a message for the data
link unitdata request primitive, we set the TLI error to TSYSERR and the
UNIX error to EAGAIN and fail the request. We could try to recover
using only timeout, but it is easier just to fail the request.

[666–671]   We call stp_buildunitdata to initialize the DL_UNITDATA_REQ
primitive. Then we call stp_buildheader to build the protocol
header. We link the header's message block on the end of the unitdata
request's message block and call stp_xmit to transmit the CONNECT
message to the peer.

[672–674]   Now we complete the local processing for the connect request. We initialize the T_OK_ACK message, save the destination address of the connect request, and free the connect request message.

```
675  stp->s_tpstate = NEXTSTATE2(stp->s_tpstate, TE_CONN_REQ,
676    TE_OK_ACK1);
677  qreply(q, bp);
678  return(DONE);
679 err:
680  if (bp != NULL)
681      freeb(bp);
682  if (hbp != NULL)
683      freeb(hbp);
684  if (stp_errorack(q, T_CONN_REQ, terr, uerr) == RETRY)
685      return(RETRY);
686  freemsg(mp);
687  return(ERR);
688 }

689 STATIC void
690 stp_buildunitdata(mblk_t *bp, struct stpaddr *ap)
691 {
692  dl_unitdata_req_t *udp;

693  bp->b_datap->db_type = M_PROTO;
694  bp->b_wptr += DL_UNITDATA_REQ_SIZE;
695  udp = (dl_unitdata_req_t *)bp->b_rptr;
696  udp->dl_primitive = DL_UNITDATA_REQ;
697  udp->dl_dest_addr_length = net.n_addrlen;
698  udp->dl_dest_addr_offset = DL_UNITDATA_REQ_SIZE;
699  udp->dl_priority = stpnopri;
```

[675–678] Finally, we change the state of the transport endpoint, send the
T_OK_ACK message upstream, and return DONE.

[679–688] On error, we jump to `err` where we free any messages we have allocated. We call `stp_errorack` to send a T_ERROR_ACK primitive
upstream. If this fails, we return RETRY, and the upper write service
procedure will put the connect message back on the queue and return.
Otherwise, we free the connect request message and return ERR.

[689–699] `stp_buildunitdata` is called to set up the data link unitdata request
so we can present messages to the data link provider for transmission
over the network. `ap` is the address of the destination transport endpoint. We set the message type to M_PROTO, increment the write
pointer by the size of a `dl_unitdata_req_t` structure, and cast a
`dl_unitdata_req_t` pointer over the message's read pointer. We
set the `dl_primitive` field to DL_UNITDATA_REQ, the
`dl_dest_addr_length` field to the size of the data link provider
address, the `dl_dest_addr_offset` field to the size of the
`dl_unitdata_req_t` structure, and the `dl_priority` field to
`stpnopri`.

```
700  if (net.n_saplen > 0) { /* sap followed by phys */
701      bcopy((caddr_t)net.n_addr, (caddr_t)bp->b_wptr,
702        net.n_saplen);
703      bp->b_wptr += net.n_saplen;
704      bcopy((caddr_t)ap->a_net, (caddr_t)bp->b_wptr,
705        NETADDRSZ);
706      bp->b_wptr += NETADDRSZ;
707  } else if (net.n_saplen < 0) { /* phys followed by sap */
708      bcopy((caddr_t)ap->a_net, (caddr_t)bp->b_wptr,
709        NETADDRSZ);
710      bp->b_wptr += NETADDRSZ;
711      bcopy((caddr_t)&net.n_addr[net.n_addrlen+net.n_saplen],
712        (caddr_t)bp->b_wptr, -net.n_saplen);
713      bp->b_wptr -= net.n_saplen;
714  } else {
715      bcopy((caddr_t)ap->a_net, (caddr_t)bp->b_wptr,
716        NETADDRSZ);
717      bp->b_wptr += NETADDRSZ;
718  }
719 }
```

[700–706] Next we copy the destination data link address into the message after the `dl_unitdata_req_t` structure. If the data link SAP identifier length is greater than 0, the format of the data link address is the SAP identifier followed by the physical network address. We copy the first `net.n_saplen` bytes from the local network address to the message, since the destination address will use the same SAP identifier. Then we increment the write pointer by the size of the SAP identifier and copy the physical network portion of the destination address to the message. Finally, we increment the write pointer by the size of the physical address.

[707–713] If the data link SAP identifier length is negative, the format of the DLSAP address is the physical network address followed by the SAP identifier. In this case, we copy the network address to the message first, then copy the SAP identifier. Since the SAP length is negative, `net.n_addrlen+net.n_saplen` gives us the offset into the local DLSAP address of the SAP identifier. Also, subtracting the SAP length from the write pointer actually advances the write pointer by the absolute value of the SAP length.

[714–719] If the data link SAP identifier length is 0, we assume we are dealing with a data link provider supporting an older version of the DLPI. In this case, the DLSAP address only contains a physical network address.

```
720 STATIC void
721 stp_buildheader(stp_t *stp, mblk_t *bp, uchar_t type,
722  uchar_t flags, uchar_t reason, ushort_t totsz,
723  ushort_t dport, int mpsize)
724 {
725  hdr_t *hp;

726  hp = (hdr_t *)bp->b_wptr;
727  hp->h_version = STPVERS;
728  hp->h_type = type;
729  hp->h_flags = flags;
730  hp->h_reason = reason;
731  hp->h_sport = htons(stp->s_lport);
732  hp->h_dport = dport; /* already in network byte order */
733  hp->h_size = htons(totsz);
734  hp->h_pad = 0;
735  hp->h_seqno = 0; /* filled in by stp_xmit */
736  bp->b_wptr += mpsize;
737 }

738 STATIC retval_t
739 stp_accept(queue_t *q, mblk_t *mp)
740 {
741  stp_t *stp, *tstp;
742  mblk_t *bp, *hbp, *dbp;
743  struct T_conn_res *resp;
744  struct T_conn_ind *indp;
745  struct stpaddr *ap;
746  int size, i, cidx;
747  long terr, uerr;
```

[720–737] `stp_buildheader` is called to initialize the protocol header in the
message, bp. We set the protocol version to its current value. Then we
set the `h_type`, `h_flags`, and `h_reason` fields to their respective
values passed to the function. The source (local) port number is stored
in the host's byte order, so we convert it to the network's byte order
before storing it in the header. The destination port number, however, is
already in the network byte order. We set `h_size` to the number of
bytes in the message after converting the value to the network byte
order. The sequence number will be filled in by `stp_xmit` when the
message is transmitted. Finally, we increment the write pointer by
`mpsize`. The difference between the `mpsize` and `totsz` parameters
is that `totsz` is the number of bytes in the message including the protocol header, and `mpsize` is this value plus any padding necessary to
meet the minimum DLSDU size requirement of the data link provider.

[738–747] `stp_accept` is called when a process accepts a transport connection.
[`t_accept(3N)` generates a `T_CONN_RES` primitive.]

```
748   stp = (stp_t *)q->q_ptr;
749   uerr = 0;
750   bp = hbp = dbp = NULL;
751   if (BADSTATE(stp->s_tpstate, TE_CONN_RES)) {
752       terr = TOUTSTATE;
753       goto err;
754   }
755   resp = (struct T_conn_res *)mp->b_rptr;
756   if ((stp->s_qlen > 1) &&
757     (resp->QUEUE_ptr == stp->s_rdq)) {
758       terr = TBADF;
759       goto err;
760   }
761   if (resp->OPT_length != 0) {
762       terr = TBADOPT;
763       goto err;
764   }
765   if (mp->b_cont != NULL) {
766       terr = TBADDATA;
767       goto err;
768   }
769   if (!canput(net.n_wrq->q_next))
770       return(RETRY);
771   for (cidx = 0; cidx < MAXCREQ; cidx++) {
772       if (stp->s_cmp[cidx] != NULL) {
773           indp = (struct T_conn_ind *)
774             stp->s_cmp[cidx]->b_rptr;
775           if (resp->SEQ_number == indp->SEQ_number)
776               break;
777       }
778   }
```

[748–760] If the state of the transport endpoint is invalid for accepting connections, we fail the attempt by setting `terr` to `TOUTSTATE` and jumping to `err`, where we send a `T_ERROR_ACK` response upstream. If there is more than one outstanding connect indication and the user specifies the transport endpoint that received the request as the one participating in the connection, we fail the connect response with the `TBADF` TLI error. You can use a listening transport endpoint for a connection only if there is just one connect indication queued.

[761–770] If the user specifies options with the connect response, or if the user attempts to transmit data with the response, we fail the request since our simple transport provider does not support these features. If the stream linked under the multiplexor is flow-controlled, we return `RETRY`.

[771–778] We search the array of connect indication messages for one with a sequence number that matches the sequence number in the connect response message.

```
779  if (cidx >= MAXCREQ) {
780      terr = TBADSEQ;
781      goto err;
782  }
783  ap = (struct stpaddr *)(stp->s_cmp[cidx]->b_rptr +
784    indp->SRC_offset);
785  bp = allocb(sizeof(struct T_ok_ack), BPRI_HI);
786  if (bp == NULL) {
787      stp_wsched(stp, sizeof(struct T_ok_ack));
788      return(RETRY);
789  }
790  size = HDRSIZE;
791  hbp = allocb(size, BPRI_HI);
792  dbp = allocb(DL_UNITDATA_REQ_SIZE+net.n_addrlen,
793    BPRI_HI);
794  if ((hbp == NULL) || (dbp == NULL)) {
795      terr = TSYSERR;
796      uerr = EAGAIN;
797      goto err;
798  }
799  for (tstp = stpendpt, i = 0; i < nstp; tstp++, i++)
800      if (tstp->s_rdq == resp->QUEUE_ptr)
801          break;
802  if (i >= nstp) {
803      terr = TBADF;
804      goto err;
805  }
```

[779–782] If we cannot find a queued connect indication corresponding to the connect response, we fail the connect response with the TBADSEQ TLI error.

[783–789] We set ap to point to the source address stored in the connect indication message. This is the address of the transport endpoint that generated the connect request. Then we attempt to allocate a message for a T_OK_ACK primitive. If the allocation fails, we call stp_wsched to recover, then return RETRY.

[790–798] Next we calculate the minimum size of the message to transmit and attempt to allocate a message for the protocol header and a message for the DLPI unitdata request. If either allocation fails, we set the TLI error to TSYSERR and the UNIX error to EAGAIN, and we fail the request.

[799–805] We search the array of transport endpoints for one with a read queue that matches the QUEUE_ptr field in the connect response message. If we do not find one, the queue pointer in the message does not belong to the transport provider, so we fail the request, setting the TLI error to TBADF.

```
806   if (tstp != stp) {
807       if (tstp->s_tpstate != TS_IDLE) {
808           terr = TBADF;
809           goto err;
810       }
811       tstp->s_tpstate = NEXTSTATE1(tstp->s_tpstate,
812         TE_PASS_CONN);
813   }

814   tstp->s_faddr = *ap;/* structure assignment */
815   freeb(stp->s_cmp[cidx]);
816   stp->s_cmp[cidx] = NULL;
817   stp->s_qlen--;

818   stp_buildunitdata(dbp, &tstp->s_faddr);
819   stp_buildheader(tstp, hbp, ACCEPT, EOM, 0, sizeof(hdr_t),
820     tstp->s_faddr.a_port, size);
821   dbp->b_cont = hbp;
822   stp_xmit(tstp, dbp, 0);
823   stp_buildokack(bp, T_CONN_RES);
824   freemsg(mp);
```

[806–813] If we find a match but the endpoint is not the same as the one used to accept the connection, we make sure it is in the proper state (TS_IDLE). If it is not, we fail the request with the TBADF TLI error. Otherwise, we place the endpoint to be used in the connection in the proper state. TE_PASS_CONN is the event used when a connection is being accepted on a different endpoint than the one used to listen for connect indications. It transitions an endpoint in the idle state to the data-transfer state.

[814–817] We store the transport address of the peer in the s_faddr field of the stp_t structure. Then we free the connect indication message and clear the corresponding pointer in the s_cmp array. This allows us to decrement the number of outstanding connect indications.

[818–824] Next we call stp_buildunitdata to construct the data link unitdata request, and we call stp_buildheader to initialize the protocol header. We link the protocol header's message on the end of the unitdata request message and transmit the packet to the peer. Then we create a T_OK_ACK acknowledgement primitive and free the connect response message. Note that when we call stp_xmit, we use tstp instead of stp. This will result in the acknowledgement message being delivered to the new endpoint instead of the endpoint used for listening.

```
825  if (stp->s_qlen == 0) {
826      if (stp == tstp)
827          stp->s_tpstate = NEXTSTATE2(stp->s_tpstate,
828              TE_CONN_RES, TE_OK_ACK2);
829      else
830          stp->s_tpstate = NEXTSTATE2(stp->s_tpstate,
831              TE_CONN_RES, TE_OK_ACK3);
832  } else {
833      stp->s_tpstate = NEXTSTATE2(stp->s_tpstate,
834          TE_CONN_RES, TE_OK_ACK4);
835  }
836  qreply(q, bp);
837  return(DONE);

838 err:
839  if (bp != NULL)
840      freeb(bp);
841  if (hbp != NULL)
842      freeb(hbp);
843  if (dbp != NULL)
844      freeb(dbp);
845  if (stp_errorack(q, T_CONN_RES, terr, uerr) == RETRY)
846      return(RETRY);
847  freemsg(mp);
848  return(ERR);
849 }
```

[825–837] A different event is used to change the state of the transport endpoint,
depending on whether there are more connect indications queued and
whether the endpoint used for the connection is different from the one
used to receive the connect indication. When no more connect indications are queued, TE_OK_ACK2 is used to place the transport endpoint
in the data-transfer state if the endpoint is to be used in the connection;
otherwise, TE_OK_ACK3 is used to place the endpoint in the idle state.
If there are more connect indications queued, TE_OK_ACK4 is used to
keep the endpoint in the state where it is waiting for responses to the
connect indications.

After the state is changed, we send the T_OK_ACK acknowledgement
primitive upstream to inform the user that the connect response has been
processed successfully. Then we return DONE.

[838–849] If we encounter an error, we jump to err, where we free any messages
we might have allocated. If we cannot send a T_ERROR_ACK primitive
upstream, we return RETRY. Otherwise, we free the connect response
message and return ERR.

```
850 STATIC int
851 stp_sameaddr(struct stpaddr *a1, struct stpaddr *a2)
852 {
853   int i;

854   for (i = 0; i < NETADDRSZ; i++)
855       if (a1->a_net[i] != a2->a_net[i])
856           return(0);
857   if (a1->a_port != a2->a_port)
858       return(0);
859   return(1);
860 }

861 STATIC retval_t
862 stp_discon(queue_t *q, mblk_t *mp)
863 {
864   stp_t *stp;
865   mblk_t *bp, *hbp, *dbp;
866   struct T_discon_req *reqp;
867   struct T_conn_ind *indp;
868   struct stpaddr addr;
869   int size, i, s;
870   long terr, uerr;

871   stp = (stp_t *)q->q_ptr;
872   uerr = 0;
873   bp = hbp = dbp = NULL;
874   if (BADSTATE(stp->s_tpstate, TE_DISCON_REQ)) {
875       terr = TOUTSTATE;
876       goto err;
877   }
878   if ((mp != NULL) && (mp->b_cont != NULL)) {
879       terr = TBADDATA;
880       goto err;
881   }
```

[850–860] `stp_sameaddr` is a little function we use to compare two transport
addresses. It returns 0 if the addresses differ, and 1 if they are the same.

[861–870] `stp_discon` is called to break an existing connection or to reject a
pending one.

[871–881] If the state is invalid for a disconnect request, we fail the request, setting
the TLI error to `TOUTSTATE`. We allow the caller to pass in a NULL
message pointer to disconnect an existing connection. We use this capability internally by the driver, but only when the endpoint is in the data-
transfer state. If a message is provided and it has a non-NULL `b_cont`
field, then the user has attempted to send data along with the disconnect
request, so we fail the request with the `TBADDATA` TLI error.

```
882  if (!canput(net.n_wrq->q_next))
883      return(RETRY);
884  bp = allocb(sizeof(struct T_ok_ack), BPRI_HI);
885  if (bp == NULL) {
886      stp_wsched(stp, sizeof(struct T_ok_ack));
887      return(RETRY);
888  }
889  size = HDRSIZE;
890  hbp = allocb(size, BPRI_HI);
891  dbp = allocb(DL_UNITDATA_REQ_SIZE+net.n_addrlen,
892    BPRI_HI);
893  if ((hbp == NULL) || (dbp == NULL)) {
894      terr = TSYSERR;
895      uerr = EAGAIN;
896      goto err;
897  }
898  if (mp != NULL)
899      reqp = (struct T_discon_req *)mp->b_rptr;
900  if (stp->s_tpstate == TS_WRES_CIND) {
901      for (i = 0; i < MAXCREQ; i++) {
902          if (stp->s_cmp[i] != NULL) {
903              indp = (struct T_conn_ind *)
904                stp->s_cmp[i]->b_rptr;
905              if (reqp->SEQ_number == indp->SEQ_number)
906                  break;
907          }
908      }
909      if (i >= MAXCREQ) {
910          terr = TBADSEQ;
911          goto err;
912      }
```

[882–897] If we cannot send messages down the data link provider's stream because of flow control, we return RETRY. As with the past few functions, we allocate three messages: one for the interface acknowledgement, one for the protocol header, and one for the DL_UNITDATA_REQ message.

[898–899] If a non-NULL message pointer is passed to the function, we cast a pointer to a T_discon_req structure over the read pointer in the message.

[900–912] If the transport provider is waiting for responses to connect indications, we step through the array of connect indication messages looking for one that has a sequence number that matches the sequence number specified in the disconnect request. If we do not find a match, then we fail the request by setting the TLI error to TBADSEQ and jump to err, where we send a T_ERROR_ACK primitive upstream.

```
913        bcopy((caddr_t)stp->s_cmp[i]->b_rptr+indp->SRC_offset,
914          (caddr_t)&addr, STPADDRSZ);
915        freeb(stp->s_cmp[i]);
916        stp->s_cmp[i] = NULL;
917        stp->s_qlen--;
918        if (stp->s_qlen == 0)
919            stp->s_tpstate = NEXTSTATE2(stp->s_tpstate,
920                TE_DISCON_REQ, TE_OK_ACK2);
921        else
922            stp->s_tpstate = NEXTSTATE2(stp->s_tpstate,
923                TE_DISCON_REQ, TE_OK_ACK4);
924    } else {
925        if (stp->s_tpstate == TS_DATA_XFER) {
926            if (putctl1(RD(q)->q_next, M_FLUSH, FLUSHRW) ==
927                0) {
928                freeb(bp);
929                freeb(hbp);
930                freeb(dbp);
931                if (!(stp->s_flag&(WRECBCALL|WRECTOUT))) {
932                    stp->s_wrecid = timeout(stp_wcont,
933                        (caddr_t)stp, drv_usectohz(HALFSEC));
934                    s = splstr();
935                    stp->s_flag |= WRECTOUT;
936                    splx(s);
937                }
938                return(RETRY);
939            }
940            addr = stp->s_faddr; /* structure assignment */
941        }
942        stp->s_tpstate = NEXTSTATE2(stp->s_tpstate,
943            TE_DISCON_REQ, TE_OK_ACK1);
944    }
```

[913–923] If we find a match, we copy the source address from the connect indication message to the stack. We then free the connect indication message,
clear the message pointer in the s_cmp array, decrement the count of
queued connect indications, and place the transport endpoint in the new
state. If connect indications are still queued, the TE_OK_ACK4 event
will leave the endpoint in the TS_WRES_CIND state. Otherwise, the
TE_OK_ACK2 event transitions the endpoint to the idle state.

[924–944] If the transport endpoint is in the data-transfer state when the disconnect
request is received, we attempt to flush both sides of the stream. If
putctl1 returns 0, then it could not allocate a message, so we free the
messages we have allocated and recover by calling timeout if
recovery is not already enabled. Then we return RETRY. If we are able
to flush the stream, we save the address of the other end of the connection and place the transport endpoint in the next state (idle).

```
945   stp_buildunitdata(dbp, &addr);
946   stp_buildheader(stp, hbp, DISCON, EOM, DIS_USER,
947     sizeof(hdr_t), addr.a_port, size);
948   dbp->b_cont = hbp;
949   stp_xmit(stp, dbp, 0);
950   stp_buildokack(bp, T_DISCON_REQ);
951   if (mp != NULL)
952       freemsg(mp);
953   qreply(q, bp);
954   bzero((caddr_t)&stp->s_faddr, STPADDRSZ);
955   return(DONE);
956 err:
957   if (bp != NULL)
958       freeb(bp);
959   if (hbp != NULL)
960       freeb(hbp);
961   if (dbp != NULL)
962       freeb(dbp);
963   if (stp_errorack(q, T_DISCON_REQ, terr, uerr) == RETRY)
964       return(RETRY);
965   if (mp != NULL)
966       freemsg(mp);
967   return(ERR);
968 }

969 STATIC retval_t
970 stp_send(queue_t *q, mblk_t *mp)
971 {
972   stp_t *stp;
973   mblk_t *bp, *hbp, *dbp, *pbp;
974   int size, psize, s;
975   struct T_data_req *reqp;
976   uchar_t flags = 0;
```

[945–952] Next we construct a data link unitdata request and a protocol header, link them together, and call stp_xmit to transmit the message. Then we free the message containing the disconnect request if mp is not NULL.

[953–955] We acknowledge the disconnect request by sending a T_OK_ACK primitive upstream. We only call stp_discon with a NULL message pointer when we are closing down the stream, so it does not matter if we send an acknowledgement message upstream even if the user is not expecting it in this case. The message will just be discarded. Before returning, we clear the foreign address field in the stp_t structure.

[956–968] As before, if we encounter an error, we jump to err where we free any messages we have allocated, send an error acknowledgement upstream, free the disconnect message, and return ERR.

[969–976] stp_send is called to send user data to the peer.

```
977   stp = (stp_t *)q->q_ptr;
978   s = splstr();
979   if (stp->s_flag & NOXMIT) {
980       splx(s);
981       return(RETRY);
982   }
983   splx(s);

984   if (stp->s_tpstate == TS_IDLE) {
985       freemsg(mp);
986       return(ERR);
987   }
988   if (BADSTATE(stp->s_tpstate, TE_DATA_REQ)) {
989       stp_fatal(q, mp);
990       return(ERR);
991   }

992   if (!canput(net.n_wrq->q_next))
993       return(RETRY);
994   size = msgdsize(mp) + sizeof(hdr_t);
995   psize = 0;
996   if (size < net.n_minsdu) {
997       psize = net.n_minsdu - size;
998       size = net.n_minsdu;
999   }
```

[977–983]   If the NOXMIT flag is set, we return RETRY. This can happen if the peer flow-controls on the read side of its stream and subsequently tells us to stop transmitting. Note that we have to protect the check of the NOXMIT flag with splstr because the flag can be set from interrupt level.

[984–991]   If the state of the transport endpoint is idle, then the TPI directs us to discard the data silently, so we free the message and return ERR. We return ERR instead of DONE to force the upper write service procedure to continue processing messages on its queue instead of simply returning. (If we had returned DONE, the upper write service procedure would have assumed we transmitted a message when we did not.) If the transport endpoint is in the wrong state to transmit data, we call stp_fatal to place the stream in error mode, thereby rendering it useless.

[992–999]   If the data link provider stream is flow-controlled, we return RETRY. Otherwise, we calculate the size of the message to be sent as the size of the M_DATA blocks contained in mp plus the size of the protocol header. If this is less than the minimum size required by the data link provider, we set the pad size (psize) to the amount needed to reach the minimum and set size to the minimum.

```
1000      hbp = allocb(sizeof(hdr_t), BPRI_MED);
1001      if (hbp == NULL) {
1002          stp_wsched(stp, sizeof(hdr_t));
1003          return(RETRY);
1004      }
1005      dbp = allocb(DL_UNITDATA_REQ_SIZE+net.n_addrlen,
1006        BPRI_MED);
1007      if (dbp == NULL)
1008          goto allocfail;
1009      if (psize != 0) {
1010          pbp = allocb(psize, BPRI_MED);
1011          if (pbp == NULL)
1012              goto allocfail;
1013          pbp->b_wptr += psize;
1014          linkb(mp, pbp);
1015      }
1016      if (mp->b_datap->db_type == M_PROTO) {
1017          reqp = (struct T_data_req *)mp->b_rptr;
1018          if (reqp->MORE_flag != 0)
1019              flags |= MORE;
1020          bp = mp;
1021          mp = mp->b_cont;
1022          freeb(bp);
1023      }
1024      stp_buildunitdata(dbp, &stp->s_faddr);
1025      stp_buildheader(stp, hbp, DATA, flags, 0, size-psize,
1026        stp->s_faddr.a_port, sizeof(hdr_t));
1027      hbp->b_cont = mp;
1028      dbp->b_cont = hbp;
1029      stp_xmit(stp, dbp, 0);
1030      return(DONE);
```

[1000–1008] If we cannot allocate a message block for the protocol header, we call stp_wsched to recover, then return RETRY. If we cannot allocate a message block for the data link unitdata request, we jump to allocfail, where we try to recover using only timeout.

[1009–1015] If the pad size is nonzero, we allocate a message to hold the pad. If this fails, we go to allocfail. Otherwise, we increment the write pointer by the pad size and call linkb(D3DK) to link the message block on the end of the message to be transmitted.

[1016–1023] If the message type is M_PROTO, the message contains a T_data_req structure. In this case, if the MORE_flag field is nonzero, we set the MORE flag in the protocol header. Then we free the first message block in the message, leaving just the user data.

[1024–1030] We initialize the unitdata request and the protocol header, link the messages together, and call stp_xmit to transmit the packet.

```
1031 allocfail:
1032     freeb(hbp);
1033     if (dbp != NULL)
1034         freeb(dbp);
1035     if (!(stp->s_flag&(WRECBCALL|WRECTOUT))) {
1036         stp->s_wrecid = timeout(stp_wcont, (caddr_t)stp,
1037             drv_usectohz(HALFSEC));
1038         s = splstr();
1039         stp->s_flag |= WRECTOUT;
1040         splx(s);
1041     }
1042     return(RETRY);
1043 }

1044 STATIC retval_t
1045 stp_restart(stp_t *stp)
1046 {
1047     mblk_t *hbp, *dbp;
1048     int size;

1049     if (net.n_state != UP)
1050         return(ERR);
1051     if (!(stp->s_flag & DORESTART))
1052         return(ERR);
1053     if (!canput(net.n_wrq->q_next))
1054         return(RETRY);
1055     if (stp->s_rxmp != NULL)
1056         return(RETRY);
1057     size = HDRSIZE;
1058     hbp = allocb(size, BPRI_MED);
1059     if (hbp == NULL)
1060         return(RETRY);
```

[1031–1043]   If we encounter an allocation failure, we jump to allocfail, where we try to recover. We cannot use bufcall here because multiple messages are needed, so we rely solely on timeout.

[1044–1048]   stp_restart is called to send a RESTART message to the peer when the read side is no longer flow-controlled. We have to undo the effect of previously sending the peer an acknowledgement with the STOP flag set.

[1049–1056]   stp_restart can be called from a timeout routine, so we check that the network is up first. If the DORESTART flag has been shut off, we return ERR. If the data link provider stream is flow-controlled, or if a message is awaiting retransmission, we return RETRY.

[1057–1060]   We calculate the minimum message size needed and try to allocate a message for the protocol header. If this fails, we return RETRY.

```
1061      dbp = allocb(DL_UNITDATA_REQ_SIZE+net.n_addrlen,
1062        BPRI_MED);
1063      if (dbp == NULL) {
1064          freeb(hbp);
1065          return(RETRY);
1066      }
1067      stp_buildunitdata(dbp, &stp->s_faddr);
1068      stp_buildheader(stp, hbp, RESTART, EOM, 0,
1069        sizeof(hdr_t), stp->s_faddr.a_port, size);
1070      dbp->b_cont = hbp;
1071      stp_xmit(stp, dbp, 0);
1072      stp->s_flag &= ~DORESTART;
1073      return(DONE);
1074 }

1075 STATIC retval_t
1076 stp_optmgmt(queue_t *q, mblk_t *mp)
1077 {
1078      stp_t *stp;
1079      struct T_optmgmt_req *reqp;  /* we know these */
1080      struct T_optmgmt_ack *ackp;  /* are the same size */
1081      long flags, terr;

1082      stp = (stp_t *)q->q_ptr;
1083      if (BADSTATE(stp->s_tpstate, TE_OPTMGMT_REQ)) {
1084          terr = TOUTSTATE;
1085          goto err;
1086      }
1087      reqp = (struct T_optmgmt_req *)mp->b_rptr;
1088      if (reqp->OPT_length != 0) {
1089          terr = TBADOPT;
1090          goto err;
1091      }
```

[1061–1066] Next we try to allocate a message for the DL_UNITDATA_REQ primitive. If this fails, we return RETRY. We do not need to establish a recovery mechanism because the caller takes care of it.

[1067–1074] We initialize the unitdata request and the protocol header, link them together, and transmit the packet by calling stp_xmit. Before returning, we shut off the DORESTART flag.

[1075–1091] stp_optmgmt is called to handle options management requests. The TPI does not specify a way to fail these requests when no options are supported, so we must respond with the appropriate primitives. If stp_optmgmt is called from an invalid state, we set the TLI error to TOUTSTATE and fail the request. If the options length is nonzero, then the user mistakenly assumed that this transport provider supports options, so we fail the request with the TBADOPT TLI error.

```
1092        flags = reqp->MGMT_flags;
1093        terr = 0;
1094        switch (flags) {
1095        case T_NEGOTIATE:
1096        case T_CHECK:
1097            break;

1098        case T_DEFAULT:
1099            flags |= T_SUCCESS;
1100            break;

1101        default:
1102            terr = TBADFLAG;
1103        }
1104        if (terr != 0)
1105            goto err;
1106        mp->b_datap->db_type = M_PCPROTO;
1107        ackp = (struct T_optmgmt_ack *)mp->b_rptr;
1108        ackp->PRIM_type = T_OPTMGMT_ACK;
1109        ackp->OPT_length = 0;
1110        ackp->OPT_offset = 0;
1111        ackp->MGMT_flags = flags;
1112        qreply(q, mp);
1113        return(DONE);
1114 err:
1115        if (stp_errorack(q, T_OPTMGMT_REQ, terr, 0) == RETRY)
1116            return(RETRY);
1117        freemsg(mp);
1118        return(ERR);
1119 }
```

[1092–1105] Next we check the flags specified in the options management request. If the T_DEFAULT flag is set, we add the T_SUCCESS flag to the flags specified by the user, as required by the TPI. If the user flags field contains an invalid value, we fail the request by setting the TLI error to TBADFLAG and jump to err, where we respond with an error acknowledgement.

[1106–1113] We convert the T_OPTMGMT_REQ into a T_OPTMGMT_ACK primitive. The corresponding data structures are the same size (indeed, they are identical), so a new message is not needed. We set the PRIM_type field to T_OPTMGMT_ACK, the options length and offset to 0, and the MGMT_flags field to the flags we have calculated. Then we send the message upstream and return DONE.

[1114–1119] On error, we jump to err, where we attempt to send a T_ERROR_ACK primitive upstream. If stp_errorack returns RETRY, then we return RETRY to the caller. Otherwise, we free the options management request message and return DONE.

```
1120 STATIC retval_t
1121 stp_errorack(queue_t *q, long prim, long terr, long uerr)
1122 {
1123     mblk_t *bp;
1124     stp_t *stp;
1125     struct T_error_ack *ackp;

1126     stp = (stp_t *)q->q_ptr;
1127     bp = allocb(sizeof(struct T_error_ack), BPRI_HI);
1128     if (bp == NULL) {
1129         stp_wsched(stp, sizeof(struct T_error_ack));
1130         return(RETRY);
1131     }
1132     bp->b_datap->db_type = M_PCPROTO;
1133     bp->b_wptr += sizeof(struct T_error_ack);
1134     ackp = (struct T_error_ack *)bp->b_rptr;
1135     ackp->PRIM_type = T_ERROR_ACK;
1136     ackp->ERROR_prim = prim;
1137     ackp->TLI_error = terr;
1138     ackp->UNIX_error = uerr;
1139     qreply(q, bp);
1140     return(DONE);
1141 }

1142 STATIC void
1143 stp_fatal(queue_t *q, mblk_t *mp)
1144 {
1145     if (mp->b_cont != NULL) {
1146         freemsg(mp->b_cont);
1147         mp->b_cont = NULL;
1148     }
```

[1120–1141] stp_errorack is called to send a T_ERROR_ACK primitive upstream. q is a pointer to the upper write queue, prim is the TPI primitive in error, terr is the TLI error code, and uerr is the UNIX error code. If we cannot allocate a message large enough to hold a T_error_ack structure, we call stp_wsched to recover and return RETRY. Otherwise, we set the type of the message to M_PCPROTO, increment the write pointer by the size of the T_error_ack structure, and initialize the structure with the function parameters. We send the message upstream and return DONE.

[1142–1148] stp_fatal is called to send an M_ERROR message upstream. This makes the stream unusable. We will convert the request message (mp) representing the primitive into an M_ERROR message. We start by freeing any message blocks linked to the message's b_cont pointer.

```
1149        mp->b_datap->db_type = M_ERROR;
1150        mp->b_rptr = mp->b_datap->db_base;
1151        *mp->b_rptr = EPROTO;
1152        mp->b_wptr = mp->b_rptr + 1;
1153        qreply(q, mp);
1154 }

1155 STATIC void
1156 stp_xmit(stp_t *stp, mblk_t *mp, int retransmit)
1157 {
1158        mblk_t *dupmp, *bp, *pbp;
1159        hdr_t *hp;
1160        int s, size, skip, maxsz;

1161        s = splstr();
1162        if (mp != NULL) {
1163            stp->s_rxmp = mp;
1164            stp->s_nretr = 0;
1165            stp->s_totxmitsz = 0;
1166            hp = (hdr_t *)mp->b_cont->b_rptr;
1167            stp->s_msgxmitsz = ntohs(hp->h_size);
1168        } else {
1169            if (!retransmit)
1170                stp->s_nretr = 0;
1171            if ((stp->s_rxmp == NULL) ||
1172              !canput(net.n_wrq->q_next)) {
1173                splx(s);
1174                return;
1175            }
1176            hp = (hdr_t *)stp->s_rxmp->b_cont->b_rptr;
1177        }
```

[1149–1154] We change the message type to M_ERROR, reset the read pointer to the base of the data buffer, store EPROTO in the first byte of the buffer, and set the write pointer to one byte past the read pointer. We know that the one-byte M_ERROR message is smaller than all TPI request messages, so the conversion is safe. q points to the write queue, so we call qreply to send the M_ERROR message upstream.

[1155–1167] stp_xmit is called to transmit a message. If mp is non-NULL, then we are transmitting a message for the first time, so we save it in the s_rxmp field of the stp_t structure and clear the retry count. Then we save the original size of the message in the s_msgxmitsz field.

[1168–1177] If mp is NULL, then stp_xmit is being called either to retransmit a message or to send the next fragment in a message that was originally too large to transmit in a single DLSDU. If the latter case, we set the retransmit count to 0. If there is no message to transmit or the data link provider stream is flow-controlled, we simply return.

```
1178        dupmp = dupmsg(stp->s_rxmp);
1179        splx(s);
1180        if (dupmp == NULL)
1181            return;
1182        if (stp->s_msgxmitsz > net.n_maxsdu) {
1183            pbp = dupmp->b_cont;
1184            bp = pbp->b_cont;
1185            size = sizeof(hdr_t);
1186            while (size < (int)stp->s_totxmitsz) {
1187                skip = stp->s_totxmitsz - size;
1188                if ((bp->b_wptr - bp->b_rptr) <= skip) {
1189                    size += bp->b_wptr - bp->b_rptr;
1190                    pbp->b_cont = bp->b_cont;
1191                    freeb(bp);
1192                    bp = pbp->b_cont;
1193                } else {
1194                    size += skip;
1195                    bp->b_rptr += skip;
1196                }
1197            }
1198            size = sizeof(hdr_t);
1199            while ((size < net.n_maxsdu) && (bp != NULL)) {
1200                maxsz = net.n_maxsdu - size;
1201                if ((bp->b_wptr - bp->b_rptr) <= maxsz) {
1202                    size += bp->b_wptr - bp->b_rptr;
1203                    bp = bp->b_cont;
1204                } else {
1205                    bp->b_wptr = bp->b_rptr + maxsz;
1206                    size += maxsz;
1207                }
1208            }
```

[1178–1181] We duplicate the message to be transmitted. If dupmsg fails, we just return and try again the next time the retransmit function runs.

[1182–1197] If the original message size is greater than the maximum DLSDU size, we can only transmit part of the message. (This only happens with DATA packets. Their format is a data link unitdata request message block linked to a message block containing the protocol header, followed by message blocks containing the user data.) s_totxmitsz contains the amount of data from the message that we have transmitted so far. Each message fragment must include a protocol header. The message we just duplicated is a copy of the entire original message, so we skip the amount of data in the message that we have already transmitted.

[1198–1208] Next we adjust the message to reflect the amount of data that can be transmitted.

```
1209              if ((bp != NULL) && (bp->b_cont != NULL)) {
1210                      freemsg(bp->b_cont);
1211                      bp->b_cont = NULL;
1212              }
1213              size = msgdsize(dupmp);
1214              hp->h_size = htons(size);
1215              if (size < net.n_minsdu) {
1216                      size = net.n_minsdu - size;
1217                      bp = allocb(size, BPRI_HI);
1218                      if (bp == NULL) {
1219                              freemsg(dupmp);
1220                              return;
1221                      }
1222                      bp->b_wptr += size;
1223                      linkb(dupmp, bp);
1224              }
1225      }
1226      if (!retransmit) {
1227              s = splstr();
1228              stp->s_totxmitsz += ntohs(hp->h_size);
1229              if (mp == NULL)
1230                      stp->s_totxmitsz -= sizeof(hdr_t);
1231              splx(s);
1232              hp->h_seqno = htonl(stp->s_seqno++);
1233              if (stp->s_totxmitsz == stp->s_msgxmitsz)
1234                      hp->h_flags |= EOM;
1235      } else {
1236              stp->s_nretr++;
1237      }
1238      drv_getparm(LBOLT, &stp->s_txtime);
1239      putnext(net.n_wrq, dupmp);
1240 }
```

[1209–1225] If message blocks remain after we reach the limit, we free them and clear the b_cont pointer. We calculate the size of this fragment and store it in the packet header. If this is the last fragment in the message, there might not be enough data present to satisfy the minimum DLSDU size requirement. In this case, we append a message block for padding to the end of the message.

[1226–1234] If this is not a retransmission, we increment the amount of data sent by the size of the packet. If mp is NULL, we subtract the header size from the count since the first fragment already accounted for it. Then we store the sequence number in the message, incrementing the sequence number. If the data transmit count equals the original message size, we set the end-of-message flag in the packet header.

[1235–1240] If this is a retransmission, we increment the retry count. In either case, we save the message transmit time and transmit the message.

```
1241 STATIC int
1242 stpursrv(queue_t *q)
1243 {
1244     mblk_t *mp;
1245     stp_t *stp;
1246     queue_t *rq;
1247     hdr_t *hp;
1248     int wasflowctled, s;

1249     stp = (stp_t *)q->q_ptr;
1250     s = splstr();
1251     wasflowctled = stp->s_flag & FLOWCTL;
1252     stp->s_flag &= ~FLOWCTL;
1253     splx(s);
1254     while ((mp = getq(q)) != NULL) {
1255         if (!canput(q->q_next)) {
1256             putbq(q, mp);
1257             s = splstr();
1258             stp->s_flag |= FLOWCTL;
1259             splx(s);
1260             break;
1261         }
1262         hp = (hdr_t *)mp->b_cont->b_rptr;
1263         switch (hp->h_type) {
1264         case DATA:
1265             if (stp_rcvdata(q, mp) == RETRY) {
1266                 putbq(q, mp);
1267                 goto checkfc;
1268             }
1269             break;
```

[1241–1253] The upper read service procedure is called both when the lower half of the multiplexor enqueues messages on the upper read queue and as a result of backenabling when the read side of the stream is no longer flow-controlled. First we remember if the FLOWCTL flag is set and then shut it off. We might flow-control during the execution of the service procedure, so we do not want to lose this information.

[1254–1263] We process messages on the queue until either the queue is empty or the read side of the upper stream flow-controls. In the latter case, we place the message back on the queue and set the FLOWCTL flag. The only messages placed on the upper read queue are data link unitdata indications. stplrput guarantees that they have the same format: a unitdata indication linked to a message block containing the packet.

[1264–1269] For a DATA packet, we call stp_rcvdata. If it returns RETRY, we place the message back on the queue and jump to checkfc to perform flow-control checks before returning. Otherwise, we continue processing messages on the queue.

```
1270            case CONNECT:
1271                if (stp_rcvconnect(q, mp) == RETRY) {
1272                    putbq(q, mp);
1273                    goto checkfc;
1274                }
1275                break;

1276            case ACCEPT:
1277                if (stp_rcvaccept(q, mp) == RETRY) {
1278                    putbq(q, mp);
1279                    goto checkfc;
1280                }
1281                break;

1282            case DISCON:
1283                if (stp_rcvdiscon(q, mp) == RETRY) {
1284                    putbq(q, mp);
1285                    goto checkfc;
1286                }
1287                break;

1288            case RESTART:
1289                freemsg(mp);
1290                s = splstr();
1291                stp->s_flag &= ~NOXMIT;
1292                splx(s);
1293                qenable(WR(q));
1294                break;

1295            default:
1296                freemsg(mp);
1297            }
1298        }
```

[1270–1287] For a CONNECT packet, we call stp_rcvconnect to convert the packet into a connect indication. If the packet is an ACCEPT message, we call stp_rcvaccept to convert the packet into a connect confirmation primitive. For a DISCON packet, we call stp_rcvdiscon to convert the packet into a disconnect indication.

[1288–1294] The processing for a RESTART packet is different from that for the other types. First, we free the message because we do not need it. Then we shut off the NOXMIT flag in the stp_t structure. If the upper write queue has messages on it, we enable its service procedure so it can continue transmitting messages.

[1295–1298] ACK packets are handled entirely by the lower read put procedure. Any other packet types constitute illegal messages, so we free them.

```
1299 checkfc:
1300     if (wasflowctled && !(stp->s_flag & FLOWCTL)) {
1301         if (net.n_state == UP) {
1302             rq = RD(net.n_wrq);
1303             if (rq->q_first != NULL)
1304                 qenable(rq);
1305         }

1306         if (stp_restart(stp) == RETRY) {
1307             s = splstr();
1308             stp->s_flag |= DORESTART;
1309             splx(s);
1310             timeout((void (*)())stp_restart, (caddr_t)stp,
1311                 drv_usectohz(HALFSEC));
1312         }
1313     }
1314     return(0);
1315 }

1316 STATIC void
1317 stp_rsched(stp_t *stp, int size)
1318 {
1319     ulong_t id;
1320     int s;
```

[1299–1305]   We reach `checkfc` when either the queue is empty or the read side of the stream flow-controls. If the read-side of the stream was flow-controlled when we began the service procedure but is not flow-controlled now, we need to enable the delivery of more packets. First, if the network is still up, we need to enable the lower read service procedure if messages are queued there. Some might be for this transport endpoint. This illustrates one of the classic problems with multiplexors. If messages destined for this endpoint are on the lower read queue, but the first message on the queue is for a different endpoint that is flow-controlled on the read side, then enabling the lower read service procedure is useless. This endpoint cannot receive any more messages until the other endpoint is no longer flow-controlled.

[1306–1315]   The second step we take to enable the delivery of more packets is to call `stp_restart` to send a RESTART message to the peer so that the peer can begin sending us packets again. If `stp_restart` returns RETRY, we set the DORESTART flag in the `stp_t` structure and schedule `stp_restart` to run again in half a second.

[1316–1320]   `stp_rsched` is just like `stp_wsched`, but it operates on the upper read side of the multiplexor instead of the upper write side.

```
1321     if (stp->s_flag & (RRECBCALL|RRECTOUT))
1322         return;
1323     id = bufcall(size, BPRI_HI, stp_rcont, stp);
1324     s = splstr();
1325     if (id == 0) {
1326         id = timeout(stp_rcont, (caddr_t)stp,
1327             drv_usectohz(HALFODO)));
1328         stp->s_flag |= RRECTOUT;
1329     } else {
1330         stp->s_flag |= RRECBCALL;
1331     }
1332     splx(s);
1333     stp->s_rrecid = id;
1334 }

1335 STATIC void
1336 stp_rcont(stp_t *stp)
1337 {
1338     if (stp->s_rdq != NULL) {
1339         stp->s_flag &= ~(RRECBCALL|RRECTOUT);
1340         qenable(stp->s_rdq);
1341     }
1342 }

1343 STATIC int
1344 stplrput(queue_t *q, mblk_t *mp)
1345 {
1346     union DL_primitives *dp;
1347     hdr_t *hp;
1348     stp_t *stp;
1349     int didack;
1350     ulong_t seqno;
```

[1321–1334] If recovery is already scheduled, we just return. Otherwise, we call bufcall to schedule stp_rcont to run when it has a good chance of allocating a message size bytes long. If bufcall fails, we use timeout to schedule stp_rcont to run in half a second. In either case, we remember the recovery method by setting the corresponding flag in the stp_t structure and storing the ID of the request in the s_rrecid field.

[1335–1342] stp_rcont is called to enable the upper read queue's service procedure when we have a better chance of allocating a message needed to process a packet.

[1343–1350] stplrput is the lower read put procedure. Its job is to accept all messages from the data link provider.

```
1351        switch (mp->b_datap->db_type) {
1352        case M_PROTO:
1353        case M_PCPROTO:
1354            dp = (union DL_primitives *)mp->b_rptr;
1355            switch (dp->dl_primitive) {
1356            case DL_INFO_ACK:
1357                stp_rcvinfo(mp);
1358                break;

1359            case DL_UNITDATA_IND:
1360                if (net.n_state != UP)
1361                    goto drop;
1362                if (!pullupmsg(mp->b_cont, -1))
1363                    goto drop; /* source will retransmit */

1364                hp = (hdr_t *)mp->b_cont->b_rptr;
1365                stp = stp_findport(ntohs(hp->h_dport));
1366                if (stp == NULL)
1367                    goto drop;
1368                seqno = ntohl(hp->h_seqno);
```

[1351–1358] The DLPI primitives are implemented as M_PROTO and M_PCPROTO messages. We only care about two of the DLPI primitives. If we receive a DL_INFO_ACK in response to the DL_INFO_REQ we generated when the multiplexor link was first made, then we call stp_rcvinfo to process the acknowledgement and complete the ioctl processing.

[1359–1363] If we get a DL_UNITDATA_IND, then we need to process the packet attached to it. If the network is not up, we just free the message, break out of the switch statement, and return. Otherwise, we call pullupmsg to align and copy the contents of the data portion of the message. If pullupmsg fails, we free the message and return. We can get away with this because the sender will retransmit the packet when it does not receive the acknowledgement in time.

[1364–1368] The beginning of the packet contains the protocol header. We call stp_findport to map the destination port number into the corresponding stp_t structure. Note we convert the port number from the network byte order to the host byte order first. If the destination port number is not bound, then stp_findport will return NULL and we will free the message and return. Next we convert the sequence number in the message to the host's byte order.

```
1369                if (hp->h_type == ACK) {
1370                    if (seqno == (stp->s_seqno - 1)) {
1371                        stp->s_rcvack = seqno;
1372                        if (stp->s_totxmitsz ==
1373                          stp->s_msgxmitsz) {
1374                            freemsg(stp->s_rxmp);
1375                            stp->s_rxmp = NULL;
1376                        }
1377                        if (hp->h_flags & STOP)
1378                            stp->s_flag |= NOXMIT;
1379                        else
1380                            qenable(WR(stp->s_rdq));
1381                    }
1382                    goto drop;
1383                }
1384                if (stp->s_tpstate == TS_DATA_XFER) {
1385                    if (seqno == stp->s_ackno) {/* lost ack */
1386                        if (stp->s_flag & FLOWCTL)
1387                            stp_sendack(stp, mp, 1);
1388                        else
1389                            stp_sendack(stp, mp, 0);
1390                        goto drop;
1391                    } else if (seqno != (stp->s_ackno + 1)) {
1392                        goto drop;
1393                    }
1394                }
```

[1369–1383] If the message is an ACK packet and the sequence number is the expected one, we save the sequence number received in s_rcvack. If the entire message has been sent and acknowledged, we free the message saved for retransmission and set the s_rxmp field to NULL. If the STOP flag is set in the acknowledgement header, we set the NOXMIT flag in the stp_t structure. Otherwise, we enable the upper write queue so the next message can be sent. In any event, we go to drop, where we free the ACK message and return.

[1384–1390] If the message is not an ACK packet and the transport endpoint is in the data-transfer state, we compare the sequence number in the packet with the last one we acknowledged. If they match, then we must assume that our acknowledgement got lost, so we call stp_sendack to resend the acknowledgement packet to the peer. If the read side of the upper stream is flow-controlled, we call stp_sendack with the third parameter set to 1 so that it will cause the peer to stop transmitting. Then we go to drop, where we free the received message and return.

[1391–1394] If the sequence number does not match the next expected number, we jump to drop to free the message and return.

```
1395              if (!canput(stp->s_rdq->q_next)) {
1396                  stp->s_flag |= FLOWCTL;
1397                  didack = stp_sendack(stp, mp, 1);
1398              } else {
1399                  didack = stp_sendack(stp, mp, 0);
1400              }
1401              if (!didack)
1402                  freemsg(mp);
1403              else
1404                  putq(q, mp);
1405              break;

1406         default:
1407 drop:
1408              freemsg(mp);
1409          }
1410          break;

1411      case M_FLUSH:
1412          if (*mp->b_rptr & FLUSHR) {
1413              flushq(q, FLUSHALL);
1414              *mp->b_rptr &= ~FLUSHR;
1415          }
1416          if (*mp->b_rptr & FLUSHW)
1417              qreply(q, mp);
1418          else
1419              freemsg(mp);
1420          break;
```

[1395–1400] If the read side of the upper stream is flow-controlled, then we set the FLOWCTL flag in the transport endpoint's `stp_t` structure and send an acknowledgement asking the transmitter to stop sending messages. If the upper stream is not flow-controlled, we still transmit the acknowledgement, but the STOP flag will be shut off in the packet header.

[1401–1405] If we were able to acknowledge the packet, we place the received message on the read queue. Otherwise, we free the message. Then we return.

[1406–1410] Any unknown DLPI primitives that we receive are freed.

[1411–1420] The lower read put procedure acts as the stream head, as far as flushing the stream is concerned. If the FLUSHR flag is set, we flush the lower read queue and shut off the FLUSHR flag. If FLUSHW is set, we send the message down the write queue. Otherwise, we free the M_FLUSH message. We do not need to flush the lower write queue because we never place any messages there.

```
1421    case M_ERROR:
1422            freemsg(mp);
1423            net.n_state = DOWN;
1424            stp_disconall(DIS_NETERR);
1425            putctl1(WR(q)->q_next, M_FLUSH, FLUSHRW);
1426            break;

1427    default:
1428            freemsg(mp);
1429    }
1430    return(0);
1431 }

1432 STATIC int
1433 stp_sendack(stp_t *stp, mblk_t *mp, uchar_t stop)
1434 {
1435     hdr_t *hp;
1436     mblk_t *hbp, *dbp;
1437     dl_unitdata_ind_t *indp;
1438     struct stpaddr addr;
1439     int size;
1440     ulong_t seqno;
1441     uchar_t flags = EOM;

1442     hp = (hdr_t *)mp->b_cont->b_rptr;
1443     seqno = hp->h_seqno;
1444     indp = (dl_unitdata_ind_t *)mp->b_rptr;
1445     stp_buildaddr(&addr, (caddr_t)mp->b_rptr+
1446         indp->dl_src_addr_offset, hp->h_sport);
```

[1421–1426] If we receive an M_ERROR message, we free it and mark the network as being DOWN. Then we call stp_disconall to send disconnect indications up all the active streams. We use DIS_NETERR for the reason for the disconnects. Finally, we send an M_FLUSH message down the lower write stream to mimic what the stream head does when it receives an M_ERROR message.

[1427–1431] We free any unknown messages that we receive.

[1432–1441] stp_sendack is used to transmit an acknowledgement packet to the peer. Its three parameters are a pointer to the transport endpoint's stp_t structure, a pointer to the message being acknowledged, and a flag controlling whether or not we ask the peer to stop transmitting.

[1442–1446] We find the protocol header in the message and save its sequence number. Then we call stp_buildaddr to create a transport address from the source address and the source port number stored in the message. We will use this address as the destination for the acknowledgement message.

```
1447      size = HDRSIZE;
1448      hbp = allocb(size, BPRI_HI);
1449      if (hbp == NULL)
1450          return(0);
1451      dbp = allocb(DL_UNITDATA_REQ_SIZE+net.n_addrlen,
1452        BPRI_HI);
1453      if (dbp == NULL) {
1454          freeb(hbp);
1455          return(0);
1456      }
1457      stp_buildunitdata(dbp, &addr);
1458      if (stop)
1459          flags |= STOP;
1460      stp_buildheader(stp, hbp, ACK, flags, 0, sizeof(hdr_t),
1461        addr.a_port, size);
1462      hp = (hdr_t *)hbp->b_rptr;
1463      hp->h_seqno = seqno;
1464      dbp->b_cont = hbp;
1465      stp->s_ackno = ntohl(seqno);
1466      putnext(net.n_wrq, dbp);
1467      return(1);
1468 }

1469 STATIC void
1470 stp_buildaddr(struct stpaddr *ap, caddr_t nap,
1471      ushort_t port)
1472 {
1473      caddr_t p = nap;

1474      ap->a_port = port;
1475      if (net.n_saplen > 0)     /* sap followed by phys */
1476          p += net.n_saplen;
1477      bcopy(p, (caddr_t)ap->a_net, NETADDRSZ);
1478 }
```

[1447–1468] If we cannot allocate messages for the protocol header and unitdata request, we return 0 to indicate that the acknowledgement was not sent. Otherwise, we construct the unitdata request and the protocol header. If the stop parameter is nonzero, we set the STOP flag in the protocol header. We store the sequence number of the message being acknowledged in the protocol header. Note that we use putnext to transmit the acknowledgement instead of stp_xmit, because ACK messages are not acknowledged and are not retransmitted using the same mechanism as other packet types. We return 1 to indicate the acknowledgement was sent.

[1469–1478] stp_buildaddr is called to construct a transport address. The results are stored in the stpaddr structure to which ap points. nap points to a DLSAP address, and port is the port number.

```
1479 STATIC void
1480 stp_rcvinfo(mblk_t *mp)
1481 {
1482     dl_info_ack_t *ackp;
1483     struct iocblk *iocp;
1484     struct linkblk *lp;
1485     mblk_t *bp;

1486     bp = net.n_mp;
1487     net.n_mp = NULL;
1488     iocp = (struct iocblk *)bp->b_rptr;
1489     lp = (struct linkblk *)bp->b_cont->b_rptr;
1490     if ((iocp->ioc_cmd == I_PLINK) &&
1491         !stp_qinuse(lp->l_qtop)) {
1492         freemsg(bp);
1493         freemsg(mp);
1494         net.n_state = DOWN;
1495         return;
1496     }
1497     ackp = (dl_info_ack_t *)mp->b_rptr;
1498     if ((ackp->dl_service_mode != DL_CLDLS) ||
1499         (ackp->dl_current_state != DL_IDLE)) {
1500         iocp->ioc_error = EPROTO;
1501         goto nak;
1502     }
1503     if (ackp->dl_addr_length > (NETADDRSZ+MAXNETSAPSZ)) {
1504         iocp->ioc_error = ENAMETOOLONG;
1505         goto nak;
1506     }
```

[1479–1489] stp_rcvinfo is called when the lower read put procedure receives a DL_INFO_ACK primitive in response to the DL_INFO_REQ primitive generated during I_LINK and I_PLINK ioctl processing. The M_IOCTL message is saved in the n_mp field of the network structure. We save the message pointer, clear the n_mp field, and identify the iocblk and linkblk structures in the message.

[1490–1496] If the link is persistent, we call stp_qinuse to verify that the queue is still in use. (Recall that a persistent link survives the closing of the upper stream, so the queue pointer that we saved in l_qtop might no longer be valid.) If the queue is no longer in use, we free the messages, mark the network as being down, and return.

[1497–1506] If the data link service is not connectionless, or the data link provider is not already bound, we convert the M_IOCTL message into an M_IOCNAK message and fail the ioctl with EPROTO, indicating a protocol error. If the length of the DLSAP address is incorrect, we fail the ioctl, setting ioc_error to ENAMETOOLONG.

```
1507     if (ackp->dl_max_sdu < (sizeof(hdr_t)+1)) {
1508          iocp->ioc_error = E2BIG;
1509 nak:
1510          bp->b_datap->db_type = M_IOCNAK;
1511          qreply(lp->l_qtop, bp);
1512          freemsg(mp);
1513          net.n_state = DOWN;
1514          return;
1515     }

1516     net.n_minsdu = ackp->dl_min_sdu;
1517     net.n_maxsdu = ackp->dl_max_sdu;
1518     net.n_addrlen = ackp->dl_addr_length;
1519     net.n_saplen = ackp->dl_sap_length;
1520     bcopy((caddr_t)mp->b_rptr + ackp->dl_addr_offset,
1521         (caddr_t)net.n_addr, net.n_addrlen);

1522     iocp->ioc_count = 0;
1523     bp->b_datap->db_type = M_IOCACK;
1524     qreply(lp->l_qtop, bp);
1525     freemsg(mp);
1526     net.n_state = UP;
1527     timeout(stp_retransmit, 0, drv_usectohz(RETRTIME));
1528 }
```

[1507–1515] If the maximum packet that the data link provider can accept is smaller than the protocol header plus one byte of data, we fail the ioctl with the error E2BIG. Note that we use the l_qtop field in the linkblk structure to identify the upper write queue associated with the ioctl request. Normally this field would be NULL for a persistent link, but recall that we set it to the upper write queue in stp_ioctl.

[1516–1521] We save the minimum and maximum data link service data unit sizes in the network structure. We also save the DLSAP address length and the SAP identifier length. Then we copy the data link provider address from the message to the n_addr field in the network structure.

[1522–1528] We set the ioc_count field to 0 to prevent the linkblk structure from being copied, and we convert the M_IOCTL message into an M_IOCACK message. We send it upstream to complete the ioctl request successfully. Then we free the DL_INFO_ACK message and mark the network as being UP. To complete the establishment of the link, we start the retransmission mechanism by calling timeout.

```
1529 STATIC int
1530 stp_qinuse(queue_t *q)
1531 {
1532     int i;

1533     for (i = 0; i < nstp; i++)
1534         if (stpendpt[i].s_rdq == RD(q))
1535             return(1);
1536     return(0);
1537 }

1538 STATIC int
1539 stp_samenetaddr(uchar_t *a1, uchar_t *a2)
1540 {
1541     int i;

1542     for (i = 0; i < NETADDRSZ; i++)
1543         if (*a1++ != *a2++)
1544             return(0);
1545     return(1);
1546 }

1547 STATIC retval_t
1548 stp_rcvdata(queue_t *q, mblk_t *mp)
1549 {
1550     stp_t *stp;
1551     mblk_t *bp, *udbp;
1552     hdr_t *hp;
1553     dl_unitdata_ind_t *udp;
1554     struct T_data_ind *indp;
1555     struct stpaddr addr;
1556     int eom;

1557     stp = (stp_t *)q->q_ptr;
1558     if (stp->s_tpstate != TS_DATA_XFER) {
1559         freemsg(mp);
1560         return(ERR);
1561     }
```

[1529–1537] `stp_qinuse` is called to check if the given write queue is still associated with a transport endpoint. If so, it returns 1; otherwise, it returns 0.

[1538–1546] `stp_samenetaddr` is the function we use to compare data link provider addresses. It returns 1 if the two addresses passed to it are the same, and 0 otherwise.

[1547–1561] `stp_rcvdata` is called to process incoming data packets. If the transport endpoint is not in the data-transfer state, we free the message and return ERR.

```
1562        udp = (dl_unitdata_ind_t *)mp->b_rptr;
1563        stp_buildaddr(&addr, (caddr_t)mp->b_rptr+
1564          udp->dl_src_addr_offset, 0);
1565        if (!stp_samenetaddr(stp->s_faddr.a_net, addr.a_net)) {
1566            freemsg(mp);
1567            return(ERR);
1568        }
1569        udbp = mp;
1570        mp = mp->b_cont;
1571        hp = (hdr_t *)mp->b_rptr;
1572        eom = hp->h_flags & EOM;
1573        if ((mp->b_wptr - mp->b_rptr) != ntohs(hp->h_size))
1574            mp->b_wptr = mp->b_rptr + ntohs(hp->h_size);
1575        mp->b_rptr += sizeof(hdr_t);
1576        if (stp->s_rcvmp == NULL) {
1577            bp = allocb(sizeof(struct T_data_ind), BPRI_MED);
1578            if (bp == NULL) {
1579                mp->b_rptr -= sizeof(hdr_t);
1580                stp_rsched(stp, sizeof(struct T_data_ind));
1581                return(RETRY);
1582            }
1583            bp->b_cont = mp;
1584            indp = (struct T_data_ind *)bp->b_wptr;
1585            indp->PRIM_type = T_DATA_IND;
1586            indp->MORE_flag = hp->h_flags & MORE;
1587            bp->b_wptr += sizeof(struct T_data_ind);
1588            bp->b_datap->db_type = M_PROTO;
1589            stp->s_rcvmp = bp;
1590        } else {
1591            linkb(stp->s_rcvmp, mp);
1592        }
```

[1562–1575] We compare the foreign address stored in the `stp_t` structure with the address of the machine that sent the packet. If they do not match, we free the message and return ERR. Otherwise, we save the end-of-message flag and adjust the write pointer in the packet's message if padding is present.

[1576–1589] If no message is being held for reassembly, we allocate a message for a `T_DATA_IND` primitive. If this fails, we restore the read pointer in the message, call `stp_rsched` to recover, and return RETRY. If the allocation succeeded, we link the packet data to the message. Then we initialize the `T_data_ind` structure, setting the `MORE_flag` field to indicate if this TSDU is part of a larger logical TSDU. We save the completed message in the `s_rcvmp` field of the `stp_t` structure.

[1590–1592] If a message is being held for reassembly, we append to it the data portion of the message received.

```
1593        freeb(udbp);
1594        if (eom) {
1595            putnext(q, stp->s_rcvmp);
1596            stp->s_rcvmp = NULL;
1597        }
1598        return(DONE);
1599  }

1600  STATIC retval_t
1601  stp_rcvconnect(queue_t *q, mblk_t *mp)
1602  {
1603        stp_t *stp;
1604        mblk_t *bp, *cbp;
1605        hdr_t *hp;
1606        struct stpaddr addr;
1607        dl_unitdata_ind_t *udp;
1608        struct T_conn_ind *indp;
1609        int i, s;

1610        stp = (stp_t *)q->q_ptr;
1611        if (BADSTATE(stp->s_tpstate, TE_CONN_IND) ||
1612          (stp->s_qlen == stp->s_maxqlen)) {
1613            freemsg(mp);
1614            return(ERR);
1615        }
1616        udp = (dl_unitdata_ind_t *)mp->b_rptr;
1617        hp = (hdr_t *)mp->b_cont->b_rptr;
1618        stp_buildaddr(&addr, (caddr_t)mp->b_rptr+
1619          udp->dl_src_addr_offset, hp->h_sport);
1620        bp = allocb(sizeof(struct T_conn_ind)+STPADDRSZ,
1621          BPRI_MED);
1622        if (bp == NULL) {
1623            stp_rsched(stp, sizeof(struct T_conn_ind)+
1624                STPADDRSZ);
1625            return(RETRY);
1626        }
```

[1593–1599] We free the message block containing the unitdata indication. If the packet just received was the last in the TSDU, we send the transport data indication upstream and clear the s_rcvmp field.

[1600–1619] stp_rcvconnect is called to process incoming connection requests. If the transport endpoint is in the wrong state to receive connect indications, or if the maximum number of indications is already queued, we free the message and return ERR. Otherwise, we copy the source transport address to the stpaddr structure on the stack.

[1620–1626] We attempt to allocate a message large enough to hold a T_conn_ind structure and a transport address. If the allocation fails, we call stp_rsched to recover and return RETRY.

```
1627        cbp = dupb(bp);
1628        if (cbp == NULL) {
1629            freeb(bp);
1630            if (!(stp->s_flag & (RRECBCALL|RRECTOUT))) {
1631                stp->s_rrecid = timeout(stp_rcont,
1632                    (caddr_t)stp, drv_usectohz(HALFSEC));
1633                s = splstr();
1634                stp->s_flag |= RRECTOUT;
1635                splx(s);
1636            }
1637            return(RETRY);
1638        }
1639        freemsg(mp);
1640        indp = (struct T_conn_ind *)bp->b_wptr;
1641        indp->PRIM_type = T_CONN_IND;
1642        indp->SRC_length = STPADDRSZ;
1643        indp->SRC_offset = sizeof(struct T_conn_ind);
1644        indp->OPT_length = 0;
1645        indp->OPT_offset = 0;
1646        indp->SEQ_number = stp->s_conseq++;
1647        bp->b_wptr += sizeof(struct T_conn_ind);
1648        bcopy((caddr_t)&addr, (caddr_t)bp->b_wptr,
1649            STPADDRSZ);
1650        bp->b_wptr += STPADDRSZ;
1651        bp->b_datap->db_type = M_PROTO;
```

[1627–1638] We attempt to duplicate the message block to be used for the connect indication. If dupb fails, we free the message block we tried to duplicate and, if recovery is not already enabled, call timeout to schedule stp_rcont to run in half a second. We protect the modification to the s_flag field with splstr. Then we return RETRY.

[1639–1651] If we were able to duplicate the connect indication message, we free the data link unitdata message and initialize the T_CONN_IND primitive. We set the SRC_length field to the size of a transport address, and we set the SRC_offset field to the location in the message where we will place the address of the transport endpoint requesting the connection. We set the OPT_length and OPT_offset fields to zero since we do not support options. Then we assign a unique connection sequence number to the connect indication and increment the sequence number in the stp_t structure. We complete the initialization of the primitive by incrementing the write pointer of its message by the size of the T_conn_ind structure, copying the source address into the message, incrementing the write pointer by the size of the address, and setting the message type to M_PROTO.

```
1652        cbp->b_wptr += (bp->b_wptr - bp->b_rptr);
1653        for (i = 0; i < MAXCREQ; i++)
1654            if (stp->s_cmp[i] == NULL)
1655                break;
1656        stp->s_cmp[i] = cbp;
1657        stp->s_qlen++;
1658        stp->s_tpstate = NEXTSTATE1(stp->s_tpstate,
1659            TE_CONN_IND);
1660        putnext(q, bp);
1661        return(DONE);
1662 }

1663 STATIC retval_t
1664 stp_rcvaccept(queue_t *q, mblk_t *mp)
1665 {
1666        stp_t *stp;
1667        mblk_t *bp;
1668        hdr_t *hp;
1669        struct stpaddr addr;
1670        dl_unitdata_ind_t *udp;
1671        struct T_conn_con *conp;

1672        stp = (stp_t *)q->q_ptr;
1673        if (BADSTATE(stp->s_tpstate, TE_CONN_CON)) {
1674            freemsg(mp);
1675            return(ERR);
1676        }
1677        udp = (dl_unitdata_ind_t *)mp->b_rptr;
1678        stp_buildaddr(&addr, (caddr_t)mp->b_rptr+
1679            udp->dl_src_addr_offset, 0);
1680        if (!stp_samenetaddr(stp->s_faddr.a_net, addr.a_net)) {
1681            freemsg(mp);
1682            return(ERR);
1683        }
```

[1652–1662] Since we duplicated the connect indication message before we initialized it, we need to update the write pointer in the copy of the message to reflect the amount of data stored in it. Then we search the array of connect indications awaiting response from the user to find an empty slot. When we find one, we store the duplicate message there. We change the state of the transport endpoint to reflect the arrival of a connect indication and send the T_CONN_IND primitive upstream.

[1663–1683] stp_rcvaccept is called to process an ACCEPT packet as part of connection establishment. If the transport endpoint is in the wrong state for a connect confirmation to be sent, we free the message and return ERR. If the ACCEPT packet did not come from the same machine to which we sent the connect request, we also free the message and return ERR.

```
1684        bp = allocb(sizeof(struct T_conn_con)+STPADDRSZ,
1685          BPRI_MED);
1686        if (bp == NULL) {
1687            stp_rsched(stp, sizeof(struct T_conn_con)+
1688              STPADDRSZ);
1689            return(RETRY);
1690        }
1691        hp = (hdr_t *)mp->b_cont->b_rptr;
1692        conp = (struct T_conn_con *)bp->b_wptr;
1693        conp->PRIM_type = T_CONN_CON;
1694        conp->RES_length = STPADDRSZ;
1695        conp->RES_offset = sizeof(struct T_conn_con);
1696        conp->OPT_length = 0;
1697        conp->OPT_offset = 0;
1698        bp->b_wptr += sizeof(struct T_conn_con);
1699        addr.a_port = hp->h_sport;
1700        freemsg(mp);
1701        bcopy((caddr_t)&addr, (caddr_t)bp->b_wptr,
1702          STPADDRSZ);
1703        stp->s_faddr.a_port = addr.a_port;
1704        bp->b_wptr += STPADDRSZ;
1705        bp->b_datap->db_type = M_PROTO;
1706        stp->s_tpstate = NEXTSTATE1(stp->s_tpstate,
1707          TE_CONN_CON);
1708        putnext(q, bp);
1709        return(DONE);
1710 }
```

[1684–1698] We attempt to allocate a message for the connect confirmation primitive. If this fails, we call stp_rsched to recover and return RETRY. To initialize the T_conn_con structure stored in the message, we set the PRIM_type field to T_CONN_CON, the RES_length field to the length of the address of the responding transport endpoint (the endpoint used in the connection on the other machine), and the RES_offset field to the location in the message where we will place the address. We set the OPT_length and OPT_offset fields both to zero because we do not support options. Then we increment the write pointer in the message by the size of the T_conn_con structure.

[1699–1710] We copy the port number of the peer to the stpaddr structure stored on the stack and free the data link unitdata indication message. Then we copy the address to the connect confirmation message immediately following the T_conn_con structure. We save the port number of the peer, increment the write pointer by the size of the address, and set the message type to M_PROTO. Finally, we place the transport endpoint in the new state dictated by the arrival of a connect confirmation, send the message upstream, and return DONE.

```
1711 STATIC retval_t
1712 stp_rcvdiscon(queue_t *q, mblk_t *mp)
1713 {
1714      stp_t *stp;
1715      mblk_t *bp;
1716      hdr_t *hp;
1717      struct stpaddr addr;
1718      dl_unitdata_ind_t *udp;
1719      struct T_conn_ind *cindp;
1720      struct T_discon_ind *indp;
1721      int i;

1722      stp = (stp_t *)q->q_ptr;
1723      bp = allocb(sizeof(struct T_discon_ind), BPRI_MED);
1724      if (bp == NULL) {
1725          stp_rsched(stp, sizeof(struct T_discon_ind));
1726          return(RETRY);
1727      }

1728      indp = (struct T_discon_ind *)bp->b_wptr;
1729      indp->PRIM_type = T_DISCON_IND;
1730      bp->b_wptr += sizeof(struct T_discon_ind);
1731      bp->b_datap->db_type = M_PROTO;
1732      hp = (hdr_t *)mp->b_cont->b_rptr;
1733      udp = (dl_unitdata_ind_t *)mp->b_rptr;
1734      stp_buildaddr(&addr, (caddr_t)mp->b_rptr +
1735        udp->dl_src_addr_offset, hp->h_sport);
1736      indp->DISCON_reason = hp->h_reason;
1737      freemsg(mp);
```

[1711–1721] stp_rcvdiscon is called to process a DISCON message intended to either reject a connection request or break an existing connection.

[1722–1727] We attempt to allocate a message large enough to hold a T_discon_ind structure. If this fails, we call stp_rsched to recover, and we return RETRY.

[1728–1737] If the allocation succeeds, we start to initialize the T_discon_ind structure by setting the PRIM_type field to T_DISCON_IND, incrementing the write pointer by the size of the T_discon_ind structure, and setting the message type to M_PROTO. We will complete the initialization after we search the array of pending connect indications. Next we copy the source address from the data link unitdata indication to the stack. Before freeing the unitdata message, we copy the disconnect reason from the packet header to the DISCON_reason field in the T_discon_ind structure.

```
1738      if (stp->s_tpstate == TS_WRES_CIND) {
1739          for (i = 0; i < MAXCREQ; i++) {
1740              if (stp->s_cmp[i] == NULL)
1741                  continue;
1742              cindp = (struct T_conn_ind *)
1743                stp->s_cmp[i]->b_rptr;
1744              if (stp_sameaddr(&addr,
1745                (struct stpaddr *)(stp->s_cmp[i]->b_rptr +
1746                cindp->SRC_offset))) {
1747                  indp->SEQ_number = cindp->SEQ_number;
1748                  freeb(stp->s_cmp[i]);
1749                  stp->s_cmp[i] = NULL;
1750                  stp->s_qlen--;
1751                  break;
1752              }
1753          }
1754          if (i >= MAXCREQ) {
1755              freeb(bp);
1756              return(ERR);
1757          }
1758          if (stp->s_qlen == 0)
1759              stp->s_tpstate = NEXTSTATE1(stp->s_tpstate,
1760                  TE_DISCON_IND2);
1761          else
1762              stp->s_tpstate = NEXTSTATE1(stp->s_tpstate,
1763                  TE_DISCON_IND3);
```

[1738–1753] If the transport endpoint is waiting for the user to respond to connect indications, we search the array of queued connect indication messages for one that contains a source address that matches the address of the transport endpoint that requested the disconnect. If we find a match, we copy the connect sequence number to the SEQ_number field in the T_discon_ind structure, free the saved connect indication message, clear the slot in the array of messages, and decrement the number of connect indications queued.

[1754–1763] If we are unable to find a connect indication with a matching address, then we free the message that we allocated for the disconnect indication and return ERR. Otherwise, we place the transport endpoint in the appropriate state. If no more connect indications are queued, TE_DISCON_IND2 will transition the endpoint into the idle state. If connect indications remain, TE_DISCON_IND3 will leave the transport endpoint in the TS_WRES_CIND state.

```
1764        } else {
1765            if (!stp_samenetaddr(stp->s_faddr.a_net,
1766              addr.a_net)) {
1767                freeb(bp);
1768                return(ERR);
1769            }
1770            if (BADSTATE(stp->s_tpstate, TE_DISCON_IND1)) {
1771                freeb(bp);
1772                return(ERR);
1773            }
1774            indp->SEQ_number = -1;
1775            if (stp->s_tpstate == TS_DATA_XFER)
1776                putctl1(q->q_next, M_FLUSH, FLUSHRW);
1777            stp->s_tpstate = NEXTSTATE1(stp->s_tpstate,
1778              TE_DISCON_IND1);
1779        }
1780        putnext(q, bp);
1781        return(DONE);
1782 }

1783 STATIC int
1784 stplrsrv(queue_t *q)
1785 {
1786        mblk_t *mp;
1787        stp_t *stp;
1788        hdr_t *hp;

1789        if (net.n_state != UP)   {
1790            flushq(q, FLUSHALL);
1791            return(0);
1792        }
```

[1764–1779] If the transport endpoint is not in the TS_WRES_CIND state, we make
             sure that the DISCON packet came from the transport endpoint at the
             other end of the connection and that the local endpoint is in the proper
             state to receive a disconnect indication. If either condition is false, we
             free the message that we allocated and return ERR. Otherwise, we set
             the SEQ_number field to −1 to indicate an existing connection is
             being broken. If the transport endpoint is in the data-transfer state, we
             flush the read and write sides of the stream, as required by the TPI.
             Then we place the endpoint in the new state (idle).

[1780–1782] Regardless of the state of the endpoint, if we do not encounter any
             errors, we send the disconnect indication upstream and return DONE.

[1783–1792] The lower read service procedure is called to demultiplex messages
             received from the data link provider, placing them on the proper upper
             read queues. If the network is not up, we flush the queue and return.

```
1793        while ((mp = getq(q)) != NULL) {
1794                hp = (hdr_t *)mp->b_cont->b_rptr;
1795                stp = stp_findport(ntohs(hp->h_dport));
1796                if (stp == NULL) {
1797                        freemsg(mp);
1798                } else if (canput(stp->s_rdq)) {
1799                        putq(stp->s_rdq, mp);
1800                } else {
1801                        putbq(q, mp);
1802                        break;
1803                }
1804        }
1805        return(0);
1806 }

1807 STATIC int
1808 stplwsrv(queue_t *q)
1809 {
1810        int i;
1811        queue_t *wq;

1812        for (i = net.n_nextsend; i < nstp; i++) {
1813                if (stpendpt[i].s_rdq != NULL) {
1814                        wq = WR(stpendpt[i].s_rdq);
1815                        if (wq->q_first != NULL)
1816                                qenable(wq);
1817                }
1818        }
```

[1793–1806]   We process every message on the queue until either we flow-control
              or the queue is empty. For each message retrieved, we locate the pro-
              tocol header and call `stp_findport` to translate a destination port
              number into an `stp_t` structure pointer. If `stp_findport` returns
              NULL, no active port was found that matched the destination port
              number stored in the protocol header, so we just free the message.
              Otherwise, we place it on the appropriate upper read queue if it is not
              flow-controlled.

[1807–1811]   The lower write service procedure is called when the write side of the
              stream linked under the multiplexor is no longer flow-controlled.

[1812–1818]   We search the array of `stp_t` structures in two passes, starting with
              the index stored in the `n_nextsend` field of the `network` structure.
              For every active endpoint we find, we enable its upper write service
              procedure if messages are queued. On the first pass, we search from
              `net.n_nextsend` to the end of the array.

```
1819        for (i = 0; i < net.n_nextsend; i++) {
1820            if (stpendpt[i].s_rdq != NULL) {
1821                wq = WR(stpendpt[i].s_rdq);
1822                if (wq->q_first != NULL)
1823                    qenable(wq);
1824            }
1825        }
1826        if ((++net.n_nextsend) == nstp)
1827            net.n_nextsend = 0;
1828        return(0);
1829 }

1830 STATIC stp_t *
1831 stp_findport(ushort_t port)
1832 {
1833        int i;
1834        stp_t *stp;

1835        stp = stpendpt;
1836        for (i = 0; i < nstp; i++, stp++)
1837            if ((stp->s_rdq != NULL) &&
1838                (stp->s_lport == port))
1839                    return(stp);
1840        return(NULL);
1841 }

1842 STATIC ushort_t
1843 stp_getuport(void)
1844 {
1845        int i;

1846        for (i = 1; i < MAXPORT; i++)
1847            if (stp_findport(i) == NULL)
1848                    return(i);
1849        return(0);
1850 }
```

[1819–1829] On the second pass, we search from the beginning of the array to net.n_nextsend. To be fair, we use a round-robin policy in deciding the first queue to enable. We increment the n_nextsend field each time the lower write service procedure runs. If we hit the end of the array, we reset n_nextsend to 0.

[1830–1841] stp_findport converts a port number into the transport endpoint bound to it. We search the endpoint array until we find an active entry with a port number that matches port. If we find a match, we return a pointer to the stp_t structure. Otherwise, we return NULL.

[1842–1850] stp_getuport finds a free port number. We call stp_findport until it returns NULL. Then we return the unused port number.

```
1851 STATIC void
1852 stp_retransmit(void)
1853 {
1854     int i;
1855     ulong_t now;

1856     if (net.n_state != UP)
1857         return;
1858     for (i = net.n_nextsend; i < nstp; i++) {
1859         if (stpendpt[i].s_rxmp != NULL) {
1860             drv_getparm(LBOLT, &now);
1861             if ((now - stpendpt[i].s_txtime) >=
1862                 drv_usectohz(RETRTIME)) {
1863                 if (stpendpt[i].s_nretr == MAXRETR) {
1864                     stp_discon1(&stpendpt[i],
1865                         DIS_TIMEOUT);
1866                 } else {
1867                     stp_xmit(&stpendpt[i], NULL, 1);
1868                 }
1869             }
1870         }
1871     }
1872     for (i = 0; i < net.n_nextsend; i++) {
1873         if (stpendpt[i].s_rxmp != NULL) {
1874             drv_getparm(LBOLT, &now);
1875             if ((now - stpendpt[i].s_txtime) >=
1876                 drv_usectohz(RETRTIME)) {
1877                 if (stpendpt[i].s_nretr == MAXRETR) {
1878                     stp_discon1(&stpendpt[i],
1879                         DIS_TIMEOUT);
1880                 } else {
1881                     stp_xmit(&stpendpt[i], NULL, 1);
1882                 }
1883             }
1884         }
1885     }
```

[1851–1885] stp_retransmit is called to retransmit a message. If the network
is not up, we just return. We search the stpendpt array in two
passes. If we find an endpoint with a message held awaiting an
acknowledgement, we call drv_getparm to get the current number
of clock ticks since the system started. If the difference between this
and the value of lbolt when the message was last transmitted is at
least as large as the retransmit interval, we need to retransmit the message. If, however, the maximum number of retransmit attempts has
been reached, we call stp_discon1 to send a disconnect indication
to the transport user, assuming that the other transport endpoint's
machine is down. If we have not yet reached the maximum retry
count, we call stp_xmit to retransmit the message.

```
1886        if (++net.n_nextsend == nstp)
1887            net.n_nextsend = 0;
1888        timeout(stp_retransmit, 0, drv_usectohz(RETRTIME));
1889 }

1890 STATIC void
1891 stp_discon1(stp_t *stp, uchar_t reason)
1892 {
1893     mblk_t *bp;
1894     struct T_discon_ind *indp;

1895     if (stp->s_rdq == NULL)
1896         return;
1897     if ((stp->s_tpstate == TS_DATA_XFER) ||
1898       (stp->s_tpstate == TS_WCON_CREQ)) {
1899         if ((stp->s_tpstate == TS_DATA_XFER) && putctl1(
1900           stp->s_rdq->q_next, M_FLUSH, FLUSHRW) == 0)
1901             return;
1902         bp = allocb(sizeof(struct T_discon_ind), BPRI_HI);
1903         if (bp == NULL)
1904             return;
1905         stp->s_tpstate = NEXTSTATE1(stp->s_tpstate,
1906           TE_DISCON_IND1);
1907         bp->b_datap->db_type = M_PROTO;
1908         bp->b_wptr += sizeof(struct T_discon_ind);
1909         indp = (struct T_discon_ind *)bp->b_rptr;
1910         indp->PRIM_type = T_DISCON_IND;
1911         indp->DISCON_reason = reason;
1912         indp->SEQ_number = -1;
1913         putnext(stp->s_rdq, bp);
1914     }
```

[1886–1889] When we are through searching the entire array, we calculate the entry to begin the search with the next time, according to a round-robin policy. Finally, we call `timeout` to schedule `stp_retransmit` to be run again when the next retransmit interval has elapsed.

[1890–1894] `stp_discon1` is called to send a disconnect indication primitive to the local transport user associated with the given transport endpoint.

[1895–1914] If the transport endpoint is not in use, we just return. If the endpoint is in the data-transfer state or is waiting for a connect request to complete, we proceed to send it a disconnect indication. For the data-transfer state, we flush the stream, as required by the TPI. If `putctl1` fails, we simply return. Similarly, if we cannot allocate a message to hold the `T_discon_ind` structure, we return. The next time `stp_retransmit` runs it will try again to break the connection. If the allocation succeeds, we initialize the `T_discon_ind` structure and send the message upstream.

```
1915      if (stp->s_rxmp != NULL) {
1916          freemsg(stp->s_rxmp);
1917          stp->s_rxmp = NULL;
1918      }
1919      if (stp->s_rcvmp != NULL) {
1920          freemsg(stp->s_rcvmp);
1921          stp->s_rcvmp = NULL;
1922      }
1923  }

1924  STATIC void
1925  stp_disconall(uchar_t reason)
1926  {
1927      mblk_t *bp, *mp;
1928      stp_t *stp;
1929      struct T_discon_ind *indp;
1930      int i;

1931      bp = allocb(sizeof(struct T_discon_ind), BPRI_HI);
1932      if (bp == NULL)
1933          return;
1934      bp->b_datap->db_type = M_PROTO;
1935      bp->b_wptr += sizeof(struct T_discon_ind);
1936      indp = (struct T_discon_ind *)bp->b_rptr;
1937      indp->PRIM_type = T_DISCON_IND;
1938      indp->DISCON_reason = reason;
1939      indp->SEQ_number = -1;
1940      for (i = 0, stp = stpendpt; i < nstp; i++, stp++) {
1941          if ((stp->s_rdq != NULL) && ((stp->s_tpstate ==
1942            TS_DATA_XFER) || (stp->s_tpstate ==
1943            TS_WCON_CREQ))) {
1944              if ((stp->s_tpstate == TS_DATA_XFER) &&
1945                putctl1(stp->s_rdq->q_next, M_FLUSH,
1946                FLUSHRW) == 0)
1947                  continue;
```

[1915–1923] Before returning, we free any message held for retransmission and any message held for reassembly.

[1924–1947] stp_disconall is called to send disconnect indications up all streams associated with active transport endpoints in the proper state. This is necessary when the network goes down or is unlinked. We allocate a message for the disconnect indication, initialize it, and then step through the array of transport endpoints looking for ones that need to be disconnected. When we find an endpoint in either the data-transfer state or the state waiting for the confirmation of a connect request, we need to generate a disconnect indication. If the endpoint is in the data-transfer state, we flush its stream. If putctl1 fails, we skip the endpoint and continue searching.

```
1948              mp = dupb(bp);
1949              if (mp == NULL)
1950                   continue;
1951              stp->s_tpstate = NEXTSTATE1(stp->s_tpstate,
1952                 TE_DISCON_IND1);
1953              putnext(stp->s_rdq, mp);
1954              if (stp->s_rxmp != NULL) {
1955                   freemsg(stp->s_rxmp);
1956                   stp->s_rxmp = NULL;
1957              }
1958              if (stp->s_rcvmp != NULL) {
1959                   freemsg(stp->s_rcvmp);
1960                   stp->s_rcvmp = NULL;
1961              }
1962          }
1963      }
1964      freeb(bp);
1965 }
```

[1948–1965] We attempt to duplicate the disconnect indication message. If dupb fails, we skip the endpoint and continue the search. Otherwise, we change the state of the endpoint and send the message up its stream. Then we free any messages that are held for retransmission or are in the process of being reassembled for this endpoint. After searching the array, we free the original message that we allocated and then return.

Summary

We have discussed how STREAMS multiplexing drivers work. We have studied a simple transport provider for two reasons. First, it illustrates a working STREAMS multiplexor and the techniques a multiplexing driver uses to route messages and propagate flow control. Second, the example displays the mechanics involved with supporting connection-oriented transport services under the TPI service interface.

Exercises

12.1 In stpclose, we do not wait around for the acknowledgement of the disconnect indication. What type of anomalous behavior can this create in user-level applications? How would you fix it?

12.2 The TPI defines precedence rules for enqueueing input primitives as well as output primitives. Output-primitive precedence processing was illustrated in stpuwput. Modify the transport provider to honor the precedence rules for input primitives.

12.3 What strategy can you design to prevent one flow-controlled upper read queue from affecting the delivery of messages to other endpoints, as discussed in the description of lines 1299 to 1305 of the example?

12.4 What modifications would be necessary for the example transport provider to be able to be used over two different network devices at the same time? What kinds of problems do you run into? Is a network layer really necessary?

Bibliographic Notes

The TPI specification is available from Unix International. (UI also publishes the NPI.) The TPI is also documented in *STREAMS Modules and Drivers* [USL 1992a].

Bellovin [1988] introduces the session TTY. Holzmann [1991] discusses protocol design and validation. Israel [1988] discusses aspects of how several communication protocols are implemented in the STREAMS framework.

Part 4
Design Project

13

Design Project:
Implementing SLIP

This chapter presents the design of a software package for UNIX SVR4 that enables IP datagrams to be transmitted over serial communication lines. Many of the facilities discussed in previous chapters are used here, including mounted streams, polling, nonblocking I/O, file descriptor passing, the Data Link Provider Interface (DLPI), STREAMS modules, and multiplexing.

13.1 INTRODUCTION TO SLIP

SLIP, serial line IP, is a de facto standard protocol that defines how IP packets are framed to allow their transmission over point-to-point serial connections. SLIP provides a cost-effective way to gain access to the Internet, so it has become very popular. The SLIP protocol is defined in RFC 1055.

The protocol is very simple. It defines two special characters, END and ESC. END is octal 300 and ESC is octal 333 (not the ASCII ESC character). At the end of each packet, the END character is transmitted. Each byte in the packet is inspected before transmission. If a data byte equals END, it is replaced with the two-byte sequence ESC 334 (octal). If a data byte equals ESC, it is replaced by the two-byte sequence ESC 335 (octal).

Some implementations also begin each packet with the END character as well. This frames (delimits) an invalid IP packet containing any bytes generated because of line noise. IP will discard these packets. If no line noise is present, a zero-length packet is generated, and either IP or SLIP will discard it.

Although many TCP/IP implementations also include support for SLIP, the standard TCP/IP software available with SVR4 does not. Several operating system vendors, however, are adding it themselves, and public-domain implementations are available.

SLIP has no provisions for addressing, so each side of a connection must know the other's IP address. Also, SLIP provides no error detection or correction, so line noise can corrupt packets, although these errors should be caught with the IP header checksum and the TCP and UDP packet checksums.

Since SLIP is just a simple framing protocol, it can only be used to support one network layer protocol at a time. It cannot be used, for example, to allow both IP and ISO network layer packets to be transmitted simultaneously over the same serial line.

To improve the performance of TCP/IP over serial lines, RFC 1144 describes how to compress TCP and IP headers. Of course, both ends of the connection must be running the same version of SLIP to allow header compression to be used.

Another protocol that enables IP datagrams to be transmitted over serial lines is PPP (point-to-point protocol). It was developed to compensate for the deficiencies found in SLIP. For example, PPP can transmit data from several different network layer protocols at the same time. PPP is described in RFCs 1171 and 1172. Because SLIP has existed longer and is simpler, it is more widely available than PPP.

13.2 SOFTWARE ARCHITECTURE

Since we want to use the existing Internet protocol implementation found in SVR4, the SLIP component will have to be implemented either as a STREAMS module or as a STREAMS multiplexing driver. Ultimately, the serial line must be linked under the IP multiplexor. IP expects the lower stream to support the Data Link Provider Interface (DLPI). The SLIP component will have to translate messages between the DLPI and the terminal interface (see Figure 13.1).

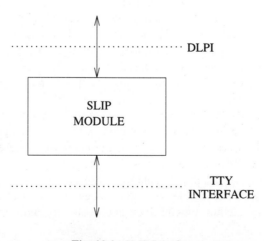

Fig. 13.1. SLIP Interfaces

Implementing SLIP as a multiplexing driver does not take advantage of the ability to multiplex messages. A SLIP connection is point-to-point, so each terminal driver acts as a separate "network" interface. If SLIP were implemented as a multiplexing driver, then a separate SLIP stream would have to be linked under IP for every serial connection. In this case, the multiplexor would route messages on a one-to-one basis between streams linked under IP and streams linked under the SLIP multiplexor. Additionally, multiplexing drivers are more complex than modules, so we will elect to implement SLIP as a STREAMS module.

Figure 13.2 shows the structure of a portion of the Internet protocol stack with SLIP included. APP is a module that works with ARP to handle address resolution between IP and the network driver. APP is not needed between IP and SLIP because SLIP connections are point-to-point and do not support addressing. Address resolution is implicit by IP's selection of the stream connected to the serial line.

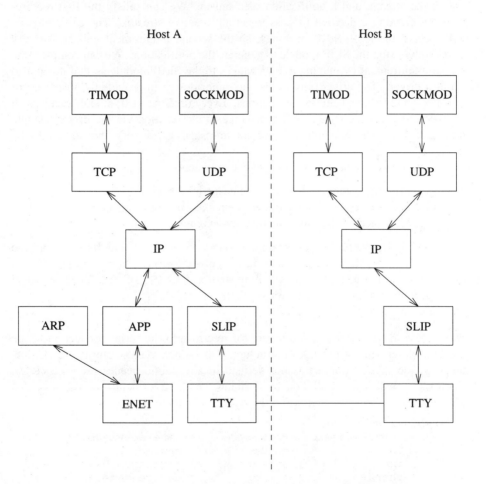

Fig. 13.2. SLIP in the Internet Protocol Stack

In addition to the kernel-level SLIP module, we need a user-level command to make the connection to the remote host, push the SLIP module, and link the stream under the IP multiplexor. A command to break the connection would be useful, too. One more component is needed, however.

Consider what happens when one end of the connection goes away. The other end's serial line driver will sense the loss of carrier and will send an M_HANGUP message upstream. From this point on, the stream cannot be used to send data, nor can it be used to receive any more data from the device. Since the stream is linked under the IP multiplexor, no process will receive notification of the hangup. Even if we could be notified of the hangup event, there is no active process to receive it.

We need two components: a process to receive the hangup notification and unlink the stream, and a notification mechanism. We can satisfy the first requirement by creating a daemon process to unlink inactive streams. The SLIP module will receive the M_HANGUP message, so the second requirement will be partially satisfied by using the SLIP module to generate the notification. We can complete the second requirement by making a few changes to the SLIP module so that it can also act as a driver. The driver only needs one minor device to provide the interface for the daemon to receive hangup notifications. Every time the SLIP module receives an M_HANGUP message, it can send a message to the daemon via the driver's single minor device. The daemon can use the message to identify the stream to be unlinked.

In summary, we have three user-level components:

1. slconnect, a command used to create a connection
2. sldisconnect, a command used to break an existing connection
3. slipd, a daemon used to clean up after hangups

To simplify the process of creating a connection to the remote host, we can use the uucp routine, dial(3C), found in the network services library (libnsl), to make a connection using the uucp administration files (Systems, Dialers, and Devices, etc.) found in /etc/uucp.

```
int dial(CALL call);
```

On success, dial returns a file descriptor referring to the serial connection to the machine described by the CALL structure. On failure, dial returns −1. Unfortunately, the CALL structure is not defined in any public header file in SVR4.0. (SVR4.2 remedies this omission by defining the CALL structure in <dial.h>.) The structure is, however, defined in the dial(3C) manual page as:

```
typedef struct {
     struct termio   *attr;      /* line settings */
     int             baud;       /* unused */
     int             speed;      /* requested baud rate */
     char            *line;      /* device name */
     char            *telno;     /* phone # or */
                                 /* system name */
     int             modem;      /* unused */
     char            *device;    /* unused */
     int             dev_len;    /* unused */
} CALL;
```

The `baud`, `modem`, `device`, and `dev_len` fields are no longer used. The `attr` field can be set to the address of a `termio` structure to have `dial` set the transmission characteristics of the serial communications line. If `attr` is set to `NULL`, the default line characteristics are used.

The `speed` field can be set to the numeric value of the baud rate at which communication should take place. It can also be set to 0 or any negative number to indicate that any speed can be used. In this case the speed is determined by the `uucp` administration files and the modem default values.

The `line` field can be set to the name of a specific device to use for the communication. It can be set to either the full pathname of the device under `/dev` (i.e., `/dev/tty01`), or simply the filename of the device (i.e., `tty01`).

The `telno` field should be set to either the name of the system to be contacted, in which case the entry is taken from the `Systems` file, or a string representing the phone number to be dialed. In our case, we will always use a system name.

Note that in SVR4.2, the implementation of `dial` has changed to interact with the connection server. Nonetheless, compatibility has been maintained with applications using the interface as described. Besides connecting to the specified machine, `dial` also creates a lock file to indicate that the device is in use. To close the file descriptor and remove the lock file, an application can call `undial(3C)`:

```
void undial(int fd);
```

`fd` is the file descriptor returned by `dial`.

We have two choices in designing the process of creating a connection. Either the `slconnect` command can call `dial`, or the `slconnect` command can send a request to `slipd` to make the call on its behalf. An unfortunate side effect of the design of `dial` will force us to choose the former alternative.

`dial` installs a signal handler for `SIGALRM` and calls `alarm(2)` to schedule the handler to run every so often to touch the lock file so that the `uucp` `cron` jobs do not mistakenly think the lock file is no longer in use and thus delete it. The SLIP daemon will also have to use `alarm` and `SIGALRM` to avoid blocking indefinitely during some system calls. To avoid having to reset the proper handler after each call to `dial`, we will choose to connect to the remote host in `slconnect`. Then we will pass the file descriptor for our end of the connection to the SLIP daemon and let the SLIP daemon link the file descriptor under IP.

As it turns out, as long as the stream for the serial device is linked under a multiplexor, the serial device is effectively inaccessible to user-level processes. Thus, the lock file really is not needed. This is convenient because it allows us to design `slconnect` to exit instead of hanging around for the lifetime of the connection.

To access the `uucp` data files when calling `dial`, `slconnect` will have to be owned by `uucp` and have its set-user-ID bit enabled. This is the one drawback to performing connection establishment in `slconnect` instead of `slipd`.

While allowing applications to use the `uucp` database files to connect to remote machines is useful, the networking libraries are deficient in that they do not provide access to the *chat scripts* found in the `Systems` file. The chat scripts describe the communication between the local and remote hosts that must occur in order to log in and execute a service. `uucp` works by using special login names that cause `uucp` programs to be run instead of a shell after logging in to the computer. A typical `uucp` entry in `/etc/passwd` might look like

```
nuucp:x:10:10:uucp:/var/spool/uucppublic:/usr/lib/uucp/uucico
```

It specifies that anyone trying to log in as user `nuucp` will execute `/usr/lib/uucp/uucico` instead of a shell. See `passwd(4)` for more information about the format of the password file.

We will require each server machine to add an entry to `/etc/passwd` for the SLIP service, as follows:

```
slip:x:10:10:slip setup:/:/usr/local/bin/slconnect
```

Of course, a corresponding entry needs to be made to `/etc/shadow` and a password selected for the `slip` login.

Since we cannot use the chat scripts from the `uucp Systems` file, we will have to implement our own. For this, we will create a new database file, `/etc/slipsys`. In addition, we will use it to specify the local and remote IP addresses for each connection.

White space in the file is ignored. Lines that begin with a pound sign (#) are treated as comments and are also ignored. Each entry in the file contains four fields: the local IP address, the foreign host name, the foreign IP address, and the chat script. A sample file containing one entry is shown below.

```
#
#  local       foreign    foreign      chat
#  address     host name  address      script
#
192.102.88.33 abc 192.102.88.200 "" \r\d in:--in: slip\sxyz word: fubar
```

The foreign host name is `abc` and the local host name is `xyz`. The password for the `slip` login is `fubar`.

The chat script defines the conversation between the local and remote systems in the following way. Expected input strings (called *expect strings*) are separated from resulting output strings (called *send strings*) by white space. The local process reads data until the expect string is received. Then the local process transmits the send string, usually followed by a carriage return. (The carriage return can be suppressed by terminating the string with the pattern `\c`.) This continues until the end of the chat script has been reached.

The expect strings only need to describe a portion of the desired input. For example, when expecting a password prompt, it is sufficient to use `word:` for the expect string. This increases the flexibility of the script because it will match `Password:`, `password:`, `Enter password:`, and any other string ending in `word:`.

An expect string can optionally contain a subsend–subexpect pair of strings. If a `read` times out, the subsend string will be transmitted and the subexpect string will become the new expect string. If this string is not received, then the conversation has failed. The subsend and subexpect strings are separated by dashes. The string `in:--in:` means expect the string `in:`, but if it is not received, transmit nothing except a carriage return, and expect `in:` again.

There are several special character sequences that can be used in the chat script to describe the expect and send strings. They are described in Table 13.1. Our implementation of chat scripts is close to that used by `uucp`, but does not match it exactly. One difference is that the `uucp` chat scripts support several other special character strings.

First we will study the user-level components of the SLIP communication software. Then we will study the kernel-level components.

Table 13.1. Special Chat Script Strings

String	Description
`" "`	Expect the null string.
`\b`	Backspace.
`\c`	Do not send a carriage return after the string.
`\d`	Delay for one second.
`\K`	Insert a break.
`\n`	Send a newline.
`\N`	Send a NULL.
`\p`	Pause for less than one second.
`\r`	Send a carriage return.
`\s`	Send a space.
`\t`	Send a tab.
`\\`	Send a \.
`\ooo`	Send the ASCII character whose value is the octal number ooo.

13.3 USER-LEVEL COMPONENTS

Before we look at the three user-level commands, we will cover the common header file and the common routines used by the commands.

Header File

The header file used by the user-level SLIP commands is called `slipcmd.h`.

```
 1 #ifndef _SLIPCMD_H
 2 #define _SLIPCMD_H

 3 #define SLIPDEV        "/dev/slip"
 4 #define SLIPSYS        "/etc/slipsys"
 5 #define PIPEPATH       "/var/.slipipe"
 6 #define RW_USER        (S_IRUSR|S_IWUSR)
 7 #define RW_GROUP       (S_IRGRP|S_IWGRP)
 8 #define RW_OTHER       (S_IROTH|S_IWOTH)
 9 #define PIPEMODE       (RW_USER|RW_GROUP|RW_OTHER)
10 #define IFCONFIGPATH  "/usr/sbin/ifconfig"
11 #define IFCONFIG       "ifconfig"

12 /*
13  * Structure used to communicate with slip daemon.
14  */
15 struct slcommand {
16    int     opcode;
17    char    arg[MAXHOSTNAMELEN];
18 };

19 /*
20  * Opcodes.
21  */
22 #define CONNECT       1    /* create a connection */
23 #define DISCONNECT    2    /* break a connection */
```

[1–11]   SLIPDEV defines the pathname of the administrative device for the SLIP
         driver. SLIPSYS is the pathname of the SLIP database file. PIPEPATH
         is the pathname of the mounted pipe used by the SLIP daemon.
         PIPEMODE defines the permissions of the mounted pipe.
         IFCONFIGPATH and IFCONFIG define the pathname and filename,
         respectively, of the command used to configure Internet network interfaces
         [see ifconfig(1M)].

[12–23] The slcommand structure defines the format of messages sent to the
         SLIP daemon from user-level commands. The first field identifies the type
         of request. The second field is a buffer used for whatever arguments the
         operation might require. The buffer usually contains a host name.

         Only two operations are currently defined, CONNECT, and DISCONNECT.
         The first is used during connection establishment, and the second is used
         during connection release.

```
24 /*
25  * Structure that represents a line in /etc/slipsys.
26  */
27 struct conninfo {
28    char     *laddr;          /* local IP address */
29    char     *fhost;          /* foreign host name */
30    char     *faddr;          /* foreiqn IP address */
31    char     *chatscript;     /* chat script used to log in */
32 };

33 extern void error(const char *, ...); /* from Chapter 2 */
34 extern void fatal(const char *, ...); /* from Chapter 2 */
35 extern int initlog(const char *);     /* from Chapter 2 */
36 extern void log(const char *, ...);   /* from Chapter 2 */
37 extern void daemonize(const char *);  /* from Chapter 2 */
38 extern struct conninfo *getcinfo(char *);
39 extern void freecinfo(struct conninfo *);

40 #endif /* _SLIPCMD_H */
```

[24–32] The `conninfo` structure is used to represent the contents of entries from
          `/etc/slipsys`. It contains four fields: the local IP address, the foreign
          (remote) host name, the foreign IP address, and the chat script.

[33–40] Many of the functions used by the commands were presented in Chapter 2.
          Two new ones are defined: one to create a `conninfo` structure, and one
          to free a `conninfo` structure. (`error` and `fatal` are from Example
          2.4.5. `initlog` is from Example 2.4.8, and `log` is from Example 2.4.9.
          `daemonize` is from Example 2.4.16.)

Common Routines

Now we will look at the two functions (`getcinfo` and `freecinfo`) used by the
user-level commands to access the SLIP database file, `/etc/slipsys`.

```
 1 #include <sys/types.h>
 2 #include <string.h>
 3 #include <stdio.h>
 4 #include <stdlib.h>
 5 #include <errno.h>
 6 #include <netdb.h>
 7 #include <ctype.h>
 8 #include <slipcmd.h>

 9 #define BUFSZ 1024

10 static char buf[BUFSZ];

11 struct conninfo *
12 getcinfo(char *host)
13 {
14    struct conninfo *cip;
15    int found, idx, start;
16    FILE *fp;
17    char name[MAXHOSTNAMELEN];

18    cip = calloc(1, sizeof(struct conninfo));
19    if (cip == NULL)
20        return(NULL);
21    fp = fopen(SLIPSYS, "r");
22    if (fp == NULL)
23        goto err;
24    found = 0;
25    while (fgets(buf, sizeof(buf), fp) != NULL) {
26        buf[strlen(buf)-1] = '\0'; /* get rid of newline */
27        if ((strlen(buf) == 0) || (buf[0] == '#'))
28            continue;
```

[1–17]   The getcinfo routine is called to return information from /etc/slipsys about the given host. The length of the host name is limited by MAXHOSTNAMELEN, defined in <netdb.h>.

[18–23] If we cannot allocate enough memory for a conninfo structure, we return NULL. Otherwise, we open /etc/slipsys for reading. If fopen fails, we jump to err, where we clean up and return NULL.

[24–28] We initialize found to 0, indicating that we have not found an entry for the given host name. Then we read one line at a time from the database file until we find an entry for the host or we reach the end of the file. For each entry, we remove the newline at the end of the string. We ignore blank lines and comment lines.

```
29          if (sscanf(buf, "%*s %s", name) != 1)
30              continue;
31          if (strcmp(name, host) == 0) {
32              found = 1;
33              break;
34          }
35      }
36  if (found) {
37      idx = 0;
38      while (isspace(buf[idx]))
39          idx++;
40      start = idx;
41      while (isdigit(buf[idx]) || (buf[idx] == '.'))
42          idx++;
43      buf[idx++] = '\0';
44      cip->laddr = strdup(&buf[start]);
45      if (cip->laddr == NULL)
46          goto err;
47      cip->fhost = strdup(name);
48      if (cip->fhost == NULL)
49          goto err;
50      while (isspace(buf[idx]))
51          idx++;
52      idx += strlen(name);
53      while (isspace(buf[idx]))
54          idx++;
```

[29–35] When we come across a nonempty, noncomment line, we call `sscanf` to copy the host name field to the character array, `name`. The host name is the second field in the database file. (The pattern `%*s` specifies that `sscanf` should parse the first string, but avoid copying it anywhere.) If the name matches the one passed to the function, we set `found` to 1 and break out of the loop.

[36–46] After the loop completes, if `found` is nonzero, then we have found an entry for the requested host. We skip any leading white space and set `start` to the first character in the local address field. Then we increment `idx` until we reach the first character after the address. Since this will be a white-space character, we can set it to 0 without any problems. This allows us to use `strdup` to make a copy of the string representing the local address. If `strdup` fails because it cannot allocate enough memory, we jump to `err`.

[47–54] The next field is the host name. Since we already know what it is, we call `strdup` using the name passed to `getcinfo` and then skip over the white space between the address and the name. We also skip over the name and any white space following it.

```
55          if (buf[idx] == '\0')
56              goto err;
57          start = idx;
58          while (isdigit(buf[idx]) || (buf[idx] == '.'))
59              idx++;
60          if (buf[idx] == '\0')
61              goto err;
62          buf[idx++] = '\0';
63          cip->faddr = strdup(&buf[start]);
64          if (cip->faddr == NULL)
65              goto err;
66          while (isspace(buf[idx]))
67              idx++;
68          if (buf[idx] == '\0')
69              goto err;
70          cip->chatscript = strdup(&buf[idx]);
71          if (cip->chatscript == NULL)
72              goto err;
73          fclose(fp);
74          return(cip);
75      } else {
76          errno = EINVAL;
77      }
78  err:
79      if (fp != NULL)
80          fclose(fp);
81      if (cip != NULL)
82          freecinfo(cip);
83      return(NULL);
84  }
```

[55–74] If we have reached the end of the string, we go to err. Otherwise, we save the index of the first character of the foreign address in start. Then we find the first character after the end of the address. If it is a NULL byte, we jump to err. A properly formed entry will contain white space here, so we terminate the foreign address with a NULL byte and duplicate the string with strdup. Then we skip any white space that follows and if we have not reached the end of the string, we duplicate the chat script string. Finally, we close the file and return the address of the conninfo structure we just constructed.

[75–77] If we were not able to find the given host name in the database file, we set errno to EINVAL to indicate that the argument was invalid.

[78–84] If we encounter an error, we jump to err, where we close the file if it is open and free any memory associated with the conninfo structure. Then we return NULL to indicate failure.

```
85 void
86 freecinfo(struct conninfo *cip)
87 {
88   if (cip->laddr != NULL)
89       free(cip->laddr);
90   if (cip->fhost != NULL)
91       free(cip->fhost);
92   if (cip->faddr != NULL)
93       free(cip->faddr);
94   if (cip->chatscript != NULL)
95       free(cip->chatscript);
96   free(cip);
97 }
```

[85–97] freecinfo is called to free the memory associated with a conninfo
         structure. For each non-NULL field, we free the memory to which the field
         points. Then we free the memory that was used for the conninfo struc-
         ture itself.

slconnect

slconnect is the command used to create a connection. On the client machine, a
user invokes it to connect to the server machine. On the server machine,
slconnect is run as a replacement shell for the slip login name. In this mode it
will not attempt to make a connection, since one already exists. It merely sends the
connect command and file descriptor for the serial line to the SLIP daemon to initialize the network interface.

On the client side, a user would invoke slconnect with a single
argument: the host name of the remote machine. On the server side, slconnect is
invoked without any arguments. It identifies the name of the host making the connection through the environment. The client host name is stored in the environment
variable named L0.

To set the environment variable, we use a feature of the login command [see
login(1)]. When we send the login name slip to the remote computer, we
append a space followed by the client host name. login will take the additional
parameter and place it in the environment variable L0. Multiple shell variables can
be set this way, each one named Ln, where n is an integer that starts at 0 and is incremented by 1 for each parameter specified.

Different implementations of SLIP require that the connection be set up in different ways. For example, one might require the user to set up the connection by
using cu(1) and executing a special command on the remote machine, then returning to the local computer and executing a similar command to complete the connection. The chat script functionality built into slconnect should allow this version
of SLIP software to work with other implementations.

```
 1 #include <sys/types.h>
 2 #include <stdlib.h>
 3 #include <unistd.h>
 4 #include <stdio.h>
 5 #include <string.h>
 6 #include <errno.h>
 7 #include <stropts.h>
 8 #include <termios.h>
 9 #include <netdb.h>
10 #include <signal.h>
11 #include <fcntl.h>
12 #include <poll.h>
13 #include <ctype.h>
14 #include <slipcmd.h>

15 #define CHATBUFSZ     4096

16 #define isoctal(X)     (isdigit(X) && ((X) < '8'))
17 #define tooctal(N, X) (((N) * 8) + ((X) - '0'))

18 typedef struct {
19    struct termio    *attr;        /* terminal line settings */
20    int              baud;         /* unused */
21    int              speed;        /* -1 or 0 for any speed */
22    char             *line;        /* device name */
23    char             *telno;       /* phone # or system name */
24    int              modem;        /* unused */
25    char             *device;      /* unused */
26    int              dev_len;      /* unused */
27 } CALL;
```

[1–17] CHATBUFSZ is the size of the buffer used when processing the chat script. isoctal is a macro that identifies whether or not a character represents an octal digit. tooctal is a macro that is used to convert an ASCII character representing an octal digit to an integer, which is then added to a variable containing the numeric value of the preceding portion of the octal string. Note that macros like isoctal have to be used carefully because the argument is evaluated twice in the expression, which can lead to undesired side effects.

[18–27] We have to define the CALL structure here because it is not defined in any public header file in SVR4.0. As stated earlier, the CALL structure is defined in <dial.h> in SVR4.2.

```
28 /* dial error codes */
29 #define INTRPT    -1   /* interrupted */
30 #define D_HUNG    -2   /* dialer hung */
31 #define NO_ANS    -3   /* no answer */
32 #define ILL_BD    -4   /* illegal baud rate */
33 #define A_PROB    -5   /* device open failed */
34 #define L_PROB    -6   /* device open failed */
35 #define NO_Ldv    -7   /* can't open Devices file */
36 #define DV_NT_A   -8   /* device unavailable */
37 #define DV_NT_K   -9   /* device unknown */
38 #define NO_BD_A  -10   /* baud rate for device unavailable */
39 #define NO_BD_K  -11   /* baud rate for device unknown */
40 #define DV_NT_E  -12   /* speed doesn't match */
41 #define BAD_SYS  -13   /* unknown system name */
42 #define CS_PROB  -14   /* connection server error */

43 static char *cmd;

44 extern int dial(CALL);
45 extern void undial(int);

46 static void dialerr(int);
47 static void timeout(int);
48 static void cleanup(int);
49 static void nop(int);
50 static int chat(int, char *);
51 static int parse(char **, char **, char **, char **,
52    char **);
53 static int doexpect(int, const char *);
54 static int dosend(int, const char *);
```

[28–42] Like the CALL structure, the return values from dial are also defined in
         <dial.h> in SVR4.2, but since this header file is missing in SVR4.0, we
         define the return values as described in the manual page for dial. The
         CS_PROB error code is only returned in SVR4.2. It indicates an inability
         to communicate with the connection server.

[43–45] cmd is a global variable we will use to point to the basename of the path-
         name used to invoke slconnect. The dial and undial functions are
         in libnsl. We declare their function prototypes here because of the lack
         of a public header file that describes them.

[46–54] The function prototypes for slconnect's procedures are declared next.

```
55 void
56 main(int argc, char *argv[])
57 {
58   int fd, pfd, n, err, server;
59   CALL call;
60   char *otherhost;
61   struct termios t;
62   struct conninfo *cip;
63   struct slcommand slcmd;
64   struct sigaction sa;

65   cmd = strrchr(argv[0], '/');
66   if (cmd == NULL)
67       cmd = argv[0];
68   else
69       cmd++;
70   err = server = 0;
71   if (argc == 1) {
72       server = 1;
73   } else if (argc != 2) {
74       fprintf(stderr, "usage: %s [system]\n", cmd);
75       exit(1);
76   }
77   if (server != 0) {
78       otherhost = getenv("L0");
79       if (otherhost == NULL)
80           exit(1);
81       close(1);
82       close(2);
83       if ((open("/dev/null", O_WRONLY) != 1) ||
84         (dup(1) != 2))
85           exit(1);
```

[55–69]   We use strrchr to find the last occurrence of / in the first argument. If none exists, we set cmd to point to argv[0]. Otherwise, we set it to the character after the slash. This gives us the last component of the pathname used to invoke the command.

[70–76]   We set server to 0, assuming slconnect is being invoked from a client machine. If only one command-line argument is supplied, we set server to 1 since the command will be acting as a server. If more than two arguments are supplied, we print a usage statement and exit.

[77–85]   If the command is invoked as a server, we call getenv(3C) to obtain the value of the L0 environment variable. If L0 is not set, getenv will return NULL, and we simply exit. Otherwise, since the command is being executed as a server, we close the file descriptors for the standard output and the standard error, and reopen them to /dev/null. This will cause any output the program might generate to be discarded silently.

```
86   } else {
87       otherhost = argv[1];
88   }

89   /*
90    * Get the information from /etc/slipsys.
91    */
92   cip = getcinfo(otherhost);
93   if (cip == NULL)
94       fatal("%s: can't get system information", cmd);

95   sigemptyset(&sa.sa_mask);
96   sa.sa_flags = 0;
97   if (server == 0) {
98       /*
99        * Create a connection to the remote host.
100       */
101      sa.sa_handler = cleanup;
102      sigaction(SIGINT, &sa, NULL);
103      sigaction(SIGQUIT, &sa, NULL);
104      sigaction(SIGTERM, &sa, NULL);
105      call.telno = otherhost;
106      call.attr = NULL;
107      call.speed = 0;
108      call.line = NULL;
109      fd = dial(call);
110      if (fd < 0) {
111          dialerr(fd);
112          exit(1);
113      }
```

[86–88]   If the command is running as a client, we set `otherhost` to the host name specified on the command line instead of getting it from the environment.

[89–94]   We call `getcinfo` to get the connection information for the specified host from `/etc/slipsys`. If the information cannot be obtained, we print an error message and exit.

[95–113]   If the command is acting as a client, then we catch the signals that typically are used to interrupt the execution of a program, so that we can remove the `uucp` lock file if we are interrupted unexpectedly. We initialize the CALL structure so that `dial` will attempt to use the Systems entries for the given host. All other values are derived from the `uucp` database files. We then call `dial` to connect to the remote host. If `dial` fails, we call `dialerr` to print the appropriate error message and then we exit.

```
114   } else {
115        fd = 0;
116   }

117   /*
118    * Set the line characteristics.
119    */
120   tcgetattr(fd, &t);
121   t.c_cflag &= ~(CSIZE|PARENB|PARODD|CLOCAL|CSTOPB);
122   t.c_cflag |= CREAD|HUPCL|CS8;
123   t.c_lflag &= ~ECHO;
124   tcsetattr(fd, TCSANOW, &t);

125   if (server == 0) {
126        /*
127         * Complete connection protocol with remote host.
128         */
129        if (chat(fd, cip->chatscript) < 0) {
130             undial(fd);
131             fatal("%s: chat failed", cmd);
132        }
133   }

134   /*
135    * Get rid of unnecessary modules.
136    */
137   n = ioctl(fd, I_LIST, NULL);
```

[114–116] If `slconnect` is invoked from the server machine, we set `fd` to 0, the
file descriptor that will be passed to the SLIP daemon to be linked under
the IP multiplexor.

[117–124] Regardless of how the command is used, we want to make sure that the
transmission characteristics are correct. We get the current line settings,
force the character size to 8 bits, disable parity, enable the receiver, and
make sure that a hangup message will be generated when the carrier is
dropped. We also disable echoing so that the line discipline does not
copy the input and send it back to the other host.

[125–133] If the command is running as a client, we call `chat` to log in and execute `slconnect` on the remote host. If `chat` fails, we call `undial`
to close the file descriptor and remove the lock file. Then we print an
error message and exit.

[134–137] The next step is to remove all of the modules from the stream. The
`I_LIST` `ioctl` command with a `NULL` argument will return the
number of modules on the given stream, plus 1 for the driver.

```
138    while (n > 1) {
139        ioctl(fd, I_POP, 0);
140        n--;
141    }

142    /*
143     * Prevent the driver from doing more than we want it to.
144     */
145    t.c_lflag = 0;
146    t.c_iflag = 0;
147    t.c_oflag = 0;
148    tcsetattr(fd, TCSANOW, &t);

149    /*
150     * Now send the request to the slip daemon.
151     */
152    slcmd.opcode = CONNECT;
153    strcpy(slcmd.arg, otherhost);
154    pfd = open(PIPEPATH, O_RDWR);
155    if (pfd < 0) {
156        if (server == 0)
157            undial(fd);
158        fatal("%s: can't open pipe to slip daemon", cmd);
159    }
160    n = write(pfd, &slcmd, sizeof(struct slcommand));
161    if (n != sizeof(struct slcommand)) {
162        if (server == 0)
163            undial(fd);
164        if (n < 0)
165            fatal("%s: can't write to slipd pipe", cmd);
166        else
167            fatal("%s: short write to slipd pipe", cmd);
168    }
```

[138–141] We use the I_POP ioctl command to remove each module from the
stream. Since the stream is attached to a serial line driver, usually at
least LDTERM will be present.

[142–148] Next we disable any input or output processing that the serial line driver
might perform on the characters received and transmitted. This prevents
the driver from attempting to interpret special characters, for example.

[149–168] We create a CONNECT message for the SLIP daemon and open the
daemon's mounted pipe. If the open fails and we are a client, we call
undial to remove the lock file. Regardless of whether we are acting as
a client or a server, we call fatal to print an error message and exit. If
the open succeeds, we write the CONNECT message to the daemon. If
the entire message is not written, or if an error occurred, we call
undial if we are a client. Then we print an error message and exit.

```
169  if (ioctl(pfd, I_SENDFD, fd) < 0) {
170      if (server == 0)
171          undial(fd);
172      fatal("%s: can't send fd to slip daemon", cmd);
173  }

174  sa.sa_handler = timeout;
175  sigaction(SIGALRM, &sa, NULL);
176  alarm(30);
177  n = read(pfd, &err, sizeof(int));
178  alarm(0);

179  if (server == 0)
180      undial(fd); /* remove uucp lock file */
181  if (n != sizeof(int)) {
182      if (n < 0)
183          fatal("%s: can't read from slipd pipe", cmd);
184      else
185          fatal("%s: short read from slipd pipe", cmd);
186  }
187  if (err == 0)
188      printf("connection established\n");
189  else
190      fatal("%s: no connection: %s", cmd, strerror(err));
191  exit(0);
192  }
```

[169–173] We use the `I_SENDFD` `ioctl` command to send the file descriptor
connected to the other machine to the SLIP daemon. If this fails, we
clean up as before and exit.

[174–178] Once the request has been sent to the daemon, we install a signal handler
for `SIGALRM` and call `alarm` to schedule `SIGALRM` to be sent to the
process after 30 seconds have elapsed. This is necessary to prevent the
`read` from blocking indefinitely. We read the completion status of the
request and then cancel the alarm.

[179–192] If we were invoked as a client program, we call `undial` now to remove
the lock file. It does not matter that `undial` will close the file descriptor, because it will be held open as long as it is linked under the IP multiplexor. If `read` failed or did not read enough for an integer, we print
an error message and exit. The SLIP daemon sends an integer describing the request's success back over the pipe. The integer will be 0 on
success and an error number on failure. We print a message in either
case and exit.

```
193 static void
194 dialerr(int code)
195 {
196  switch (code) {
197  case INTRPT:
198      fprintf(stderr, "%s: call interrupted\n", cmd);
199      break;

200  case D_HUNG:
201      fprintf(stderr, "%s: call hung\n", cmd);
202      break;

203  case NO_ANS:
204      fprintf(stderr, "%s: no answer\n", cmd);
205      break;

206  case ILL_BD:
207      fprintf(stderr, "%s: invalid baud rate\n", cmd);
208      break;

209  case A_PROB:
210  case L_PROB:
211      fprintf(stderr, "%s: can't open device\n", cmd);
212      break;

213  case NO_Ldv:
214      fprintf(stderr, "%s: can't open uucp files\n", cmd);
215      break;

216  case DV_NT_A:
217      fprintf(stderr, "%s: device in use\n", cmd);
218      break;

219  case DV_NT_K:
220  case NO_BD_K:
221      fprintf(stderr, "%s: device not found\n", cmd);
222      break;

223  case NO_BD_A:
224      fprintf(stderr, "%s: no available devices\n", cmd);
225      break;

226  case DV_NT_E:
227      fprintf(stderr, "%s: unsupported speed\n", cmd);
228      break;
```

[193–228] `dialerr` is called to print an error message when `dial` fails. For each
value, we print the appropriate error message.

```
229  case BAD_SYS:
230      fprintf(stderr, "%s: unknown system\n", cmd);
231      break;

232  case CS_PROB:
233      fprintf(stderr, "%s: can't reach connection server\n",
234        cmd);
235      break;

236  default:
237      fprintf(stderr, "%s: dial error (%d)\n", cmd, code);
238  }
239 }

240 static void
241 timeout(int signo)
242 {
243  undial(-1);
244  fatal("%s: request timed out", cmd);
245 }

246 static void
247 cleanup(int signo)
248 {
249  undial(-1);
250  fatal("%s: interrupt (signal %d)", cmd, signo);
251 }
```

[229–239] Recall that CS_PROB applies only to the SVR4.2 version of dial. If dial returns an undocumented error code, we can do nothing but print a less informative error message.

[240–245] timeout is the signal handler that is called when an alarm fires. In this case, we call undial to remove the lock file, passing it −1 for the file descriptor. This will prevent undial from closing the file descriptor, but will not impede its ability to remove the lock file. undial just removes all lock files created by the process. Then we print an error message and exit. When we exit, the file descriptor will be closed automatically.

[246–251] cleanup is the signal handler called when the process is interrupted, probably by the user hitting the interrupt or quit key. Like timeout, it calls undial with an invalid file descriptor, prints an error message, and exits. We only bother to clean up if we are interrupted by signals we expect to receive. Any unexpected signals that terminate the program will leave the lock file around. We could try to clean up after any signal, but some signals, such as SIGKILL, cannot be caught, so it does not make sense to try.

```
252 static int
253 chat(int fd, char *script)
254 {
255   char *expectstr, *sendstr, *subexpectstr, *subsendstr;
256   struct sigaction sa;

257   sigemptyset(&sa.sa_mask);
258   sa.sa_handler = nop;
259   sa.sa_flags = 0;
260   sigaction(SIGALRM, &sa, NULL);
261   while (parse(&script, &expectstr, &sendstr, &subexpectstr,
262     &subsendstr)) {
263       if (doexpect(fd, expectstr)) {
264           if (dosend(fd, sendstr) < 0)
265               return(-1);
266       } else if (subexpectstr) {
267           if (dosend(fd, subsendstr) < 0)
268               return(-1);
269           if (doexpect(fd, subexpectstr)) {
270               if (dosend(fd, sendstr) < 0)
271                   return(-1);
272           } else {
273               return(-1);
274           }
275       } else {
276           return(-1);
277       }
278   }
279   return(0);
280 }
```

[252–262] chat is called to communicate with another host according to a chat script. We start by catching SIGALRM. If we wait too long without matching the expected input, an alarm will fire and we will send the sub-send string, if present. We call parse repeatedly to break up the chat script into separate strings, until the entire script has been consumed.

[263–274] We call doexpect to wait for the expect string. If it arrives, we call dosend to transmit the send string. If this fails, we return failure (−1). If doexpect fails and a subsend string is present, we transmit it with dosend. If dosend fails, we return −1; otherwise, we use doexpect to wait for the subexpect string. If it arrives, we transmit the send string. If we do not receive the subexpect string, we return failure.

[275–280] If the expect string is not received and no subexpect string is provided, then we return failure. Each time we call parse, it updates the chat script pointer (script). As long as work remains, parse returns 1. When the entire chat script has been processed, parse returns 0. Then we return 0 to indicate that the conversation completed successfully.

```
281 static int
282 parse(char **chstrpp, char **expp, char **sndpp,
283  char **subexpp, char **subsndpp)
284 {
285  char *s, *p;
286  int first;

287  *subexpp = NULL;
288  *subsndpp = NULL;
289  *expp = NULL;
290  *sndpp = NULL;
291  s = *chstrpp;
292  while (isspace(*s))
293      s++;
294  if (*s == '\0')
295      return(0);   /* done */
296  *expp = s;
297  while ((*s != '\0') && !isspace(*s))
298      s++;
299  if (*s == '\0') {
300      *chstrpp = s;
301  } else {
302      *chstrpp = s + 1;
303      *s = '\0';
304  }
305  first = 1;
```

[281–290] parse is called to parse the chat script and return the next expect string, send string, subexpect string, and subsend string, if they exist. Initially we set all these string pointers to NULL so if we return prematurely, the caller can tell if a particular string was found by checking if its pointer is non-NULL.

[291–298] We start at the beginning of the chat script and ignore any leading white space. If we reach the end of the string, we return 0 to indicate that there is no more work to do. Otherwise s will point to the beginning of the next expect string in the chat script, so we set the expect string pointer in the argument list to point to it. Then we search for the end of the expect string.

[299–305] If we reach the end of the chat script, we update the chat script string pointer to refer to the end of the script. Otherwise, we set the chat script string pointer to the next character where the search will continue and convert the white-space character to a NULL byte, thus terminating the expect string.

```
306   for (p = *expp; *p != '\0'; p++) {
307       if (*p == '-') {
308           *p = '\0';
309           if (first) {
310               *subsndpp = p + 1;
311               first = 0;
312           } else {
313               *subexpp = p + 1;
314           }
315       }
316   }
317   if (*++s == '\0')
318       return(1);
319   *sndpp = s;
320   while ((*s != '\0') && !isspace(*s))
321       s++;
322   if (*s == '\0') {
323       *chstrpp = s;
324   } else {
325       *chstrpp = s + 1;
326       *s = '\0';
327   }
328   return(1);
329 }

330 static int
331 doexpect(int fd, const char *s)
332 {
333   int i, n, len;
334   char ebuf[CHATBUFSZ];
```

[306–316] Once we have found the expect string, we check if it contains a subsend–subexpect string pair. We step through the string until we reach the terminating NULL byte. If we find a dash, then we have reached a substring. The first substring is the subsend string and the second one is the subexpect string. We convert the dash to a NULL byte and save the substring address in the proper argument pointer.

[317–329] s was left at the terminating NULL byte of the expect string before we checked for the presence of substrings. We increment s and if we have reached the end of the chat script, we return 1 to indicate to the caller that we have found strings for it to process. Otherwise, the next string is the send string, so we store its address in the send string pointer argument. We finish by searching for the end of the send string, terminating it with a NULL byte if necessary, updating the chat script string pointer with the next location to start searching, and returning 1.

[330–334] doexpect is called to wait for either an expect string or a subexpect string.

```
335   len = strlen(s);
336   if (len == 0)     /* null string */
337       return(1);
338   if ((len == 2) && (s[0] == '"') &&
339     (s[1] == '"')) /* null string */
340       return(1);
341   errno = 0;
342   alarm(60);
343   n = 0;
344   for (i = 0; i < CHATBUFSZ; i++) {
345       if (read(fd, &ebuf[i], 1) != 1) {
346           alarm(0);
347           return(0);
348       }
349       if (i < (len-1))
350           continue;
351       if (strncmp(s, &ebuf[n], len) == 0) {
352           alarm(0);
353           return(1);
354       }
355       n++;
356       if (errno == EINTR)
357           return(0);
358   }
359   alarm(0);
360   return(0);
361 }
```

[335–342] If the length of the string is 0, then we return 1 to indicate that the string has been received. If the string is the alias for the empty string, as specified in Table 13.1, then we also return 1. Otherwise, we call alarm so that the read does not block indefinitely.

[343–355] We read one byte at a time into ebuf. If read does not return one byte, we cancel the alarm and return 0 to indicate that the expect string was not received. We continue to read one byte at a time until len bytes have been read. Once we have reached this point, we compare the received data with the expect string. If they match, we cancel the alarm and return 1. Otherwise, we increment the location in the receive buffer from which we should start the comparison in the next iteration of the loop.

[356–361] If errno gets set to EINTR by the signal handler, then the alarm went off while we were not blocking in the call to read, so we just return 0. If we read CHATBUFSZ bytes without a match, we cancel the alarm and return 0.

```
362 static int
363 dosend(int fd, const char *s)
364 {
365  int docr;
366  uchar_t n;

367  docr = 1;
368  while (*s != '\0') {
369      switch (*s) {
370      case '\\':
371          s++;
372          switch (*s) {
373          case 'b':   /* send a backspace */
374              if (write(fd, "\b", 1) != 1)
375                  return(-1);
376              break;

377          case 'c':   /* don't send a carriage return */
378              if (*(s + 1) == '\0')
379                  docr = 0;
380              break;

381          case 'd':   /* delay 1 second */
382              sleep(1);
383              break;

384          case 'K':   /* send a break */
385              tcsendbreak(fd, 0);
386              break;

387          case 'n':   /* send a newline */
388              if (write(fd, "\n", 1) != 1)
389                  return(-1);
390              break;
```

[362–390] dosend is called to transmit a send or subsend string. After the string is sent, a carriage return is usually transmitted, even if the string is empty. We set docr to 1 to indicate that we should transmit a carriage return. Then we check each character in the string for special characters. If we find a backslash, we check the next character. If it is a b, we transmit a backspace. If the next character is a c and is the last character in the string, we set docr to 0 to suppress the transmission of the carriage return. Otherwise, the c is just ignored. If the next character is a d, we sleep for one second and continue processing the string. If the next character is a K, we send a break by calling tcsendbreak [see termios(2)]. If the next character is an n, we transmit a newline.

```
391              case 'N':    /* send a null */
392                  if (write(fd, "\0", 1) != 1)
393                      return(-1);
394                  break;

395              case 'p':    /* pause for part of a second */
396                  poll(NULL, 0, 300); /* 300 ms */
397                  break;

398              case 'r':    /* send a carriage return */
399                  if (write(fd, "\r", 1) != 1)
400                      return(-1);
401                  break;

402              case 's':    /* send a space */
403                  if (write(fd, " ", 1) != 1)
404                      return(-1);
405                  break;

406              case 't':    /* send a tab */
407                  if (write(fd, "\t", 1) != 1)
408                      return(-1);
409                  break;

410              case '0':    /* send a byte */
411              case '1':    /* with the given */
412              case '2':    /* octal value */
413              case '3':
414                  if (isoctal(*(s+1)) && isoctal(*(s+2))) {
415                      n = tooctal(0, *s++);
416                      n = tooctal(n, *s++);
417                      n = tooctal(n, *s);
418                      if (write(fd, &n, 1) != 1)
419                          return(-1);
420                      break;
421                  }
422              /* else fall through */
```

[391-422] If the next character is an N, we send a NULL byte. If the next character
           is a p, we delay for 300 milliseconds. We use poll(2) as a high-
           resolution timer by specifying that there are no file descriptors to poll
           and setting the delay to the desired time. If the character is an r, we
           transmit a carriage return. If the character is an s, we send a space. If
           the character is a t, we send a tab. If the character is the first digit of a
           three-digit octal number, we calculate the number that the digits
           represent and transmit its value. Otherwise, we fall through to the
           default case.

```
423           default:     /* send the escaped character */
424               if (write(fd, s, 1) != 1)
425                   return(-1);
426           }
427           s++;
428           break;

429       default:     /* send the character */
430           if (write(fd, s, 1) != 1)
431               return(-1);
432           s++;
433       }
434   }
435   if (docr) {
436       if (write(fd, "\r", 1) != 1)
437           return(-1);
438   }
439   return(0);
440 }

441 static void
442 nop(int signo)
443 {
444   errno = EINTR;
445 }
```

[423–428] In the default case, any other character that follows the backslash is transmitted as is. Then we increment the pointer to the next character to transmit.

[429–440] If the original character we found was not a backslash, then we transmit the character and increment the pointer. Whenever we try to transmit a character and `write` fails, we return failure (−1) to the caller. When we have reached the end of the string, if we need to transmit a carriage return, we do so. Then we return success (0).

[441–445] nop is the signal handler for SIGALRM used during doexpect. It sets errno to EINTR so that doexpect can tell that the time for waiting for the expected string has expired. Because the alarm can go off while doexpect is not blocked in read, we have to resort to setting a global variable and having doexpect check its status on each iteration of its main loop. Another alternative would be to use sigsetjmp in doexpect, and then call siglongjmp from the signal handler.

sldisconnect

sldisconnect is the command used to break an existing connection. It takes a
single argument: the name of the host to which a connection exists. It does some of
the same things that slconnect does, but is much simpler. sldisconnect only
has to send a request to the SLIP daemon to unconfigure the interface and unlink the
stream associated with the connection.

```
 1 #include <sys/types.h>
 2 #include <stdlib.h>
 3 #include <unistd.h>
 4 #include <stdio.h>
 5 #include <string.h>
 6 #include <errno.h>
 7 #include <netdb.h>
 8 #include <signal.h>
 9 #include <fcntl.h>
10 #include <slipcmd.h>

11 static char *cmd;

12 static void timeout(int);

13 void
14 main(int argc, char *argv[])
15 {
16    int pfd, n, err;
17    struct conninfo *cip;
18    struct slcommand slcmd;
19    struct sigaction sa;

20    cmd = strrchr(argv[0], '/');
21    if (cmd == NULL)
22        cmd = argv[0];
23    else
24        cmd++;
25    if (argc != 2) {
26        fprintf(stderr, "usage: %s system\n", cmd);
27        exit(1);
28    }
```

[1–12]   As in slconnect, we use cmd to store the basename of the command
         used to invoke the program. timeout is the only function other than
         main contained in this file.

[13–28] We find the last component in the pathname of the command used to
         invoke the program and store a pointer to it in cmd. Then we check the
         number of command-line arguments provided. If it is incorrect, we print a
         usage statement and exit.

```
29    /*
30     * Get the information from /etc/slipsys.
31     */
32    cip = getcinfo(argv[1]);
33    if (cip == NULL)
34        fatal("%s: can't get system information", cmd);

35    /*
36     * Send the request to the slip daemon.
37     */
38    slcmd.opcode = DISCONNECT;
39    strcpy(slcmd.arg, argv[1]);
40    pfd = open(PIPEPATH, O_RDWR);
41    if (pfd < 0)
42        fatal("%s: can't open pipe to slip daemon", cmd);
43    n = write(pfd, &slcmd, sizeof(struct slcommand));
44    if (n != sizeof(struct slcommand)) {
45        if (n < 0)
46            fatal("%s: can't write to slipd pipe", cmd);
47        else
48            fatal("%s: short write to slipd pipe", cmd);
49    }
50    sigemptyset(&sa.sa_mask);
51    sa.sa_handler = timeout;
52    sa.sa_flags = 0;
53    sigaction(SIGALRM, &sa, NULL);
54    alarm(30);
55    n = read(pfd, &err, sizeof(int));
56    alarm(0);
57    if (n != sizeof(int)) {
58        if (n < 0)
59            fatal("%s: can't read from slipd pipe", cmd);
60        else
61            fatal("%s: short read from slipd pipe", cmd);
62    }
```

[29–34] The only argument is a host name. If it is not in /etc/slipsys, or if an error occurs while the database file is processed, then getcinfo will return NULL and we will call fatal to print an error message and exit.

[35–49] We create the DISCONNECT message and open the daemon's mounted pipe. If open fails, we print an error message and exit. Otherwise, we send the disconnect request to the daemon. If write is unable to transmit the message, we print an error and exit.

[50–62] Next we install a signal handler for SIGALRM and set a 30-second alarm so that we do not block indefinitely. We read the response code from the daemon and cancel the alarm. If read returns an invalid value, we print an error message and exit.

```
63   if (err == 0)
64       printf("disconnected\n");
65   else
66       fatal("%s: can't break connection: %s", cmd,
67           strerror(err));
68   exit(0);
69 }

70 static void
71 timeout(int signo)
72 {
73   fatal("%s: request timed out", cmd);
74 }
```

[63–69] err is set to 0 if the daemon satisfied the request. Otherwise, err is set to an error code from <sys/errno.h>. In either case, we print a message indicating the result of the request and then exit.

[70–74] timeout will be invoked if we do not receive a response from the daemon in 30 seconds. We print an error message and exit.

slipd

The SLIP daemon handles requests from the user-level SLIP commands and cleans up after receiving hangup notifications from the SLIP driver. The SLIP daemon takes no command-line arguments.

```
 1 #include <sys/types.h>
 2 #include <sys/stat.h>
 3 #include <sys/socket.h>
 4 #include <sys/sockio.h>
 5 #include <net/if.h>    /* depends on <sys/socket.h> */
 6 #include <stdlib.h>
 7 #include <stdio.h>
 8 #include <unistd.h>
 9 #include <fcntl.h>
10 #include <stropts.h>
11 #include <poll.h>
12 #include <wait.h>
13 #include <netdb.h>
14 #include <errno.h>
15 #include <signal.h>
16 #include <string.h>
17 #include <slipcmd.h>
```

[1–17] The socket ioctl commands are listed in <sys/sockio.h>. <net/if.h> contains the structure used with these commands.

```
18 typedef struct seriallink slink_t;

19 struct seriallink {
20    slink_t *next;        /* next entry in list */
21    slink_t *prev;        /* previous entry in list */
22    dev_t   dev;          /* dev # of driver at end of stream */
23    int     id;           /* link ID */
24    char    hostname[MAXHOSTNAMELEN]; /* foreign host */
25 };

26 static slink_t *slist;
27 static int netfd;

28 static void svc_pipe(int);
29 static void svc_driver(int);
30 static int doconn(int, struct slcommand *);
31 static int dodiscon(struct slcommand *);
32 static int setifname(int);
33 static int ifup(int, struct conninfo *);
34 static int ifdown(int);
35 static int _discon(slink_t *);
36 static void timeout(int);

37 void
38 main()
39 {
40    int fd, fl;
41    int pfd[2];
42    struct pollfd pary[2];
43    struct sigaction sa;

44    daemonize("slipd");
```

[18–25] We use the `seriallink` structure (type `slink_t`) to represent each active SLIP connection. The `next` and `prev` fields are used to link the structures on a doubly linked list. The `dev` field identifies each connection by the device number of the serial line driver at the end of the stream. The `id` field is the multiplexor ID that can be used to unlink the stream from under the IP multiplexor. The `hostname` field contains the name of the host at the other end of the connection.

[26–36] `slist` is the head of the linked list of `slink_t` structures. `netfd` is the file descriptor open to the IP multiplexor. The function prototypes for the subroutines defined in the daemon's source file are listed next.

[37–44] The first thing we do is call `daemonize` to become a daemon. We pass it the name of the daemon, `slipd`. `daemonize` will use the name to create a log file, `/tmp/slipd.log`.

```
45    fd = open(SLIPDEV, O_RDWR|O_NONBLOCK);
46    if (fd < 0) {
47        log("can't open %s: %s", SLIPDEV, strerror(errno));
48        exit(1);
49    }
50    netfd = open("/dev/ip", O_RDWR);
51    if (netfd < 0) {
52        log("can't open /dev/ip: %s", strerror(errno));
53        exit(1);
54    }

55    if (pipe(pfd) < 0) {
56        log("can't create pipe: %s", strerror(errno));
57        exit(1);
58    }
59    if ((fl = fcntl(pfd[1], F_GETFL, 0)) < 0) {
60        log("can't get pipe file flags: %s", strerror(errno));
61        exit(1);
62    }
63    if (fcntl(pfd[1], F_SETFL, fl|O_NONBLOCK) < 0) {
64        log("can't set pipe file flags: %s", strerror(errno));
65        exit(1);
66    }
67    if (ioctl(pfd[0], I_PUSH, "connld") < 0) {
68        log("can't push CONNLD: %s", strerror(errno));
69        exit(1);
70    }
71    close(creat(PIPEPATH, PIPEMODE));
72    if (fattach(pfd[0], PIPEPATH) < 0) {
73        log("can't attach pipe to %s: %s", PIPEPATH,
74            strerror(errno));
75        exit(1);
76    }
```

[45–54] We open the SLIP driver using the O_NONBLOCK flag. The driver open
routine will not sleep, but we need the O_NONBLOCK flag set for the file
descriptor, and specifying it here saves us from having to use fcntl to set
it later. Then we open the IP multiplexor. If either open fails, we log a
message and exit. Note that the driver will only allow one process to open
it at any given time, so multiple SLIP daemons are prevented from running
at the same time.

[55–76] We create a pipe and place one end in nonblocking mode. Then we push
CONNLD on the other end. We use creat(2) to create the file on
which we will mount the pipe. If the file already exists, creat will truncate it. Then we close the file descriptor returned by creat. Finally, we
call fattach(3C) to mount the end of the pipe containing CONNLD on
/var/.slipipe.

```
 77  sigemptyset(&sa.sa_mask);
 78  sa.sa_handler = timeout;
 79  sa.sa_flags = 0;
 80  sigaction(SIGALRM, &sa, NULL);
 81  pary[0].events = POLLIN;
 82  pary[0].fd = fd;
 83  pary[1].events = POLLIN;
 84  pary[1].fd = pfd[1];
 85  while (poll(pary, 2, INFTIM) >= 0) {
 86      if (pary[0].revents & (POLLERR|POLLHUP|POLLNVAL)) {
 87          log("poll driver revents %x", pary[0].revents);
 88          exit(1);
 89      }
 90      if (pary[1].revents & (POLLERR|POLLHUP|POLLNVAL)) {
 91          log("poll pipe revents %x", pary[1].revents);
 92          exit(1);
 93      }
 94      if (pary[0].revents & POLLIN)
 95          svc_driver(pary[0].fd);
 96      if (pary[1].revents & POLLIN)
 97          svc_pipe(pary[1].fd);
 98  }
 99  log("poll failed: %s", strerror(errno));
100  exit(1);
101  }

102  static void
103  svc_pipe(int pipefd)
104  {
105      struct strrecvfd piprecv;
106      struct slcommand slcmd;
107      int n, err;
```

[77–84]   We install a signal handler for SIGALRM and initialize the pollfd
          array. The first element in the array contains the file descriptor open to
          the SLIP driver, and the second element contains the file descriptor of
          the other end of the mounted pipe. The only events of interest are input
          events.

[85–101] We block indefinitely in poll, waiting for input from either the driver
          or the pipe. If poll returns, we check for errors on either file descrip-
          tor. If one of the streams is in error mode or hangup mode, or if either
          file descriptor is invalid, we log a message and exit. Otherwise, if data
          are present from the driver, we call svc_driver to process them. If
          data are present in the pipe, we call svc_pipe to process them. If
          poll fails, we log a message and exit.

[102–107] svc_pipe is called when there are data in the pipe to be read. It is
          passed the file descriptor of the unmounted end of the pipe.

```
108   while (ioctl(pipefd, I_RECVFD, &piprecv) == 0) {
109       alarm(30);
110       n = read(piprecv.fd, &slcmd,
111         sizeof(struct slcommand));
112       alarm(0);
113       if (n != sizeof(struct slcommand)) {
114           if (n < 0)
115               log("can't read from received pipe: %s",
116                 strerror(errno));
117           else
118               log("only read %d bytes from pipe", n);
119       } else {
120           err = 0;
121           switch (slcmd.opcode) {
122           case CONNECT:
123               log("received connect request");
124               if (doconn(piprecv.fd, &slcmd) < 0)
125                   err = errno;
126               break;

127           case DISCONNECT:
128               log("received disconnect request");
129               if (dodiscon(&slcmd) < 0)
130                   err = errno;
131               break;

132           default:
133               err = EINVAL;
134               log("unknown opcode: %d", slcmd.opcode);
135           }
136           write(piprecv.fd, &err, sizeof(int));
137       }
138       close(piprecv.fd);
139   }
```

[108–118]   Since CONNLD is on the other end of the pipe, only M_PASSFP messages can be on this end's stream head read queue. We use the I_RECVFD ioctl command to retrieve a file descriptor. If successful, we call alarm to avoid blocking indefinitely and then attempt to read the slcommand structure from the new file descriptor to determine what the client wants. On error, we log a message, close the received file descriptor, and continue trying to receive more file descriptors.

[119–139]   If we read the correct amount, we process the requested operation. For a CONNECT, we log a message and call doconn to do the work. If it fails, we save the error code in err. We write the results back to the user via the pipe file descriptor we received, close this file descriptor, and continue. We take similar steps for a DISCONNECT, except we call dodiscon to handle the request. We log unknown requests.

```
140  if (errno == EAGAIN)
141      return;
142  log("error receiving fd on mounted pipe: %s",
143    strerror(errno));
144  }

145 static int
146 doconn(int pipefd, struct slcommand *cmdp)
147 {
148  struct strrecvfd slrecv;
149  struct conninfo *cip;
150  struct stat sbuf;
151  slink_t *slp;
152  int id;

153  cip = getcinfo(cmdp->arg);
154  if (cip == NULL) {
155      log("can't find info on host %s", cmdp->arg);
156      return(-1);
157  }
158  alarm(30);
159  if (ioctl(pipefd, I_RECVFD, &slrecv) < 0) {
160      log("can't receive slfd: %s", strerror(errno));
161      return(-1);
162  }
163  alarm(0);
164  slp = NULL;
165  if (fstat(slrecv.fd, &sbuf) < 0) {
166      log("can't stat slfd: %s", strerror(errno));
167      goto err;
168  }
```

[140–144] Since `pipefd` is in nonblocking mode, when no more M_PASSFP messages are left, the I_RECVFD ioctl will return EAGAIN. Then we
return. Any other failure results in a message being logged.

[145–157] doconn is called to process a connect request. We call `getcinfo` to
obtain the information about the host name stored in the `slcommand`
structure. If `getcinfo` fails, we log a message and return failure (−1).

[158–168] For a connect request, the client is supposed to send us the file descriptor
connected to the remote machine after sending the `slcommand` structure. We set a 30-second alarm and use the I_RECVFD ioctl command to try to receive the file descriptor. If this fails, we log a message
and return −1. Otherwise, we cancel the alarm and call `fstat(2)` to
obtain information about the received file descriptor. If `fstat` fails, we
log a message and jump to `err`, where we clean up and return.

```
169  slp = malloc(sizeof(slink_t));
170  if (slp == NULL) {
171      log("can't allocate slink_t structure: %s",
172        strerror(errno));
173      goto err;
174  }
175  if (ioctl(slrecv.fd, I_PUSH, "slip") < 0) {
176      log("can't push slip module: %s", strerror(errno));
177      goto err;
178  }
179  id = ioctl(netfd, I_PLINK, slrecv.fd);
180  if (id < 0) {
181      log("link failed: %s", strerror(errno));
182      goto err;
183  }
184  if (setifname(id) < 0) {
185      log("can't set interface name: %s", strerror(errno));
186      ioctl(netfd, I_PUNLINK, id);
187      goto err;
188  }
189  if (ifup(id, cip) < 0) {
190      log("can't ifconfig");
191      ioctl(netfd, I_PUNLINK, id);
192      goto err;
193  }
194  slp->dev = sbuf.st_rdev;
195  slp->id = id;
196  slp->next = slist;
197  slp->prev = NULL;
198  strcpy(slp->hostname, cip->fhost);
199  if (slist != NULL)
200      slist->prev = slp;
201  slist = slp;
```

[169–183] We attempt to allocate enough memory for an slink_t structure, but if malloc fails, we log an error message and jump to err to clean up. Otherwise, we push the SLIP module on the file descriptor for the serial connection and use the I_PLINK ioctl command to link the stream under the IP multiplexor. We use persistent links instead of normal ones so that the connections survive if the SLIP daemon should die. If the link failed, we log an error message and jump to err.

[184–201] We then call setifname to initialize the name of the network interface, and we call ifup to initialize the interface addresses and mark the interface as active. If either function fails, we log an error message, unlink the stream, and go to err. Otherwise, we initialize the slink_t structure and place it at the front of the linked list of active slink_t structures.

```
202   log("link dev 0x%x ID %d created", slp->dev, id);
203   close(slrecv.fd);
204   return(0);

205 err:
206   close(slrecv.fd);
207   if (slp != NULL)
208       free(slp);
209   return(-1);
210 }

211 static int
212 setifname(int id)
213 {
214   struct strioctl strioc;
215   struct ifreq req;

216   sprintf(req.ifr_name, "sl%d", id);
217   req.ifr_metric = id;
218   strioc.ic_cmd = SIOCSIFNAME;
219   strioc.ic_timout = INFTIM;
220   strioc.ic_len = sizeof(struct ifreq);
221   strioc.ic_dp = (caddr_t)&req;
222   return(ioctl(netfd, I_STR, &strioc));
223 }
```

[202–204]   Finally, we log a message to record the existence of the link, close the
file descriptor for the connection, and return success (0).

[205–210]   We jump to `err` if we encounter an error after we have received the file
descriptor for the connection. We close the received file descriptor, and
if we have allocated memory for an `slink_t` structure, we free it.
Then we return −1 to indicate that the connect request failed.

[211–223]   `setifname` is called to give the link a network interface name. Historically, interface names have been built by concatenating a short string
with a number, where the string identifies the type of interface and the
number identifies the particular instance of that type of interface. The
numbers usually start at 0 and are incremented by 1 for each interface.
For simplicity, we use the link ID for the number. We could have used
some zero-based consecutive numbering scheme, such as the entry
number in the `slipsys` file, but that would have required more work.

The IP multiplexor needs to associate the interface name with the link
ID, so it expects the link ID to be stored in the `ifr_metric` field of
the `ifreq` structure (defined in <net/if.h>). We use the `I_STR`
`ioctl` command to perform the `SIOCSIFNAME` `ioctl` operation to
set the interface name.

```
224 static int
225 ifup(int id, struct conninfo *cip)
226 {
227   pid_t pid;
228   int status;
229   char ifname[IFNAMSIZ];

230   sprintf(ifname, "sl%d", id);
231   if ((pid = fork()) < 0) {
232       log("fork failed: %s", strerror(errno));
233       return(-1);
234   }
235   if (pid == 0) {        /* child */
236       execl(IFCONFIGPATH, IFCONFIG, ifname, "inet",
237         cip->laddr, cip->faddr, "up", NULL);
238       log("unexpected return from exec");
239       exit(1);
240   }
241   /* parent */
242   while (waitpid(pid, &status, 0) != pid)
243       ;
244   if (WIFEXITED(status) && (WEXITSTATUS(status) == 0)) {
245       return(0);
246   } else {
247       errno = EPROTO; /* as good as any */
248       return(-1);
249   }
250 }
```

[224–230] ifup is called to mark the interface as being active and initialize the source and destination addresses. IFNAMSIZ is the maximum size of an interface name. It is defined in <net/if.h>. We begin by creating the interface name from the string sl and the link ID.

[231–240] We call fork(2) to make a copy of the existing process. If fork fails, we log a message and return −1 to indicate failure. Otherwise, the child process uses execl to execute the ifconfig command. If execl returns, then ifconfig could not be run for some reason, so we log a message and exit.

[241–250] The parent process calls waitpid in a loop until the child exits and its status can be obtained. If the child exited normally and succeeded (indicated by an exit status of 0), then we return success (0). Otherwise, we set errno to EPROTO and return −1. There is no easy way to get the error code from the child since we do not have control over the design of the ifconfig command.

```
251 static int
252 dodiscon(struct slcommand *cmdp)
253 {
254   slink_t *slp;

255   for (slp = slist; slp != NULL; slp = slp->next)
256       if (strcmp(slp->hostname, cmdp->arg) == 0)
257           break;
258   if (slp == NULL) {
259       log("no slink_t structure for host %s", cmdp->arg);
260       errno = EINVAL;
261       return(-1);
262   }
263   return(_discon(slp));
264 }

265 static int
266 _discon(slink_t *slp)
267 {
268   if (ifdown(slp->id) < 0) {
269       log("can't mark interface down");
270       return(-1);
271   }
272   if (ioctl(netfd, I_PUNLINK, slp->id) < 0) {
273       log("unlink failed: %s", strerror(errno));
274       return(-1);
275   }
276   if (slp == slist)
277       slist = slp->next;
278   else
279       slp->prev->next = slp->next;
280   if (slp->next != NULL)
281       slp->next->prev = slp->prev;
282   log("ID %d unlinked", slp->id);
283   free(slp);
284   return(0);
285 }
```

[251–264] dodiscon is called to process disconnect requests. We search the linked list of slink_t structures until either we hit the end of the list or we find an entry with a host name that matches the one sent by the user. If we do not find a match, we log a message, set errno to EINVAL, and return −1. Otherwise, we call _discon to finish the work.

[265–285] _discon disables a network interface and unlinks the stream associated with its connection. We call ifdown to perform the former task, and we use the I_PUNLINK ioctl command to do the latter. We remove the slink_t structure from the linked list, record the disconnect in the log, free the structure's memory, and return 0 to indicate success.

```
286 static int
287 ifdown(int id)
288 {
289  pid_t pid;
290  int status;
291  char ifname[IFNAMSIZ];

292  sprintf(ifname, "sl%d", id);
293  if ((pid = fork()) < 0) {
294      log("fork failed: %s", strerror(errno));
295      return(-1);
296  }
297  if (pid == 0) {      /* child */
298      execl(IFCONFIGPATH, IFCONFIG, ifname, "down", NULL);
299      log("unexpected return from exec");
300      exit(1);
301  }
302  /* parent */
303  while (waitpid(pid, &status, 0) != pid)
304      ;
305  if (WIFEXITED(status) && (WEXITSTATUS(status) == 0)) {
306      return(0);
307  } else {
308      errno = EPROTO; /* as good as any */
309      return(-1);
310  }
311 }

312 static void
313 svc_driver(int drvfd)
314 {
315  slink_t *slp;
316  dev_t dev;
317  int n;
```

[286–291] ifdown is called to disable a network interface.

[292–301] We create the interface name from the string sl and the link ID. Then
           we call fork to create a child process. If the fork fails, we log an
           error message and return failure (−1). If the fork succeeds, the child
           proceeds to execute the command

                   ifconfig sl*n* down

           where *n* is the link ID. If execl fails, we log an error message and exit.

[302–311] Just as in ifup, the parent process calls waitpid to obtain the exit
           status of the child process. If the child succeeded, we return 0 to indi-
           cate success. Otherwise, we return −1.

[312–317] svc_driver is called when there are data to be read from the driver.

```
318  for (;;) {
319      n = read(drvfd, &dev, sizeof(dev_t));
320      if (n < 0) {
321          if (errno == EAGAIN) {
322              break;
323          } else {
324              log("read from driver failed: %s",
325                  strerror(errno));
326              exit(1);
327          }
328      }
329      log("read dev 0x%x from driver", dev);
330      for (slp = slist; slp != NULL; slp = slp->next)
331          if (slp->dev == dev)
332              break;
333      if (slp == NULL)
334          log("no slink_t found");
335      else
336          _discon(slp);
337  }
338  }

339  static void
340  timeout(int signo)
341  {
342    log("request timed out");
343  }
```

[318–328] We expect the driver to send the daemon the device number of any SLIP
stream that enters hangup mode. We repeatedly read device numbers
from the driver file descriptor until we encounter an error. Recall that
the driver file descriptor is in nonblocking mode. If read fails with
errno set to EAGAIN, then we know we are done servicing the driver,
so we break out of the loop and return. If we encounter any other type
of failure, we log an error message and exit.

[329–338] For each device number we read, we log a message to record the event
and search the linked list of slink_t structures to find an entry with a
matching device number field. If we do not find a match, we log a message. Otherwise, we call _discon to break the connection.

[339–343] timeout is called when SIGALRM is sent to the process. We log a
message and return. The system call that was interrupted will subsequently fail, preventing the daemon from blocking indefinitely.

13.4 KERNEL-LEVEL COMPONENTS

Now that we have looked at the user-level components of the SLIP communication software, we will discuss the kernel-level components. These consist of the SLIP module C source file and header file, as well as the master and system files needed by the system configuration software.

Installation

The following section discusses the driver installation and configuration method on an Intel 80x86-based SVR4 system.

After the SLIP module is compiled, the driver should be renamed `Driver.o`. The master file entry is stored in a file named `Master`, and the system file entry is stored in a file called `System`. The `idinstall(1M)` command can be used to install the driver, as in

```
/etc/conf/bin/idinstall -akmso slip
```

The `a` flag directs `idinstall` to add the module. The `k` flag prevents `idinstall` from deleting the driver files in the current directory. The `m` flag indicates there is a master file entry, the `s` flag indicates there is a system file entry, and the `o` flag indicates there is a `Driver.o` file. The string `slip` is used to identify the module.

After installation, check `/etc/conf/cf.d/mdevice` to find the major device selected for the SLIP driver. Then you can either make the `/dev/slip` node by hand, or create a file in `/etc/conf/node.d` to make the node automatically. See `idmknod(1M)` for more details.

Configuration Files

The master file [see `mdevice(4)`] describes the characteristics of the module. The SLIP master file is shown below.

```
slip -    Smciof  slip    0    0    0    0    -1
```

The first field is the name of the module. The second field is used for a list of global functions. The SLIP module does not have any, so we place a dash in this field. The third field further describes the module. The `S` indicates the module is a STREAMS module or driver. The `m` indicates it is a STREAMS module. The `c` indicates that it is also a character device. The `i` specifies that the module is installable. The `o` specifies that the module may have only one `sdevice` entry. The `f` indicates that the module routines follow the SVR4-style calling syntax.

The fourth field is the module prefix, which we set to `slip`. The next two fields are the block and character major numbers. Since this is not a block driver, the block major number is set to 0. The character major number is set to 0, too, but it will be modified by `idinstall` when we install the module. The last three fields specify the minimum number of minor devices, the maximum number of minor devices, and the DMA channel, respectively. All are unused and set accordingly.

The system file [see `sdevice(4)`] describes the local-site configurable values for the module. The SLIP system file is shown below.

```
slip Y   0   0   0   0   0   0   0   0
```

The first field corresponds to the first field of the master file. The second field controls whether or not the driver is included the next time the operating system is built (`Y` includes the driver and `N` excludes it). The third field is the number of minor devices configured. Since the SLIP driver only supports one minor device and the number is not tunable, we set this field to 0. The fourth field is the interrupt priority level at which the driver's interrupt handler will run. Software drivers and modules set this field to 0. The fifth and sixth fields specify the type of interrupt and the interrupt vector, respectively. The last four fields describe addressing information about the hardware controlled by the driver.

The driver and module configuration details have changed in SVR4.2, but compatibility has been maintained with prior installation file formats.

Header File

```
 1 #ifndef _SYS_SLIP_H
 2 #define _SYS_SLIP_H
 3 /*
 4  * SLIP - Serial Line IP module/driver (a la RFC 1055)
 5  */

 6 #define MAXSDUSZ  1006      /* maximum user data per packet */
 7 #define MINSDUSZ  1         /* minimum user data per packet */
 8 #define ADMINDEV  0         /* for administrative daemon */
 9 #define SLIPSAPSZ 4         /* size of SAP identifier */

10 #define END       0300      /* end of packet */
11 #define ESC       0333      /* next byte is real */
12 #define ESC_END   0334      /* ESC ESC_END is END */
13 #define ESC_ESC   0335      /* ESC ESC_ESC is ESC */

14 #endif /* _SYS_SLIP_H */
```

[1–9]   `MAXSDUSZ` is the maximum service data unit size supported by the SLIP module. It was chosen based on historical information contained in RFC 1055. `MINSDUSZ` is the minimum service data unit size and is required to be at least 1 byte by the DLPI. `ADMINDEV` is the minor device number for the SLIP driver. `SLIPSAPSZ` is the size of the service access point identifier for the SLIP module.

[10–14] The definitions for the special bytes are taken directly from RFC 1055. `END` is used to frame IP packets. `ESC ESC_END` is used to represent a data byte equal to `END` (0300). `ESC ESC_ESC` is used to represent a data byte equal to `ESC` (0333).

The SLIP Module/Driver

Figure 13.3 summarizes the SLIP module functions. There are put and service procedures on both the read and write sides. On the read side, most messages are simply enqueued for the service procedure to handle. The write-side put procedure acts in a similar manner, but handles M_FLUSH and M_IOCTL messages immediately.

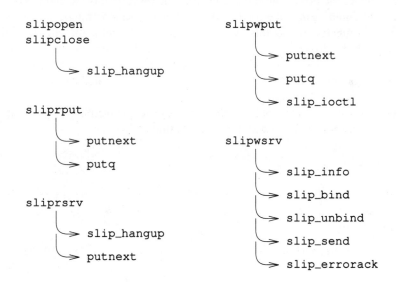

Fig. 13.3. SLIP Module Function Diagram

If the SLIP module is opened as a driver, then the write-side put procedure will free unknown messages instead of passing them downstream. When opened as a SLIP driver, the stream is used only to retrieve hangup notifications. When used as a SLIP module, the read-side service procedure will convert from the TTY service interface to the DLPI, and the write-side service procedure will convert from the DLPI to the TTY interface.

The SLIP module supports two versions of the DLPI: Version 1.2 and Version 2.0. For the most part, these versions are compatible. Version 2.0 is a superset of Version 1.2, including more primitives and extending several existing ones. Most primitives that changed between the two versions did so through the use of fields that were reserved in Version 1.2, so structure sizes and existing structure member offsets remained the same. There are exceptions, however, such as the growth of the information-acknowledgement primitive. The SLIP module can be compiled to work with either version of the DLPI. If the symbol DLPIV2 is defined, then Version 2.0 is used; otherwise, Version 1.2 is used. Most existing software uses Version 1.2.

As in the examples presented in the last three chapters, most comments have been removed to decrease the size of the example SLIP module.

```
 1 /*
 2  * SLIP - Serial Line IP module/driver (a la RFC 1055)
 3  */
 4 #include <sys/types.h>
 5 #include <sys/param.h>
 6 #include <sys/systm.h>
 7 #include <sys/stream.h>
 8 #include <sys/stropts.h>
 9 #include <sys/errno.h>
10 #include <sys/kmem.h>
11 #include <sys/cred.h>
12 #include <sys/dlpi.h>
13 #include <sys/socket.h>
14 #include <sys/sockio.h>
15 #include <net/if.h>
16 #include <netinet/in.h>
17 #include <sys/cmn_err.h>
18 #include <sys/ddi.h>
19 #include <slip.h>

20 #undef STATIC

21 #ifdef DEBUG
22 #define STATIC
23 #else
24 #define STATIC static
25 #endif

26 #define HALFSEC        500000  /* in microseconds */

27 /* interface flags */
28 #define IFF_SLIPFLAGS (IFF_POINTOPOINT|IFF_RUNNING)
```

[1–19]   Most of the header files used by the module should be familiar. We need
         <netinet/in.h> to be able to process the ioctl commands that pass
         through the IP multiplexor.

[20–25] We define STATIC as we usually do for kernel files so that private sym
         bols are made global during development and debugging.

[26–28] HALFSEC represents the number of microseconds in half a second. It is
         used during recovery of buffer allocation failures. IFF_SLIPFLAGS is a
         bitmask of the interface flags set only by the SLIP module.
         IFF_POINTOPOINT indicates that the interface is one end of a connec-
         tion between two machines. IFF_RUNNING indicates that the interface
         has been initialized.

```
29 typedef struct slip slip_t;

30 struct slip {
31    queue_t      *s_rdq;       /* read queue */
32    slip_t       *s_next;      /* linked list */
33    ulong_t      s_sap;        /* sap bound */
34    ulong_t      s_rid;        /* read bufcall and timeout ID */
35    ulong_t      s_wid;        /* write bufcall and timeout ID */
36    ulong_t      s_flag;       /* see below */
37    mblk_t       *s_udmp;      /* unitdata indication */
38                              /* being assembled */
39    mblk_t       *s_hupmp;     /* used to notify daemon of */
40                              /* hangup */
41    dev_t        s_dev;        /* device number of TTY driver */
42    ushort_t     s_dlstate;    /* DLPI state */
43    struct ifstats s_ifstats; /* for netstat(1) */
44    ulong_t      s_ifflag;     /* interface flags */
45    struct ifaddr s_ifaddr;   /* interface addresses */
46    char         s_ifname[IFNAMSIZ]; /* interface name */
47 };

48 /* flags */
49 #define RDBCALL    0x01      /* read-side bufcall pending */
50 #define RDTOUT     0x02      /* read-side timeout pending */
51 #define WRBCALL    0x04      /* write-side bufcall pending */
52 #define WRTOUT     0x08      /* write-side timeout pending */
53 #define GOTESC     0x10      /* received an escape */
54 #define LOCADDR    0x20      /* local address set */
55 #define REMADDR    0x40      /* remote address set */
```

[29–47] The slip_t structure describes each instance of the module. All
         instances are linked together via the s_next field. While an IP packet is
         being assembled, a pointer to the message containing it is held in the
         s_udmp field. The s_hupmp field is used to save a message so that we
         can reliably notify the daemon when the device has hung up. The
         s_ifstats field contains statistics used by netstat(1). The
         s_ifflag field contains the interface flags, defined in <net/if.h>.
         The s_ifaddr field contains the local and remote IP addresses, and the
         s_ifname field contains the name of the interface.

[48–55] The flags that can be set in the s_flag field include ones used to indicate
         that recovery functions are scheduled to run, similar to the other modules
         and drivers described in this text. The GOTESC flag is used to remember if
         an ESC character has been received. LOCADDR is set when the local
         address has been initialized via the SIOCSIFADDR ioctl command.
         REMADDR is set when the remote address has been initialized via the
         SIOCSIFDSTADDR ioctl command.

```
56 STATIC slip_t slipadmin;
57 STATIC slip_t *sliplist;

58 int slipdevflag = 0;

59 extern struct ifstats *ifstats;    /* global kernel list */

60 typedef enum retval {
61    DONE,    /* function completed its job */
62    RETRY,   /* temporary failure; try again later */
63    ERR      /* permanent error */
64 } retval_t;

65 STATIC int slipopen(queue_t *, dev_t *, int, int, cred_t *);
66 STATIC int slipclose(queue_t *, int, cred_t *);
67 STATIC int slipwput(queue_t *, mblk_t *);
68 STATIC int slipwsrv(queue_t *);
69 STATIC int sliprput(queue_t *, mblk_t *);
70 STATIC int sliprsrv(queue_t *);
71 STATIC void slip_ioctl(queue_t *, mblk_t *);
72 STATIC void slip_hangup(queue_t *);
73 STATIC retval_t slip_info(slip_t *, mblk_t *);
74 STATIC retval_t slip_bind(slip_t *, mblk_t *);
75 STATIC retval_t slip_unbind(slip_t *, mblk_t *);
76 STATIC retval_t slip_send(slip_t *, mblk_t *);
77 STATIC retval_t slip_errorack(slip_t *, mblk_t *, ulong_t);
78 STATIC void slip_wsched(slip_t *, int);
79 STATIC void slip_wcont(slip_t *);
80 STATIC void slip_rsched(slip_t *, int);
81 STATIC void slip_rcont(slip_t *);
```

[56–57] slipadmin is the slip_t structure used for the single minor device supported by the driver. sliplist is the head of the linked list of active slip_t structures. sliplist pertains only to module slip_t structures; slipadmin is never placed on the list.

[58–59] slipdevflag is the driver flag needed by the system to indicate the capabilities of the driver or module. We set it to 0, thereby indicating that the module supports the SVR4 calling syntax. The ifstats pointer is a global pointer to a list of ifstats structures in the kernel. Drivers and modules that provide network interfaces for the Internet protocols can make themselves visible to users by linking their ifstats structures onto this global list.

[60–64] The retval_t enumeration defines the possible return values from functions that can fail because of buffer allocation failures.

[65–81] The functions defined by the driver are declared next. Figure 13.3 summarizes the major ones.

```
82 STATIC struct module_info slip_minfo = {
83  0x534c, "slip", MINSDUSZ, MAXSDUSZ, 8*MAXSDUSZ, 2*MAXSDUSZ
84 };

85 STATIC struct qinit slip_rinit = {
86  sliprput, sliprsrv, slipopen, slipclose, NULL,
87  &slip_minfo, NULL
88 };

89 STATIC struct qinit slip_winit = {
90  slipwput, slipwsrv, NULL, NULL, NULL, &slip_minfo, NULL
91 };

92 struct streamtab slipinfo = {
93  &slip_rinit, &slip_winit, NULL, NULL
94 };

95 STATIC int
96 slipopen(queue_t *q, dev_t *devp, int flag, int sflag,
97  cred_t *crp)
98 {
99  slip_t *slp;
100  mblk_t *bp;

101  switch (sflag) {
102  default:
103       return(EINVAL);
```

[82–94]   We select 0x534c for the module ID. This is the hexadecimal ASCII value of the string SL. The minimum packet size of the module is set to the minimum service data unit size. Similarly, the module's maximum packet size is set to the maximum service data unit size. The high-water mark is set to allow at least eight IP packets to be queued. The low-water mark is set so that flow-control restraints will be lifted when at most two IP packets are left on the queue.

The SLIP module has a read put procedure and a read service procedure. On the write side, it has a put procedure and a service procedure, too. Only the first two fields in the streamtab structure are initialized since this is not a multiplexing driver.

[95–103]   slipopen is called when the driver is opened and when the module is pushed on a stream. The way we tell the difference between the two cases is by checking the sflag parameter. If sflag contains an invalid value (such as CLONEOPEN), then we enter the default case of the switch statement and return EINVAL.

```
104   case MODOPEN:
105       if (q->q_ptr != NULL)    /* not first open */
106           return(0);
107       bp = allocb(sizeof(dev_t), BPRI_HI);
108       if (bp == NULL)
109           return(EAGAIN);
110       slp = (slip_t *)kmem_zalloc(sizeof(slip_t), KM_SLEEP);
111       slp->s_hupmp = bp;
112       slp->s_next = sliplist;
113       sliplist = slp;
114       break;

115   case 0:
116       if (geteminor(*devp) == ADMINDEV) {
117           slp = &slipadmin;
118           if (slp->s_rdq != NULL)
119               return(EBUSY);  /* one at a time */
120       } else {
121           return(ENXIO);
122       }
123       slp->s_hupmp = NULL;
124       break;
125   }
126   slp->s_rdq = q;
127   slp->s_dlstate = DL_UNBOUND;
128   slp->s_flag = 0;
129   slp->s_ifflag = IFF_POINTOPOINT;
130   slp->s_udmp = NULL;
```

[104–114] If sflag is set to MODOPEN, then this is a module open. If this is not the first call for this instance of the module, we simply return success (0). Otherwise (when the module is being pushed in the stream), we allocate a message large enough to hold a device number. If this fails, we return EAGAIN. We call kmem_zalloc to allocate a new instance of a slip_t structure, set s_hupmp to the message we have just allocated, and link the slip_t structure onto the active list.

[115–125] For a driver open, if the minor device is invalid, we return ENXIO. If the driver is currently active, we fail the open by returning EBUSY. Only one process can open the single administrative minor device at a time. We clear the s_hupmp pointer because hangup notifications are not performed on the driver; they apply only to modules.

[126–130] For first-open initialization for both the module and the driver, we set the s_rdq field of the slip_t structure to the address of the read queue. We set the initial DLPI state to DL_UNBOUND, the module flags to 0, the interface flags to IFF_POINTOPOINT, and the unitdata message pointer to NULL.

```
131  slp->s_dev = *devp;
132  slp->s_ifstats.ifs_name = slp->s_ifname;
133  slp->s_ifstats.ifs_mtu = MAXSDUSZ;
134  slp->s_ifstats.ifs_addrs = &slp->s_ifaddr;
135  slp->s_ifaddr.ifa_ifs = &slp->s_ifstats;
136  q->q_ptr = (caddr_t)slp;
137  WR(q)->q_ptr = (caddr_t)slp;
138  return(0);
139  }

140 STATIC int
141 slipclose(queue_t *q, int flag, cred_t *crp)
142 {
143  slip_t *slp, *tslp, *pslp;
144  struct ifstats *ifp, *pifp;

145  slp = (slip_t *)q->q_ptr;
146  if (slp->s_flag & RDTOUT)
147      untimeout(slp->s_rid);
148  else if (slp->s_flag & RDBCALL)
149      unbufcall(slp->s_rid);
150  if (slp->s_flag & WRTOUT)
151      untimeout(slp->s_wid);
152  else if (slp->s_flag & WRBCALL)
153      unbufcall(slp->s_wid);
154  if (slp != &slipadmin)
155      slip_hangup(q);
156  pifp = NULL;
157  ifp = ifstats;
158  while ((ifp != NULL) && (ifp != &slp->s_ifstats)) {
159      pifp = ifp;
160      ifp = ifp->ifs_next;
161  }
```

[131–139] We store the device number of the driver at the end of the stream in the
s_dev field. Next we initialize the ifstats and ifaddr structures.
Finally, we store a pointer to the slip_t structure in both the read and
write queues and return success.

[140–155] slipclose is called when the stream is closed or when the module is
popped off the stream. If a timeout is pending on the read side, we
call untimeout to cancel it. Otherwise, if a bufcall is pending on
the read side, we call unbufcall to cancel it. Then we do the same
thing for the write side. If this is a module being closed, we call
slip_hangup to notify the daemon that this connection is no longer in
use.

[156–161] We search the linked list of ifstats structures until we hit the end of
the list or we find one that belongs to the module instance being closed.

```
162  if (ifp != NULL) {
163      if (pifp != NULL)
164          pifp->ifs_next = ifp->ifs_next;
165      else
166          ifstats = ifp->ifs_next;
167  }
168  tslp = sliplist;
169  pslp = NULL;
170  while ((tslp != NULL) && (tslp != slp)) {
171      pslp = tslp;
172      tslp = tslp->s_next;
173  }
174  if (tslp == slp) {
175      if (pslp != NULL)
176          pslp->s_next = slp->s_next;
177      else
178          sliplist = slp->s_next;
179      kmem_free(slp, sizeof(slip_t));
180  } else {
181      slp->s_rdq = NULL;
182  }
183  q->q_ptr = NULL;
184  WR(q)->q_ptr = NULL;
185  return(0);
186  }

187  STATIC int
188  slipwput(queue_t *q, mblk_t *mp)
189  {
190   slip_t *slp;
```

[162–167] If this instance of the module has its `ifstat` structure still on the
           linked list, we unlink it from the list. If there is no previous `ifstats`
           pointer (i.e., if `pifp` is NULL), then this `ifstat` structure was on the
           front of the list, so we set `ifstats` to point to the next structure in the
           list.

[168–182] Next we need to take the `slip_t` structure off the module's linked list.
           We search the list until we either reach the end or find a match. If we
           find a match, then we remove the structure from the list and call
           `kmem_free` to free its underlying memory. Otherwise, we simply clear
           the `s_rdq` pointer to indicate that the structure is no longer in use. A
           match will not be made if this is the close for the driver's minor device.

[183–186] We complete the close processing by clearing the private pointers in the
           read and write queues and returning 0 to indicate success.

[187–190] `slipwput` is called when messages are passed to the module (or
           driver) for transmission downstream.

```
191   slp = (slip_t *)q->q_ptr;
192   if (slp == &slipadmin) {
193       if (mp->b_datap->db_type == M_IOCTL) {
194           mp->b_datap->db_type = M_IOCNAK;
195           qreply(q, mp);
196       } else {
197           freemsg(mp);
198       }
199       return(0);
200   }

201   switch (mp->b_datap->db_type) {
202   case M_FLUSH:
203       if (*mp->b_rptr & FLUSHW)
204           flushq(q, FLUSHALL);
205       if (*mp->b_rptr & FLUSHR)
206           flushq(RD(q), FLUSHALL);
207       putnext(q, mp);
208       break;

209   case M_DATA:
210       freemsg(mp);
211       break;

212   case M_PROTO:
213   case M_PCPROTO:
214       putq(q, mp);
215       break;
```

[191–200] If the slip_t structure associated with the queue is the same as the driver structure, then we need to process messages as a driver would. If we receive an M_IOCTL message, we convert it into an M_IOCNAK message and send it back upstream. All other message types are freed. The driver is not supposed to be used for anything other than receiving hangup notifications. Thus, it is unnecessary to process M_FLUSH messages in the driver. The only reason we even bother to reply to M_IOCTL messages is so that applications do not block indefinitely.

[201–208] The remainder of the write put procedure is used by the module only. If we get an M_FLUSH message, we flush the read and write queues as directed. Then we forward the message on downstream.

[209–215] We free any M_DATA messages we receive, because they are not part of the DLPI interface. If we receive any M_PROTO or M_PCPROTO messages, we place them on the queue for processing by the write service procedure.

```
216  case M_IOCTL:
217      slip_ioctl(q, mp);
218      break;

219  default:
220      putnext(q, mp);
221      break;
222  }
223  return(0);
224  }

225 STATIC void
226 slip_ioctl(queue_t *q, mblk_t *mp)
227 {
228  slip_t *slp;
229  struct iocblk *iocp;
230  struct iocblk_in *iniocp;
231  struct ifreq *reqp;
232  int i;
233  ushort_t unit;

234  slp = (slip_t *)q->q_ptr;
235  iocp = (struct iocblk *)mp->b_rptr;
236  switch (iocp->ioc_cmd) {
237  case SIOCGIFFLAGS:
238      if ((mp->b_cont == NULL) ||
239        (iocp->ioc_count == TRANSPARENT)) {
240         mp->b_datap->db_type = M_IOCNAK;
241      } else {
242          reqp = (struct ifreq *)mp->b_cont->b_rptr;
243          reqp->ifr_flags = slp->s_ifflag;
244          mp->b_datap->db_type = M_IOCACK;
245      }
246      break;
```

[216–224] If we receive an M_IOCTL message, we call slip_ioctl to process the request immediately. We pass all other messages downstream.

[225–233] slip_ioctl is called to process M_IOCTL messages. There are several socket ioctl commands we need to support so that we can operate within the Internet protocol stack.

[234–246] The SIOCGIFFLAGS command is a request to obtain the interface flags. If the message is improperly formed or was generated as a transparent ioctl, then we change the message type to M_IOCNAK to fail the request. Otherwise, the data buffer in the second block in the message contains an ifreq structure, so we store the interface flags in the ifr_flags field and change the message type to M_IOCACK. Then we break out of the switch statement.

```
247  case SIOCSIFFLAGS:
248      if ((mp->b_cont == NULL) ||
249        (iocp->ioc_count == TRANSPARENT)) {
250          mp->b_datap->db_type = M_IOCNAK;
251      } else {
252          reqp = (struct ifreq *)mp->b_cont->b_rptr;
253          slp->s_ifflag = reqp->ifr_flags |
254            (slp->s_ifflag & IFF_SLIPFLAGS);
255          mp->b_datap->db_type = M_IOCACK;
256      }
257      break;

258  case SIOCSIFNAME:
259      if ((mp->b_cont == NULL) ||
260        (iocp->ioc_count == TRANSPARENT) ||
261        (slp->s_ifname[0] != '\0')) {
262          mp->b_datap->db_type = M_IOCNAK;
263      } else {
264          reqp = (struct ifreq *)mp->b_cont->b_rptr;
265          for (i = 0; i < IFNAMSIZ; i++)
266              if ((reqp->ifr_name[i] == '\0') ||
267                ((reqp->ifr_name[i] >= '0') &&
268                (reqp->ifr_name[i] <= '9')))
269                  break;
270              else
271                  slp->s_ifname[i] = reqp->ifr_name[i];
272          for (unit = 0; i < IFNAMSIZ; i++)
273              if (reqp->ifr_name[i] == '\0')
274                  break;
275              else
276                  unit = unit * 10 + reqp->ifr_name[i] - '0';
277          slp->s_ifstats.ifs_unit = unit;
278          mp->b_datap->db_type = M_IOCACK;
279      }
280      break;
```

[247–257] The SIOCSIFFLAGS command is used to set the interface flags. We validate the message as before and then update the s_ifflags field with the flags specified in the message, making sure we retain the current interface flags that are set only by the module.

[258–280] The SIOCSIFNAME command is used to set the interface name. If the message format is invalid or the interface name is the null string, we set the message type to M_IOCNAK. Otherwise, we search the interface name for the first character that represents a digit. As we search, we copy any nondigit characters to the s_ifname field in the slip_t structure. When we have reached the first digit character, we calculate its decimal value and save it in the ifs_unit field in the ifstats structure. Then we change the message type to M_IOCACK.

```
281   case SIOCSIFADDR:
282       if ((slp->s_flag & LOCADDR) || (mp->b_cont == NULL) ||
283           (iocp->ioc_count == TRANSPARENT)) {
284           mp->b_datap->db_type = M_IOCNAK;
285       } else {
286           reqp = (struct ifreq *)mp->b_cont->b_rptr;
287           slp->s_ifaddr.ifa_addr = reqp->ifr_addr;
288           slp->s_flag |= LOCADDR;
289           mp->b_datap->db_type = M_IOCACK;
290           if ((slp->s_flag & (LOCADDR|REMADDR)) ==
291               (LOCADDR|REMADDR)) {
292               slp->s_ifstats.ifs_next = ifstats;
293               ifstats = &slp->s_ifstats;
294               slp->s_ifflag |= IFF_RUNNING;
295               slp->s_ifstats.ifs_active = 1;
296           }
297       }
298       break;

299   case SIOCSIFDSTADDR:
300       if ((slp->s_flag & REMADDR) || (mp->b_cont == NULL) ||
301           (iocp->ioc_count == TRANSPARENT)) {
302           mp->b_datap->db_type = M_IOCNAK;
303       } else {
304           reqp = (struct ifreq *)mp->b_cont->b_rptr;
305           slp->s_ifaddr.ifa_dstaddr = reqp->ifr_dstaddr;
306           slp->s_flag |= REMADDR;
307           mp->b_datap->db_type = M_IOCACK;
308           if ((slp->s_flag & (LOCADDR|REMADDR)) ==
309               (LOCADDR|REMADDR)) {
310               slp->s_ifstats.ifs_next = ifstats;
311               ifstats = &slp->s_ifstats;
312               slp->s_ifflag |= IFF_RUNNING;
313               slp->s_ifstats.ifs_active = 1;
314           }
315       }
316       break;
```

[281–298]   The SIOCSIFADDR command is used to set the local address. If the local address is already set or the message format is invalid, we change the message type to M_IOCNAK. Otherwise, we store the local IP address in the ifa_addr field of the ifstats structure for this instance of the module. Then we set the LOCADDR flag and change the message type to M_IOCACK. If the local and remote addresses have been set, we link the ifstats structure on the head of the ifstats list, set the IFF_RUNNING flag, and mark the interface as active.

[299–316]   The SIOCSIFDSTADDR command is used to set the remote address. The code is similar to that of the SIOCSIFADDR command.

```
317  case SIOCGIFNETMASK:
318  case SIOCSIFNETMASK:
319  case SIOCGIFADDR:
320  case SIOCGIFDSTADDR:
321  case SIOCGIFMETRIC:
322      mp->b_datap->db_type = M_IOCACK;
323      break;

324  default:
325      putnext(q, mp);
326      return;
327  }

328  if ((mp->b_datap->db_type == M_IOCACK) &&
329     ((mp->b_wptr - mp->b_rptr) >= sizeof(struct iocblk_in))) {
330      iniocp = (struct iocblk_in *)mp->b_rptr;
331      iniocp->ioc_ifflags = slp->s_ifflag;
332  }
333  qreply(q, mp);
334  }
```

[317–323] The SIOCGIFNETMASK command is used to obtain the subnet mask. The SIOCSIFNETMASK command is used to set the subnet mask. The SIOCGIFADDR command is used to get the local address of the interface. The SIOCGIFDSTADDR command is used to get the address of the machine at the other end of the connection. The SIOCGIFMETRIC command is used to get the routing metric for the connection. These commands are ultimately handled by IP, but IP sends them down to the network driver and waits for a response before completing the command.

[324–327] For unknown ioctl commands, we pass the M_IOCTL messages downstream and return.

[328–334] If we are going to respond successfully to the ioctl request and the message is large enough to contain an iocblk_in structure, we set the ioc_ifflags field to the value of the interface flags for this instance of the module. This way IP can stay informed of the status of this network interface. (IP modified the message to contain extra, private information. The iocblk_in structure is a superset of the iocblk structure and is used as a side-door means of communication between IP and the network drivers.) Finally, we send the response message upstream.

```
335 STATIC int
336 slipwsrv(queue_t *q)
337 {
338   mblk_t *mp;
339   slip_t *slp;
340   union DL_primitives *dlp;
341   retval_t ret;

342   if ((slp =. (slip_t *)q->q_ptr) == NULL)
343       return(0);
344   while ((mp = getq(q)) != NULL) {
345       dlp = (union DL_primitives *)mp->b_rptr;
346       switch (dlp->dl_primitive) {
347       case DL_UNITDATA_REQ:
348           ret = slip_send(slp, mp);
349           break;

350       case DL_INFO_REQ:
351           ret = slip_info(slp, mp);
352           break;

353       case DL_BIND_REQ:
354           ret = slip_bind(slp, mp);
355           break;

356       case DL_UNBIND_REQ:
357           ret = slip_unbind(slp, mp);
358           break;

359       default:
360           ret = slip_errorack(slp, mp, DL_BADPRIM);
361           break;
362       }
```

[335–344] slipwsrv is the module write service procedure. It handles all DLPI primitives. We pick up a pointer to the slip_t structure from the queue and if it is no longer valid, we just return. Otherwise, we remove messages from the queue and process them until we run into an allocation failure, the stream flow-controls on the write side, or the queue is empty.

[345–362] We call slip_send to handle DL_UNITDATA_REQ primitives, slip_info to handle DL_INFO_REQ primitives, slip_bind to handle DL_BIND_REQ primitives, and slip_unbind to handle DL_UNBIND_REQ primitives. If we receive an unrecognized primitive, we respond by sending a DL_ERROR_ACK primitive back upstream.

```
363        if (ret == RETRY) {
364            putbq(q, mp);
365            break;
366        }
367    }    /* while */
368    return(0);
369 }

370 STATIC retval_t
371 slip_info(slip_t *slp, mblk_t *mp)
372 {
373    dl_info_ack_t *ackp;
374    mblk_t *bp;

375    bp = allocb(DL_INFO_ACK_SIZE+SLIPSAPSZ, BPRI_HI);
376    if (bp == NULL) {
377        cmn_err(CE_WARN, "slip: can't ack DL_INFO_REQ");
378        return(ERR);
379    }
380    freemsg(mp);
381    bp->b_datap->db_type = M_PCPROTO;
382    ackp = (dl_info_ack_t *)bp->b_wptr;
383    ackp->dl_primitive = DL_INFO_ACK;
384    ackp->dl_max_sdu = MAXSDUSZ;
385    ackp->dl_min_sdu = MINSDUSZ;
386    ackp->dl_addr_length = sizeof(ulong_t);
387 #ifdef DLPIV2
388    ackp->dl_mac_type = DL_OTHER;
389 #else
390    ackp->dl_mac_type = DL_ETHER;
391 #endif
```

[363–369] If we get a RETRY return from any of the functions, then we put the message back on the queue and return. The functions will have scheduled the queue to be enabled at some point in the future.

[370–379] slip_info is called to respond to DL_INFO_REQ primitives. We try to allocate a message for the response, but if allocb fails, we print a warning on the console and return ERR. We cannot return RETRY because slipwsrv would then put the message back on the queue, and information requests are implemented as M_PCPROTO messages.

[380–391] We free the message for the request primitive because we no longer need it. The DL_INFO_ACK response is implemented as an M_PCPROTO message. We initialize the primitive type, the maximum and minimum service data unit sizes, and the address length field. For Version 2.0 of the DLPI, we set the type of medium access control to DL_OTHER. For earlier versions, no appropriate type is defined, so we fake an Ethernet interface.

```
392   ackp->dl_reserved = 0;
393   ackp->dl_current_state = slp->s_dlstate;
394 #ifdef DLPIV2
395   ackp->dl_sap_length = sizeof(ulong_t);
396 #else
397   ackp->dl_reserved2 = 0;
398 #endif
399   ackp->dl_service_mode = DL_CLDLS;
400   ackp->dl_qos_length = 0;
401   ackp->dl_qos_offset = 0;
402   ackp->dl_qos_range_length = 0;
403   ackp->dl_qos_range_offset = 0;
404   ackp->dl_provider_style = DL_STYLE1;
405   bp->b_wptr += DL_INFO_ACK_SIZE;
406   if (slp->s_dlstate == DL_IDLE) {
407       ackp->dl_addr_offset = DL_INFO_ACK_SIZE;
408       *(long *)bp->b_wptr = slp->s_sap;
409       bp->b_wptr += SLIPSAPSZ;
410   } else {
411       ackp->dl_addr_offset = 0;
412   }
413 #ifdef DLPIV2
414   ackp->dl_version = DL_VERSION_2;
415   ackp->dl_brdcst_addr_length = 0;
416   ackp->dl_brdcst_addr_offset = 0;
417 #endif
418   ackp->dl_growth = 0;
419   putnext(slp->s_rdq, bp);
420   return(DONE);
421 }
```

[392–412]   We set the current state of the DLSAP to the contents of the
s_dlstate field of the slip_t structure. For Version 2.0 of the
DLPI, we set the length of the SAP identifier to the size of an
unsigned long. For other versions, we set the dl_reserved2
field to 0. We set the service mode to indicate that we support connectionless data link service. We do not support quality-of-service parameters, so we set them all to 0. We set the dl_provider_style field to
DL_STYLE1 since we do not support physical point of attachment
(PPA) primitives (see Section 10.3). Then we increment the write
pointer by the size of a dl_info_ack_t structure and if the DLSAP is
in the idle state, we copy the SAP identifier into the message. Otherwise, we set the location of the address in the message to 0.

[413–421]   For Version 2.0 of the DLPI, we indicate the version of the DLPI that
we support, and then set the broadcast address length and offset to 0
since serial lines do not support broadcasts. Finally, we send the message upstream and return DONE.

```
422 STATIC void
423 slip_wsched(slip_t *slp, int size)
424 {
425   ulong_t id;

426   if (slp->s_flag & (WRBCALL|WRTOUT))
427       return;
428   id = bufcall(size, BPRI_HI, slip_wcont, slp);
429   if (id == 0) {
430       id = timeout(slip_wcont, (caddr_t)slp,
431         drv_usectohz(HALFSEC));
432       slp->s_flag |= WRTOUT;
433   } else {
434       slp->s_flag |= WRBCALL;
435   }
436   slp->s_wid = id;
437 }

438 STATIC void
439 slip_wcont(slip_t *slp)
440 {
441   qenable(WR(slp->s_rdq));
442   slp->s_flag &= ~(WRBCALL|WRTOUT);
443 }

444 STATIC retval_t
445 slip_bind(slip_t *slp, mblk_t *mp)
446 {
447   slip_t *tslp;
448   dl_bind_req_t *reqp;
449   dl_bind_ack_t *ackp;
450   mblk_t *bp;
```

[422–437]   slip_wsched is called to recover from message allocation failures. If recovery is already scheduled, we return. Otherwise, we call bufcall to schedule slip_wcont to be run when a message of the specified size can be allocated. If bufcall fails, we fall back to using timeout with a half-second interval. In either case, we save the recovery information in the slip_t structure so that it can be canceled from the close routine.

[438–443]   slip_wcont is called to enable the service procedure as part of recovery. After calling qenable, we shut off the flags in the s_flag field of the slip_t structure that indicate that recovery is active.

[444–450]   slip_bind is called to bind an address to a DLSAP.

```
451  if (slp->s_dlstate != DL_UNBOUND) {
452      if (slip_errorack(slp, mp, DL_OUTSTATE) == RETRY)
453          return(RETRY);
454      return(DONE);
455  }
456  reqp = (dl_bind_req_t *)mp->b_rptr;
457  /* don't check dl_service_mode -- IP doesn't set it */
458  for (tslp = sliplist; tslp != NULL; tslp = tslp->s_next) {
459      if (tslp->s_sap == reqp->dl_sap) {
460          if (slip_errorack(slp, mp, DL_NOADDR) == RETRY)
461              return(RETRY);
462          return(DONE);
463      }
464  }
465  bp = allocb(DL_BIND_ACK_SIZE+SLIPSAPSZ, BPRI_HI);
466  if (bp == NULL) {
467      slip_wsched(slp, DL_BIND_ACK_SIZE+SLIPSAPSZ);
468      return(RETRY);
469  }
470  slp->s_sap = reqp->dl_sap;
471  freemsg(mp);
472  bp->b_datap->db_type = M_PCPROTO;
473  ackp = (dl_bind_ack_t *)bp->b_wptr;
474  ackp->dl_primitive = DL_BIND_ACK;
475  ackp->dl_sap = slp->s_sap;
476  ackp->dl_addr_length = SLIPSAPSZ;
477  ackp->dl_addr_offset = DL_BIND_ACK_SIZE;
478  ackp->dl_max_conind = 0;
```

[451–469]   If the data link state is not unbound, we send an error acknowledgement upstream to indicate that the endpoint is in the wrong state. If slip_errorack fails, we return RETRY; otherwise, we return DONE. We do not bother to validate the requested mode of service, because IP neglects to set it. We search the list of active SLIP endpoints to make sure one does not exist with the same SAP identifier that is specified in the request. If a duplicate is found, we respond with an error acknowledgement. Otherwise, we try to allocate a message large enough to hold the bind acknowledgement and the SAP identifier.

[470–478]   We store the requested SAP identifier in the slip_t structure and free the bind request message. We set the type of the bind acknowledgement message to M_PCPROTO and initialize the dl_bind_ack_t structure. For the purposes of the SLIP module, an address is only made up of the SAP identifier, so we set the dl_addr_length field to the size of the SAP identifier and the dl_addr_offset field to the size of the dl_bind_ack_t structure.

```
479 #ifdef DLPIV2
480   ackp->dl_xidtest_flg = 0;
481 #else
482   ackp->dl_growth = 0;
483 #endif
484   bp->b_wptr += DL_BIND_ACK_SIZE;
485   *(ulong_t *)bp->b_wptr = slp->s_sap;
486   bp->b_wptr += SLIPSAPSZ;
487   slp->s_dlstate = DL_IDLE;
488   putnext(slp->s_rdq, bp);
489   return(DONE);
490 }

491 STATIC retval_t
492 slip_unbind(slip_t *slp, mblk_t *mp)
493 {
494   mblk_t *bp;
495   dl_ok_ack_t *ackp;

496   if (slp->s_dlstate != DL_IDLE) {
497       if (slip_errorack(slp, mp, DL_OUTSTATE) == RETRY)
498           return(RETRY);
499       return(DONE);
500   }
501   if ((bp = allocb(DL_OK_ACK_SIZE, BPRI_HI)) == NULL) {
502       slip_wsched(slp, DL_OK_ACK_SIZE);
503       return(RETRY);
504   }
505   freemsg(mp);
506   putctl1(slp->s_rdq->q_next, M_FLUSH, FLUSHRW);
```

[479–483] For Version 2.0 of the DLPI, we set the `dl_xidtest_flg` field to 0 since the SLIP module does not support automatic responses to XID or TEST packets. In older versions of the DLPI, the field at this offset is reserved for future growth, thus we initialize the `dl_growth` field to 0.

[484–490] We increment the write pointer by the size of the `dl_bind_ack_t` structure and then store the SAP identifier in the message immediately following the `dl_bind_ack_t` structure. Then we increment the write pointer by the size of the SAP identifier, set the data link provider state to idle, send the acknowledgement message upstream, and return DONE.

[491–506] `slip_unbind` is called to unbind an address from a DLSAP. If an address is not bound, we call `slip_errorack` to send an error-acknowledgement message upstream. If this fails, we return RETRY; otherwise, we return DONE. If the DLSAP is in the idle state, we allocate an acknowledgement message. If `allocb` fails, we call `slip_wsched` to recover, and return RETRY. Otherwise, we free the unbind request message and flush the stream, as required by the DLPI.

```
507   bp->b_datap->db_type = M_PCPROTO;
508   ackp = (dl_ok_ack_t *)bp->b_wptr;
509   ackp->dl_primitive = DL_OK_ACK;
510   ackp->dl_correct_primitive = DL_UNBIND_REQ;
511   bp->b_wptr += DL_OK_ACK_SIZE;
512   slp->s_dlstate = DL_UNBOUND;
513   slp->s_sap = 0;
514   putnext(slp->s_rdq, bp);
515   return(DONE);
516 }

517 STATIC retval_t
518 slip_send(slip_t *slp, mblk_t *mp)
519 {
520   mblk_t *bp, *omp;
521   int size;

522   if (slp->s_dlstate != DL_IDLE) {
523       freemsg(mp);
524       return(DONE);
525   }
526   if (!canput(WR(slp->s_rdq)->q_next))
527       return(RETRY);
528   size = msgdsize(mp);
529   if ((size < MINSDUSZ) || (size > MAXSDUSZ)) {
530       freemsg(mp);
531       slp->s_ifstats.ifs_oerrors++;
532       return(DONE);
533   }
```

[507–516]   We set the type of the acknowledgement message to M_PCPROTO. Then we initialize the dl_ok_ack_t structure contained in the message by setting the dl_primitive field to DL_OK_ACK and the dl_correct_primitive field to DL_UNBIND_REQ, the primitive that we are acknowledging. We complete the unbind processing by incrementing the write pointer by the size of the dl_ok_ack_t structure, changing the state of the data link provider to unbound, clearing the SAP identifier for this DLSAP, sending the acknowledgement message upstream, and returning DONE.

[517–533]   slip_send is called to transmit a packet. If the endpoint is not in the proper state for data transfer, we free the message and return DONE. If the stream is flow-controlled on the write side, we return RETRY. The write service procedure will be backenabled when the flow-control restrictions are lifted. If we can send the message, we calculate the number of bytes of data to be transmitted. If the size is invalid, we free the message, increment the count of the number of output errors encountered by the interface, and return DONE.

```
534  size = 2*size + 2;   /* worst case */
535  bp = allocb(size, BPRI_MED);
536  if (bp == NULL) {
537      slip_wsched(slp, size);
538      return(RETRY);
539  }
540  omp = mp;
541  mp = mp->b_cont;
542  freeb(omp);
543  omp = mp;
544  *bp->b_wptr++ = END;
545  while (mp != NULL) {
546      while (mp->b_rptr < mp->b_wptr) {
547          if (*mp->b_rptr == END) {
548              *bp->b_wptr++ = ESC;
549              *bp->b_wptr++ = ESC_END;
550          } else if (*mp->b_rptr == ESC) {
551              *bp->b_wptr++ = ESC;
552              *bp->b_wptr++ = ESC_ESC;
553          } else {
554              *bp->b_wptr++ = *mp->b_rptr;
555          }
556          mp->b_rptr++;
557      }
558      mp = mp->b_cont;
559  }
560  *bp->b_wptr++ = END;
```

[534–539] The worst-case largest message size we will need is if every byte needs
to be escaped. Then we will require two bytes for every byte of input,
plus one byte for the END byte in the beginning of the packet, and one
byte for the one at the end of the packet. If we cannot allocate a large
enough message, we call `slip_wsched` to recover and return RETRY.

[540–543] We save a pointer to the original message and set `mp` to the second message block in the message. We free the first message block, discarding
the `dl_unitdata_req_t` header. Then we save a pointer to the
remaining message in `omp`.

[544–560] We begin the message to be transmitted by storing in it an END byte as
suggested by RFC 1055. Then we check every byte in the input message. If we come across a byte equal to END, we store two bytes in the
output message: ESC and ESC_END. If we find a byte equal to ESC,
we store ESC and ESC_ESC in the output message. We copy all other
bytes to the output message unmodified. When we reach the end of the
current message block, we continue with the next block in the message
until the entire message has been copied. Then we terminate the output
packet with an END byte.

```
561   freemsg(omp);
562   putnext(WR(slp->s_rdq), bp);
563   slp->s_ifstats.ifs_opackets++;
564   return(DONE);
565   }

566   STATIC retval_t
567   slip_errorack(slip_t *slp, mblk_t *mp, ulong_t err)
568   {
569   union DL_primitives *dp;
570   dl_error_ack_t *errp;
571   mblk_t *bp;

572   bp = allocb(DL_ERROR_ACK_SIZE, BPRI_HI);
573   if (bp == NULL) {
574       slip_wsched(slp, DL_ERROR_ACK_SIZE);
575       return(RETRY);
576   }
577   bp->b_datap->db_type = M_PCPROTO;
578   errp = (dl_error_ack_t *)bp->b_wptr;
579   errp->dl_primitive = DL_ERROR_ACK;
580   dp = (union DL_primitives *)mp->b_rptr;
581   errp->dl_error_primitive = dp->dl_primitive;
582   errp->dl_errno = err;
583   errp->dl_unix_errno = 0;
584   bp->b_wptr += DL_ERROR_ACK_SIZE;
585   freemsg(mp);
586   putnext(slp->s_rdq, bp);
587   return(DONE);
588   }
```

[561–565] We free the input message and pass the output message downstream. Then we increment the count of the number of packets transmitted from the interface and return DONE.

[566–576] slip_errorack is called to send an error acknowledgement upstream. mp is the message containing the erroneous primitive, and err is the DLPI error code. If we cannot allocate a message for the primitive, we call slip_wsched to recover, and return RETRY.

[577–588] We set the type of the message to M_PCPROTO and initialize the dl_error_ack_t structure. We set the dl_primitive field to DL_ERROR_ACK, the dl_error_primitive field to the primitive in the message passed to us, the dl_errno field to the given error code, and the dl_unix_errno field to 0. Here we have hard-coded knowledge that the SLIP module never generates DL_SYSERR errors. We increment the write pointer by the size of the dl_error_ack_t structure, free the message containing the primitive in error, and send the error-acknowledgement message upstream. Finally, we return DONE.

```
589 STATIC void
590 slip_hangup(queue_t *q)
591 {
592   slip_t *slp;
593   mblk_t *bp;

594   slp = (slip_t *)q->q_ptr;
595   if (slp->s_udmp != NULL) {
596       freemsg(slp->s_udmp);
597       slp->s_udmp = NULL;
598   }
599   if ((bp = slp->s_hupmp) == NULL)
600       return;
601   slp->s_hupmp = NULL;
602   if (slipadmin.s_rdq == NULL) {
603       freeb(bp);
604   } else {
605       *(dev_t *)bp->b_wptr = slp->s_dev;
606       bp->b_wptr += sizeof(dev_t);
607       putnext(slipadmin.s_rdq, bp);
608       flushq(slp->s_rdq, FLUSHALL);
609       flushq(WR(slp->s_rdq), FLUSHALL);
610   }
611 }

612 STATIC int
613 sliprput(queue_t *q, mblk_t *mp)
614 {
```

[589–611]   slip_hangup is called when the SLIP module receives an M_HANGUP
            message from downstream. We need to mark the device as having hung
            up and notify the daemon. We pick up a pointer to the slip_t struc-
            ture from the queue and if there is a packet being assembled for delivery
            upstream, we free it. If no message is available to send the daemon
            notification of the hangup, then we just return. Otherwise, we clear the
            hangup message pointer in the slip_t structure. If the administrative
            minor device of the SLIP driver is inactive, we cannot notify the dae-
            mon, so we free the message. Otherwise, we store the device number of
            the driver at the end of the stream in the message and increment the
            write pointer by the size of the device number. We send the message up
            the stream associated with the SLIP driver, and then flush the read and
            write queues of the SLIP module.

[612–614]   sliprput is called when messages are passed to the SLIP module
            from the serial line driver.

```
615  switch (mp->b_datap->db_type) {
616  case M_FLUSH:
617      if (*mp->b_rptr & FLUSHR)
618          flushq(q, FLUSHALL);
619      if (*mp->b_rptr & FLUSHW)
620          flushq(WR(q), FLUSHALL);
621      putnext(q, mp);
622      break;

623  case M_ERROR:
624  case M_HANGUP:
625  case M_DATA:
626      putq(q, mp);
627      break;

628  case M_CTL:
629      freemsg(mp);
630      break;

631  default:
632      putnext(q, mp);
633      break;
634  }
635  return(0);
636  }

637  STATIC int
638  sliprsrv(queue_t *q)
639  {
640    mblk_t *mp, *udbp, *bp, *omp;
641    slip_t *slp;
642    dl_unitdata_ind_t *dp;

643    slp = (slip_t *)q->q_ptr;
```

[615–636] If we receive an M_FLUSH message, we flush our queues as dictated by the flags in the message. Then we pass the message upstream. If we receive an M_HANGUP, M_ERROR, or M_DATA message, we place it on the queue for the read service procedure to handle. If we receive an M_CTL message, we free it. (Recall from Chapter 11 that the TTY service interface allows serial line drivers to generate M_CTL messages in response to queries from LDTERM. We should not receive M_CTL messages by the time the SLIP module is in place, but if one should be received, we want to avoid forwarding it upstream, because M_CTL messages usually only have significance between neighboring components in a stream.) We pass all other types of messages upstream.

[637–643] sliprsrv is the read service procedure of the module. It is called to process incoming IP packets and handle errors.

```
644    while ((mp = getq(q)) != NULL) {
645        if ((mp->b_datap->db_type == M_HANGUP) ||
646          (mp->b_datap->db_type == M_ERROR)) {
647            flushq(q, FLUSHALL);
648            slip_hangup(q);
649            putnext(q, mp);
650            return(0);
651        }
652        if (!canput(q->q_next)) {
653            putbq(q, mp);
654            return(0);
655        }
656        if (slp->s_udmp == NULL) {
657            udbp = allocb(DL_UNITDATA_IND_SIZE, BPRI_MED);
658            if (udbp == NULL) {
659                slip_rsched(slp, DL_UNITDATA_IND_SIZE);
660                putbq(q, mp);
661                return(0);
662            }
663            bp = allocb(MAXSDUSZ, BPRI_MED);
664            if (bp == NULL) {
665                freeb(udbp);
666                slip_rsched(slp, 0);
667                putbq(q, mp);
668                return(0);
669            }
```

[644–651] We process each message on the queue until the queue is empty or we encounter a failure. If we retrieve an M_HANGUP or M_ERROR message, then the stream is effectively unusable, so we flush the queue, call slip_hangup to notify the daemon, forward the message upstream, and return. Note that since we call slip_hangup from the service procedure instead of the put procedure, hangup processing is automatically serialized with normal input message processing.

[652–669] Any other message we get off the queue must be a data message. If we cannot send messages upstream, we put the message back on the queue and return. Otherwise, we assemble the IP packet. If no unitdata indication is currently being assembled, we need to allocate one. If allocb fails, we call slip_rsched to schedule the service procedure to be run when there is a better chance that the allocation will succeed, put the message back on the queue, and return. If the allocation succeeds, we then try to allocate a message for the data portion of the primitive. We have no way of knowing how big the packet is, so we allocate a message large enough to hold the largest packet we support. If allocb fails, we free the previously allocated message, enable recovery, and return. The 0 size passed to slip_rsched will be explained shortly.

```
670                udbp->b_datap->db_type = M_PROTO;
671                dp = (dl_unitdata_ind_t *)udbp->b_wptr;
672                dp->dl_primitive = DL_UNITDATA_IND;
673                dp->dl_dest_addr_length = 0;
674                dp->dl_dest_addr_offset = 0;
675                dp->dl_src_addr_length = 0;
676                dp->dl_src_addr_offset = 0;
677 #ifdef DLPIV2
678                dp->dl_group_address = 0;
679 #else
680                dp->dl_reserved = 0;
681 #endif
682                udbp->b_wptr += DL_UNITDATA_IND_SIZE;
683                udbp->b_cont = bp;
684                slp->s_udmp = udbp;
685         }
686     omp = mp;
687     udbp = slp->s_udmp->b_cont;
688     while (mp != NULL) {
689         while (mp->b_rptr < mp->b_wptr) {
690             if (slp->s_flag & GOTESC) {
691                 if (*mp->b_rptr == ESC_END)
692                     *mp->b_rptr = END;
693                 else if (*mp->b_rptr == ESC_ESC)
694                     *mp->b_rptr = ESC;
695                 else
696                     slp->s_ifstats.ifs_ierrors++;
```

[670–685]   We initialize the unitdata indication next, setting the message type to M_PROTO and the primitive type to DL_UNITDATA_IND. We clear the rest of the fields in the dl_unitdata_ind_t structure because the IP multiplexor will just discard the header without further inspection. (Note that the field reserved in previous versions of the DLPI is used in Version 2.0 to indicate whether or not the source address is multicast.) Then we increment the write pointer to reflect the size of the primitive and link the message to be used to contain the IP packet to the unitdata indication message. We store a pointer to the resulting message in the s_udmp field of the slip_t structure.

[686–696]   We save a pointer to the message we took off the queue and set udbp to the address of the message block used to hold the IP packet. We need to remove the framing information and special escape characters from the received message, so we inspect every byte. If the last byte was ESC, then the GOTESC flag will be set in the s_flag field of the slip_t structure. If the next byte is ESC_END, we overwrite it with END. Otherwise, if the byte is ESC_ESC, we overwrite it with ESC. Any other value constitutes a protocol error, so we increment the number of input errors.

```
697                    if ((udbp->b_wptr - udbp->b_rptr) ==
698                      MAXSDUSZ)
699                         mp->b_rptr++;
700                    else
701                         *udbp->b_wptr++ = *mp->b_rptr++;
702                    slp->s_flag &= ~GOTESC;
703               } else if (*mp->b_rptr == END) {
704                    mp->b_rptr++;
705                    if (udbp->b_rptr != udbp->b_wptr) {
706                         putnext(q, slp->s_udmp);
707                         slp->s_ifstats.ifs_ipackets++;
708                         slp->s_udmp = NULL;
709                         if (msgdsize(omp) != 0)
710                              putbq(q, omp);
711                         else
712                              freemsg(omp);
713                         omp = mp = NULL;
714                         break;
715                    }
716               } else if (*mp->b_rptr == ESC) {
717                    slp->s_flag |= GOTESC;
718                    mp->b_rptr++;
719               } else {
720                    if ((udbp->b_wptr - udbp->b_rptr) ==
721                      MAXSDUSZ) {
722                         mp->b_rptr++;
723                         slp->s_ifstats.ifs_ierrors++;
724                    } else {
725                         *udbp->b_wptr++ = *mp->b_rptr++;
726                    }
```

[697–702] If the IP packet has reached the maximum size we support, then we skip
the input byte. Otherwise, we copy the byte from the input message to
udbp, incrementing the read pointer in the input message and the write
pointer in udbp. Then we shut off the GOTESC flag.

[703–715] If the input byte is END, we increment the read pointer. If udbp is not
empty, we send the unitdata indication upstream, increment the count of
the number of received packets, and clear the s_udmp field in the
slip_t structure. The next time around the loop we will allocate new
messages for the unitdata indication. If more data remain in the message
we removed from the queue, then we put the message back on the front
of the queue. Otherwise, we free the message. Then we set mp and omp
to NULL so that we will process the next message on the queue.

[716–726] If we come across an ESC byte in the input, we set the GOTESC flag and
skip the byte. Any other value is a normal data byte, so we copy it to
udbp if there is room. We increment the count of input errors if we
reach the maximum service data unit size and input still remains.

```
727                   }
728               }
729               if (mp != NULL)
730                   mp = mp->b_cont;
731           }
732       if (omp != NULL)
733           freemsg(omp);
734   }
735   return(0);
736 }

737 STATIC void
738 slip_rsched(slip_t *slp, int size)
739 {
740   ulong_t id;

741   if (slp->s_flag & (RDBCALL|RDTOUT))
742       return;
743   if (size == 0)
744       id = 0;
745   else
746       id = bufcall(size, BPRI_HI, slip_rcont, slp);
747   if (id == 0) {
748       id = timeout(slip_rcont, (caddr_t)slp,
749         drv_usectohz(HALFSEC));
750       slp->s_flag |= RDTOUT;
751   } else {
752       slp->s_flag |= RDBCALL;
753   }
754   slp->s_rid = id;
755 }
```

[727–736] When we finish checking every message block in the message, we free
the input message, using the pointer we saved before we started processing it. When no more messages are left on the queue, we return.

[737–755] `slip_rsched` is called to recover from an allocation failure during the
execution of the read service procedure. If recovery is already enabled,
we just return. If the `size` is 0, we avoid using `bufcall` and use
`timeout` instead. Otherwise, we call `bufcall` to schedule
`slip_rcont` to be run when a message of the given size has a good
chance of being allocated. If `bufcall` fails, we use `timeout` to
schedule `slip_rcont` to be run in a half second. We set the appropriate flag in the `s_flag` field of the `slip_t` structure to indicate the
recovery method. Before returning, we save the identifier returned from
`bufcall` or `timeout` so that the recovery can be canceled when the
module is popped off the stream.

```
756 STATIC void
757 slip_rcont(slip_t *slp)
758 {
759   qenable(slp->s_rdq);
760   slp->s_flag &= ~(RDBCALL|RDTOUT);
761 }
```

[756–761] `slip_rcont` is called via a `bufcall` or a `timeout` to enable the
read queue. Accordingly, we call `qenable` and then clear the flags that
indicate recovery is active.

Summary

This completes the design project. We have studied both the user-level and kernel-
level components of a SLIP communication package designed for SVR4. By implementing the SLIP protocol as a STREAMS module, we can integrate it smoothly into
the existing SVR4 Internet protocol stack. By placing all connection-establishment
details at user level, the SLIP module is simplified. The chat script functionality
built into `slconnect` should provide the needed flexibility to create SLIP connections to systems running alternate SLIP packages and even to systems running different operating systems.

Exercises

13.1 Write a command and the related daemon function to print a list of the serial
devices currently in use, along with their corresponding interface names,
local addresses, foreign addresses, and foreign host names.

13.2 In `slip_unbind`, what would you do if `putctl1` returned 0?

13.3 Obtain RFC 1144 and modify the SLIP driver to support TCP/IP header
compression.

13.4 If the SLIP daemon is not running, hangup notifications are lost. What
design changes can you make to prevent this?

Bibliographic Notes

O'Reilly and Todino [1989] and Nowitz [1990] discuss the ins and outs of adminis-
tering uucp. Hunt [1992] covers interface configuration using `ifconfig` and
discusses the installation and configuration of several SLIP implementations.

RFC 1055 [Romkey 1988] presents the SLIP protocol. RFC 1144 [Jacobson 1990] specifies the algorithms to be used to compress TCP/IP headers when using SLIP. RFC 1171 [Perkins 1990] contains the proposed PPP standard, and RFC 1172 [Perkins and Hobby 1990] specifies the PPP initial configuration options.

Bibliography

ANSI. 1989. "American National Standard for Information Systems — Programming Language C." X3.159–1989.

> ANSI standard C language specification.

AT&T. 1986. *UNIX System V Release 3 STREAMS Programmer's Guide*. AT&T.

> The first documentation regarding the commercial version of STREAMS.

Bach, M. J. 1986. *The Design of the UNIX Operating System*. Prentice-Hall, Englewood Cliffs, NJ.

> Describes the algorithms that make up UNIX SVR2.

Bellovin, S. M. 1988. "The Session Tty Manager," *Proceedings of the 1988 Summer USENIX Conference*. San Francisco, CA, pp. 339–354.

> Describes the application of a STREAMS multiplexor to isolate login sessions.

Black, U. 1991. *OSI: A Model for Computer Communications Standards*. Prentice-Hall, Englewood Cliffs, NJ.

> More readable than the OSI standards themselves, but less detailed.

Comer, D. E. 1991. *Internetworking with TCP/IP, Volume 1: Principles, Protocols, and Architectures*. Second edition, Prentice-Hall, Englewood Cliffs, NJ.

> A good overview of the TCP/IP protocol suite.

Corbin, J. R. 1991. *The Art of Distributed Applications: Programming Techniques for Remote Procedure Calls*. Springer-Verlag, New York, NY.

> A good overview of the Sun RPC, on which SVR4's RPC is based.

Diffie, W., and M. E. Hellman. 1976. "New Directions in Cryptography," *IEEE Transactions on Information Theory*. Vol. IT-22 (November 1976), pp. 644–654.

>   Introduces the public key encryption mechanism eventually adopted for use in secure RPC.

Holzmann, G. J. 1991. *Design and Validation of Computer Protocols*. Prentice-Hall, Englewood Cliffs, NJ.

>   How to design communication protocols and verify that they work properly.

Hunt, C. 1992. *TCP/IP Network Administration*. O'Reilly & Associates, Sebastopol, CA.

>   How to administer TCP/IP networks, including interface configuration and use of several SLIP packages.

IEEE. 1990. "Information Technology — Portable Operating System Interface (POSIX) — Part 1: System Application Program Interface." IEEE Std. 1003.1-1990. ISO/IEC 9945-1:1990.

>   The C language interface to operating systems. The interface was based on the UNIX system.

IEEE. 1992. "Information Technology — Portable Operating System Interface (POSIX) — Part xx: Protocol Independent Interfaces." P1003.12, Draft 1.2 (September 1992).

>   The C language interface to protocol-independent, process-to-process network communication services.

ISO. 1984. "Open Systems Interconnection — Basic Reference Model." DIS 8072.

>   A description of the OSI reference model.

ISO. 1986. "Open Systems Interconnection — Transport Service Definition." DIS 8072.

>   A description of the services provided by the transport layer.

ISO. 1987. "Data Link Service Definition for Open Systems Interconnection." DIS 8886.

>   A description of the services provided by the data link layer.

Israel, R. K. 1988. "Implementing Network Services under Unix System V Release 3.0," *UniForum 1988 Conference Proceedings*. Dallas, TX, pp. 185–198.

>   Descriptions of several protocol implementations under the STREAMS framework.

Jacobson, V. 1990. "Compressed TCP/IP Headers for Low-Speed Serial Links." RFC 1144.

>   Changes to SLIP that improve performance by compressing TCP/IP headers.

Kernighan, B. W., and R. Pike. 1984. *The UNIX Programming Environment.* Prentice-Hall, Englewood Cliffs, NJ.

>   An excellent introduction to the UNIX programming environment.

Kernighan, B. W., and D. M. Ritchie. 1978. *The C Programming Language.* First edition, Prentice-Hall, Englewood Cliffs, NJ.

>   A description of K&R C by its originators.

Kernighan, B. W., and D. M. Ritchie. 1988. *The C Programming Language.* Second edition, Prentice-Hall, Englewood Cliffs, NJ.

>   An update to the first edition, based on the ANSI draft standard.

Kogure, H., and R. McGowan. 1987. "A UNIX System V STREAMS TTY Implementation for Multiple Language Processing," *Proceedings of the 1987 Summer USENIX Conference.* Phoenix, AZ, pp. 323–336.

>   How international (multibyte) characters are supported by STREAMS-based TTYs.

Lathi, B. P. 1983. *Modern Digital and Analog Communication Systems.* Holt, Rinehart & Winston, New York, NY.

>   For those interested in communication theory.

Leffler, S. J., M. K. McKusick, M. J. Karels, and J. S. Quarterman. 1989. *The Design and Implementation of the 4.3BSD UNIX Operating System.* Addison-Wesley, Reading, MA.

>   A description of the socket framework and the network protocols implemented in 4.3BSD, amidst other information about this UNIX variant.

Lennert, D. 1987. "How to Write a UNIX Daemon," *;login:.* Vol. 12, No. 4 (July/August 1987), pp. 17–23.

>   Just what it says. Reprinted with modifications in the December 1988 issue of *UNIX World.*

Martin, J., with K. K. Chapman. 1989. *Local Area Networks: Architectures and Implementations.* Prentice-Hall, Englewood Cliffs, NJ.

>   An overview of local area networking products and protocols.

Metcalfe, R. M., and D. R. Boggs. 1976. "Ethernet: Distributed Packet Switching for Local Computer Networks," *Communications of the ACM*. Vol. 19, No. 7 (July 1976), pp. 395–404.

> The original paper describing the Ethernet.

Mills, D. L. 1992. "Network Time Protocol (Version 3) Specification, Implementation and Analysis." RFC 1305.

> Describes the protocol used to maintain a consistent notion of time between machines on a network.

Mockapetris, P. 1987a. "Domain Names — Concepts and Facilities." RFC 1034.

> Introduces the domain name service.

Mockapetris, P. 1987b. "Domain Names — Implementation and Specification." RFC 1035.

> Details about the domain name service and protocol.

NBS. 1977. "Data Encryption Standard." Federal Information Processing Standards Publication 46 (January 1977). National Bureau of Standards.

> The data encryption standard used with secure RPC.

Nowitz, D. A. 1990. "Uucp Administration," *Unix Research System Papers, Tenth Edition*. Vol. 2, Saunders College Publishing, Fort Worth, TX, pp. 563–580.

> How to administer honey-dan-ber uucp, by dan.

Olander, D. J., G. J. McGrath, and R. K. Israel. 1986. "A Framework for Networking in System V," *Proceedings of the 1986 Summer USENIX Conference*. Atlanta, GA, pp. 38–45.

> Describes the port of Streams to System V and the work done to support service interfaces.

O'Reilly, T., and G. Todino. 1989. *Managing uucp and Usenet*. O'Reilly & Associates, Sebastopol, CA.

> How to administer different versions of uucp on different versions of the UNIX system.

Perkins, D. 1990. "The Point-to-Point Protocol for the Transmission of Multi-Protocol Datagrams Over Point-to-Point Links." RFC 1171.

> The protocol intended to replace SLIP eventually.

Perkins, D., and R. Hobby. 1990. "The Point-to-Point Protocol (PPP) Initial Configuration Options." RFC 1172.

> PPP allows for protocol options to be negotiated. Their initial values are described in this specification.

Pike, R., and B. W. Kernighan. 1984. "Program Design in the UNIX Environment," *AT&T Bell Laboratories Technical Journal*. Vol. 63, No. 8 (October 1984), pp. 1595–1605.

>   Read this before adding another option to your favorite command.

Presotto, D. L., and D. M. Ritchie. 1985. "Interprocess Communication in the Eighth Edition Unix System," *Proceedings of the 1985 Summer USENIX Conference*. Portland, OR, pp. 309–316.

>   A description of the IPC facilities built on top of Streams in the Research UNIX System.

Presotto, D. L., and D. M. Ritchie. 1990. "Interprocess Communication in the Ninth Edition Unix System," *Unix Research System Papers, Tenth Edition*. Vol. 2, Saunders College Publishing, Fort Worth, TX, pp. 523–530.

>   A version of the USENIX paper updated to match the Ninth Edition UNIX System.

Rago, S. A. 1989. "Out-of-Band Communications in STREAMS," *Proceedings of the 1989 Summer USENIX Conference*. Baltimore, MD, pp. 29–37.

>   Describes changes made in SVR4 to allow multiple bands of data flow within a stream.

Ritchie, D. M. 1984. "A Stream Input–Output System," *AT&T Bell Laboratories Technical Journal*. Vol. 63, No. 8 (October 1984), pp. 1897–1910.

>   The original introduction to the Streams mechanism.

Ritchie, D. M. 1990. "A Stream Input–Output System," *Unix Research System Papers, Tenth Edition*. Vol. 2, Saunders College Publishing, Fort Worth, TX, pp. 503–511.

>   Mostly a reprint of the classic 1984 paper.

Ritchie, D. M., and K. Thompson. 1974. "The UNIX Time-Sharing System," *Communications of the ACM*. Vol. 17, No. 7 (July 1974), pp. 365–375.

>   The historic paper describing the Research UNIX System (Fourth Edition). Reprinted in the *The Bell System Technical Journal*, Vol. 57, No. 6 (July-August 1978).

Rochkind, M. J. 1985. *Advanced UNIX Programming*. Prentice-Hall, Englewood Cliffs, NJ.

>   One of the few places you can find a decent description of System V IPC.

Romkey, J. 1988. "A Nonstandard for Transmission of IP Datagrams Over Serial Lines: SLIP." RFC 1055.

>   Describes the SLIP framing protocol.

Stevens, W. R. 1990. *UNIX Network Programming*. Prentice-Hall, Englewood Cliffs, NJ.

> A good introduction to IPC and network programming, with examples mainly from BSD, but also from System V. Contains real (working) source code.

Stevens, W. R. 1992. *Advanced Programming in the UNIX Environment*. Addison-Wesley, Reading, MA.

> Excellent coverage of the most recent UNIX programming environments. Includes lots of examples, and notes differences between SVR4 and 4.4BSD.

Sun Microsystems. 1987. "XDR: External Data Representation Standard." RFC 1014.

> Describes the XDR language.

Sun Microsystems. 1988. "RPC: Remote Procedure Call Protocol Specification, Version 2." RFC 1057.

> Describes the RPC protocol.

Tanenbaum, A. S. 1989. *Computer Networks*. Second edition, Prentice-Hall, Englewood Cliffs, NJ.

> A broad overview of computer networks, with detailed discussions concerning design issues and protocols.

Thompson, K. 1978. "UNIX Implementation," *The Bell System Technical Journal*. Vol. 57, No. 6 (July-August 1978), pp. 1931–1946.

> A description of the implementation of the Research UNIX System, somewhere between the Sixth Edition and the Seventh Edition.

USL. 1990a. *UNIX System V Release 4 Programmer's Reference Manual*. Prentice-Hall, Englewood Cliffs, NJ.

> Most manual pages for programmers.

USL. 1990b. *UNIX System V Release 4 Programmer's Guide: STREAMS*. Prentice-Hall, Englewood Cliffs, NJ.

> Information about STREAMS internals, including the STREAMS-based TTY subsystem.

USL. 1990c. *UNIX System V Release 4 System Administrator's Guide*. Prentice-Hall, Englewood Cliffs, NJ.

> Included among the administrivia are descriptions of the network selection facility and basic networking utilities (uucp).

USL. 1990d. *UNIX System V Release 4 Programmer's Guide: Networking Interfaces*. Prentice-Hall, Englewood Cliffs, NJ.

> An overview of the networking interfaces found in SVR4.

USL. 1990e. *UNIX System V/386 Release 4 Integrated Software Development Guide*. Prentice-Hall, Englewood Cliffs, NJ.

> How to build and install kernel-level software, among other things.

USL. 1992a. *UNIX System V Release 4.2 STREAMS Modules and Drivers*. Prentice-Hall, Englewood Cliffs, NJ.

> Covers STREAMS internals and documents both the Data Link Provider Interface and the Transport Provider Interface.

USL. 1992b. *UNIX System V Release 4.2 Device Driver Programming*. Prentice-Hall, Englewood Cliffs, NJ.

> An overview of how to create and configure device drivers.

Vessey, I., and G. Skinner. 1990. "Implementing Berkeley Sockets in System V Release 4," *Proceedings of the 1990 Winter USENIX Conference*. Washington, DC., pp. 177–194.

> A description of how sockets are built on top of STREAMS in SVR4.

Williams, T. 1989. "Session Management in System V Release 4," *Proceedings of the 1989 Winter USENIX Conference*. San Diego, CA, pp. 365–375.

> How job control is implemented in SVR4.

Xerox Corp., et al. 1982. *The Ethernet: A Local Area Network*.

> The specification for the data link and physical layers of Ethernet, developed by Xerox Corporation, Digital Equipment Corporation, and Intel Corporation.

Index

Most functions and constants necessary for UNIX System V network programming are listed in this index. The "definition of" entries for functions listed here refer to places in the book where the function prototypes can be found. Similar entries are provided to identify structure definitions. References have been omitted to places where common functions, such as exit, are used. Page numbers printed in boldface refer to the location in the book where the source code implementing the corresponding function can be found.

abortive release, 157, 200, 594
absolute pathname, 23
abstract syntax, 17
accept library routine, 304, 325, 333, 344
  definition of, 303
access method, 6, 8
access rights, 308, 317
address
  DLSAP, 490, 500, 514–515, 517, 519–520,
    529, 603, 629
  Ethernet, 497, 504, 535
  Ethernet broadcast, 497, 504, 516
  Example 5.3.3, universal, 238–240
  format, 218
  multicast, 497
  physical, 428, 497
  private, 267, 274, 285
  shared, 267, 285
  structure, socket, 291
  universal, 238–240, 375
  virtual, 428
address family, 294–295
Address Resolution Protocol, see ARP
AF_INET constant, 342, 348–349
AF_UNIX constant, 295, 317, 319
alarm system call, 119, 170, 199, 202, 280,
    282, 311, 409, 411, 696, 702, 707, 712–713
Albert, S., xiv
alias
  anyhost, 345
  host name, 231
  localhost, 345
allocb kernel function, 514, 519–520,
    525–526, 528, 533, 557, 564–565, 567, 572,
    607, 612, 617, 621, 624, 627, 632, 636,
    640–642, 644, 647, 656, 660–661, 664–665,
    671–672, 727, 736, 739–740, 742–743, 746
  definition of, 448–449

Amegadzie, G., xv
application layer, 12, 18
APP module, 679
architecture, STREAMS, 96–101
argument processing, 27–39
    Example 2.4.1, 27–29
arm of a discriminated union, 368
ARP (Address Resolution Protocol), 679
ASSERT kernel function, 510, 514
asynchronous I/O, see nonblocking I/O
atoi library routine, 35, 64, 71
  definition of, 37
authdes_getucred library routine, definition
    of, 417
authdes_seccreate library routine,
    definition of, 417
auth_destroy library routine, 414
  definition of, 412
authentication, 412–417
  DES, 412, 416
  null, 412
  RPC, 383
  UNIX-style, 412, 414, 421
AUTH_NONE constant, 412
authnone_create library routine, definition
    of, 412–413
AUTH_REJECTEDCRED constant, 416
AUTH_REJECTEDVERF constant, 416
AUTH_SHORT constant, 412
AUTH_SYS constant, 413, 415
authsys_create_default library routine,
    414
  definition of, 413
authsys_create library routine, definition
    of, 413
authsys_parms structure, definition of, 415
autopush command, 264, 543
autopush mechanism, 146, 539

B0 constant, 548, 562–563
B9600 constant, 548, 558
Bach, M., xiv
backenabling, 461–462, 584, 648
    definition of, 443
background, 26
    process group, 21
backlog, *see* queue length
backoff, exponential, 176
band, *see* priority band
bandwidth, 7
baseband transmission, 7
basename, 31
baud rate flags, 548
bcanput kernel function, 487
    definition of, 463
bcopy kernel function, 523, 629, 637, 656, 662, 664
    definition of, 438–439
Berkeley Software Distribution, *see* BSD
big-endian byte order, 360
binding addresses to UNIX domain sockets, Example 7.5.1, 315–317
bind library routine, 297, 317, 331, 342
    definition of, 295
Bittner, G., xiv
blocking, 16
block-special file, 22, 479
bounded media, 4
BPRI_HI constant, 449, 453
BPRI_LO constant, 448, 453
BPRI_MED constant, 448, 453
break condition, definition of, 549
broadband transmission, 7
broadcast, 4
    address, Ethernet, 497, 504, 516
    RPC, 420–421
broadcast RPC, response function, 421
BSD (Berkeley Software Distribution), xii, 291
BSD compatibility library, libucb, 293
btop kernel function, definition of, 436
btopr kernel function, definition of, 436
bufcall ID, 454, 503
bufcall kernel function, 524, 557–558, 619, 651, 738, 749
    definition of, 453
bufcall routine, 484
buffers, externally supplied, 454
bug, flow control, 115–116
Buroff, S., xiv
bus topology, 4–5
busy-wait, definition of, 437
byte order, 252, 359, 602, 622–623, 630
    big-endian, 360
    Ethernet, 498
    little-endian, 360
byte stream mode, read modes, 143, 471
bzero kernel function, 564–565, 608, 638
    definition of, 438

callback RPC, 418–420
callback RPC, Example 8.6.3, 419–420
calloc library routine, 190, 686
CALL structure, definition of, 680–681
canonical mode, *see* cooked mode
canput kernel function, 462, 486, 514, 530, 533, 565, 627, 631, 636, 639, 641, 645, 648, 654, 668, 741, 746
    definition of, 463
Carrier Sense Multiple Access with Collision Detection, *see* CSMA/CD
catching, signals, 60
catmap function, **48–49**
catreg function, 45, **46**, 48, 116
cattostream function, 116, **118–119**
CBAUD constant, 547, 562–563
CCITT (International Telegraph & Telephone Consultative Committee), 14
CE_CONT constant, 439
CE_NOTE constant, 439
CE_PANIC constant, 439
CE_WARN constant, 439, 511, 513, 521, 617, 736
channel, definition of, 4
character-special file, 22, 479
chat function, 694, **699**
chat script, 681–683, 689–690, 699–701
    special characters, 683
chdir system call, 22, 86, 340
    definition of, 85
checking for modules, Example 3.7.1, 147
child process, 73
chmod system call, 136, 272
chown system call, 272
    definition of, 53
chroot system call, 22
circuit-switched network, 9
cleanup function, 696, **698**
CLGET_FD constant, 385
CLGET_RETRY_TIMEOUT constant, 385
CLGET_SVC_ADDR constant, 385
CLGET_TIMEOUT constant, 385
client–server networking model, 11
client-side authentication, Example 8.6.1, 413–414
client-side connection establishment, Example 4.4.1, 176–179
client-side connection establishment (socket version), Example 7.3.1, 301–302
client-side of datagram-based application, Example 7.4.1, 310–313
CLIENT type, *see* RPC client handle
clist mechanism, 95, 146, 555
clnt_call library routine, 388, 402, 406, 418
    definition of, 386
clnt_control library routine, definition of, 385
clnt_create library routine, 388, 401, 406, 413
    definition of, 383–384

`clnt_dg_create` library routine, definition of, 383–384
`clnt_freeres` library routine, definition of, 387
`clnt_pcreateerror` library routine, definition of, 384
`clnt_perrno` library routine, definition of, 377
`clnt_perror` library routine, 389
    definition of, 386
`clnt_spcreateerror` library routine, 388, 401, 406, 414
    definition of, 384
`clnt_sperrno` library routine, 379, 402
    definition of, 377
`clnt_sperror` library routine, 407
    definition of, 386
`clnt_tli_create` library routine, definition of, 383–384
`clnt_tp_create` library routine, definition of, 383–384
`clnt_vc_create` library routine, definition of, 383–384
CLOCAL constant, 547, 694
clone, 102
    driver, 488
    open, 431, 488–489, 507, 607–608
CLONEOPEN constant, 483, 488, 507, 607–608
`closedir` library routine, 347
close-on-exec flag, 52, 77, 89, 114
close routine
    driver, 480, 483–484
    module, 543
`close` system call, definition of, 45
CLSET_FD_CLOSE constant, 385
CLSET_FD_NCLOSE constant, 385
CLSET_RETRY_TIMEOUT constant, 385
CLSET_TIMEOUT constant, 385
`cmn_err` kernel function, 442, 511, 513, 521, 617, 736
    definition of, 439
collision, 8
command-line options processing, 33–39
    Example 2.4.4, 34–39
commands, 26
common header files, 26
common kernel header files, 428
common `typedefs`, 429
communication, peer-to-peer, 13
communication domain, 294
    Internet, 294
    UNIX, 294, 308, 313–322
complex message, 447, 449
    diagram of, 450
composite filter, XDR, 372
concatenating messages, *see* pulling up messages
concatenation, 17
concrete syntax, *see* transfer syntax
configuration script, 262–264
`connect` function, **177–178**, 198, 233

connectionless client, Example 4.3.1, 169–172
connectionless mode state diagram, 165
connectionless server, Example 4.3.2, 172–174
connectionless service, 10
connectionless transport primitives, diagram, 168
connection-oriented data transfer
    Example 4.4.5, 197–200
    Example 4.4.6, 200–203
connection-oriented mode state diagram, 206
connection-oriented service, 10
connection-oriented state machine, 205–207
connection server, 235, 681
`connect` library routine, 302, 308, 325, 332–333, 349
    definition of, 301
connect queue length, definition of, 178
`conn` function, **232–234**, 287
CONNLD module, 139–140, 710, 712
context, process, 426, 436–437, 442, 483–484, 487, 542–543, 545
controlling
    stream, 582
    terminal, 22, 84, 472–473, 557
control message, 463–464
conventions, RPC, 375–376, 403, 405
cooked mode, 546
`copyb` kernel function, 451
    definition of, 452
`copymsg` kernel function, definition of, 452
`copyreq` structure, definition of, 468
`copyresp` structure, 468
    definition of, 469
`crash` command, 506
CREAD constant, 547, 558, 694
creation mask, file, 43, 87
`creat` system call, 141, 277, 341, 351, 710
credentials, definition of, 412
critical regions, 63, 117, 432, 442, 511, 562–563, 620, 662
critical sections, *see* critical regions
CS8 constant, 547–548, 558, 694
CSIZE constant, 547, 694
CSMA/CD (Carrier Sense Multiple Access with Collision Detection), 8, 496
CSTOPB constant, 547, 694
`ctime` library routine, 56
    definition of, 57
cu command, 268–269, 318, 551, 689
current working directory, 22, 84–85

daemonize function, **85–87**, 276, 340, 381, 395, 398, 709
daemons, 26, 84
DARPA (Defense Advanced Research Projects Agency), 294
Data Encryption Standard, *see* DES
data message, 464
`datab` structure, 446
    definition of, 447

datagram, *see* connectionless service
datagram socket, *see* SOCK_DGRAM socket type
data link layer, 12, 15, 496
Data Link Provider Interface, *see* DLPI
Data Link Service Access Point, *see* DLSAP
Data Link Service Data Unit, *see* DLSDU
data types, XDR, 364–365
DDI/DKI (Device Driver Interface/Driver-Kernel
    Interface), 427, 458
debugging, 502, 506, 510, 554, 723
Defense Advanced Research Projects Agency,
    see DARPA
delay kernel function, definition of, 437
dequeueing messages, 460–461
DES authentication, 412, 416
DES (Data Encryption Standard), 412
deserializing, 361
DES key, 416–417
device number, 101, 273, 429–431, 542
    external, 429–430
    internal, 429–430
    major, 101, 429
    minor, 101, 429
Device Driver Interface/Driver-Kernel Interface,
    see DDI/DKI
devices, minor, 102
/dev/kmem, 276–277
/dev/null, 86–87, 89, 213, 692
/dev/slip, 720
/dev/tty, 22
dialerr function, 693, **697–698**
dial library routine, 693
    definition of, 680
Diffie-Hellman encryption, 416–417
Direct Memory Access, *see* DMA
directory, 22
    current working, 22, 84–85
    root, 22
directory server, 243
directory service, 218
_discon function, **717**, 719
disconnect, *see* abortive release
discriminant, 368
discriminated union, 368
dispatching, definition of, 389
disposition, signals, 59
distance, operating, 8–9
DL_BADADDR DLPI error, 522
DL_BADDATA DLPI error, 523
DL_BADPRIM DLPI error, 513, 735
DL_BIND_ACK constant, 490, 492, 519, 739
dl_bind_ack_t structure, definition of, 492
DL_BIND_REQ constant, 490, 492, 512,
    517–518, 735
dl_bind_req_t structure, definition of, 492
DL_CLDLS constant, 515, 518, 657, 737
DL_ERROR_ACK constant, 490, 493, 525, 743
dl_error_ack_t structure, definition of, 493
DL_ETHER constant, 515, 736

DL_IDLE DLPI state, 516, 519–520, 522,
    527–528, 530, 533, 657, 737, 740–741
DL_INFO_ACK constant, 490–491, 515, 652,
    736
dl_info_ack_t structure, definition of, 491
DL_INFO_REQ constant, 490, 511, 613, 735
dl_info_req_t structure, definition of, 490
DL_NOADDR DLPI error, 518, 739
DL_NOAUTO DLPI error, 518
DL_NOTSUPPORTED DLPI error, 512
DL_OK_ACK constant, 490, 493, 521, 741
dl_ok_ack_t structure, definition of, 493
DL_OTHER constant, 736
DL_OUTSTATE DLPI error, 517, 520, 522,
    739–740
DLPI (Data Link Provider Interface), 479,
    489–495, 585, 678, 722
DLPI connectionless state diagram, 496
DLSAP (Data Link Service Access Point), 490
    address, 490, 500, 514–515, 517, 519–520,
    529, 603, 629
DLSDU (Data Link Service Data Unit), 15, 494,
    599
DL_STYLE1 constant, 515, 737
DL_UDERROR_IND constant, 490, 494, 526
dl_uderror_ind_t structure, definition of,
    495
DL_UNBIND_REQ constant, 490, 493, 512, 520,
    735, 741
dl_unbind_req_t structure, definition of,
    493
DL_UNBOUND DLPI state, 507–508, 517, 521,
    531, 727, 739, 741
DL_UNITDATA_IND constant, 490, 494, 529,
    534, 652, 747
dl_unitdata_ind_t structure, definition of,
    494
DL_UNITDATA_REQ constant, 490, 494, 511,
    628, 735
dl_unitdata_req_t structure, definition of,
    494
DL_UNSUPPORTED DLPI error, 518
DL_VERSION_2 constant, 516, 737
DMA (Direct Memory Access), 428–429, 435,
    535
DMAC (DMA Controller), 435
doconfig library routine, 274
    definition of, 264
doconn function, 712, **713–715**
dodiscon function, 558, 562–563, **572**, 712,
    717
doexpect function, 699, **701–702**
dosend function, 699, **703–705**
dowinch function, 569–570, **571**
Drechsler, R., xv
driver, 439
    clone, 488
    close routine, 480, 483–484
    definition of, 19

hardware, 97, 479
init routine, 480
open routine, 480–481, 483
processing rules, 485–486
put procedure, 484
service procedure, 486
software, 97, 479
start routine, 480
driver canonical
flushing algorithm, 485
service procedure algorithm, 486–487
drv_getparm kernel function, 647, 670
definition of, 433
drv_hztousec kernel function, definition of, 434
drv_priv kernel function, 531
definition of, 437
drv_usectohz kernel function, 524, 556–558, 620, 624, 637, 641, 651, 662, 670–671, 738, 749
definition of, 434
drv_usecwait kernel function, definition of, 437
dupb kernel function, 450, 662, 673
definition of, 451
duplicating messages, 450
diagram of, 451
dupmsg kernel function, 646
definition of, 451
dup system call, 87, 213, 272, 319, 692
definition of, 89
dynamic kernel memory allocator, 438
dynamic shared library, 219

EACCES error, 139
EAGAIN error, 73–74, 102, 113, 123, 178, 305, 328, 558, 564–565, 567, 572, 607, 612, 627, 632, 636, 713, 719, 727
EBADMSG error, 105, 143
EBUSY error, 317, 531, 612, 727
ECHILD error, 74
ECHO constant, 694
EDESTADDRREQ error, 308
EEXIST error, 315
EFAULT error, 107
EIA (Electronic Industry Association), 14
EINPROGRESS error, 325, 328
EINTR error, 83, 121–122, 211, 320, 556–557, 702, 705
EINVAL error, 51, 287, 507, 556, 582, 607, 688, 712, 717, 726
EIO error, 113, 473
EISCONN error, 308
Electronic Industry Association, *see* EIA
enableok kernel function, definition of, 462
enabling a queue, 462
enabling asynchronous I/O on a socket, Example 7.6.2, 329–330

enabling nonblocking I/O on a socket, Example 7.6.1, 327–328
ENAMETOOLONG error, 316, 657
encoding an array using XDR, Example 8.2.1, 367
encoding a structure using XDR, Example 8.2.2, 370–372
encryption
Diffie-Hellman, 416–417
public key, 416–417
endhostent library routine, 345
definition of, 335
endnetconfig library routine, 236
definition of, 220–221
endnetent library routine, definition of, 336
endnetpath library routine, 233–234
definition of, 225
endprotoent library routine, definition of, 337
endservent library routine, definition of, 337
enet_bind function, 512, **517–520**
enetclose function, **508**
enet_errorack function, 517–518, 520, **525–526**
enet_free function, **534**
enet_info function, **514–517**
enetinit function, **506**
enetintr function, **527–530**
enet_ioctl function, 509, **531–532**
enet_loop function, 523–524, **533–534**
enetopen function, **507**
enetrsrv function, **513–514**
enet_send function, 511, **521–524**
enet_uderr function, 522–523, **526–527**
enet_unbind function, 512, **520–521**
enet_wcont function, 524, **525**
enetwput function, **509**
enet_wsched function, 519–520, **524**, 525
enetwsrv function, **510–513**
ENOBUFS error, 306
ENODEV error, 305
ENOENT error, 316, 341
ENOMEM error, 306
ENONET error, 614
ENOSPC error, 208, 305
ENOSR error, 178, 305
ENOTCONN error, 308
enqueueing messages, 459–460
environment variable
HOME, 268
ISTATE, 265
L0, 689, 692
MPREFIX, 268, 271–272
NETPATH, 225, 227–229, 234, 374, 377, 379, 382
NLSADDR, 268
NLSOPT, 268
NLSUDATA, 268
PATH, 77

PMTAG, 266
environment variables, shell, 32
environ variable, 25, 77
ENXIO error, 306, 473, 507, 607, 727
EPERM error, 437
EPROTO error, 106, 108, 166, 208, 320, 574,
        645, 657, 716, 718
errno variable, 36, 38, 49, 86, 108, 152, 271,
        275, 278, 302, 304–305, 340–344, 346–351,
        712–714, 716–719
error function, **40**, 45–46, 48–49, 78, 82, 116,
        126–127
error handling, 40–41
error logging, 50
    Example 2.4.8, 50–53
    Example 2.4.9, 55–58
error mode, of a stream, 112–113, 473, 639
error-reporting functions, Example 2.4.5, 40–41
errors
    permanent, 306
    temporary, 306
esballoc kernel function, 528, 535
    definition of, 454
esbbcall kernel function, 454
    definition of, 455
ESRCH error, 66
/etc/hosts, 334–335, 338–339, 344–345
/etc/inittab, 262, 274
/etc/netconfig, 218, 220, 228–230, 234,
        314, 335, 379, 382
    and interaction with RPC, 374
    format of, 218–219
/etc/networks, 334–336
/etc/protocols, 334, 336–337
/etc/services, 334, 337–338
/etc/slipsys, 682, 685–686, 693, 707
/etc/ttysrch, 273
/etc/uucp, 680
/etc/uucp/Devconfig, 270
/etc/uucp/Devices, 270, 680
/etc/uucp/Systems, 270, 680–681
Ethernet, 496–498
    address, 497, 504, 535
    broadcast address, 497, 504, 516
    byte order, 498
    packet format, 497
    packet header, 500
ETIME error, 178, 302
etoimajor kernel function, definition of, 431
E2BIG error, 658
EUC (Extended Unix Code), 550
EUC ioctl commands, 554, 566
EUC_IXLOFF ioctl command, 549, 566
EUC_IXLON ioctl command, 549, 566
EUC_MREST ioctl command, 549, 566
EUC_MSAVE ioctl command, 549, 566
EUC_OXLOFF ioctl command, 549, 566
EUC_OXLON ioctl command, 549, 566
EWOULDBLOCK error, 328
execle system call, definition of, 76

execlp system call, definition of, 76
execl system call, 78, 83, 272, 716, 718
    definition of, 76
exec system call, 74, 76, 318
execution semantics, 357–359
    at-least-once, 357–358
    at-most-once, 357–358
    exactly-once, 357
    simulated at-most-once, 402
execve system call, definition of, 76
execvp system call, 213, 320
    definition of, 76
execv system call, definition of, 76
exit library routine, definition of, 29
_exit system call, definition of, 29
exit values, 25
expect string, 682, 699–702
expedited data, 145, 196
expiration window, timestamp, 416
exponential backoff, 176
extended socket example, Example 7.8.1,
        338–352
Extended Unix Code, *see* EUC
external device number, 429–430
externally supplied buffers, 454

FASYNC constant, 328–329
fatal function, **41**, 78, 81–83, 85–86, 116,
        118, 120, 122–123, 141, 162–163, 297,
        310–311, 322, 372, 693–696, 698, 707–708
fattach library routine, 136, 141, 278, 710
    definition of, 135
fchown system call, 51
    definition of, 53
fclose library routine, 36, 256–258, 363, 688
    definition of, 38
fcntl operations, 52
fcntl system call, 51, 120, 279, 324, 327–329,
        472, 710
    definition of, 52
FD_CLOEXEC constant, 51
FD_CLR macro, definition of, 325
fdetach library routine, definition of, 137
FD_ISSET macro, 343, 411
    definition of, 325
FD_SET macro, 343
    definition of, 325
FD_SETSIZE constant, 325
F_DUPFD constant, 52, 89
FD_ZERO macro, 343
    definition of, 325
ferror library routine, 38
FEXCL constant, 481–482
fflush library routine, 81, 363
    definition of, 82
F_GETFD constant, 51–52
F_GETFL constant, 52, 120, 279, 327–329, 710
fgets library routine, 78, 81, 173, 255, 257,
        686

definition of, 78–79
FIFO, 99
  diagram of, 100
file, 20
  creation mask, 43, 87
  locking, 23
  mapping, 46–50
  ownership, 43
  permissions, 23
file descriptor, 25
file descriptor passing, 137–143, 274
  Example 3.6.2, 138–139
file descriptor passing using sockets, 317–322
  Example 7.5.2, 318–322
file mapping, Example 2.4.7, 47–50
files, interpreter (#!), 76
file system, 22
  identifier, 273
filter, XDR, 363, 386, 389, 393–394, 396, 403, 405
FIOASYNC ioctl command, 328, 330
FIONBIO ioctl command, 327–328
FIOSETOWN ioctl command, 324, 328, 330
flow control, 102, 113, 117, 314–315, 443–444, 457–458, 460, 462–463, 487, 514, 584, 601, 615, 627, 636, 639, 645, 648, 650, 653–654, 668, 674, 726, 735, 741
  bug, 115–116
flow-controlled, definition of, 443
FLUSHALL constant, 461, 509, 611, 615, 654, 667, 730, 744–746
FLUSHBAND constant, 474–475, 485, 545
flushband kernel function, 485, 545
  definition of, 461
FLUSHDATA constant, 461, 485, 544–545, 579
flushing algorithm
  driver canonical, 485
  module canonical, 544
  multiplexor (lower half) canonical, 579
flushing data, 112
  in a pipe, 134–135, 545
  in a stream, 474–476
flushq kernel function, 485, 509, 544–545, 579, 611, 615, 667, 730, 744–746
  definition of, 461
FLUSHR constant, 112, 134, 279, 474–476, 485, 509, 544–545, 579, 611, 654, 730, 745
FLUSHRW constant, 112, 134, 474, 476, 521, 545, 624, 637, 655, 667, 671–672, 740
FLUSHW constant, 112, 134, 474–476, 485, 509, 544–545, 579, 611, 654, 730, 745
FNDELAY constant, 327–328, 481–482, 484, 543
FNONBLOCK constant, 481–482, 484, 543
fopen library routine, 36, 255, 257, 371, 686
  definition of, 37–38
foreground, 26
  process group, 21, 472–473
fork system call, 78, 82, 86, 186, 192, 209, 305, 318–319, 409, 716, 718

definition of, 73
fpathconf system call, 133
  definition of, 54
fprintf library routine, 30, 35–36, 41, 80, 171, 178, 198–199, 302, 310, 312, 322, 371, 378–379, 388, 401–402, 406–407, 410, 413–414, 692, 697–698, 706
  definition of, 31
framing, 7, 15, 496, 677, 742
FREAD constant, 481–482
fread library routine, 202
freeb kernel function, 523, 528, 567, 609, 614, 623, 628, 633–634, 637–638, 640–642, 646, 656, 661–662, 666–667, 742, 744, 746
  definition of, 449
freecinfo function, 688, **689**
free library routine, 105, 247–248, 250–251, 254–255, 689, 715, 717
freemsg kernel function, 449, 485, 509, 511, 513, 517–520, 523–524, 530, 533, 559–565, 569–570, 573–574, 579, 608–611, 617, 623–625, 627–628, 633–634, 638–639, 643–644, 647, 649, 653–655, 658–665, 668, 672–673, 730, 736, 739, 741, 743–745, 748–749
  definition of, 450
freenetconfigent library routine, 408
  definition of, 221
free_rtn structure, 454, 505
F_SETFD constant, 51–52
F_SETFL constant, 52, 120, 279, 327–329, 710
F_SETOWN constant, 324, 328–329
fstat system call, 48, 56, 271, 713
  definition of, 49
ftruncate system call, 56
  definition of, 58
full-duplex transmission, 7
FWRITE constant, 481–482

getack function, **107–108**, 131
getcinfo function, **686–688**, 693, 707, 713
getc library routine, 39
  definition of, 39
getdents system call, 102
getemajor kernel function, 507, 608
  definition of, 430
geteminor kernel function, 607, 727
  definition of, 430
getenv library routine, 33, 271, 408, 692
getgrnam library routine, 51
  definition of, 53
gethostbyaddr library routine, definition of, 335
gethostbyname library routine, definition of, 335
gethostent library routine, 345
  definition of, 335
getmajor kernel function, definition of, 430
getminor kernel function, 507

definition of, 430
getmsg system call, 102, 105, 108, 163, 473
    definition of, 106
getmsg usage, Example 3.3.4, 107–108
getnetbyaddr library routine, definition of,
    336
getnetbyname library routine, definition of,
    336
getnetconfigent library routine, 239, 241,
    408
    definition of, 221
getnetconfig library routine, 222, 236
    definition of, 221
getnetent library routine, definition of, 336
getnetpath library routine, 226, 233
    definition of, 225–226
getopt library routine, 35
    definition of, 34
getpeername library routine, 165
    definition of, 323
getpid system call, 65, 67–68, 72, 329–330
    definition of, 66
getpmsg system call, 102
    definition of, 145
getprotobyname library routine, definition
    of, 337
getprotobynumber library routine, definition
    of, 337
getprotoent library routine, definition of,
    337
getq kernel function, 461–462, 486–487, 510,
    514, 615, 648, 668, 735, 746
    definition of, 460
getrlimit system call, 25, 86, 411
    definition of, 87–88
getservbyname library routine, 342
    definition of, 337–338
getservbyport library routine, definition of,
    337–338
getservent library routine, definition of, 337
getsockname library routine, 165
    definition of, 323
getsockopt library routine, 308, 332–333
    definition of, 300–301
getutent library routine, 372
Gitlin, J., xiv
Gomes, R., xiv
group ID, 21
    effective, 21
    real, 21
    saved-set, 21
    supplementary, 21
group structure, definition of, 53

half-duplex transmission, 6
Hamilton, D., xv
handle, XDR, 362
handler, signal, 60
hangup mode, of a stream, 113, 473, 719

hard links, 24
hardware driver, 97, 479
Harris, G., xiv, 584
header files
    common, 26
    common kernel, 428
h_errno variable, definition of, 335
high-level client RPC functions, Example 8.3.1,
    377–379
high-level server RPC functions, Example 8.3.2,
    380–382
high-water mark, 444, 471–472, 505, 555,
    557–558, 606, 608, 726
    definition of, 443
HOME environment variable, 268
Honeyman, P., xiv
HOST_ANY constant, 231, 246
HOST_BROADCAST constant, 231, 246
hostent structure, definition of, 334
host name alias, see alias, host name
HOST_NOT_FOUND constant, 335
HOST_SELF constant, 231, 236, 246
htons macro, 623, 630, 647
HUPCL constant, 547, 558, 694

I_ATMARK ioctl command, 110, 446
I_CANPUT ioctl command, 110, 119
I_CKBAND ioctl command, 110
ICMP (Internet Control Message Protocol), 294
idempotent procedures, 358
identifier, file system, 273
idinstall command, 720
IEEE (Institute of Electrical and Electronics
    Engineers), xiii
ifconfig command, 684, 716, 718
I_FDINSERT ioctl command, 110
ifdown function, 717, **718**
IFF_POINTOPOINT constant, 723, 727
IFF_RUNNING constant, 723, 733
I_FIND ioctl command, 110
I_FLUSHBAND ioctl command, 110, 474
I_FLUSH ioctl command, 110, 112, 134,
    279, 474
IFNAMSIZ constant, 716, 732
ifstats global kernel list, 725, 728–729
ifup function, 714, **716**
I_GETBAND ioctl command, 110
I_GETCLTIME ioctl command, 110
I_GETSIG ioctl command, 110
I_GRDOPT ioctl command, 110, 143
I_GWROPT ioctl command, 110, 143
I_LINK ioctl command, 110, 579–580, 582,
    612, 657
I_LIST ioctl command, 110, 147, 444, 694
I_LOOK ioctl command, 110, 408
INADDR_ANY constant, 342–343
in_addr structure, definition of, 238, 297–298
inetd daemon, 421
INFPSZ constant, 555

INFTIM constant, 111, 711, 715
initclient function, **154–155**, 169, 198, 233
initlog function, **50–51**, 85, 271
init routine
  driver, 480
  module, 542
initserver function, **159–160, 155–156, 158–159**, 172
inode, 22
  number, 22, 273
I_NREAD ioctl command, 110
insq kernel function, 462
  definition of, 460
installation of kernel-level software, 720
Institute of Electrical and Electronics Engineers, *see* IEEE
interactive programs
  Example 2.4.15, 80–84
  and signals, 79
internal device number, 429–430
International Organization for Standardization, *see* ISO
International Telegraph & Telephone Consultative Committee, *see* CCITT
Internet communication domain, 294
Internet address, *see* in_addr structure
Internet Control Message Protocol, *see* ICMP
Internet Protocol, *see* IP
interpreter (#!) files, 76
interrupt, spurious, 506, 530
interrupt handler, 426, 431–432, 480–481
interrupt priority mask, *see* processor priority level
interrupts, 431–433
interrupt service routine, *see* interrupt handler
interrupt stack, 441–442
interrupt vector, 432, 480–481
I/O
  I/O-mapped, 435
  memory-mapped, 435
  multiplexing, 325
  nonblocking, 113–125, 280, 326–330, 472
  timing results, nonblocking, 124
iocblk_in structure, 734
iocblk structure, 465, 657
  definition of, 466
ioctl
  I_STR, 109–111, 467, 469, 566, 715
  processing, 465–469
  transparent, 109–111, 467, 469, 566, 569–570
ioctl system call, 118–119, 121, 139, 141–142, 147, 211, 213, 278–279, 328, 330, 407, 473, 546, 694, 696, 710, 712–715, 717
  definition of, 109
I/O-mapped I/O, 435
iovec structure, definition of, 307–308
I_PEEK ioctl command, 110
IP (Internet Protocol), 294, 577–578, 679
I_PLINK ioctl command, 110, 585, 612–613, 657, 714

I_POP ioctl command, 109–110, 211, 408, 539–540, 543, 558, 695
IPPROTO_ICMP constant, 295
IPPROTO_TCP constant, 295
IPPROTO_UDP constant, 295
I_PUNLINK ioctl command, 110, 585, 613, 714, 717
I_PUSH ioctl command, 109–110, 141, 213, 408, 539, 710, 714
I_RECVFD ioctl command, 110, 137–139, 142, 279, 476, 712–713
isastream library routine, 116
  definition of, 117
isdigit library routine, 687–688, 690
I_SENDFD ioctl command, 110, 137, 139, 142, 476, 696
I_SETCLTIME ioctl command, 110
I_SETSIG ioctl command, 110, 113–114, 118, 121, 278–279, 474
isgroupaddr function, 529, **535**
ISO (International Organization for Standardization), 11
isprint library routine, 39
  definition of, 39
Israel, R., xiv
I_SRDOPT ioctl command, 110, 143, 470
isspace library routine, 687–688, 700–701
ISTATE environment variable, 265
I_STR ioctl, 109–111, 467, 469, 566, 715
I_SWROPT ioctl command, 110, 143
itoemajor kernel function, definition of, 431
I_UNLINK ioctl command, 110, 581, 585, 613

job control, 22

kernel
  definition of, 19
  stack, 426
kernel-level software, installation of, 720
_KERNEL symbol, 498
Kernighan, B., xiv
keyserv daemon, 416
keywords, RPC, 403–404
kill system call, 65, 67–68, 72
  definition of, 66
kmem_alloc kernel function, definition of, 438
kmem_free kernel function, 557, 559, 729
  definition of, 438
kmem_zalloc kernel function, 556, 727
  definition of, 438
KM_NOSLEEP constant, 438, 556
KM_SLEEP constant, 438, 727

L0 environment variable, 689, 692
LAN (Local Area Network), 9

LBOLT constant, 434, 647, 670
lchown system call, definition of, 53
LDTERM module, 268–270, 476, 539, 544,
    546–551, 559–560, 578, 695, 745
libnls, network listener service library, 273
libnsl, network services library, 151
library
    dynamic shared, 219
    libnls, network listener service, 273
    libnsl, network services, 151
    libsocket socket, 293
    libucb, BSD compatibility, 293
    RPC, 359
    XDR, 359–373
libsocket socket library, 293
libucb, BSD compatibility library, 293
limits, resource, 88
line discipline, 95, 539, 546
linkb kernel function, 640, 647, 660
linkblk structure, 585, 603, 612–613,
    657–658
    definition of, 580
link ID, *see* multiplexor ID
links
    hard, 24
    symbolic, 24
listen daemon, *see* listener process
listener process, 261, 265, 267, 421
listen library routine, 297, 331, 342
    definition of, 302
little-endian byte order, 360
LLC (Logical Link Control), 15
LLCLOOP driver, 479
Local Area Network, *see* LAN
LOCALNAME constant, 164
locking
    file, 23
    record, 23
LOG driver, 479
log function, **56–57**, 86–87, 155–156, 158–160,
    172–173, 181, 185, 190, 192, 195, 201–202,
    210, 213, 271, 275, 277–278, 283, 304,
    340–351, 381, 395, 398–399, 710–719
Logical Link Control, *see* LLC
login command, 261, 273, 689
longjmp library routine, 79
low-level client RPC functions, Example 8.4.1,
    387–389
low-level I/O, Example 2.4.6, 45–46
low-level server RPC functions, Example 8.4.2,
    394–396
low-water mark, 444, 461, 471–472, 505, 555,
    557–558, 606, 608, 726
    definition of, 443
lseek system call, 276, 283, 348
    definition of, 44
lstat system call, definition of, 49

MAC (Medium Access Control), 15

major device number, 101, 429
makedevice kernel function, 488, 507, 608
    definition of, 431
making daemons, Example 2.4.16, 85–89
malloc library routine, 104, 244, 247–248,
    250, 253–254, 256–257, 277, 319, 345, 714
MAN (Metropolitan Area Network), 9
MAP_FIXED constant, 47
mapping, file, 46–50
MAP_PRIVATE constant, 47–48
MAP_SHARED constant, 47
master file, 720
maximum packet size, 102, 444, 455, 471, 505,
    555, 606, 726
M_BREAK message type, 448, 474, 575
MC_CANONQUERY constant, 560
MC_DO_CANON constant, 560
MC_NO_CANON constant, 560
M_COPYIN message type, 448, 467–468, 568
M_COPYOUT message type, 448, 467–468, 567
MC_PART_CANON constant, 560
M_CTL message type, 448, 476, 554, 560, 745
M_DATA message type, 101, 103, 105–108, 114,
    129, 144, 448, 464–465, 585, 593, 610–611,
    615, 730, 745
M_DELAY message type, 448, 464, 474, 561
media
    bounded, 4
    transmission, 4
    unbounded, 4
Medium Access Control, *see* MAC
memcmp library routine, 156, 159–160, 237
memcpy library routine, 105, 156, 158, 170
Memory Management Unit, *see* MMU
memory-mapped I/O, 435
memset library routine, 406, 410
M_ERROR message type, 448, 473, 645, 655,
    745–746
mesh topology, 5
message
    control, 463–464
    data, 464
    priority, 101, 456, 459
    TEST, 518
    types, 101
    XID, 518
message block, 101, 447
message coalescing, 472
message discard mode, read modes, 143, 471
message nondiscard mode, read modes, 144, 471
message priority, and ordering, 457
messages on a queue, diagram of, 457
message-switched network, 9
message type, 447
Metropolitan Area Network, *see* MAN
M_FLUSH message type, 112, 134, 448,
    473–476, 509, 521, 611, 624, 637, 654–655,
    667, 671–672, 730, 740, 745
M_HANGUP message type, 448, 473, 574, 680,
    744–746

midpoint, pipe, 132
minimum packet size, 444, 455, 471, 555, 606, 726
min kernel function, 536
minor
    device number, 101, 429
    devices, 102
minor macro, 271
M_IOCACK message type, 448, 466, 532, 563–566, 568, 570–573, 614, 731–734
M_IOCDATA message type, 448, 469, 559, 571
M_IOCNAK message type, 448, 467, 486, 532, 562–569, 574, 614, 658, 730–733
M_IOCTL message type, 448, 465, 485–486, 509, 544, 559, 575, 611, 730–731
mknod system call, 271
mmap system call, 48, 102
    definition of, 47
MMU (Memory Management Unit), 428
modes of service, 10
    connectionless, 10
    connection-oriented, 10
MODOPEN constant, 483, 507, 542, 556, 607, 727
module, 439
    definition of, 98
    close routine, 543
    init routine, 542
    open routine, 542
    processing rules, 544
    put procedure, 544
    service procedure, 545
    start routine, 542
module canonical flushing algorithm, 544
module_info structure, 505, 541, 555, 606, 726
    definition of, 444
module on a stream, diagram of, 98
module prefix, 445, 480, 542, 720
modules on pipes, 132–133
MORECTL constant, 107
MOREDATA constant, 107
mounted streams, 135
    Example 3.6.1, 135–137
mounted streams facility, 99
M_PASSFP message type, 137–138, 448, 476, 712–713
M_PCPROTO message type, 101, 103, 105–108, 129, 131, 144, 448, 464–465, 509–510, 514, 519, 521, 525, 573, 585, 610, 613, 618, 623, 625, 643–644, 652, 730, 736, 739, 741, 743
M_PCRSE message type, 448, 476–477
M_PCSIG message type, 448, 474
MPREFIX environment variable, 268, 271–272
M_PROTO message type, 101, 103, 105–108, 129, 144, 448, 464–465, 509–510, 514, 526, 529, 534, 572, 574, 585, 610, 628, 640, 652, 660, 662, 664–665, 671–672, 730, 747
M_READ message type, 448, 476
M_RSE message type, 448, 476–477

M_SETOPTS message type, 448, 469, 557, 608
MSG_ANY constant, 145–146
MSG_BAND constant, 145–146
msgb structure, definition of, 446
MSGDELIM constant, 446, 472
MSG_DONTROUTE constant, 307
msgdsize kernel function, 522, 639, 647, 741, 748
msghdr structure, definition of, 307
MSG_HIPRI constant, 145–146
MSGMARK constant, 446
MSG_MAXIOVLEN constant, 308
MSG_OOB constant, 307–308, 324
MSG_PEEK constant, 308, 351–352
M_SIG message type, 448, 473, 571
M_STARTI message type, 448, 474
M_START message type, 448, 474
M_STOPI message type, 448, 474
M_STOP message type, 448, 474
multibyte processing, 550
multicast address, 497
multiple processes, Example 2.4.14, 77–79
multiple versions of an RPC function, Example 8.4.3, 397–402
multiplexing driver, *see* multiplexor
multiplexing, I/O, 325
multiplexor, 98, 440, 679
    diagram of, 99
    routing criteria, 582
multiplexor ID, 580–581, 585
multiplexor (lower half) canonical flushing algorithm, 579
multipoint connection, 4
    and switching style, 9
munmap system call, 49
    definition of, 47
MUXID_ALL constant, 581–582, 585

named pipe, *see* FIFO
named streams, *see* mounted streams
NAMEFS file system, 135
name server, *see* directory server
name-to-address mapping, *see* name-to-address translation
name-to-address translation, 218, 229–243, 334–352
    library design, 243–259
name-to-address translation library design, Example 5.4.1, 245–259
NC_NOFLAG constant, 220
nc_perror library routine, 222, 226
    definition of, 223
nc_sperror library routine, definition of, 223
NC_TPI_CLTS constant, 220
NC_TPI_COTS constant, 220, 233, 236
NC_TPI_COTS_ORD constant, 220, 233, 236
NC_TPI_RAW constant, 220
NC_VISIBLE flag, 220
ND_ADDRLIST constant, 232–234, 236

nd_addrlist structure, 234, 248
  definition of, 231
ND_BADARG network directory error, 249,
  252–253
ND_CHECK_RESERVEDPORT constant, 240
_nderror variable, 245–254
ND_HOSTSERVLIST constant, 232
nd_hostservlist structure, definition of,
  232
nd_hostserv structure, definition of, 230
ND_MERGEADDR constant, 240–241, 243, 251
nd_mergearg structure, definition of, 241
ND_NOCTRL network directory error, 252
ND_NOHOST network directory error, 246–247,
  250
ND_NOMEM network directory error, 247–248,
  250–251, 253–254
ND_NOSERV network directory error, 247, 249
ND_OK constant, 246, 249, 251–253
ND_SET_BROADCAST constant, 240
ND_SET_RESERVEDPORT constant, 240
ND_SYSTEM network directory error, 246–247,
  249
netbuf structure, definition of, 153, 385
netconfig structure, definition of, 219–220
netdir_free library routine, 233–234, 236
  definition of, 232
netdir_getbyaddr library routine, definition
  of, 231–232
_netdir_getbyaddr library routine,
  249–251
  definition of, 244
netdir_getbyname library routine, 231,
  233–234, 236
  definition of, 230
_netdir_getbyname library routine,
  246–248
  definition of, 244
netdir_options library routine, 243
  definition of, 240
_netdir_options library routine, **251–252**
  definition of, 244
netdir_options ND_MERGEADDR
  command, Example 5.3.4, 241–243
netdir_perror library routine, 242–243
  definition of, 231
netdir_sperror library routine, definition
  of, 231
netent structure, definition of, 336
netname, 416
NETPATH environment variable, 225, 227–229,
  234, 374, 377, 379, 382
NETPATH library routines, 219, 225–229
  Example 5.2.2, 226–229
netstat command, 724
netty program, **270–272**
network
  definition of, 3
  circuit-switched, 9
  message-switched, 9

  packet-switched, 9
  topology, 4–6
network configuration library routines, 219–225
  Example 5.2.1, 222–225
network identifier
  tpi_clts, 219
  tpi_cots, 219
  tpi_cots_ord, 219
  tpi_raw, 219
network-independent, client-side connection
  establishment, Example 5.3.1, 232–234
network-independent, server-side connection
  establishment, Example 5.3.2, 235–238
networking model
  client–server, 11
  transparency, 11
network layer, 12, 15–16
network listener process, *see* listener process
Network Listener Protocol Service, *see* NLPS
network listener service library, libnls, 273
Network Provider Interface, *see* NPI
network selection, 217
network services library, libnsl, 151
Network Time Protocol, *see* NTP
news command, 338
nickname, 416
nlist library routine, 276
NLPS (Network Listener Protocol Service), 267
  protocol message, 285
  protocol strings, 286
NLPS client, Example 6.6.1, 286–287
NLPS server, 285–288
NLSADDR environment variable, 268
nlsadmin command, 267, 274, 285
  example of, 275
NLSDISABLED constant, 286
NLSFORMAT constant, 286
nlsgetcall library routine, definition of, 273
_nlslog variable, 286
NLSOPT environment variable, 268
NLSPROVIDER environment variable, 268, 408
nlsprovider library routine, definition of,
  273
nlsrequest library routine, definition of, 286
_nlsrmsg variable, 286
NLSSTART constant, 286
NLSUDATA environment variable, 268
NLSUNKNOWN constant, 286
NOASSIGN constant, 264, 274
NO_DATA constant, 335
node, definition of, 4
NODEV constant, 431
noenable kernel function, definition of, 462
NOERROR constant, 473
nonblocking
  I/O, 113–125, 280, 326–330, 472
  I/O timing results, 124
  RPC, 417–418
nonblocking I/O, Example 3.4.1, 114–125
nonidempotent procedures, 358

nop function, 699, **705**
NO_RECOVERY constant, 335
normal protocol mode, read modes, 144, 471
NORUN constant, 264, 274
NPI (Network Provider Interface), 596
NSTRPUSH tunable parameter, 540
nteclose function, **558–559**
nteioccont function, 559, **569–570**
nteioctl function, 559, **561–569**
NTE module, 268–269, 550–551
nteopen function, **556–558**
nterput function, **572–574**
ntewput function, **559–561**
ntohl macro, 652, 656
ntohs macro, 622, 645, 660
NTP (Network Time Protocol), 416
null authentication, 412
null procedure, 376, 380
number
    device, 101, 273, 429–431, 542
    external device, 429–430
    inode, 22, 273
    internal device, 429–430
    major device, 101, 429
    minor device, 101, 429
    sequence, 596, 653

O_APPEND constant, 42, 51
O_CREAT constant, 42–43, 51
octet, definition of, 238
O_EXCL constant, 42–43
Olander, D., xiv
O_NDELAY constant, 42, 113, 279, 327, 472
one-shot server, 267–274
    Example 6.4.1, 268–273
O_NOCTTY constant, 42–43, 84
O_NONBLOCK constant, 42, 113, 120, 279, 472
opaque_auth structure, definition of, 414
open, clone, 431, 488–489, 507, 607–608
opendir library routine, 346
open routine
    driver, 480–481, 483
    module, 542
open system call, 45, 48, 51, 86, 101, 116, 138,
    213, 272, 276, 322, 348, 472, 692, 695, 707,
    710
    definition of, 42
operating distance, 8–9
optarg variable, definition of, 34
opterr variable, 35
    definition of, 34
optind variable, 36
    definition of, 34
options processing, command-line, *see*
    command-line options processing
optopt variable, definition of, 34
orderly release, 157, 200, 594
O_RDONLY constant, 42, 45, 48, 116, 213, 276,
    348

O_RDWR constant, 42, 86, 138, 154–155,
    158–159, 162, 185, 237, 242, 272, 322
OSI reference model, 11–18
O_SYNC constant, 42–43
OTHERQ kernel function, 464
    definition of, 456
O_TRUNC constant, 42–43
out-of-band data, 145, 307–308, 324
ownership, file, 43
O_RDONLY constant, 692
O_WRONLY constant, 42, 51
O_NONBLOCK constant, 710
O_RDWR constant, 695, 707, 710

packet format, Ethernet, 497
packet header
    Ethernet, 500
    simple transport protocol, 599
packet header format, simple transport protocol,
    597
packet size
    maximum, 102, 444, 455, 471, 505, 555, 606,
        726
    minimum, 444, 455, 471, 555, 606, 726
packet-switched network, 9
PARENB constant, 547, 694
parent process, 73
PARODD constant, 547, 694
parse function, 699, **700**
PATH environment variable, 77
pathconf system call, 133
    definition of, 54
pathname
    absolute, 23
    relative, 23
pause system call, 60, 62, 278
    definition of, 61
PCATCH constant, 437, 483–484, 542, 556–557
_PC_CHOWN_RESTRICTED constant, 54
_PC_LINK_MAX constant, 54
pclose library routine, 173, 202
_PC_MAX_CANON constant, 54
_PC_MAX_INPUT constant, 54
_PC_NAME_MAX constant, 54
_PC_NO_TRUNC constant, 54
_PC_PATH_MAX constant, 54
_PC_PIPE_BUF constant, 54
_PC_VDISABLE constant, 54
peer-to-peer communication, 13
permanent errors, 306
permissions, file, 23
perror library routine, 40, 332, 409
persistent links, 582, 584–585, 613
PF_INET constant, 295
PF_UNIX constant, 295
physical address, 428, 497
physical layer, 12, 14, 496
Physical Point of Attachment, *see* PPA

pipe
  anonymous, 99
  diagram of, 100, 132
  midpoint, 132
  nonblocking semantics, 133
  structure, 132
PIPE_BUF constant, 132–133
PIPEMOD module, 134, 545
pipe-special file, 22
pipe system call, 101, 136, 141, 277, 313, 710
  definition of, 131
pmadm command, 266
  example of, 269, 275
PMTAG environment variable, 266
point-to-point connection, 4, 9, 678
Point-to-Point Protocol, *see* PPP
POLLERR constant, 125–127, 711
pollfd structure, definition of, 125
POLLHUP constant, 125–127, 711
POLLIN constant, 126–127, 237, 280, 282, 333,
    711
polling, 125, 431
  Example 3.4.2, 125–127
POLLNVAL constant, 125–127, 711
POLLOUT constant, 126
POLLPRI constant, 126
POLLRDBAND constant, 126
POLLRDNORM constant, 126, 333
poll system call, 126, 279, 282–283, 325, 704,
    711
  definition of, 125
  used as a high resolution timer, 704
POLLWRBAND constant, 126
POLLWRNORM constant, 126
popen library routine, 173, 201
Portable Operating System Interfaces, *see*
    POSIX
port monitor, 261, 265–266
POSIX (Portable Operating System Interfaces),
    xii–xiii, 546
POSIX_PIPE_BUF constant, 133
PPA (Physical Point of Attachment), 489–490,
    737
PPP (Point-to-Point Protocol), 678
precedence rules, 673
prefix, *see* module prefix
presentation layer, 12, 17–18
Presotto, D., 318
primitives, service interface, 129
fprintf library routine, 169
printf library routine, 28, 33, 61–62, 65,
    67–68, 72, 78, 80–81, 163, 222–223,
    226–227, 239, 242–243, 379, 388, 402, 407,
    696, 708
  definition of, 28–29
priocntl system call, 79
priority, message, 101, 456, 459
priority band, 145–146, 446, 456–459, 461, 463,
    472, 485, 487, 545
private address, 267, 274, 285

procedure number, RPC, 359, 375, 380, 404
process exit status, *see* process termination status
process, 20–22
  child, 73
  context, 426, 436–437, 442, 483–484, 487,
    542–543, 545
  parent, 73
  termination status, 74
process attributes, and exec, 77
process group, 21
  background, 21
  foreground, 21, 472–473
process ID, 21
processing rules
  driver, 485–486
  module, 544
processor priority level, 432–434, 481, 542
program interface, 25
program number, RPC, 359, 375, 380, 384, 391,
    404, 418–420
PROT_EXEC constant, 47
PROT_NONE constant, 47
protocol, definition of, 12
protocol data mode, read modes, 144, 471
protocol data unit, 13
protocol discard mode, read modes, 144, 471
protocol family, 294–295
  table of IDs, 296
protocol message, NLPS, 285
protocol migration, 130
protocol replacement, 129
protocol specification, RPC, 403
protocol strings, NLPS, 286
protoent structure, definition of, 336
PROT_READ constant, 47–48
PROT_WRITE constant, 47
pseudo-driver, *see* software driver
PTM driver, 479
ptob kernel function, 435, 536
  definition of, 436
PTS driver, 479
public key encryption, 416–417
Pulijal, H., xiv
Pulijal, U., xiv
pulling up messages, 452–453
  diagram of, 453
pullupmsg kernel function, 652
  definition of, 452
pushing and popping modules using ioctl,
    Example 3.3.5, 109
putbq kernel function, 459, 462, 486–487,
    511–514, 617, 648–649, 668, 736, 746, 748
  definition of, 460
putbuf kernel variable, 439
putchar library routine, 39
  definition of, 39
putc library routine, 41
putctl1 kernel function, 463, 521, 571, 624,
    637, 655, 667, 671–672, 740
  definition of, 464

`putctl` kernel function, 463
  definition of, 464
`putmsg` system call, 102, 105, 162, 473
  definition of, 103
`putmsg` usage, Example 3.3.2, 104–105
`putnext` kernel function, 464, 486–487, 514,
  517, 520–521, 526–527, 544–545, 558, 561,
  569–570, 572–574, 583, 608, 613, 647, 656,
  661, 663–664, 667, 671, 673, 730–731, 734,
  737, 740–741, 743–746, 748
  definition of, 463
`putpmsg` system call, 102
  definition of, 145
put procedure, 441, 445
  driver, 484
  module, 544
`putq` kernel function, 462, 485, 509, 530, 534,
  583, 611, 654, 668, 730, 745
  definition of, 459
`PZERO` constant, 437, 558

`QCOUNT` constant, 458
`qenable` kernel function, 525, 527–528, 620,
  649–651, 653, 668–669, 738, 750
  definition of, 462
`QFIRST` constant, 458
`QFLAG` constant, 458
`QFULL` constant, 455
`QHIWAT` constant, 458–459
`qinit` structure, 444, 455, 485, 505–506, 555,
  606, 726
  definition of, 445
`QLAST` constant, 458
`QLOWAT` constant, 458–459
`QMAXPSZ` constant, 458–459
`QMINPSZ` constant, 458–459
`QPCTL` constant, 464, 486–487
`QREADR` constant, 455
`qreply` kernel function, 485, 509, 532, 560,
  562–571, 579, 611, 619, 623, 625, 628, 634,
  643–644, 654, 658, 730, 734
  definition of, 464
queue length, 297, 302
queue scheduling, 461–462
`queue` structure, definition of, 455
quoting conventions, shell, 28

Rago, L., xv
raw socket, *see* `SOCK_RAW` socket type
raw mode, 546
RD kernel function, 485, 544, 565, 571, 650, 730
  definition of, 456
`readdir` library routine, 346
reading from a stream, Example 3.3.3, 106
read modes, 143–144, 470–471
  byte stream mode, 143, 471
  message discard mode, 143, 471
  message nondiscard mode, 144, 471

normal protocol mode, 144, 471
  protocol data mode, 144, 471
  protocol discard mode, 144, 471
`read` system call, 46, 105–106, 122, 127, 277,
  283, 306, 333, 349, 472–473, 696, 702, 707,
  712, 719
  definition of, 44
read/write over a transport connection, Example
  4.5.1, 208–214
`realloc` library routine, 281
reassembling, 16, 601, 660
record locking, 23
`recvfrom` library routine, 311, 333
  definition of, 309
`recv` library routine, 333, 351–352
  definition of, 308
`recvmsg` library routine, 321, 333
  definition of, 309
relative pathname, 23
relay nodes, 14
release
  abortive, 157, 200, 594
  orderly, 157, 200, 594
reliably delivered message socket, *see*
  `SOCK_RDM` socket type
`REMOTENAME` constant, 164
remote procedure call, definition of, 356
remote program interface specification, *see* RPC
  protocol specification
reserved ports, 323
resource limits, 88
response function, broadcast RPC, 421
results, nonblocking I/O timing, 124
retransmission, 601, 615, 653, 656, 670
ring topology, 5
Ritchie, D., xii, xiv, 96, 318
`RLIMIT_INFINITY` constant, 86
`RLIMIT_NOFILE` constant, 86, 88, 411
RMSGD, *see* message discard mode
RMSGN, *see* message nondiscard mode
`rmvq` kernel function, 462, 610–611
  definition of, 461
RNORM, *see* byte stream mode
root directory, 22
routing criteria, multiplexor, 582
RPC
  authentication, 383
  broadcast, 420–421
  callback, 418–420
  client handle, 382
  conventions, 375–376, 403, 405
  keywords, 403–404
  library, 359
  nonblocking, 417–418
  procedure number, 359, 375, 380, 404
  program number, 359, 375, 380, 384, 391,
    404, 418–420
  protocol specification, 403
  server dispatching function, 391–393
  server handle, 389

version number, 359, 375, 380, 384, 391, 404, 419–420
RPC and port monitors, 421
RPC_ANYFD constant, 384, 391, 419
RPC_AUTHERROR constant, 416
rpcb_getaddr library routine, definition of, 384–385
rpcbinder, *see* rpcbind server
rpcbind server, 359, 375, 379, 385, 389–392, 418, 420–421
rpc_broadcast library routine, definition of, 420–421
rpcb_set library routine, 419
   definition of, 418
rpcb_unset library routine, 395, 398–399, 419
   definition of, 392
rpc_call library routine, 378
   definition of, 376–377
RPC_CLNT symbol, 411
rpc_createerr variable, 401–402
rpcgen comments, 411
rpcgen output, Example 8.5.1, 405–411
rpcgen pass-through mode, 411
rpcgen translator, 359, 403–412
RPC_HDR symbol, 411
rpc_reg library routine, 381
   definition of, 379–380
RPC_SUCCESS constant, 377, 386, 402, 406
RPC_SVC symbol, 411
RPC_TBL symbol, 411
RPC_TIMEDOUT constant, 418, 421
RPC_VERSMISMATCH constant, 400–401
RPC_XDR symbol, 411
RPROTDAT, *see* protocol data mode
RPROTDIS, *see* protocol discard mode
RPROTNORM, *see* normal protocol mode
RS_HIPRI constant, 103, 105, 107, 114, 146, 162

SAC (Service Access Controller), 262, 265–266
sacadm command, 262
SAD driver, 479
SAF (Service Access Facility), 261
sameaddr function, 524, **535**
SAMESTR kernel function, 545
SA_NOCLDSTOP constant, 70, 209
SA_NOCLDWAIT constant, 70
SA_NODEFER constant, 70
SA_ONSTACK constant, 70
SAP identifier, 490, 516, 519, 529, 629, 737, 739–741
SA_RESETHAND constant, 70
SA_RESTART constant, 70
SA_SIGINFO constant, 70
S_BANDURG constant, 114
_SC_ARG_MAX constant, 55
_SC_CHILD_MAX constant, 55

_SC_CLK_TCK constant, 55
Scheer, M., xiv
_SC_JOB_CONTROL constant, 55
_SC_LOGNAME_MAX constant, 55
_SC_NGROUPS_MAX constant, 55
_SC_OPEN_MAX constant, 55
_SC_PAGESIZE constant, 55
_SC_PASS_MAX constant, 55
_SC_SAVED_IDS constant, 55
_SC_VERSION constant, 55
_SC_XOPEN_VERSION constant, 55
secure rpc, *see* DES authentication
SEEK_CUR constant, 44
SEEK_END constant, 44
SEEK_SET constant, 44–45, 276, 283, 348
segmenting, 16
select library routine, 333, 343
   definition of, 325
senddata function, **104–105**, 130
send library routine, 308, 333, 349–350
   definition of, 306
sendmsg library routine, 322, 333
   definition of, 307
send string, 682, 699–701, 703
sendto library routine, 311, 333
   definition of, 307
separation, 17
sequence number, 596, 653
sequenced packet socket, *see*
    SOCK_SEQPACKET socket type
serializing, 361
Serial Line IP, *see* SLIP
S_ERROR constant, 114
servent structure, definition of, 337
server
   connection, 235, 681
   Example 6.4.1, one-shot, 268–273
   Example 6.5.1, standing, 275–285
   one-shot, 267–274
   standing, 267, 274–285
server dispatching function, RPC, 391–393
server-side authentication use, Example 8.6.2, 415–416
server-side connection establishment
   Example 4.4.2, 181–183
   Example 4.4.3, 183–187
   Example 4.4.4, 188–195
server-side connection establishment (socket version), Example 7.3.2, 304–306
Service Access Controller, *see* SAC
Service Access Facility, *see* SAF
service data unit, 13
service interface, 108, 128–131
   definition of, 128
   diagram of, 128
   Example 3.5.1, 130–131
   primitives, 129
service procedure, 441, 443, 445, 459, 463
   driver, 486

module, 545
service procedure algorithm, driver canonical,
    486–487
session, 21, 84
session layer, 12, 17
session leader, 22, 88, 472
setgid system call, 21
set-group-ID, 21
sethostent library routine, definition of, 335
setifname function, 714, **715**
setjmp library routine, 79
setnetconfig library routine, 222, 236
    definition of, 220–221
setnetent library routine, definition of, 336
setnetpath library routine, 226, 233–234
    definition of, 225
setprotoent library routine, definition of,
    337
setrlimit system call, 25, 88
setservent library routine, definition of,
    337–338
setsid system call, 86, 409
    definition of, 84
setsockopt library routine, 301, 332
    definition of, 299–300
setuid system call, 21
set-user-ID, 21, 681
S_HANGUP constant, 114
shared address, 267, 285
shell, 20
    environment variables, 32
    quoting conventions, 28
shell environment variables, Example 2.4.3,
    32–33
S_HIPRI constant, 114
shutdown library routine, 334
    definition of, 298–299
S_IFCHR constant, 271
S_IFIFO constant, 315
S_IFSOCK constant, 315
sigaction structure, definition of, 70
sigaction system call, 71, 81–83, 116, 118,
    121, 170, 199, 202, 209–210, 278, 311, 693,
    696, 699, 707, 711
    definition of, 69
sigaddset library routine, 72, 81, 118, 130,
    209, 278
    definition of, 69
SIGALRM signal, 59, 170–171, 199, 202, 278,
    280, 311, 409, 696, 699, 707, 711
SIG_BLOCK constant, 70, 72, 119, 130, 209
SIGCHLD signal, 59, 209–211
    ignoring, 76
sigdelset library routine, definition of, 69
SIG_DFL constant, 60, 210
sigemptyset library routine, 71–72, 81–82,
    115, 118, 121, 130, 170, 199, 202, 209–210,
    278, 311, 693, 699, 707, 711
    definition of, 69
SIG_ERR constant, 60

sigfillset library routine, definition of, 69
SIG_HOLD constant, 62
sighold system call, 68
    definition of, 63
SIGHUP signal, 59, 86, 88
SIG_IGN constant, 60, 67, 86
sigignore system call, definition of, 63
SIGINT signal, 59–62, 64–65, 67–68, 71–72,
    79, 81–83, 693
SIGIO signal, 326
sigismember library routine, definition of, 69
SIGKILL signal, 59, 698
siglongjmp library routine, 81
    definition of, 79
signal handler, 60
signal handling
    Example 2.4.10, 60–61
    Example 2.4.11, 62–63
signal mask, 62, 70
signals, 58–73, 77
    catching, 60
    disposition, 59
    and interactive programs, 79
    terminology, 58–59
    timing windows, 60–62
signals and critical regions
    Example 2.4.12, 63–69
    Example 2.4.13, 71–73
signal system call, 60–61, 409
    definition of, 60
signal-to-noise ratio, 8
sigpause system call, definition of, 63
sigpending system call, definition of, 71
SIGPIPE signal, 59, 133, 144
SIGPOLL signal, 59, 113–114, 116–118,
    121–122, 130, 278–279, 326, 473–474
sigprocmask system call, 72, 119, 130–131,
    209–210
    definition of, 70
SIGQUIT signal, 59, 79, 81–83, 693
sigrelse system call, 68
    definition of, 63
sigsetjmp library routine, 80–81
    definition of, 79
SIG_SETMASK constant, 70, 72, 130–131
sigset system call, 61–62, 64, 67
    definition of, 62
sigsuspend system call, 119, 122
    definition of, 71
SIGTERM signal, 59, 693
SIG_UNBLOCK constant, 70, 119, 210
SIGURG signal, 324
SIGUSR1 signal, 59
SIGUSR2 signal, 59
SIGWINCH signal, 571
simple stream, diagram of, 96
simple error handling, Example 2.4.2, 30–32
simple message, 101, 447
    diagram of, 449
simple transport protocol

packet header, 599
packet header format, 597
simplex transmission, 6
simplified DLPI connectionless state diagram, 497
S_INPUT constant, 114, 278–279
SIOCATMARK ioctl command, 324
SIOCGIFADDR ioctl command, 734
SIOCGIFDSTADDR ioctl command, 734
SIOCGIFFLAGS ioctl command, 731
SIOCGIFMETRIC ioctl command, 734
SIOCGIFNETMASK ioctl command, 734
SIOCSIFADDR ioctl command, 733
SIOCSIFDSTADDR ioctl command, 733
SIOCSIFFLAGS ioctl command, 732
SIOCSIFNAME ioctl command, 715, 732
SIOCSIFNETMASK ioctl command, 734
SIOCSPGRP ioctl command, 324, 328
S_IRGRP constant, 43, 50, 141, 339, 684
S_IROTH constant, 43, 141, 339, 684
S_IRUSR constant, 43, 50, 135, 141, 271, 339, 684
S_ISFIFO macro, 277
S_ISGID constant, 43
S_ISREG macro, 347
S_ISUID constant, 43
S_IWGRP constant, 43, 50, 135, 141, 684
S_IWOTH constant, 43, 141, 684
S_IWUSR constant, 43, 50, 135, 141, 271, 339, 684
S_IXGRP constant, 43
S_IXOTH constant, 43
S_IXUSR constant, 43
Skinner, G., xiv, 584
slconnect command, 680, **689–705**
SL_CONSOLE constant, 443
sldisconnect command, 680, **706–708**
sleep kernel function, 483, 556–558
    definition of, 436–437
sleep library routine, 61, 63, 178, 302, 703
    definition of, 61
SL_ERROR constant, 443
SL_FATAL constant, 443
slip_bind function, 735, **738–740**
slipclose function, **728–729**
slipd daemon, 680, **708–719**
slip_errorack function, 735, 739–740, **743**
slip_hangup function, 728, **744**, 746
SLIP header file, 721
slip_info function, 735, **736**
slip_ioctl function, 731, **731–734**
SLIP module, 714
slipopen function, **726–728**
slip_rcont function, 749, **750**
sliprput function, **744–745**
slip_rsched function, 746, **749**
sliprsrv function, **745–749**
slip_send function, 735, **741–743**
SLIP (Serial Line IP), 677
slip_unbind function, 735, **740–741**

slip_wcont function, **738**
slipwput function, **729–731**
slip_wsched function, **738**, 739–740, 742–743
slipwsrv function, **735–736**
SL_NOTE constant, 443
SL_NOTIFY constant, 443
SL_TRACE constant, 443
SL_WARN constant, 443
S_MSG constant, 114
SNAcP (Subnet Access Protocol), 16
SNDCP (Subnet Dependent Convergence Protocol), 16
SNDPIPE write mode, 144
SNDZERO write mode, 144
SNICP (Subnet Independent Convergence Protocol), 16
SO_ALL constant, 470
SO_BAND constant, 470, 472
SO_BROADCAST socket option, 300
sockaddr_in structure, 238, 298
    definition of, 239
sockaddr structure, definition of, 295
sockaddr_un structure, definition of, 315
SOCK_DGRAM socket type, 294, 308, 310, 314
socket
    address structure, 291
    definition of, 294
    library, libsocket, 293
    mechanism, 291–353
socket architecture
    diagram of BSD, 292
    diagram of SVR4, 293
socket implementation, differences between 4BSD and SVR4, 295–296, 299, 303, 308, 312–317, 325–326, 329, 333
socket interface, compared to the TLI, 302–303, 306, 312, 330–334, 338
socket library routine, 297, 311, 317, 331, 342, 349
    definition of, 294
socketpair library routine, 319
    definition of, 313
socket version of initserver function, Example 7.2.1, 296–298
SOCKMOD module, 292, 303, 314, 324, 578, 585, 679
SOCK_RAW socket type, 294
SOCK_RDM socket type, 294
SOCK_SEQPACKET socket type, 294, 303, 333
SOCK_STREAM socket type, 294, 303, 308, 310, 314, 319, 342, 349–350
SO_DEBUG socket option, 300
SO_DELIM constant, 470, 472
SO_DONTROUTE socket option, 300
SO_ERROR socket option, 301, 308, 333
software driver, 97, 479
SO_HIWAT constant, 470–471, 557, 608
SO_ISNTTY constant, 470, 472
SO_ISTTY constant, 470, 472, 557

SO_KEEPALIVE socket option, 300
SO_LINGER socket option, 299–300
SO_LOWAT constant, 470–471, 557, 608
SOL_SOCKET constant, 300
SOMAXCONN, 303, 343
SO_MAXPSZ constant, 470–471
SO_MINPSZ constant, 470–471
SO_MREADOFF constant, 470, 472
SO_MREADON constant, 470, 472
SO_NDELOFF constant, 470, 472
SO_NDELON constant, 470, 472
SO_NODELIM constant, 470, 472
SO_OOBINLINE socket option, 300
SO_PROTOTYPE socket option, 300
SO_RCVBUF socket option, 300, 312
SO_RCVLOWAT socket option, 300
SO_RCVTIMEO socket option, 300
SO_READOPT constant, 470–471
SO_REUSEADDR socket option, 300
SO_SNDBUF socket option, 300
SO_SNDLOWAT socket option, 300
SO_SNDTIMEO socket option, 300
SO_STRHOLD constant, 470, 472
SO_TONSTOP constant, 470, 472
SO_TOSTOP constant, 470, 472
SO_TYPE socket option, 301
SO_USELOOPBACK socket option, 300
S_OUTPUT constant, 114, 118
SO_WROFF constant, 470–471
speed, transmission, 7–8
splhi kernel function, 432
    definition of, 433
spl kernel functions, 432
splstr kernel function, 511, 562–563, 620,
    624–625, 639, 641, 645, 648–651, 662
    definition of, 442
splx kernel function, 511, 562–563, 620,
    624–625, 639, 641, 645–646, 648–651, 662
    definition of, 433
sprintf library routine, 40, 85, 195, 253, 271,
    287, 388, 716, 718
spurious interrupt, 506, 530
S_RDBAND constant, 114
S_RDNORM constant, 114
sscanf library routine, 253, 256–257, 687
stack, kernel, 426
standard error, 25
standard input, 25
standard output, 25
standing server, 267, 274–285
    Example 6.5.1, 275–285
star topology, 5–6
start routine
    driver, 480
    module, 542
state diagram
    connectionless mode, 165
    connection-oriented mode, 206
    DLPI connectionless, 496

simplified DLPI connectionless, 497
stat system call, 271, 277, 316, 341, 346–347
    definition of, 49
Stevens, R., xiv
stp_accept function, 616, **630–634**
stp_bind function, 616, **620–623**
stp_buildaddr function, 655, **656**, 660–661,
    663, 665
stp_buildheader function, 627, **630**, 633,
    638, 640, 642, 656
stp_buildeback function, 625, 627, 630,
    638
stp_buildunitdata function, 627,
    628–629, 633, 638, 640, 642, 656
stpclose function, **608–609**
stp_connect function, 616, **626–628**
stp_discon1 function, 670, **671–672**
stp_disconall function, 614, **672–673**
stp_discon function, 609, 616, **635–638**
stp_errorack function, 623–624, 628, 634,
    638, 643, **644**
stp_fatal function, 617, 639, **644–645**
stp_findport function, 622, 652, 668, **669**
stp_getuport function, **669**
stp_info function, 616, **617–619**
stpinit function, **606**
stp_ioctl function, 611, **612–614**
stplrput function, **651–655**
stplrsrv function, **667–668**
stplwsrv function, **668–669**
stpopen function, **607–608**
stp_optmgmt function, 616, **642–643**
stp_qinuse function, 655, **659**
stp_rcont function, 651, 662
stp_rcvaccept function, 649, **663–664**
stp_rcvconnect function, 649, **661–663**
stp_rcvdata function, 648, **659–661**
stp_rcvdiscon function, 649, **665–667**
stp_rcvinfo function, 652, **657–658**
stp_restart function, 615, **641–642**, 650
stp_retransmit function, 658, **670–671**
stp_rsched function, **650–651**, 660–661,
    664–665
stp_sameaddr function, **635**, 666
stp_samenetaddr function, **659**, 660, 663,
    667
stp_sendack function, 653–654, **655–656**
stp_send function, 615, **638–641**
stp_unbind function, 616, **624–625**
stpursrv function, **648–650**
stpuwput function, **610–611**
stpuwsrv function, **614–617**
stp_wcont function, 619–620, 624, 637, 641
stp_wsched function, **619–620**, 621, 624,
    627, 632, 636, 640, 644
stp_xmit function, 615, 627, 633, 638, 640,
    642, **645–647**, 670
strbuf structure, definition of, 103
strcat library routine, 56, 170, 198, 311

definition of, 58
strcmp library routine, 246, 258, 345–346,
    408, 687, 717
strcpy library routine, 57, 170, 198, 208,
    256–257, 311, 317, 396, 399, 695, 707, 714
strdup library routine, 250–251, 253, 687–688
stream socket, *see* SOCK_STREAM socket type
stream
    controlling, 582
    definition of, 96
    XDR, 361–362
stream head, 96
    definition of, 97
STREAMS, xii, 95–148
    architecture, 96–101
    drivers, 479–537
    messages, 95, 446–455
    modules, 95, 539–576
    multiplexors, 577–674
    pipes, 98–100, 131–143
    queues, 97, 440, 455–462
    scheduler, 441
streamtab structure, 506, 555, 606, 726
    definition of, 445
strerror library routine, 36, 41, 86, 271, 275,
    278, 304–305, 340–344, 346–351, 708, 710,
    712–714, 716–719
    definition of, 38
strioctl structure, 110
    definition of, 111
strlen library routine, 57, 170, 173, 198, 208,
    212, 287, 316–317, 349, 687, 702
    definition of, 58
strlog kernel function, 442
    definition of, 443
STRMSGSZ tunable parameter, 103
strncmp library routine, 702
strncpy library routine, 56, 351
    definition of, 57
stroptions structure, 469
    definition of, 470
strqget kernel function, definition of, 458
strqset kernel function, 458
    definition of, 459
strrchr library routine, 30, 212, 319, 692, 706
    definition of, 31
strrecvfd structure, definition of, 138
structure, socket address, 291
subexpect string, 682, 699–701
subnet, 14
subsend string, 682, 699–701, 703
supplementary group ID, 21
svc_create library routine, 395, 398, 409
    definition of, 390
svc_destroy library routine, 419
    definition of, 394
svc_dg_create library routine, definition of,
    390
svc_dg_enablecache library routine,
    definition of, 402

svc_driver function, 711, **718–719**
svcerr_auth library routine, 394, 415
svcerr_decode library routine, 394, 410
svcerr_noproc library routine, 394, 410
svcerr_systemerr library routine, 394,
    396, 400, 410
svcerr_weakauth library routine, 394, 415
svc_fd_create library routine, 421
svc_freeargs library routine, definition of,
    393
svc_getargs library routine, 410
    definition of, 393
svc_noproc library routine, 396, 399
svc_pipe function, 711, **711–713**
svc_reg library routine, 391, 408, 418–419,
    421
    definition of, 392
svc_req structure, 414
    definition of, 393
svc_run library routine, 381, 393, 395, 398,
    409, 421
    definition of, 380
svc_sendreply library routine, 396,
    399–400, 409–410, 415, 418
    definition of, 394
svc_tli_create library routine, 408, 419,
    421
    definition of, 390
svc_tp_create library routine, definition of,
    390
svc_unreg library routine, definition of, 392
svc_vc_create library routine, definition of,
    390
SVCXPRT type, *see* RPC server handle
switching style, 9
    circuit-switched, 9
    message-switched, 9
    packet-switched, 9
S_WRBAND constant, 114
S_WRNORM constant, 114
symbolic links, 24
sysconf system call, 54
    definition of, 55
sysinfo structure, 276
syslog library routine, 380, 391, 410
system clock, 433–434
system file, 721
system options and limits, 54–55

t_accept library routine, 182, 186, 191, 331,
    333, 630
    definition of, 179
taddr2uaddr library routine, 239, 242
    definition of, 238
_taddr2uaddr library routine, **252–253**
    definition of, 244–245
T_ADDR constant, 154, 156, 158–159, 237, 242
T_ALL constant, 154, 156, 170, 172, 182, 185,
    190

t_alloc library routine, 156, 158–159, 166, 170, 172, 177, 182, 185, 190, 237, 242, 312, 332
   definition of, 153
TBADADDR TLI error, 621–622, 626
TBADDATA TLI error, 196, 626, 631, 635
TBADFLAG TLI error, 643
TBADF TLI error, 631–633
TBADOPT TLI error, 626, 631, 642
TBADSEQ TLI error, 632, 636
T_BIND_ACK constant, 586, 588, 623
T_bind_ack structure, definition of, 588
T_BIND constant, 154, 156, 158–160, 237, 242
t_bind library routine, 155–156, 158, 160, 185, 237, 242, 331
   definition of, 152
T_BIND_REQ constant, 586–587, 616, 623
T_bind_req structure, definition of, 587
t_bind structure, 302
   definition of, 153
TBUFOVFLW TLI error, 167
T_CALL constant, 154, 177–178, 182, 185, 190
t_call structure, 273
   definition of, 175
TCGETA ioctl command, 548–549, 564
tcgetattr library routine, 694
TCGETS ioctl command, 548–549, 565
T_CHECK constant, 164, 643
t_close library routine, 155, 185, 187, 192, 194, 211, 234, 237, 242, 281, 287, 334
   definition of, 156–157
T_CLTS constant, 161, 411
T_CONN_CON constant, 586, 591, 664
T_conn_con structure, definition of, 592
t_connect library routine, 177, 332
   definition of, 174–175
T_CONNECT TLI event, 188
T_CONN_IND constant, 586, 590, 662
T_conn_ind structure, definition of, 590
T_CONN_REQ constant, 586, 589, 610–611, 616, 627–628
T_CONN_RES constant, 616
T_conn_req structure, definition of, 590
T_CONN_RES constant, 586, 591, 633–634
T_conn_res structure, definition of, 591
T_COTS constant, 161, 197, 619
T_COTS_ORD constant, 161, 197
TCP address, *see* sockaddr_in structure
TCP (Transmission Control Protocol), 129, 161, 294, 324, 577–578, 679
TCSBRK ioctl command, 549, 566
tcsendbreak library routine, 703
TCSETAF ioctl command, 548–549, 563, 573
TCSETA ioctl command, 548–549, 563, 573
tcsetattr library routine, 694–695
TCSETAW ioctl command, 548–549, 563, 573
TCSETSF ioctl command, 548–549, 561
TCSETS ioctl command, 548–549, 561
TCSETSW ioctl command, 548–549, 561
T_DATA_IND constant, 586, 593, 660

T_data_ind structure, definition of, 593
T_DATA_REQ constant, 585–586, 592, 610, 615
T_data_req structure, definition of, 592
T_DATA TLI event, 188
T_DATAXFER TLI state, 205, 408
T_DEFAULT constant, 164, 643
T_DISCON_IND constant, 552, 574, 586, 593–594, 665, 671–672
T_discon_ind structure, definition of, 552, 594
T_DISCONNECT TLI event, 188, 194
T_DISCON_REQ constant, 552, 572–574, 586, 593–594, 610, 616, 638
T_discon_req structure, definition of, 552, 594
T_DIS constant, 154, 190
t_discon structure, definition of, 176
TE_BIND_ACK TPI event, 623
TE_BIND_REQ TPI event, 621, 623
TE_CONN_CON TPI event, 663–664
TE_CONN_IND TPI event, 661, 663
TE_CONN_REQ TPI event, 626, 628
TE_CONN_RES TPI event, 631, 634
TE_DATA_REQ TPI event, 639
TE_DISCON_IND1 TPI event, 667, 671, 673
TE_DISCON_IND2 TPI event, 666
TE_DISCON_IND3 TPI event, 666
TE_DISCON_REQ TPI event, 637
TE_DISCON_RES TPI event, 635
temporary errors, 306
TE_OK_ACK1 TPI event, 628, 637
TE_OK_ACK2 TPI event, 634, 637
TE_OK_ACK3 TPI event, 634
TE_OK_ACK4 TPI event, 634, 637
TE_OPTMGMT_REQ TPI event, 642
TE_PASS_CONN TPI event, 633
terminal, controlling, 22, 84, 472–473, 557
terminal interface, 546–550
termination status, process, 74
termios structure, definition of, 546–547
termio structure, definition of, 548
t_errlist array, 152
t_errno variable, 152, 170, 173, 177–178, 182, 186, 191
T_ERROR_ACK constant, 553, 574, 586, 588, 590, 593, 644
T_error_ack structure, definition of, 553, 588
T_ERROR constant, 188, 195
t_error library routine, 154–155, 170–171, 177, 199, 209, 242, 332
   definition of, 152
TEST message, 518
TE_UNBIND_REQ TPI event, 624
T_EXDATA TLI event, 188
T_EXPEDITED constant, 196
TFLOW TLI error, 166, 196, 203
t_free library routine, 159–160, 177–178, 237, 254, 332
   definition of, 157

t_getinfo library routine, 332, 411
  definition of, 160
t_getname library routine, definition of, 164
t_getstate library routine, 332, 408
  definition of, 205
Thompson, K., xiv
TICLTS driver, 313–314, 479
TICOTS driver, 314–315, 479
TICOTSORD driver, 314, 479
T_IDLE TLI state, 205
TIDU size, 161, 196, 600, 619
TIDU (Transport Interface Data Unit), 592–593
TIME constant, 434
timeout function, 696, **698**, 707, **708**, 711,
  719
timeout ID, 503
timeout kernel function, 524, 556–558, 620,
  624, 637, 641, 650–651, 658, 662, 671, 738,
  749
  definition of, 434
timeout routine, 433, 484
timestamp expiration window, 416
time system call, 56
  definition of, 57
timeval structure, definition of, 326, 386
timing results, nonblocking I/O, 124
timing windows, signals, 60–62
TIMOD module, 128–129, 150, 164, 264, 268,
  274, 550–551, 578, 679
T_INCON TLI state, 205
T_INFO_ACK constant, 586, 618
T_info_ack structure, definition of, 586
T_INFO constant, 154
T_INFO_REQ constant, 162, 586, 594, 616
T_info_req structure, definition of, 586
T_INREL TLI state, 205
TIOCGWINSZ ioctl command, 549, 566, 569
TIOCSTI ioctl command, 549, 565
TIOCSWINSZ ioctl command, 549, 568, 570
TIRDWR module, 207–208, 214, 268–269, 282,
  331, 333, 539, 550–551, 559–560
ti_statetbl kernel variable, 604
TLI (Transport Layer Interface), xii, 149–215
  architecture, 150
t_listen library routine, 182, 186, 191, 194,
  273, 333
  definition of, 179
T_LISTEN TLI event, 188, 194
t_look library routine, 194, 332
  definition of, 188
TLOOK TLI error, 167, 170, 173, 177, 182, 186,
  188, 191, 331
T_MORE constant, 167, 196–197
T_NEGOTIATE constant, 164, 643
t_nerr variable, 152
TNOADDR TLI error, 622
TNODATA TLI error, 167, 175, 179, 197
T_OK_ACK constant, 552, 573, 586, 588–590,
  593–594, 625
T_ok_ack structure, definition of, 552, 589

t_open library routine, 154–155, 158–159,
  185, 219, 237, 242, 331
  definition of, 151
topology
  bus, 4–5
  mesh, 5
  network, 4–6
  ring, 5
  star, 5–6
  tree, 5–6
T_OPT constant, 154
T_OPTMGMT_ACK constant, 643
T_OPTMGMT constant, 154
t_optmgmt library routine, 332
  definition of, 163–164
T_OPTMGMT_REQ constant, 616, 643
t_optmgmt structure, definition of, 163–164
T_ORDREL TLI event, 188, 204
T_OUTCON TLI state, 205
T_OUTREL TLI state, 205
T_OUTSTATE TLI error, 205
TOUTSTATE TLI error, 588, 621, 624, 626, 631,
  635, 642
TPDU (Transport Protocol Data Unit), 17
TP_EXPINLINE constant, 619
TPI (Transport Provider Interface), 128, 150,
  550, 552–553, 585–596
  precedence rules, 610
  states, 596
  state diagram, 595
tpi_clts network identifier, 219
tpi_cots network identifier, 219
tpi_cots_ord network identifier, 219
tpi_raw network identifier, 219
TP_SNDZERO constant, 619
transfer syntax, 17
transmission
  baseband, 7
  broadband, 7
  full-duplex, 7
  half-duplex, 6
  media, 4
  method, 6–7
  simplex, 6
  speed, 7–8
Transmission Control Protocol, *see* TCP
transparency networking model, 11
transparent ioctl, 109–111, 467, 469, 566,
  569–570
TRANSPARENT constant, 466–467, 531,
  567–568, 731–733
transport connection
  connection release, 203–204
  data transfer, 195–203
  establishment, 174–195
transport endpoint
  definition of, 151
  initialization of, 151
transport endpoint initialization
  Example 4.2.1, 154–156

Example 4.2.2, 157–160
Transport Interface Data Unit, *see* TIDU
transport layer, 12, 17
Transport Layer Interface, *see* TLI
transport provider, 150, 160–161
Transport Provider Interface, *see* TPI
Transport Service Data Unit, *see* TSDU
t_rcvconnect library routine, 333
  definition of, 175–176
t_rcvdis library routine, 182, 186, 194, 334
  definition of, 176–177
t_rcv library routine, 199, 201, 209, 212, 333
  definition of, 197
t_rcvrel library routine, 334
  definition of, 204
t_rcvudata library routine, 170, 173, 333
  definition of, 166–167
t_rcvuderr library routine, 171, 173, 312,
  333
  definition of, 167
tree topology, 5–6
truncate system call, definition of, 58
TS_DATA_XFER TPI state, 609, 637, 653, 659,
  671–672
TSDU size, 161, 196–197, 618
  zero-length, 174, 619
TSDU size and TIDU size, Example 4.2.3,
  162–163
TSDU (Transport Service Data Unit), 592–593,
  599, 660
TS_IDLE TPI state, 633, 639
t_snddis library routine, 186, 191–192, 209,
  211, 281, 333–334
  definition of, 183
t_snd library routine, 199, 202, 287, 333, 585
  definition of, 196
t_sndrel library routine, 334
  definition of, 203
t_sndudata library routine, 170, 173, 333
  definition of, 166
T_STATECHNG TLI error, 205–206
T_SUCCESS constant, 643
TS_UNBND TPI state, 608
TS_WCON_CREQ TPI state, 671–672
TS_WRES_CIND TPI state, 636, 666
t_sync library routine, definition of, 205–206
TSYSERR TLI error, 152, 166, 178, 211, 553,
  588, 627, 632, 636
TTCOMPAT module, 264, 541
TTIPRI constant, 556–557
ttyadm command, 266
TTYHOG constant, 555
ttymon command, 261, 265
ttyname library routine, 136, 272–273
T_UDATA constant, 154
T_UDERROR constant, 154
t_uderr structure, definition of, 167
T_UDERR TLI event, 188
tunable parameter
  NSTRPUSH, 540

STRMSGSZ, 103
t_unbind library routine, 331
  definition of, 157
T_UNBIND_REQ constant, 586, 588, 616,
  624–625
T_unbind_req structure, definition of, 588
T_UNBND TLI state, 205
T_UNITDATA constant, 154, 170, 172
t_unitdata structure, definition of, 165
type-ahead, 197
types, message, 101

uaddr2taddr library routine, definition of,
  238
_uaddr2taddr library routine, **253–254**
  definition of, 244–245
UDP address, *see* sockaddr_in structure
UDP (User Datagram Protocol), 294, 577–578,
  679
umask system call, 85
  definition of, 87
uname system call, 246, 341, 381, 396, 399, 407
unblocking, 16
unbounded media, 4
unbufcall kernel function, 455, 508, 557,
  609, 728
  definition of, 454
undial library routine, 694–696, 698
  definition of, 681
unique pipe connections, 139–142
  diagram of, 140
  Example 3.6.3, 141–142
universal address, 238–240, 252, 375
  definition of, 238
  Example 5.3.3, 238–240
UNIX, communication domain, 294, 308,
  313–322
UNIX-style authentication, 412, 414, 421
UNIX system architecture, diagram of, 20
unlink system call, 317
unnamed pipe, *see* pipe, anonymous
untimeout kernel function, 508, 556–557,
  609, 728
  definition of, 434
urgent data, 324
urgent mark, 196, 324
User Datagram Protocol, *see* UDP
user ID, 21
  effective, 21
  real, 21
  saved-set, 21
using configuration scripts, Example 6.1.1,
  263–264
utime system call, 347
utmpname library routine, 371
utmp structure, definition of, 370
utsname structure, definition of, 382
uucp, 681–682
  administrative files, 270

command, 318
lock files, 681, 693, 698

va_end library routine, 40–41, 56
va_list type, 40–41
/var/adm/utmp, 262, 370
va_start library routine, 40–41, 56
verifier, definition of, 412
version number, RPC, 359, 375, 380, 384, 391,
    404, 419–420
vfprintf library routine, 41
    definition of, 41
virtual address, 428
virtual circuit, *see* connection-oriented service
vsprintf library routine, 56
vtop kernel function, 536
    definition of, 429

Wait, J., xv
waitpid system call, 78, 83, 320, 716, 718
    definition of, 74
wait system call, definition of, 74
wakeup kernel function, 556–558
    definition of, 437
WAN (Wide Area Network), 9
WCONTINUED constant, 75
WCOREDUMP macro, 75
Wehr, L., xiv
Wheeler, G., xiv
Wide Area Network, *see* WAN
WIFCONTINUED macro, 75
WIFEXITED macro, 75, 320, 716, 718
WIFEXITSTATUS macro, 75, 320, 716, 718
WIFSIGNALED macro, 75, 320
WIFSTOPPED macro, 75
WIFTERMSIG macro, 75
window, timestamp expiration, 416
winsize structure, definition of, 550
WNOHANG constant, 75
WNOWAIT constant, 75
write modes, 144
write offset, 471
write system call, 46, 49, 57, 123, 127, 171,
    199, 209, 282, 306, 308, 312, 333, 352,
    472–473, 585, 695, 703–705, 707, 712
    definition of, 44
    on a transport endpoint, 207–208, 282
writing to a stream, Example 3.3.1, 102–103
WR kernel function, 508, 527–528, 544, 558,
    579, 608–609, 620, 649, 653, 655, 668–669,
    727, 729, 741, 743–745
    definition of, 456
WSTOPSIG macro, 75
WUNTRACED constant, 75

XDR
    composite filter, 372

data types, 364–365
    filter, 363, 386, 389, 393–394, 396, 403, 405
    handle, 362
    library, 359–373
    stream, 361–362
xdr_array library routine, definition of, 367
xdr_bool library routine, definition of, 363
xdr_bytes library routine, 368
    definition of, 366
xdr_char library routine, 397
    definition of, 363
XDR_DECODE XDR operation, 362
xdr_destroy library routine, definition of,
    363
xdr_discrim structure, definition of, 368
xdr_double library routine, definition of, 363
XDR_ENCODE XDR operation, 362, 371
xdr_enum library routine, definition of, 363
xdr_float library routine, definition of, 363
xdr_free library routine, definition of, 369
XDR_FREE XDR operation, 362
xdr_int library routine, definition of, 363
xdr_long library routine, 372–373
    definition of, 363
xdr_opaque library routine, 368
    definition of, 366
xdr_pointer library routine, definition of,
    369
xdrproc_t type, 367
xdr_reference library routine, definition of,
    369
xdr_short library routine, 372–373
    definition of, 363
xdrstdio_create library routine, 371
    definition of, 363
xdr_string library routine, 367–369, 378,
    381, 397, 400
    definition of, 366
xdr_u_char library routine, definition of, 363
xdr_u_int library routine, definition of, 363
xdr_u_long library routine, definition of, 363
xdr_union library routine, definition of, 368
xdr_u_short library routine, definition of,
    363
xdr_utmp function, **373**
xdr_vector library routine, 368, 372–373,
    389, 397
    definition of, 366–367
xdr_void library routine, 378, 381, 388–389,
    396, 399, 402, 406, 409–410
    definition of, 366
xdr_wrapstring library routine, 406, 410
    definition of, 369
XID message, 518
X/OPEN, xii
XTI (X/OPEN Transport Interface), xii
XT multiplexor, 578

zombies, 76